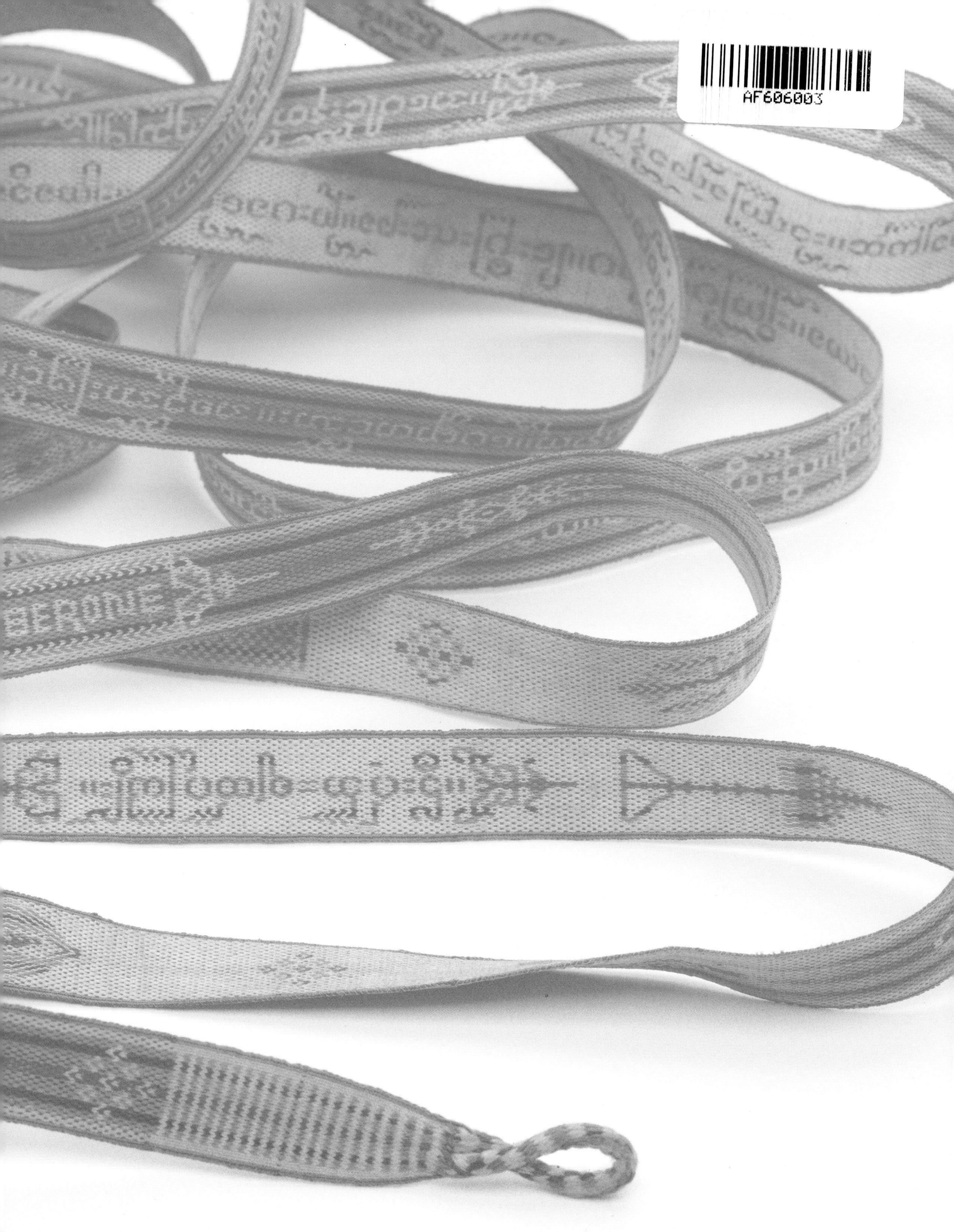

sazigyo

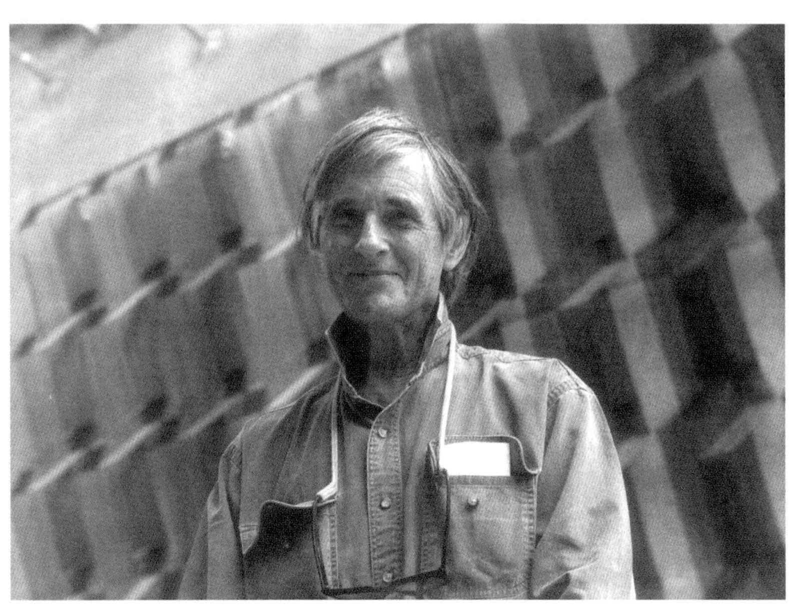

IN MEMORY OF PETER COLLINGWOOD OBE, MASTER WEAVER (1922–2008)

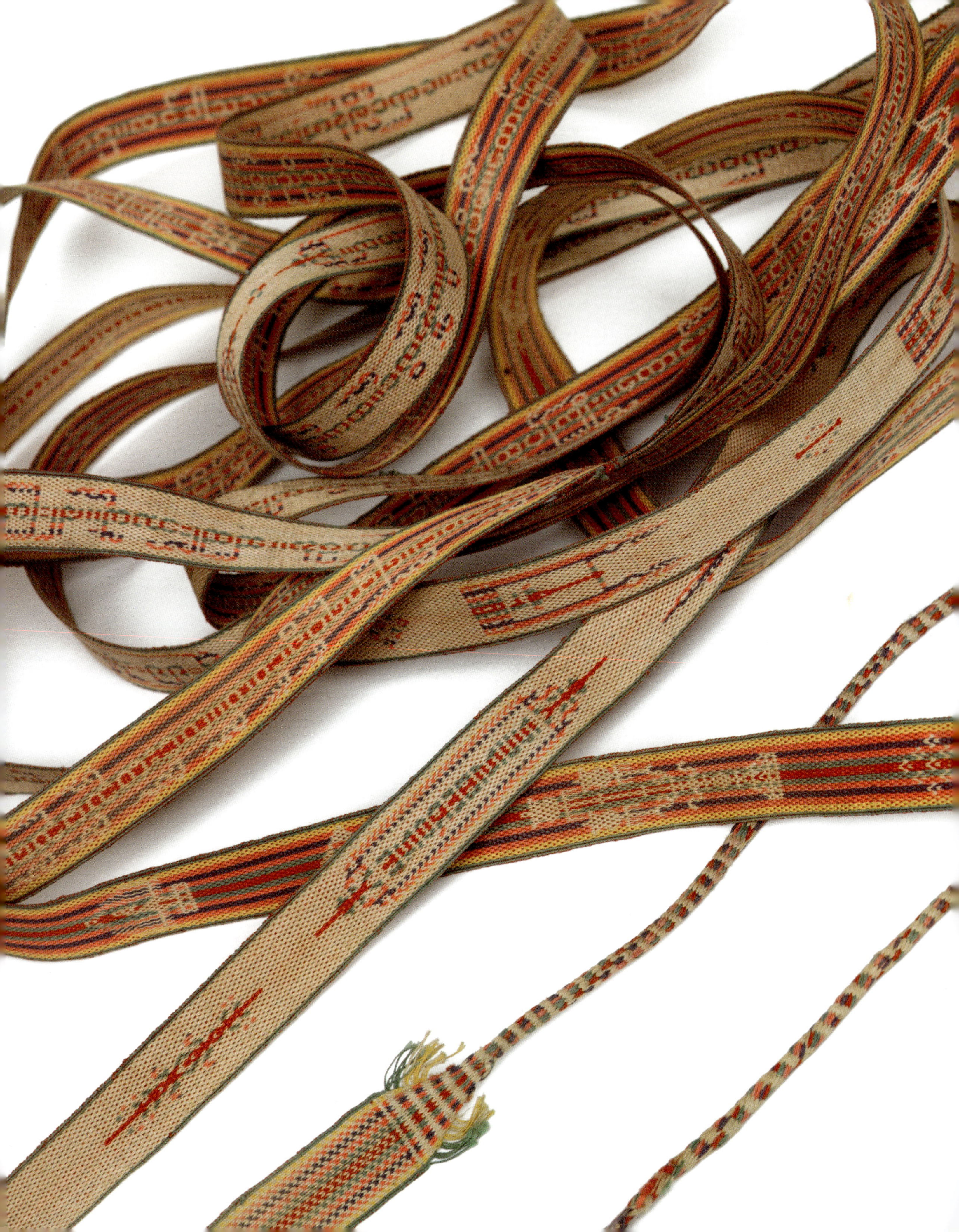

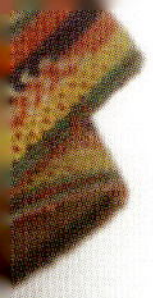

WOVEN MINIATURES OF BUDDHIST ART

sazigyo

BURMESE MANUSCRIPT BINDING TAPES

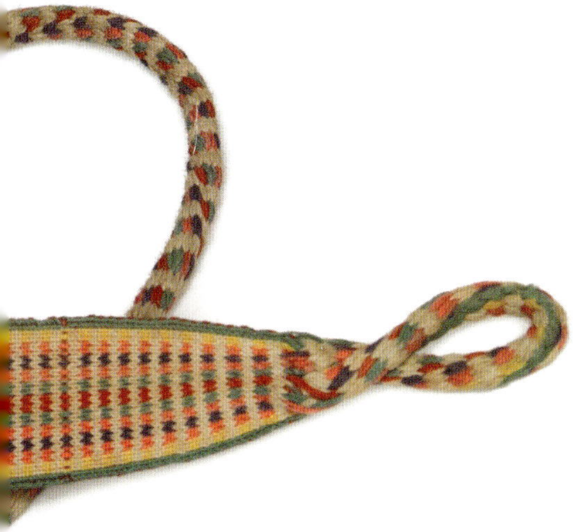

RALPH ISAACS

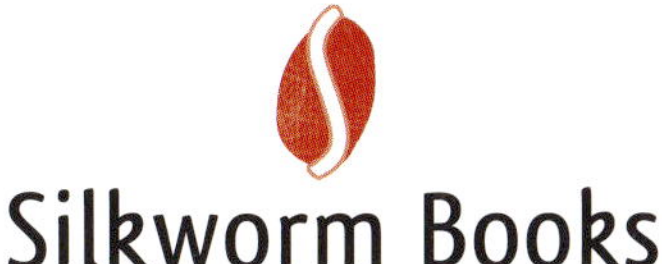

Silkworm Books

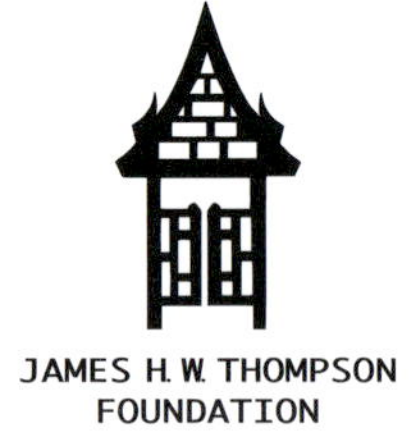

Published with a grant from the James H. W. Thompson Foundation

ISBN: 978-616-215-073-9

Published in 2014 by

Silkworm Books
6 Sukkasem Road, T. Suthep
Chiang Mai 50200 Thailand
info@silkwormbooks.com
http://www.silkwormbooks.com

Cover and book design by Nigel Cunningham
Cover image: a sazigyo from the collection of Neil and Digna Ryan (R106)
The design of the bookmark by Brian Turner Trimmings Ltd. replicates the same sazigyo.
The images of a sazigyo depicted in endpapers and chapter displays are courtesy of the Wellcome Foundation Library (W93).
The photo of Peter Collingwood is by Jason Collingwood.
Typeset in Joanna 11 pt
Printed and bound in China

5 4 3 2 1

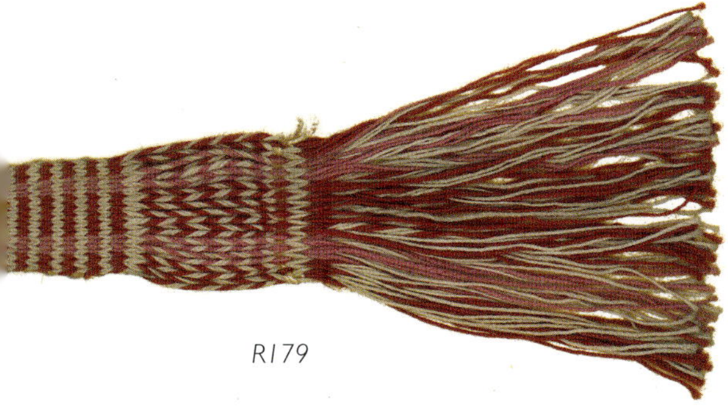

R179

R001

See appendix 6 for a list of all sazigyo illustrated in this book.

Contents

Preface

This book aims to introduce art lovers and textile enthusiasts to a little-known but fascinating textile art form. Sazigyo are Burmese bands for binding palm-leaf manuscripts. Tablet-woven in silk or cotton, they are up to six meters long but only about two centimeters wide. The sazigyo starts with a loop and ends with a cord, which together form a tie when the tape is wound around the palm-leaf manuscript in its cloth sleeve. The flat area between loop and cord carries a woven text, which names the donors who aspire to gain merit by donating the manuscript to a monastery, and this text is often interspersed with miniature images.

You do not have to be a weaver or a textile expert to appreciate these wonderful weaves. Their bright colors, long lines of rounded script, and miniature woven pictures of birds, beasts, and fish are immediately appealing. Then attraction turns to curiosity, and you begin to wonder who made these tapes, and how, and when. What were they used for? Why are there all the little woven pictures? What does the text mean? This book will offer answers. It will interest weavers, of course, and lovers of textile design; it will also appeal to admirers of supreme craftsmanship, and to art lovers aware that small can be beautiful. The sheer creative exuberance of these Burmese women weavers comes across vividly: always imaginative and occasionally quirky and witty. Several of these women artists of over a century ago signed their weaves. Some even inserted into the text they wove verses in praise of their art and skill.

The craft of weaving lettered bands flourished in Burma for a couple of centuries but never recovered from the impact of the printed book, and by the late 1970s sazigyo weaving had died out. This book is a tribute to weavers of genius and a posthumous celebration of a craft now extinct.

The book owes its inception and its main purpose to the late Peter Collingwood, master weaver and author of the standard works on the techniques of handloom weaving. His technical analysis of the sazigyo collected by the author in Burma in the early 1990s and gifted to the James Green Centre for World Art at the Brighton Museum forms part of this book. A great weaver with a maker's eye, Peter understood, admired, and analyzed the work of the world's most skillful craftsmen, but the finest sazigyo left him "gasping with admiration! They are terrific . . . so fine and beautifully woven, and so imaginative. You really must do a book devoted to them. These images should be made known. They are the work of real experts who deserve some posthumous fame."

This then is the book Peter inspired and urged me to write. Any merit it may possess is shared with him and with the Burmese sazigyo weavers. All its shortcomings and errors are mine alone. A book about sazigyo is a risky undertaking. Great length, extreme narrowness, and a tendency to get tangled—all natural in sazigyo—are fatal flaws in a book. The reader will judge how far I have side-stepped the snares.

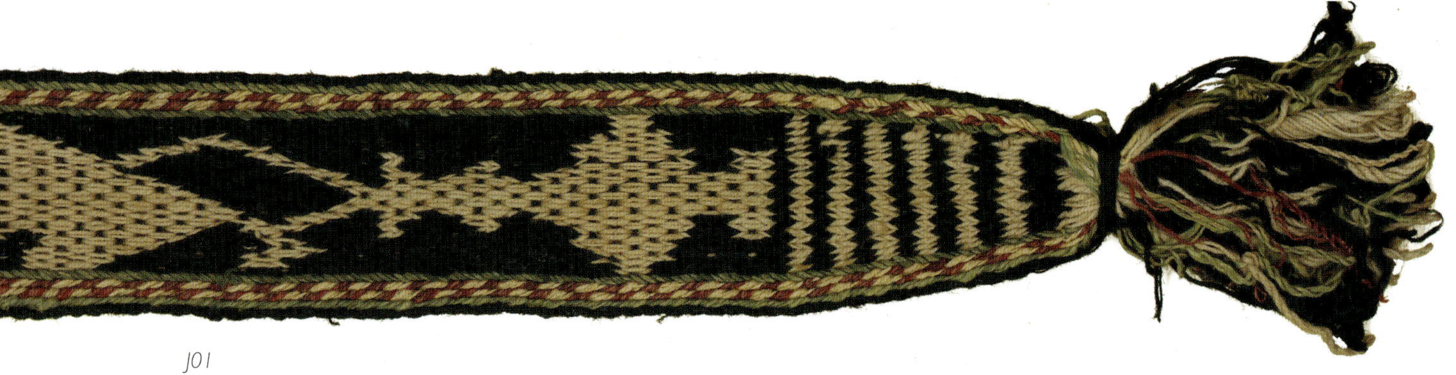

J01

Acknowledgments

Work on this book began more than a decade ago, and two people responsible more than any others for its ever being started did not live to see it appear. Shwebo Mi Mi Gyi wrote the first book on sazigyo in Burmese and encouraged my early interest. Peter Collingwood showed me the technical and artistic merit of the sazigyo weavers and urged me to put their artistry on record. I owe an enormous debt to both of them.

I have drawn copiously on eyewitness accounts of Burmese life, folk beliefs, customs, and ceremonies by observers such as Sir J. G. Scott (Shway Yoe), Max and Bertha Ferrars, Maung Htin Aung, Daw Khin Myo Chit, and Daw Mi Mi Khaing. I have relied on popular paperback accounts of Buddhism, including those by Walpola Rahula and Richard Gombrich. Readers who wish to read further about the teachings of Buddhism and the spread of the religion in Southeast Asia will find some useful works listed in the bibliography.

I should like to record my thanks to all those who have given me help and support. Dr. Elizabeth Dell, former director of the Green Centre for World Art at the Brighton Museum & Art Gallery, commissioned Peter Collingwood's technical analysis of every sazigyo in the Brighton collection, here published for the first time with the museum's permission. She also arranged for the translation of some of the woven texts, and started me writing by inviting me to contribute a section on sazigyo to the book she co-edited, *Textiles from Burma*.[1] Helen Mears, the present director of the Green Centre, has been constantly helpful, especially in providing facilities for the scanning of hundreds of sazigyo. I wish to thank the trustees of the James Henry Green Foundation as well as the James H. W. Thompson Foundation for their very generous support. Otfried Staudigel, expert tablet weaver and author of pattern books for tablet weavers, noticed tiny but significant details in the miniature pictorial images and patiently pointed them out to me. Jennie Parry checked part 5 of the text from a weaver's standpoint. Dr. Uta Weigelt traced photos by Christine Scherman in the Munich Ethnological Museum.

Neil and Digna Ryan gave me unlimited access to their large collection, its catalogue, and database. I cannot thank them sufficiently for this unique contribution. Most of the images of sazigyo in this book, including the cover and the woven bookmark, are of tapes in the Ryan collection, and many of the other illustrations are their photographs of Burmese scenes.

I wish to record my deep gratitude to the family of the late Peter Collingwood.

Museum and library staff gave their time generously in the British Library, British Museum, Crafts Council, Horniman Museum, New Walk Museum, Leicester, Munich Ethnological Museum, Royal Asiatic Society, Royal Geographical Society, and Wellcome Foundation Library.

The verses composed by weavers in praise of their art that introduce the major sections of this book are taken from the late Shwebo Mi Mi Gyi's

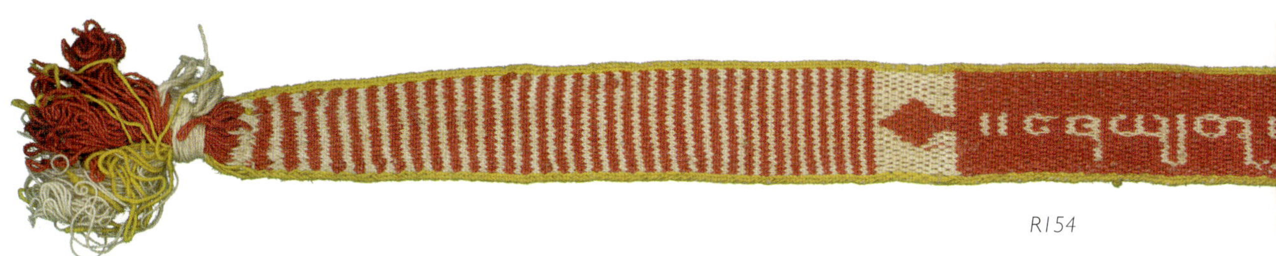

R154

1993 book in Burmese, *Collected Texts of Manuscript Binding Tapes*. Her son Dr. Ye Myint helped me translate these verses, and also translated numerous extracts from sazigyo texts in his late mother's anthology.

Vanessa Chan shared much information about the craft and its practitioners, and made freely available the translations she commissioned of Shwebo Mi Mi Gyi's book and of many sazigyo texts in her own collection. Donald Stadtner sought out images of Burmese art, life, and religious practice.

I am grateful to many sazigyo collectors who lent me weaves for study and permitted me to scan them: Herbert Haar III and Dr. Sathirakorn Pongpanich, Mrs. Kathleen Johnson, John Lafortune and Laurie De Groot, Ni Wayan Murni of Ubud Bali, James and Carrie Barker of Santa Fe, New Mexico, Mrs. Jenny Spancake, Sue and David Richardson, Mrs. Pam Gordon, Jill Morley Smith, and Deborah Deacon. The Wellcome Foundation Library kindly provided photographs of a fine silk sazigyo (W93) that appear as endpapers and decorative dividers between the parts of this book. Illustrated on the book cover is a fine sazigyo from the Ryan collection (R106) whose braids had lost their binding and were expertly rebraided by Jennie Parry. Brian Turner of Brian Turner Trimmings Ltd. gave generously of his expertise to produce the woven bookmark, which replicates the same sazigyo (R106).

Several scholars contributed translations into English of sazigyo texts. I offer thanks to the Ven. Dr. Khammai Dhammasami, director of the Oxford Buddhist Vihara, who translated many sazigyo in the Brighton collection into English, and to other translators, including John Okell, Jotika Khur-Yearn, U Kyaw Zan Tha, Dr. Ye Myint, U Toh, Dr. Sai Tin Maung, Saya Soe Kyaw Thu, Ms. Jacqueline Filliozat, Vanessa Chan, and Noel Singer.

Patricia Herbert read an early draft, pointing out the more glaring errors. John Randall offered useful suggestions. John Okell suggested many improvements, correcting many inaccuracies in the translation of Burmese expressions and in the romanization of Burmese words. All remaining errors are my own.

Prefaces often declare how fortunate the author feels to have had this editor, or that book designer. Having chosen both myself, I have both luck and my own judgment to thank.

My debt to book designer Nigel Cunningham is huge. Readers will readily appreciate the results of his technical knowledge and sense of beauty, but can only guess at the closeness of the working relationship between author and designer. Nigel's patience with the esoteric subject matter and sometimes impatient author was endless.

Nina Shandloff's fund of experience with authors of the British Museum Press was quite invaluable in keeping this book consistent, stylish, straight, taut, untangled—like a good sazigyo. Lisa Keary brought her flair and energy to the vital task of seeing the book text through its final stages

My heartfelt thanks to my wife Ruth, who from the inception of this book to its completion a decade later, has constantly comforted, supported, and encouraged a sometimes snarling author and tolerated sazigyo creeping snake-like out of my study and infiltrating other rooms.

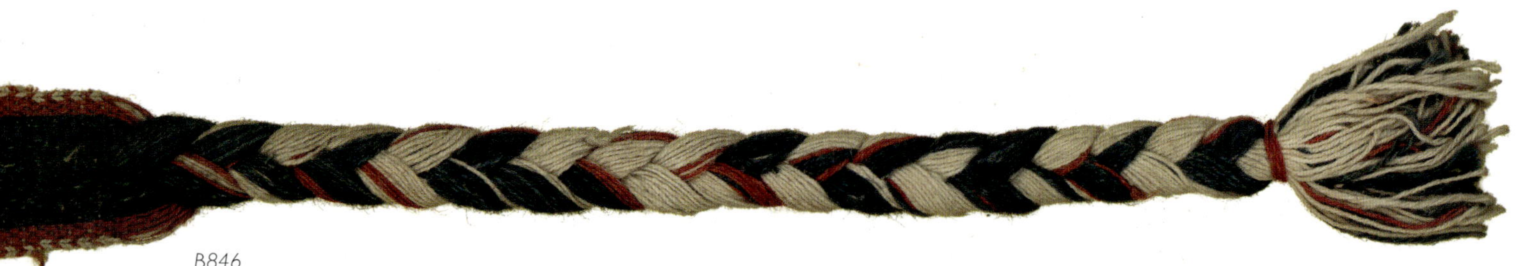

B846

Note on the Illustrations

The illustrations of sazigyo, which form a large part of the attraction of this book and its value as a resource for further study, are the product of the skill and patience of Rob Cunningham. It took over a year to scan hundreds of sazigyo on a high-resolution flatbed scanner and to convert these raw scans to more than a thousand "book-ready" images. These are reproduced at actual size to enable readers to appreciate the weavers' accuracy and skill. There are two exceptions, one technical, one artistic: a few images have been blown up to illustrate points of weaving technique, and others have been enlarged as decorative details, including the woven beasts employed as illuminated capitals in the style of medieval manuscripts. Where an image of a sazigyo is twice natural size, "x2" is added to its reference number.

Images of sazigyo are juxtaposed with other illustrations, such as folios from Burmese painted manuscripts and photographs of scenes and ceremonies. The text and captions accompanying these illustrations place the images and the woven texts in the social and religious context of Burmese life and beliefs.

The book is not aimed primarily at the specialist academic, but the author hopes the illustrations will be a stimulus for further study. To help researchers locate sazigyo and obtain access to them, every sazigyo illustrated in the plates or mentioned or quoted in the text has its individual reference number. Appendix 6 lists all the sazigyo and gives the museum acquisition number in public collections or catalogue number in private collections, the dimensions of the weave, and the date when it was woven. Analogous information for the "non-sazigyo" illustrations is provided in a separate list of illustrations, which gives source references, bibliographical details, accession numbers of museum objects, photographic credits, and acknowledgments. Appendix 7 lists some areas of further research that might usefully draw on the text and illustrations of this book.

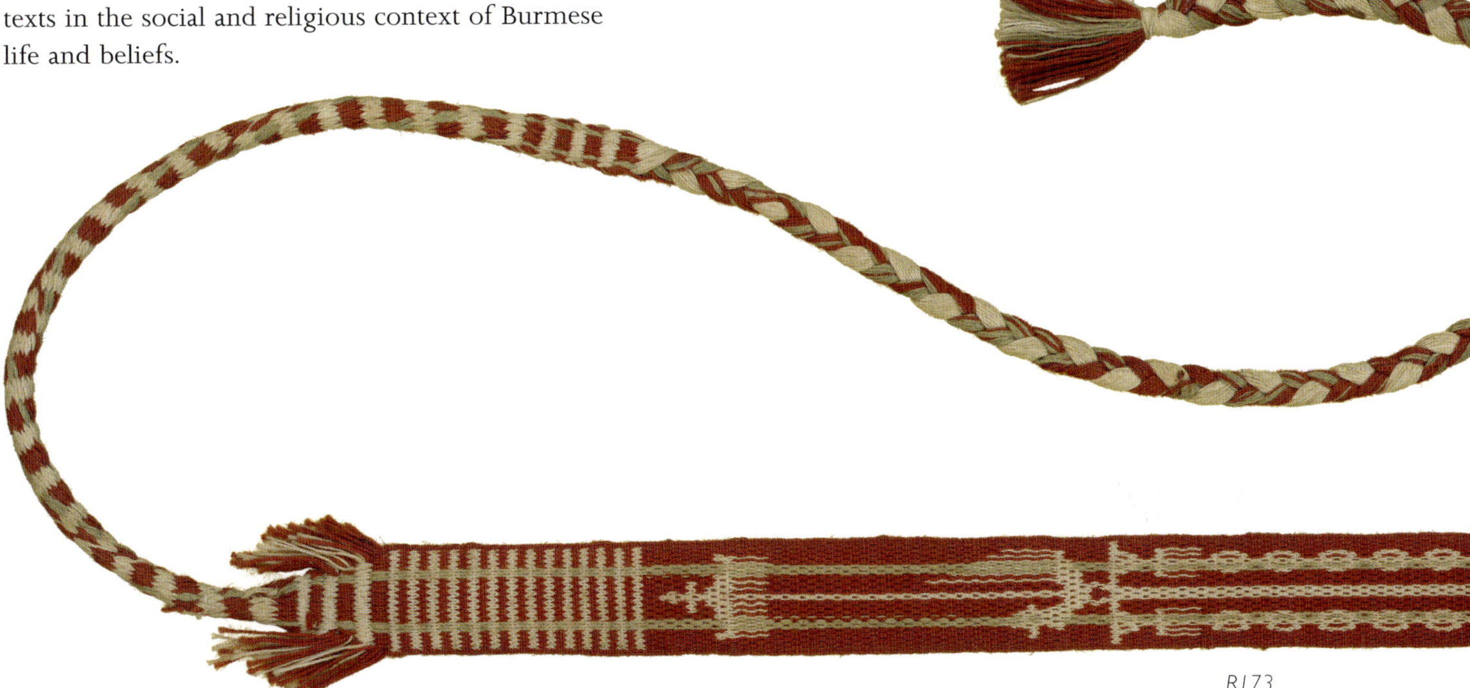

R173

First we prepare red yarn and white,
Ten skeins in a bundle
We fix them firmly on the post of the loom,
Gather them evenly, stretch them out straight.
We weaving women of North Mandalay
Work delicate bands, fit for the palace.
Turning the tablets in varying groups
That is our art of weaving verses.

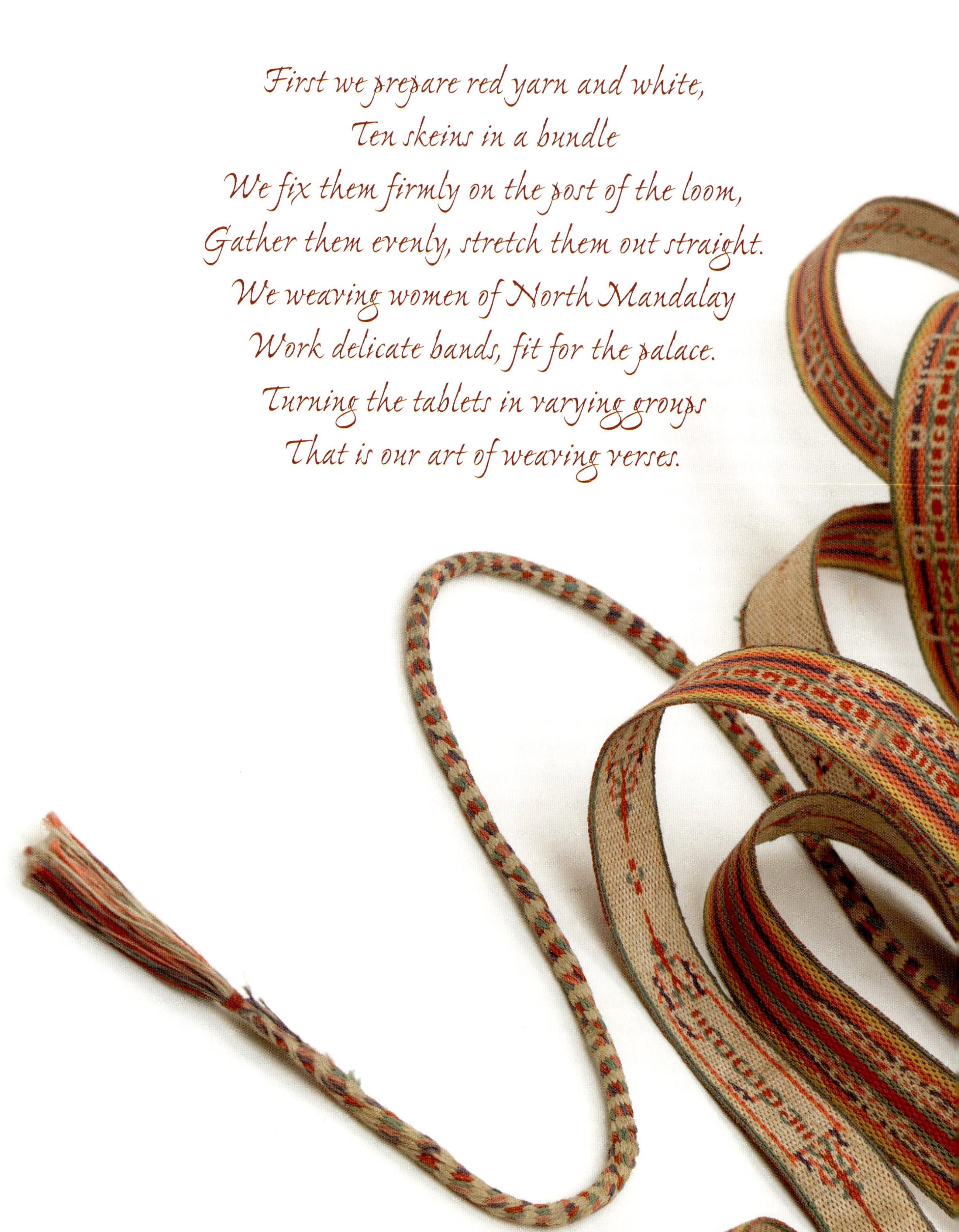

Part I
THE SAZIGYO IN CONTEXT

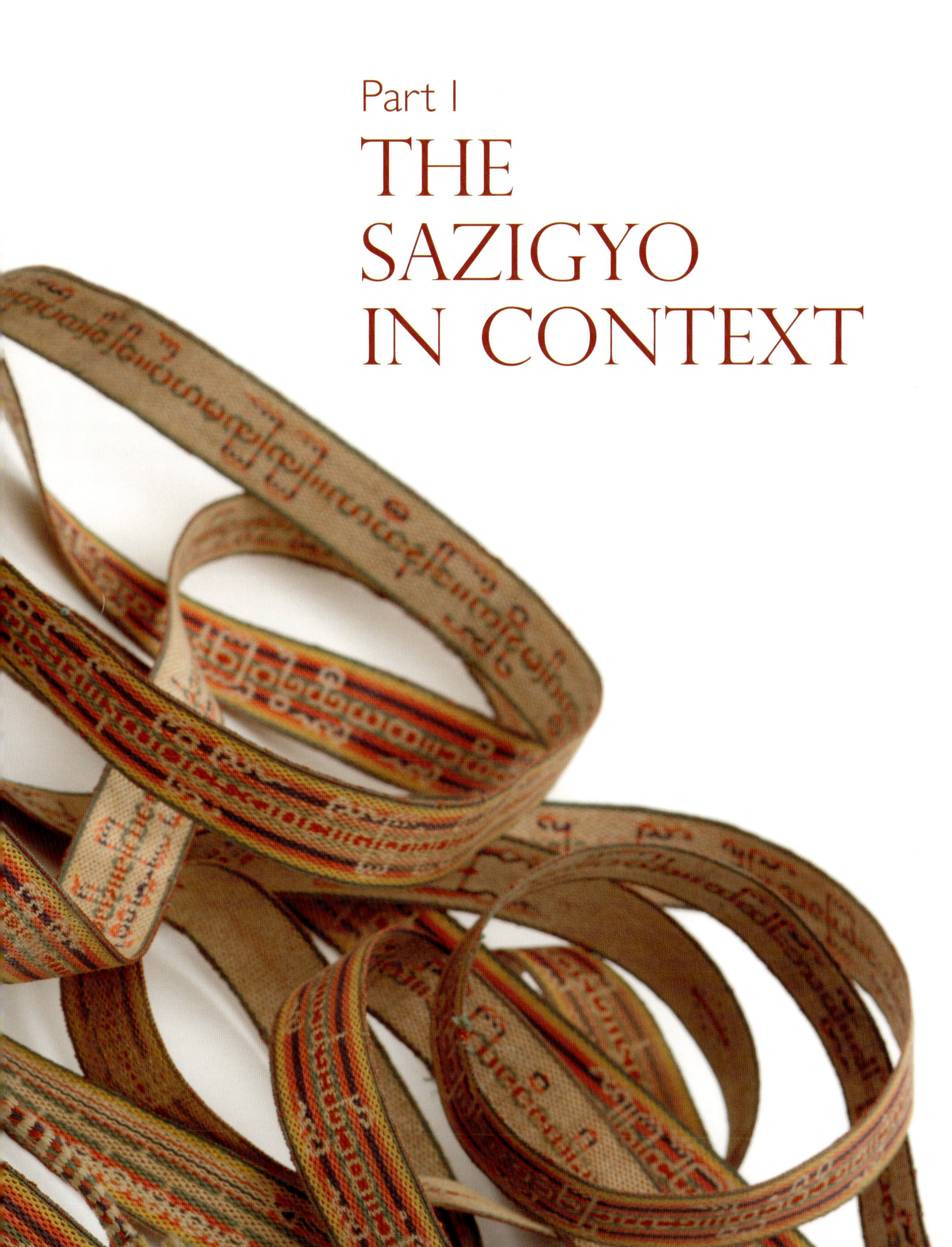

Part I Chapter I

Snared by Sazigyo on the Shwedagon Steps

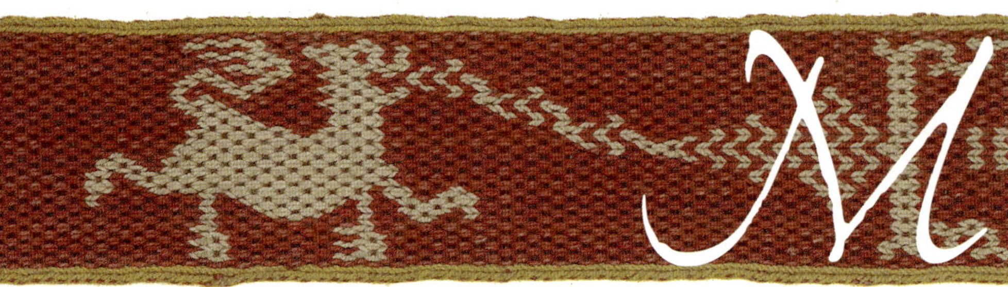

R024

Midway up the approach steps of the Shwedagon pagoda in Rangoon in 1991, my fascination with sazigyo began. I peered into an old plastic bag hanging on a nail outside a curio stall and saw a tangle of dirty cotton tapes, mixed with lumps of termite earth and candle grease. I had no idea what these textiles could be, but glimpsing woven script and little images of birds and beasts, I bought the lot.

Burmese friends identified the tapes as sazigyo, manuscript binding tapes. Cleaning, sorting, and photographing them took many months of mixed puzzlement and delight. Insects and mold must have invaded the lacquered teak manuscript chests in some derelict monastery and attacked the flimsy palm-leaf manuscripts, reducing them to dust but leaving more or less intact their tough woven cotton binding tapes.

The term sazigyo is made up of three Burmese words: *sa*, anything written; *si* or *zi*, to tie into bundles; and *gyo*, a rope or cord. Sometimes they are called *sa-htok-gyo*, which means exactly the same: a cord or tape for tying manuscript leaves into bundles. The sazigyo starts with a loop and ends in a cord, to fit it for its function as a tie. The long flat area between loop and cord may be "textless"—quite plain or very simply patterned. But almost all the tapes I bought on the Shwedagon steps were "lettered bands," with stretches of woven text interspersed with miniature images. The closer I looked at these, the more I felt challenged to decipher them. With help from books and Burmese informants I learned to read bits of the texts, to pick out the names of the donors and the dates of their donations. Gradually my understanding grew of the Buddhist social and religious context in which these weaves were commissioned, woven, donated, and used.

Each manuscript that the donor commissioned from the scribe was provided with its own sazigyo, woven by a specialist weaver. The long area of flat tape between loop and cord was woven with the text of a prayer composed for the donor, and with appropriate geometric and pictorial motifs. So the sazigyo had two functions: as textile, it bound the manuscript securely in its cloth bag, and as text, it recorded the donor's deed of merit. This dual role, as textile and text, cord and record, gives the sazigyo a complex appeal and makes it such an intriguing artifact and rewarding subject of study.

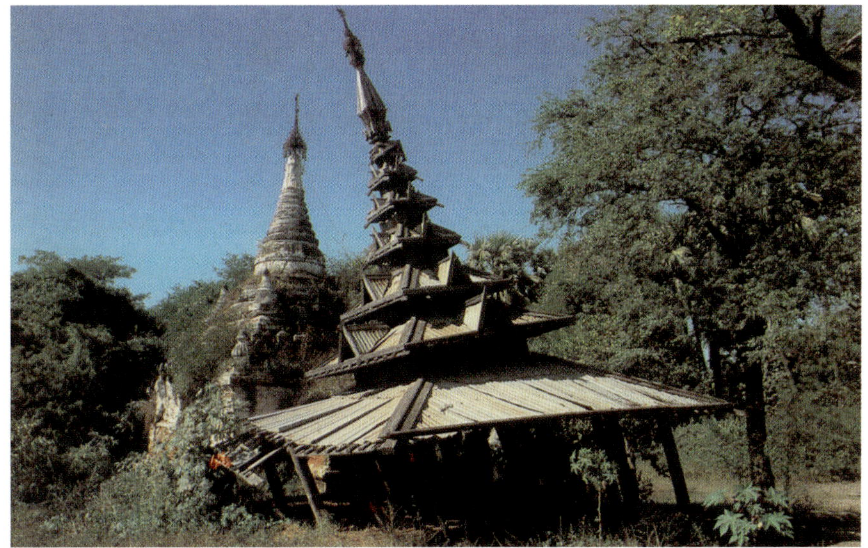

Plate 1 RIGHT
Nothing is permanent. Monasteries decay, and insects and mold invade the lacquered teak *sadaik* manuscript chests to reduce the flimsy palm-leaf manuscripts to dust. But their tough woven cotton binding tapes may be left more or less intact.

Sazigyo are textiles, many of them remarkably neatly woven, colorful, and decorative. But they are also texts, crying out to be read—and I can never resist trying to decipher an inscription. Success may not make the inscribed object any more beautiful, but it means more to me, and goes up in my estimation. The beauty of a well-crafted object lies partly in its design, its fitness for purpose, and partly in its power to convey something of the way of life of the men and women who made and used it. Far from being lifeless, some inanimate objects seem to retain and exude the creative energy of the craftsmen who made them and even the beliefs and affections of the people who handled and cherished them. This signal is greatly amplified when an object carries inscriptions added by the maker or owner. When it was made and first changed hands, an inscribed object formed a message between members of a group with a common language and culture. Inscriptions, properly interpreted, enable us to tap into this dialogue and to learn directly from real people about the beliefs and values they shared in a distinct culture separated from ours in space and time.

Sazigyo are much more than a length of narrow cotton tape: their woven messages and pictorial symbols carry a wealth of information about Burmese Buddhist beliefs and practice, and about the life and aspirations of the Burmese people who made and valued them. The novelist Hilary Mantel describes the "shock of the past," the thrill of realizing that people of the past "were as alive as I am." Her task as an historical novelist is "to unfreeze antique feeling, unlock the emotion stored and packed tight in paper, brick and stone."[1] Tablet-woven cotton sazigyo, once unwound and their tightly woven messages decoded, also have something of human value to reveal, to earn them respect in the ranks of ordinary objects. The reader will surely grant the sazigyo promotion to that higher order, dignified by T. S. Eliot: "Even the humblest material artefact, which is the product and symbol of a particular civilisation, is an emissary of the culture out of which it comes."[2]

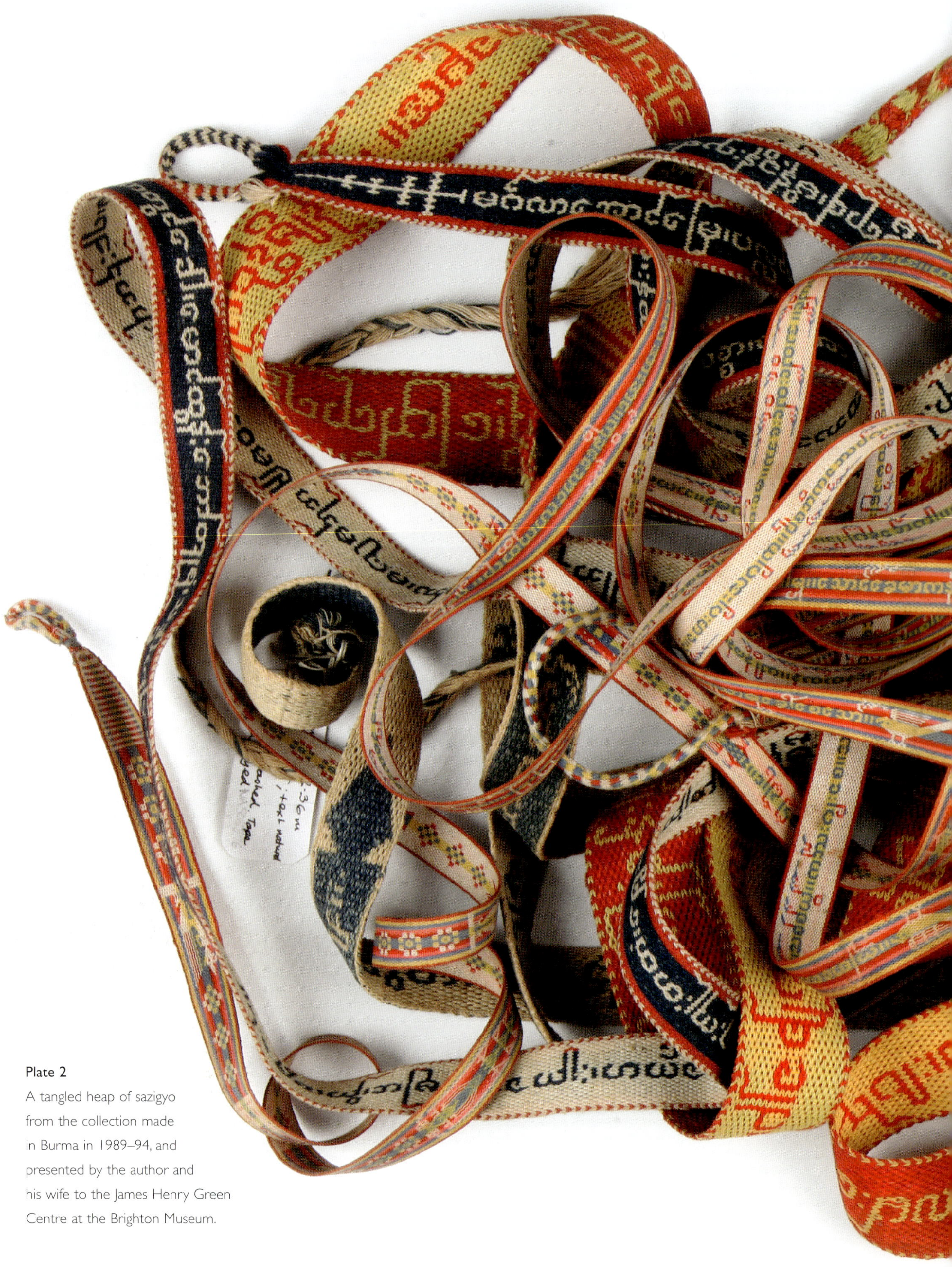

Plate 2

A tangled heap of sazigyo from the collection made in Burma in 1989–94, and presented by the author and his wife to the James Henry Green Centre at the Brighton Museum.

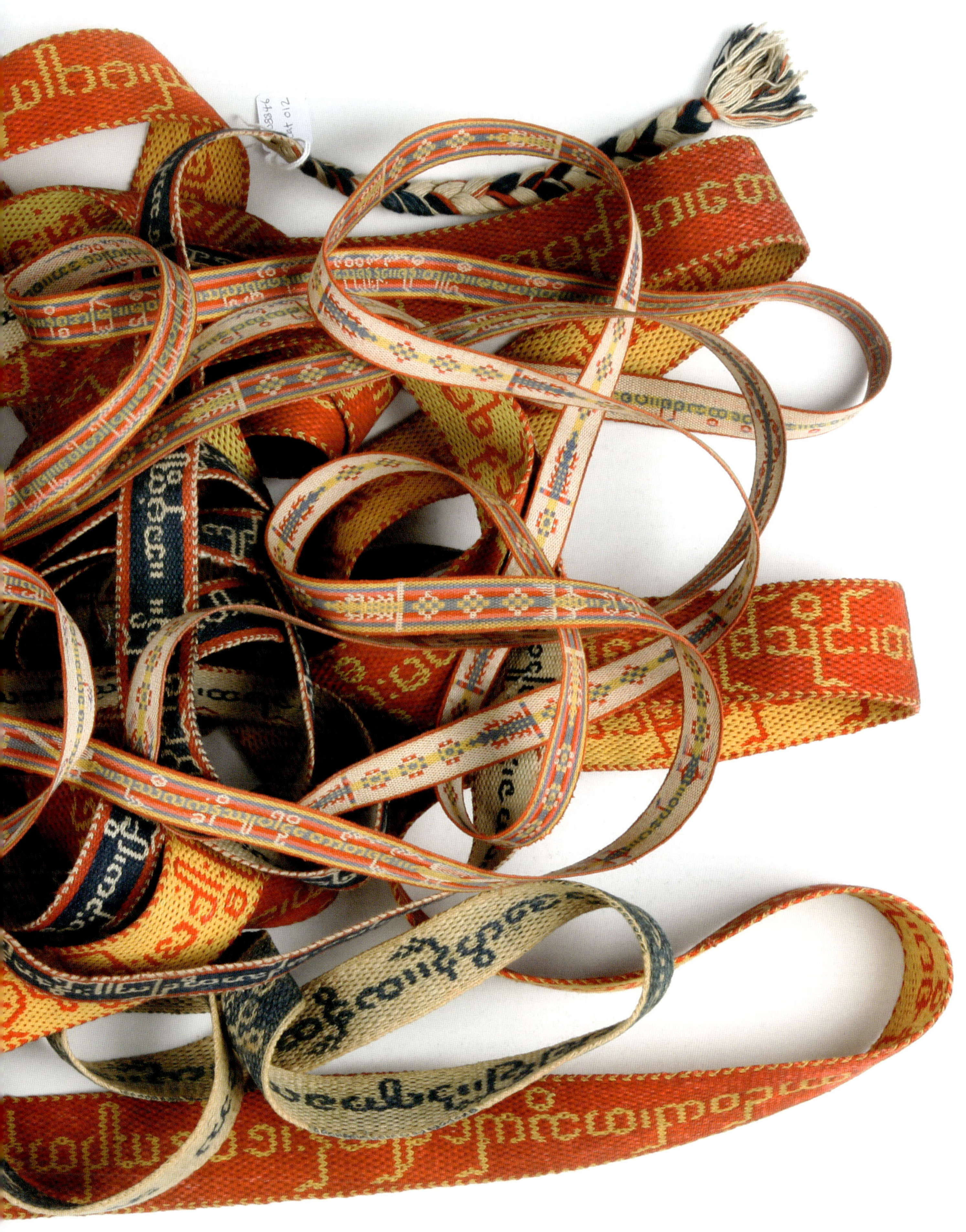

Part I Chapter 2

Buddhism, Monks, and Monasteries in Burma

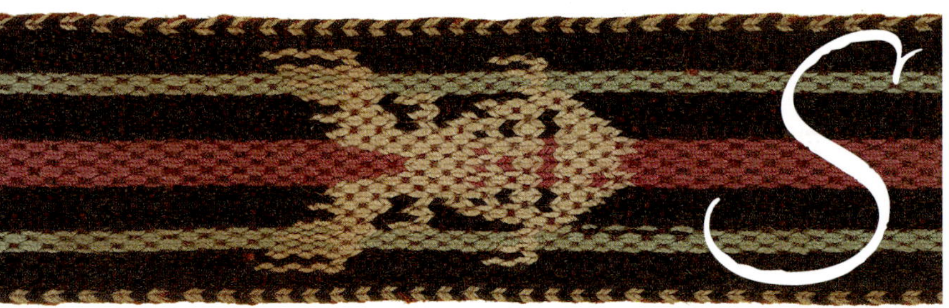
R246

Some understanding of Theravada Buddhism is needed to appreciate the meaning and purpose of the sazigyo's woven texts, which were commissioned and produced by devout Burmese Buddhists in a particular social and religious context. To ease the way of the reader who may be unacquainted with Buddhism I have provided this brief introduction, inevitably oversimplified.

The religion and philosophy of Buddhism was founded by a historical figure who probably lived in the sixth and fifth centuries BCE. (Various incidents from his life story are illustrated here by folios from a fine painted book [*parabaik*].) The man who was to become the Buddha was born into a princely family in northern India in 563 BCE. His family name was Gotama, and his personal name was Siddhattha. Brought up in sheltered luxury, he saw on an outing from the palace the "Four Signs": an aged man, a sick man, a dead man, and a mendicant (plate 3). Realizing that nothing could protect him from life's harsh realities, he left his wife and baby son asleep and stole out of the palace. He made for the forest, where he cut off his hair, exchanged his rich garments for a yellow robe, and became a wandering ascetic mendicant.

Various teachers all left him unsatisfied, and he resolved to seek himself the answer to his questions about the nature of life. Seated beneath a peepul tree in deep and prolonged meditation, he overcame all the distractions of the senses, realized in physical form by the terrifying army of the demon-king Mara, and attained enlightenment, becoming a Buddha or Awakened One.[3] The peepul tree at Gaya later became known as the Bodhi tree, the tree of enlightenment. (The Bo tree is a frequent motif on sazigyo.) He called on the Earth to witness his enlightenment, and the Earth Goddess Vasundhara responded by wringing out her long wet hair and drowning the hosts of Mara (plate 5). (An image of the Earth Goddess [Burmese: Waythondaye] appears on most sazigyo.)

The fully enlightened Buddha now considered whether or not it would be possible to communicate his spiritual insight to others. He walked to Varanasi and delivered his First Sermon in a deer park at nearby Sarnath (plate 6). (Images of the stag occur on many sazigyo.) In this and in many other discourses he taught the Middle Way, avoiding the two extremes of sensual indulgence and of mortification. The Buddha taught the Four Noble Truths. Suffering is the basic condition of human existence: birth is suffering; growing old is suffering; sickness is suffering; sorrow, pain, grief, and despair are suffering; association with the unpleasant is suffering; dissociation from the pleasant is suffering; not to get what one wants is suffering. Suffering is caused by desire, and desire can be eliminated, and this can be done by leading a life according to certain moral precepts.

Crucially, Buddha accepted the ancient Indian idea of reincarnation and the law of karma. In *samsara*, the endless round of birth, death, and rebirth to which all conditioned beings are subject, actions committed for good or ill during the course of each earthly life affect one's "account balance" at the time of death. This determines future destiny, and the state into which one is reborn—animal or human, poor or rich, male or female. Merit can be made, and lost, by ordinary men. (Thus acts of charity, such as the gift to a monastery of a manuscript with its sazigyo, help the donor to accumulate merit for a favorable rebirth.)

Release from *samsara* comes only through knowledge attained by austere discipline. Practically, only those prepared to abandon all ties, including family ties, and become itinerant monks could follow these moral precepts. The ideal was thus to be a monk, supported by the lay community. The followers of the Buddha quickly elevated three elements to represent the summation of their beliefs: the Buddha himself; the Dhamma, his teaching; and the Sangha, the body of monks who followed his teachings and taught them. These are the Three Gems, or the Triple Gem, which all Buddhists honor. Buddhists begin any ritual or religious ceremony by saying three times that they "take refuge" in the Three Gems. (Numerous motifs on sazigyo represent these Three Gems.)

The Buddha preached "The Noble Eightfold Path, of right view, right thought, right speech, right action, right livelihood, right effort, right mindfulness, and right concentration, which leads to calm, to insight, to enlightenment, to nirvana."[4] Nirvana means "blowing out"—extinguishing the triple fire of greed, hatred, and delusion.

The Buddha taught in many parts of eastern India. His many disciples memorized his sayings, which were only much later written down. When the Buddha died in 483 BCE at the age of eighty, having in his final life accumulated enough merit through his attainment of enlightenment and Buddhahood, he entered the void, nirvana: he had escaped the tyranny of *samsara*.

The Buddha did not leave behind him a fully recognized canon of religious writings. It was only after his death, when his ashes were enshrined in hemispherical solid tumuli or stupas, that a cult of the Buddha slowly developed based on the stupa as a symbol of the nirvana of the Buddha. (Woven images of stupas occur on sazigyo.) These doctrines spread dramatically within India during the reign of the emperor Ashoka (272–232 BCE) and then outside India.

FOLLOWING PAGES

SCENES FROM THE LIFE OF THE BUDDHA

Illustrations from a *parabaik*, a Burmese folding painted book.

Plate 3

Prince Siddhattha, the Buddha-to-be, sees the "Four Signs": a poor old man, a sick man, a dead man, and a mendicant.

Plate 4

The "Great Departure": the Prince, mounted on his horse Kanthaka, leaves the luxurious life of the palace to seek enlightenment as a wandering mendicant.

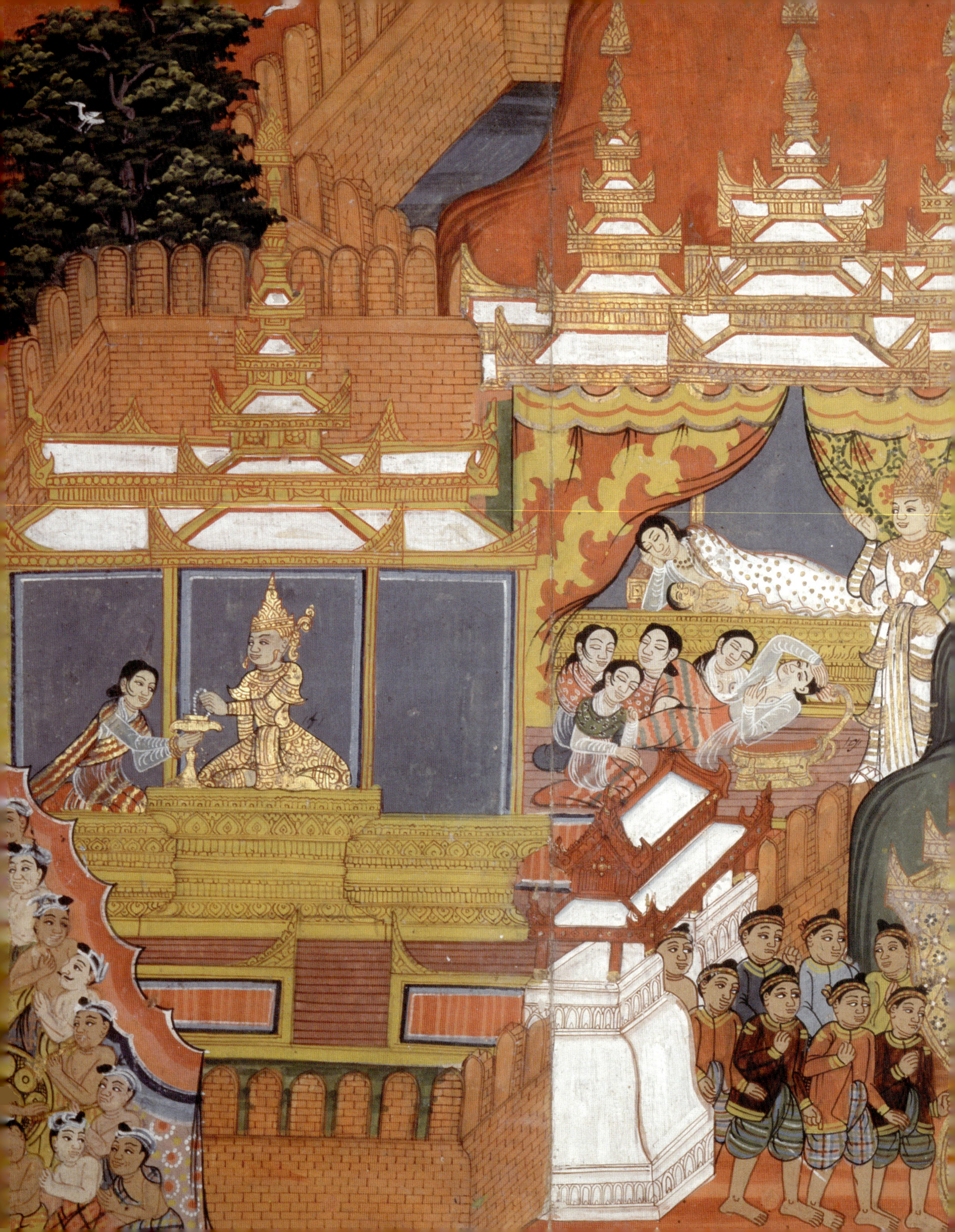

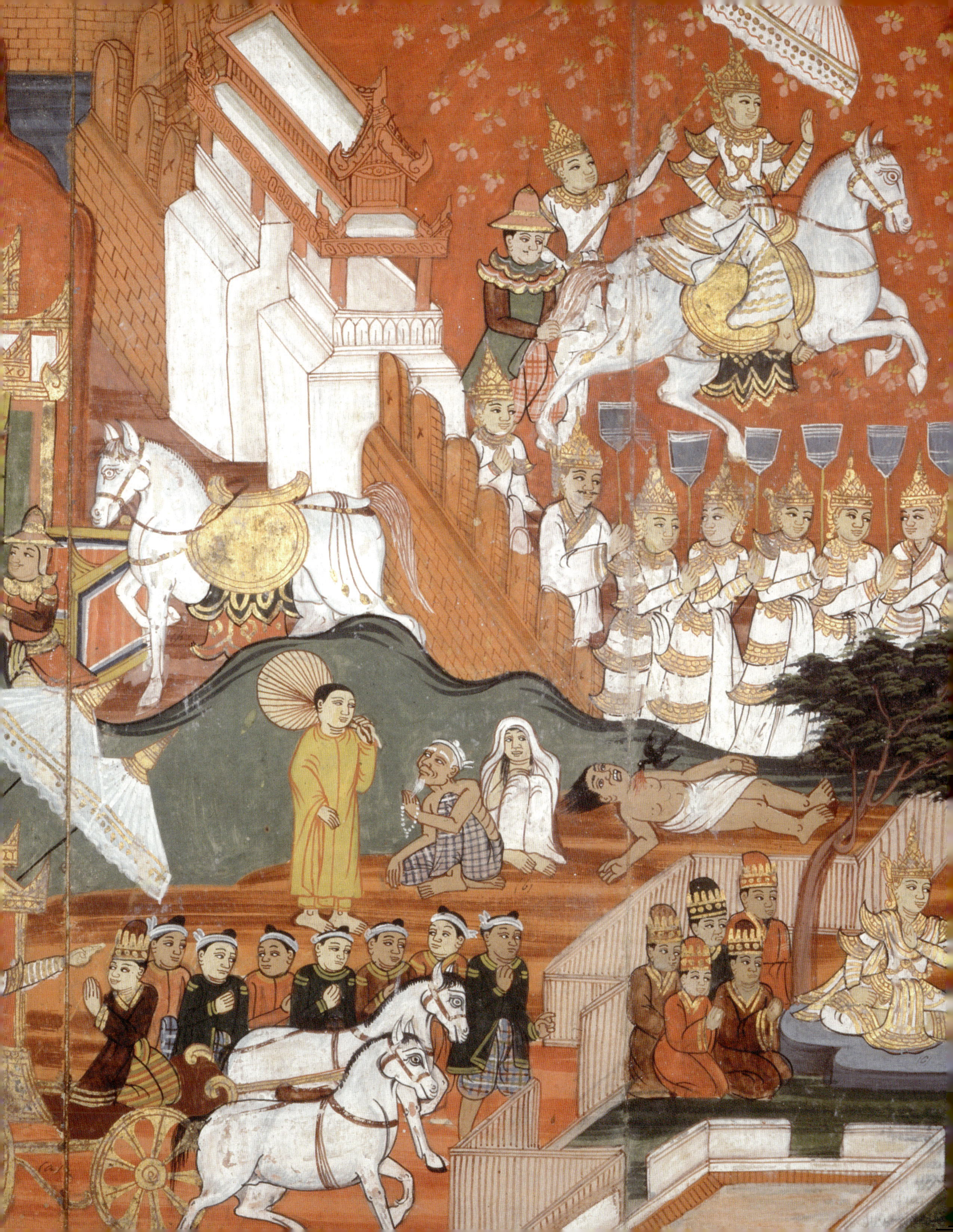

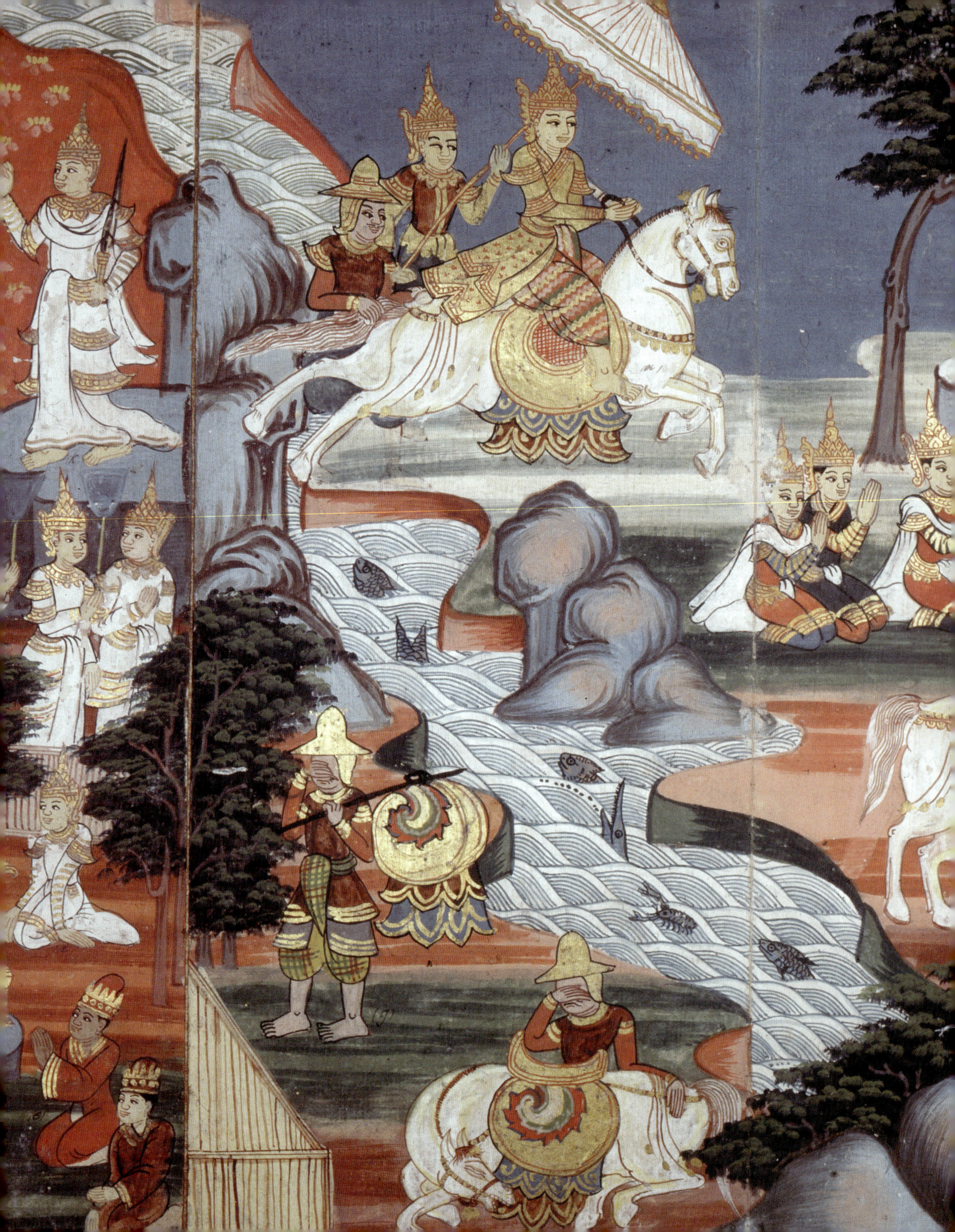

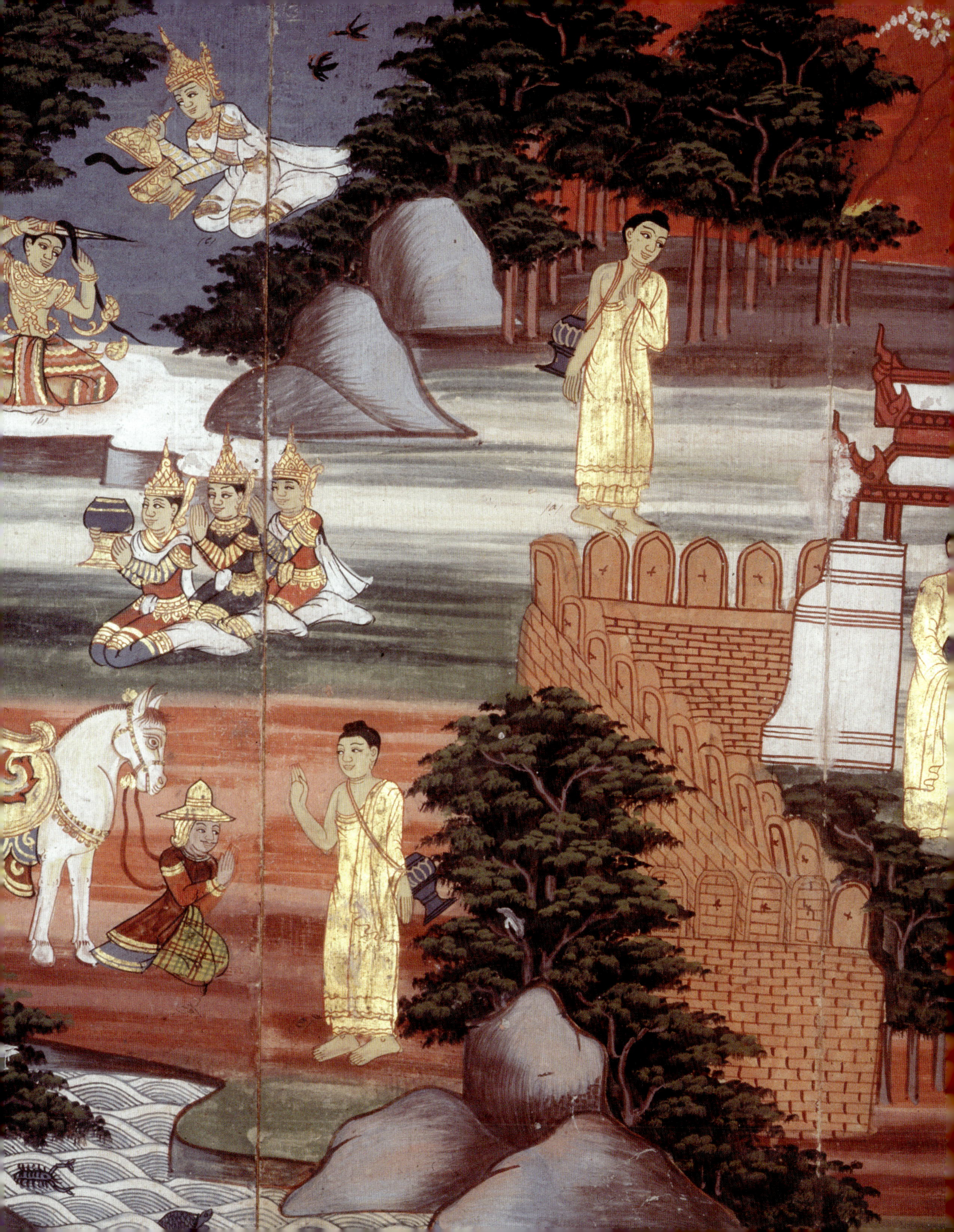

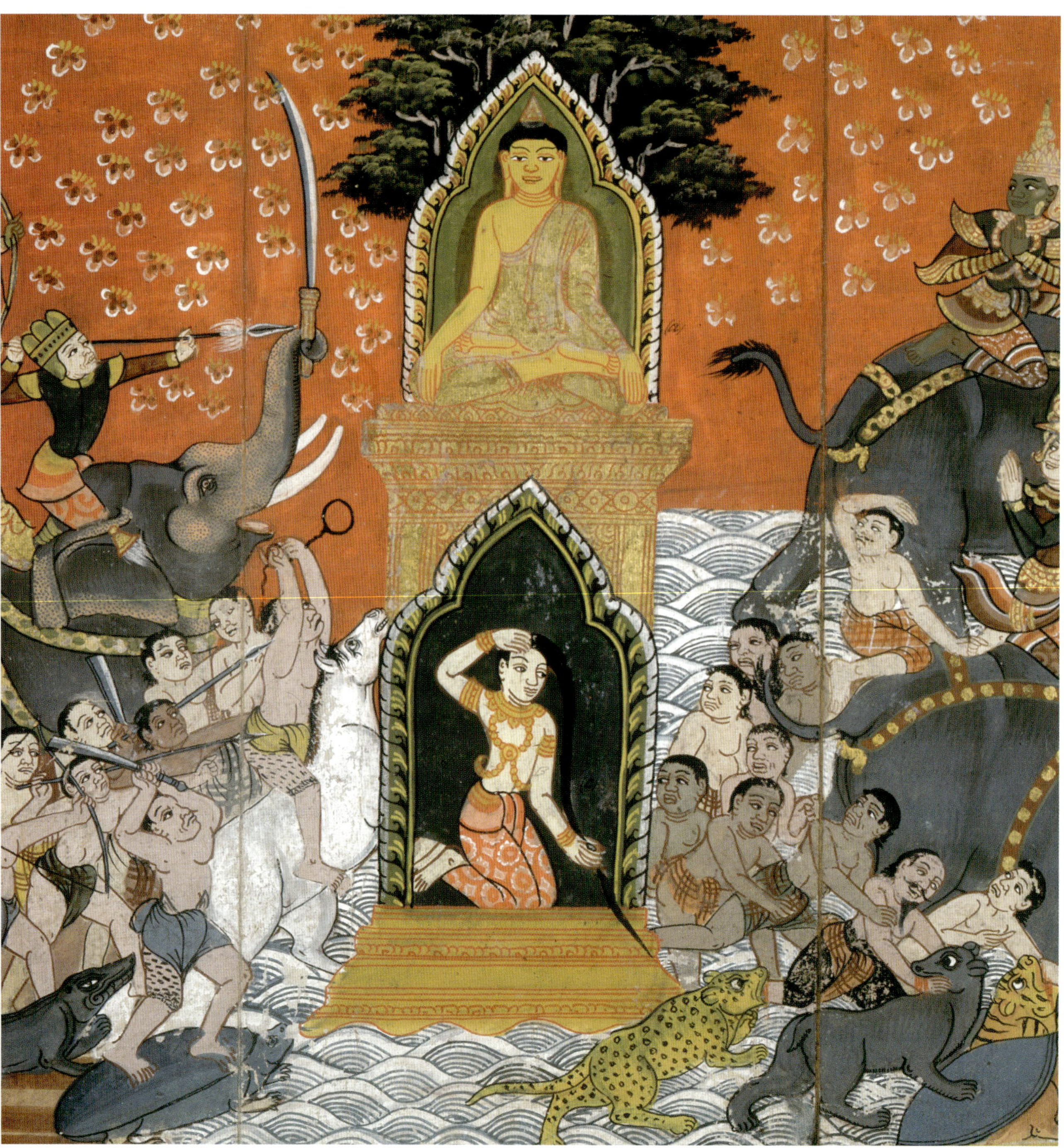

Plate 5 ABOVE
Seated under a fig tree, Prince Siddhattha was assailed by the demon Mara and a vast army of seducers and devils. But he resisted distraction, attained enlightenment, and called upon the earth as witness. The Earth Goddess Vasundhara responded by wringing out her long wet hair, and the hosts of Mara perished in the flood.

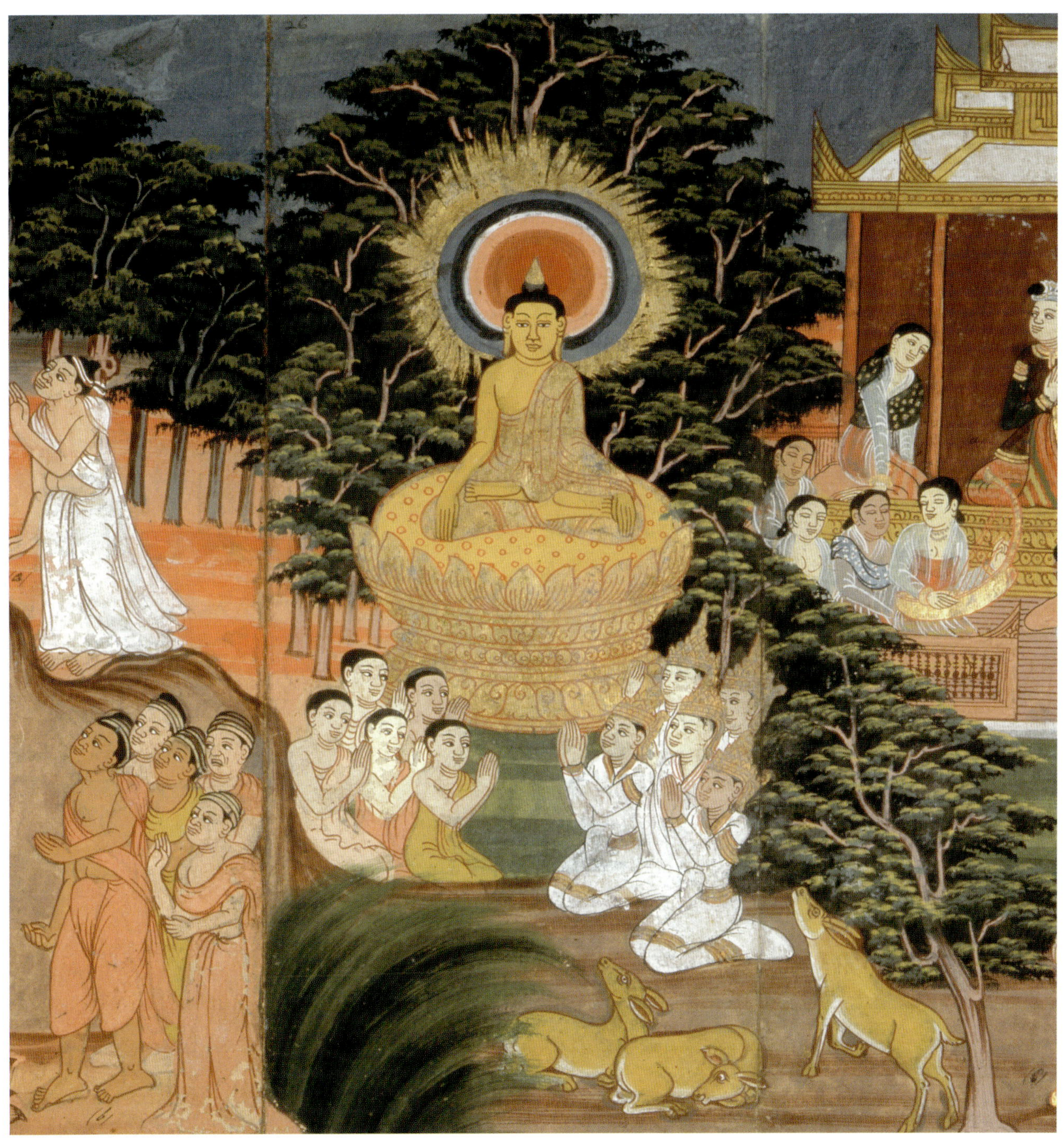

Plate 6 ABOVE
The fully enlightened Buddha preached his First Sermon in a deer park near Varanasi.

Following his death, his previous existences began to be elaborated in a sequence of stories, the Jataka tales. In Burma, especially, these are a rich source of narrative art, for dramatic performances, and for depiction in paintings and sculpture (see plate 20).

Immediately following the Buddha's death a degree of unanimity prevailed among his disciples and their descendants, but in the succeeding centuries divisions developed within the Sangha. Some related to doctrine, some to monastic discipline. About the time of the beginning of the Christian era, two basic branches of Buddhism began to diverge. Buddhism was transformed by the rise of the movement known as the Mahayana, or self-proclaimed "Greater Vehicle" (of salvation). Its adherents used the pejorative term Hinayana, or "Lesser Vehicle," for other schools of Indian Buddhism. Of many Hinayana schools only the Theravada survives, and is practiced in Sri Lanka, Thailand, and Burma today. Theravada means in Sanskrit the "Doctrine of the Elders," the Elders being that group of the Buddha's disciples who immediately following his death convened the First Great Council to recite the Buddha's teachings in order to agree on a definitive version. Theravada Buddhists refer to their religion as the Sasana, the "Teaching" (sazigyo donors often pray: "May the Sasana long endure!").

For the next twenty-five centuries Theravada Buddhism emphasized discipline. Theravada monks submit to 227 rules of conduct that contain precise instructions about all aspects of the religious life. They are required to beg for food, to abstain from eating after midday, and to own no more than eight specified possessions: namely a three-part robe, a loin cloth, a begging bowl, a water filter, a razor, and a needle. Essentially, the code of morality and conduct at the heart of Theravada Buddhism is one for the monastic life and contains little addressed to the layman.

A hallmark of Theravada Buddhism is the use, as its main sacred language, of Pali, an ancient derivative of Sanskrit. By 250 BCE the Buddha's teachings had been arranged into three divisions. The Tipitaka, the "three baskets" or collections of texts. The Vinaya Pitaka, the "basket of discipline," which contains the rules of the Sangha. The Sutta Pitaka, the "basket of discourses," which contains the Buddha's sermons and religious poetry, and is by far the largest "basket." The third division, the Abhidhamma Pitaka, the "basket of higher doctrine," contains detailed psycho-philosophical analysis of the Dhamma. When the term "Tipitaka" occurs in sazigyo texts it is usually a respectful title for any scriptural manuscript. Only rarely does it mean that the donor has donated the whole Tipitaka, which would take many months to copy: it is a dozen times longer than the Christian Bible.

Traditions and sparse archaeological evidence suggest that Buddhism arrived in Burma from southern India as early as the fifth century CE. Archaeological finds from the Pyu city of Sri Ksetra near modern Prome (now called Pyay) in central Burma include the Maunggun gold plates, which date from the fifth century CE. Shaped like folios from a palm-leaf book, they record the Buddhist creed. The language is Pali and the script is closely related to a south Indian one.

Burma is a Buddhist country, but the complex Burmese belief system embraces an almost infinite range of pre-Buddhist deities, astrological forces, and magical powers. Alongside Buddhism is a cult of the Nats, whose presence is assumed everywhere in Burma. That great interpreter of Burmese customs Daw Khin Myo Chit warns: "It is almost incomprehensible to foreigners that animism and Buddhism should exist side by side in Burmese society and in the Burmese personality. For an ordinary Burmese Buddhist it is natural to believe in the existence of Nats and to give offerings to them if he wishes."[5] These are often local spirits of the place—the house, tree, hill, or pool—who are invoked for protection or propitiated with offerings. Some are associated with historical events, often violent. Some have their own wild *pwe*, or ceremonial performances, where alcohol flows and license prevails. When the great King Anawrahta of Pagan united the whole of Burma into a single kingdom in the eleventh century CE and made Theravada Buddhism the national religion, he was obliged to recognize the existing cult of the Thirty-Six Lords. He skillfully added the guardian god of Buddhism, whose name was Sakra in Pali and Thagya in Burmese, to the list, thus making it the cult of the "Thirty-Seven Lords." To this day Thagya Min, "King of the Nats," is invoked at every Burmese Buddhist ceremony, and his woven image often appears on sazigyo.

THE MONKS

In Theravada Buddhist countries the community of monks, the Sangha, forms the basis of religious life. Almost every Burmese boy becomes a novice monk, if only for a few days. His novitiate is celebrated whenever the parents or better-off relatives can afford it. This, the *shinbyu* ceremony, is a hugely important family event, and the occasion for donations by wealthy parents. The whole performance is modeled on the life of the Buddha, who as Prince Siddhattha renounced the life of luxury and rode out of the royal palace on his horse Kanthaka to become a shaven-headed mendicant. Once the novice would have been about nine years old, but nowadays the boy or youth can be anything from five to his late teens. Dressed in princely finery glittering with tinsel, crowned, mounted on horses, and shaded by white umbrellas, the boys ride to the pagoda. Here prayers are said and the procession then proceeds to the monastery, where each boy has his head shaved and exchanges his golden costume for the saffron robes of monkhood.

Most young novices stay only a few days or weeks in the monastery, but a few poor or devout children may remain for life. Novice monks who stay on in the monastery observe a set of rules including the following three, which are fundamental. They renounce

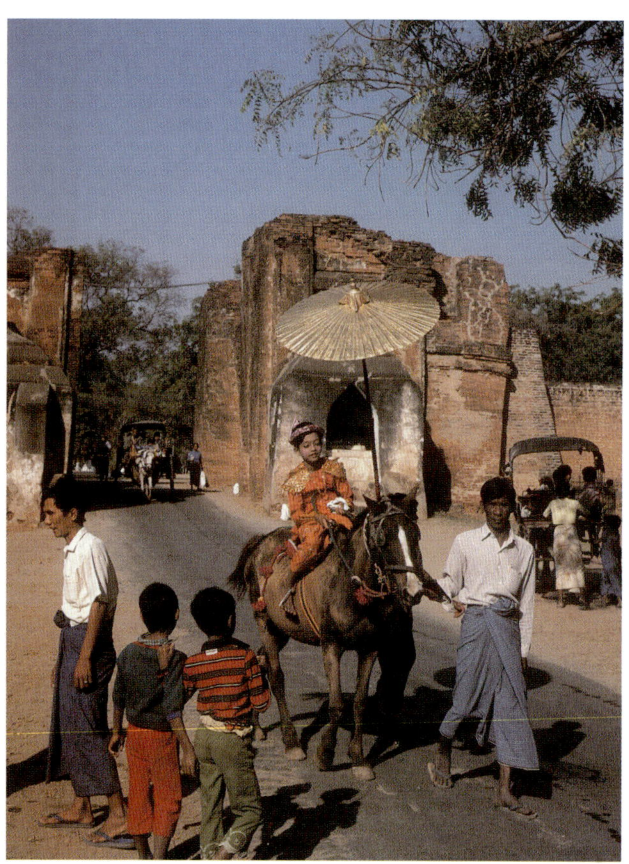

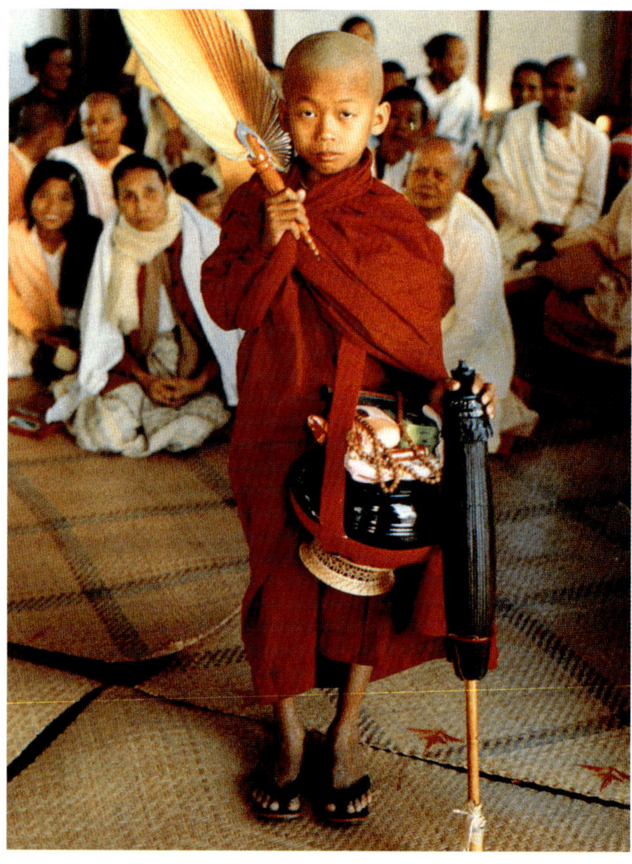

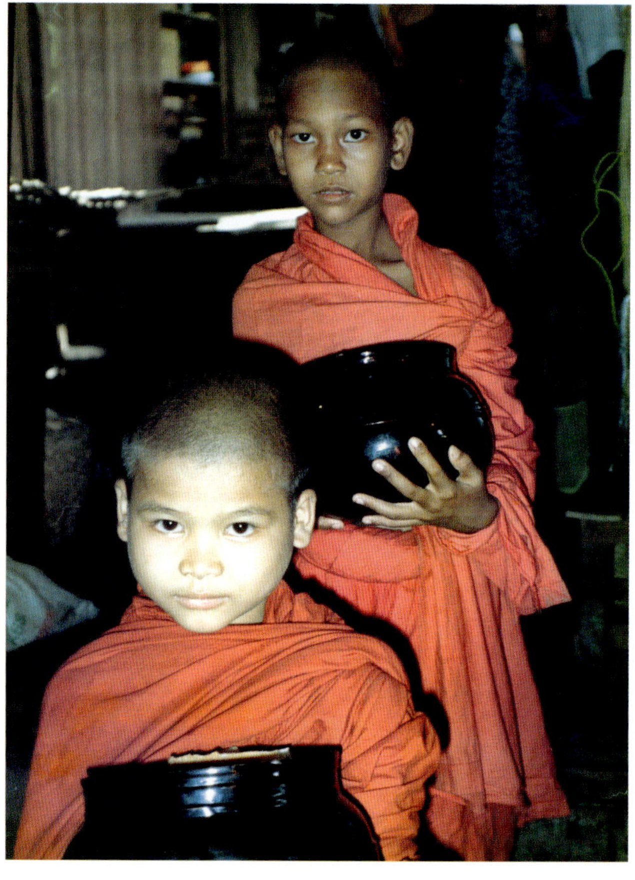

Plate 7 ABOVE
A *shinbyu* boy rides through the city gates of Pagan.

Plate 8 ABOVE RIGHT
This shaven-headed new novice has been provided by his adoring family with a complete set of monk's equipment, all brand new.

Plate 9 RIGHT
Novice monks carrying their black lacquered alms bowls.

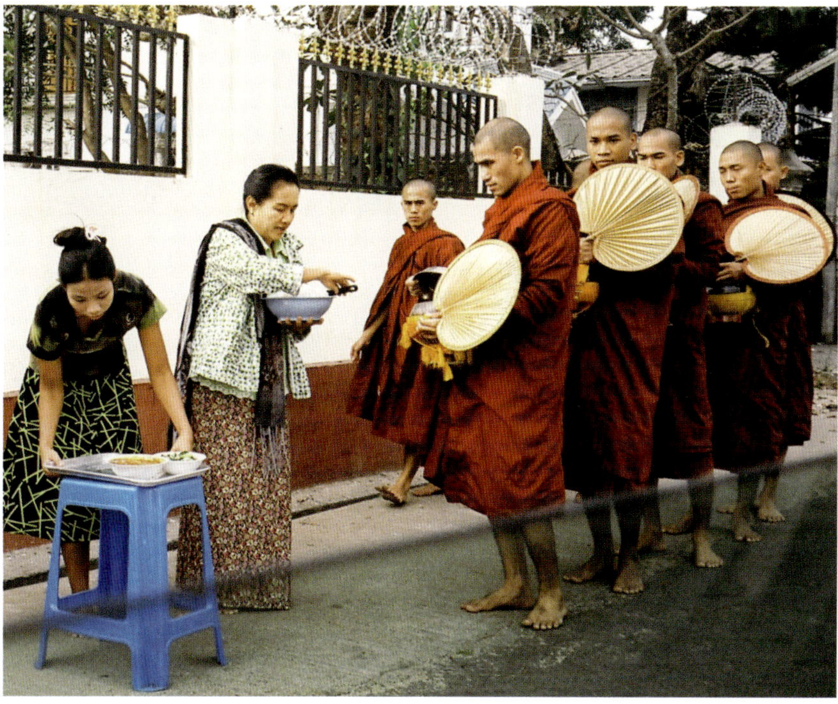

Plate 10 RIGHT
Monks receive alms food from a housewife and her daughter.

all possessions, with the exception of the eight items allowed to monks. They vow to injure nothing and to offend no one, and they take a vow of celibacy. They breakfast at dawn and leave the monastery in procession every morning, walking barefoot and carrying their alms bowls to the houses of lay donors. Monks do not give thanks for the food given in alms, since it is they who are doing the favor by giving the laity a chance to earn merit. The food received in alms is eaten before noon and is their last meal of the day.

A monk cannot attain full ordination before the age of twenty, when he can submit to the discipline of the Vinaya or first "basket" of the Theravada Buddhist scriptures. The rest of his life will be devoted to meditation, study of scripture, and instruction of the laity. Over two hundred Vinaya rules govern all aspects of life in a monastic community, but at its core lie the Five Precepts, the basic code of ethical conduct to which every practicing Buddhist subscribes: refraining from killing, stealing, sexual misconduct, lying, and using intoxicants.

The vast majority of laymen do not actively pursue the goal of the extinction of self, nirvana, in their lifetime. Rather, they seek a more pleasurable rebirth, a reduction of suffering, and avoidance of calamities in this life and in future lives. To this end they try to refrain from sinful acts that violate the five precepts, and to preserve their store of merit by avoiding acts that create greed, anger, or delusion. They seek to add gradually to their prospects of favorable rebirth by engaging in merit-making activities, such as donation. Monks commonly refer to laymen as *daga* (donors). All the sazigyo illustrated in this book were donated to make merit.

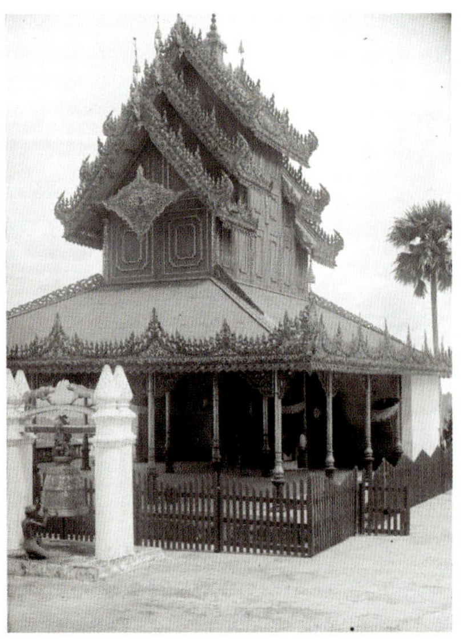

MONASTERIES

Before the British conquest of Lower Burma in 1852 CE every village had its own monastery. Even a hamlet had at least a one-room structure with a single monk in residence.[6] This was still the case in 1882, when Sir J. G. Scott's encyclopedic account of Burmese life, culture, custom, and belief, *The Burman, His Life and Notions*, appeared under the pen name Shway Yoe (Golden Elephant). The village monastery might house only one or two resident monks, whose food was given in alms by villagers grateful for this daily opportunity to make merit. The building was oblong, of wood, raised a few feet above the ground on posts of teak. The roof had a stepped spire.

In the cities monastic buildings were of remarkable size and splendor, particularly those of Mandalay, the center of Burmese Buddhist fervor and scholarship. The Royal Monastery, the Kyaung Daw Gyi, extended over many acres. "Every building in it is magnificent, every inch carved with the ingenuity of a Chinese toy; the whole ablaze with gold-leaf and a mosaic of fragments of mirror-glass . . . The huge posts are gilt all over, or covered with red lacquer; the eaves and gables represent all kinds of fantastic and grotesque figures."[7] The special multi-tiered roofs, called *pyatthat*, were exclusive to royal palaces and monastic buildings. They are often represented in the woven images on sazigyo.

Plate 11 ABOVE
A village monastery may have only one or two monks.

Plate 12 BELOW
Mandalay, the Queen's Silver Kyaung.

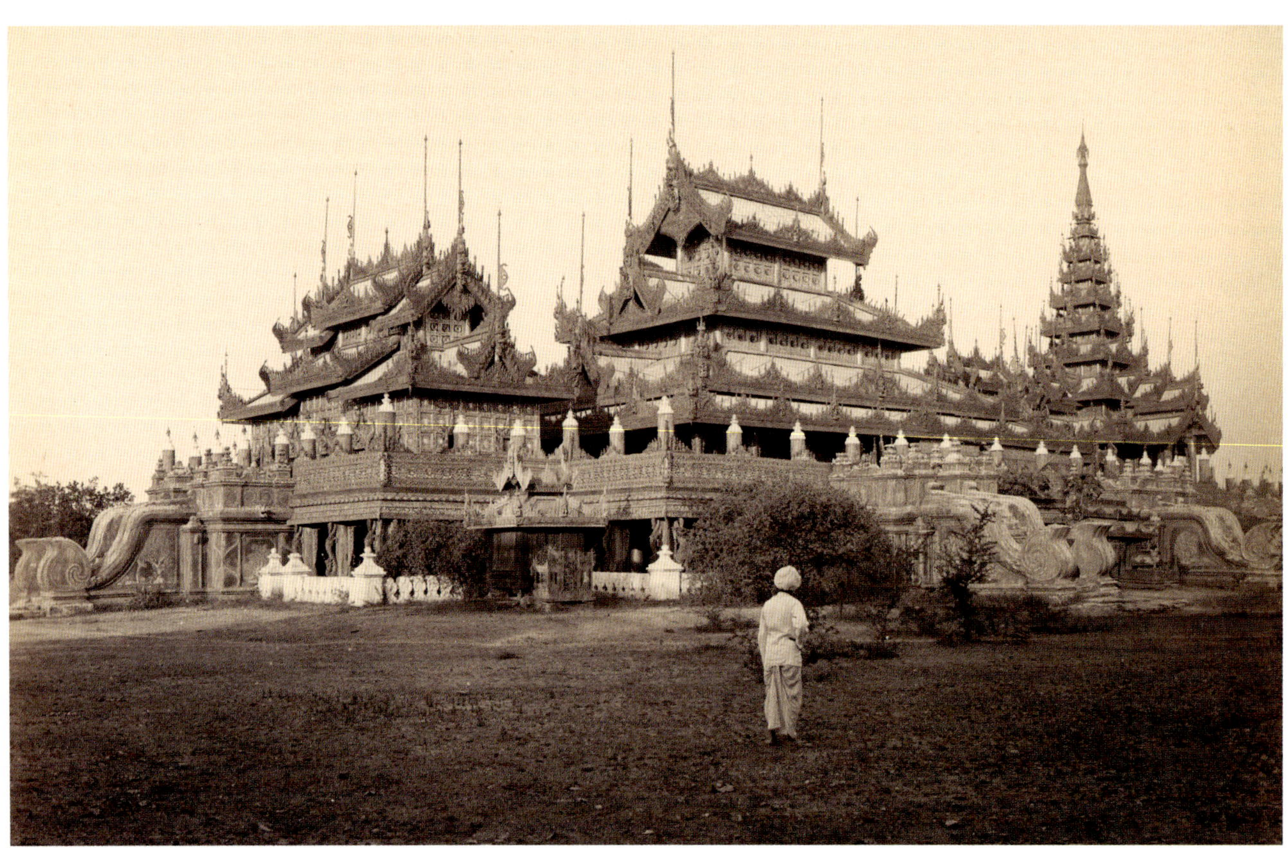

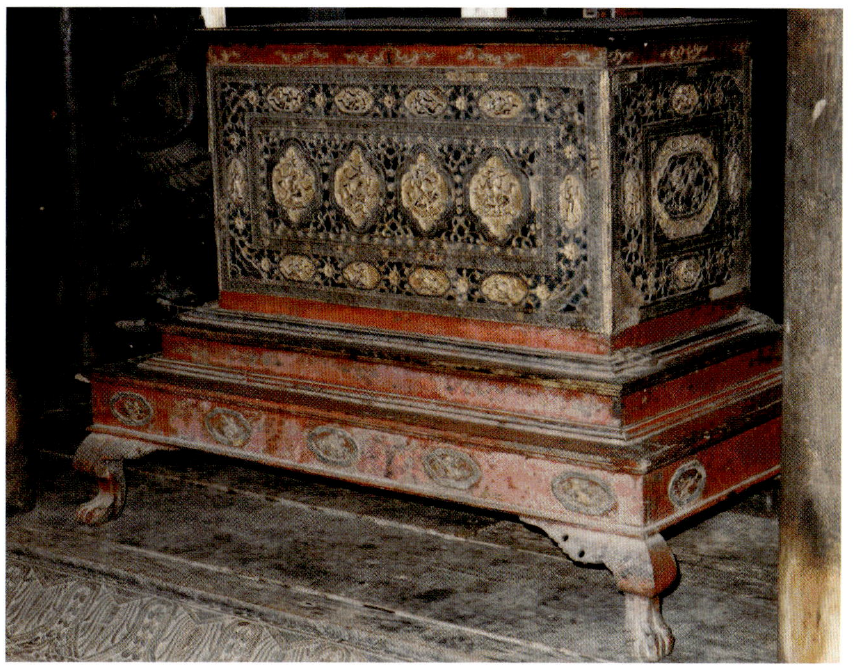

Plate 13 RIGHT
An old *sadaik* (manuscript chest) in the Bagaya monastery, Inwa.

In the great central hall of the main building of the monastery, the Buddha images were ranged, usually on the east side. In Scott's time the palm-leaf book was still universal, and many monasteries had large libraries. The library chests, *sadaik*, made of teak, lacquered and gilded, were arranged in three rows on a tiered platform according to the subject matter of the manuscripts they contained. The lower chests held the "*thuts* and *zats*," the Suttas and Jatakas, sermons and birth stories of the Buddha. Above these were the commentaries and exegeses, mostly by Sinhalese scholars, in Pali. The top row held Burmese translations from the Pali and explanations of scripture composed in Burmese by learned *hsayadaw*, senior monks of this and other monasteries.

But following the British annexation of Lower Burma this wealth of religious learning was unevenly distributed. Scott wrote:

> In Lower Burma the majority of the monks do not even possess a complete copy of the three parts of the Bitaghat [Tipitaka], the Buddhist Bible, and some few have nothing beyond a copy of the Kammavaca . . . Many others have no doubt valuable collections, but the monks are ignorant, they cannot read the books themselves, and they do not care to exhibit them to those who can . . . Consequently, the books moulder away in the bottom of the sadaik, crushed away into the darkest corner of the main room of the monastery.[8]

Some of the sazigyo illustrated in this book may have come from such a neglected chest, after decay and insects had destroyed their contents of palm-leaf manuscripts.

Part I Chapter 3

From Palm Tree to Palm-Leaf Manuscript

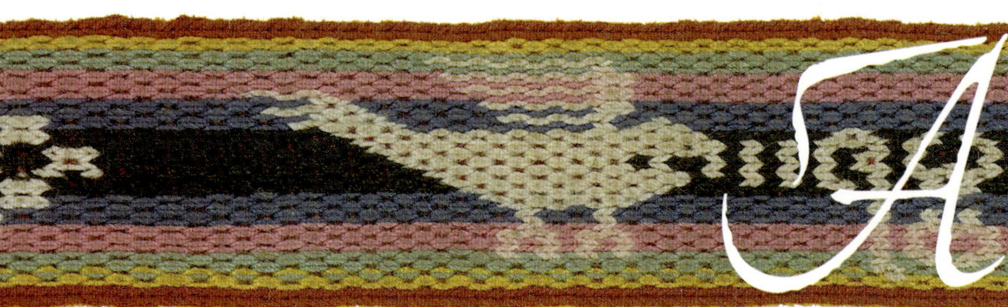

BM246

A Burmese proverb credits palm-leaf manuscripts with lasting a thousand years. But the harsh monsoon climate, insects, rodents, fire, and war have ensured that no manuscripts older than about three hundred years have survived. Still, gold plates excavated in the ancient Pyu city of Sri Ksetra in central Burma are good evidence for the use of palm leaves for writing nearly two thousand years ago. They are shaped like palm leaves and bear inscriptions in the Pali language in Gupta lettering. Some are even pierced with two holes in each plate.[9]

In Burma, as elsewhere in Southeast Asia, the cured leaves of the talipot palm *Corypha umbraculifera* were used for writing the Tipitaka ("three baskets"), the sacred scriptures of Theravada Buddhism. The art of preparing palm leaves for use as manuscripts may have reached Burma from Sri Lanka in the early centuries CE.

> The leaves are taken whilst still tender, and after separating the central ribs, they are cut into strips and boiled in spring water. They are first dried in the shade and then in the sun, then made into rolls, which can be stored. Before they are fit for writing upon they are subjected to a second process, of smoothing. A smooth plank of the areca palm is tied horizontally between two trees. Each leaf is then damped, and a weight being attached to one end of it, it is drawn backwards and forwards across the edge of the wooden plank till the surface becomes perfectly smooth and polished.The smoothing of a single leaf will occupy from fifteen to twenty minutes.[10]

Now the smoothed leaves were piled up, clamped tightly together. All four edges of this bundle were singed with a hot iron, to trim all the leaves to the same size and to repel insects. A hot iron needle or spike was used to bore two holes through every leaf in the pile, to be used later for stringing the written leaves together into a palm-leaf book.

Plate 14 RIGHT
The talipot palm *Corypha umbraculifera*, whose leaves were used for writing the sacred scriptures of Theravada Buddhism.

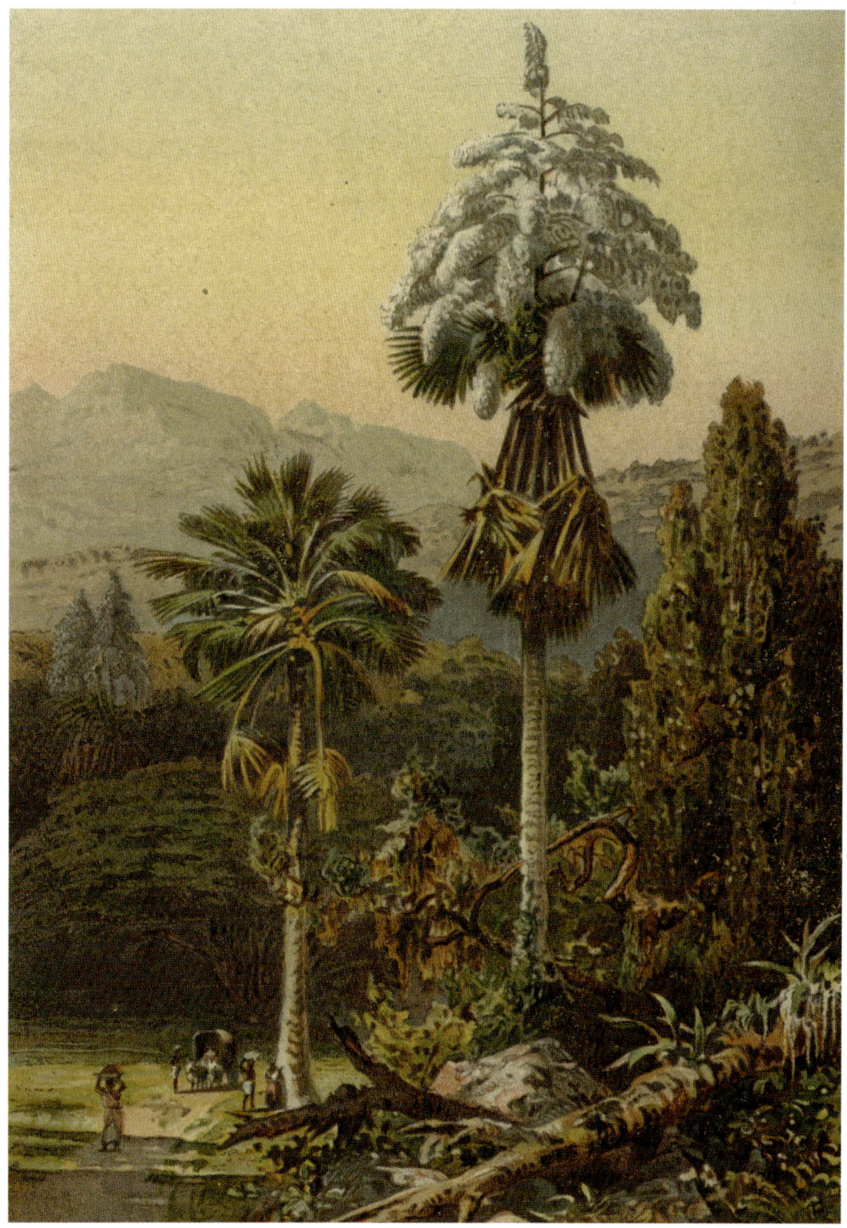

The scribe wrote using a stylus with an iron or steel point. The engraved letters were colorless. "Inking," rubbing with charcoal powder mixed with resinous oil, made the script on the palm leaf dark brown or black and the words easy to read. Student monks might carry loose palm leaves from lesson to lesson rolled up in the equivalent of a school satchel, a special cloth woven with a warp of stout splints of bamboo to stiffen it and protect the flimsy leaves. Such manuscript-wrapping cloths were known as *sapalway* or *gabalway*.

A finished manuscript book might have from a few dozen to several hundred folios, about 40 cm long by 10 cm wide. These were strung together through the two holes pierced in each leaf, and often sandwiched between wooden covers. Sometimes the bundle was

wrapped in a cotton or silk cloth sleeve or bag. For important palm-leaf books these *gabalway* could be very beautiful. If it also had a sazigyo, this was wound round and round the whole parcel, and tied by means of the loop at one end and cord at the other.

A blade-shaped spatula of palm leaf, used to help turn the thin leaves of the book, might be tucked under the sazigyo. These book knives, called *gabyidan*, often bear the title of the manuscript, a useful aid for readers searching through a library chest for a particular manuscript (see appendix 2). It should be emphasized, however, that by no means all manuscript books were furnished with fancy cloth wrappers, sazigyo, and *gabyidan*.

The Kammava, an anthology of excerpts from the Vinaya, the rules for monks, was often commissioned by relatives or sponsors of a monk, to be read aloud at the ceremony of his full ordination. *Kammavaca* manuscripts were especially ornate, lacquered, and gilt. They were much broader than the standard palm leaf, so if a foundation of palm leaves were used, two palm leaves were needed side by side, welded together by the thick lacquer coating. The folios of many *kammavaca* manuscripts have a foundation not of palm leaves, but of sheets of lacquered cloth, lavishly gilt, and the most expensive are written on lacquered sheets of copper or even thin slivers of ivory.[11] Donors proudly referred to their gift as "a complete set": the gilt manuscript itself, wrapped in its cloth sleeve and bound around with its woven sazigyo, and the whole bundle fitted into a gilt and glass-inlaid box.

Plate 15 ABOVE
Each palm-leaf folio was about 40 cm long by 10 cm wide. A manuscript book could comprise hundreds of folios, strung together through the holes in each leaf.

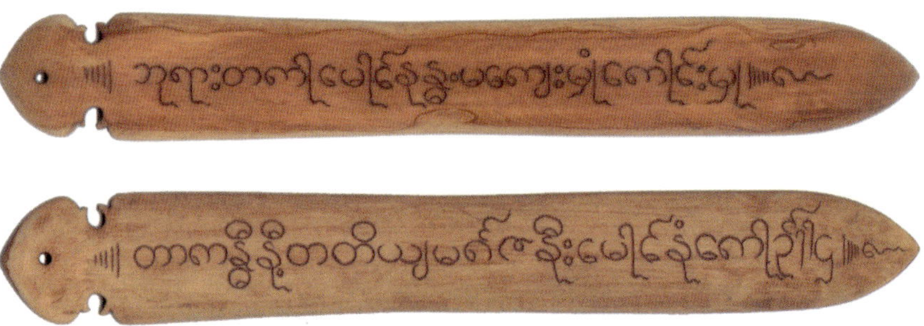

Plate 16 RIGHT
A blade-shaped spatula or "book knife" of palm leaf, wood, or ivory was used to turn the thin leaves of the book. When not in use it was tucked under the sazigyo. Some bear the title of the manuscript and the name of the donor. This one reads: "The deed of merit of pagoda builder Maung Nanda and [his wife] Ma Kyay Hmon," and on the other side the same but in Mon, not Burmese.

Plate 17 RIGHT
A *sapalway*, manuscript sleeve, laid flat. Its cloth ends will be tucked up over the ends of the manuscript.

Plate 18 CENTER RIGHT
The same *sapalway* rolled around its manuscript, and the bundle tied with a sazigyo.

Plate 19 BELOW
A "complete set," consisting of a palm-leaf manuscript with lacquered and gilt wooden covers, its *sapalway* cloth wrapper, its sazigyo, and its gilt and glass-inlaid box.

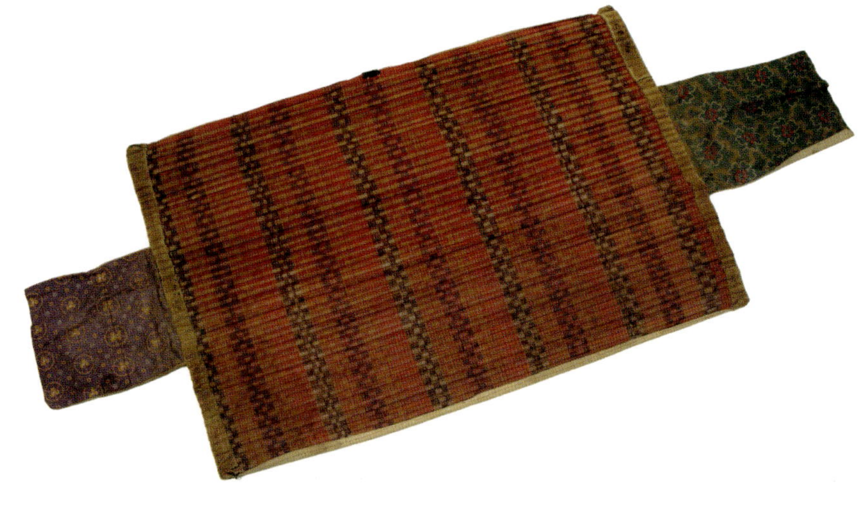

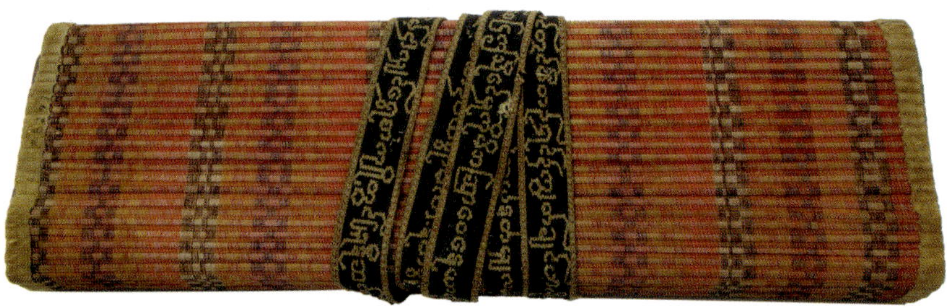

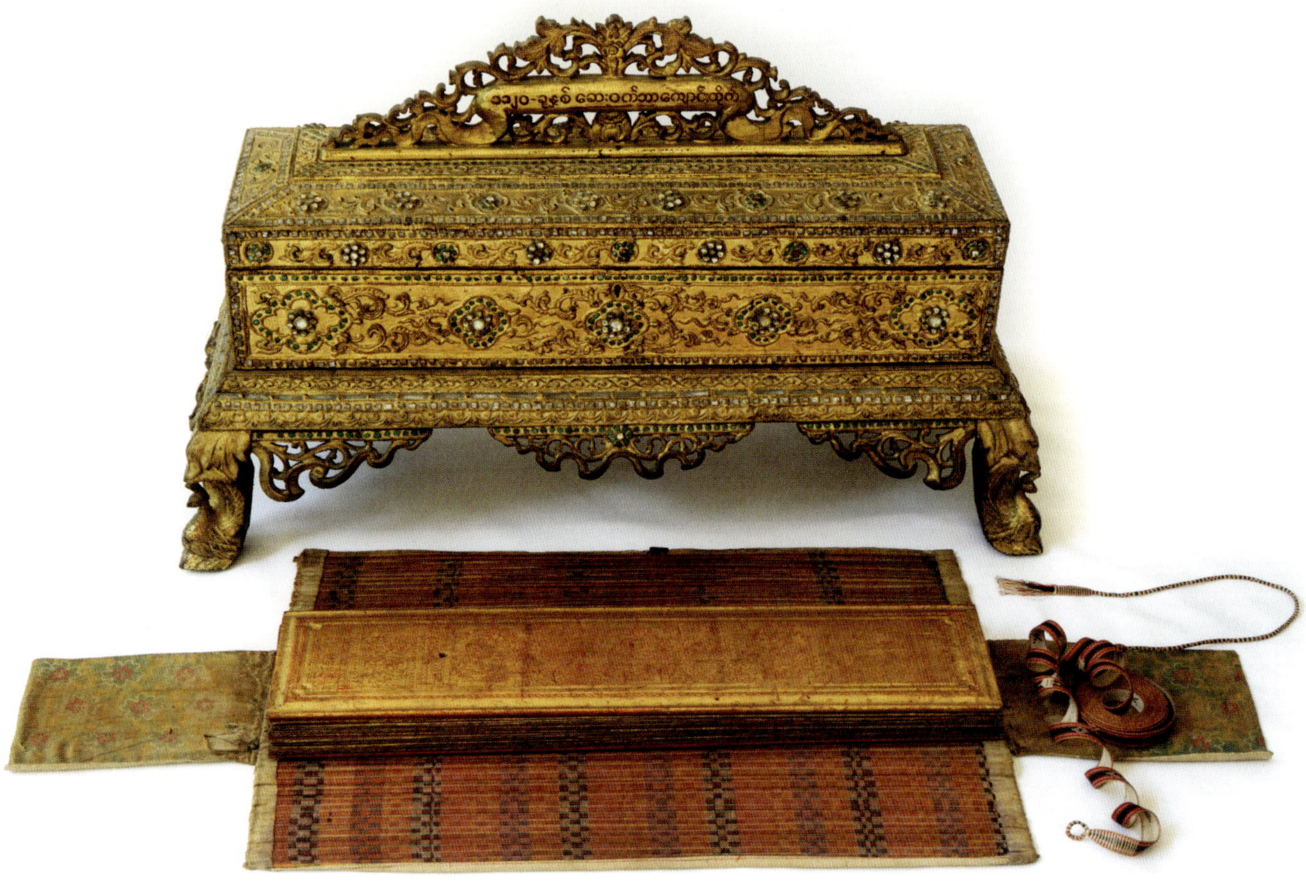

Part I Chapter 4

Donation as a Way of Life

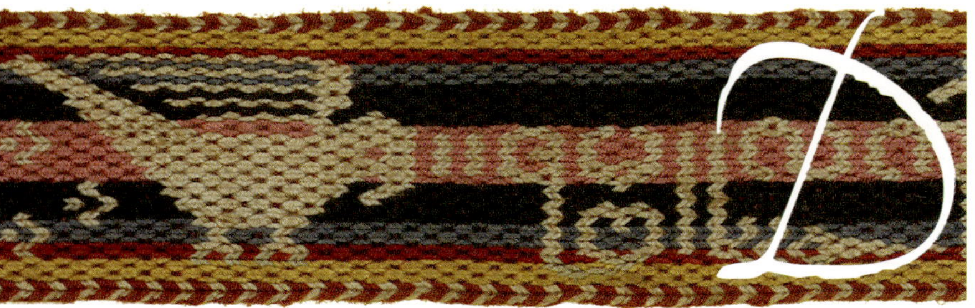

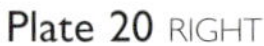

J07

Donating to the Sangha, the Buddhist order of monks, is a way of life in Burma. Well-to-do households cook food daily to give alms to visiting lines of monks, who thus provide the laity with daily opportunities to add to their store of merit. Less prosperous folk content themselves with smaller and less frequent donations.

Every donation is a merit-seeking deed, its motive the accumulation of merit for a favorable rebirth. Wealthy donors may give the materials and labor for the building of a pagoda, an ordination hall (*thein*), or an entire monastery. They may pay for the casting of a bronze bell, or for an image of the Buddha. Common sense and human nature suggest that "monastery donors," having built a monastery, would wish to see its library properly equipped. They would be inclined to use their resources to donate manuscripts with their sazigyo, and perhaps also *sadaik*, teak manuscript chests, to hold them. Royalty and a few very wealthy folk might donate a full set of the Tipitaka, the "three baskets" of the Theravada Buddhist scriptures, paying numerous scribes for many months' work. King Mindon's munificent donations, meticulously recorded in word and picture, included manuscripts of the scriptures (plate 21).[12]

Every sazigyo illustrated or cited in this book was donated by Burmese Buddhists, usually a married couple. Generosity (*dana*) is the

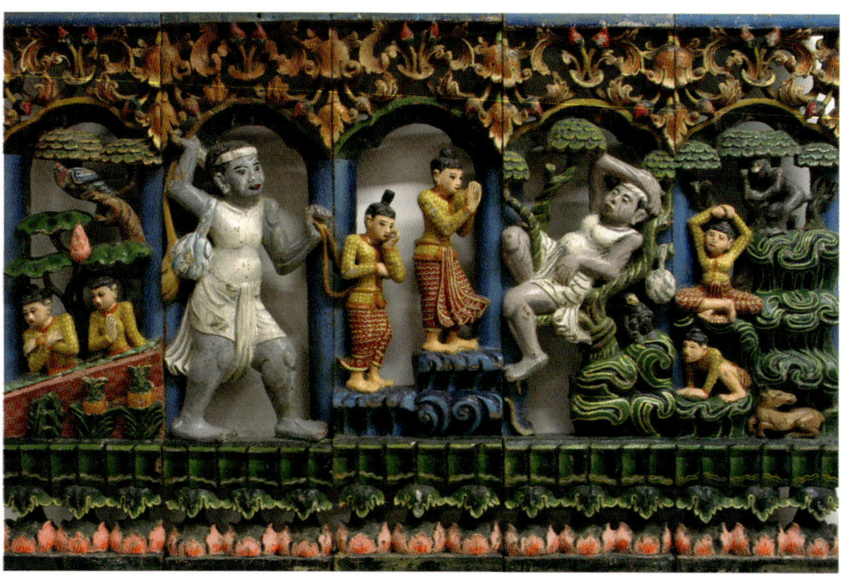

Plate 20 RIGHT

The Buddha-to-be, in his last incarnation as Prince Vessantara, gave away in his boundless generosity all the treasures of the royal palace and everything he possessed, even his son and daughter. This carved and painted panel shows the children being led away and maltreated by the wicked Brahmin Jujaka.

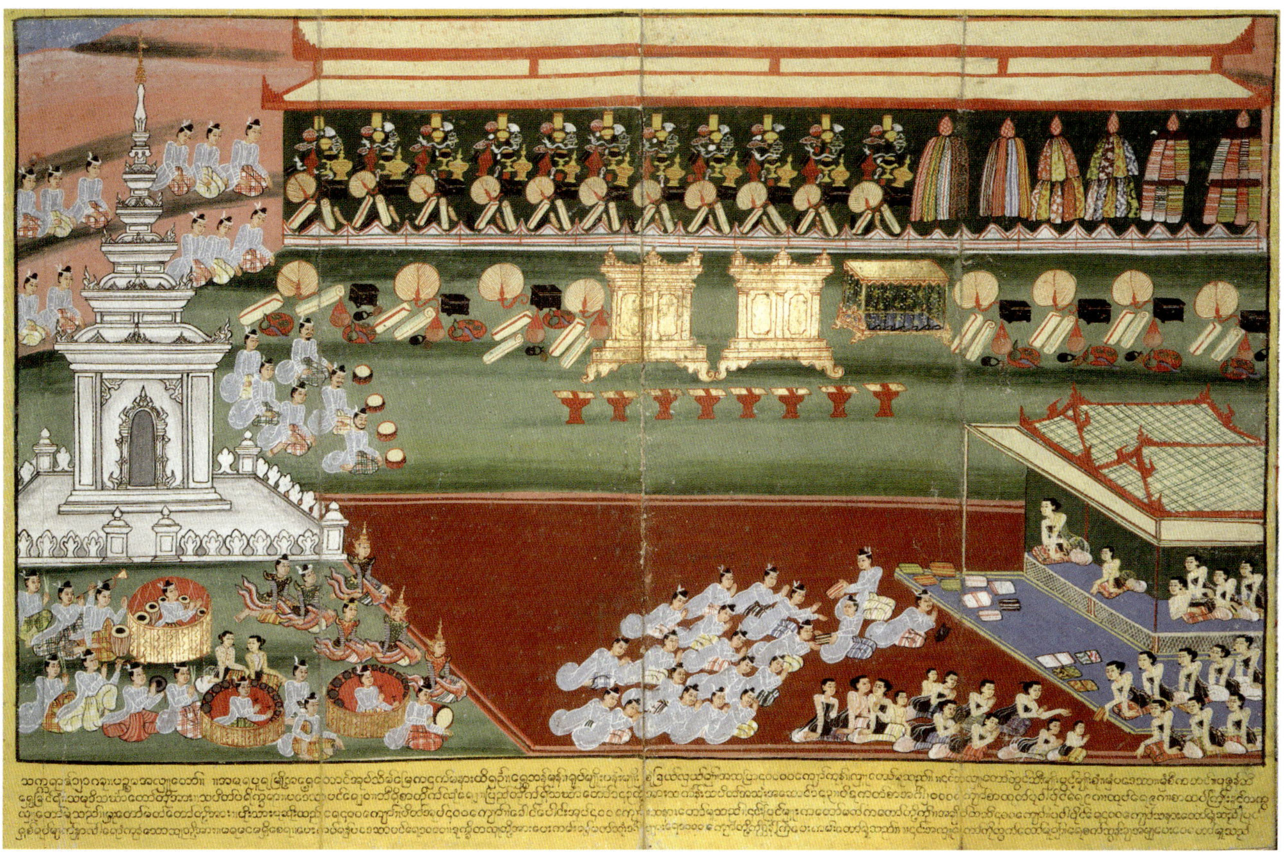

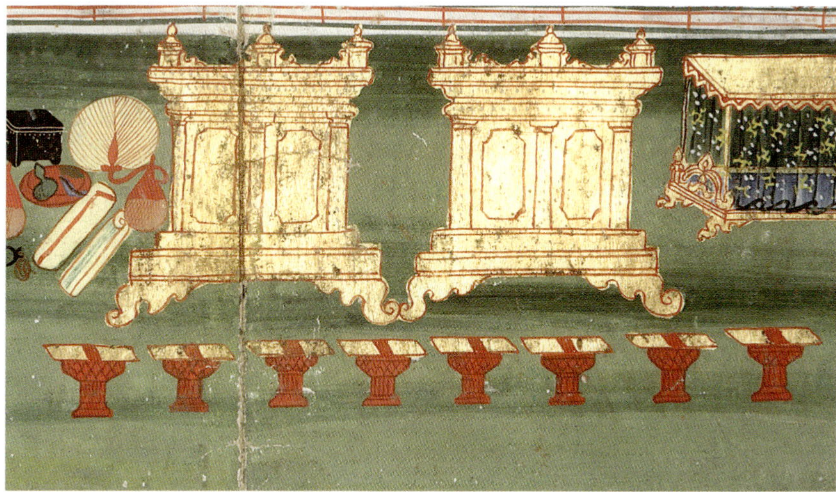

Plate 21 TOP AND ABOVE RIGHT
King Mindon's munificent donations were meticulously recorded. This donation included large gilt library cupboards and scriptural manuscripts, each on its *kalat* tray and bound with a red sazigyo.

most admirable of the "ten acts of perfection" listed in the Sutta of Blessings, one of the best known of all the Buddha's sermons: "Making offerings and giving abundant alms, these are blessed things."

The embodiment of *dana-paramita*, the perfection of giving, is Prince Vessantara, the last incarnation of the Buddha-to-be before his appearance on earth as Prince Siddhattha. All Burmese Buddhists know how Vessantara in his boundless generosity gave away all his royal treasures, the royal rain-bringing elephant, and everything he possessed, even his own son and daughter. Some donors like U Sein Ko

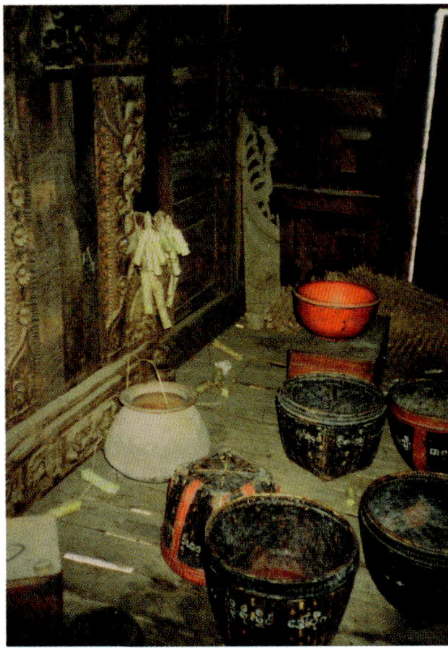

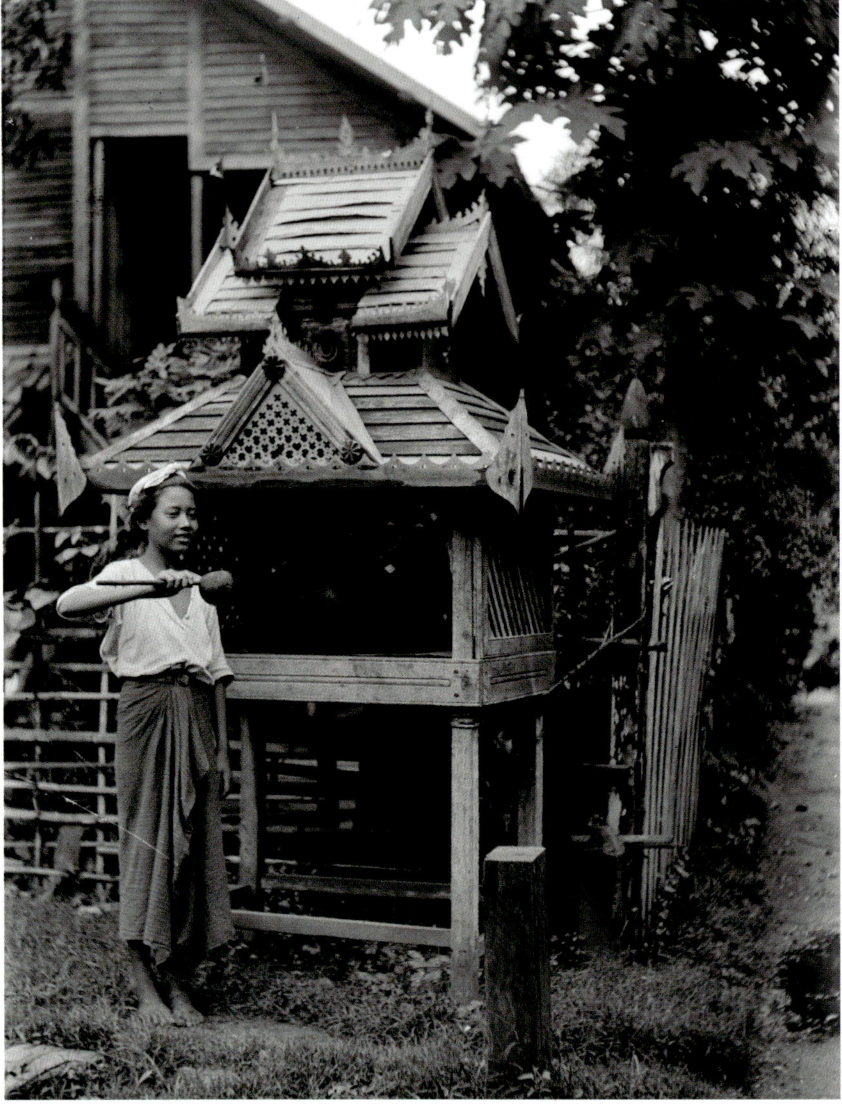

and Ma Pyu thought of their donation as emulating the generosity of Prince Vessantara and his wife Maddi, and in the text of their sazigyo even compared their village to the Buddha-to-be's forest retreat:

> We perform this meritorious deed out of the overflowing generosity we feel in our hearts. We even wish to compare our donation with that of King Vessantara, the Buddha-to-be, who practiced the virtue of giving. Likewise, our home village of Kyakan should be likened to the hill of Winkaba in the jungle of Himalaya, the forest retreat where King Vessantara and his consort Queen Maddideva lived as recluses, having practiced the virtue of giving. (VC)

Plate 22 ABOVE LEFT
Every little donation adds to the donor's balance of merit. These old water bowls in the corner of a Pagan village monastery are all inscribed with donors' names. The couples who gave them did not consider themselves too poor to be donors.

Plate 23 ABOVE RIGHT
A wayside water stand in the city brings merit to the donor.

But a single manuscript with its sazigyo is not a negligible gift. No donation is negligible. Every little counts. The less well-off can still, by small donations, increase their nest egg of merit in this life and their chances in the next life of possessing more resources for merit-making. A water shelf, for example, is often donated for merit. It may consist of a board fixed to the trunk of a shady wayside tree, with porous clay pots and a long-stemmed ladle cup made from a coconut shell, to offer a cooling drink to thirsty travelers.

Twenty years ago my wife and I were walking up Sagaing Hill, across the river from Mandalay, the site of innumerable religious foundations, monasteries, temples, and nunneries. We saw no one on the covered pathway but a silver-haired old lady. We stopped to greet her and to buy some of the roasted bean snacks she was selling. In answer to my questions, she said she had been coming to the same spot daily, for over thirty years. On some days she sold all her snacks, but even on days when she sold nothing, her daughter who sat on the other side of the hill might sell some packets. We noticed, on the path near her feet, a little heap of cooked rice, less than half a handful, and asked her what it was. "Oh," she said, "that's for the ants. You can see them coming. They know where to find it, because I always put it in the same place." She had nothing, but she did not consider that her poverty disqualified her from being a donor, and found something to give every day. Too poor to give daily alms to a line of brown-robed monks, she was content in this life to feed a line of brown ants.

Donating scriptures to a monastery was a sure way to earn merit. To quote from a sazigyo text: "Of all kinds of offerings, the result of which assuredly follow the donor, the offering of the Tipitaka, which is the wheel of truth, gives an instant reward."[13] Such donations are made to the Sangha, the whole universal monastic community, but, of course, are lodged in one particular monastery.

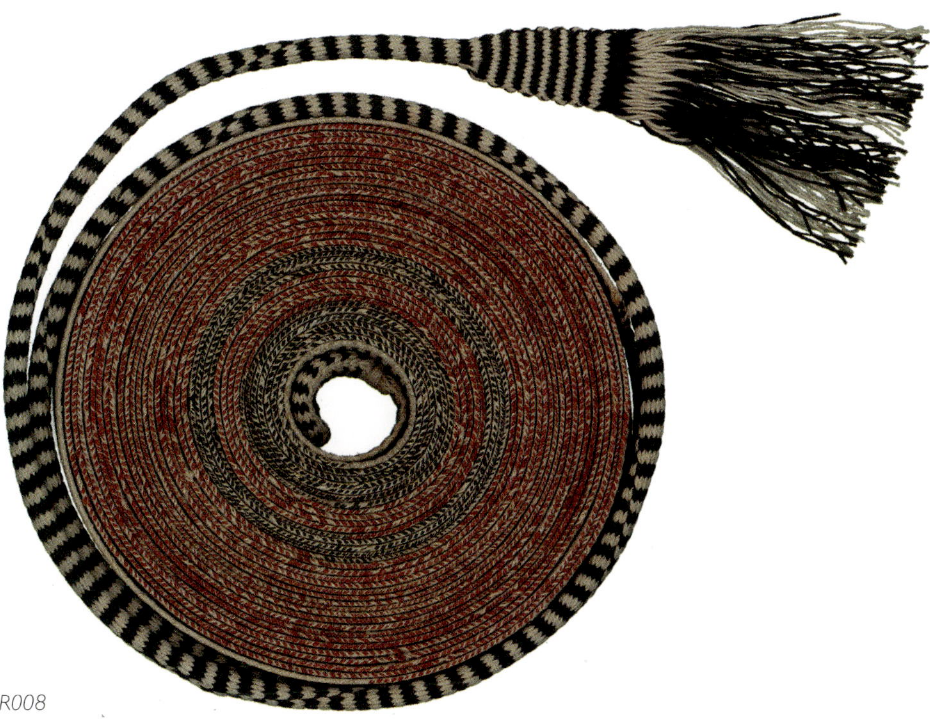

R008

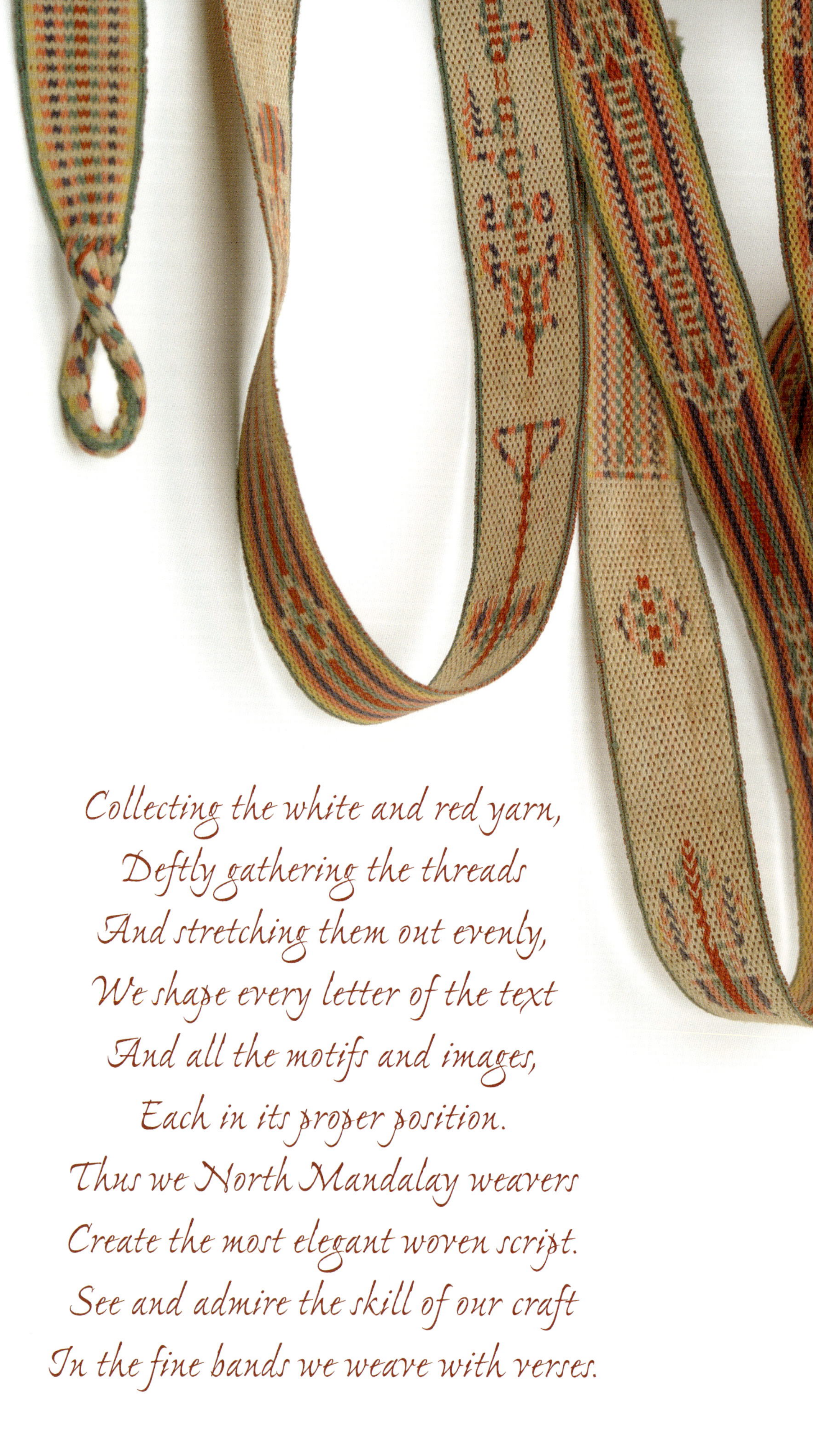

Collecting the white and red yarn,
Deftly gathering the threads
And stretching them out evenly,
We shape every letter of the text
And all the motifs and images,
Each in its proper position.
Thus we North Mandalay weavers
Create the most elegant woven script.
See and admire the skill of our craft
In the fine bands we weave with verses.

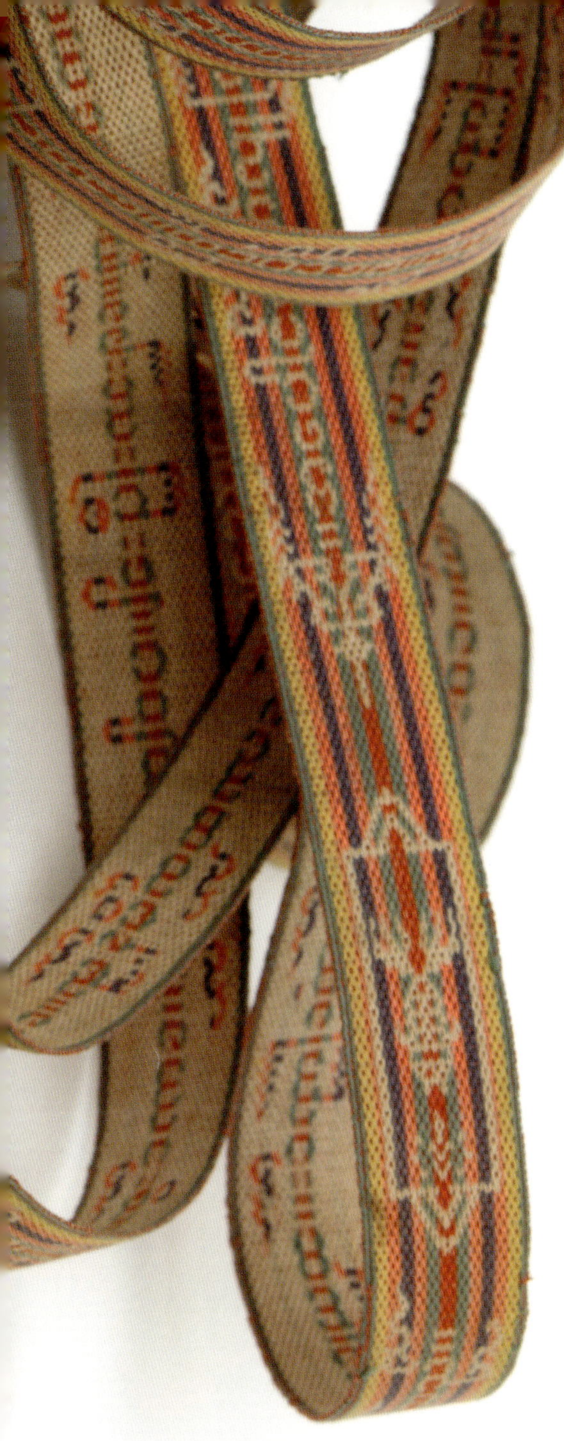

Part II
THE SAZIGYO AS TABLET-WOVEN TEXTILE BAND

Part II Chapter 5

A Brief History of Tablet Weaving

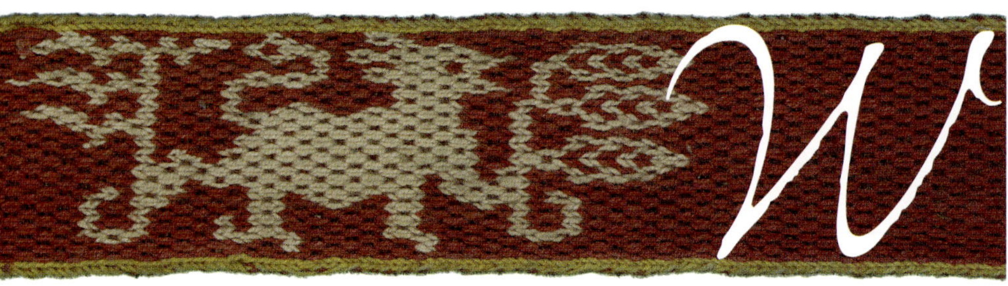

R086

Weaving with tablets is an ancient craft. Bone tablets, sometimes with warp threads still in place, were found preserved in peat bogs in northwestern Europe and have been dated to the Iron Age of two thousand years ago. Others are known from early medieval Germany, Greece, Spain, and England. Textiles found in the seventh-century CE Sutton Hoo ship burial in East Anglia included a four-hole tablet weave, perhaps a shoe strap.[1] The use of tablets for weaving lettered bands is also at least a thousand years old. Latin lettering adorns the borders of St. Cuthbert's vestments in Durham Cathedral, woven between 905 and 916 CE. Scripts that have been woven in the past include Greek, Latin, Arabic, Persian, and several Indian scripts. Illuminated books of hours from the fifteenth century CE show the Virgin Mary at her tablet loom.

By the seventeenth century the craft was in decline in Western Europe. A popular souvenir of visits to the Holy Land was a pair of tablet-woven silk garters inscribed with the city name, Jerusalem or Damascus, the year of the journey, and the name of the lady who would wear them. The only place in Western Europe where the craft survived was Iceland, where it was rediscovered in the late nineteenth century by German researcher Margarethe Lehman-Filhes. She read of Icelandic bands called *spjaldofid* (made with tablets) and in a Danish museum saw a band with attached tablets. She taught herself the technique and brought tablet weaving to the attention of weavers and scholars in a book still considered an excellent source of ethnological material.[2] She has many disciples today in Europe and America, weavers who proudly turn the tablet pack.

Thomas Wardle, a silk manufacturer and close associate of William Morris, was the first to mention the craft in English. Two entries in his catalogue of the 1886 Colonial and Indian Exhibition, Indian Silk Culture, are worth quoting:

> 239. Handloom, such as has been used for centuries at Benares, in which is woven the sacred ribbon exhibited below it. Lent by Mr Wardle. This small handloom is used by probably not more than three weavers, who sit in niches in the streets of Benares near the temples weaving the sacred ribbon exhibited below. This ingenious and very curious little loom evidently foreshadowed the application of cards in the Jacquard loom. In this case the cards are little squares of horn, each having four

Plate 24 RIGHT
Illuminated books of hours from the fifteenth century show the Virgin Mary at her tablet loom.

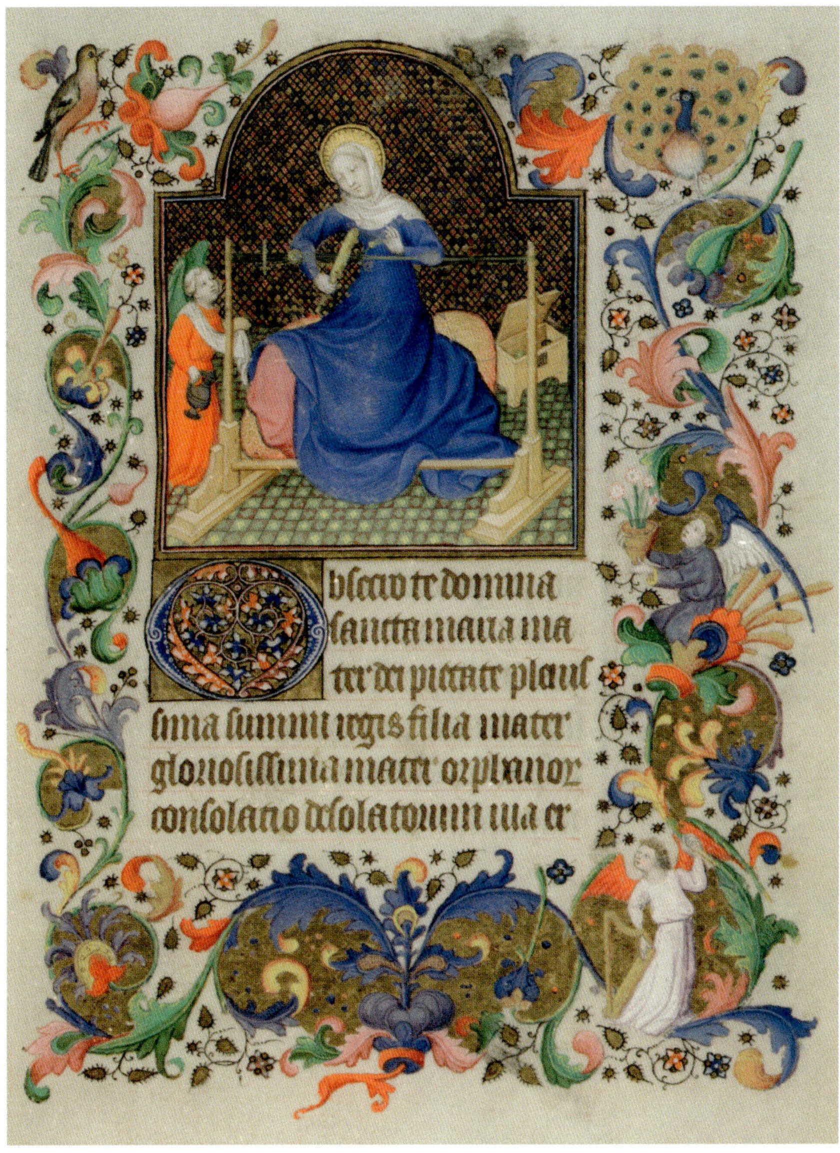

perforations through which four of the warp threads pass and are guided at will to help in forming the intricate pattern. There are in all forty-six horns [sic], indicating 184 warp threads. Colours of warp green, white and crimson. Colours of weft crimson, which is knocked up by a small knife-shaped hand-beam.

> Length of loom.......4 ft 4 in.
> Height.....................9 in.
> Breadth....................2½ in.

It is made of wood, and consists only of a base of a carved piece of teak wood, having an upright peg at one end and the woven tape attached to the other. The only harness is a wooden comb, six inches in length, having 72 teeth, which holds the warp threads sufficiently apart for the horns which are 1½ in. square to be worked.

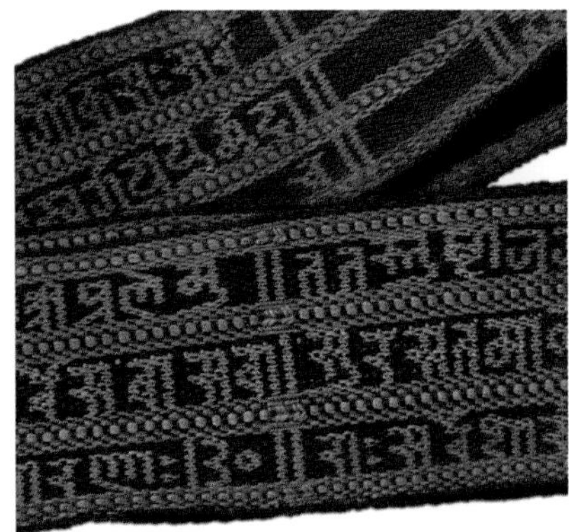

> 240. Sacred Ribbon or Tape woven at Benares in the little loom exhibited above it. It contains, in ornamental borders, twenty-nine names of Vishnu written in Sanscrit, some of them having Gujarati terminations.[3]
> Another tape below is intended for Shiva worshippers, and contains only a repetition of 'Om Namha Shivaja', 'I bow to Shiva'. These tapes are worn at worship in the Hindoo temples, and at home. Lent by Mr. Wardle.

Wardle was unaware that "this very curious little loom" had been used in England a thousand years before and was still widely used in nineteenth-century Scandinavia.

THE DOUBLE-FACED WEAVE IN BURMA

Much further study is needed to establish when double-faced weaving and woven lettering arrived in Burma, and whether they came from India. Researchers might find a study of Arakanese weaves offers clues as to the route taken. Arakan in the far west of Burma lies closest to India, and Indian influences are numerous in Buddhism in Arakan. The oldest dateable sazigyo are mid-eighteenth century, only 250 years old.

In Britain there is a brown-background tape associated with a manuscript dateable to 1792 in the collections of the Royal Asiatic Society.[4] The earliest woven date I have found, 1798, is on an indigo and white sazigyo in the Pitt Rivers Museum in Oxford.[5]

The oldest sazigyo in the Ryan collection with a woven date, an indigo and white tape (R162) dated 1216 BE (1854 CE), is illustrated in plate 35. The most recent (R274) is dated 1327 BE (1965 CE) and illustrated in plate 47. The Brighton collection includes an important tape dateable by its text to 1874, and many with woven dates from 1892 to 1928.

As printed books replaced palm-leaf manuscripts, the market for sazigyo declined, and the craft of weaving lettering was generally thought to have died out completely in the early 1970s. According to Noel Singer,[6] the last few ribbons produced by a professional weaver were made in the early 1970s by an eighty-two-year-old called Daw Hsint of Oakshitkon Village near Monywa. Nevertheless, an attempt seems to have been made to revive the craft, for in September 1994, about a year after the publication of Shwebo Mi Mi Gyi's anthology of sazigyo texts, a training workshop on sazigyo weaving, led by Daw Thein Htay, was held at the Saunders Weaving Institute in Amarapura near Mandalay. And as recently as October 2010, when Shwebo Mi Mi Gyi's son Dr. Ye Myint visited the Saunders Institute, he found several weavers competent in the weaving of traditional round script, and a group of monks at the nearby Mahagandayone monastery who knew how to weave lettering and use their skill to weave personalized

Plate 25 ABOVE
The double-faced technique could have reached Burma from India in the eighteenth century. This Devanagari script band was collected in 1910 by Lucian Scherman, director of the Munich Ethnological Museum.

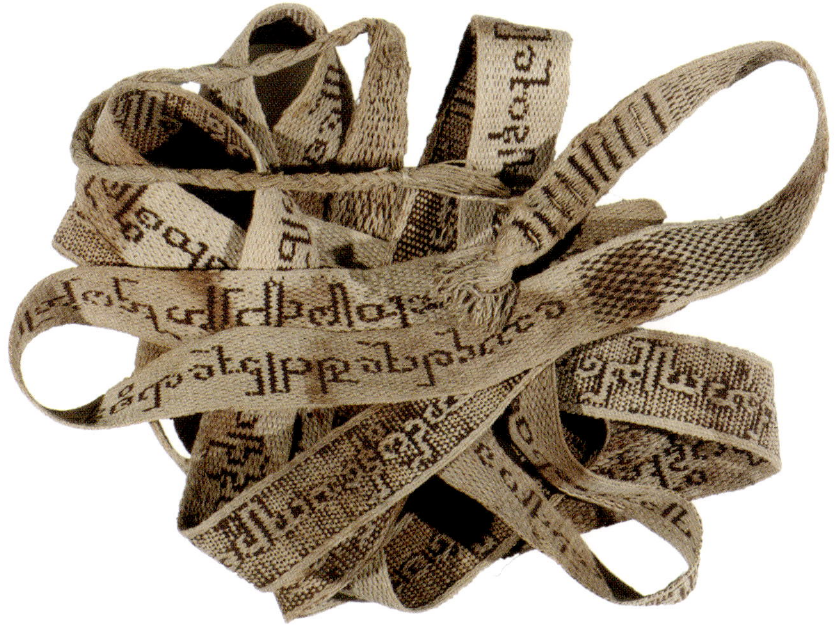

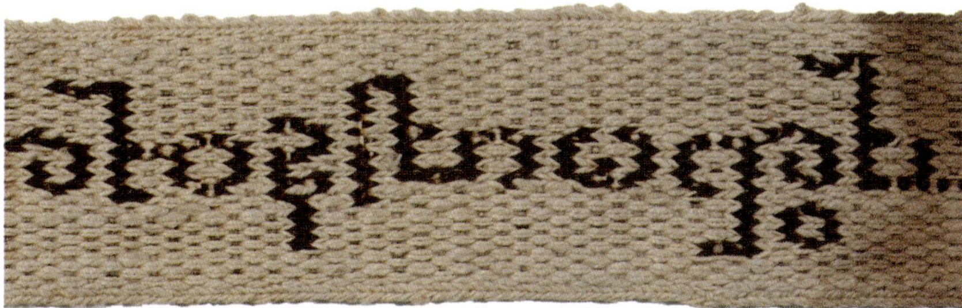

Obverse

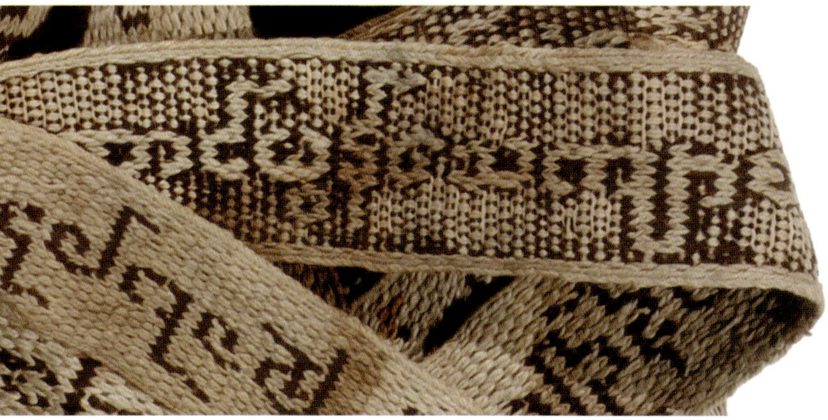

Reverse

Plate 26 RIGHT, CENTER, AND BELOW RIGHT This old brown sazigyo in the Royal Asiatic Society (RAS) is associated with a manuscript dated 1792. It is in need of conservation. Decomposition of the brown dye has progressed further on the obverse than on the reverse.

monks' waistbands.[7] A training course in sazigyo weaving was held in June 2013 at the Saunders Institute for weavers from Rakhine state.

Although tablet weavers no longer weave sazigyo, they still find plenty of work making other articles for monks such as waist girdles and alms bowl slings. Their customers include mothers kitting out their young sons as novice monks for their *shinbyu* initiation (see plate 8) and other devout Buddhists seeking merit through bulk donations to a monastery.

Part II Chapter 6

The Craft, Its Tools, and Techniques

LOOM AND TOOLS

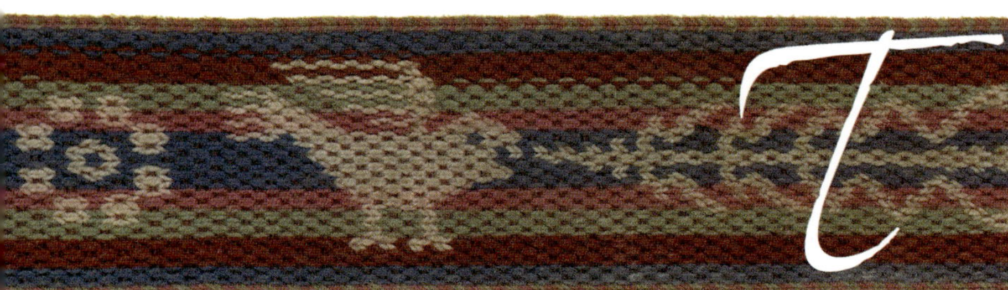

B877

The tablet loom used in Burma for weaving sazigyo consists of a 1.5-meter-long plank, fitted at each end with a movable block of wood. One of these blocks incorporates a peg around which the warp ends are wound, and the other has a roller for winding up the finished part of the tape. It is very similar to the Benares loom described above by Thomas Wardle in his 1886 catalogue. In Mandalay in 1911 Professor Lucian Scherman, director of the Royal Bavarian Ethnological Museum in Munich, and his wife Christine photographed a sazigyo weaver at her loom, a close-up of tablets and beater, and a woman engaged in lacquering the square leather tablets.[8] Scherman noted that weavers used thirty-eight tablets of lacquered deerskin and a flat beater of polished *padauk*, a hard and heavy wood.

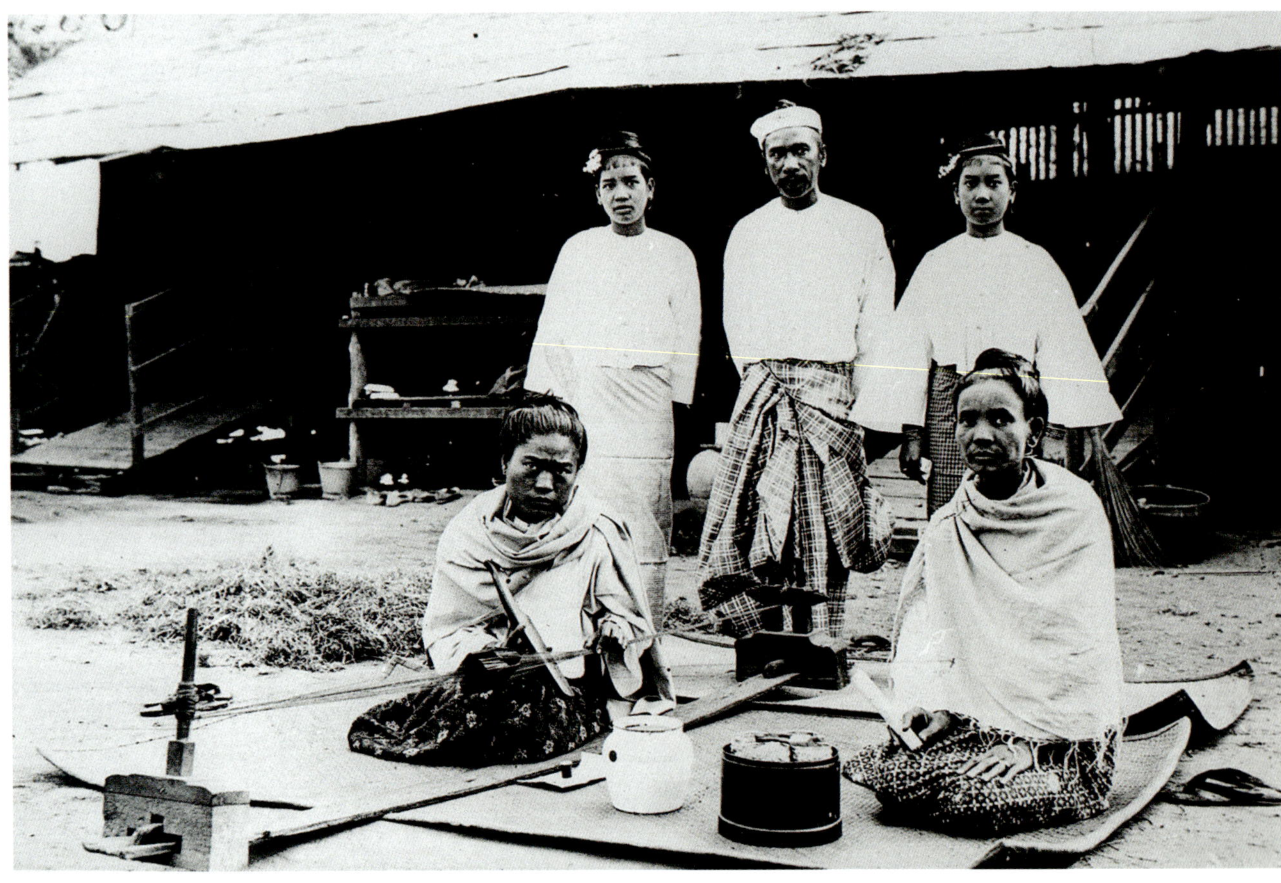

Plate 27 PREVIOUS PAGE BELOW
This photograph of a sazigyo weaver at her loom in Mandalay was taken in 1911 by Christine Scherman, wife of the great ethnographer Lucian Scherman, director of the Munich Ethnological Museum. Peter Collingwood writes:

> It shows a woman (a magistrate's daughter) weaving a sazigyo. She sits on a mat beside her loom; this consists of a long plank resting on the ground, with a large movable wooden block at either end. At the far end (from the weaver's point of view) the block has a vertical post to which the warp, wound round a stick, is attached. At the near end, a nicely carved block supports a horizontal roller, acting like a cloth beam for the woven band. The band carries thirty-eight square tablets, made of lacquered leather, clearly arranged in two packs . . . A piece of paper, weighted down by some heavy object, is on the ground in front of her; perhaps it is the written text which she is copying on to the woven band.

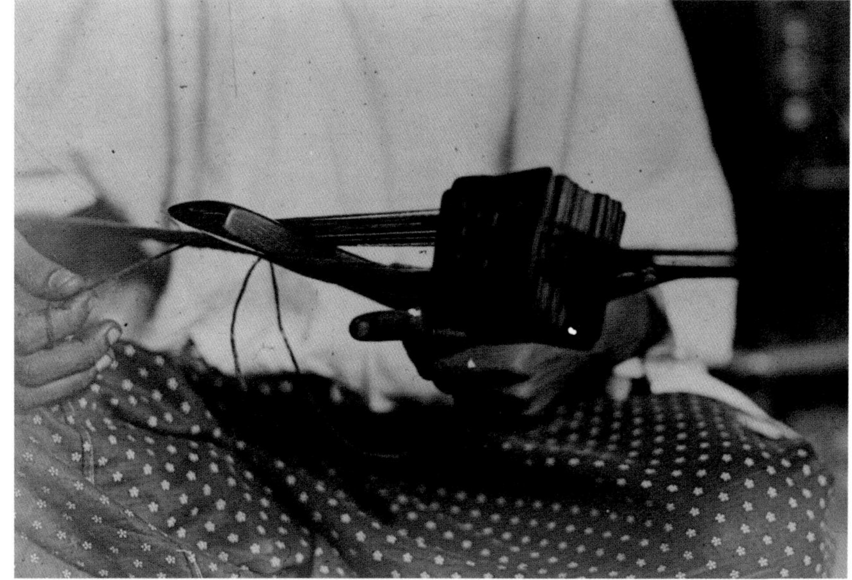

Plate 28 TOP RIGHT
Close-up view of tablets and beater. Scherman noted that weavers used thirty-eight tablets of lacquered deerskin and a flat beater of polished *padauk* wood.

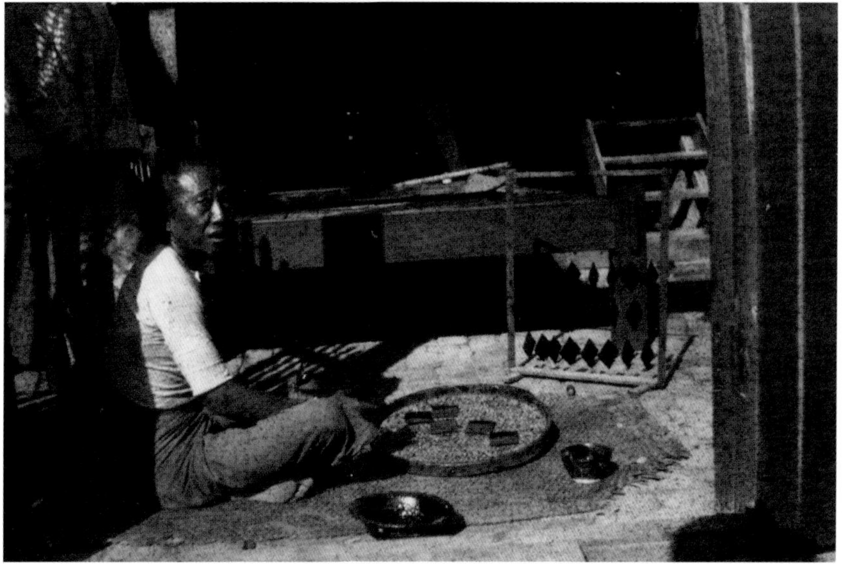

Plate 29 ABOVE RIGHT
A woman lacquering leather tablets.

THE TECHNIQUES OF SAZIGYO WEAVING IN A NUTSHELL

I am not a weaver. My knowledge of the structure of sazigyo I owe to reading Peter Collingwood's standard work on the techniques of tablet weaving[9] and his survey report on the Brighton collection of sazigyo. This latter is available at the James Green Centre for World Art at the Brighton Museum & Art Gallery, and slightly abridged forms part 5 of this book. I enjoyed a third resource, Peter's e-mails in our "museum-through-the-letterbox" collaboration. His critiques of the sazigyo I sent him reflect a master weaver's enjoyment of the skill and artistry of the sazigyo weavers.[10] They also amounted to a series of informal tutorials. A brief description of the techniques employed by the sazigyo weavers is offered here for the reader's convenience.

Plate 30 RIGHT AND NEXT PAGE
DOUBLE-FACED WEAVE
In the double-faced weave the weaver can create images by turning her pack of tablets and changing colors. If the images on the obverse of the weave are symmetrical then they will appear identical on the reverse of the band, but with colors reversed (right).
Text created in the double-faced weave will appear in mirror-image on the reverse of the weave (next page).

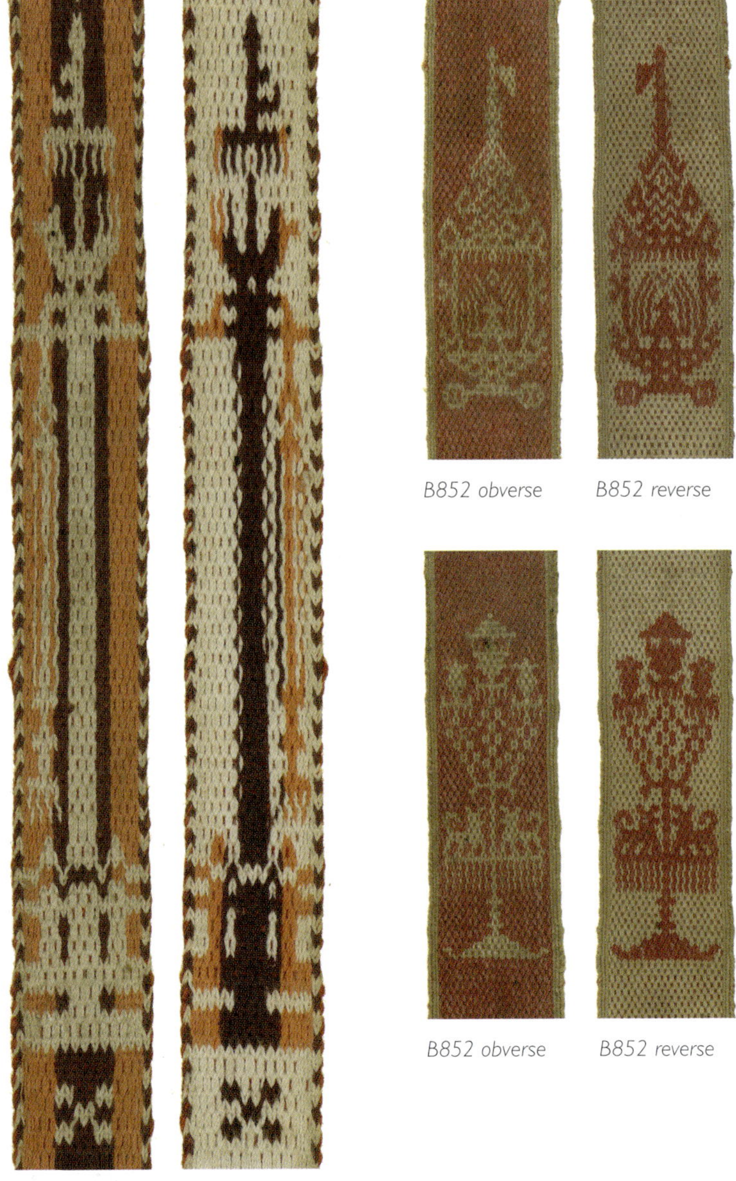

B852 obverse *B852 reverse*

B852 obverse *B852 reverse*

R227 obverse *R227 reverse*

Every sazigyo begins with a loop and ends in a cord. All sazigyo are tablet-woven, using from twenty-eight to fifty-two tablets, each with four holes, through which the warp is threaded. Of the many possible techniques, only two are used: warp-twining and double-faced weave. The former ensures tightness, and used in the selvage prevents fraying at edges. It is also used for the warp-twined cross-stripes, which are an efficient way to encourage the band to acquire its full width after the initial loop. At this stage, at the start of the flat area the second of the two textile structures used in sazigyo takes over. This, the double-faced weave, makes possible the two most striking features of the tapes: the text lettering and the images of beasts, birds, bells, and other ritual objects. To make patterns, script, and images in the double-faced weave, the tablets are turned individually or in groups, not as a whole pack.

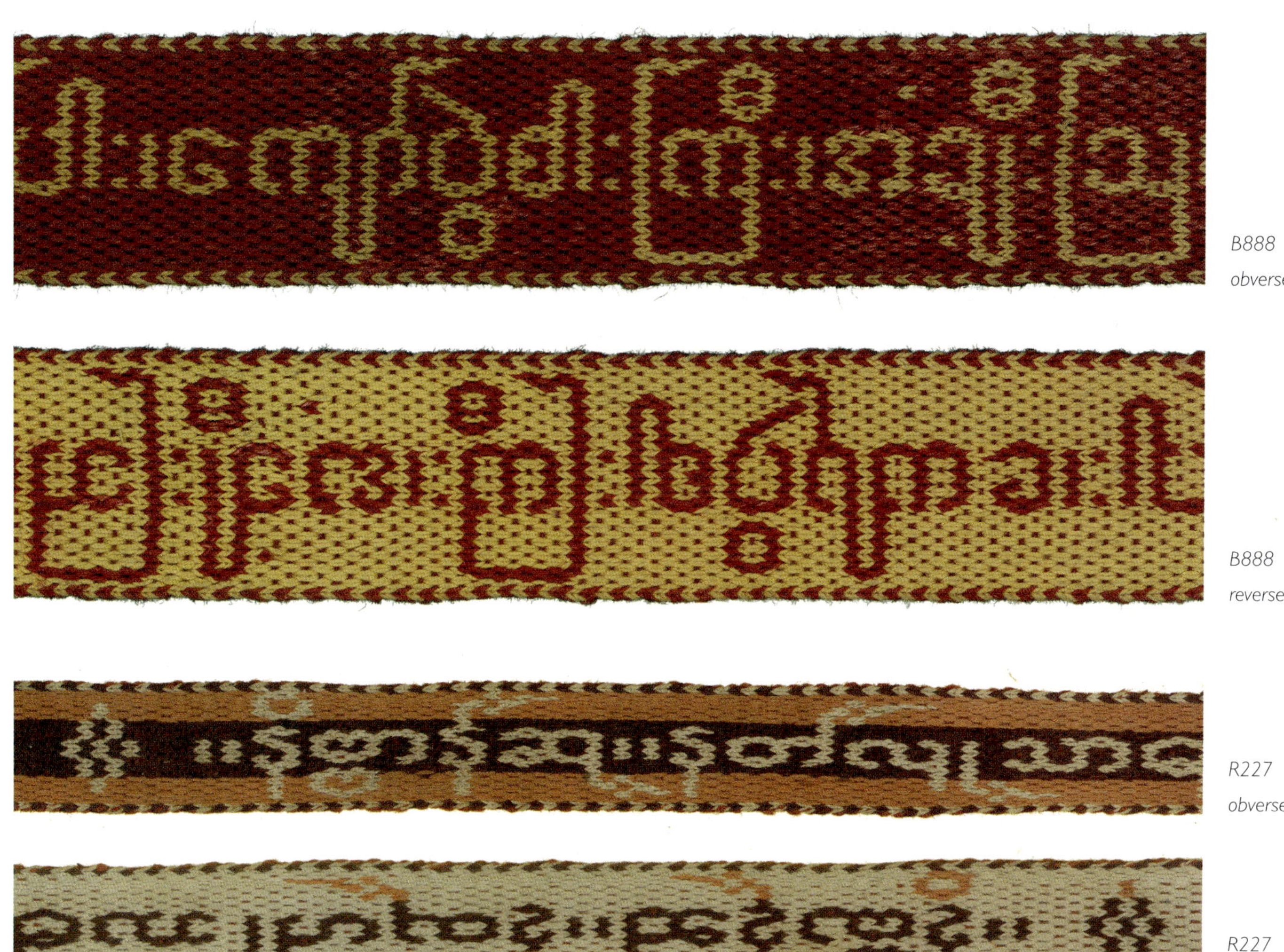

B888 obverse

B888 reverse

R227 obverse

R227 reverse

Examples of silk sazigyo are known,[11] but all the tapes in the Brighton collection use cotton yarn. This varies in thickness. In the coarsest tapes uneven thickness of the yarn indicates hand-spun, but all the finer tapes use machine-made yarn, imported from Britain and Europe. Fineness of the work varies widely. The number of warp-ends (lengthwise threads) per centimeter of width ranges from 38 to 123.

One very narrow tape with tiny lettering (R106) particularly fascinated me. But apparently small size was nothing to marvel at:

> One feature of tablet weaving is that it is really no more difficult to weave with fine threads than with coarse. You handle the tablets (which are always the same size) to make the images in exactly the same way whatever the size of the yarn. It's not like braiding with your fingers where finer threads would be more difficult to deal with, or even to see. So a finer sazigyo is really nothing to be too amazed at![12]

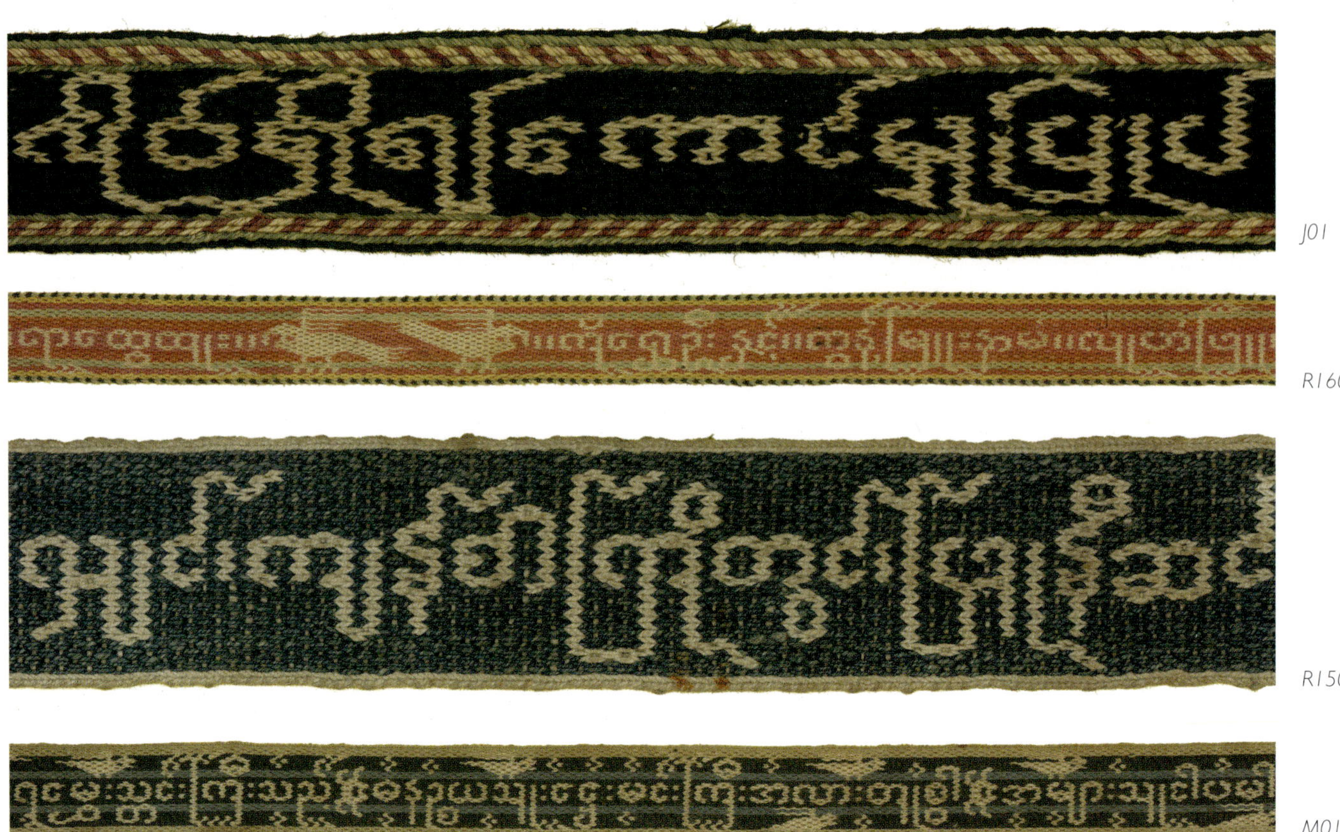

CLARITY OF THE WOVEN SCRIPT

Weavers and donors of sazigyo took pride in the clarity of the woven Burmese script. Its legibility and beauty are mentioned in the woven text of some sazigyo, **"So that the text can be easily read we have had the words copied on to palm leaves and woven on the cotton ribbon clearly, like glass balls well-arranged."** (VC49)

"The deeply meaningful words of my wish are woven on the cotton ribbon. The words are not only noteworthy but also as easily legible as if written with a [white] steatite stylus [on black paper]." (VC32) **"I donate these golden palm leaves with script as clear as the figure of the rabbit on the surface of the moon."** (MMG ch. 2, no. 9)

Two nineteenth-century British male observers admired Burmese sazigyo weavers' neatly woven script and rated it vastly superior to the efforts of English ladies. Sir Henry Yule noticed in Ava in 1855:

> . . . a woman carrying on another curious art, indirectly connected with ecclesiastical objects. The Buddhist monks are very careful of their books, looking on them with even a religious veneration, and keep them not only shut up in handsome chests, but carefully wrapt in chintz covers . . . These covers are tied on with a peculiar style of ribbon, bearing a long inscription of a religious character. These

Plate 31 ABOVE
WIDTH AND FINENESS
Early sazigyo woven in homespun yarn may be over 30 mm wide, while those woven with imported hard cotton could be as narrow as 11 mm, with correspondingly tiny script.

Plate 32 BELOW
KNITTED LOOK
Sazigyo are woven, not knitted. But the pattern of little paired chevrons formed by the warp in the double-faced weave at the start of some sazigyo undoubtedly has a knitted look.

> ribbons are worked either in silk or cotton, and are a common present from devout ladies to their spiritual guides. The beauty and accuracy with which the round Burmese character is formed on these ribbons had before struck me, and is indeed quite remarkable. It might give a lesson to our fair countrywomen, whose alphabetical attempts . . . seldom come nearer the intended inscription than . . . its reflection on the agitated surface of water.[13]

Sir J. G. Scott (Shway Yoe), writing in 1882, followed Yule in aiming a jibe at his female compatriots' needlework skills: "The *sa-si-gyo*, a riband, about two fingers' breadth, and upwards of a yard in length . . . is knitted or crocheted in a peculiarly close fashion, which puzzles English ladies. They are very neat, and quite easy to read, an advantage which does not always characterise Berlin wool work."[14]

Shway Yoe had for many years almost biblical authority, and in many respects still remains a useful and reliable source of information. But Scott certainly slipped in his description of the sazigyo. Knitted? Crocheted? All innocently I sent this snippet to Peter Collingwood, world expert on hand-weaving techniques. He reacted as though stung:

> Seriously, "knitted or crocheted" are utterly incorrect descriptions! Shockingly so to a textile structuralist! Those techniques use ONE element (thread) and create a coherent fabric from it by pulling loops through loops. They are "one-element structures." No other thread is needed. One ball of wool can give one sock. Sazigyo are definitely woven; they meet the definition "TWO SETS of elements interlaced at right angles," i.e. there is an initial warp (one set of longitudinal threads) through which a weft (a long continuous second set) is progressively interlaced, in some over/under sequence

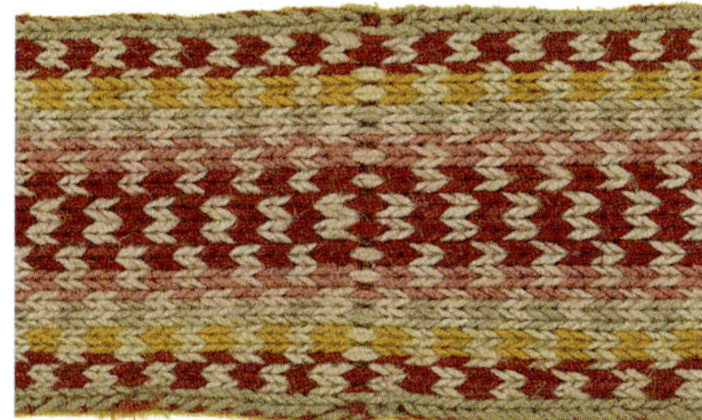

B873 (x2)

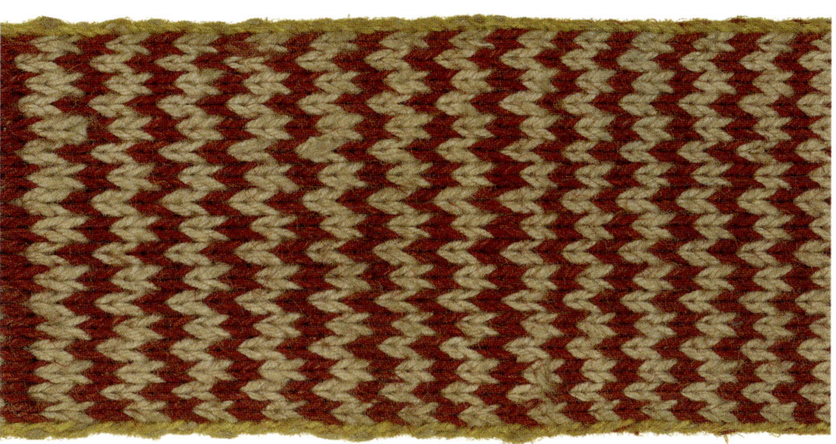

R223 (x2)

> depending on pattern required. I must admit that one frequently hears (albeit with a shudder) of the "knitted appearance" of simple tablet weaving . . . as at beginnings of sazigyos. This is because the little paired chevrons formed by warp do superficially look like a knitted surface. So Shway Yoe could be slightly forgiven. Lesson over!

HOW LONG DID IT TAKE TO WEAVE A SAZIGYO?

Those who handle a sazigyo and marvel at the detailed work often ask how long it would have taken to weave. Determined to obtain estimates, but unable to find surviving Burmese sazigyo weavers, I took my questions to a professional non-Burmese weaver, Otfried Staudigel. Drawing on a lifetime's experience of tablet weaving, he reckoned that a fast-working expert could weave forty centimeters of plain double-faced weave in an hour, but would need four or five hours to weave the same length of lettering or pictorial images. Of course, every sazigyo has its own proportion of plain weave to text and woven motifs and images. But applying Staudigel's estimates to a notional band with five meters total flat area, half plain weave and the other half in lettering, motifs, and images, we find it would require at least forty hours of concentrated work—and this is for the flat area alone. Quite recently I learned of another estimate, this time by a Burmese weaver.[15] Daw Thein Htay, leader of a workshop on tablet weaving held at the Saunders Weaving Institute at Amarapura near Mandalay in 1994, noted that an expert weaver could produce five inches of "artistic design and text weaving" in a day's work. Suppose we reckon five hours' work daily, and one inch per hour. Then 2.5 meters (roughly 93 inches) of motifs, images, and text would need about twenty days' work. Add five days' work for the other 2.5 meters of plain double-faced weave. The total work time would be about twenty-five days—for the flat area of double-faced weave alone. Additional time is needed for setting up the work, preparing and sorting the warp threads on the loom, threading them through each of forty tablets, making and binding the initial loop, making the tapers (up to full width at the start, and down to the cord at the end), and making the cord itself, whether tubular or braided. Take all these tasks into account and the estimated time taken to produce a finely woven sazigyo rises to as much as thirty days. Evidence in support of this estimate comes from the text of a sazigyo woven more than a century ago:

> **In the cool season of the year 1238 BE** [1876 CE] **on the seventh day of the waxing moon of Tazaungmon the words of the text were given to the weaver, and the band was completed on Sunday afternoon the fourth day of the waxing moon of Natdaw, on the third stroke of the time drum.** (JB6.51)

The weaver took almost exactly four whole weeks to complete this sazigyo, but it is an incredible nine meters in length and has over a hundred verses.

Few women weavers were full-time professionals: most had to fit their craft work into a busy pattern of domestic duties. A sazigyo with lengthy text and numerous woven images might easily take several months to complete. Meanwhile, the scribe was at work copying the scriptural manuscript.

Admiring the finished decorative effect, we might assume that the task of weaving script and miniature images demanded the weaver's undivided concentration. But Scherman noted in Mandalay in 1911 that sazigyo weavers sitting near each other exchanged gossip and banter while weaving complex lettering. Their fingers, like those of musicians, had developed a memory of their own.

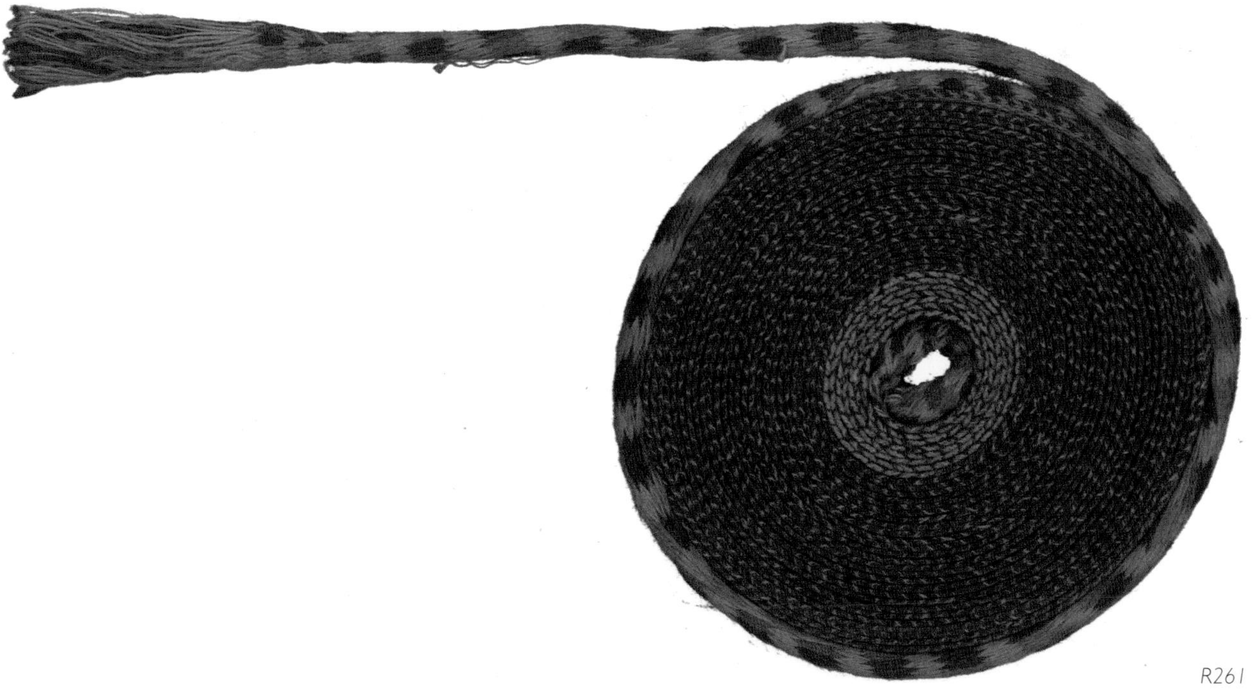

R261

Part II Chapter 7

Damage and Repairs to Sazigyo

FADING AND DYES RUNNING

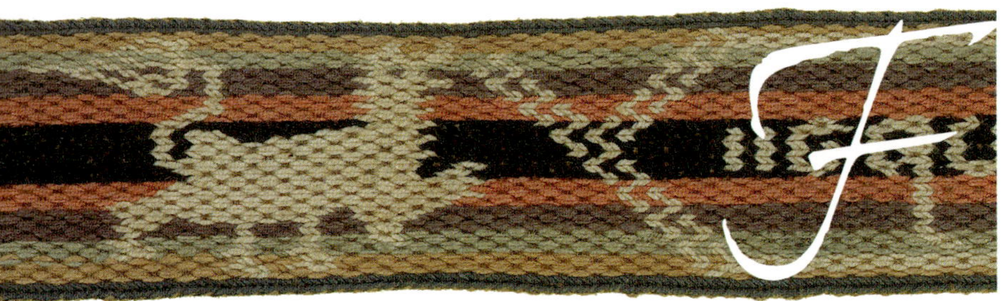

MYA055T

Few sazigyo survive in pristine condition. They were made to be used, and most are worn and faded. Frequently the fading is at intervals, caused when the manuscript with sazigyo wound around it was exposed to sunlight on one side. Old indigo sazigyo seem immune to fading, but in later sazigyo fading of colors can render text almost illegible, and virtually erase woven images. The reverse side of a sazigyo is usually less faded because it was less exposed to direct sunlight. Computer cunning can sometimes exploit this uneven damage and restore badly faded woven texts to readability, simply by scanning the reverse of the faded sazigyo and "flipping" the images.

The results of water damage and running of dyes, especially pink and red, in sazigyo woven after cheap imported yarn took the place of indigo and madder can vary from patchy to completely indistinct.

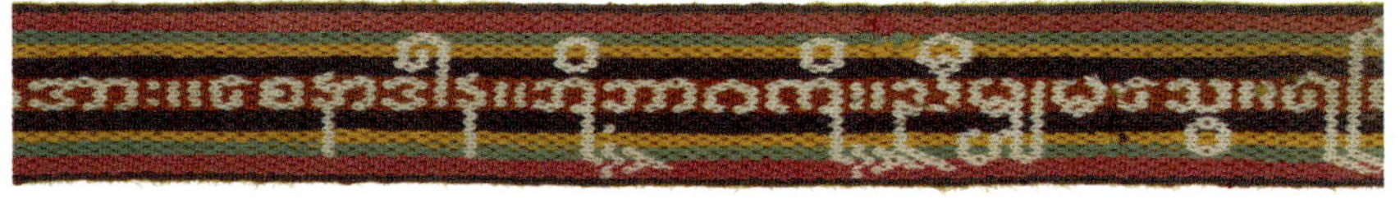

R012

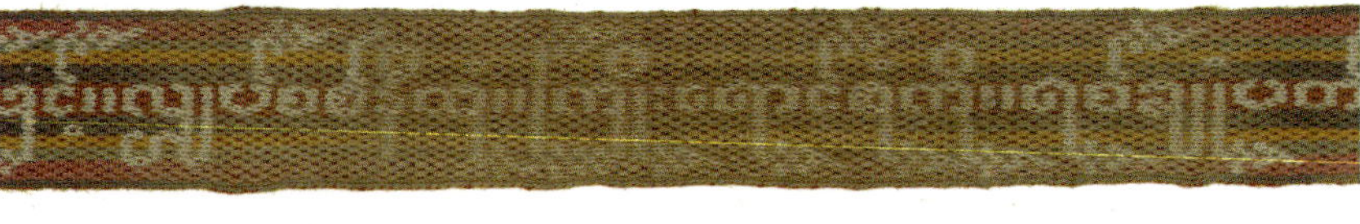

R012

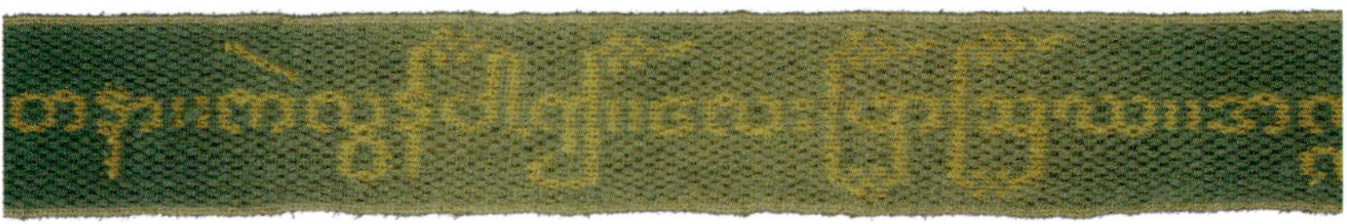

R049

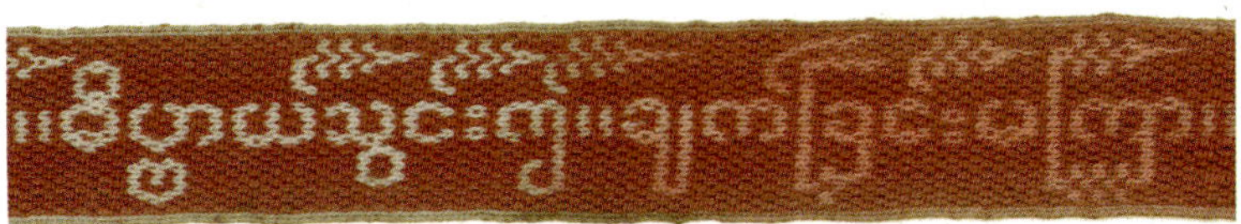

R057

Plate 33 RIGHT AND TOP NEXT PAGE

DAMAGE TO SAZIGYO

Few sazigyo survive in pristine condition. Many are faded at intervals, caused when the manuscript with sazigyo wound around it was exposed to sunlight on one side. *(R012, R049)*

Run dyes, especially pink and red, are a frequent cause of damage in sazigyo woven after cheap imported yarn took the place of indigo and madder. *(R057)*

Insect boreholes or tunnels always start on the reverse of the sazigyo, suggesting that the insects had first attacked the palm-leaf manuscript and its cloth sleeve. *(R053, B885, J07)*
Study by candlelight risks scorch marks. *(M01)*

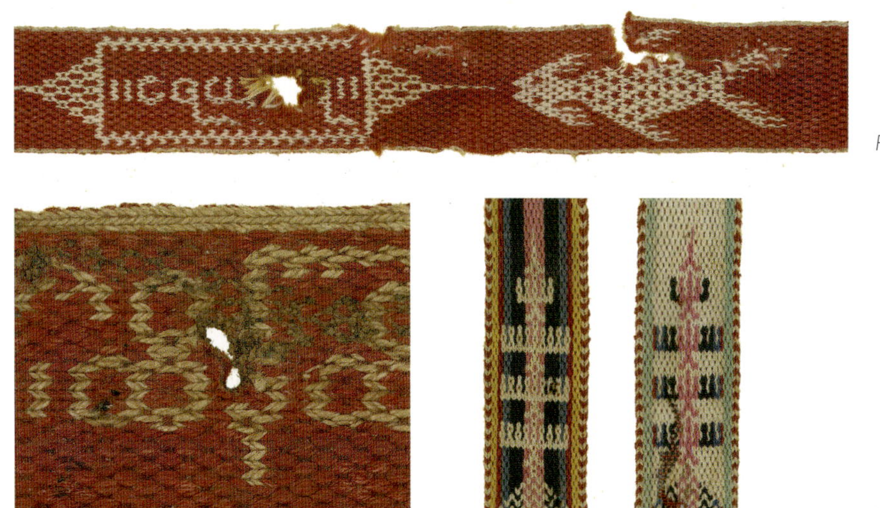

R053

B885 (x2) *J07 obverse* *J07 reverse*

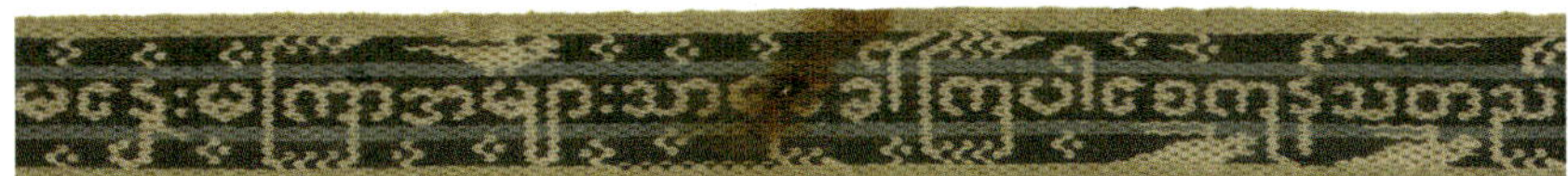

M01

DAMAGE BY INSECTS AND RODENTS

Insect damage shows in characteristic holes and tunnels, the latter almost always on the reverse of the sazigyo, suggesting that the insect larvae had reached the sazigyo from within the bundle of palm-leaf manuscript and its cloth sleeve. Rodents must also have been at work, but the evidence they leave is more ambiguous. Scorch marks and candle-wax stains are also common.

DAMAGE TO LOOP

The loop is the first part to be woven, and the first to go. Loops formed of a tubular woven cord are much more durable than those made by simply wrapping or whipping the warp threads.[16] The latter type of loop is, of course, doomed to dissolve as soon as the binding thread wears through. In about a third of all the sazigyo I have studied, the loop is largely or completely dissolved. Without a loop the sazigyo becomes unfit for purpose. Judging by their fine state of preservation, some sazigyo lost their loop early, while still fresh, whereupon they were rolled up and pushed into a chest or cupboard—forgotten, but safe from the harmful light of day.

Plate 34 BELOW AND TOP NEXT PAGE
THE LOOP
Some old sazigyo were woven without a loop. *(AZ3)*
Some have been provided with a functional loop in the form of an extra cord tied through the warp threads at the start of the band. *(R162, R177)*
The loop is the first to go, and in this sazigyo the damage to the binding of the loop has begun. *(B888)*
Unusable without a loop, some sazigyo may be rolled up and stored in a chest or cupboard while still fresh. *(R154)*

A few old sazigyo of mid-nineteenth-century date seem to have no loop. A closer look at the rounded end of the weave reveals the original "loop" perfectly preserved—but perfectly useless. It is tiny, far too small to admit the great fat cord, made with little or no reduction of warp threads. This curious defect can scarcely have been accidental. Some of these "loopless" sazigyo have been equipped with a functional loop formed with an extra cord tied through the warp threads. This can be seen in two old indigo sazigyo in the Ryan collection, one of which is dated 1854.[17]

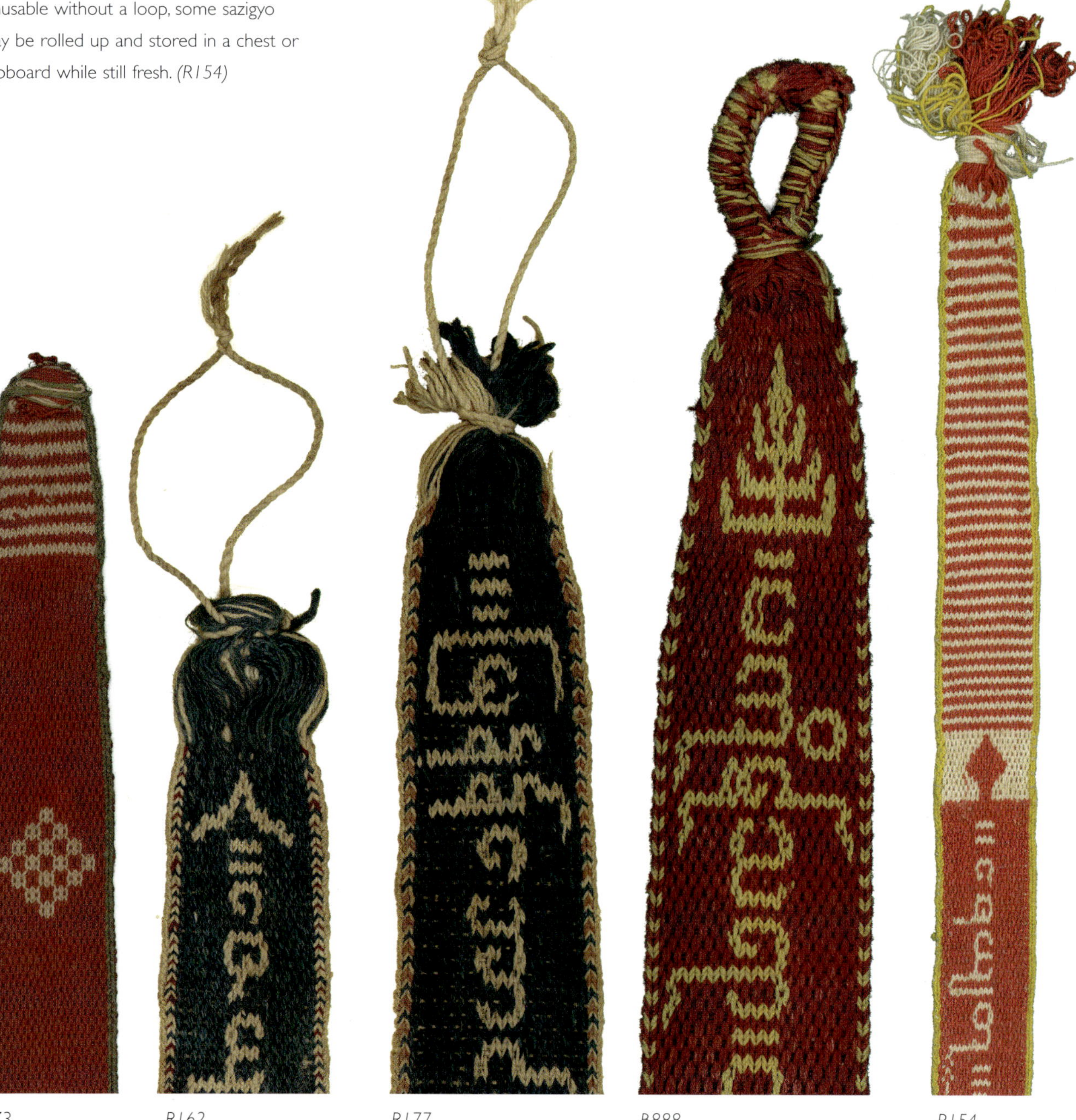

AZ3 *R162* *R177* *B888* *R154*

DAMAGE TO BODY OF BAND

This very fine old sazigyo includes many beautiful images. It must have been greatly cherished to have been sewn together in two different places. *(B852)*

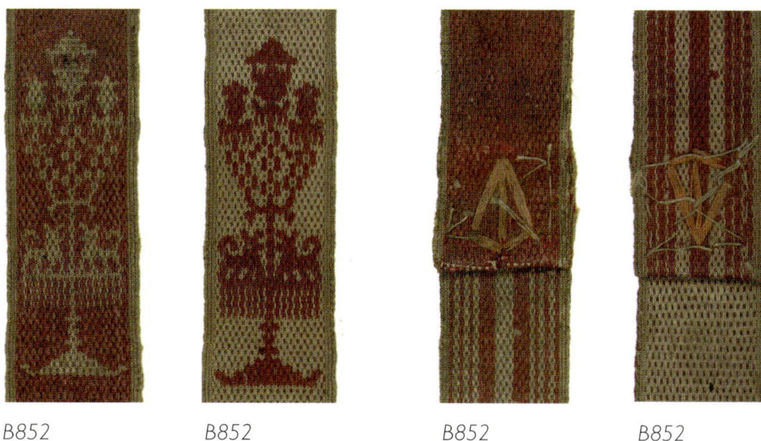

B852 *B852* *B852* *B852*

DAMAGE TO BODY OF BAND AND TO CORD

Once it has worn right through, a sazigyo is useless. The monk user of an exceptionally fine old sazigyo (B852) must have cherished it greatly, for it has been sewn together in two different places. Reluctant to discard it when it fell to pieces, he must have had it repaired with needle and thread or even sewn it together himself. But in these harsh modern times, readers shown a sazigyo stitched together with a sewing machine should suspect an antique dealer's trick.

The cord is also prone to accident. Some are cut short, and a few have been lengthened by the addition of a piece of cord from another (presumably destroyed) sazigyo, simply tied on with a tight knot.

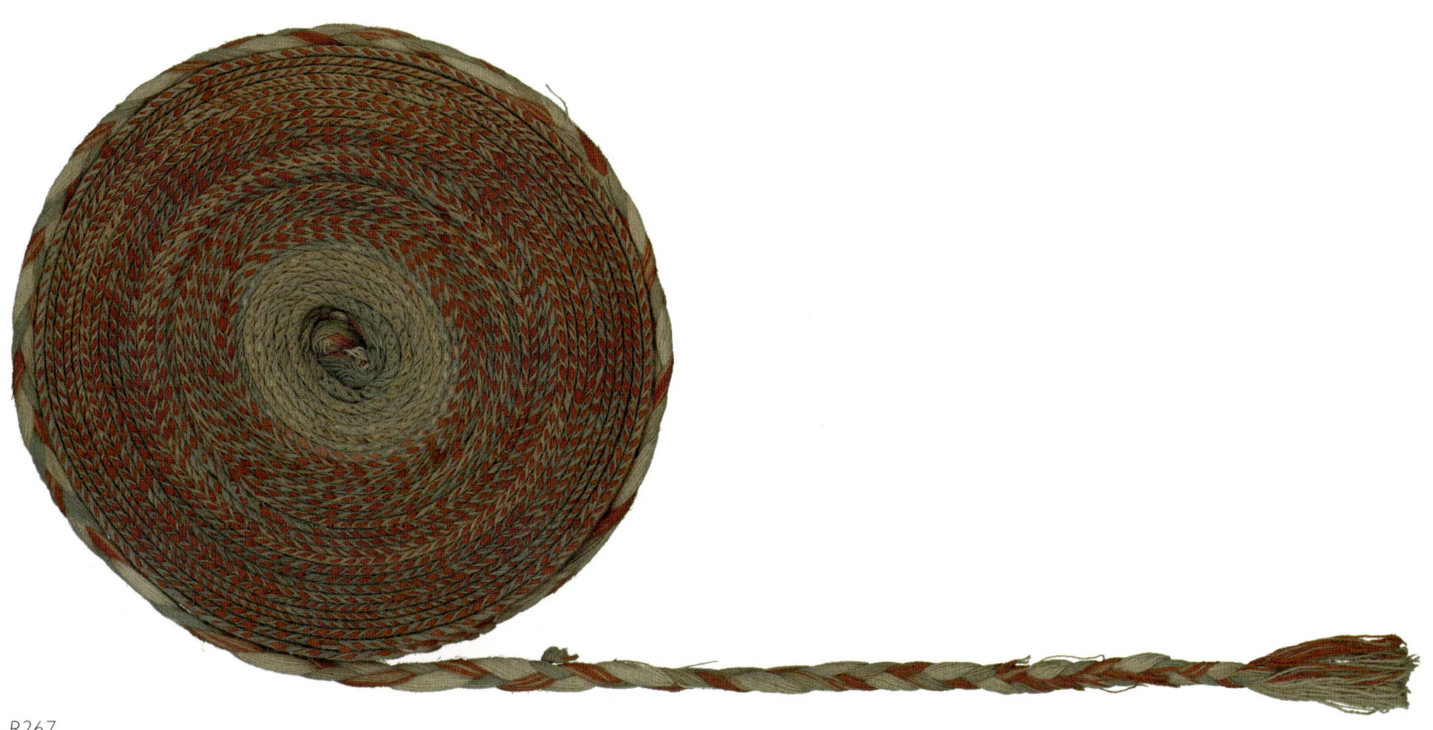

R267

Like an embroiderer with needle and gold wire thread,
So we weave the lettering of the script,
Working with the greatest care,
Moving the tablets back and forth, back and forth,
Concentrating hard and avoiding mistakes,
Grouping the tablets in packs,
Turning and returning them—
This is the whole method of our art.

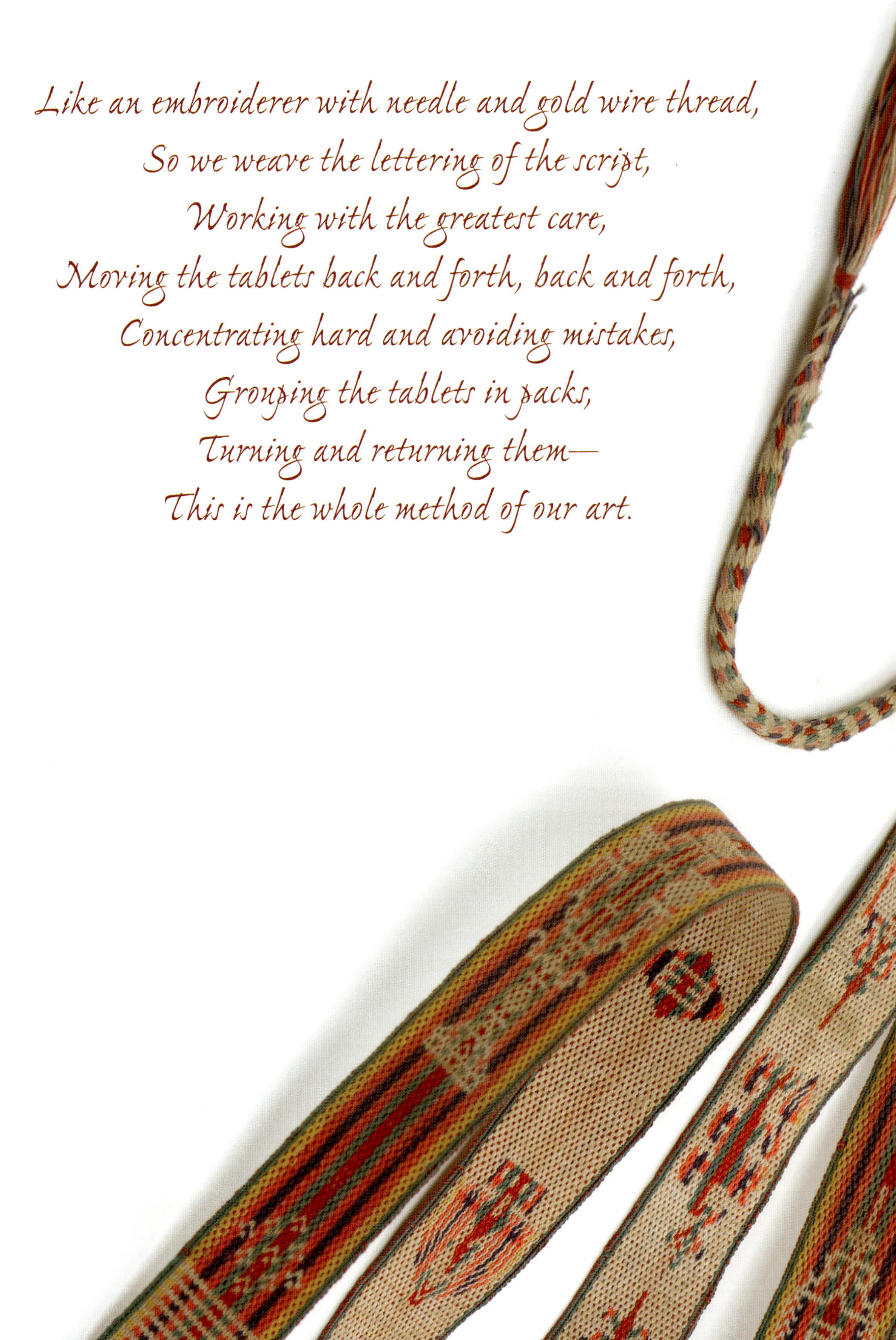

Part III

THE SAZIGYO AS WOVEN TEXT

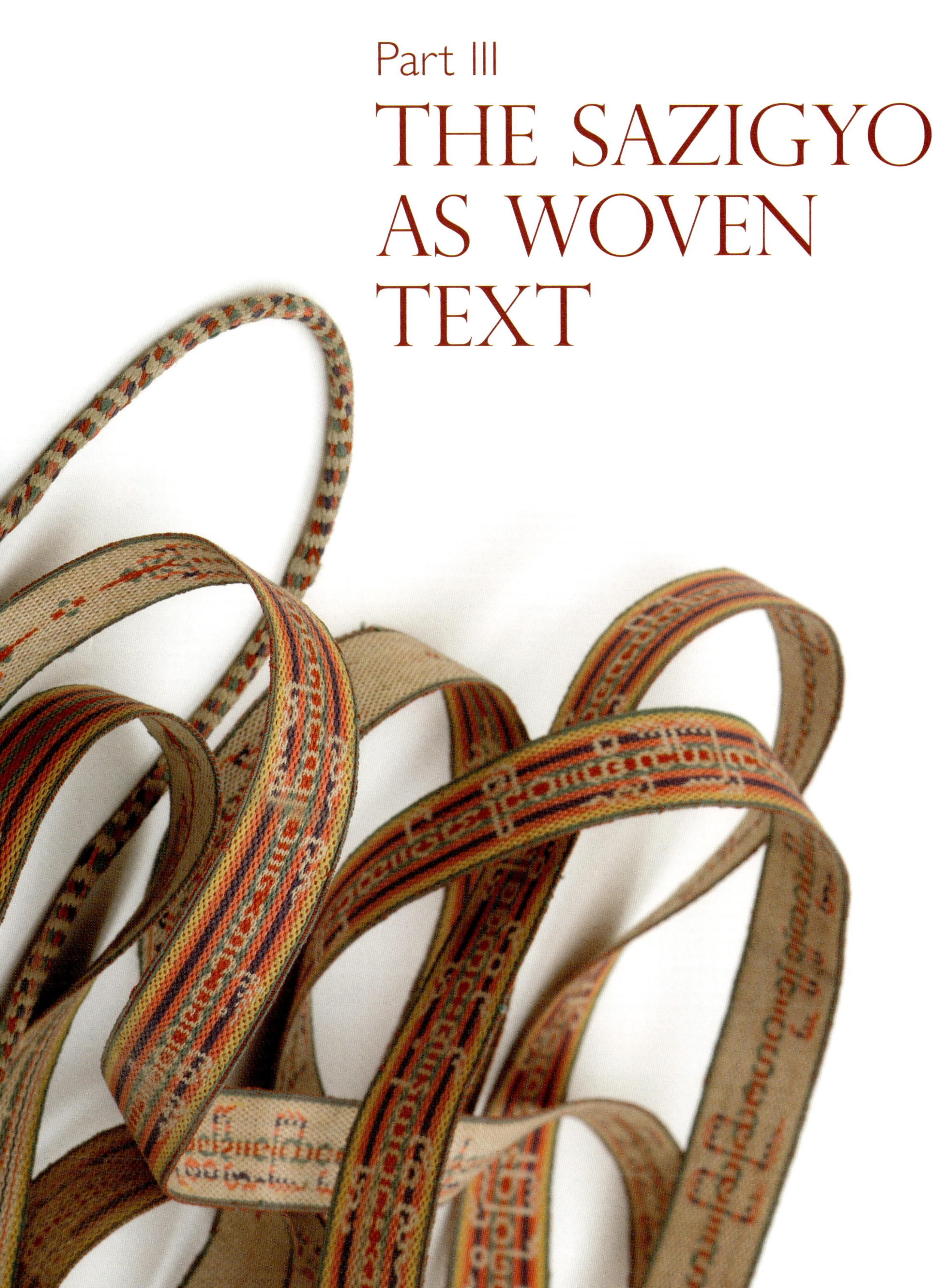

Part III Chapter 8

Text Lettering: The Look of the Script Band

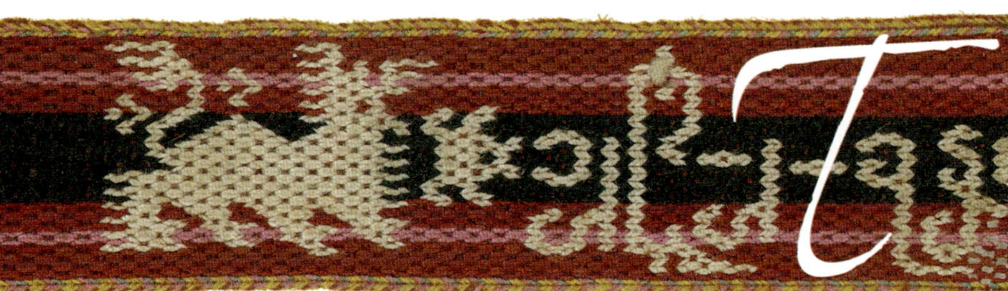

R245

The time has come to shift the focus from textile to text. Up to now we have treated the sazigyo as a textile, an artifact of the weaver's art. Here we shall look at the woven script of the text, at the color, size, and shape of the lettering, and at the pleasing patterns it makes. Then, with the help of English translations, we shall go on to consider the meaning of the various script messages and to relate them to the social and religious context in which sazigyo were made and used. These messages are the fruit of Theravada Buddhist belief and practice, but they also carry traces of other more ancient beliefs.

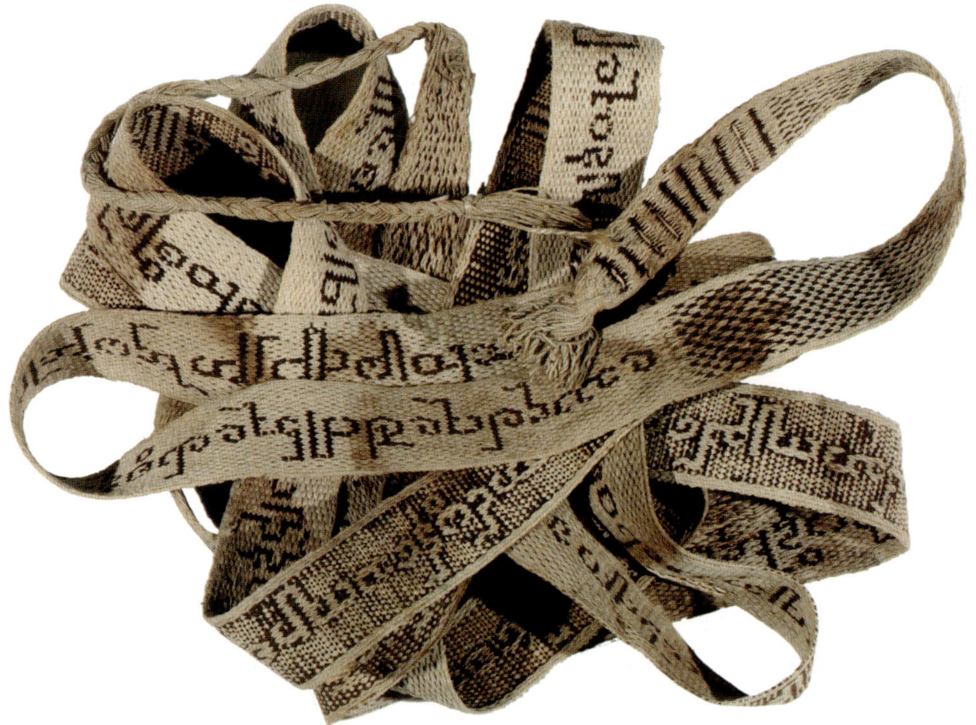

RAS

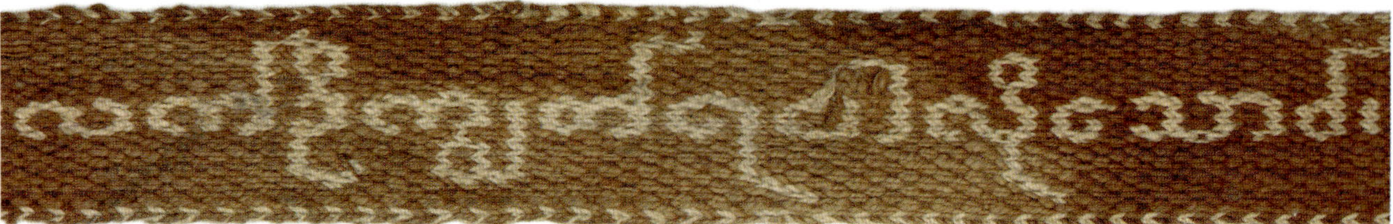

HM12220

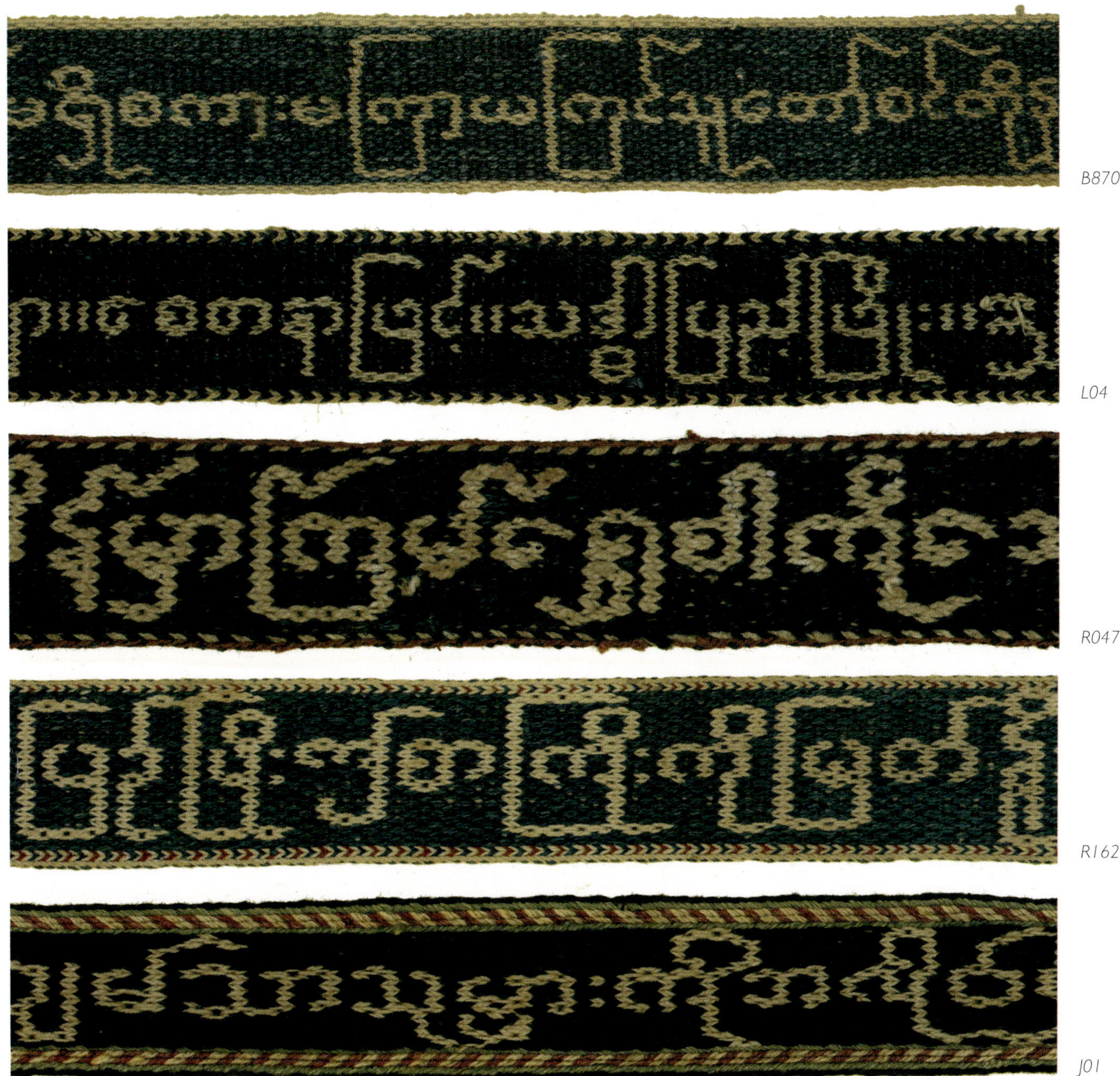

Plate 35

PREVIOUS PAGE, ABOVE, AND FOLLOWING PAGE

The oldest known sazigyo have a brown background, with a text in natural, undyed yarn. *(RAS, HM12220)*

Many nineteenth-century sazigyo are indigo blue, and the shades range from pale baby blue to deep midnight blue and near black. *(B870, L04, R047)*

Contrasting colors might appear sparingly in the selvage (edging), but not as long warp stripes. *(R162, J01)*

Totally unreadable script, if we are not struggling to decipher it, can be curiously pleasing as a two-colored pattern. The mosque-builders of Iran and other Islamic lands exploited Arabic calligraphic script for its decorative beauty as well as its sacred message. The power and beauty of the script can appeal even to the illiterate. We can look at the sazigyo's woven text as a patterned and colored textile, taking in the color, size, and shape of the script, the way the lettering fills the flat space on the woven band and how it stands out from the background color.

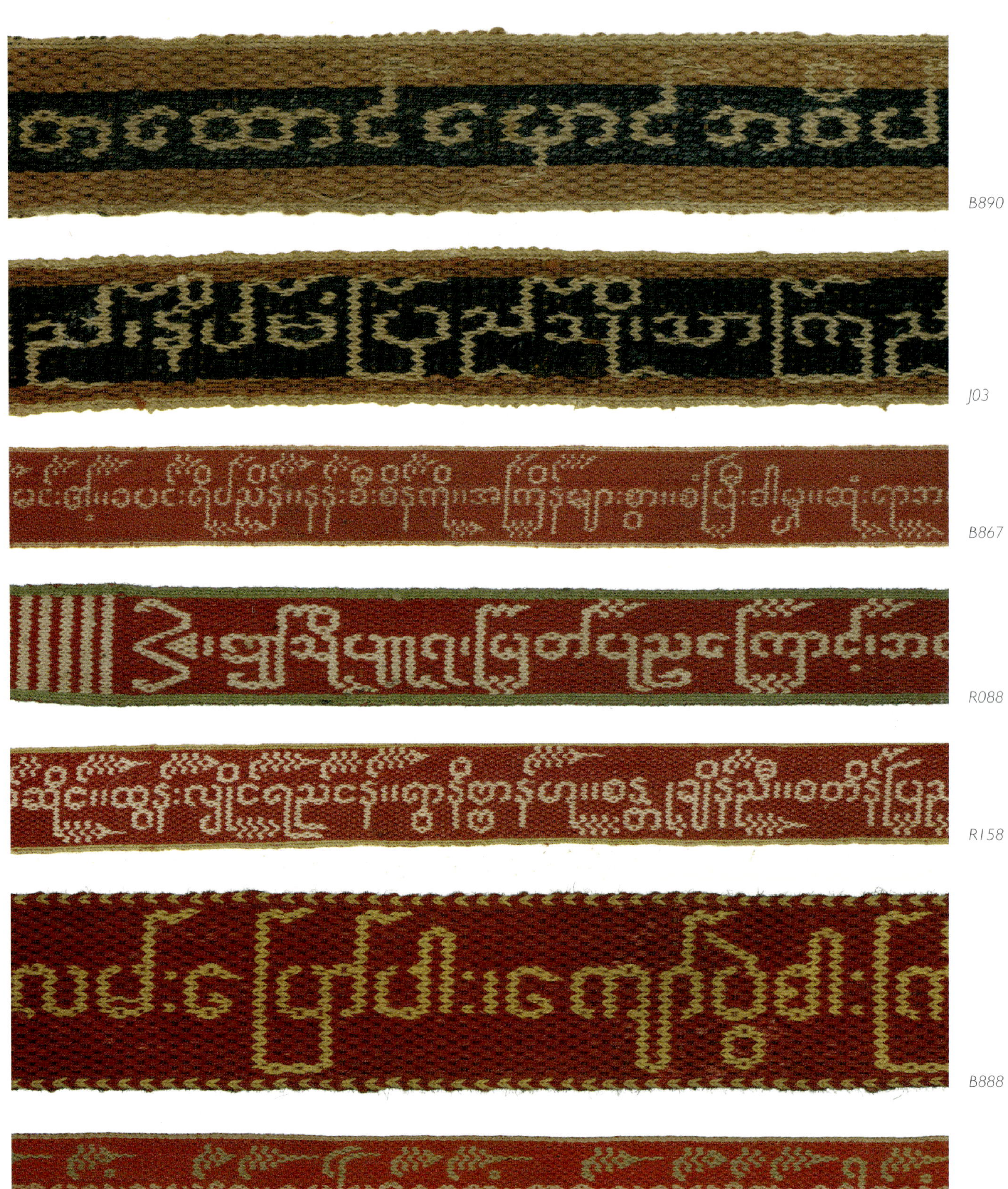

B890

J03

B867

R088

R158

B888

R272

Sometimes the warp was of both brown and indigo blue. *(B890, J03)*

Red is equally common in nineteenth- and early twentieth-century sazigyo, and red yarn and white is the stock term used by women weavers describing their craft. *(B867, R088, R158)*

Some sazigyo have a yellow text on a red ground. *(B888)*

Here the weaver retains white only for the central warp stripe, using green above and yellow below. The happy result is a three-colored script: the central portion is white, with all its upper flourishes green and all the lower ones yellow. *(R272)*

The oldest known sazigyo have a brown background, with a text in natural, undyed yarn. Two old brown sazigyo are in British collections, one in the Horniman Museum dateable to 1795, and another late eighteenth-century brown sazigyo in the Royal Asiatic Society.[1] The brown dye is from the bark of an acacia tree.

Many nineteenth-century sazigyo are indigo blue, with a text in natural, undyed yarn. Shades range from pale "baby blue" to deep midnight blue, the depth of color depending on the number of times the yarn was dipped in the indigo dye. When new and fresh these indigo tapes were beautiful: **"This ribbon is woven with excellent handiwork using pearl-white thread for the warp stretched lengthwise and sapphire-blue thread as the weft."** (VC19)

The Pitt Rivers Museum in Oxford has an early indigo sazigyo whose main text is in Pali, but the final text naming the donor is in Burmese: **"The work of merit of the nun Meh Aye. Completed on Sunday, third day of the waning moon of the month of Tazaungmon, 1160** [1798 CE]**."**[2]

In the Ryan collection a well-preserved indigo sazigyo (R162) is dated in the Burmese text 1216 BE (1854 CE). Some old sazigyo use both brown and indigo warp.

Equally common in nineteenth- and early twentieth-century sazigyo is "natural on red." The red dye was powdered lac. "Red yarn and white" is the stock term used by women weavers describing their craft and materials.

Burmese weavers of silk and cotton cloth continued to use native vegetable dyes for some time after imported yarn became generally available. Mi Mi Khaing, writing in 1946, nostalgically recalls "silks of exquisite pinks, blue-greys, gold and amber, strong reds and purples, dull dirty greens, all from the sunset skies, water-vegetation, birds and trees, never fading." Each shade was named not after the dyestuff, but from its occurrence in nature, "tender flowers, dove, wood smoke, leaf-bud, marian seed, prawn oil, amber, cock's blood, slime-moss, rotten vegetation."[3]

In Mandalay in 1911 Prof. Lucian Scherman noted that sazigyo weavers there favored yellow text on a black background. The yellow dye was prepared from the bark of the jackfruit tree. This formal fashion lasted until at least 1928, when either yellow or white yarn, or both together, were used against a black ground, mimicking the rich effect of silver and gold on black lacquer.

From about 1900, imported thread was available in hundreds of colors, and fine enough to enable the weaving of very small lettering. Sazigyo weavers were quick to exploit the new yarn, devising their own color schemes of six or more shades. The results were often arresting, some garish, some harmonious.

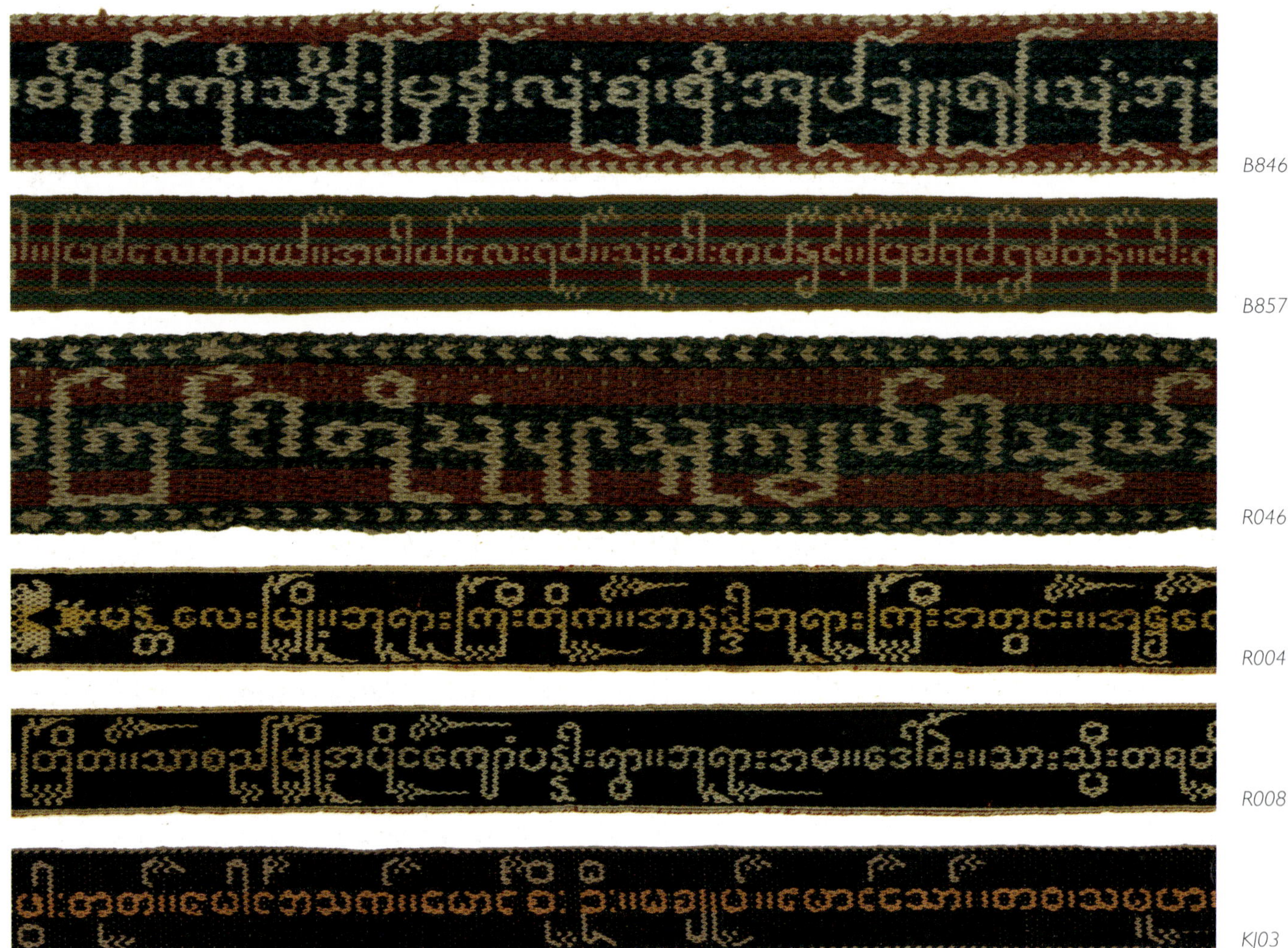

Plate 36 ABOVE

A third color began to appear in sazigyo woven about 1890. *(B846, B857, R046)* Mandalay weavers in the early twentieth century favored yellow or white text on a black background. *(R004, R008, KJ03)*

Plate 37 NEXT AND FOLLOWING PAGE

Weavers were quick to exploit the vast range of colors, devising their own color schemes of six or more shades, some garish, some harmonious. *(B840, B842, R116, H031, J06, KJ02, R027, R058, R105, R247, R026)*

LARGE AND SMALL SCRIPT

A few virtuoso weavers spangled the woven text with tiny stars and miniature parrots, crammed into every spare space above and below the lettering. They even invented parrot-shaped flourishes integral to the letters themselves. But multicolored letters could make the text less legible, and unfortunately some of the new shades, unlike the old reliable indigo, were not fast.

Most sazigyo woven before about 1890 are entirely devoted to text. Such bands have two colors: natural undyed yarn for the text, and a blue or red ground. There are no distracting woven images: the text is allocated the maximum possible space, both height and length. The "tops and tails" of the script may reach to the edges of the band, merging with the selvage. The text may start immediately after the loop, even before the band has reached full width, and it may extend to the very end of the flat area where it starts to taper down to the cord. In an indigo sazigyo woven ca. 1855 (R177), the text covers over 99 percent of the flat area: 534 cm out of a total of 539 cm.

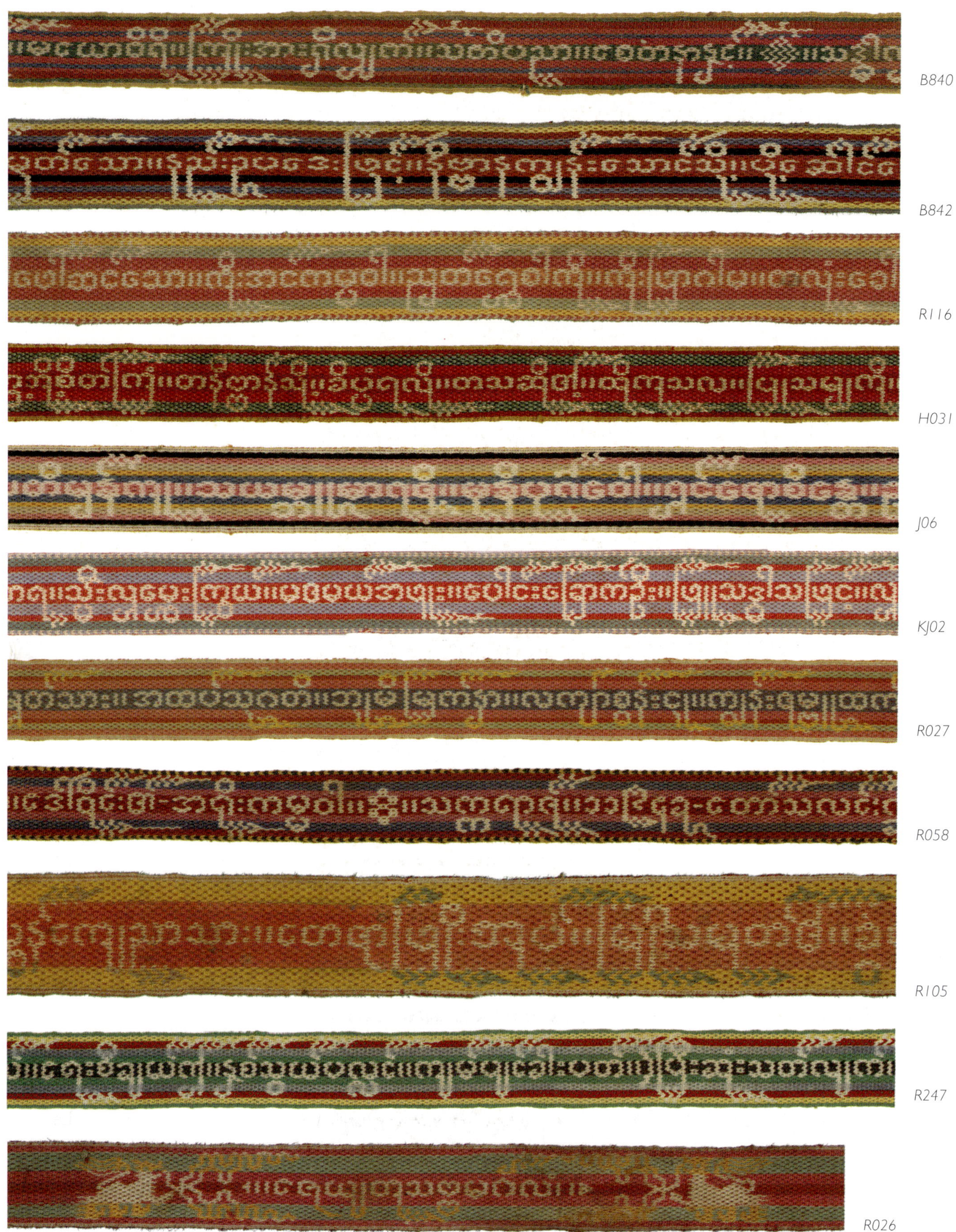

B840

B842

R116

H031

J06

KJ02

R027

R058

R105

R247

R026

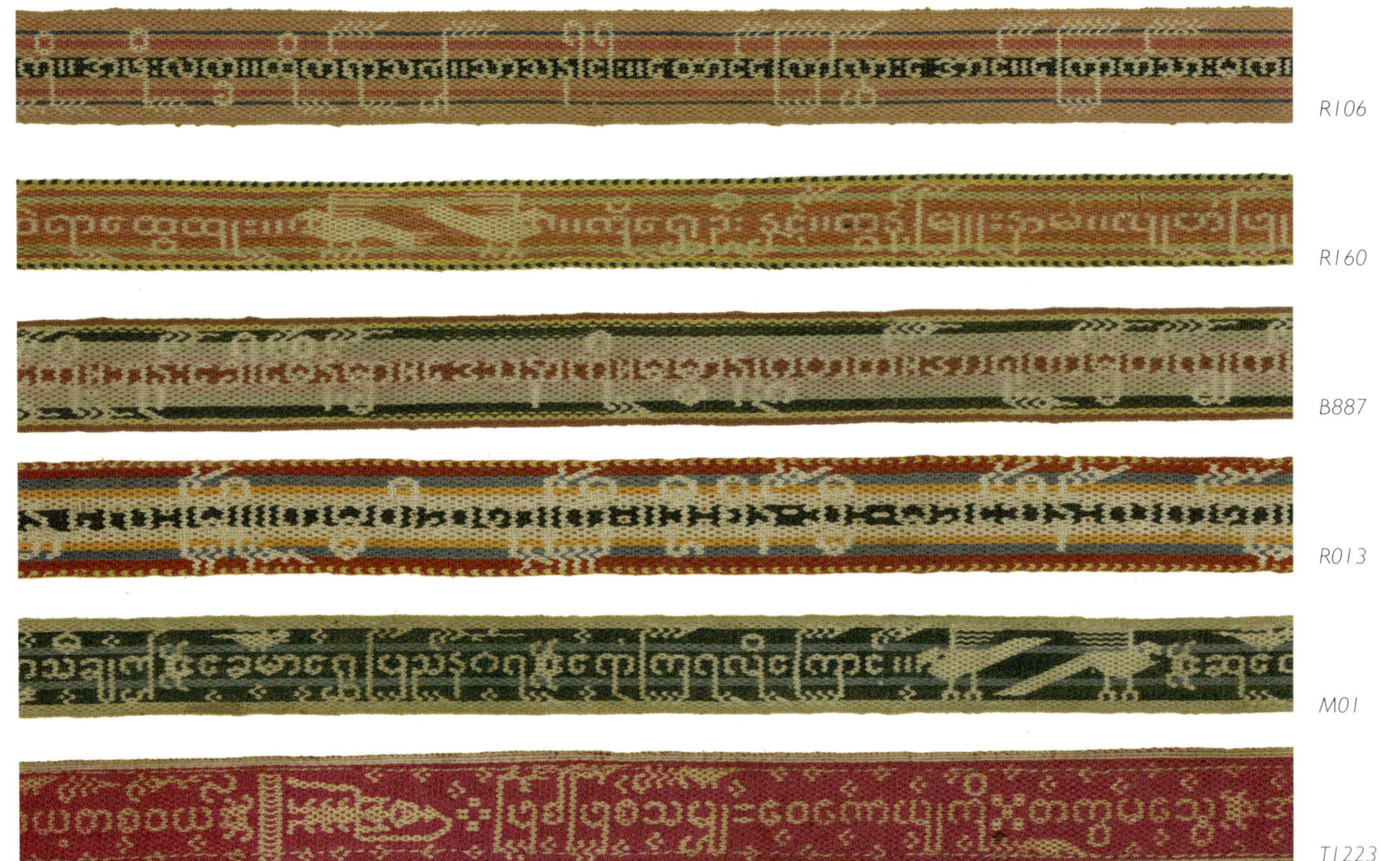

ABOVE

From about 1900, imported hard cotton thread enabled the weaving of very small lettering. *(R106, R160)*
The many different colors could detract from the legibility of the text. *(B887, R013)*
Some virtuoso weavers spangled the text with tiny woven stars and crammed miniature parrots and frogs into every spare space above and below the lettering. *(M01, T1223)*

Sazigyo woven after about 1890 have different priorities. The text may still be lengthy, but it is confined to a central warp stripe which runs between other narrow stripes of bright contrasting colors, and it is embellished with woven images. The script may be neatly woven, but it can look cramped if the letters are very small.

Written Burmese, with its predominately rounded letters, resembles a series of bubbles. For centuries before pen and ink and paper, Burmese scribes used a metal stylus to engrave the letters on palm leaves. Lines drawn lengthwise on the cured palm leaf would easily tear it, and it has been suggested that this is how the letters of the Burmese alphabet acquired their round shapes.[4]

SQUARE SCRIPT

Rectangular script, imitating lithic inscriptions, was fashionable in the first decade of the twentieth century. Several neatly woven sazigyo dated to 1907 or 1908 are entirely in this consciously archaistic square script. Meh May (the weaver of B850) wove the whole of a long text in square script—except for her own name. When she came to sign her work, Meh May reverted to round script.

"ENGRAVED" SCRIPT

A few sazigyo show a curious effect: the text is "recessed" on the obverse, and "embossed" or raised on the reverse. The white script appears engraved or sunken below the surrounding red background—and this must have been the effect sought by the weavers, mimicking engraved inscriptions on stone or bronze. The sunken script on the obverse of the weave loses in legibility, in contrast to the script on the back of the tape, where the text stands up prominently in red above the white ground. This potentially excellent way to highlight the script seems never to have been exploited for that purpose.[5]

"RULED" LINES

On two sazigyo dated 1903 the round elements of the lettering are confined between two thin yellow lines, reminiscent of the ruled lines in old-style school exercise books. In one (R029) the text is reasonably well woven, clearly legible, and signed by a male weaver "Work of Ko Khin," though his work could hardly be considered a good advertisement for the skill of male weavers. In another (B838) the effect is again rather like a lined school exercise book, for a child learning to write. Shwebo Mi Mi Gyi told me in January 2007 that men used not only to weave sazigyo, but also to instruct girls.

DOUBLE LINE OF TEXT

The National Museum in Yangon holds an amazing sazigyo, which has two lines of woven script for its entire length (see plates 38 and 75). The weaver must have had quite extraordinary skill to anticipate and allow for every riser and faller in both the upper and lower lines of text simultaneously. Indeed it is hard to imagine how this could have been achieved without working from a written text. The text has been translated by Dr. Ye Myint, who also knows of at least one other two-line sazigyo, in the Thaton Museum.[6]

NMY

Plate 38 RIGHT AND FOLLOWING PAGE
This sazigyo in the National Museum in Yangon is almost unique in having two lines of woven script for its entire length of over four meters. The weaver would have needed to anticipate and allow for every riser and faller in both the upper and lower lines of text. *(NMY)*

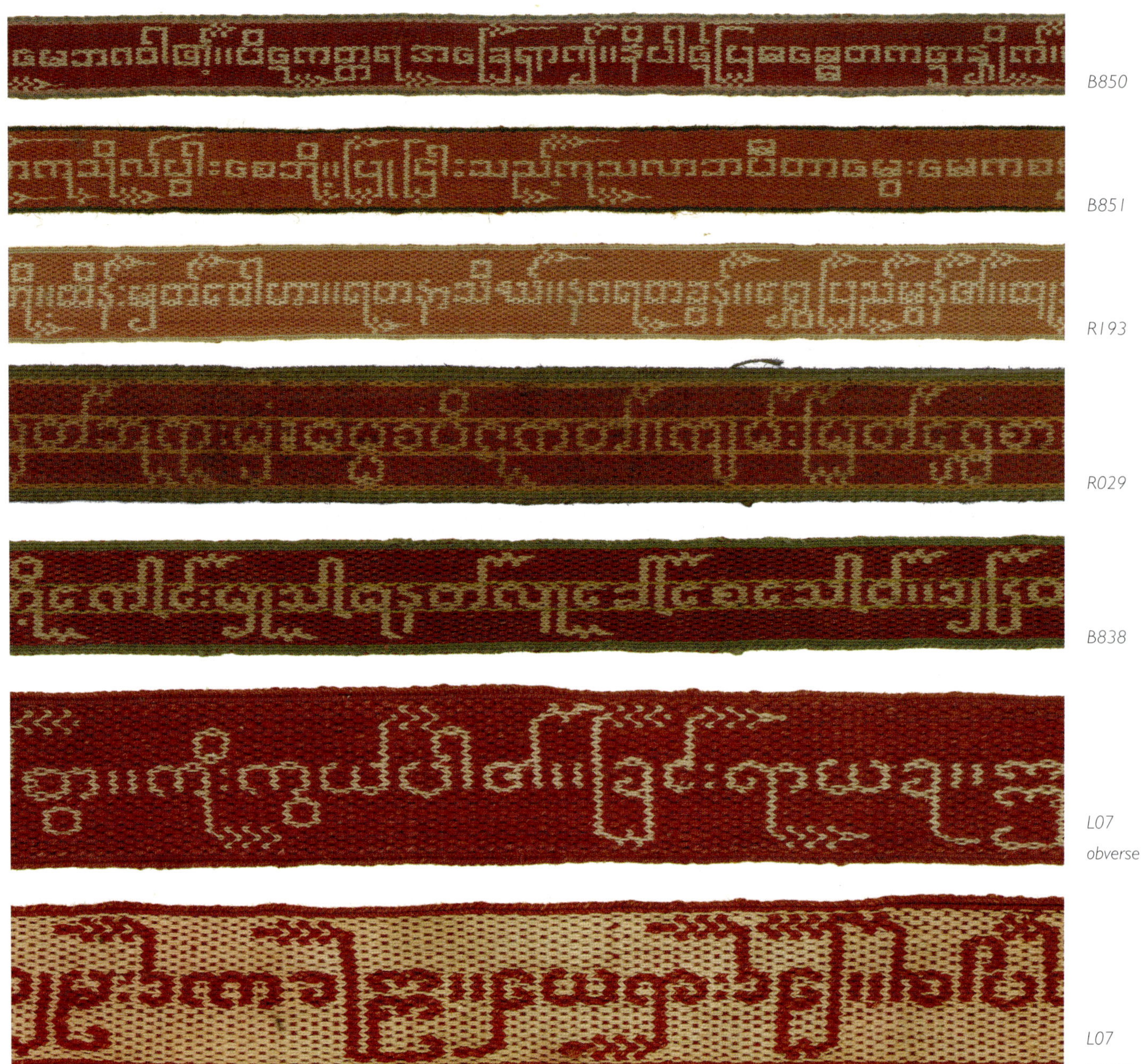

ABOVE

Square script, imitating stone inscriptions, was fashionable in the first decade of the twentieth century. *(B850, B851, R193)*
The text of two sazigyo, both dated 1903, recalls the ruled lines in old-style school exercise books. *(R029, B838)*
In a few sazigyo the white text appears sunken below the red background, as if the weavers were trying to mimic engraved inscriptions on stone or bronze. *(L07)*

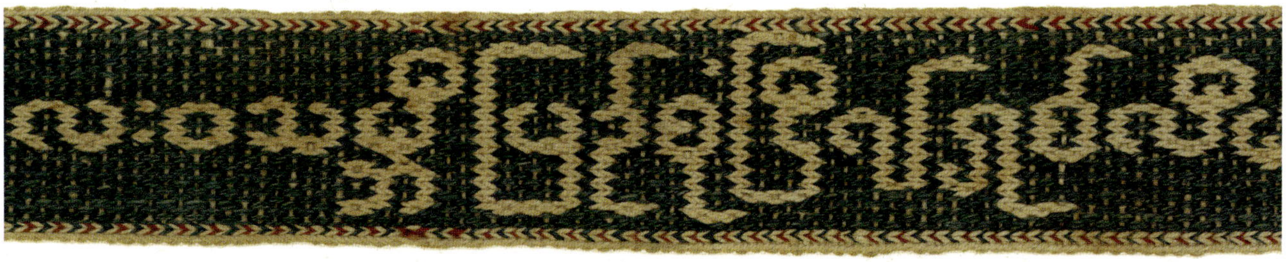

R162

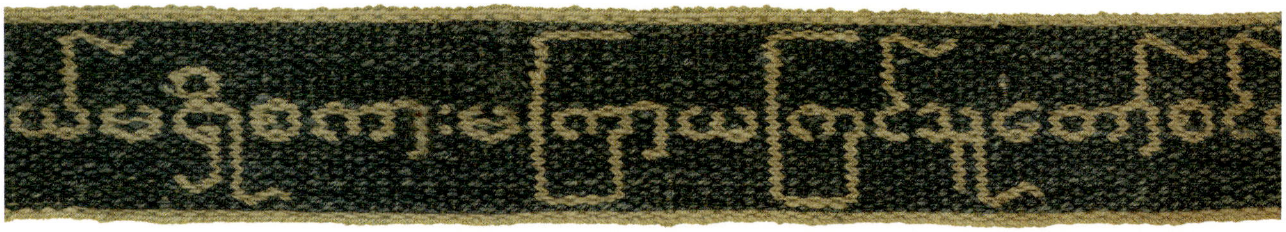

B870

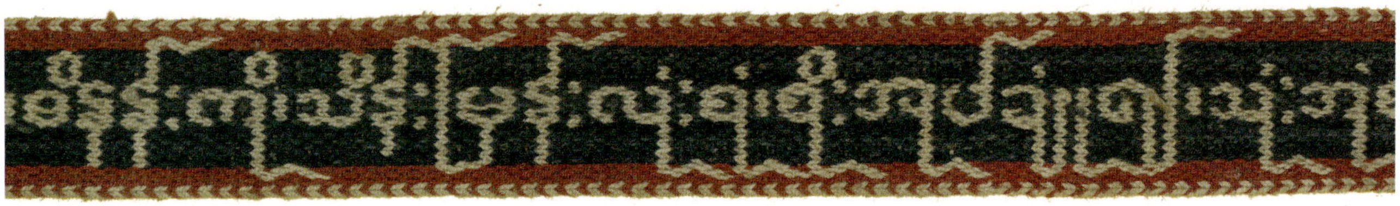

B846

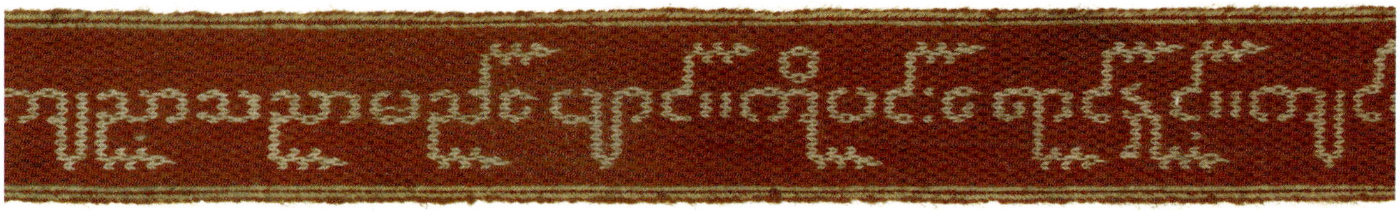

B880

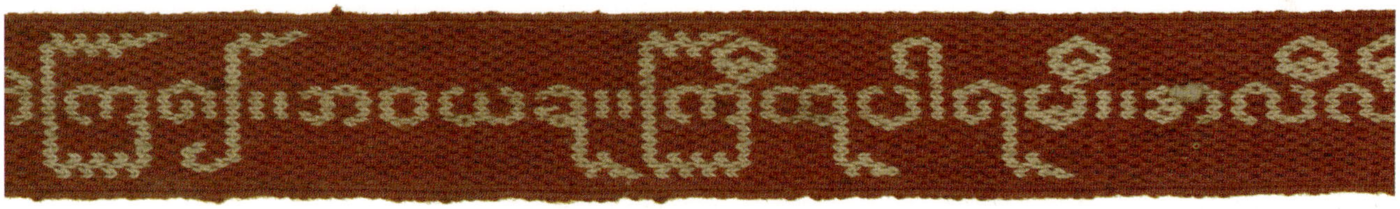

B509305

Plate 39

ABOVE, RIGHT, AND FOLLOWING PAGES

Risers and fallers grow increasingly elaborate through time. In the woven text of mid-nineteenth-century indigo sazigyo they are simple, angular, and always attached to the letter to which they belong. *(R162, B870)*

By 1890, straight arms had become simple arched curves. *(B846)*

Early twentieth-century weavers were using alternate or zig-zag projections. *(B880, B509305, R183, R205)*

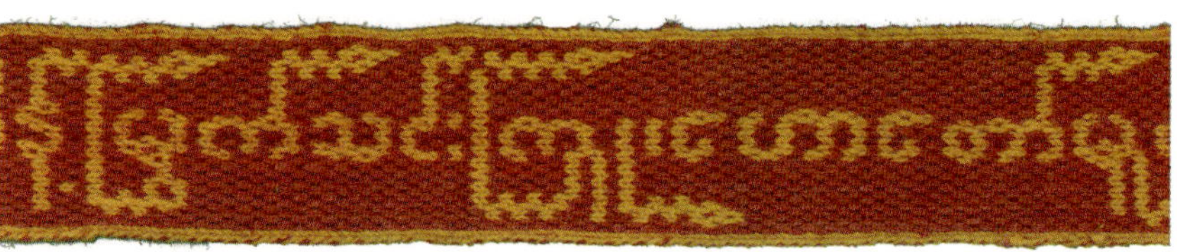

R183

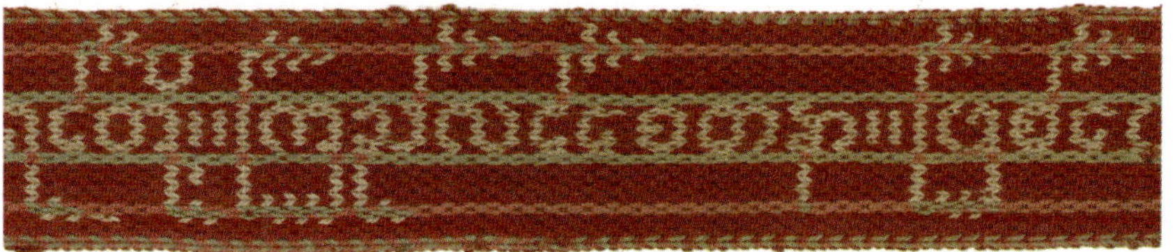

R205

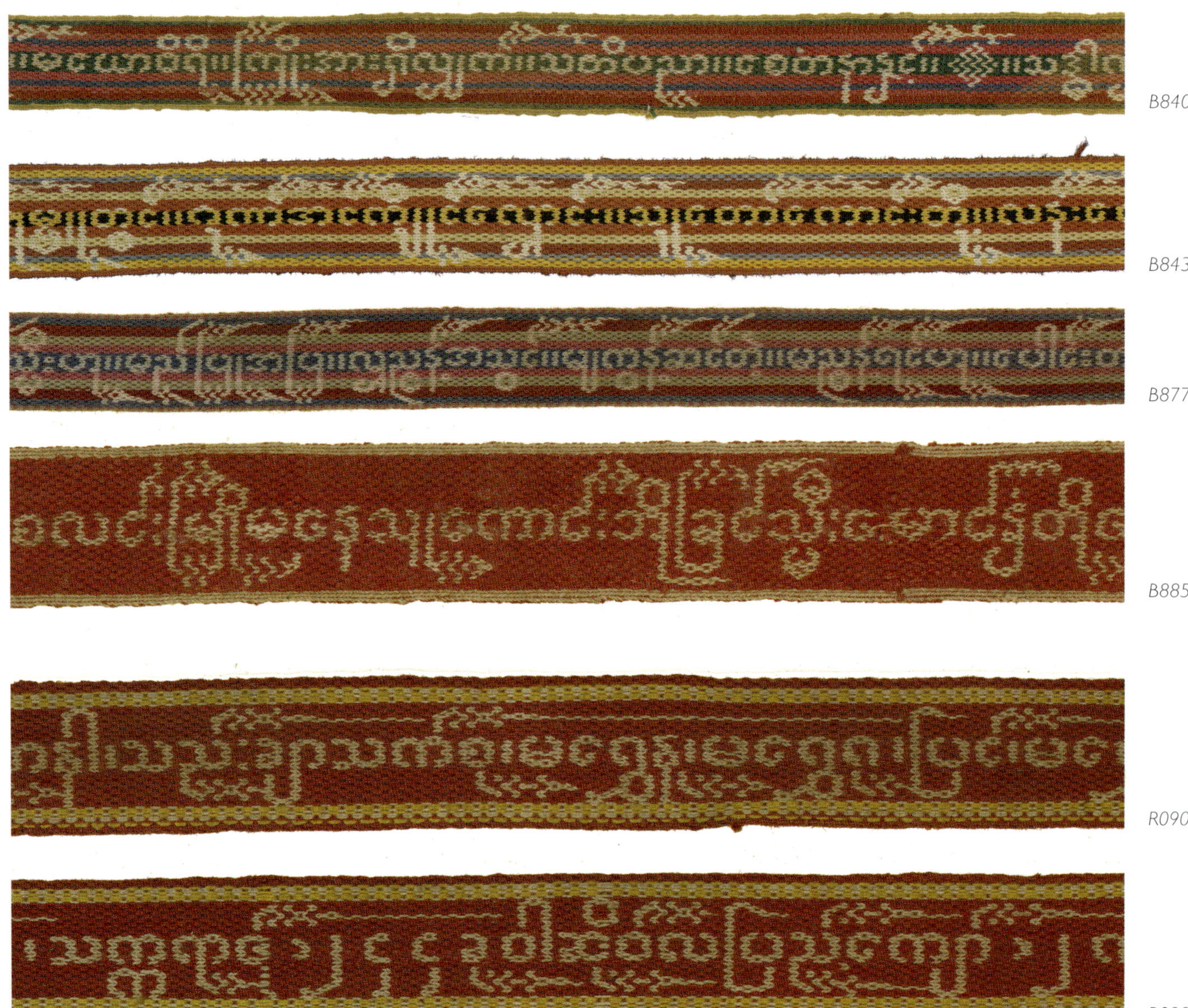

ABOVE

Risers and fallers soon became branched growths, like little Christmas trees, and developed long extensions, like boathooks or staghorn corals. *(B840, B843, B877, B885)*

Exaggerated flourishes could reach amazing lengths. *(R090)*

ASCENDERS AND DESCENDERS

In Burmese lettering the many "risers and fallers" are integral to the letter forms. They are not purely decorative flourishes as in sixteenth- and seventeenth-century European calligraphic penmanship. Nevertheless they show a steady elaboration through time. The simple, angular risers and fallers of mid-nineteenth-century indigo sazigyo are always joined to the letter to which they belong. By 1890, straight arms had become shallow concave curves. Before the turn of the

BELOW

The extensions on the last letter of the last word in the last phrase or "textlet" of the text are often particularly elaborate. *(J02, L06, R152, L08)*

One fanciful final diacritical mark is drawn out to resemble the twig of a tree, inviting a little bird to perch on it. *(B852)*

century, some weavers were using alternate or zig-zag projections, and early in the twentieth century imported fine hard thread brought an explosion of fanciful creation—elaborate branched growths, like Christmas trees, and long almost "baroque" extensions, like boathooks or staghorn corals. These tend to part company with the letters whose sound they modify, and to float above them unattached. Weavers clearly enjoyed inventing elaborate flourishes, even using several forms in a single phrase (B885). Letters end in little parrots. The last letter of the last word in the last phrase or "textlet" of the text was a prime target for their ingenuity, and often bore a particularly elaborate extension. One fanciful final diacritical mark is drawn out to resemble the twig of a growing tree, and provides a perch for a little bird.

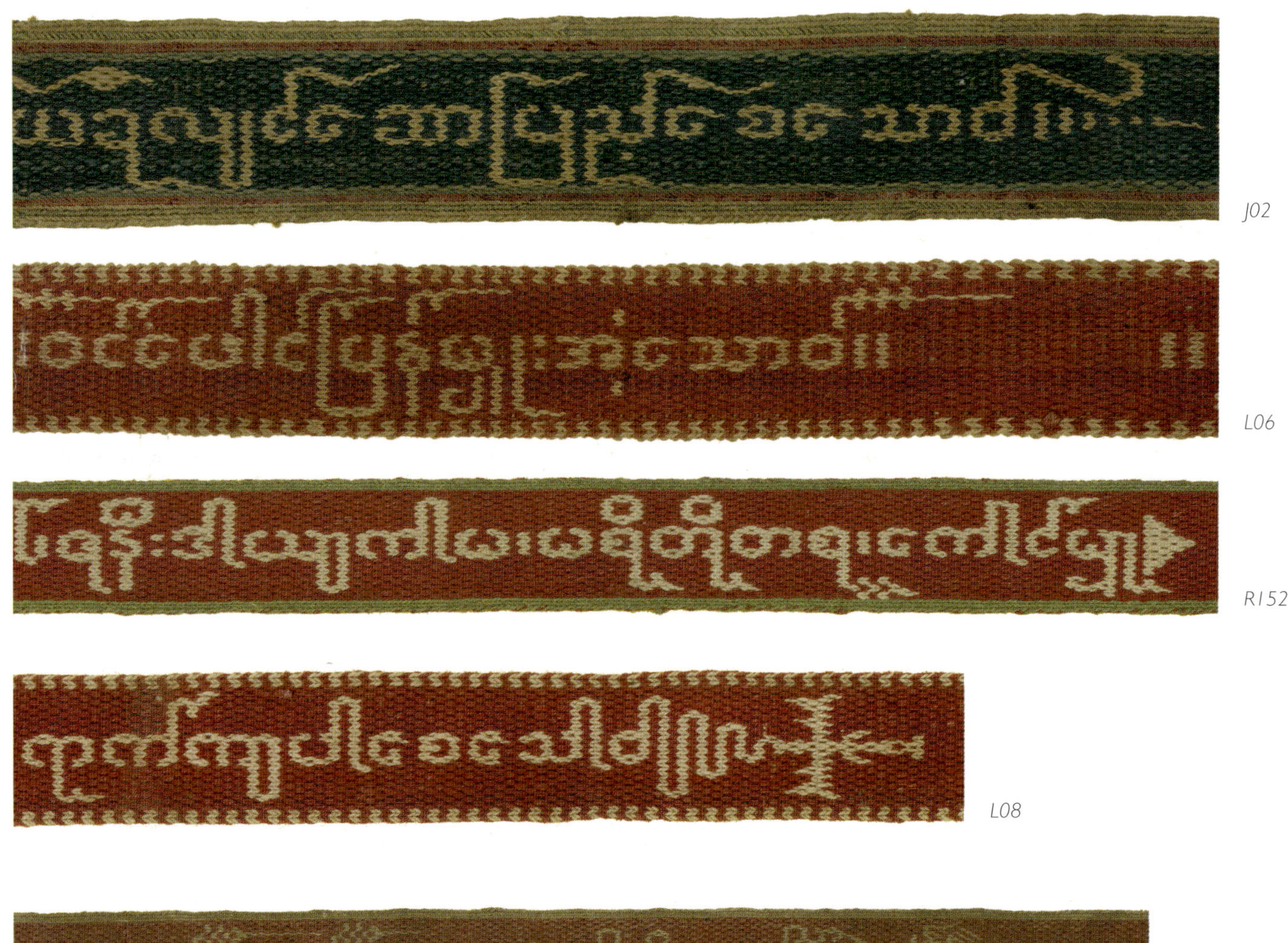

Part III Chapter 9

Sewn Corrections to the Woven Text

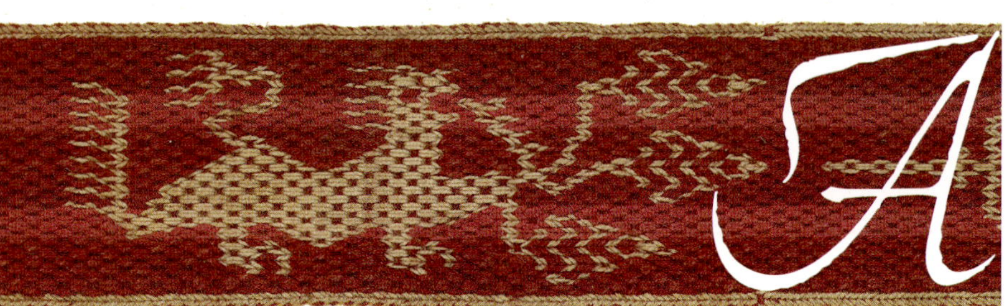

R192

A Burmese scriptural manuscript is not rendered ritually unusable by a textual error. In Burmese palm-leaf manuscripts, a letter engraved in error cannot be erased, but the scribe uses his stylus to make a dot in the middle of the letter, which indicates that it should be ignored. But in a woven sazigyo text the correction of errors presents a special problem. Weavers insist that if an error is discovered in the woven text while the tablets are still in place it can be corrected by laborious unpicking and reweaving. At this stage what is woven can be unwoven—with difficulty. But once the tablets have been removed, the only way to correct an error is with needle and thread.

Sewn corrections can be detected by touch when passing a sazigyo between finger and thumb, for the stitches stand up slightly above the flat weave. The first such correction to meet my thumb was on an indigo sazigyo dated 1854. To my eyes the correction looked just as old as the weave. A letter had been omitted from the woven text, and a large "X" carefully sewn just below the omission was clearly meant for a proofreader's insertion mark, but the editor had not supplied the missing letter: that was left to the reader of the text. Not so in a fine red and white sazigyo woven around 1900. No less than seven spelling errors have been neatly corrected with white thread or red, chosen to match the color of the woven lettering or that of the background. Missing strokes have been supplied in white thread; where a letter or a whole word has had to be erased, red yarn was used. Intriguingly, despite so many mistakes and corrections, this sazigyo shows signs of many years of use.

It is tempting to speculate on the identity of the editor. Whose eye spotted the mistakes? Whose fingers went to such trouble to correct them? Is this the work of the woman weaver? If her errors were discovered by a monk when the sazigyo and its manuscript were already in the monastery, he might have sent for the weaver, pointed out her mistakes, and instructed her to correct them. Or might he have used the needle, which is one of the eight permissible possessions of monks, to make the alterations himself? Perhaps he was the composer of the verses of the text.

In harsher modern times a blue ballpoint pen might replace the needle. (R142)

Plate 40 RIGHT

SEWN CORRECTIONS

After the tablets have been removed, errors in the woven script can only be corrected with needle and thread. A large X carefully sewn just below the woven text of a sazigyo woven about 1854 indicates where a letter is missing, but it is left to the reader to supply the missing letter. *(R177)*

Both the X above the woven script and the missing letter supplied below are sewn using thread chosen to match the color of the woven lettering, in white for (R114) and (R184).

Neat weaving but careless spelling: although missing letters or strokes have been supplied in white thread, when a letter or a whole word had to be erased, red yarn was used to match the background color of the sazigyo. The threads are clearly visible on the back. *(R184)*

Missing letters and a missing diacritical mark have here been supplied in ocher-colored thread and neat curved stitches. *(R093)*

In impatient modern times, the correction is made with a blue ballpoint pen. *(R142)*

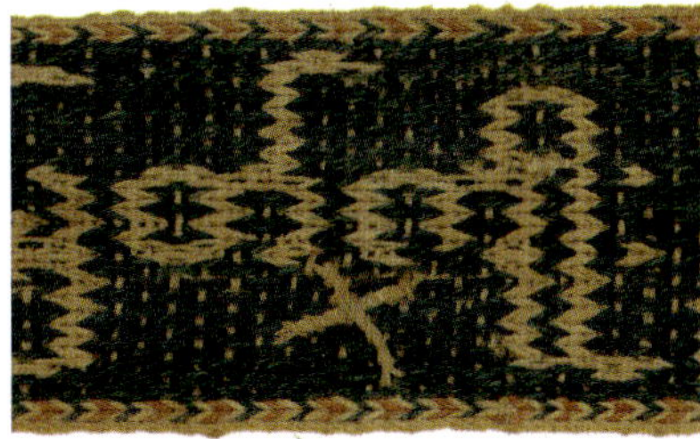

R177

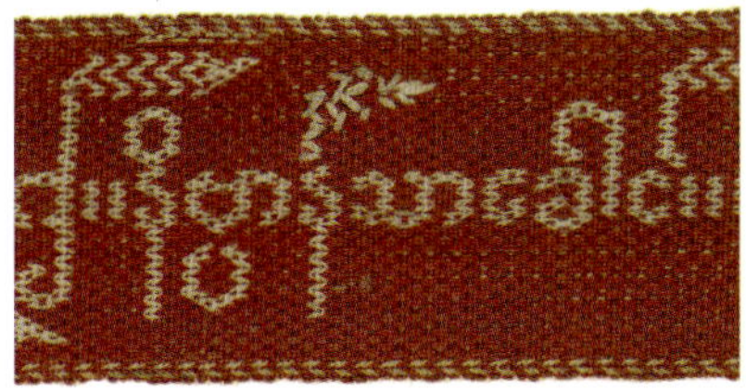

R184 obverse

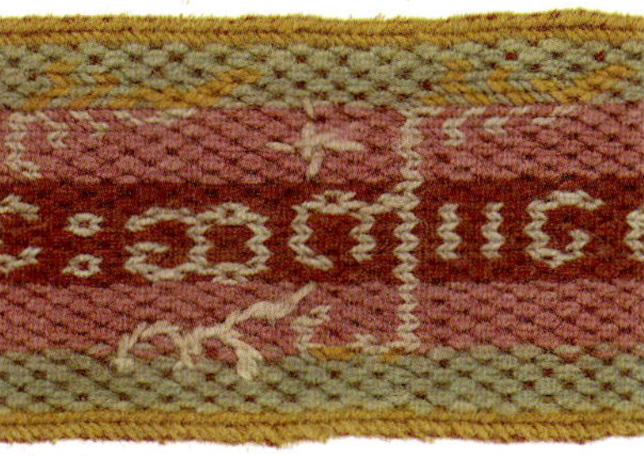

R114 (x2)

R184 reverse

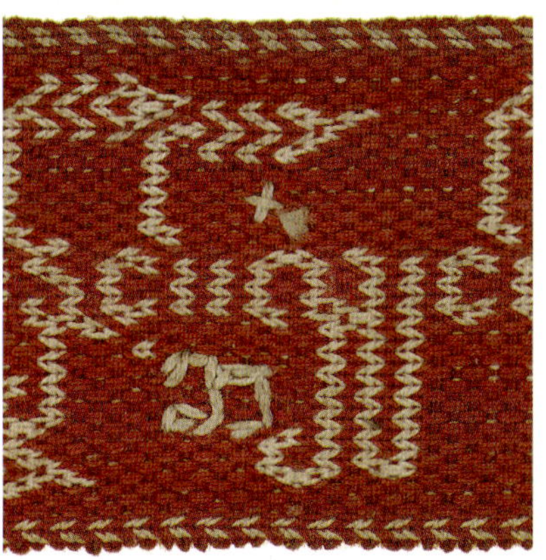

R184 (x2)

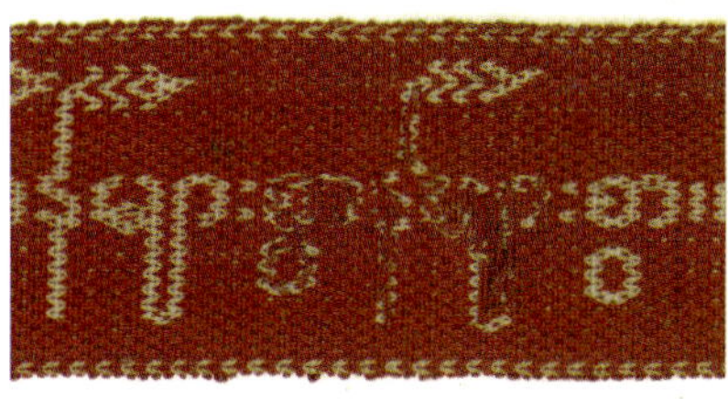

R184 obverse

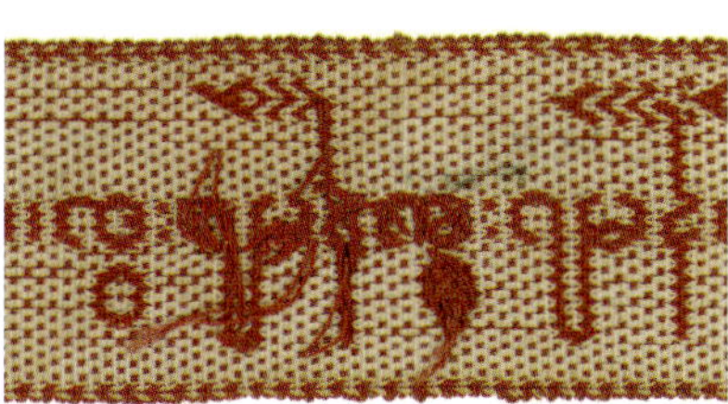

R184 reverse

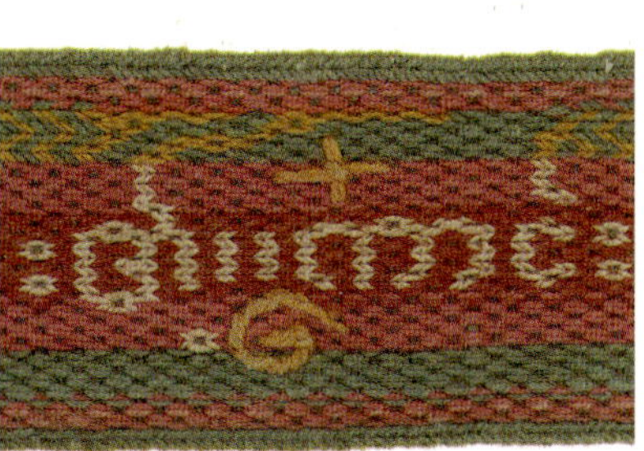

R093 (x2)

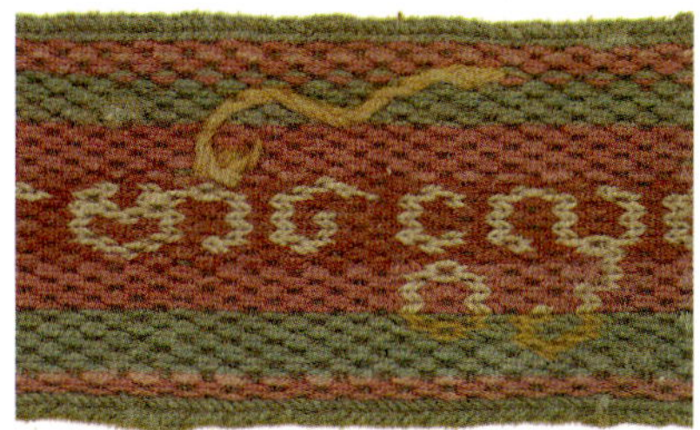

R093 (x2)

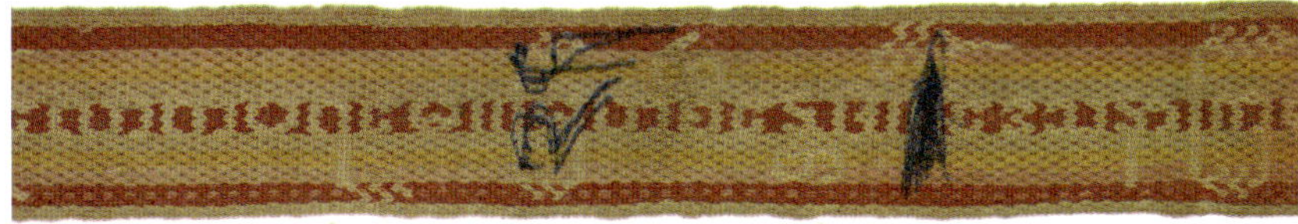

R142

Part III Chapter 10

The Woven Word: Text Messages

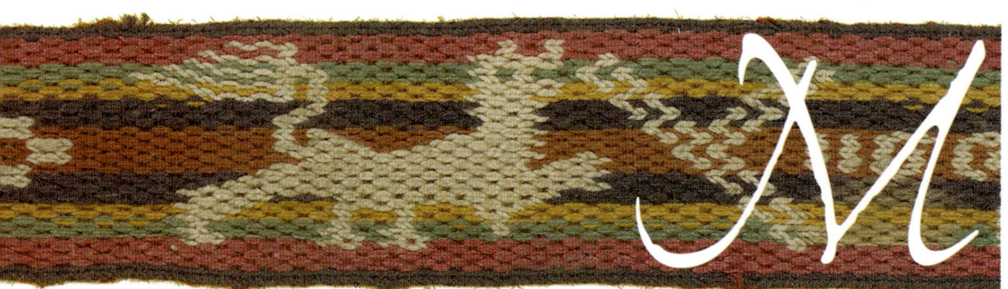

R012

Many sazigyo lack both text and images.[7] Although they are not the subject of study in this book, it would be misleading to omit all mention of them. These "textless bands" show a range of color, pattern, and texture, and can be beautifully woven.

LETTERED BANDS

The cheapest lettered sazigyo, sold ready woven, "off-the-peg," were very basic articles, the text a mere string of standard formulae, adequate in Buddhist terms but blandly impersonal. Most donors required their names in script, and were willing to pay to commission a completely new sazigyo. But there is evidence that a compromise could be negotiated, that weavers tempted customers with a special offer. Some sazigyo texts are in two distinct parts, the first formulaic and the second personal. This arrangement suggests that the weaver started a sazigyo with a text of pious formulae, and rolled it up three-quarters finished. When a paying customer appeared, the weaver added a second text naming the donor and his family.

Some weavers knew by heart whole texts of sonorous verses. The Ven. Dr. Khammai Dhammasami deduces from a study of the spellings in one poetic text[8] that the prayer was originally composed by a competent versifier with literary skills; that these verses became widely known, and were later transcribed by a scribe with indifferent spelling skills. Either this scribe copied it out for use by the weaver, or the weaver herself memorized the text, and wove it from memory, to impress a customer with such a high-sounding piece. But most of the sazigyo quoted in this book were specially commissioned by donors who got what they paid for—a woven text naming them and all their family, and recording their deed of merit.

Plate 41 NEXT PAGE
Many sazigyo have neither text nor images. These textless bands show a range of color, pattern, and texture, and some are beautifully woven. *(R234, R235, R238, R239, R240, R241, B873)*

THE THREE ESSENTIAL TEXTS

The text in a sazigyo may be over five-meters long, and may take up more than 90 percent of the flat tape between start loop and end cord. In older sazigyo the script forms a single unbroken passage, but in later sazigyo the text is divided into several distinct sections. The central

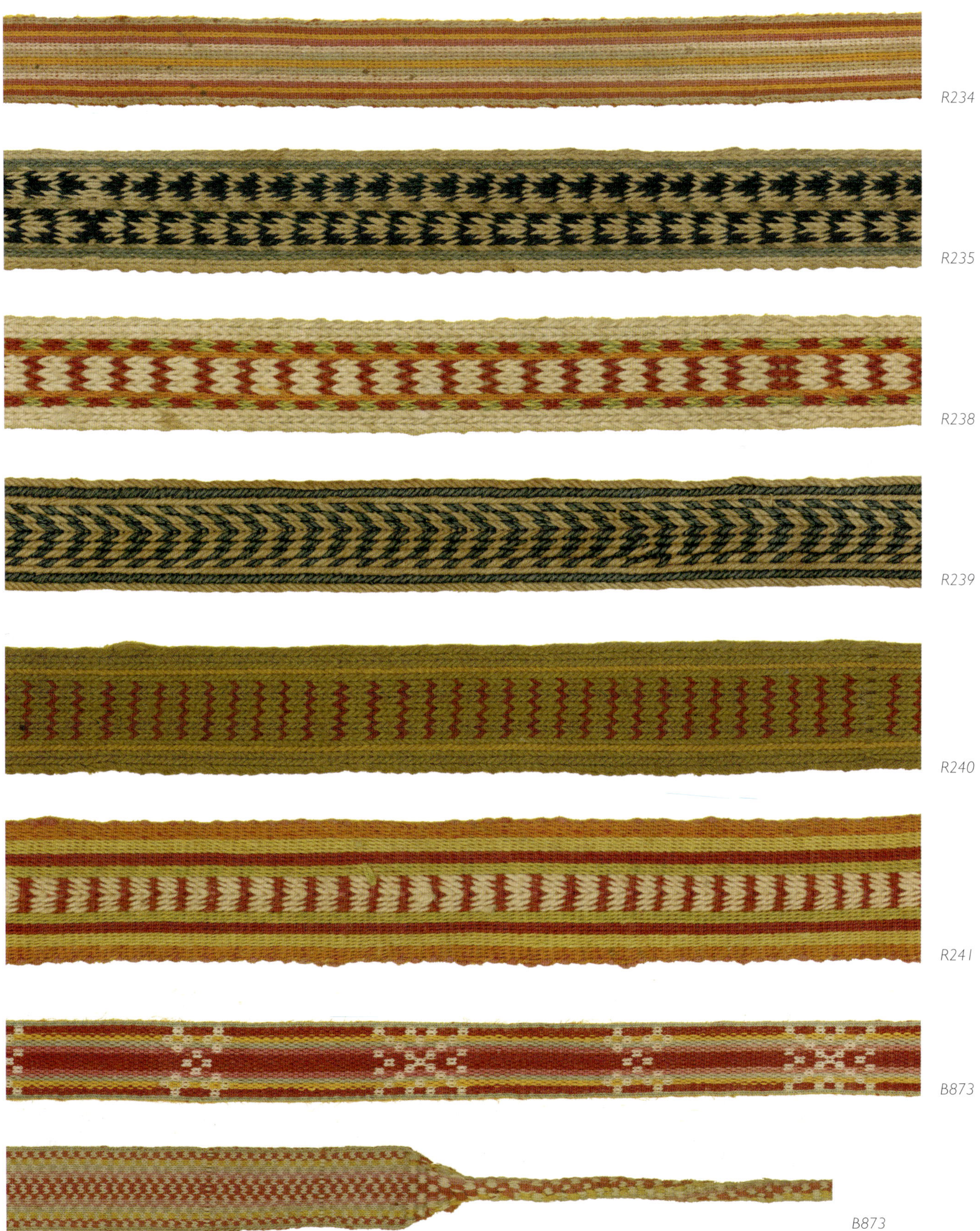

R234

R235

R238

R239

R240

R241

B873

B873

message of the sazigyo is a prayer in which the donors identify themselves, proclaim their donation, and state their motivation as the eventual attainment of nirvana. A short invocation precedes this main text and another follows it, and both are essential to the success of the donation. With the very first word on the sazigyo, ***"Zeyatu!"*** (**"Success!"**), the donors express their fervent wish for the smooth accomplishment of their religious act. After the main prayer the donors conclude their religious act with an appeal to human and celestial beings to approve and applaud their deed; they invite witnesses to call out ***"Thadu!"*** (**"Well done!"**) and offer them an equal share in the merit of the deed.

SUBSIDIARY TEXTS ("TEXTLETS")

Six or more distinct minor texts may occur, though rarely all on the same sazigyo. Each of these "textlets" conveys quite specific information about the manuscript donors and their donation—for example, the date of the donation (and so also of the weave), the number of verses in the text, the weaver's signature, the price she charged for her work, the title of the scriptural manuscript for which the sazigyo was woven, and (less frequently) the name of the monk recipient. A single example of each of these "textlets" is illustrated here. Each will be discussed fully later.

INITIAL INVOCATION "*ZEYATU!*"

The very first word on many sazigyo, ***"Zeyatu!,"*** is not Burmese but Pali, the language of the Theravada Buddhist scriptures, and means **"Victory!"** or **"Success!"**[9] In the context of the sazigyo its full meaning is **"May this our donation be a success!"** But what constitutes a success? The donors pray that conditions may remain auspicious for the performance of their religious deed, that no untoward bad influence will spoil it or prevent its fulfillment. If all goes well, the donation will earn the donors merit. But first the act itself must be correctly carried out. Another common opening phrase, ***"Thirimaha Mingala,"*** means very much the same as ***"Zeyatu!"*** The two may be combined to form a powerful double invocation, **"May this our deed be gloriously auspicious and blessed!"** Rarely ***"Zeyatu!"*** is absent, and instead the first text is a phrase in Pali, ***"Ciram titthatu saddhammo,"*** which means **"May the noble teaching long endure."** (AZ4) The donors' fervent appeal to celestial powers is the opening act in the ceremony, which will continue with the ritual of proclaiming the donation and conclude by inviting witnesses, both human and celestial, to share in the merit of the deed. On the sazigyo the initial invocation rarely leads straight into the main text. More often it stands apart in its own important space, framed between decorative brackets, or between a pair of birds, beasts, or fish, enclosed in a cartouche, or blazoned on a banner held by two heraldic beasts.

Plate 42 RIGHT AND BELOW

INITIAL AND FINAL INVOCATIONS

The first word on the sazigyo is usually the exclamation *Zeyatu!* (Success!). In this initial invocation the donors express their fervent wish that their religious act may be accomplished smoothly. *(KJ02 Zeyatu, R082 Zeyatu)*

In the concluding invocation the donors invite human beings and celestials to witness their deed, to approve and applaud it by calling out *Thadu!* (Well done!), and to share equally in the merit of the deed. *(KJ02 Thadu, R082 Thadu)*

SUBSIDIARY TEXTS ("TEXTLETS")

Here are examples of six kinds of minor texts or "textlets," each carrying distinct information:

Date of the donation and of the sazigyo: "1261" (1899 CE). *(R082)*

Final verse-count: "86 *pada* verses." Each *pada* verse has four syllables. *(BM246)*

Signature of the weaver: "Meh May's handwork." *(B850)*

Price charged by the weaver: "The price of this sazigyo is one kyat 8 pyas." *(B879)*

Title of the manuscript, in Pali: "Aggapadusaradipani Vol. 11." *(R218)*

Name of the monk recipient of the manuscript: "Ven. U Asara's sazigyo." *(B509047)*

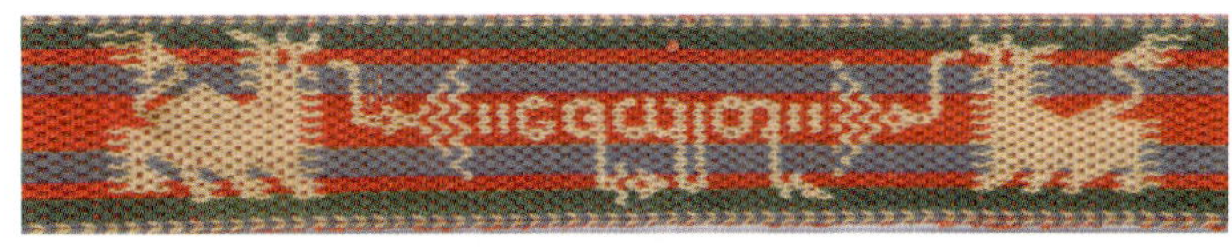

KJ02 Zeyatu

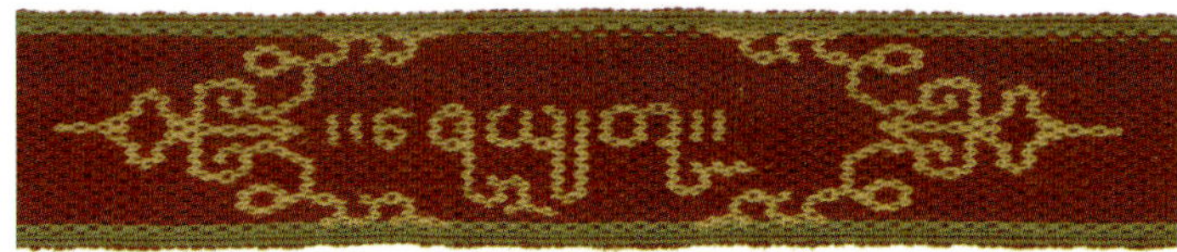

R082 Zeyatu

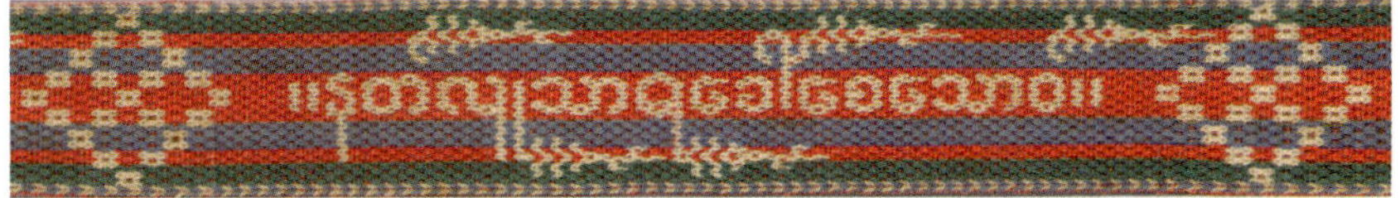

KJ02 Thadu

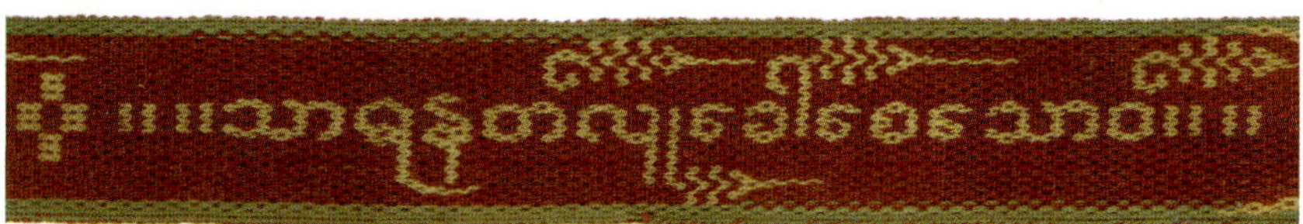

R082 Thadu

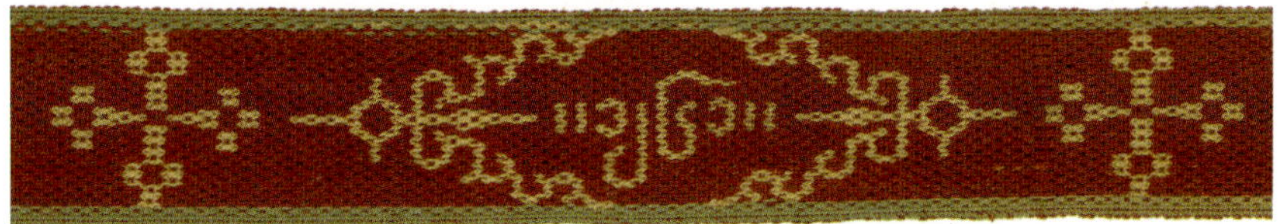

R082

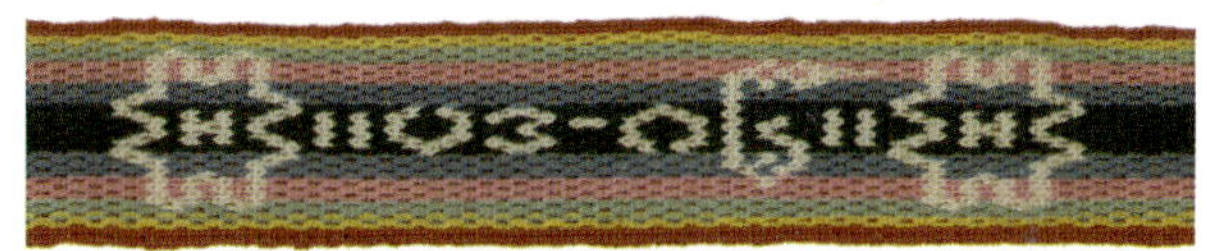

BM246

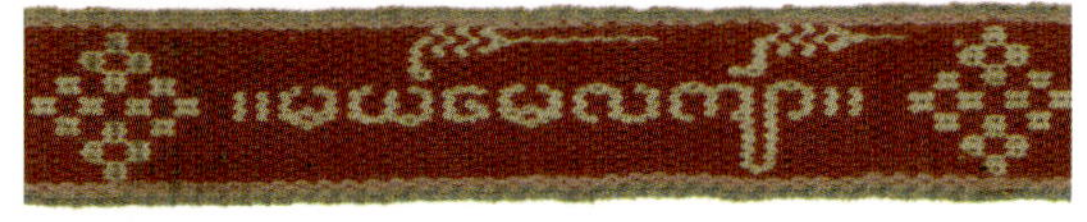

B850

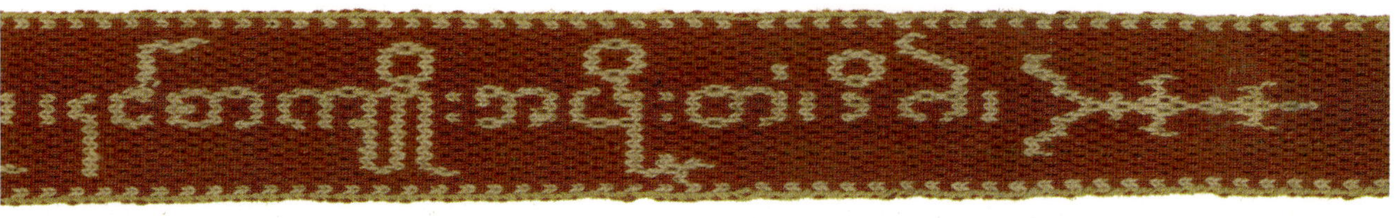

B879

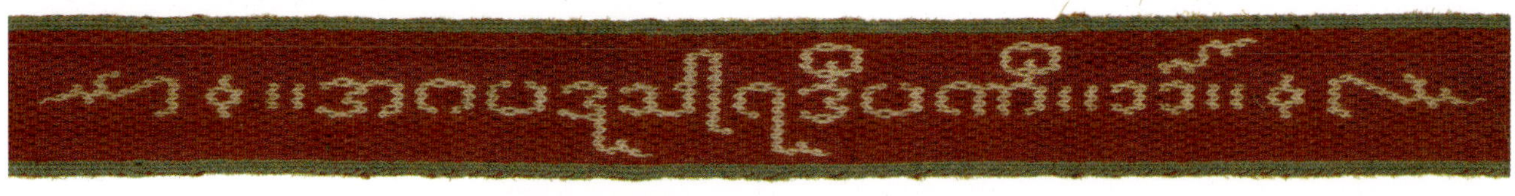

R218

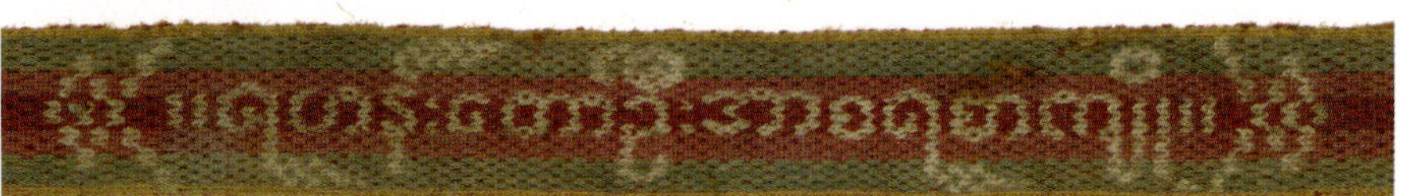

B509047

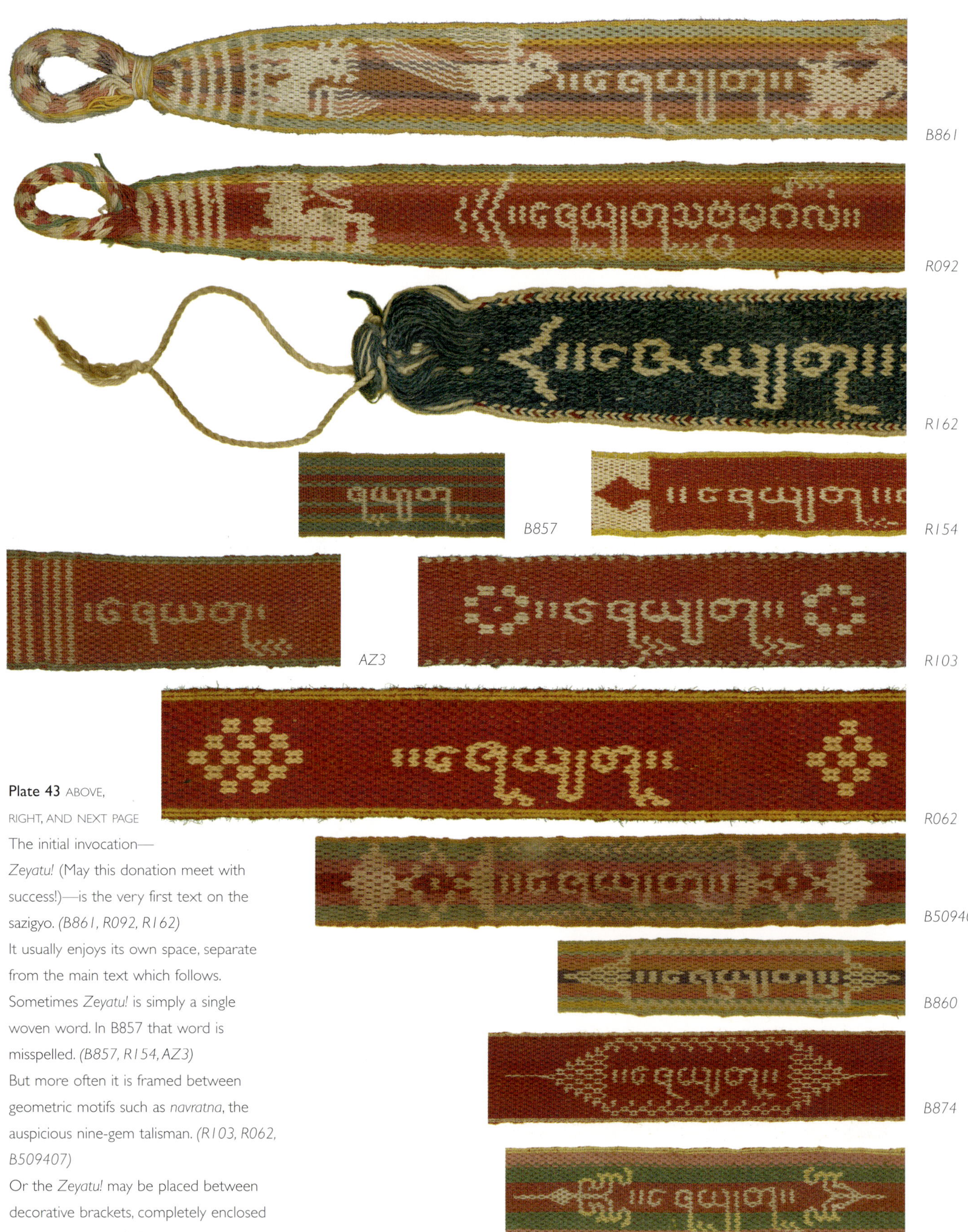

Plate 43 ABOVE, RIGHT, AND NEXT PAGE

The initial invocation—*Zeyatu!* (May this donation meet with success!)—is the very first text on the sazigyo. *(B861, R092, R162)*

It usually enjoys its own space, separate from the main text which follows. Sometimes *Zeyatu!* is simply a single woven word. In B857 that word is misspelled. *(B857, R154, AZ3)*

But more often it is framed between geometric motifs such as *navratna*, the auspicious nine-gem talisman. *(R103, R062, B509407)*

Or the *Zeyatu!* may be placed between decorative brackets, completely enclosed in a cartouche. *(B860, B874, R130)*

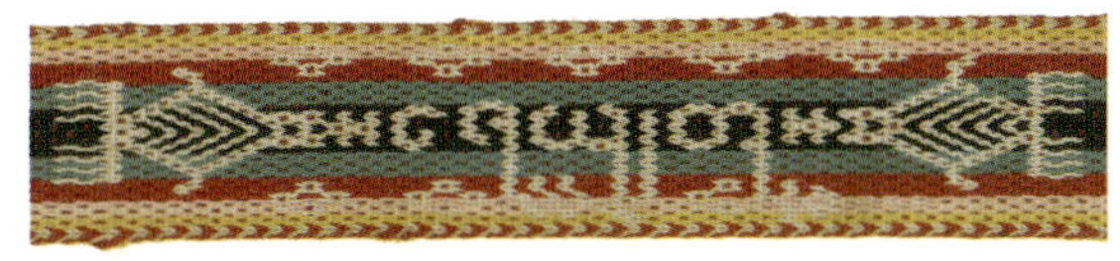
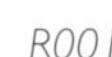
R001

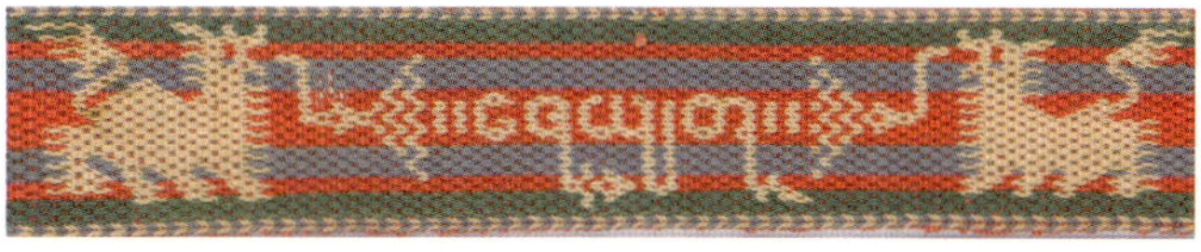
KJ02

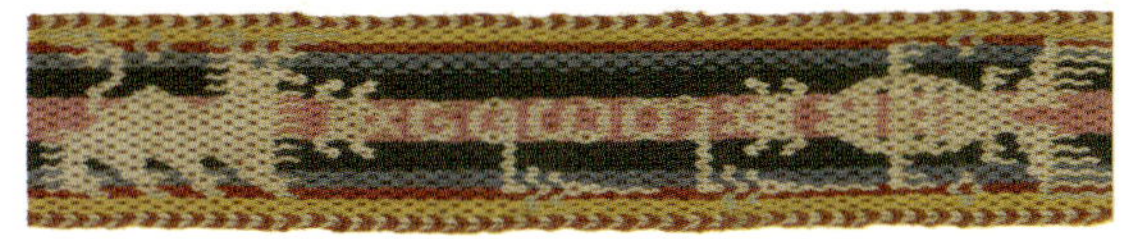
J07

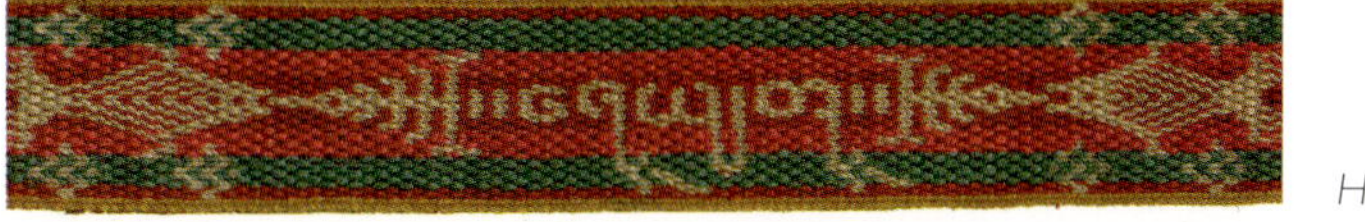
H031

ABOVE, RIGHT, AND BELOW THIS PAGE

ABOVE AND RIGHT: Often woven images of beasts, birds, or fish act as brackets. *(R001, KJ02, J07, H031, BL, B872, MYA055T)*

CENTER: Pointing hands lend emphasis. *(JBT6.49)*

BELOW: The powerful mythical beast, the *pyinsarupa*, the beast of five body forms, which is associated with physical energy and loud noise, breathes out the word *Zeyatu! (R027, R192)*

Heraldic lions carry a banner proclaiming *Zeyatu!*, the ribbon held in their mouths. *(R024)*

Zeyatu! may be followed by *"Thamba Mingala!."* Together they mean "May this our deed be gloriously auspicious and blessed, and may we succeed in gaining merit thereby!" One sazigyo weaver pulls out all the stops: she doubles the *Zeyatu!*, adds *Thamba Mingala!* (Great auspiciousness!), and enlists three vocal creatures (dog, frog, and parrot) to lend fortissimo vehemence to the whole invocation. *(B843)*

Rarely, *Zeyatu!* is absent, and instead the first text is a phrase in Pali, *"Ciram titthatu saddhammo,"* which means "May the noble teaching long endure." *(AZ4)*

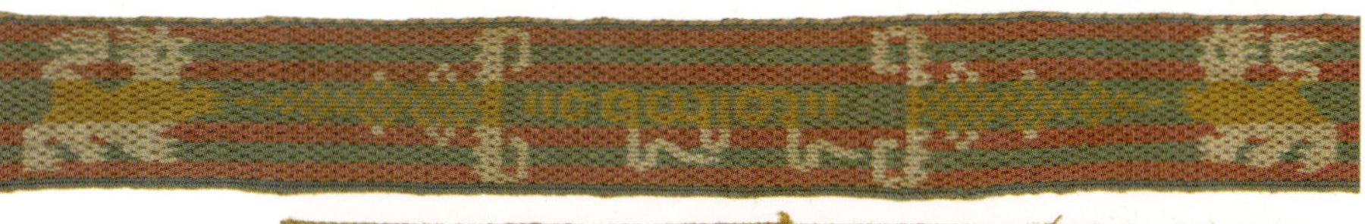
BL

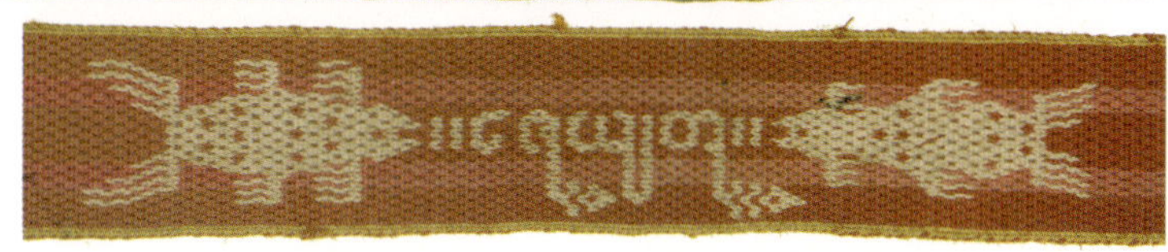
B872

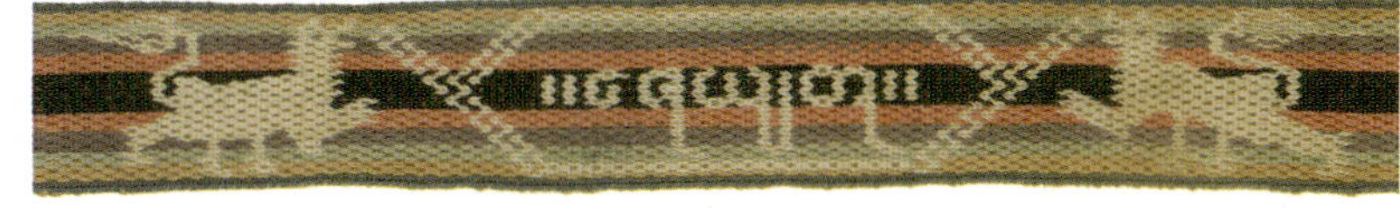
MYA055T

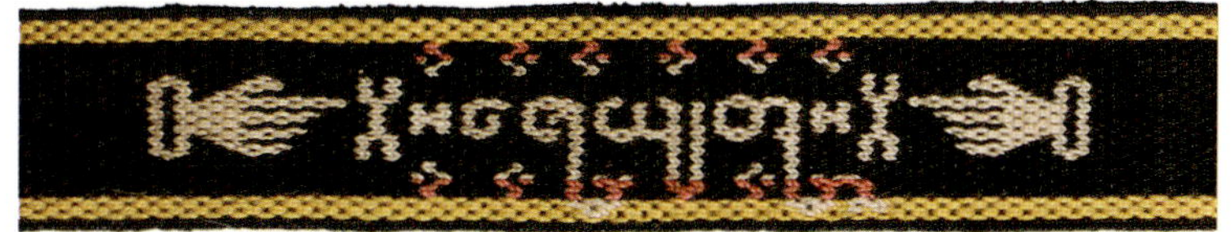
JBT6.49

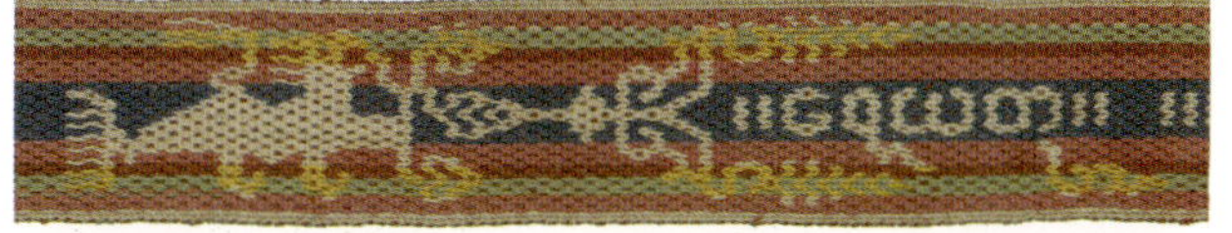
R027

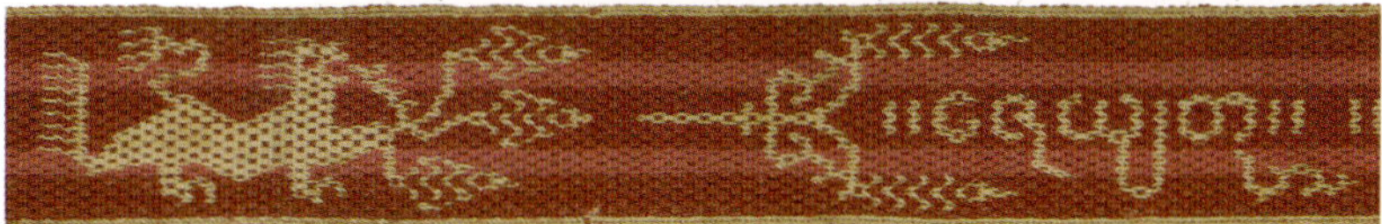
R192

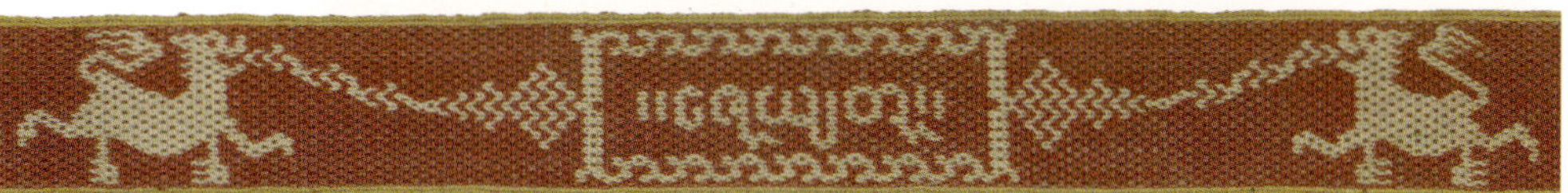
R024

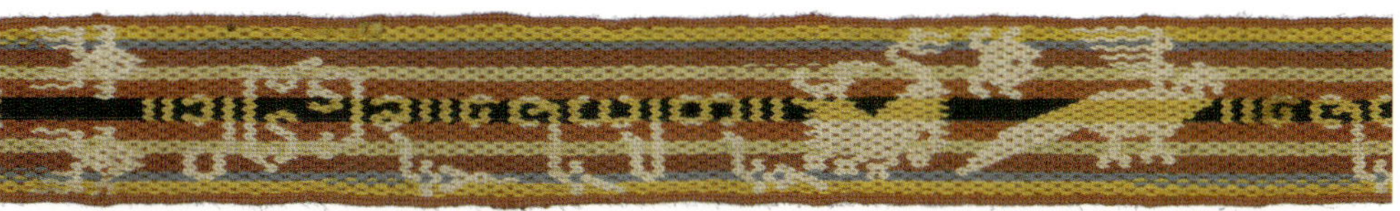
B843

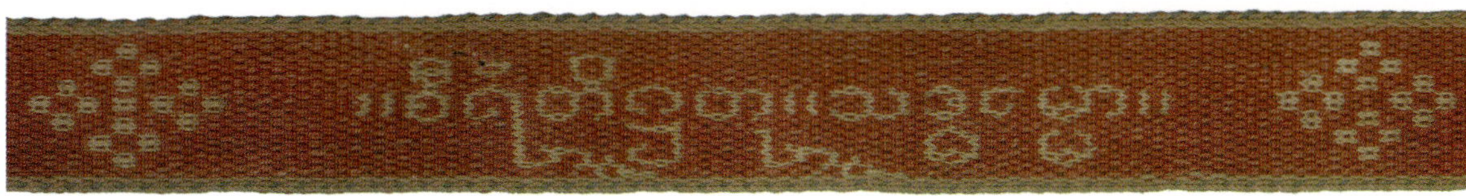
AZ4

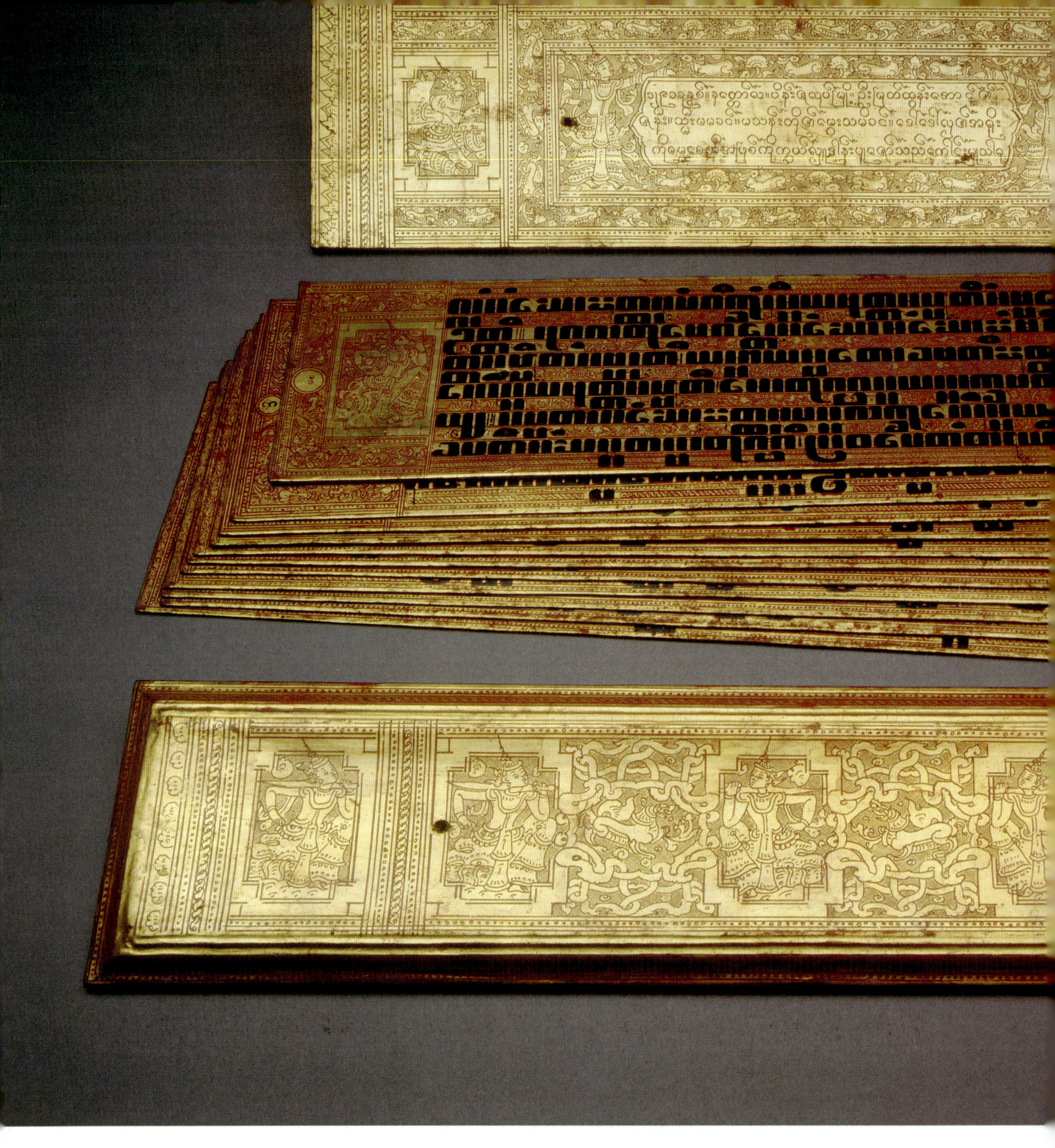

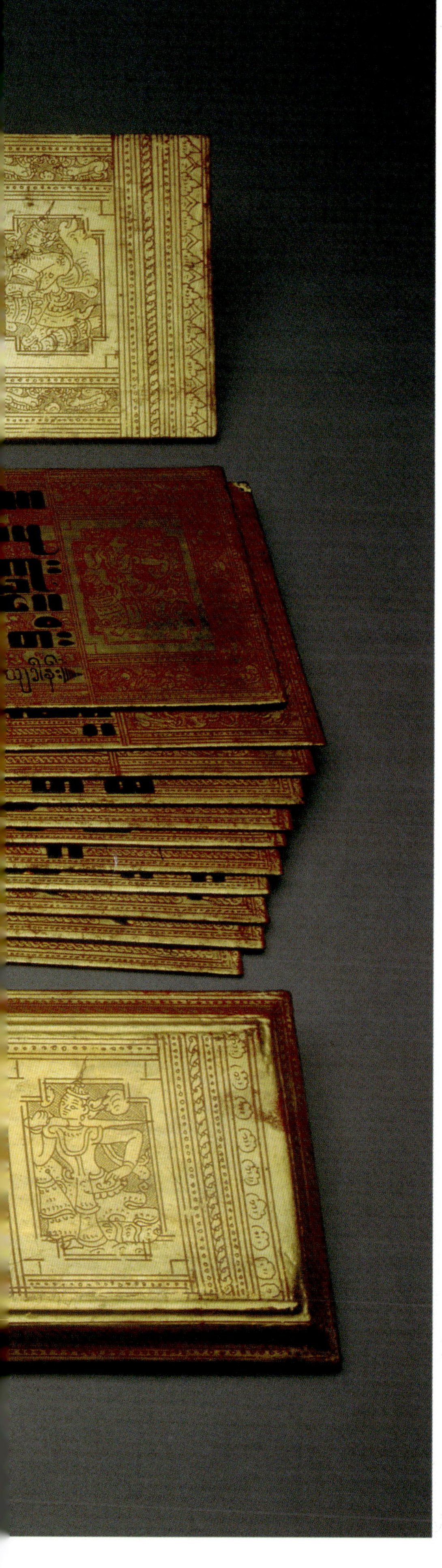

CONTENTS OF THE MAIN TEXT

Next comes the main text, which may comprise only a few words but is usually much longer, up to several hundred words in length, and often in verse. The language is Burmese, though a few old sazigyo have the text in Pali, and some sazigyo are known with a text in Mon or Arakanese. The manuscript donors, usually a married couple, identify themselves by names and titles, give their residential address, and list family members and sometimes friends and neighbors who share in the cost of the donation and in its merit. This evidence of donation was important because manuscripts were expensive prestige objects whose legal ownership could revert to the donor following the death of a monk recipient. All donors conclude by expressing the hope that their meritorious deed may help them attain nirvana.

Some texts describe the number, quality, and titles of the donated manuscripts, and record the expense incurred. A few texts read like an accountant's report: one such text is printed in full below (see pp. 122–23). Some donations, especially those of *kammavaca* manuscripts, were a "complete set"—the manuscript itself, its cloth wrapper, and specially woven sazigyo, all contained in a lacquered, gilt, and glass-inlaid box.

Politics intrudes even into sazigyo texts. One expresses nostalgic regret at the overthrow of Burmese sovereignty by the British:

> **The dynasty of the Konbaung kings, to whom the jewel of the swastika came, reigned in their palaces. But in the reign of the eleventh Konbaung king Thibaw disaster struck, and the dynasty lost its sovereignty by violence. Without the king and the palace, the entire land of Myanmar has become as dark as night. The sun has set on the Konbaung dynasty.** (VC16)

Another text is a tirade denouncing the hated colonial power as enemies of Buddhism and of the Sangha. It is included in the selection of full uncut texts. (VC62, p. 52)

MAIN TEXT: DONORS' NAMES, TITLES, AND STYLE

DONORS' NAMES

The main text names the manuscript donors, and often every member of the nuclear family. Burmese names may require some explanation. Women retain their names on marriage, and do not take their husband's name. Children do not take their father's name. There are no family names. A notable exception to this rule is Daw Aung San Suu Kyi's name, which includes that of her father, Aung San, hero of Burma's independence struggle. The first element of a Burmese name is

Plate 44 PREVIOUS PAGES
Kammavaca manuscripts, anthologies of monastic rules, were often presented to monasteries by family members when a monk relative was ordained. They are written in an archaic square script called "tamarind seed" on heavily lacquered and gilded leaves.
An inscription on the inner face of the wooden cover states that the manuscript was donated in 1929 by the widower U Myat Htun Aung and his two daughters, and that the bone ash relics of his deceased wife Daw Daw Hla "have been enshrined in this reliquary pagoda *[dhammaceti]* for worship." Some of her cremation ashes would have been mixed with liquid lacquer and used to write this manuscript.

the title, equivalent to Mr., Miss, or Mrs. For junior males the title prefix is Maung (younger brother), for those in middle years Ko (elder brother), and for seniors U (Uncle). For females Ma is Miss and Daw is a matron, with Meh something in between.

The initial title syllable of a Burmese name is followed by a further one to three words. Parents selected these, and a century ago the choice of first name was strictly governed by rules. The letters of the Burmese alphabet were traditionally shared between the planets, and a child's first name had to begin with one of the group of consonants allocated to its birthday planet. Although nowadays this system has fallen into disuse, it was strictly adhered to in the years when the oldest known sazigyo were woven. For example: U Khin (Mr. Lovable) would certainly have been a Monday child; U Than Hla (Mr. Strong and Handsome) a Friday child; and Ma Nu Nu Tint (Miss Delicate and Comely) could only have been born on a Saturday.

Every element in the name has a meaning, and few are exclusive to males or females. Common names are Shwe, Ngwe (gold, silver), Sein, Mya (diamond, emerald), Thein (glory), Lin (bright), Hla (pretty or handsome), Hmway (fragrant), Pwint (blossom), Chit (dear), Nyunt (best), Khaing (constant), Tint (comely), Nu (delicate), Aye (cool), Thin (learned), Thant (pure), and Aung (victorious).

DONORS' TITLES AND STYLE

Most donors were married couples. The sazigyo text often declares in set phrases their compatibility and mutual devotion: **"I Ko Htun Baw and my wife Ma Meh Htwe were destined to meet and marry in this existence as a reward for good deeds done together in our past lives. We are inseparable and indivisible as the two faces of a coin."** (VC05)

The husband's trade, or his post in the government bureaucracy, is usually prefixed to his name. He may be a village headman, boat owner, trader, broker, Chin goods dealer, or a senior clerk, army officer, court official, even a minister of the royal government. One career politician uses the sazigyo text to record every post he ever filled and every promotion.

The donor's spouse shares his style, "consort of chief clerk" or "consort of merchant." All donor couples enjoy titles earned by their pious donations, past or present. By virtue of their current donation they are styled "manuscript donor" and "lady donor of a manuscript." Previous works of merit may have entitled a wealthy donor to other honorifics, such as "monastery founder" or "pagoda builder." As a contributor to these pious donations, his spouse shares the distinction and enjoys the form of address "lady founder of a monastery" or "lady builder of a pagoda." Less common honorifics are "donor of an ordination hall" (*thein*), "donor of a seven-tiered *pyatthat* roof," "donor of a gilt palanquin," and "donor of a library chest" (*sadaik*). One donor couple had each founded a different monastery, perhaps in previous marriages: **"U Shwe Waing, donor of Thanyato Nagayaka monastery in Shwedaung Township, and his spouse Ma Ohn, donor of Kanhlaing Tintha monastery."** (R189)

In most cases manuscript and sazigyo were part of the same donation, but one donor couple preferred to pay separately, he for the manuscript, and she for the sazigyo: **"Manuscript donor Ko Ta Tu and Lady donor of binding tape Ma Min Ya had this sazigyo woven on the tenth waxing day of the month of Tawthalin in the year 1249** [1887 CE]**."** (R212)

A Mandalay couple increased their donation from a set of manuscripts to an entire library chest full. The arrangement of text and images on the sazigyo shows that the donors' change of mind was an afterthought. It came late in the day, when the weaver had completed not only the text recording the original donation, with an image of the Earth Goddess Waythondaye as witness of the deed of merit, but had even woven the *dagundaing*—usually the final image on the sazigyo. Now the woven postscript is introduced by prancing lions. Ko Yin Thi is promoted from "manuscript donor" to "donor of *sadaik*," literally a

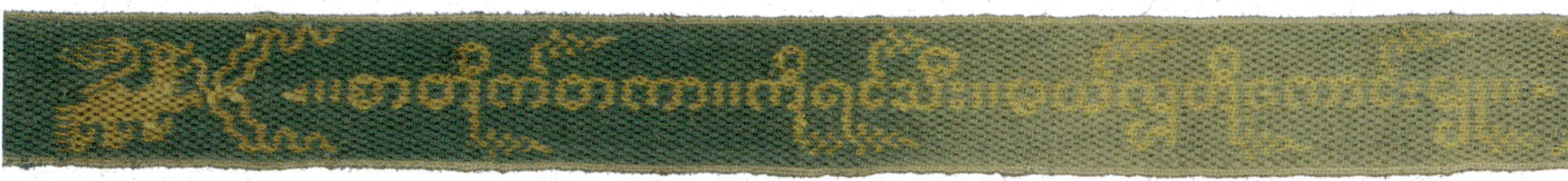

R049

library chest, but here including its contents, and the Earth Goddess is recalled to witness the enhanced donation. (R049)

A son, himself only a manuscript donor, proudly basks in the reflected merit of his pious mother's superior title, **"Deed of merit of pagoda builder Meh Htwa's son Ko Aung Mya, and his wife Ma Shin and their son Maung Tint."** (R109)

Lay people were not alone in seeking merit. A fine old indigo sazigyo presented to the Pitt Rivers Museum in Oxford by Sir Richard Carnac Temple in 1889 was woven in 1798, and donated by Meh Aye. She was a nun, *thila-shin*, literally "keeper of precepts," and her prayer runs, **"I garland my head with the gem of the Buddha, and worship my whole life long . . . I garland my head with the gem of the Dhamma . . . I garland my head with the gem of the Sangha."** (PRM 1889.29.200)

Plate 45 ABOVE
The final phrase of this (faded) sazigyo is a postscript recording the donors' late decision to increase their donation from a single manuscript to an entire library, thereby earning new honorific titles: Donor of a library chest and Lady donor of a library chest.

DONORS' ADDRESSES

Burmese names are so common that any fair-sized place of work will have several employees with the same names. The name label on the breast pocket of a civil servant's uniform might read, "U Maung

Maung No. 23." Donors of manuscripts eager to identify themselves fully and unequivocally often include their full address in the sazigyo text. Rural people name their village, and some add the "township," the administrative division or district in which it lies: "**Senior Clerk Ko Bo Gyo, his wife Ma May Yin, son Maung Ba Thit, daughters Ma Ngwe Sein, Ma Mya Yee, and Ma Thein Tin, of North Chaung Waing Gyi Village in Twante Township.**" (R244)

"**Residents of Myaynu Ward in Bokkyaung Village, in Aingthabyu Compound, Lay Myethna Quarter, Hanthawaddy District: manuscript donor U Shan Gyi, wife lady manuscript donor Daw Shwe, son Maung Shwe Ku, and daughter Meh Hla Ohn.**" (R009)

Village residents have fulsome praise for their native village, which had everything:

> **The glorious beauty of our village Cho Lay almost makes the earth tremble. The radiance covers both the upper lands and the valley lands below. The village is incomparable in peace and pleasantness, and the very mention of its name evokes respect. It is also a center of trade and commerce, where merchants in many wares from the prosperous city of Hanthawaddy transact their trade.** (VC05)

Urban dwellers name the ward or quarter of their home town: "**Minhla Township, the dwelling place of wise and good men, and the rich and prosperous Mo Nyo Quarter, where the renowned and munificent donor U Shwe Dun has his abode.**" (BM246)

"**Broker Ko Khaing and his wife Ma Chain, daughter Ma Hpwa Thin, son Maung Ba Thaw and baby daughter Ma Hpwa Shin, all of Shwe Gu Quarter in Prome Town.**"

"**Manuscript donor Ma Eh of Mill Compound, 7th Ward, Hpangabin Village, in the city of Thirikettara.**" Thirikettara is the ancient Pyu name for the modern town of Prome, or Pyay. (R040)

NAMING ALL THE FAMILY

The Master of Ceremonies at a Burmese wedding, in a lengthy lyrical oration known as the "*Mingala Yadu*," chants aloud the names of all the relatives on both sides of the family and effusively praises them. Similarly, most sazigyo texts name all the donors' immediate family, and many add a long list of members of the extended family. All those named are thereby associated with the meritorious deed, becoming co-donors, entitled to an equal share in the merit of the donation. Some lists are rather formal, but many are enlivened by an affectionate tone and pet names. On a sadly faded tape the donors' names are still legible: "**U San Htwa, wife Ma Hpu Thit, dear son Maung Tha Hsaing, precious daughters Meh Hsan and Ma Meh Than, of Salin Town.**" (R243)

A widower and proud father of six daughters praises their beauty, **"U Kyaw and his family members Ma Ma Ein, who lives up to her good reputation, Meh Meh Hpo, who is graceful and elegant, Ma Ma Shan, who is slim, slender, and beautiful like a princess, Ma Ma Oun, who is gentle with bright looks, Ma Hmoun, and his youngest daughter Ma Thoun."** (VC09)

A lady donor, perhaps a widow, lavishes loving praise on every family member:

> **My family have long lived in the region of Htanaunbin. I, Meh Meh U, am gentle in nature, and well-known in this region where my reputation is fragrant. The donors, who are all my family members, include Ko Hpwe, my nephew, and wife Ma Meh Pan, my eldest son Ko Htun Hla, my daughter Ma Kaung Pon, my middle son Ko Kyaw Hla and my youngest son Ko Kyaw Za. My nephew Ko Hpwe is a handsome man, and his wife Ma Meh Pan is of fine beauty, and she is unbelievably generous in donations. My eldest son Ko Htun Hla is a decent, handsome gem-like son. He is very gentle like wax. He really enjoys living in this region, and his name is sweet in the community. The next after Ko Htun Hla is a daughter and her name is Ma Kaung Pon. As she is the younger sister of wax-like gentle Ko Htun Hla, her limbs are soft and gentle. Her fine jet-black hair is the colour of a carpenter-bee and three cubits long** [137 cm]**. Ma Kaung Pon wears her hair coiled in a top-knot, and is demure and stable in character and appearance, charming and attractive to everyone who beholds her. Born after her is my middle son Ko Kyaw Hla. He is of fair complexion, and well-grown, in fact big for his age. All the family members love him as he loves us. Born after Ko Kyaw Hla is Ko Kyaw Za, the youngest in the family, of slender build, golden complexion, and fine appearance. As he is the youngest, he is cherished like a gold necklace with full family love.** (VC71)

At funerals, too, the family gathers to honor the deceased. In the selection of uncut sazigyo texts, the reader will find on page 127 a text (H012) naming more than thirty family members who contributed to the cost of a special *kammavaca* manuscript, made with the cremation ashes of their revered father and grandfather.

Dear departed family members are included so that they, too, may share in the merit of the donation, **"May the benefits from this great deed be shared by those who have passed away: U Bay, father, and Meh Moe, mother, to both of whom the donors owe an indescribable debt of gratitude."** (MMG Ch. 9 No. 4)

> Manuscript donor U Shwe Hman, lady manuscript donor Ma Ngwe Pwint, Law Court Clerk U Po Thein, son Maung Thaung, wife Ma May Su, granddaughter Ma Mya Yi, youngest daughter Ma Ma Lay, grandsons Maung Gyi, Maung Ba Chit, Maung Ba Thit, late grandson Maung Ba San, grandson Maung Ba Than, granddaughters Ma Nyi Ma and Ma May Pu, of Market Quarter, Letpandan Township, Tharawaddy District. (B508186)

> U Hpo Pyu, eldest son Maung Htun Win, equally loved bright daughter Ma Shwe Yin, younger sons Maung Ba Pe and Maung Ba Kyaw . . . may we finally attain nirvana. And may the merit of this deed be shared by my beloved wife who has departed this life. And I pray that I and my children may not in the future have to endure further painful separation. (VC02, translated by Dr. Ye Myint)

> ". . . Through the merit of this deed may we avoid evils, and escaping from the round of rebirth proceed directly to Heaven and at last attain nirvana. And may the merit of this deed also secure admission for our dear departed grandson Maung Pu Toe . . ." (VC01, translated by Dr. Ye Myint)

FINAL DESTINATION NIRVANA

Release from *samsara*, the weary round of birth, death, and rebirth, and the attainment of nirvana is the motive for all donations. This is most simply expressed in the rhyming tags **"*Neibban hsu, kaung hmu*" ("May the prize of nirvana reward this our deed of merit")** that follow the main text and conclude the ritual.

The desirability of a smooth, unhindered, and speedy passage to nirvana is often mentioned in the verses of the main text. Some donors may elaborate on their motivation:

> In the course of our lives we came to think of how to escape from *samsara*, the cycle of birth and death and rebirth, and realized that the Buddhas-to-be all placed the virtue of *dana*, generous giving, before all other virtues. Thinking of this we felt a surge of bliss in our minds and hearts and realized that our existences will be in vain unless we sow seeds of *dana* to benefit our future existences, even though we have already amassed a pile of property gained through our hard work. Therefore, this family of five discussed the donation of a full set of the Pitakas. (VC41)

A few donors dwell on the misery of *samsara*, on the low quality of life in the weary round of birth, death, and rebirth, dismissed as no better than **"the lives of larvae thriving in the latrine pit."** (MMG)

Or they may link their meritorious deed to their world-weariness and to the onset of age, **"U Tha Kyaw and Ma Minn Kalay of Insein District donated the Tipitaka . . . because they are now disgusted with the material possessions of the ten-thousand worlds, which they have in abundance, and because they now garland themselves with the flowers of faith."** (B850)

Donors have the same destination, but different degrees of patience, **"May we attain it** [nirvana] **quickly, in a single *hkana*."** (B849) This is a request for the fast-track service, for the dictionary defines "*hkana*" as "a measure of time spanning ten winks of the eye or ten snaps of the fingers."

Others are less impatient, **"Ko Hpo Myaing and his sister Ma Mainkalay, of Shwe Kon Village in Insein Township, who have done much merit together in their past lives, now wish they may speedily and without obstacles attain nirvana."** (B852)

And Maung Zo Nyeint and Ma May Ni of Zet Ton Village are in no hurry at all, **"May we reach it as quickly and smoothly as when picking lotus blooms whose blossoms and stalks we wind together and pluck out all in a bunch."** (B847)

Perhaps the happiest metaphor for the ultimate transition to nirvana is this, **"May we reach it as quickly and smoothly as when picking lotus blooms whose blossoms and stalks we wind together and pluck out all in a bunch."** (VC05)

SUMMONING WITNESSES AND SHARING THE MERIT

The second of the paired concluding invocations is an invitation to both celestial and human beings to witness the donors' deed of merit, to approve it, and to applaud. The most common form of words is: **"May Nats and humans alike approve this deed and applaud this deed, and call out '*Thadu! Thadu!*'** ['Well done! Well done!']**"**

To witnesses' cries of **"*Thadu!*"** donors reply **"*Ahmya!*"** (**"Equal shares!"**), accepting the applause of witnesses and disseminating the merit, undiminished. The importance of this final invocation is marked by its separation from the end of the main text, often by brackets or by woven images of vocal birds or beasts.

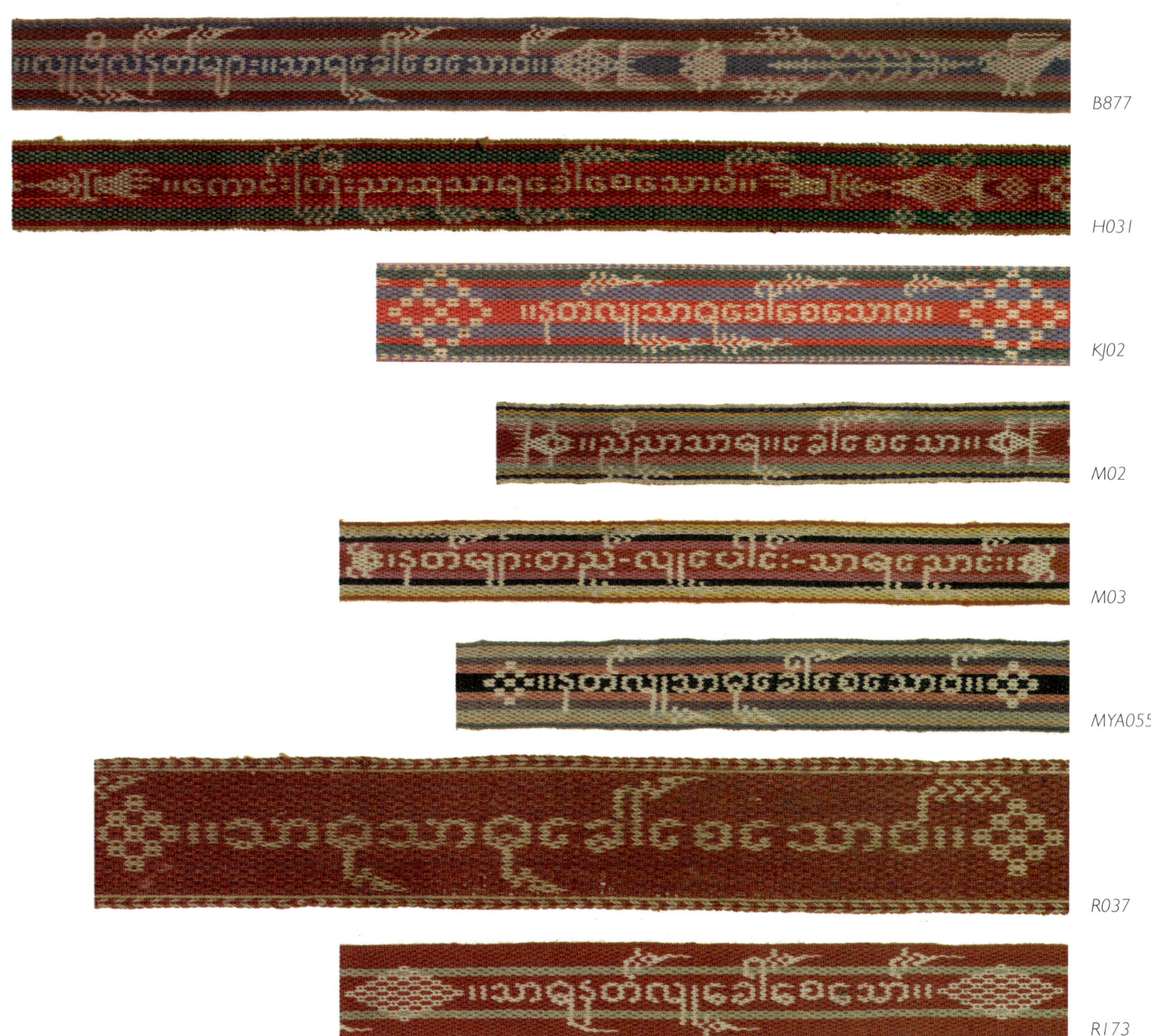

Plate 46 ABOVE

"THADU!" ("WELL DONE!")

The text ends with paired invocations, which conclude the ritual. The donors wish that the merit of their current donation may speed them on their way to nirvana; and they invite celestials and human beings to witness their deed of merit, to approve it, and to applaud, calling out *Thadu!* (Well done!). *(B877, H031, KJ02, M02, M03, MYA055T, R037, R173)*

Donors may pray that their donation of a scriptural manuscript will contribute to the enduring strength of the Buddhist dispensation: **"May the Sasana** [the Buddha's teachings] **ever endure!"**

Or they may end with an expression of the sheer joy of donation: **"Our hearts are full of gladness like the lotus bloom opening on the water."** (R123)

The Earth Goddess Waythondaye (Sanskrit: Vasundhara) may be called on as a powerful celestial witness, **"We ask Vasundhara, the guardian god of the earth, to be the witness of our deed."** (MMG5.5)

"We call this aloud for all to hear. Waythondaye, guardian god of the earth, please stand witness to this our deed." (MMG5.7)

VERSES AND RHYME SCHEMES

Many early twentieth-century sazigyo texts contain over a hundred four-syllable *pada* verses, with flowery expressions, in "poetic diction." A discussion of Burmese poetry is far outside the scope of this book (and in any case far beyond this author), but one feature of Burmese prosody should be mentioned here, since it helps us appreciate the musicality of the text and the role of the woven images of vocal or noisy birds and beasts that appear within it. The four-syllable *pada* verses that comprise the text of many sazigyo are interlinked in a complex rhyme scheme, only possible in a monosyllabic language where each syllable is a whole word, and rhymes are superabundant. In most English poetry, lines rhyme only in the last syllable: a common pattern of end rhymes in a verse of four lines is expressed in the conventional notation: (ABAB / CDCD / etc.). Contrast this with the rhyme scheme of Burmese *pada* verses, where each "verse" consists of four monosyllabic words, any of which may be linked by rhyme to the previous verse and to the verse that follows. In the example below, each capital letter represents a single syllable, and each group of four sounds is a whole "verse": (AABA / ABAA / CABB / AABD / etc.). This example is from an actual sazigyo text (B876). The chiming sonorities achieved by skillful composers of *pada* verses have more affinity with the alliterative lines of Anglo-Saxon or sixteenth-century Scots poetry than with familiar stanzas of classical English verse.

SUBSIDIARY TEXTS ("TEXTLETS")

DATES

One or more very short texts or "textlets" follow the main text, bracketed off by woven images of vocal birds or beasts. The most common of these is the date of the donation—and so also of the weave. The majority of sazigyo are dated, and since donors consulted astrologers before selecting the most auspicious date for their donation, many bear the day of the month selected for the performance of the religious act—sometimes even the exact hour when the sazigyo was completed. The year is usually given in numerals, often in decorative parentheses, but some dates are spelled out in words fitted within the verses of the woven text. **"The year 1292 BE** [1930 CE] **is the date of this donation."** (BM246) **"In the royal era, in the year one thousand two hundred and ninety six** [1934 CE]**, in the month of Tabodwe . . ."** (B887)

The Burmese "royal" or secular era is 638 years less than the Christian, or Common Era. Religious dates are reckoned from the birth of the Lord Buddha. Paired dates, secular and religious, are common on bell inscriptions but rare on sazigyo. Nevertheless a few sazigyo

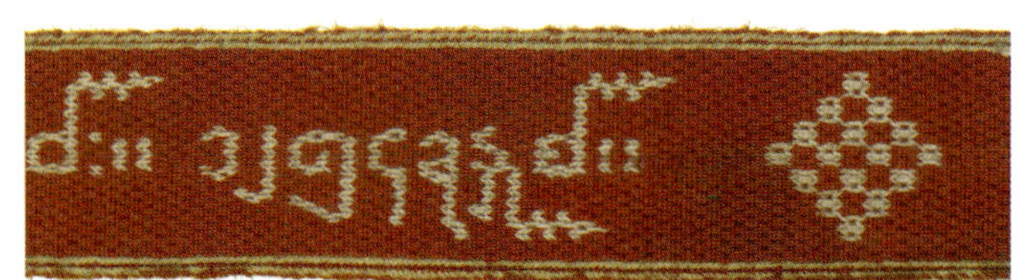

B880

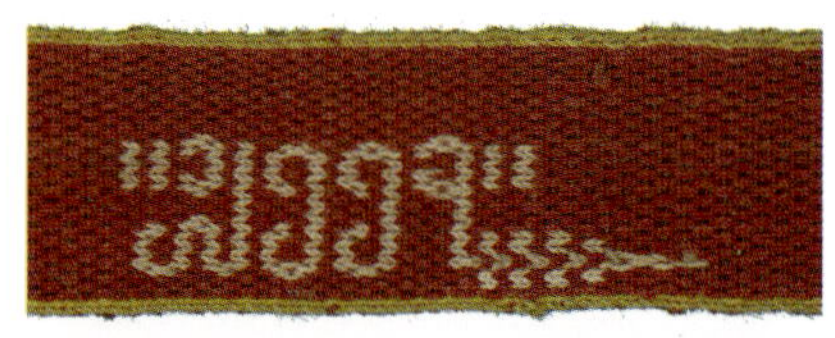

R086

R272

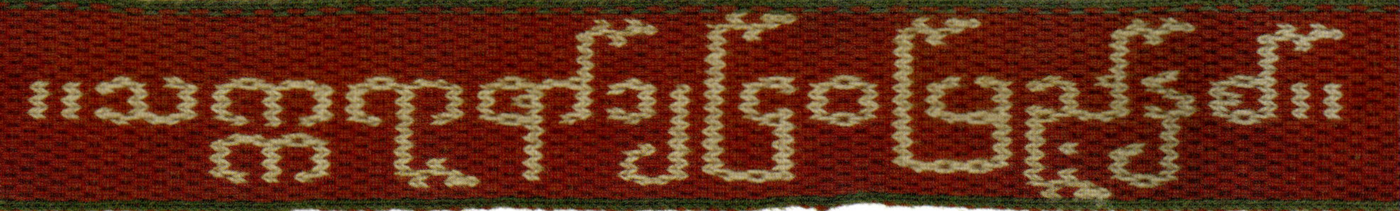

B884

BM246

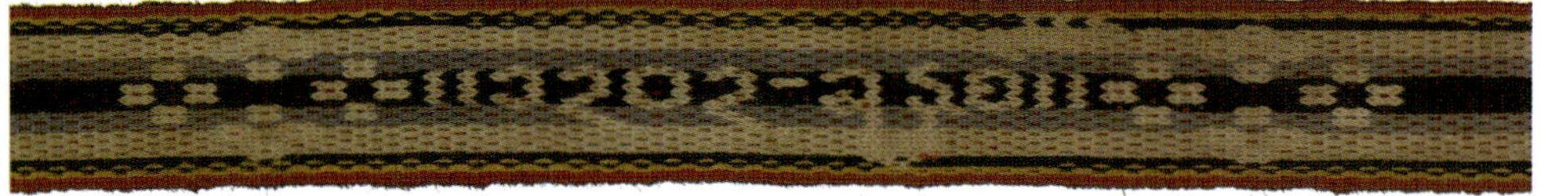

R305

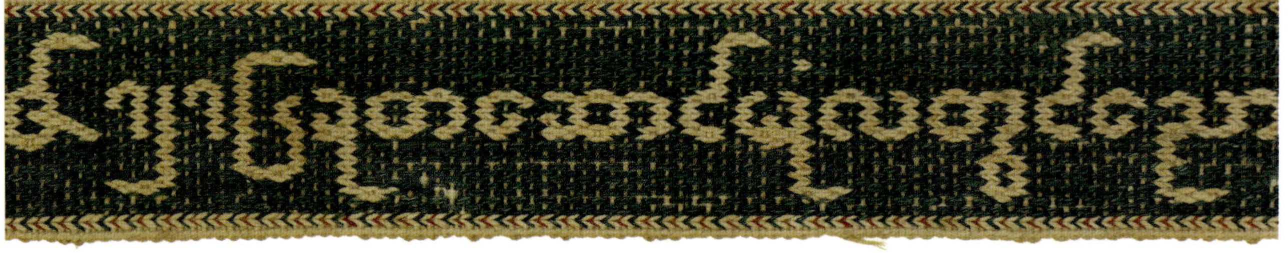

R162

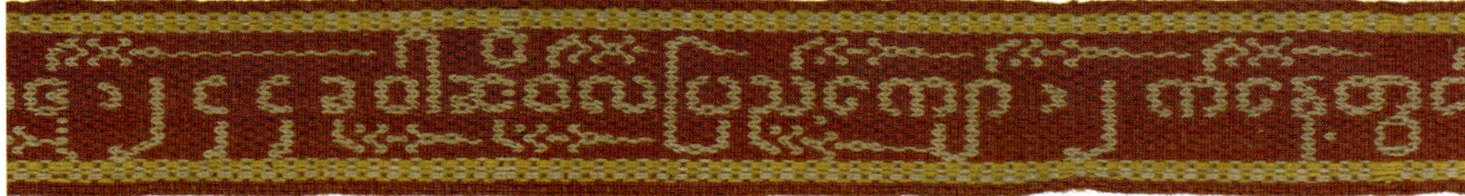

R090

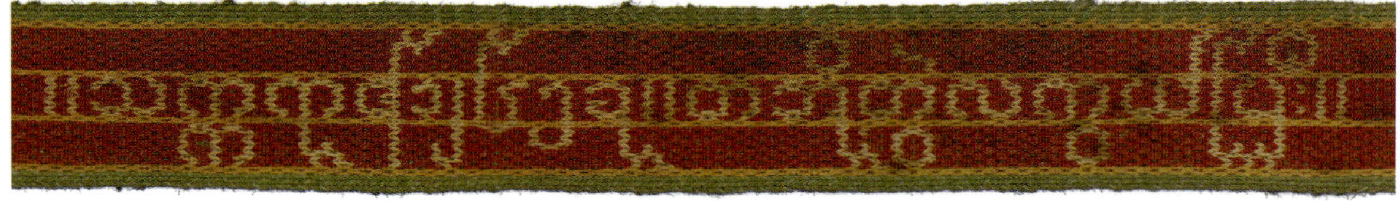

R029

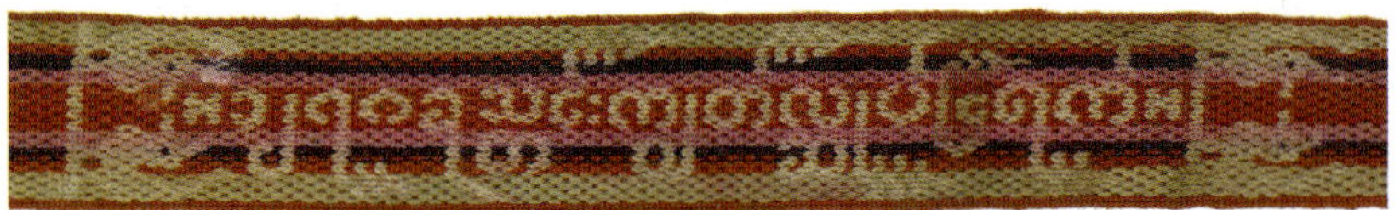

B866

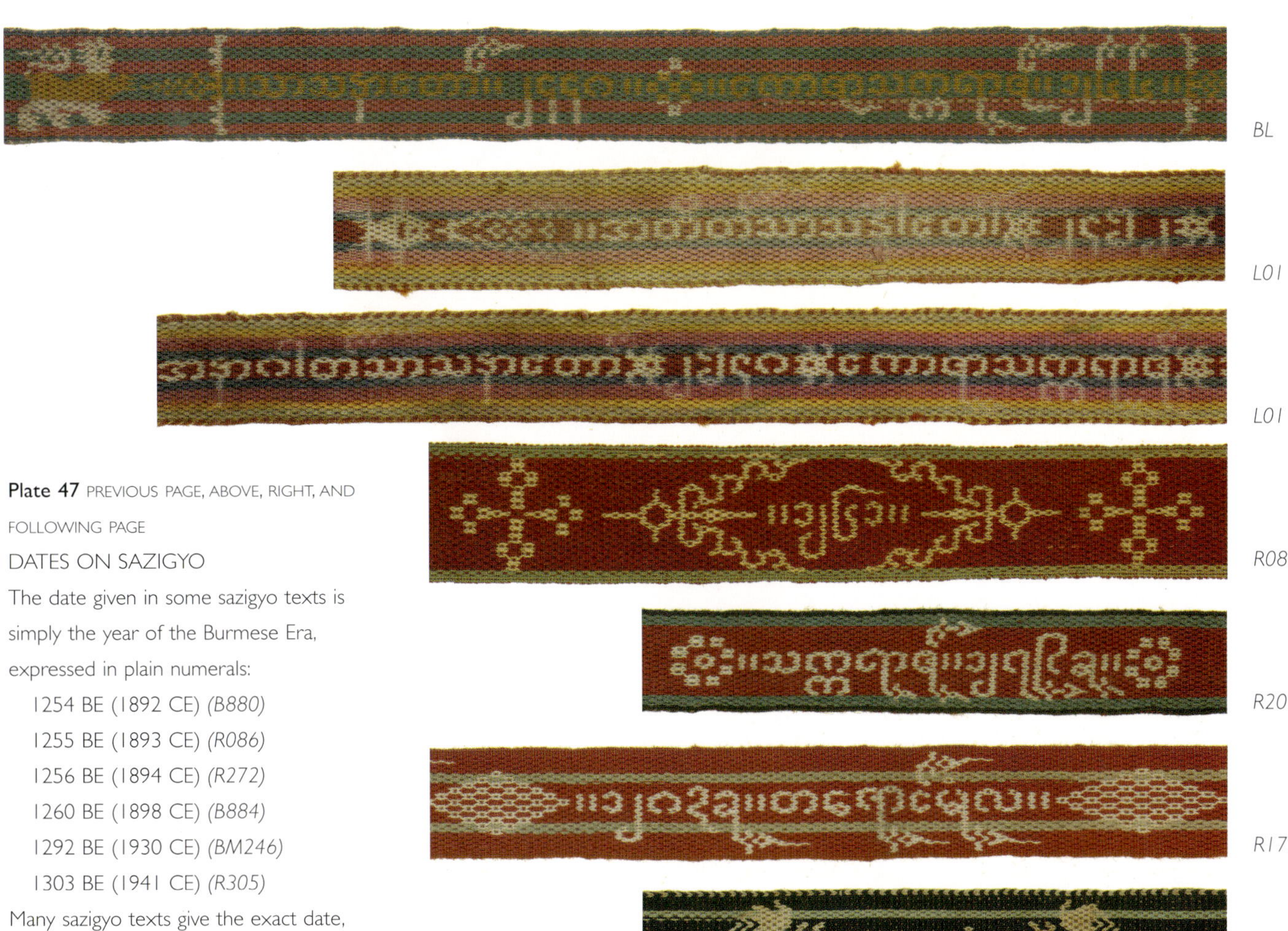

BL

L01

L01

R082

R202

R173

R246

Plate 47 PREVIOUS PAGE, ABOVE, RIGHT, AND FOLLOWING PAGE

DATES ON SAZIGYO

The date given in some sazigyo texts is simply the year of the Burmese Era, expressed in plain numerals:

1254 BE (1892 CE) *(B880)*
1255 BE (1893 CE) *(R086)*
1256 BE (1894 CE) *(R272)*
1260 BE (1898 CE) *(B884)*
1292 BE (1930 CE) *(BM246)*
1303 BE (1941 CE) *(R305)*

Many sazigyo texts give the exact date, year, month, and day, selected by astrologers as auspicious for the donation:

1216 BE (1854 CE) in the month of Tazaungmon *(R162)*
1244 BE (1882 CE), 12th waxing day of Waso *(R090)*
1265 BE (1903 CE), month of Tabodwe *(R029)*
1278 BE (1916 CE), 6th day of waning moon of Thadingyut *(B866)*

A few sazigyo texts record both the secular (or royal) date and one or more of several ecclesiastical dates calculated from the key events in the story of Buddhism. *(BL, L01)*

Dates may be framed in decorative brackets, or flanked by geometrical motifs:

1261 BE (1899 CE) *(R082)*
1276 BE (1914 CE) *(R202)*
1283 BE (1921 CE) *(R173)*
1288 BE (1926 CE) *(R246)*

(BL, L01) bear not only the secular date but also one or more ecclesiastical dates. L01 has three dates, the royal or secular date 1370 (1908 CE) and two ecclesiastical dates, 2352 and 2538.

Many sazigyo texts spell out the year, month, and day of donation:

> **In the year 1292 BE [1930 CE], on the ninth day of the waxing moon of the month of Nayon, residents of Sonkon Ward in Siku Town Ko Bo Kyeh and his wife Ma Thet Hnin, sons Ko San Tint and Ko San Shin, daughters Ma Kywe and Ma Swe, their deed of merit, seeking nirvana. May celestial and human beings approve, and call out "*Thadu!*"** (R245)

A very few give the date when the weaver was given the words, and started work, **"In the cool season of the year 1238 BE [1876 CE] on the seventh day of the waxing moon of Tazaungmon the words of the text were given to the weaver, and the band was completed on Sunday afternoon the fourth day of the waxing moon of Natdaw, on the third stroke of the time drum."** (JB6.51)

RIGHT AND BELOW

The date is often bracketed by beasts, birds, or fish:

1262 BE (1900 CE) *(KJ01)*
1265 BE (1903 CE) *(R030)*
1272 BE (1910 CE) *(R100)*
1273 BE (1911 CE) *(M01)*
1279 BE (1917 CE) *(R167)*
1280 BE (1918 CE) *(R005)*
1290 BE (1928 CE) *(R008)*

"ENGLISH" DATES

During British colonial times it was fashionable for sazigyo weavers to include the "English" date alongside the date in the Burmese Era:

1269 BE (1907 CE) *(B850)*
1269 BE (1908 CE) *(B851)*
1285 BE (1923 CE) *(R054)*

A VERY LATE DATE

The date 1327 BE (1965 CE) is one of the latest ever woven on a sazigyo. *(R274)* "In the year 1327 on the eighth waxing day of the month of Tazungmon, 1.11.65, in the town of Zalun, retired senior physician U Ba Kyaw passed away aged seventy leaving his devoted widow Daw Daw Shin and numerous family, who have donated this manuscript . . . Dated in the month of Tabodwe 1327 [1965 CE]." The date of the deceased's death is given first in traditional Myanmar form, then again, perhaps to make it thoroughly official, in the English style but in Burmese numerals "1-11-65."

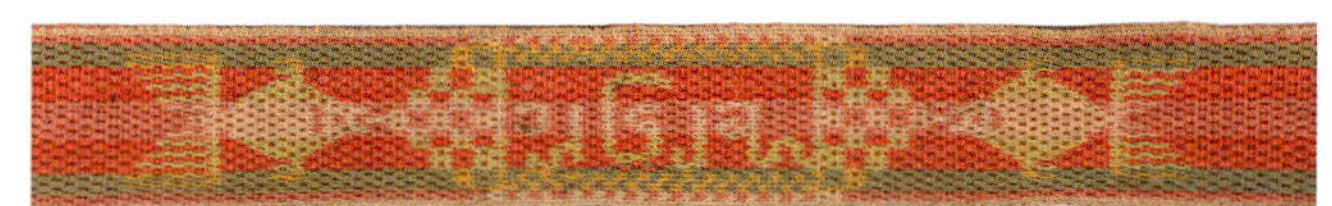

KJ01

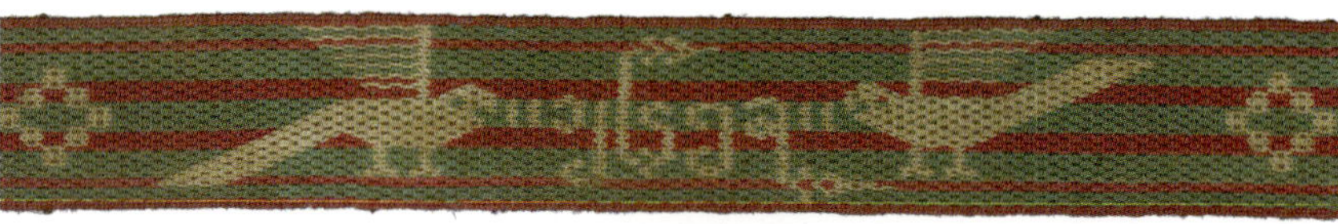

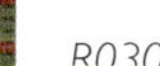

R030

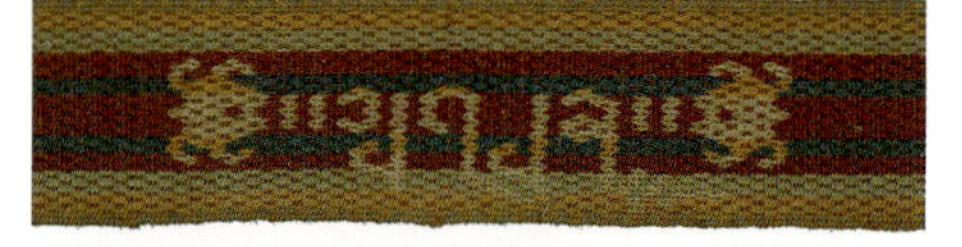

R100

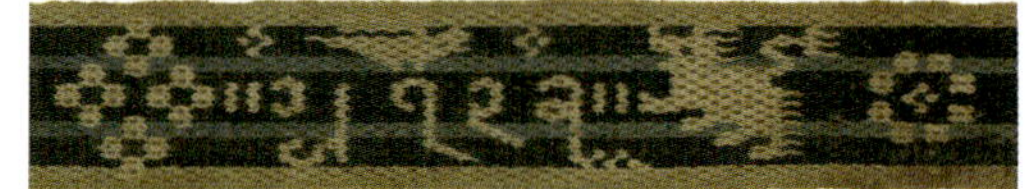

M01

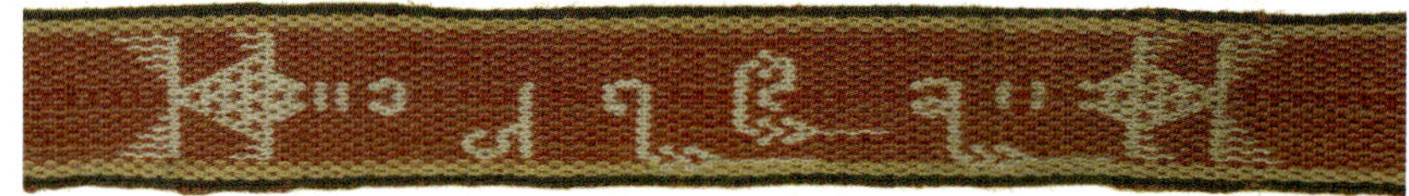

R167

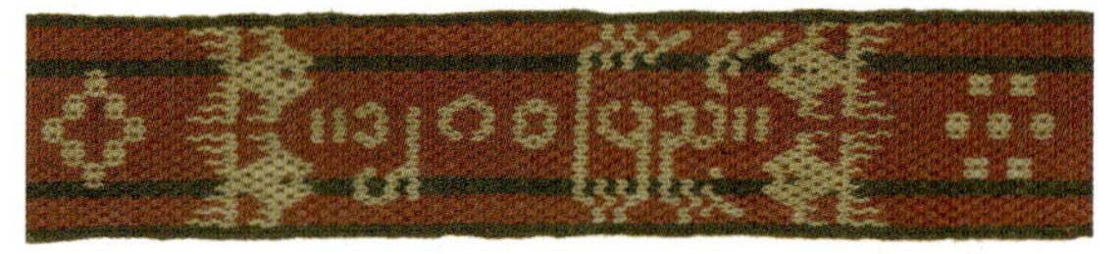

R005

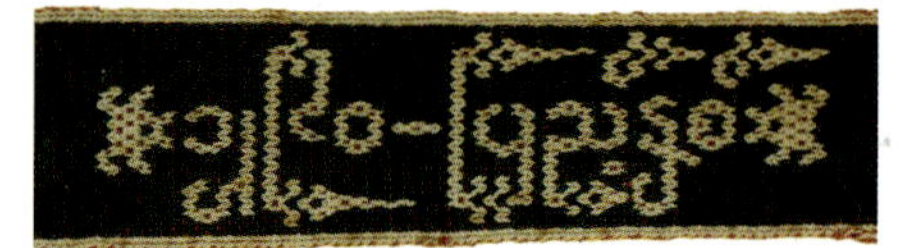

R008

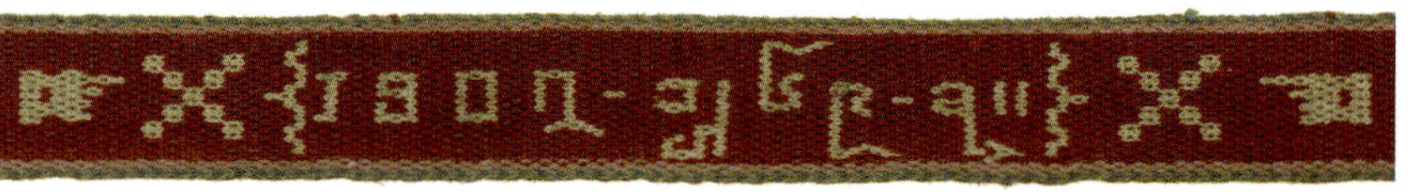

B850

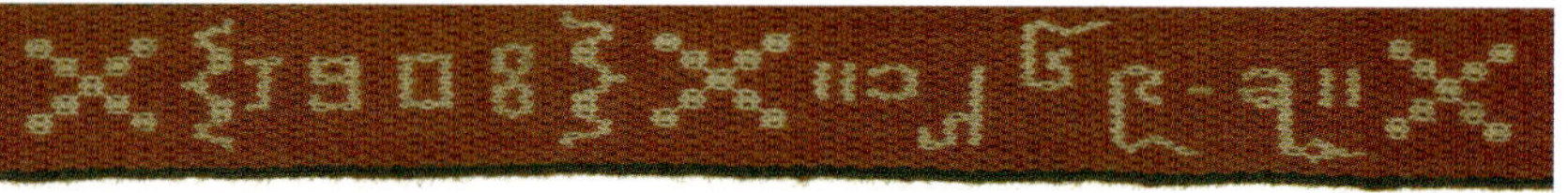

B851

R054

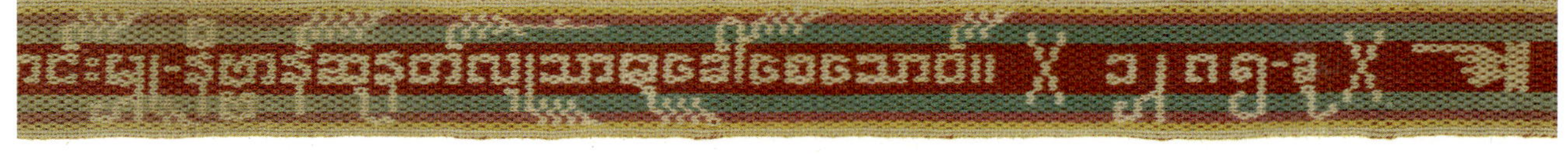

R054

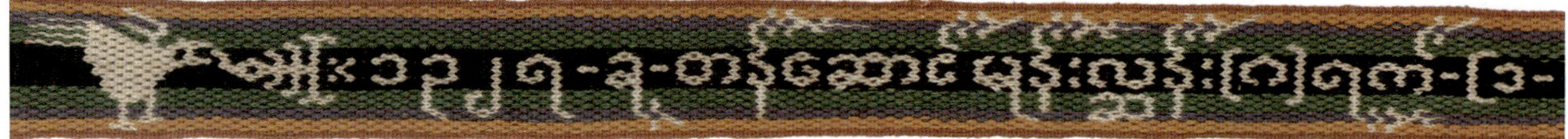

R274

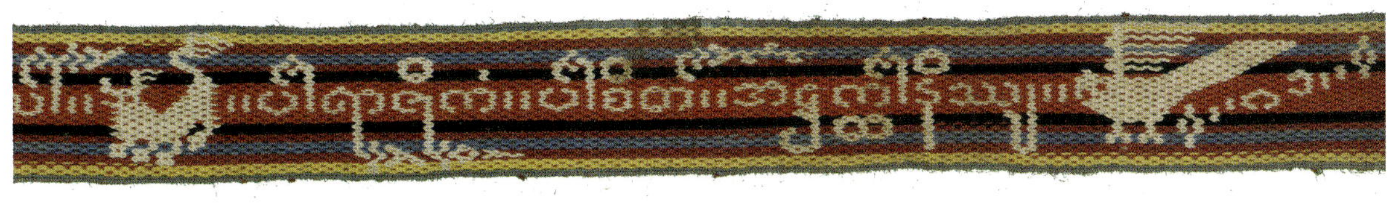

B842

R181

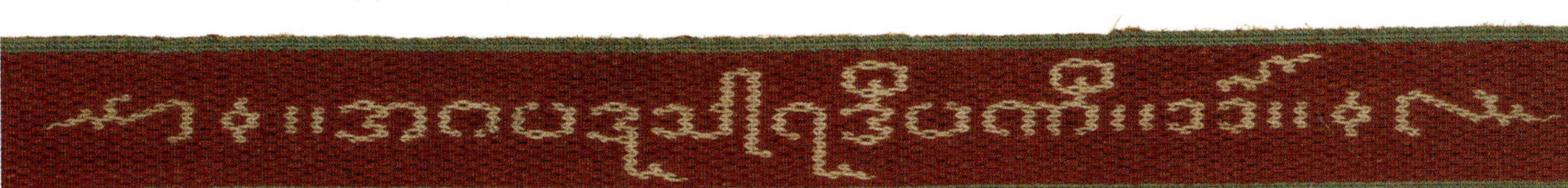

R218

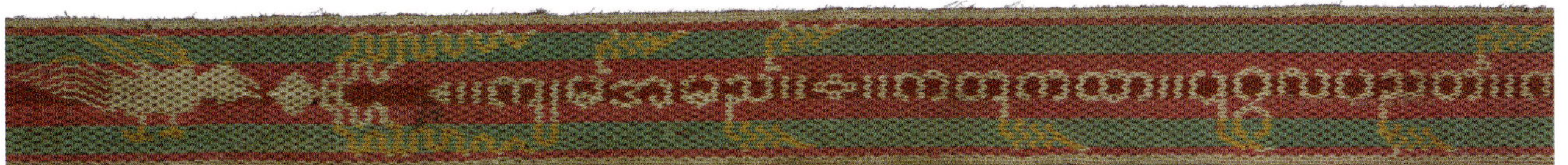

R026

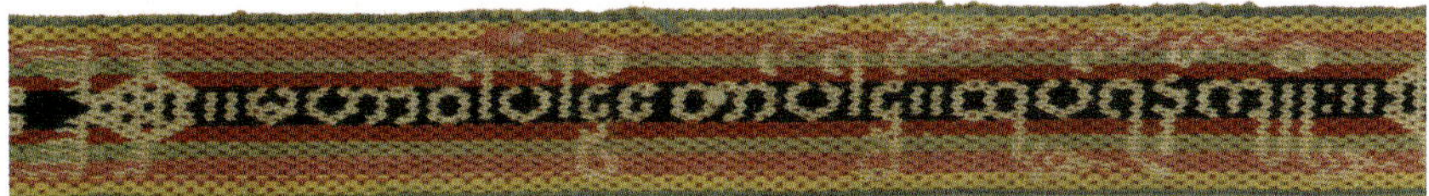

B855

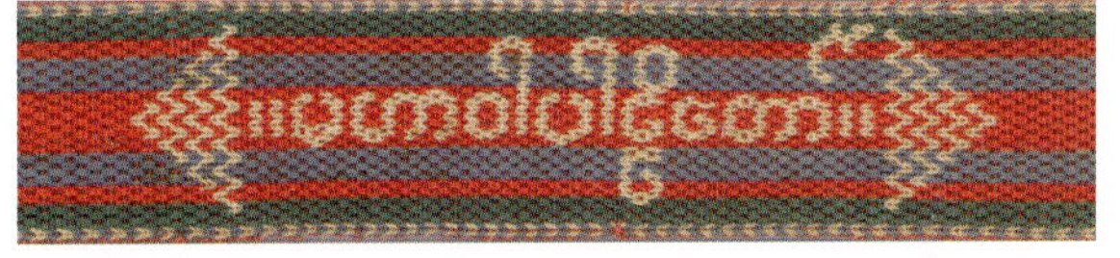

KJ02

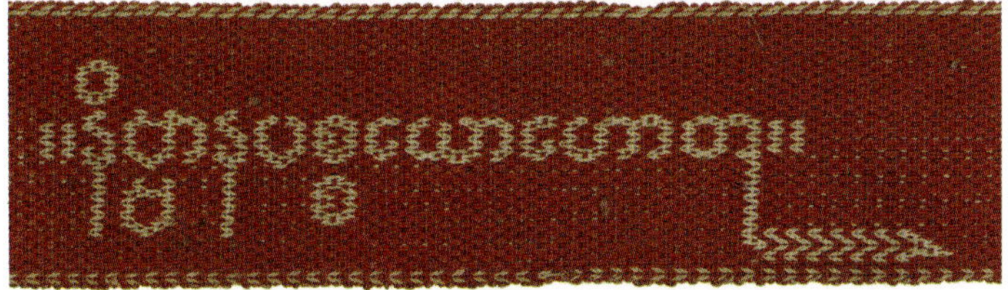

R184

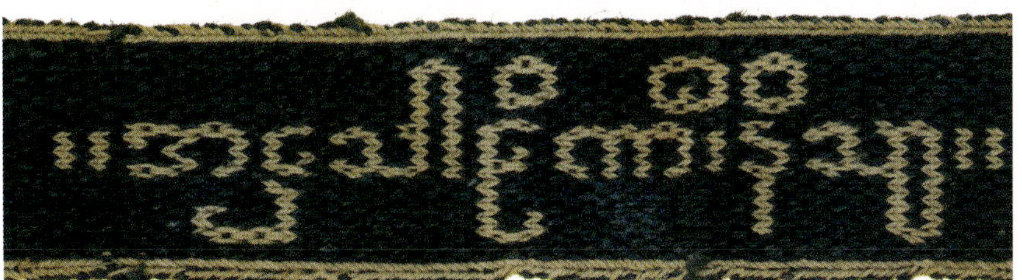

T410

Plate 48 ABOVE AND RIGHT

TITLE OF MANUSCRIPT

The title of the scriptural manuscript appears near one end of the flat weave, which helps the reader of palm-leaf manuscripts to select reading material from the manuscript chest. I am grateful to Dr. Jotika Khur-Yearn for his translations from the Pali.

Nissaya commentary on two sections of the *Books of Discipline* (Vinaya Pitaka), the Paaraajika and the Pacittiya. *(B842)*

Yamaka in Pali, pack 1. *(R181)*

Agapadusaradipani, commentary on the essence of *"agapadu"* a term in Telugu, not Pali. *(R218)*

Titles of treatises: *Discussion on Elements; A Designation of Human Types; Points of Controversy;* in Pali. *(R026)*

Tape for binding the Mahawa selection in the sacred Pali. (This sazigyo was woven for a *kammavaca* manuscript). *(B855)*

Mahavaggapali, one of the five books of the Vinaya Pitaka. *(KJ02)*

"Nibbana passaya hotu." *(R184)*

Attasalin (first of the seven books of the Abidhamma Pitaka). *(T410)*

Plate 49 NEXT PAGE
WEAVER'S SIGNATURE
The weaver's name may be added. Most signatures are those of female weavers.
"Meh May's work" *(B850)*
"Meh Aye" *(B869)*
"Meh U's work" *(R024)*
"Worked by Ma Ma Kyi" *(AZ6)*
On this sazigyo, apart from "parts 1 and 2," the only text is "Ma Htar wove this manuscript band." The rather rough weaving suggests the weaver was a young girl apprenticed to an experienced female relative. *(B845)*
The woven text claims that Ma Khin Thein wove this sazigyo for a manuscript made by her father: "Worked by Ma Khin Thein, daughter of the Mandalay master *kammavaca* manuscript maker U Sein." *(R013)*
The first male signature is that of a professional weaver: "Work of Ko Khin." *(R029)*
The second male signatory is a novice monk who wove a sazigyo for a brother novice: "Woven by Ko Shin Withuda. This sazigyo is for Ko Hpyu." *(KJ04)*

SIGNING AT THE VERY END
Signatures are usually the last text on the tape, but some witty women withheld their signatures even longer. They finish the flat area, start the tubular cord, and just before the end of the cord, switch back to double-faced weave and sign their name. *(JBT6.49)*

This information enables us to calculate that this sazigyo took almost exactly four weeks to weave. It is exceptionally long, at over nine meters, and has well over a hundred verses, so the weaver had reason to be proud.

Burmese and "English" dates appear together on some sazigyo woven about two decades after the British annexation of Upper Burma, "1269" in Burmese numerals is followed by "1907" in roman numerals. A hand emerges from a stiff English shirt cuff and points to the English date, while large crosses resemble the Union Jack.

Dates offer a potentially powerful research tool for future study of the stylistic development of the lettering and images. The style of text and images of undated sazigyo can readily be compared to examples with a woven date.

TITLE OF MANUSCRIPT

When the Pali title of the scriptural manuscript for which the sazigyo was commissioned appears near one end of the flat weave, it acts like the title and author's name on the spine of Western printed books. The reader of palm-leaf manuscripts could select his reading material without the trouble of opening the whole parcel. If he found no manuscript title on the sazigyo itself the reader could look for another aid to identification—the little book knife or *gabyidan* tucked into the wrapper or its sazigyo. This was usually a simple slip of palm leaf, but some were inscribed with the manuscript title. These book knives are described and illustrated in appendix 2.

WEAVER'S SIGNATURE

The weaver may "sign" her work by adding her name. English needlework samplers often bear the name of the girl who worked them, but on other craftwork the name of a female artist is a rarity. Sazigyo offer us the names of scores of women weavers who lived and worked a century ago. Male signatories are rarer. One is a novice monk, who wove a sazigyo to give to a brother novice (KJ04).

Every weaver's signature advertises her skills, but this one is explicitly commercial, **"Take a good look at this woven text. My residence is in Chaungu town center, my name Ma Cheint Ba, and this is an example of my skill. If you wish to purchase** [a similar sazigyo] **just step my way."** (AZ1) To impress potential customers the weaver repeats the name of her home town, this time in English capital letters.

Some signatures on sazigyo, like those on lacquerware, should be read with caution. The name may not be that of the artist craftworker, but of the workshop or business. Apparently Ma Khin Thein was not herself a weaver, but the "boss," the owner-manager of the family firm (R013).

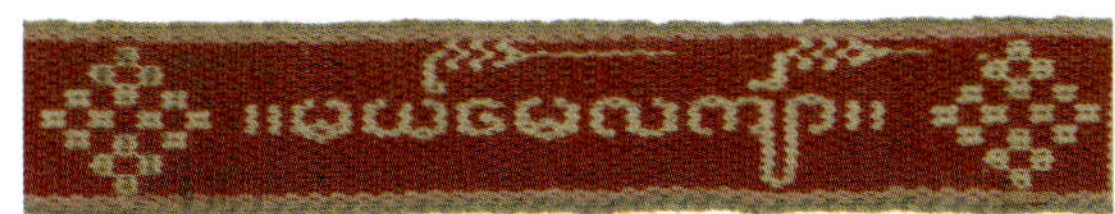
B850

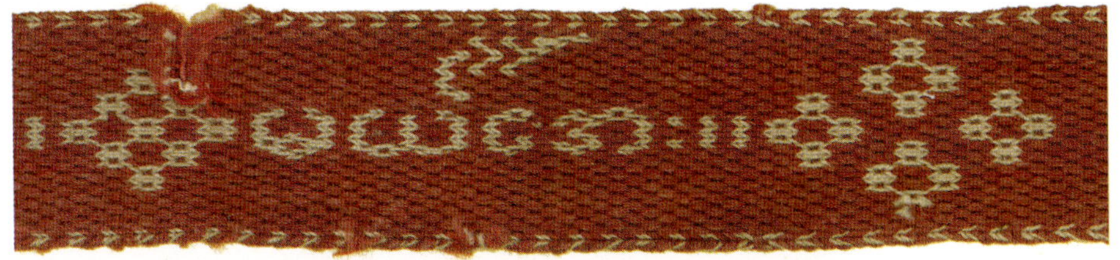
B869

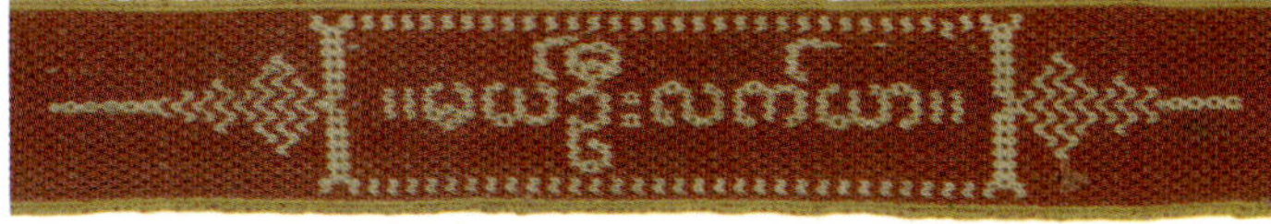
R024

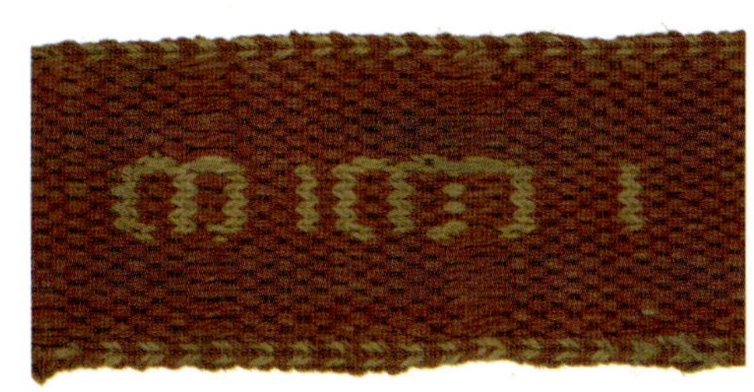
B845

AZ6

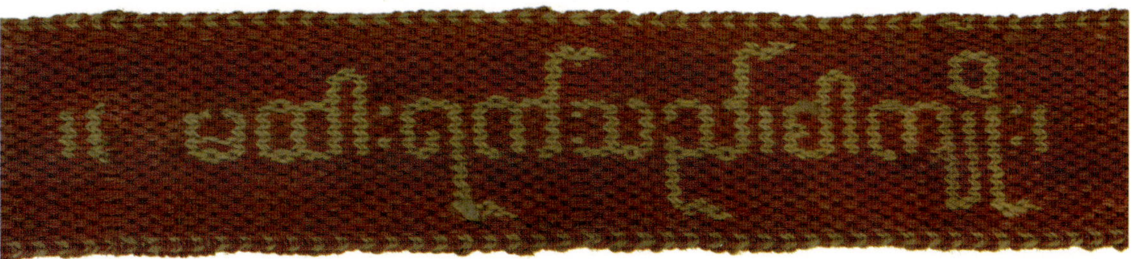
B845

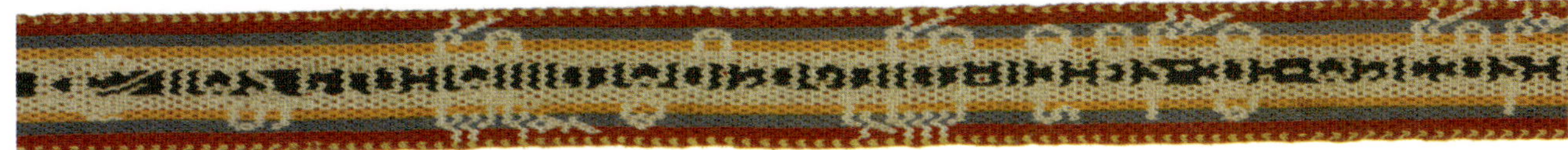
R013

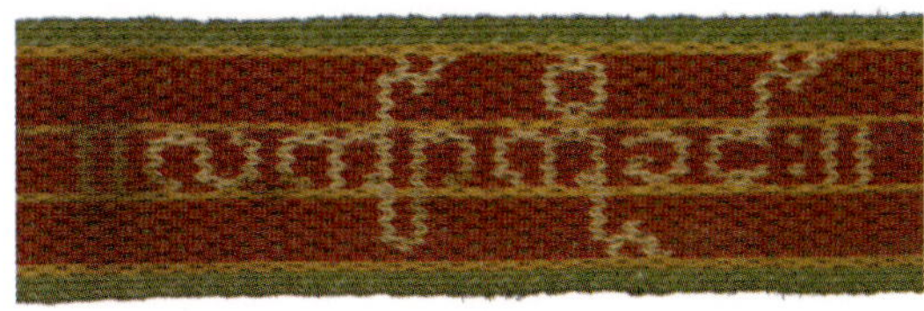
R029

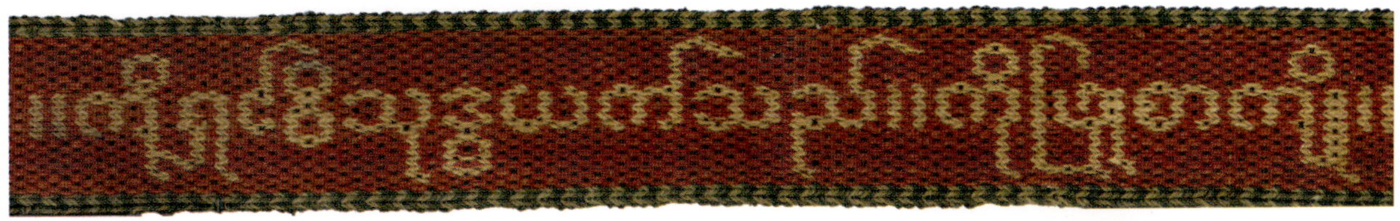
KJ04

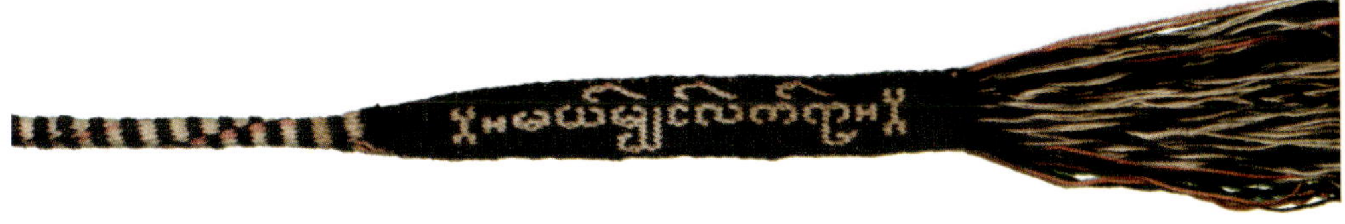
JBT6.49

Plate 50 RIGHT
SIGNING IN ENGLISH
In the British colonial period, English was fashionable among educated Burmese, and a few weavers used English lettering for their signatures. Most used block capitals *(KJ03)*, but one brave woman attempted "joined-up" writing. *(H008)*
The weaver repeats the name of her home town, Chaungu, in English block capitals. *(AZ1)*

"BEST ONE"
The English phrase "BEST ONE" is common on sazigyo woven between 1900 and 1910. *(R027, R192)*
A very superior silk sazigyo has a rare variant: "NUMBERONE." *(W93)*

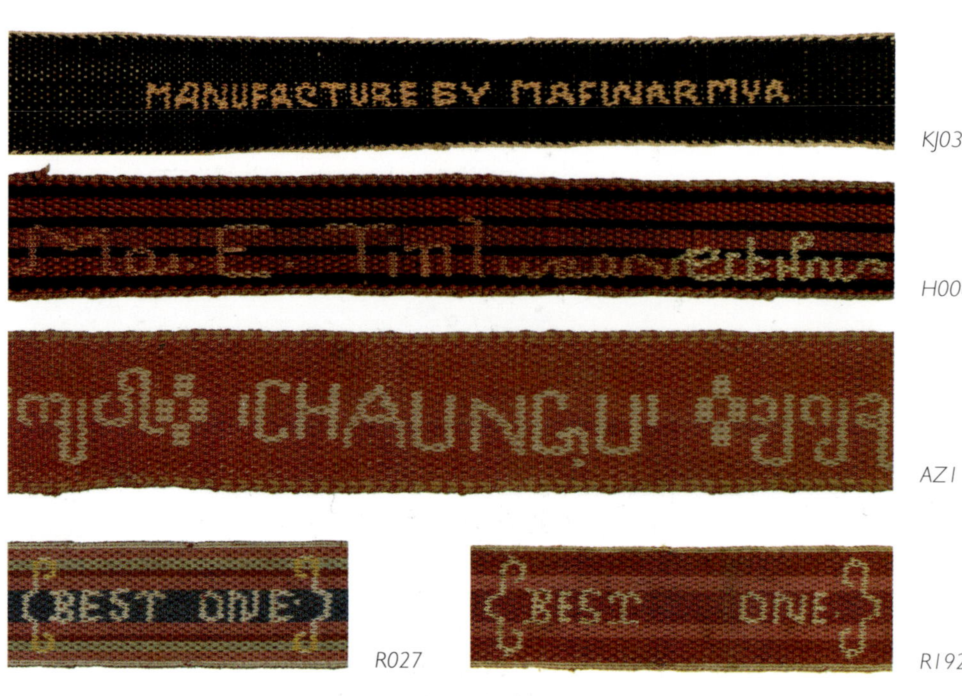

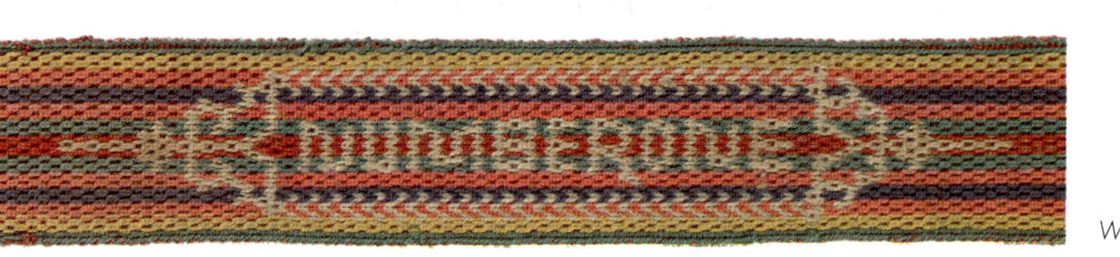

Plate 51 NEXT AND FOLLOWING PAGE
CUMULATIVE AND FINAL VERSE-COUNT
The final verse-count was proof of the weaver's skill and formed the basis for the price she charged.
"The verse count is 66" *(W93)*
"80 *pada* verses" *(M01)*
"86 *pada* verses" *(BM246)*
"96 verses" *(B844)*
"100 *pada* verses" *(R027)*
"125" *(R037)*
A parrot keeps a running count of the verses in some long texts, appearing at intervals of ten verses, often with numerals under its tail recording the cumulative total. The parrots record 10, 20, 50, 60, 70, 80 verses, and the final count of 94. *(B854)*
The running count is 70, 80, 90 verses, and final count of 96. *(B844)*

Weavers' signatures are usually the very last text on a sazigyo, but some witty women weavers withheld their signatures even longer. They finish the flat area, complete the taper, and start the tubular cord—then switch back to double-faced weave to create a flat strip long enough to sign their name, just before the fringe.

"BEST ONE"

During the British colonial period, the English language was fashionable among educated Burmese. English words were borrowed into Burmese, and some, including slang words of the moment, became "chic" usage, even among Burmese with very little English. Lacquer makers in Pagan who inscribed their wares with slogans claiming unbeatable quality began to use English words like "special," "number one," and "lottery [winner] written in Burmese script." Weavers of sazigyo followed suit, and the English phrase "BEST ONE" is common on sazigyo woven between 1900 and 1910, always in English capitals, and always enclosed in decorative brackets or in a cartouche as a separate "textlet." The variant "NUMBERONE" appears on a single very superior silk sazigyo (W93). Originally "BEST ONE"

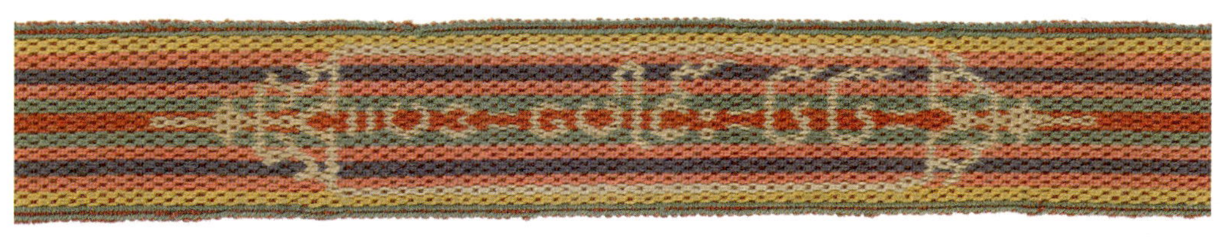

W93

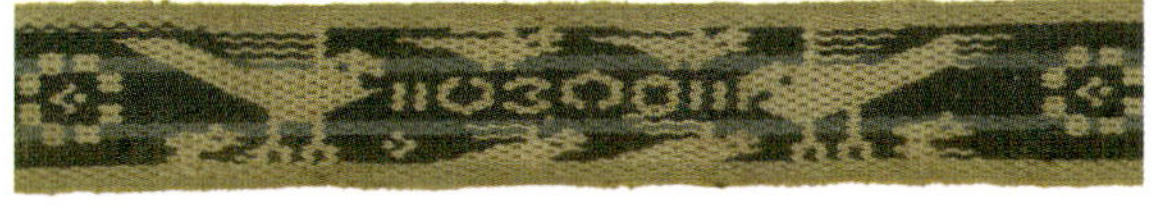

M01

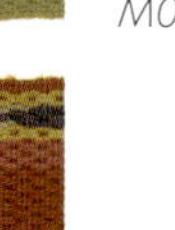

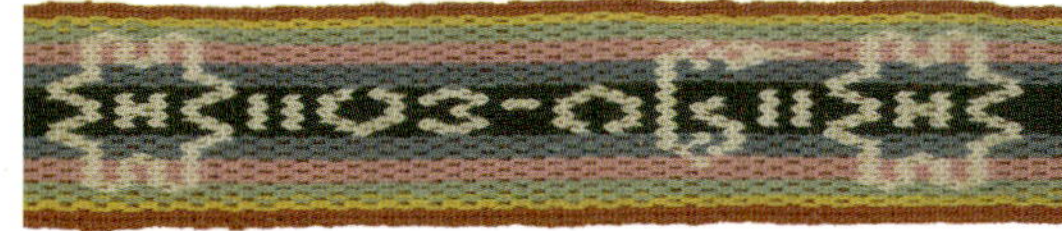

BM246

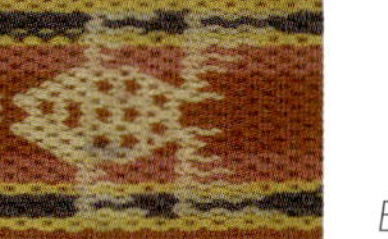

B844

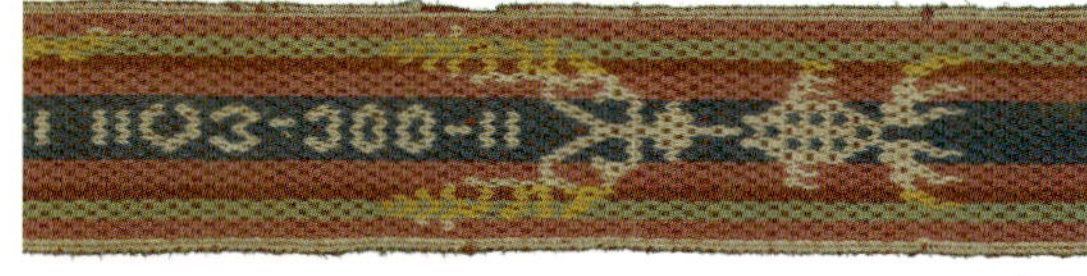

R027

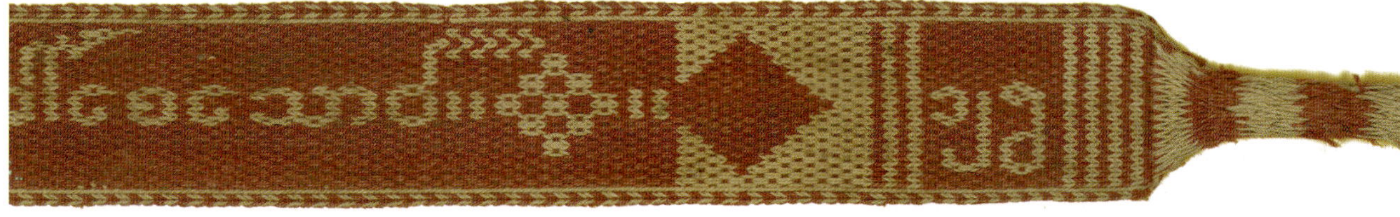

R037

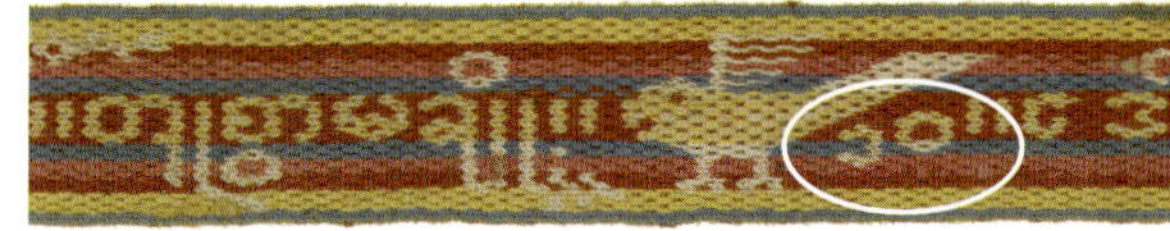

B854
10 verses

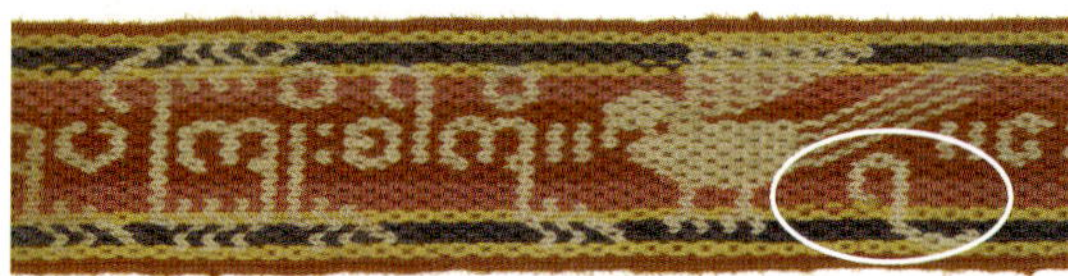

B844
7 i.e.,
70 verses

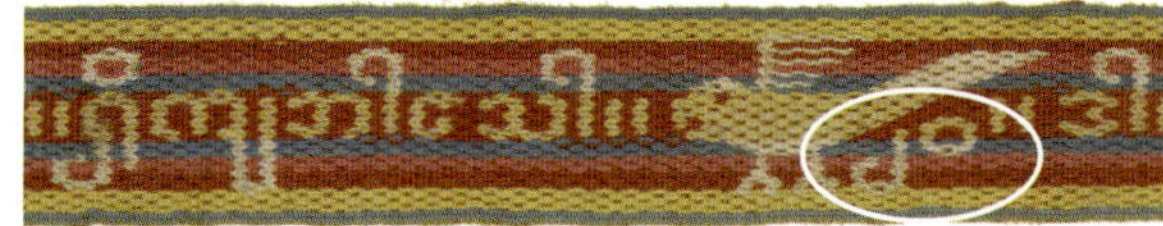

B854
20 verses

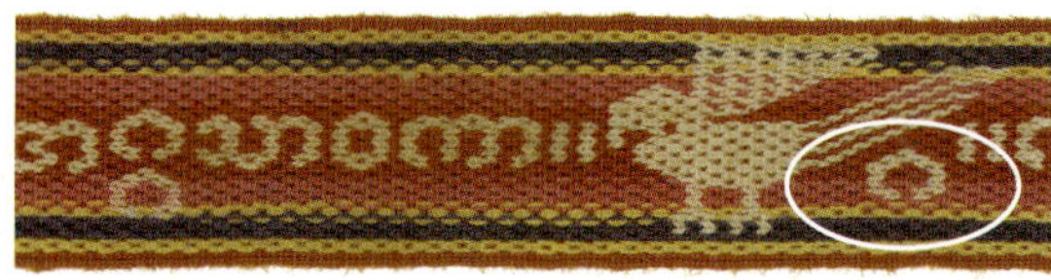

B844
8 i.e.,
80 verses

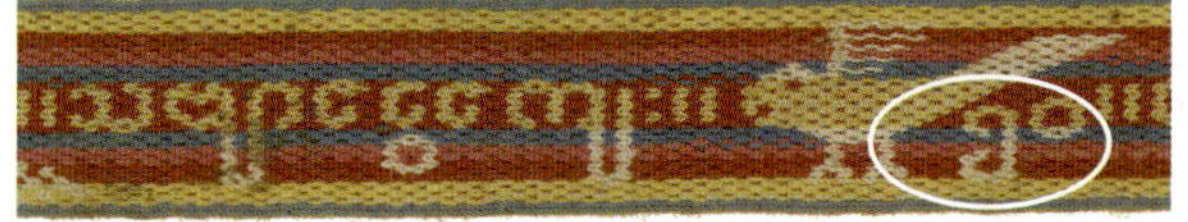

B854
50 verses

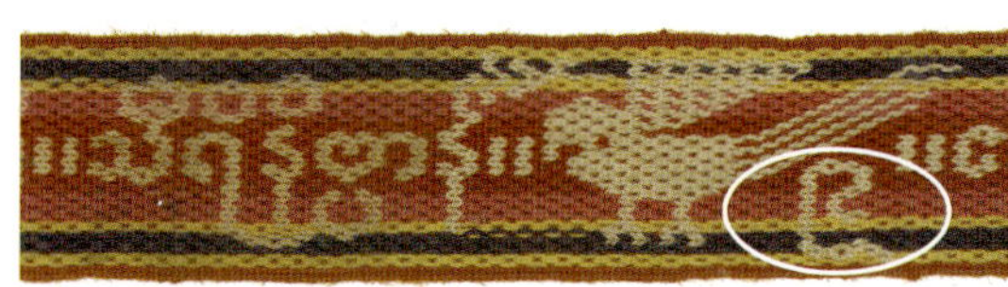

B844
9 i.e.,
90 verses

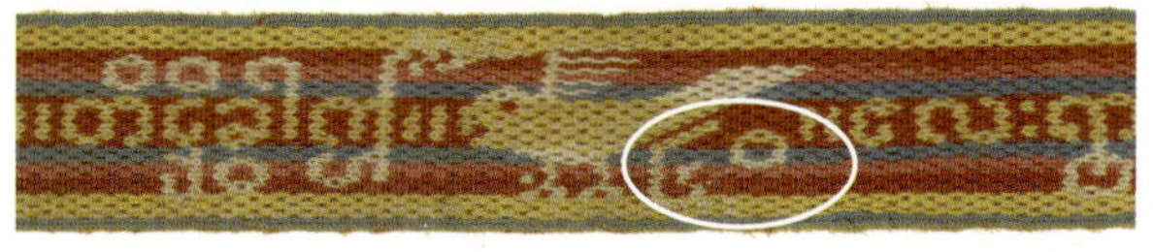

B854
60 verses

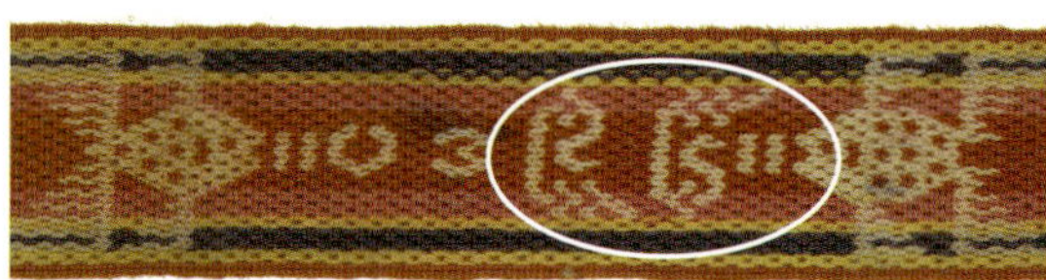

B844
Final count
96 verses

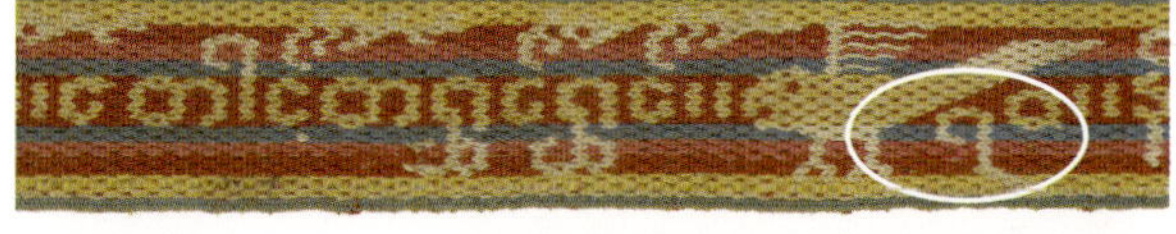

B854
70 verses

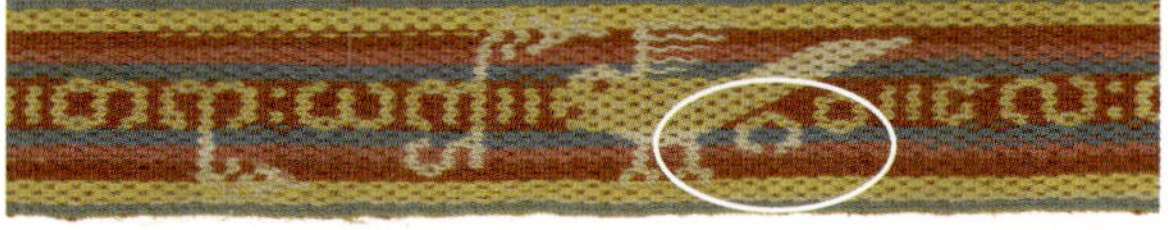

B854
80 verses

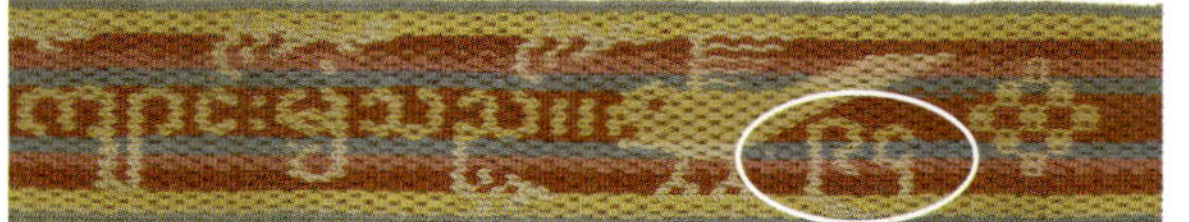

B854
final count
94 verses

BELOW

COMPACTING THE DATA

The weaver had no space to waste at the end of this fine sazigyo. She inserts a bird or a fish and numerals (20, 40, 70) above or below the text: "97 [verses] price 2 kyats 8 pyas in the year 1268 [1906 CE]." *(B861)*

FINAL VERSE-COUNT IN THE RIGGING OF A *DAGUNDAING*

Short of warp space for the usual verse-count bracketed between birds, this weaver's ingenious solution is to insert "110 *pada*" (verses) symmetrically into the rigging of the *dagundaing*, the tall teak flagpost, the final image. *(R160)*

was a seal of quality claimed by the weaver and understood by the customer, proof that the article was in the latest fashionable style, but over time the phrase became devalued, and one very indifferently woven sazigyo (R087) has "BEST ONE" as its only text. One weaver gives her address in Burmese, but repeats the name of her home town, CHAUNGU, in English block capitals (AZ1). A few weavers even used English lettering for their signatures. Most stuck to block capitals, but one brave woman even attempted "joined-up" writing.

VERSE-COUNT: RUNNING TOTAL, FINAL TALLY

The total verse-count was important to the weaver, and often recorded. A high verse-count of 70, 80, even 100, was proof of her workmanship, and formed the basis for the price she charged. Some long texts include not only a final count, but a running count. An image of a parrot, or a pair of these intelligent birds, is inserted at intervals of ten verses to keep a running count by means of numerals tucked under its tail. Whether or not the long text has been split up into "parrotgraphs," the final tally of four-syllable *pada* verses commonly appears near the end of the tape, bracketed off by parrots or other beasts. The final

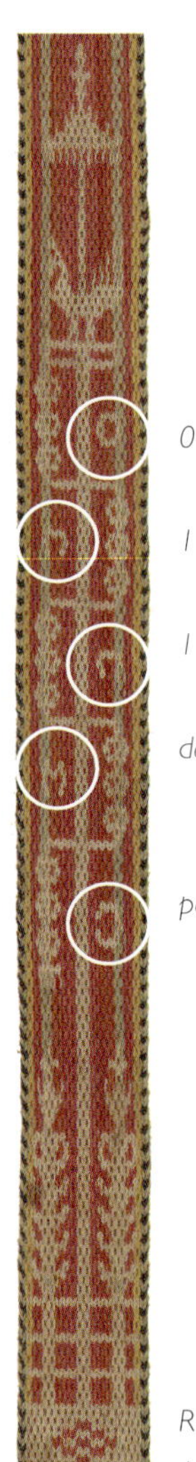

0

1

1

da

pa

R160

110 verses

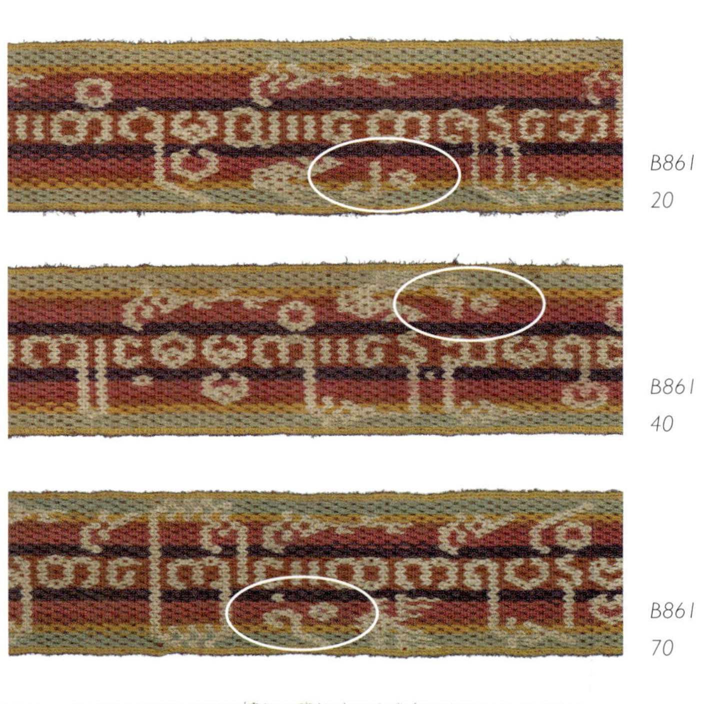

B861

20

B861

40

B861

70

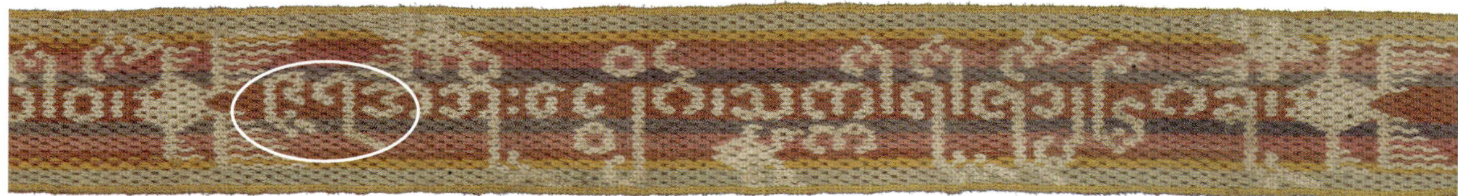

B861

final count

97 verses

invocation "*Thadu!*" may end with a parrot, under whose tail is the final verse-count (B849).

The exceptionally high verse-count of R037 needs no birds, beasts, or cartouche: the bare three digits "125" occupy a very prominent place, right at the end of the flat area, a unique arrangement. The weaver of R160 has run short of warp: there is simply no space for the usual verse-count bracketed between birds. She finds an ingenious solution, inserting the three digits "110" and the two-letter word "*pa-da*" (verses) symmetrically into the rigging of the *dagundaing*, the tall teak flagpost, the final image—with just four millimeters of warp left before the flat area ends and the taper begins.

WEAVER'S PRICE

Some weavers also insert the price they charged for their work, usually just after the total number of verses, on which they based their charges, **"67 verses, price 2 kyats 8 pyas"** (B861): **"This specially woven band is priced at 5 kyats."** (R223)

The weavers were well paid for their skills. In 1880 CE 5 kyats was a considerable sum of money: a tickal (about 6 grams) of gold cost 25 kyats. A long text and many motifs must have taken a month or more

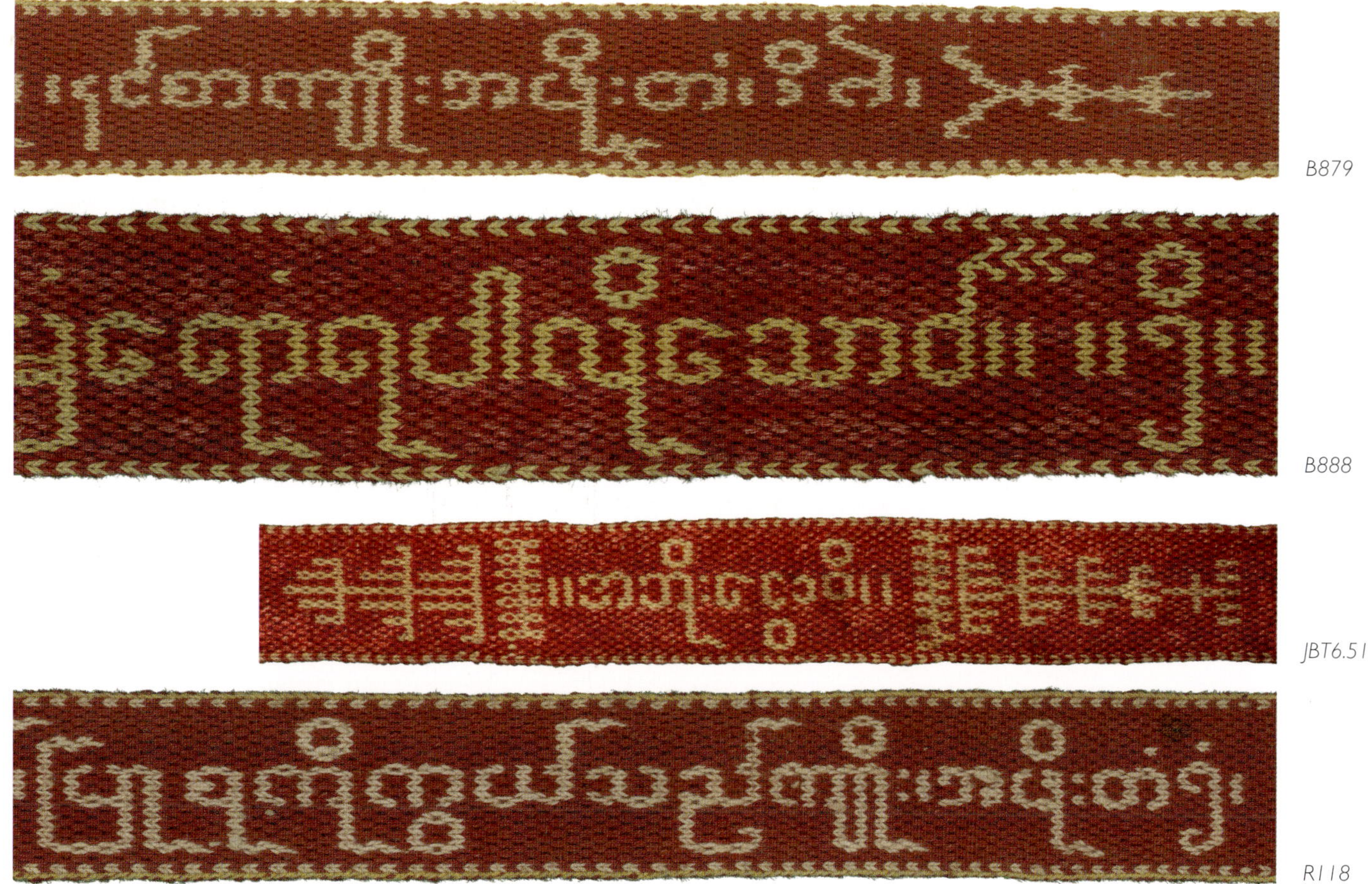

Plate 52 BELOW
Weavers based their charges on the number of verses, and their price usually appears just after the total verse-count:
"Four manuscript bands, price"
"1 kyat 8 pyas" *(B879)*
"5 kyats" *(B888)*
"price 10 kyats" *(JBT6.51)*
"In the year 1242 BE [1880 CE], this specially woven band priced 5 kyats" *(R118)*

to weave, and the prices asked for the work are not excessive. The longest sazigyo known to this author measures nine meters eighteen centimeters and is priced at 10 kyats, a considerable sum of money when it was woven in 1876 (JBT6.51). Some woven prices may have been for several sazigyo, not for a single tape.

MONK'S NAME

The Vinaya rules permit different gifts: to the entire Sangha, to the community of a single monastery collectively, or to an individual monk. More merit is earned by gifts to the whole order, but many Burmese lay donors specify a monk recipient of their donation. **"Kammava manuscript donated for use by Hsayadaw U Wunna"** (KJ01); **"Senior monk U Asara's lettered band."** (B509047)

"U Einda's band" (PG): The manuscript donor, "Great Lion" High Minister of the Shan state of Thein Ni (Hsenwi), was involved in the insurrection led by the Myinzaing prince against the British invader. U Einda, the recipient of the donated manuscript, was one of four monks who played a crucial part in the insurrection, writing and distributing the orders of the Myinzaing prince to all areas of Burma. When their plans were uncovered all were arrested by the British, detained without trial for four years, and released in December 1891.

"U Ponya's manuscript binding tape" (W93): **"On the twelfth day of the waning moon of the month of Waso in the year 1252** [1890 CE] **Ko Bo San and his wife Meh Thaing donated more than 20, almost 30 inga** [bundles of palm leaves] **to the Reverend Lord Hsayadaw** [Abbot] **of the palace, the Venerable Uthingaya."** (L08)

"We donate these palm-leaf manuscripts to the venerable monk U Thawdasara, presiding monk at the monastery of Danoundaw Kyaung." (VC61)

> **We reverently donate with our good intentions the entire bundle to Ashin Thumana, presiding monk of Boundaw monastery. A prestigious venerable monk perfectly trained in the precepts, Ashin Thumana willingly follows the two austere practices, teaching Buddhist scriptures and sitting in insight meditation, both exemplary practices for Buddhist monks."** (VC71)

The named monk may have been a revered teacher. Sir Henry Yule observed of sazigyo in 1855, "These ribbons are worked either in silk or cotton, and are a common present from devout ladies to their spiritual guides." In some cases the monk recipient may have been the author of the verses of the sazigyo text.

Plate 53 BELOW

The name of the monk recipient of the donated manuscript may appear on the sazigyo:

"Senior monk U Asara's lettered band" *(B509047)*

"U Einda's band" *(PG)*

"Donated for use by the abbot of the Tango Palace Monastery" *(R039)*

"U Ponya's manuscript binding tape" *(W93)*

"*Kammavaca* manuscript donated for use by "Hsayadaw [senior monk] U Wunna" *(KJ01)*

U Tikkindiya's" *(M01)*

The mother of a novice monk might donate a manuscript for use at her son's ordination, an occasion of great family rejoicing. Thereafter she would follow his monastic career year after year with growing pride, and might hope eventually to be entitled to use a special title of honor, **"Ma Nyein Aung, mother of a monk abbot, donates this Kammava manuscript as her deed of merit."** (JP01)

Sorrow also occasioned such gifts. An inscription on the cover of a manuscript made in 1294 BE (1932 CE) names the monk for whom the manuscript was made and his deceased mother whose ashes it contains. The donors are not named, but would probably have been children of the deceased, siblings of the monk recipient, **"This *kammavaca* manuscript reliquary enshrines the bone ash relics of Daw Hla Gaung Aye, mother of the monk U Vazavin."** (Musée des Arts Asiatiques, Nice, France)

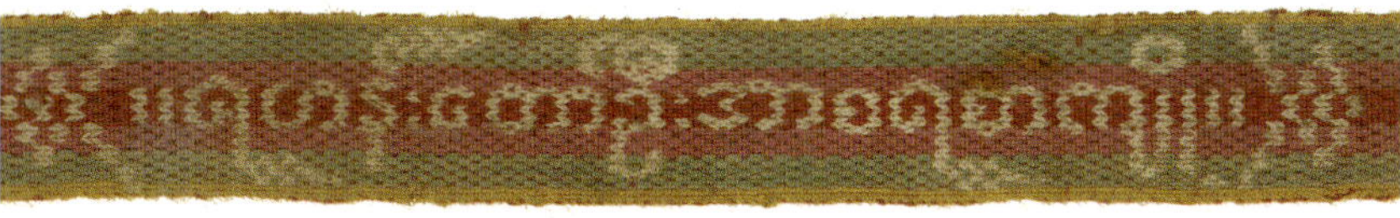

B509047

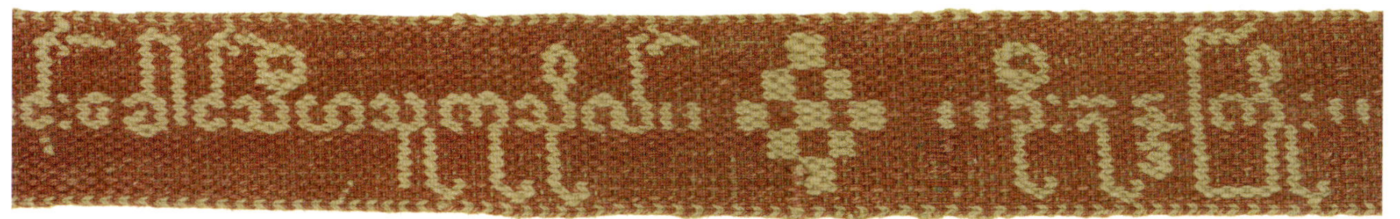

PG

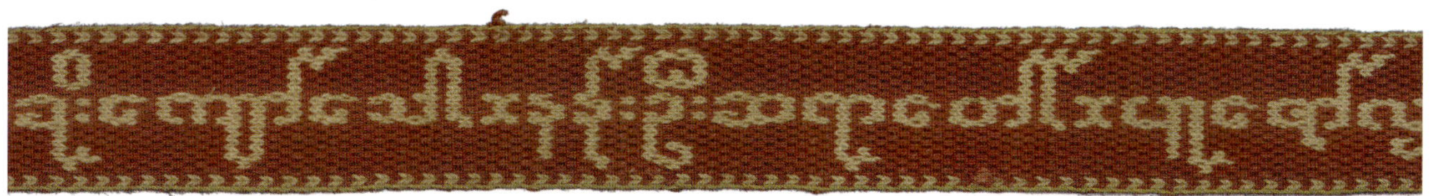

R039

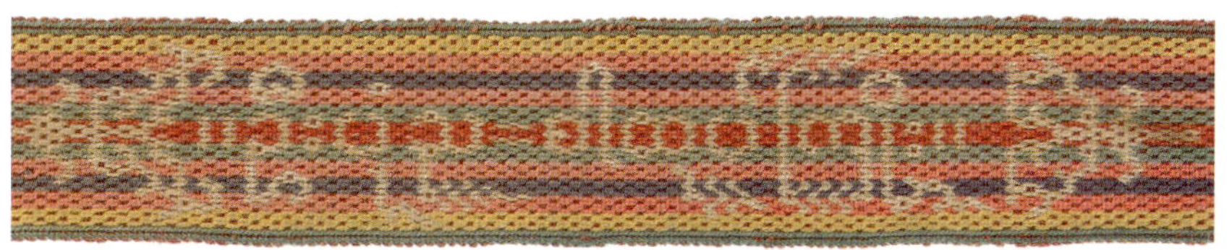

W93

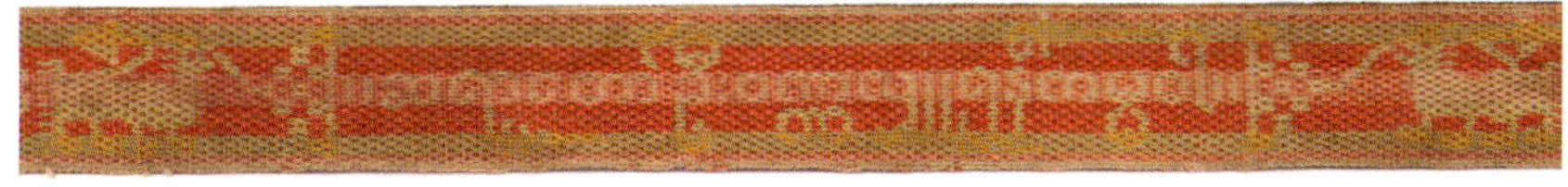

KJ01

M01

Part III Chapter 11

Selected Full Sazigyo Texts in English Translation

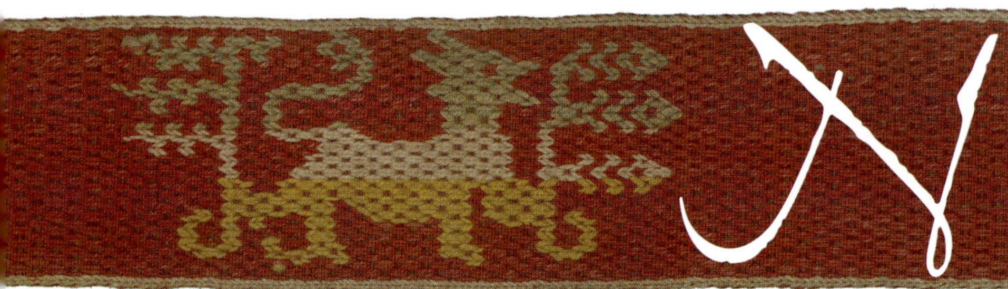

R272

Now follows a selection of full uncut sazigyo texts translated into readable modern English prose for the benefit of the general reader. The original texts are in verse, often in highly poetic language, and most required translation from archaic to modern Burmese before translation into English.

They vary greatly in length. The first few examples are of texts of unusual terseness—the bare minimum. At the bottom end of the market for lettered bands were ready-woven sazigyo, sold cheaply off the peg. Their text might be a formula of only a dozen words, **"Seeking nirvana, may Nats and humans approve and call out '*Thadu!*'"** (R227)

No donors' names appear in these impersonal articles. Who bought them? Perhaps villagers who had spent all they could spare, or more, on the manuscript itself. Obliged to economize on the sazigyo, they may have considered and rejected the cheapest option, a textless band. Even the barest minimum of lettering on the sazigyo offered close contact with the law of the Buddha, comfort to the illiterate, and good value for a few copper coins, **"The three baskets** [Tipitaka] **in the sacred Pali language."** (R134)

The great majority of donors were literate, and when they commissioned a specially woven sazigyo they expected to see their names appear in its text. The names of the donors and the motive for their donation, nirvana, could be packed into quite a short text: **"The deed of merit of Maung Bo Hla, wife, and family."** (B886)

Another, even shorter, consists of only four single-syllable Burmese words, **"Ma Hmway's deed of merit"** (H00) Ma Hmway (Miss Fragrant) may have considered this perfectly adequate: it names her as donor and records the motive for her donation.

Slightly longer texts are more common, **"Manuscript donor Ko Ba Tawt, lady manuscript donor Ma Ngwe Thaik, and family; this is their deed of merit, seeking nirvana. May Nats and humans approve and call out '*Thadu!*'** ['Well done!']**"** (R054)

Many donors insert their full address, in order to identify themselves beyond doubt, **"The manuscript donors, residents of Mye U Ward in Brick Monastery Village in Hanthawaddy District, are U**

Shan Kyi, Daw Shwe, and family. They call on Nats and humans to approve their deed of merit by calling out '*Thadu!*'" (R111)

"This is a record of the deed of merit of Pagoda builder U Hlaing and his wife Ma Ohn, residents of Thirihema Palaing Quarter in North Mandalay. They seek nirvana, and may Nats and humans approve and call out '*Thadu!*'" (H030)

Some donors give full directions to their residence, which is also their place of business, **"Mandalay City, Western District, Victory Palace Ward, Peaceful Retreat Quarter, past the Flea Market, down fish-paste seller's row, on the right hand side, Maung Eik and his wife Meh Myaing; their deed of merit, seeking nirvana. May Nats and humans approve and call out '*Thadu!*'"** (R167, R179, R194, R202, R203)

Plate 54 BELOW

The simplest woven texts were a mere formula, impersonal.

"Ma Hmway's deed of merit" *(KJ01)*

"Seeking nirvana, may Nats and humans approve and call out "*Thadu!*" *(R227)*

"Deed of merit of retired Chief Clerk U Seik, and Chief Clerk's consort Ma Hpyu Saing" *(R112)*

"Deed of merit in the year 1257 [1895 CE] of donor U Shwe Maung and his wife lady donor Ma Soe, residents of Say Yay [Painters'] road in Ma Taw Quarter of Prome Town" *(R152)*

Plate 55 FOLLOWING PAGES

The entire woven text of a fine red and white sazigyo. *(L08)*

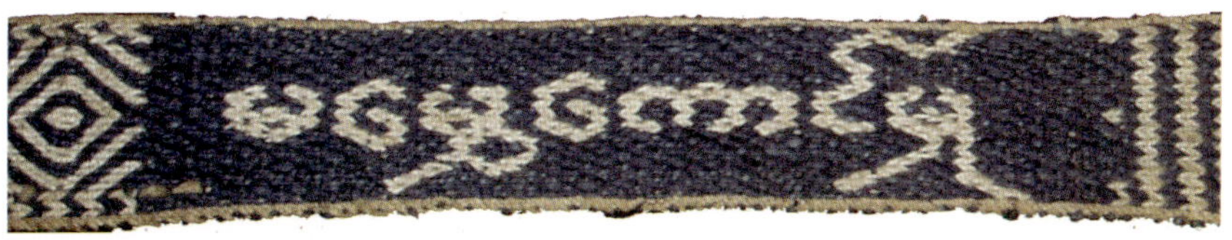

KJ01

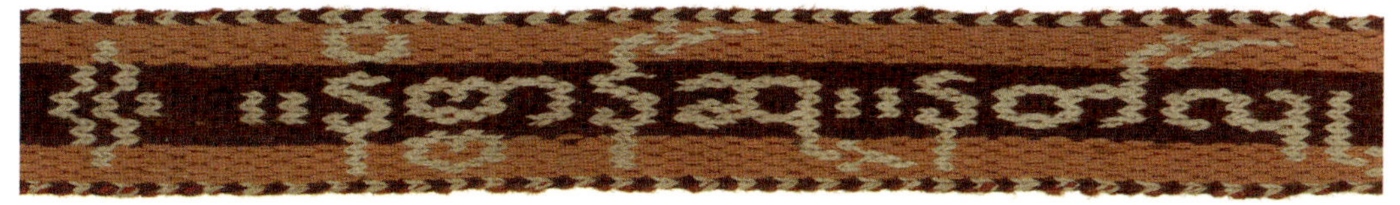

R227

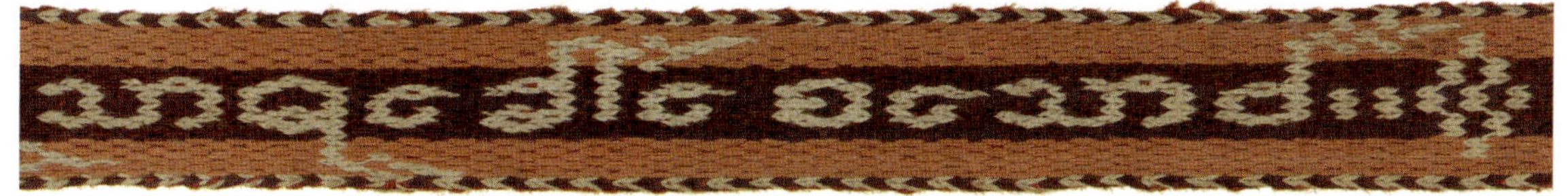

R227

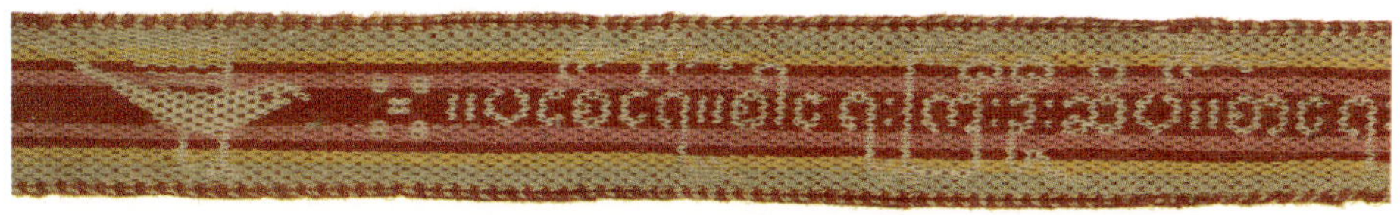

R112

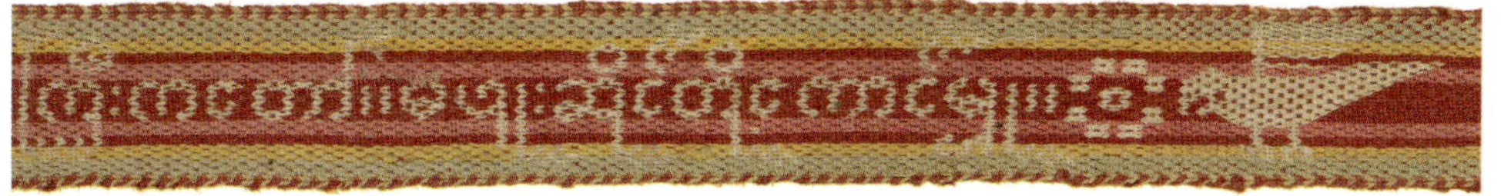

R112

R152

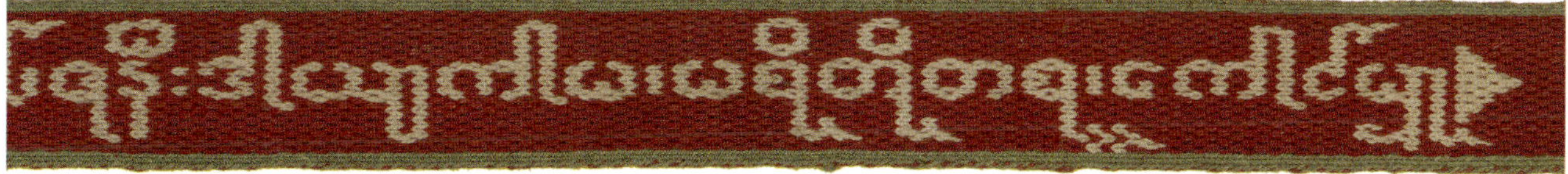

R152

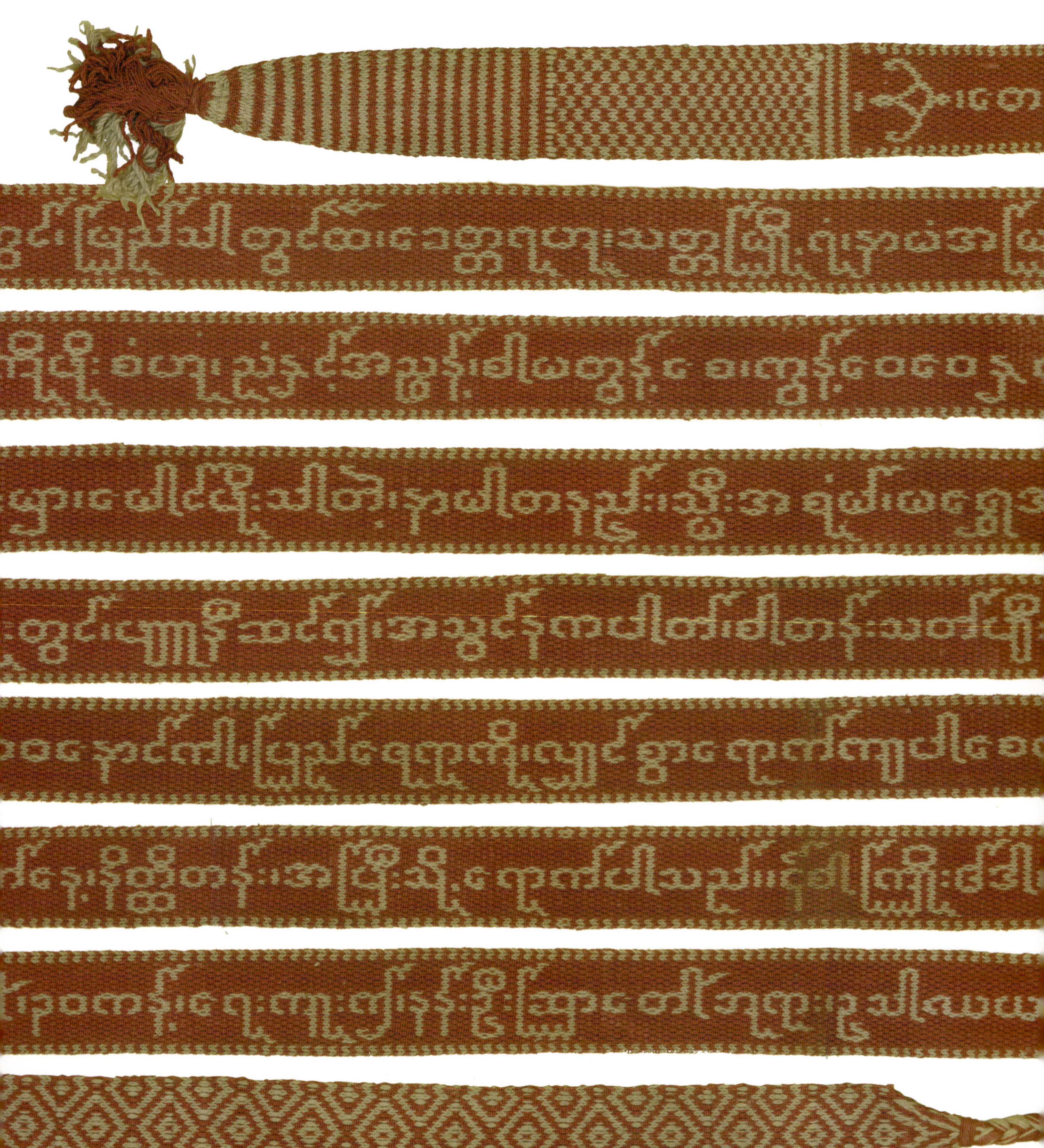

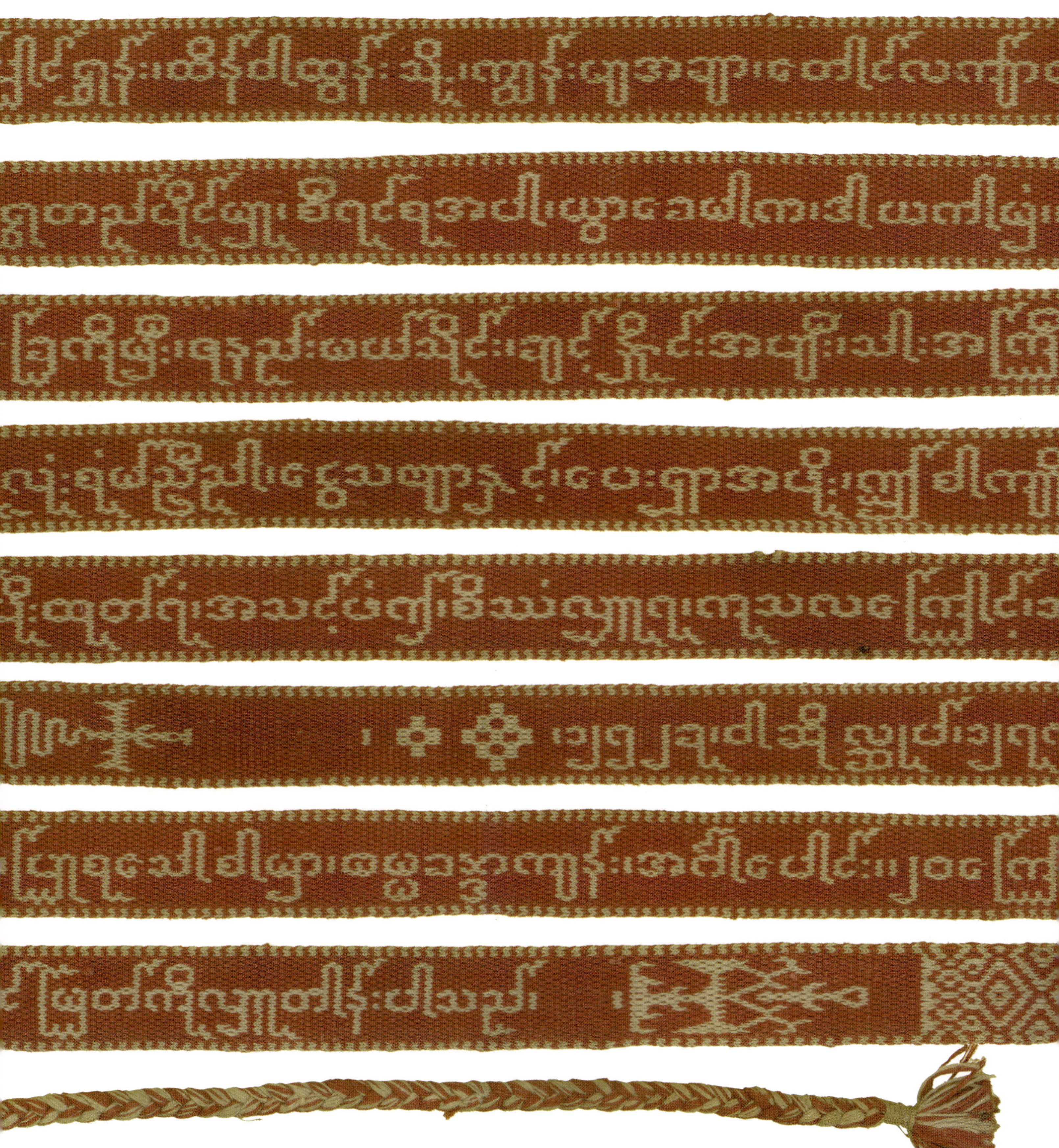

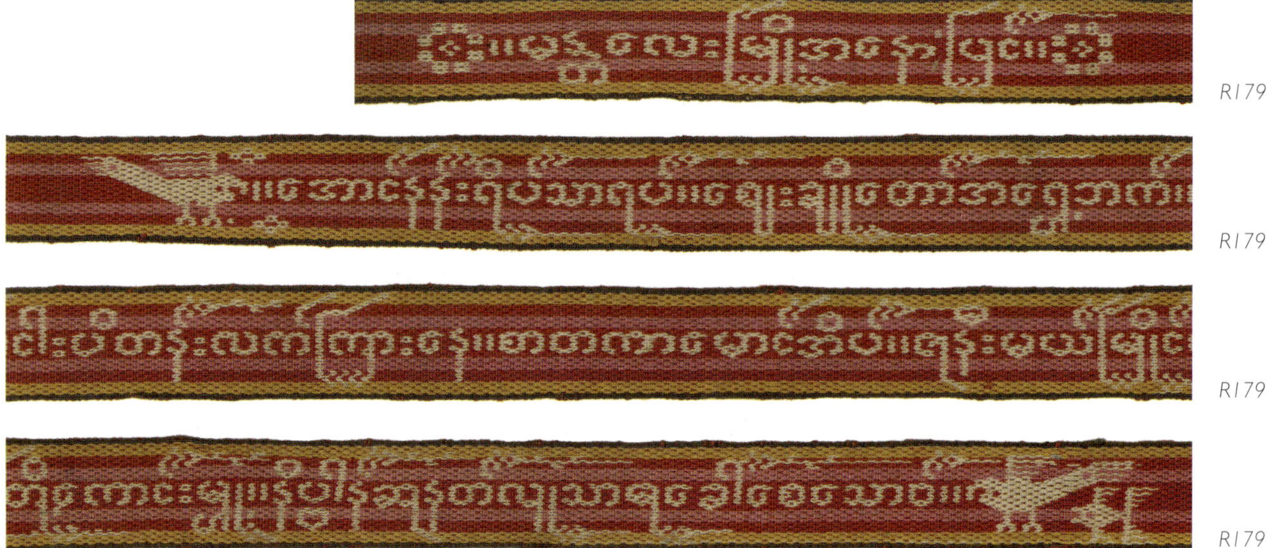

The same text occurs on at least five sazigyo, which suggests a sizeable donation. Clearly there was money in the fish-paste trade.

"Mandalay City, Western District, Victory Palace Ward, Peaceful Retreat Quarter, past the Flea-Market, down the fish-paste seller's row, on the right hand side, live Maung Eik and his wife Meh Myaing; this is their deed of merit, seeking Nirvana. May Nats and humans approve and call out '*Thadu!*'" (R179). Whether innocently or not, one weaver chose images of fish to introduce and end this text.

Each of the longer texts that follow is preceded by a brief explanatory note giving the date of the weave and the collection to which it now belongs, and offering explanations of terms of Buddhist doctrine employed by the composer of the verses. The English translations may succeed in reflecting the sense of the verse, but not its sonority. Monk poets used poetic diction, and their compositions may be pious effusions, recitals of Buddhist principles in strings of sounding phrases, full of learned allusions. All these texts would have been recited aloud. Some are deliberately composed with a succession of numbers acting as a mnemonic.

Some texts are more family-centered. Nirvana is the ultimate objective of all donors, but the immediate timing of the donation can be influenced by family events, such as the birth of a child or grandchild, or the *shinbyu* initiation of a son.

Wider politics may also be reflected in the sazigyo text. A high official in the service of the Burmese king details every post he ever filled and every promotion in his career. Another donor sees the British colonial power as the enemy of Buddhism and uses the sazigyo text to deplore the damage done to the Sangha by the foreign occupiers.

The selection ends with some texts of sazigyo woven for *dhammaceti* manuscripts, made with the sifted cremation ashes of a dead relative. In Burma the guiding rule was, "In joy, donate, and in grief, donate."

Plate 56 ABOVE
The same wording, giving full directions to the donors' residence and place of business in the fish-paste trade, is the only text on this and at least four other sazigyo. *(R179)*

The texts that follow from a wide sampling of sazigyo can be dipped into, as an anthology, or with some concentration read straight through. May the reader's undertaking be blessed with success!

This fine old indigo sazigyo was donated by the nun Meh Aye to a monastery in 1798, and to the Pitt Rivers Museum by Sir Richard Carnac Temple in 1889. It is unusual in that the main text is in lyrical Pali verse, although the last sentence, which names the donor, is in Burmese. For some 1,500 years the Sangha included both male and female monks, nuns, and novices, but the female ordination tradition was lost around 1000 CE. In modern Burma there are women who dress and behave like nuns, but they are not reckoned as members of the Sangha. (Pitt Rivers Museum 1889.29.200; translation from Pali and Burmese by Jotika Khur-Yearn)

May the Triple Gems long endure!

I garland my head with the past and future Gems of the Buddhas.
To them I pay homage as long as I live.
Through the merit of this my good deed may I overcome suffering.

I garland my head with the past and future Gems of the Dhamma.
To them I pay homage as long as I live.
Through the merit of this my good deed may I overcome suffering.

I garland my head with the past and future Gems of the Sangha.
To them I pay homage as long as I live.
Through the merit of this my good deed may I overcome suffering.

By the grace of this merit that I have acquired,
May I associate with noble people in this and every life.
May I attain nirvana and bliss beyond this world.

The work of merit of the nun Meh Aye, completed on Sunday, third day of the waning moon of Tazaungmon in the year 1160 [1798 CE].

The next text was commissioned by royalty. Sons of the *sawbwas*, rulers of the Shan princely states, were sent to Mandalay palace to learn the ways of the court as page boys, a sort of tribute in exchange for the powerful protection of the Mandalay throne, and daughters were offered to the Burmese monarch. The donor of this sazigyo is one of two sisters, daughters of the Shan Sawbwa of Hsenwi, who became consorts of King Mindon. At least three other sazigyo in Vanessa Chan's collection have almost identical texts, so the Shan queens must have donated many manuscripts.

Some princesses had actually learned to weave sazigyo. Princess Natmauk Hteik Khaung Tin, daughter of King Mindon, declares **"she has personally handmade this sazigyo for binding the stack of palm leaves of Tipitaka, being full of generosity and noble sentiments. The Princess prays that as a reward she be set on the path of nirvana, unimpeded, with her arrival ensured in the land of utmost bliss."**[18] Other women of the palace and daughters of ministers and court officials must also have learned the craft.

The six female flaws referred to in the text are being too tall, too short, too fat, too thin, too pale-skinned, and too dark-skinned. The five womanly virtues are having an excellent complexion, excellent structure, excellent hair, excellent figure, and excellent youthfulness.

The reference to the rabbit on the surface of the moon relates to a Jataka story that tells how a monkey, an otter, a jackal, and a rabbit resolved to perform a deed of charity on the day of the full moon, believing that this demonstration of great virtue (*dana*) would earn a great reward. When an old man begged them for food, the monkey gathered fruits and the otter collected fish, while the jackal offered a lizard and a pilfered pot of milk-curd. The rabbit knew only how to gather grass, so it offered its own body, throwing itself into a fire the man had built. The rabbit, however, was not burnt. The old man revealed himself to be Thagya Min, Sakra or Indra, King of the Nats. Touched by the rabbit's virtue, the god drew the likeness of the rabbit on the moon for all to see. (VC14)

> **May all know this auspiciousness!**
>
> **The king** [King Mindon] **who has established his new palace in the city of Mandalay on his authority as a descendant from the Sun is the lord of the noble lords of ten thousand universes. In the royal palace of Mandalay I receive the love and kindness of the king, the chief queen, and eighty thousand ladies-in-waiting.**
>
> **My father is the noble and prosperous Shan chief of Hsenwi, lord of one hundred and one kings using royal regalia, whose throne is in the Golden Haw** [Palace] **in the city of Hsenwi in the territory of Thiwirahta, and who rules and possesses the town of Thounze and many other towns, villages, and tributary territories. I am a beloved daughter, cherished like a ruby by my father, whose title is Thiwirahtta Mahawunthapawartheihta Thudamaraja and who is famous everywhere in the territory, by my mother, his right-hand consort the Mahadevi who enjoys the title of Shwe** [Gold], **and by my grandmother.**

> **In the palace of Mandalay I have been granted the city of Kyaukpadaung with the title of Shwe** [Gold] **under the name of Thu Thiri Yadana as I am so loved by the king and the chief queen. I, who am a beautiful lady free of the six female flaws and having the five womanly virtues, am well aware of the truth of *samsara*. Therefore, I donate these golden palm leaves with script as clear as the figure of the rabbit on the surface of the moon, on which I have had copied the Pali of the Pitakas as preached by the Buddha Himself.**
>
> **Through this donation I wish to attain nirvana as soon as possible, ending the cycle of rebirths just as the white tipped rolling waves come to an end when they reach the broad pearl-colored sand bank. All humans, Nats, and Brahmas are requested to say "Well done!" in approval of my donation.**

This sazigyo has an indigo blue ground with text in white. The text lacks punctuation, and the script has simple, angular "risers and fallers" like those of sazigyo woven in the 1850s. The absence of donors' names suggests that this sazigyo was woven to be sold ready-made, and judging from the emphasis on the avoidance of disaster, it may have been woven in uncertain times. The translator, the Ven. Dr. Khammai Dhammasami, comments that the verses are sonorous and well composed. (B870)

> **May the merit of donating this manuscript help us avoid the four woeful states of *apaya*** [hell, rebirth as beast, insatiable craving, and persecution] **and three kinds of calamitous times** [famine, epidemics, and lawlessness]. **May the merit also reward us with divine and human lives and finally with the attainment of nirvana. May we never know hunger. May we be endowed with faith, morality, knowledge, generosity, wisdom, shame in doing evil, and fear of doing evil deeds.**
>
> **We share the merit of this donation with all beings, beginning with parents and teachers. May all beings equally receive their share.**

This red and white sazigyo probably dates from the late nineteenth century. The English translator, Ven. Dr. Khammai Dhammasami, deduces from the high-flown verses but wayward spellings of the text that this prayer was originally composed by a competent versifier, and widely known, but at some stage was transcribed by a scribe with indifferent spelling skills, and either copied out by him for use by the weaver, or memorized by the weaver and woven from memory. (B839)

> **This scriptural manuscript of the Tipitaka** [the three baskets of the scriptures], **the Vinaya, the Sutta, and the Abhidhamma, all uttered by the jeweled mouth of the Buddha, the fully Self-Enlightened One, the Incomparable and the Conqueror, the Well-Gone, the holiest teacher, King of the Three Worlds with nine qualities, is offered with a beautiful binding ribbon with a prayer inscribed on it, and a covering sleeve made of finest cloth from Khoma** [India]. **May this offering help us avoid the four woeful states of *apaya*, the three kinds of calamity, and the eight realms of suffering; may I without seeking them be empowered with all means; may the merit of this deed truly transport me to a place of happiness, for which I fervently pray; and may all divine and celestial beings approve and rejoice in this act, and say "*Thadu!*"** ["Well done!"].
>
> **Offered by broker Ko Khaing and his wife Ma Chain, daughter Ma Hpwa Thin, son Maung Ba Thaw, and baby daughter Ma Hpwa Shin of Shwe Gu Quarter in the town of Prome.**

The indigo blue and white homespun yarn of this sazigyo suggests a mid-nineteenth-century date. The translator, Ven. Dr. Khammai Dhammasami, comments that the short text is well-written in verse (*kabya*). The high-sounding poetic style of the verses and the absence of donors' names suggest that this text (like that of B839 above) was passed from hand to hand among weavers, who learned it by heart and sold it ready-made. (B876)

> **As the result of these acts of perfection** [*parami*], **such as generosity** [*dana*] **and moral conduct** [*sila*], **which are ten in number, may I be endowed with wisdom; may I be powerful; may my wish be fulfilled; may I also receive the garlands of Dhamma, taught by the Buddha who overcame all enemies, who was unparalleled, who had six rays shining out of his physical body and who was immeasurable. May all beings share this merit of mine.**

This red and white weave from around 1880, now in poor condition, dirty, faded, stained, and tunnelled by insects, was once clearly cherished, for even after long use and severe damage it was twice mended with needle and thread (quite possibly by a monk) and used again till its cord was lost. The images of *padaythathabin* (trees of plenty) and a peacock in a chariot are outstanding in their lacy elegance. The lettering has elaborate branching flourishes, and the last element of the very last letter is teased out into a twig, to form a perch for a tiny bird. The translation by Ven. Dr. Khammai Dhammasami shows the donors were not the usual married couple but brother and sister, wealthy, devout, and devoted to each other. They lived in Insein, near Rangoon, where the sazigyo may well have been woven. (B852)

> **May there be success!**
>
> **Residents of the village called Shwe Kone, in the town of Insein, a place endowed with four fulfillments, Ko Hpo Myaing and his sister Ma Meingalay, who have done much merit together in their past lives, and are now blessed with wealth, offer with three kinds of pure generosity the Tipitaka, the elements of Dhamma, with a binding tape and a cover cloth. May this merit free them from the bondage of *samsara* and, when Maitreya Buddha comes, may they get the opportunity to listen to him first, and may they ultimately and quickly attain nirvana, where there are no five aggregates.**[19]

In 1929, U Shwe Dun and his wife Daw Htar donated to a monastery a gilt *kammavaca* manuscript with this specially woven sazigyo. The praise for the donor, his spouse, and their home town may strike us as rather fulsome—considering that they themselves commissioned and paid for the verses—but it is altogether typical of this genre of verse. In this English translation by U Kyaw Zan Tha we learn of the happy family event, which immediately motivated their act of generosity.

Visakha was a Buddhist matron who generously supported the monks during the lifetime of the Buddha. In Burma she personifies female generosity and fecundity. A model hard to emulate, she is credited by legend with producing numerous offspring, living to the age of 120, never looking older than eighteen, and possessing the strength of five elephants. (BM246, British Museum 1998,0723.246.2, donated by Ralph and Ruth Isaacs)

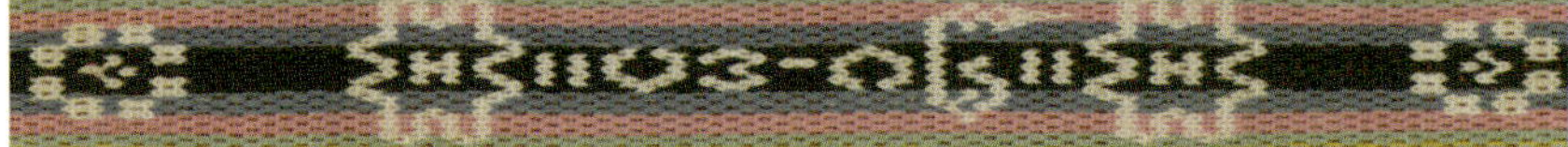

Plate 57 ABOVE
The full text on a sazigyo woven in 1929. *(BM246)*

"Zeyatu!"

At the center of the South Island of Jampati lies a famous spot comparable to the Tavatimsa Heaven in the sky—Tharawaddy District, and there lies Minhla Township, the dwelling place of wise and good men, and the rich and prosperous Mo Nyo Quarter, where the renowned and munificent donor U Shwe Dun has his abode, united in this life, as a reward for deeds of merit in a previous existence, with Daw Htar, a radiant beacon of goodwill, comparable in generosity to Visakha. Their bright and beautiful daughter Ma Mya Yi and her husband Maung Po Meik have given them a lovely baby granddaughter, Ma Thein Nyunt. Inspired by the impulse to donate, they have commissioned the writing of this manuscript, paying the salary of the scribe, and providing a fine gilt and glass-inlaid box to hold the *kammavaca* in its own wrapping sleeve and specially woven binding ribbon, a complete set. Their wish is to escape the world of suffering and the cycle of rebirth and to attain nirvana. They share the merit of this deed with parents, teachers, family, and with all denizens of the spirit world, even to Yama, Lord of Hell. May all beings in the round of existence witness this deed of merit and applaud, calling out "*Thadu! Thadu!*" ["Well done! Well done!"]

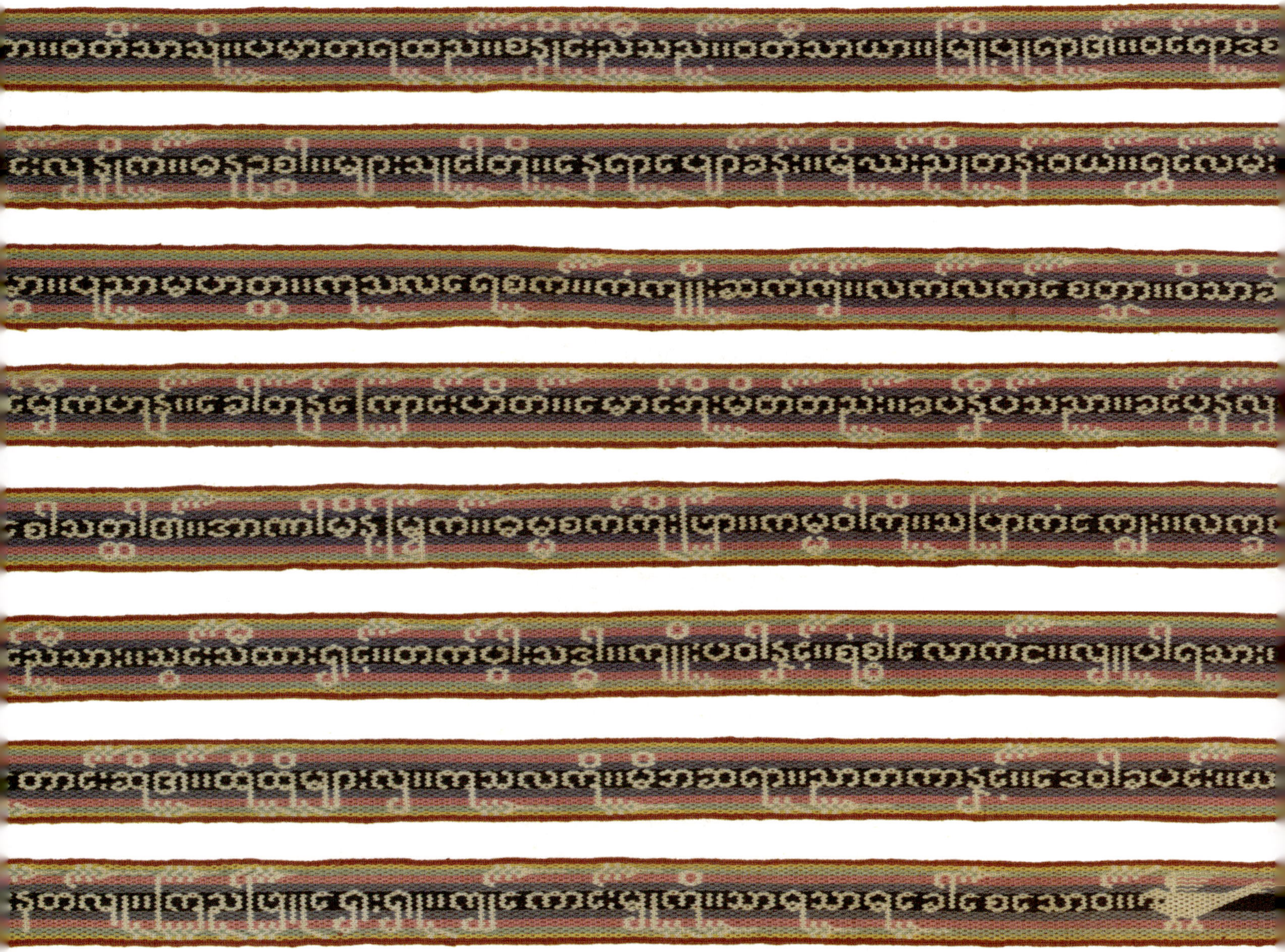

This red and white sazigyo records the donation of the entire Tipitaka by a powerful national figure—the jurist and statesman U Kaung, the Kinwun Mingyi (1822–1908). From the donor's royal titles listed in the text, Noel Singer dates this donation to the period 1874–78, when the Kinwun Mingyi was very close to King Mindon, and at the height of his power. He had visited Europe in 1872, and kept a diary, recently published in a new English translation.[20] U Kaung's influence declined under King Mindon's successor Thibaw. But he survived to see Thibaw overthrown by the British, who came to value his counsel and awarded him the CSI (Companion of the Most Exalted Order of the Star of India). As a poet U Kaung was the author of secular and topical verses, and as a devout Buddhist he composed the verses for many sazigyo. (B883)

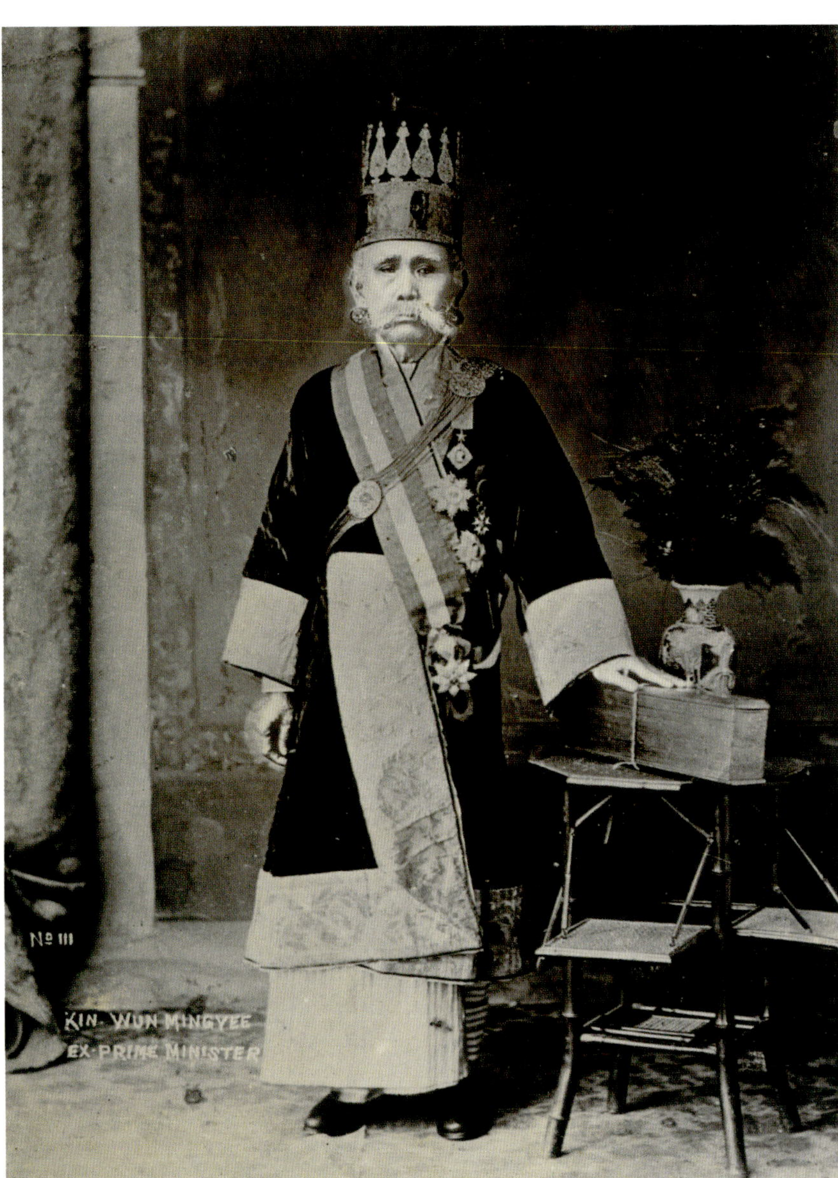

Plate 58 RIGHT
In this studio portrait of U Kaung, the Kinwun Mingyi (1822–1908), taken around 1905, some twenty years after the last king of the Konbaung dynasty was deposed by the British, his costume reflects his remarkable career. The gold-edged velvet robe, high headdress, and gold sash *(salway)* are those of a minister of the Burmese king, but pinned to his ministerial robe are the insignia of foreign decorations: the Companion of the Most Exalted Order of the Star of India, the French Legion d'Honneur, and the Couronne d'Italie. His left hand rests on a palm-leaf manuscript, representing his literary interests and donations of scripture.

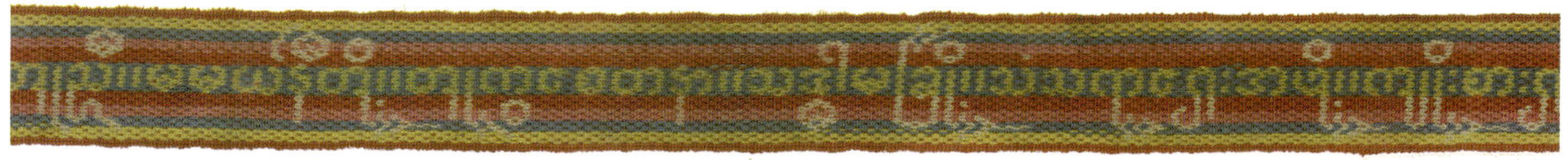

B847

B847

Woven in 1907, the sazigyo above is nearly six meters long and has a beautiful color scheme of seven colors, with text and images in yellow and white on a sky-blue ground. The text, translated by the Ven. Dr. Khammai Dhammasami, names the donors, but also celebrates the Buddha in a sequence of lyrical phrases arranged in numerical order, which served as an aid to memory. (B847)

> **May** [this deed] **be blessed with success!**
>
> **This Tipitaka scripture, the elements of the Dhamma, which is honored by all kings, has been donated by Maung Nyo Zeint and his wife, Ma May Ni of Zetton Village, Danubyu Town. The Tipitaka was preached by the Leader of the Three Worlds, the Self-Enlightened One, the King of the Doctrine, who was of Sakya stock, who had ten kinds of wisdom power, who attained nine kinds of supra-mundane spiritual achievement, who possessed eight kinds of voice, and seven factors of enlightenment, six rays of light emanating from his body, and five faculties of vision,[22] and who was the Leader of the chief clans. The donors share faith, wealth, and generosity and hope for their own betterment in *samsara*, the circle of birth. May the merit of this deed help them avoid the four woeful states of *apaya*, the eight places of failings, and the ninety-six kinds of disease; may they enjoy the pleasure of divine and human worlds many times and then reach the further shore, that is nirvana.**

The weaver Meh May, working in 1907, used fashionable archaistic square script for the whole text, but round script for her signature. The British influence shows in the "English" date, flanked by pointing hands and large crosses reminiscent of the Union Jack. The translator, the Ven. Dr. Khammai Dhammasami, comments that the verses are nicely composed. (B850)

> **May there be success! The basic truth, the foundation of the Tipitaka, preached by the Buddha, the Supreme Conqueror,**

Plate 60 ABOVE
Nearly six meters long, this sazigyo was woven in 1907, and has a lovely color scheme of seven shades. *(B847)*

has been recorded also in the commentaries by Buddhaghosa. The Tipitaka was brought from Thaton by King Anawrahta and has been preserved well to this day.

Ko Tha Kyaw and his wife, Ma Min Kalay, their sons, Maung Tha Han and Maung Tha Yan, daughters, Ma Ma Khin and Ma Ma Thin, who live in the village of Nyaung Kone, Insein District, a place famed for the four-relics pagoda, the Shwedagon, donate the Tipitaka. They do so because they are weary of the material possessions of the ten-thousand worlds, which they have in abundance, and because they now adorn themselves with the flowers of faith. Of all kinds of offerings, the result of which assuredly follow the donor, the offering of the Tipitaka, which is the wheel of truth, gives an instant reward. With the good intention of prolonging the life span of the Buddhasasana [the Buddha's dispensation] and of bringing an end to the process of birth, existence, and decay, they offer this Tipitaka literature. May all beings in the thirty-one realms of existence rejoice in the merit they share and attain nirvana.

Please say "*Thadu! Thadu!*"

Dated 1907 [CE] and 1269 BE.

The text of this sazigyo is a political polemic by a donor who sees the British colonial power as the enemy of Buddhism and of the Sangha, in particular. The Second Anglo-Burmese War of 1852 had disastrous consequences for the Buddhist religion in Burma. Mass migrations of monks to Upper Burma left many towns and villages in British-occupied Lower Burma without any resident monk. Monasteries fell into neglect and decay. Petitioned by the laity in Lower Burma to extend patronage to Buddhism, and to appoint a primate to enforce discipline among the clergy, the British governor refused. Eighty years later, resentment of British indifference to Buddhism smolders on in this sazigyo text. No date appears in the woven text, but the militant nationalist sentiment and the mention of rumors of rebellion strongly suggest the period immediately before the Saya San rebellion broke out in 1930. The forty-five-year-old Saya San, appointed in 1924 by the General Council of Buddhist Associations to survey the state of the Burmese peasantry, began inciting the peasants to revolt against British taxation and rule. In December 1930, he organized local resistance against the hated poll tax, which quickly grew into an uncoordinated national revolt. Official reports claimed that Saya San was a *minlaung*—a self-declared pretender king who would restore the Burmese monarchy and revitalize the declining Buddhist religion. It took the British colonial power massive military force and two years to crush the rebellion. Saya San was captured and executed by hanging. (VC62)

> May we triumph over our enemy! The ruby glows red, its heart color, flawless and free from blemishes. Like this precious stone with its proud hue, the light of the Buddha's teachings was truly brilliant.
>
> Theravada Buddhism, which had been flourishing since it first arrived in Myanmar, has now faded in the times of the unscrupulous ruler. During the reign of the devilish ruler the light of Buddhism has dimmed, many monks are downcast, the influence of noble Buddhist monks has been diminished. A whole body of Buddhist monks is concerned about the future of Buddhism and the present conditions that prevent them from freely serving Buddhist purposes. The heretical rulers who have annexed Myanmar without respect for the Buddhism in which the Myanmar people devotedly trust, are watching and making records, and acting against all those on their black list whom they consider dangerous to their rule. The whole country is awash with muttered prophecies and ominous rumors that "some king-to-be is emerging in such-and-such a place," so that people are expecting to recover their own sovereignty.
>
> Meiktila is a city and district where such sayings are rife. Among the many villages crammed into the city of Meiktila and kept under British rule, if one searches at a particular location and distance, one can find Pyunbauk Village, where I, U Htaik, donor of palm-leaf manuscripts of the Pitakas, blissfully do meritorious deeds with great benevolence. I seek Dharma by keeping precepts, practicing meditation and doing justice in my daily business. Lord Buddha teaches in his Parabawa Sutta that a person who cherishes Dharma is a winner and a person who detests Dharma is a loser, and that among mankind the first cause of destruction or suffering is the lack of inborn intelligence. I believe that I must have done good deeds in my previous existences as I love Dharma with all my inborn intelligence.
>
> Our family consisting of my wife, Ma Lay, destined to live with me by our shared good deeds and merit in our previous existences, our daughter, Ma Pu, our son, Maung Bo Han, who is as fine as an ear-ornament, our other daughter, Ma Seint, our son, Maung Kyo, who is as fragrant as *gadou* perfume and energetic in donations, and our son Maung Bo

> Nyunt, who has mastered both secular and spiritual literary works; together we donate the Pitakas of the Lord Buddha inscribed on palm leaves, urged by our great benevolence and generosity. The statements of the Buddha in his sermons and teachings give peace and relief from the pains and sufferings encountered by all beings eligible for nirvana. We pay the scribe for copying the Pitakas onto these palm leaves and we donate them blissfully.
>
> As a reward for our donation made in great good will and generosity we wish to be able to do homage to Maitreya the future Buddha: may the light of the teachings of Lord Buddha shine brilliantly like a ruby free from darkness!

This text is remarkable for the detailed list of expenses incurred by the donors in their current and previous deeds of merit. The cost of every item purchased for donation is recorded, and compared with expenditure by the donor's grandparents. The last entry in the ledger is the weaver's fee for the sazigyo itself. (VC22)

The Nine Deities ceremony, usually held when there is sickness in the house, is considered by many scholars to be a survival of Hindu practices, as it involves propitiation of the Nine Planets of Vedic astrology. It is popular even though frowned on by some strict Buddhists.

Kathina, the season for offering monastic robes to monks, begins on the first waning day of Thadingyut, the seventh month, and lasts till the full-moon day of the eighth month Tazaungmon.

> May success be with us! We have been looking forward to the opportunity to make another donation out of good will.
>
> We, Ko Yoe and Ma Min Zan, who together sponsored the building of a monastery, our daughter Ma Ngwe Zin, our son-in-law Maung Tha Hmat, who won our daughter's love, our first granddaughter Ma Me Yin, who gives pleasure to us all equally, Ko Pho Aung, who constantly and strenuously exerts himself in doing good deeds, and Ma Meh O, who has a heart of gold and speaks sweetly, now have the chance to make another donation of the Pitakas of the Buddha.
>
> I remember that the cost of building a monastery by our grandparents was 500 kyats. We spent 500 kyats to build a monastery. We also spent 50 kyats on the ceremony of paying homage to the Nine Deities, 100 kyats for silk, satin, and velvet robes and 50 kyats for the celebration of Kathina in

accordance with the subtle scriptures. Not content with those good deeds, worthy though they were, we did more. We paid 50 kyats for a cement floor for the monastery so that it would have a clean floor. And we paid 150 kyats for a copy of the Buddha's sacred sermons. Having the glorious Vinaya Pitakas copied, comprising two texts with nine selections, cost 60 kyats. The grand total expended was 960 kyats.

We share our great merit with our parents, teachers, and relatives. May the renown of such great merit resound everywhere on earth! If I have the prophecy of the Buddha that I myself will be a future Buddha, may I be endowed with the eight necessities for preordainment, and surely, wholly and swiftly fulfill the good deeds of the five kinds of relinquishment in my successive existences! May I save all living creatures throughout the thirty-one planes of existence from drowning in the whirlpool of the four torturing causes and help them to reach the shore of nirvana called *kheima*! May I achieve the reward that I wish for from among the four rewards, to become a lesser Buddha who attains Enlightenment but does not preach, or one of the two chief disciples of the Buddha, or one of the eighty Arahats.

This deed was fully accomplished on Friday, the thirteenth waxing day of Thadingyut in the year 1252 BE [1890 CE]. May this deed help us on our path to nirvana!

The cost of this cotton ribbon was 8 kyats and 3 ma' [75 pyas].

Sazigyo Woven for Manuscripts Made with Cremation Ashes

The sazigyo whose short prose texts are quoted pp. 125–27 (R004, R006, R013, R058, and H012) were all woven for manuscripts made with the sifted cremation ashes of a monk or layperson. Such manuscripts are known as *dhammaceti*. This term has several meanings. Literally it means "a stupa enshrining the law," but figuratively it can refer to the whole Tipitaka, or to any individual scriptural manuscript. And *dhammaceti* can also mean (as it does here) a very special sort of manuscript, one made with cremation ashes. Scott described in 1882 CE how relatives of the deceased layperson might collect the charred bone fragments and grind them down into powder. This was mixed with liquid lacquer (*thit-si*) to make a paste or putty, and molded into a small image of the Buddha, which was set in an honored place in their house. After the grand funeral ceremony for a senior monk, the monastic brethren would collect the bone fragments to be buried somewhere near the pagoda. Sometimes, in the case of a particularly saintly man, the bone ashes were pounded down, mixed into a paste with *thit-si*, and molded into an image of the Buddha, which was stored up in the monastery.[24]

The custom of saving part of a person's cremation ashes to be incorporated into an object of devotion can be traced back to the enshrinement of the bone relics of the Buddha in a stupa. The inscriptions below show that this custom continues today, and that bone ash relics of a deceased monk or layperson were sometimes incorporated into a *dhammaceti* manuscript, rather than an image of the Buddha. The lacquer putty *thayo* was used to smooth the surface of the leaves.

The sons and daughters of Daw Toke of Tabin town gave her cremation ashes to be used to make a fine gilt *kammavaca* manuscript.

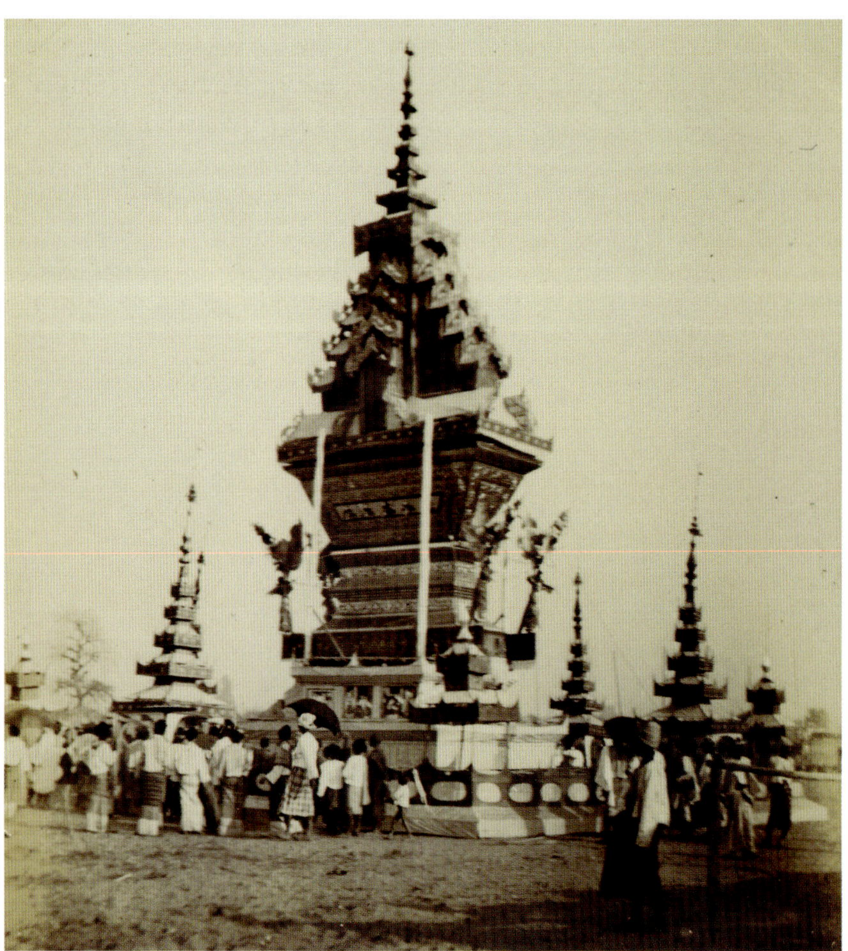

Plate 61 RIGHT
Pyre tower for the ceremonial funeral of a senior monk, the *pongyibyan*.

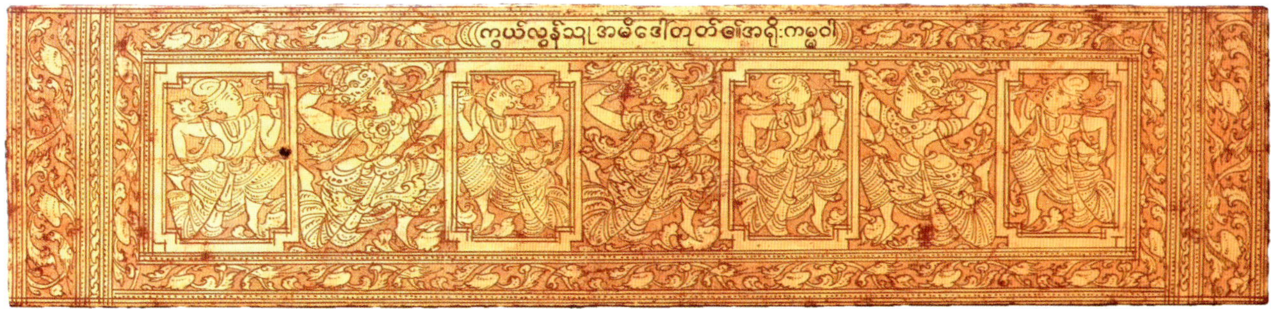

Plate 62 ABOVE
An inscription on the gilt cover of this manuscript reads: "This *kammavaca* manuscript enshrines the bone ash relics of our late mother Daw Toke."

The Burmese practice of using cremation ashes as a raw material shocked some nineteenth-century European Christians, although they would have felt no qualms about wearing a mourning locket or a brooch containing a lock of the hair of the dead, or even a miniature painted with pigment compounded with chopped-up hair. Nowadays twenty-first-century websites offer a bereaved family creative recycling of their deceased loved one. Cremation ashes can be mixed with artists' colors in a souvenir painting, or used to make a synthetic diamond, a glass paperweight, or a tea mug.

The first sazigyo in this group (R004) was woven in 1928 for a manuscript made with the bone ash relics of senior monk U Pandawuntha. The color scheme used—yellow motifs and text on a black ground—was fashionable in 1911 when Scherman visited Mandalay. The first of two short prose texts is introduced and followed by a crankshaft-handled fan and a little frog. While the fan is one of the eight possessions permitted to a monk, the monastic significance of the frog is obscure. One startling image unmistakably represents the *pongyibyan*, the grand ceremonial funeral of a senior monk. The object resembling a stout candle is the great rocket (Burmese: *doun*) fired to ignite the funeral pyre. U Pandawuntha's ashes were used to make more than one manuscript, for a second sazigyo (R008) has identical texts. Daw Weh, the lady who commissioned both manuscripts, may have been a devotee of the monk, or a family member, or both.

"[This is] **the *dhammaceti* of U Pandawuntha, senior monk of the Ok Kyaung [brick monastery] in the Ananda Temple in the cure of the Mahamuni Great Pagoda, Mandalay."** (R004)

The second text names the donor, "[This donation is] **the deed of merit of Lady pagoda-builder Daw Weh and family of Kyaukpanna Village, Thazi Township, Meiktila District."** (R004)

A similar sazigyo (R006) was woven to bind a scriptural manuscript made with the cremation ashes not of a monk, but of a layperson. The donors were probably the widower and children of the dead lady.

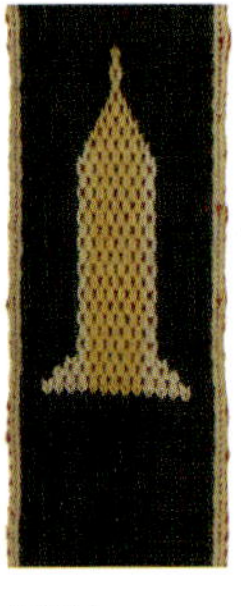

R004

"Kammava manuscript [made with] the bone ash relics of lady monastery founder Daw Kyay Hmon [who was] born on the sixth day of the waxing moon of Wagaung in the year 1235 BE [1873 CE] and died on the thirteenth day of the waxing moon of Tawthalin in the year 1286 BE [1924 CE]. [This is] the deed of merit of U Bo Tut and family."

The prose inscription on R058 reads: "[This] *kammavaca* manuscript made with the bone ash relics of Daw Waing, who was

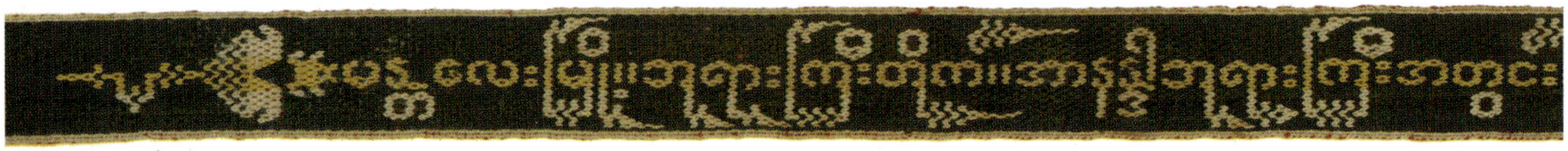

R004

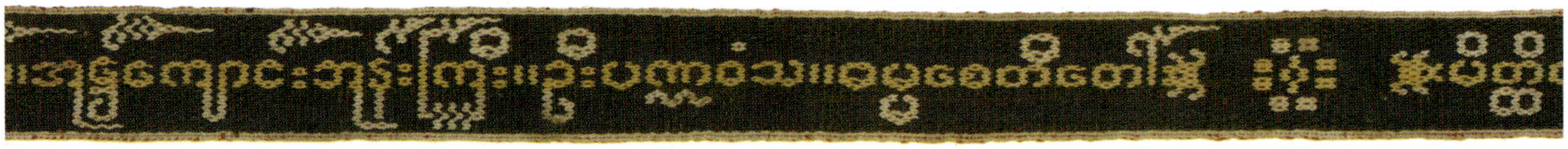

R004

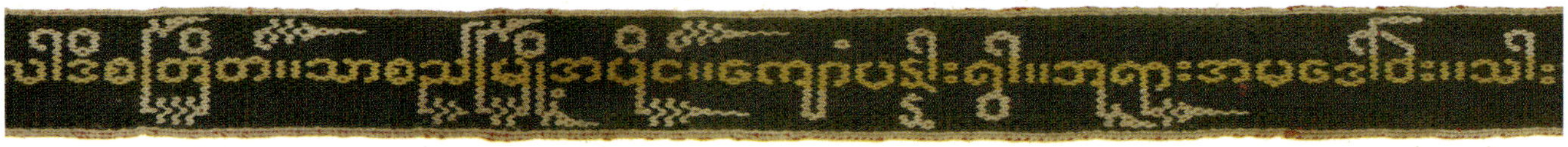

R004

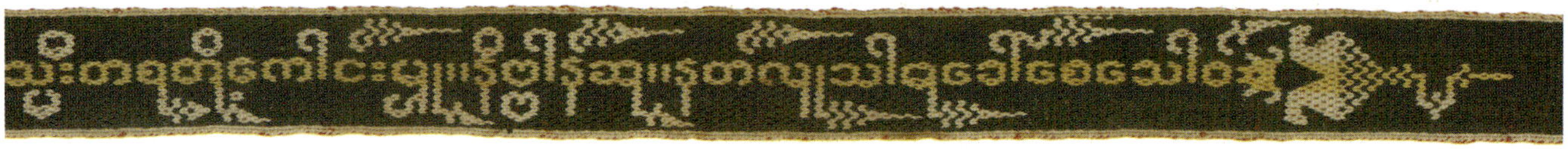

R004

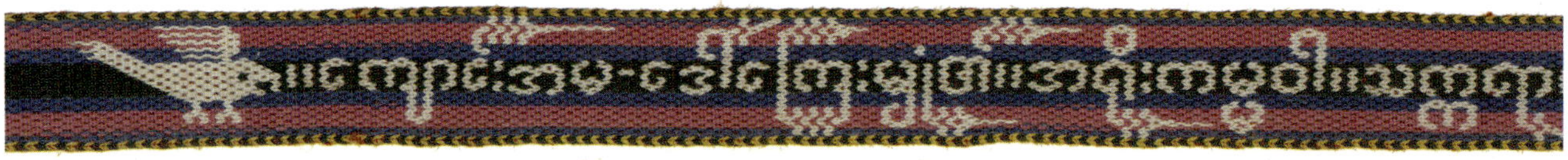

R006

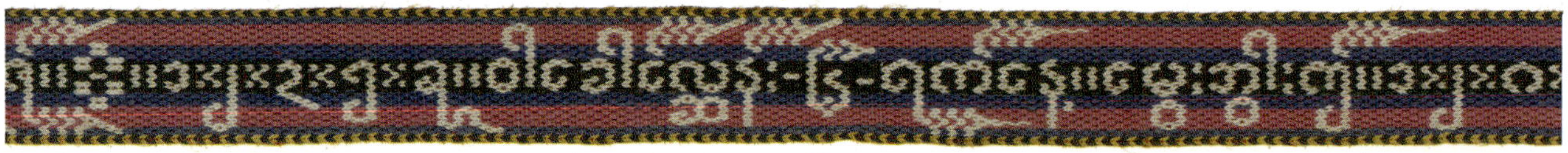

R006

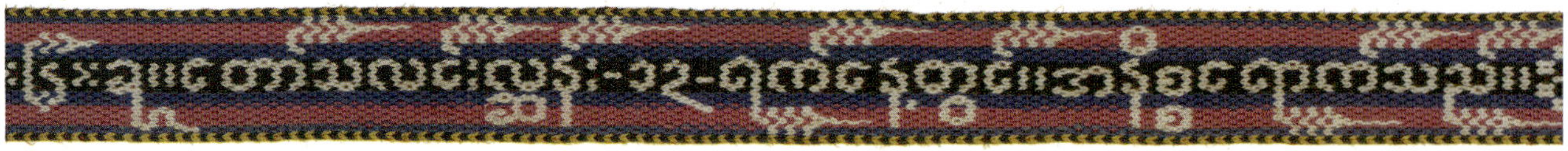

R006

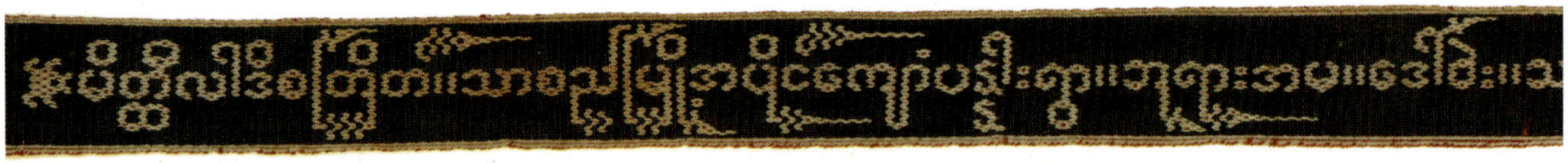

R008

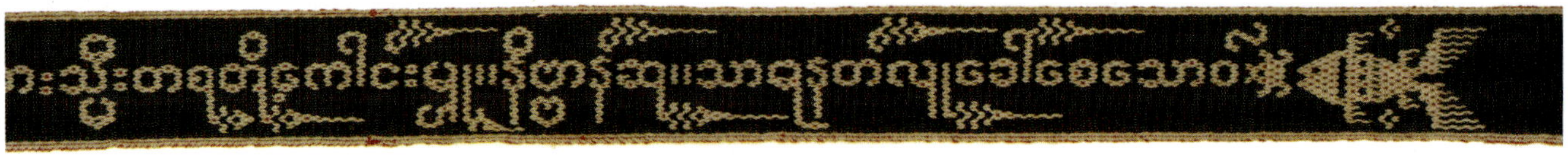

R008

Plate 63 PREVIOUS PAGE
All three sazigyo illustrated here were woven for *dhammaceti* manuscripts, which incorporate the cremation ashes of a deceased monk or lay person. The image of a rocket (Burmese: *doun*) is a clear reference to the elaborate funeral ceremony of a senior monk, the *pongyibyan*, in which rockets were fired at the funeral pyre to ignite it. *(R004, R006, R008)*

born on the seventh day of the waxing moon of Tawthalin, in the year 1194 BE [1832 CE]**, and passed away on the twelfth day of the waxing moon of Thadingyut in the year 1276 BE** [1914 CE]**. This is the deed of merit of Maung Tha Hmway and Ma Chit."**

Daw Waing was over eighty years of age at her death in 1914. The donors who earned merit for this deed may have been her grandchildren.

A sazigyo dated 1957 names the dead person whose ashes were incorporated into the manuscript, and goes on to name the maker of the manuscript and weaver of the sazigyo, who were father and daughter. Perhaps they were also the donors.

"This is a solemn record that the esteemed bone ash relics of Thakin U Htun Ok were collected and crushed to powder to be mixed [with liquid lacquer] **in order to be used to make this *kammavaca* manuscript, which is donated most reverently."**

"[This sazigyo is] **the work of Ma Khin Thein, daughter of the master *kammavaca* manuscript maker U Sein of Mandalay town."** (R013)

Ma Khin Thein and her father U Sein were still in business in 1959.

The sazigyo whose text is quoted below was woven to bind a lacquered and gilded manuscript made with the cremation ashes of a distinguished man, Thakin Yazawut Wun U Khin, who had been an inspector of police in the British colonial era. The text names more than thirty members of several generations of his family who came together in family solidarity and contributed to the cost of donating the manuscript. (Translation by Ralph Isaacs)

> **In the year 1321 BE** [1959 CE] **the bone ash relics of the late Thakin Yazawut Wun U Khin were given to be made into a *kammavaca* manuscript of the Dhamma, by his entire posterity, all his descendants together: his sons and daughters, sons-in-law and daughters-in law, U Maung Maung and Daw Than Yin; U Thet and Daw Than Kyi; U Nyunt Maung and Daw Htwe Yin; U Hla Maung and Daw Aye Kyu; U Kyaw Sein and Daw Tin Tin; Daw Tin Tin Myint, Daw Khin Mu; all his grandchildren** [and their spouses]**, U Win Maung and Daw Khin Khin Yi; U Tin Maung Aye and Daw Khin Sein Yin; U Tin Maung Kyi and Daw Khin Ma Kyi** [unmarried grandchildren]**; Maung Myo Kyaw, Maung Myo Zin, Maung Myo Than, Ma Khin Myo Myint; other younger descendants Tin Zaw Win, Tin Zi Win, Tin Mu Win, Tin Sein Aye, Tin Thein Aye, Tin Lin Kyi, Tin Win Kyi, Tin Min Kyi Taik; all the above charitably donate this manuscript reverently.**
>
> **Worked by Ma Khin Thein, daughter of the famous master Kammava manuscript maker U Sein of Mandalay City.**
> (H012)

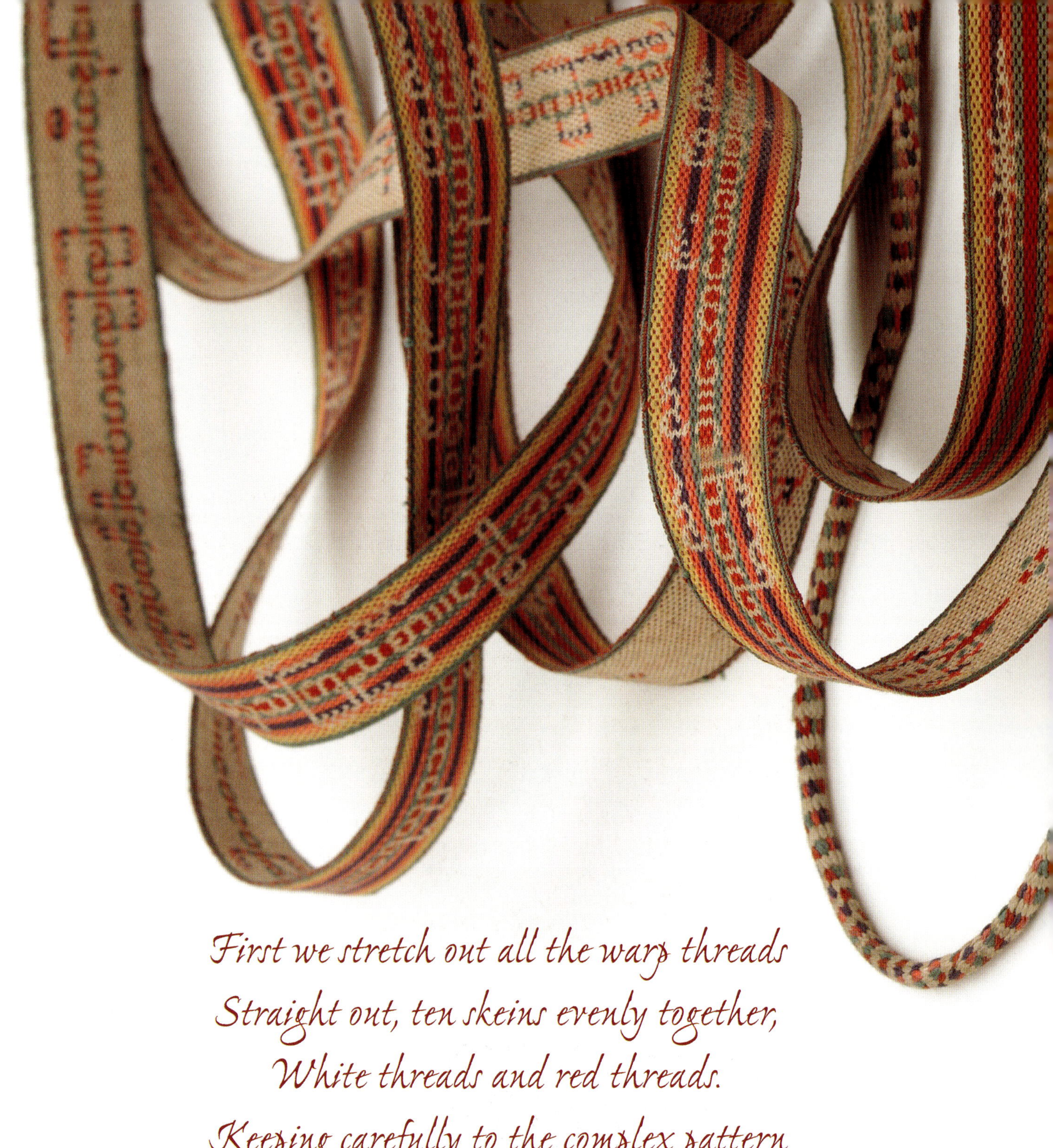

First we stretch out all the warp threads
Straight out, ten skeins evenly together,
White threads and red threads.
Keeping carefully to the complex pattern
We cunning girls of North Mandalay
Skilled in the subtle script of Pali verses,
Deftly weave our golden bands
Long lines of fine shapely lettering.

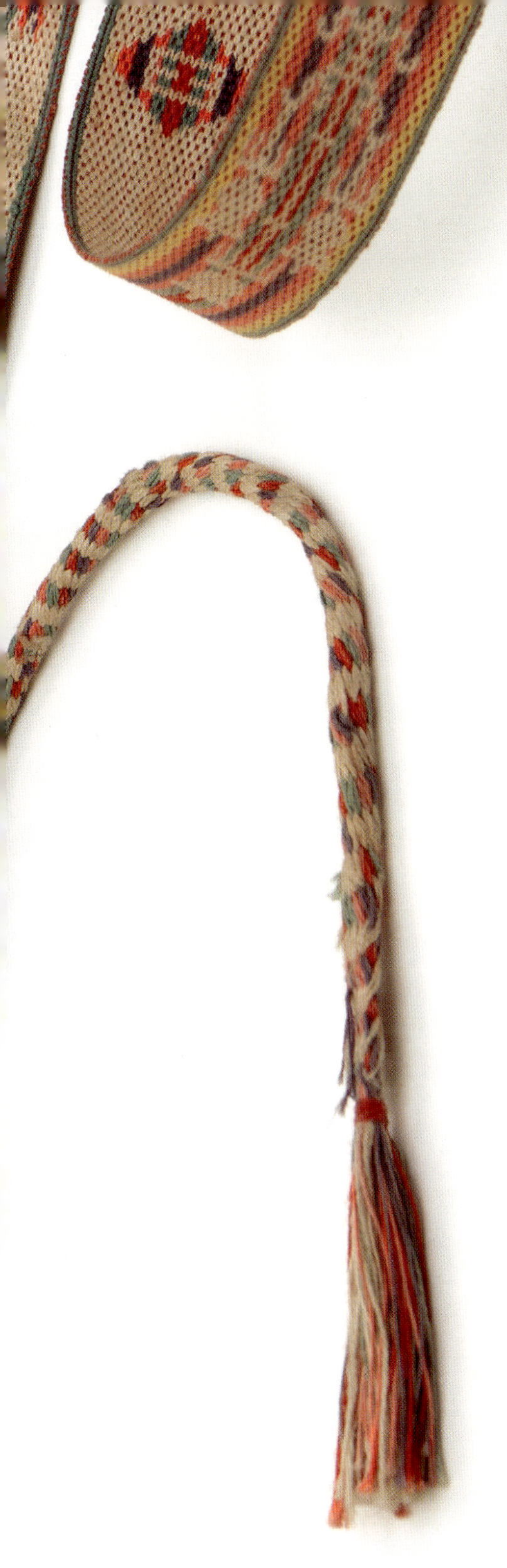

Part IV

PATTERN AND PICTURE: WOVEN MOTIFS AND IMAGES

Part IV Chapter 12

Geometric Motifs as Pattern and Symbol

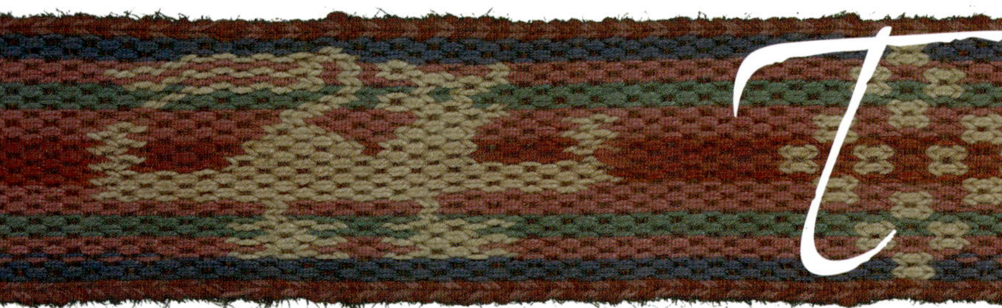

R304

The woven text of the sazigyo bears the main load of meaning, but there are other colorful carriers in the caravan—the many non-verbal devices that embellish the text. Geometric motifs composed of tiny "blocks" of color may seem purely decorative, but their shape and arrangement can convey quite specific meanings. The miniature pictorial images, often considered the sazigyo's crowning glory artistically, are also "non-text messages," full of symbolic significance. This section of the book will identify woven motifs and pictorial images and explore their relationship to each other and to the woven text.

An attractive diamond pattern often appears at both ends of the flat area. Near the end of the sazigyo the diamond pattern has a technical utility: its constant twining reverses prevent the buildup of twist beyond the tablets, which the short remaining warp could not absorb.

On many older sazigyo the first shape to emerge from the cross-stripes at the start of the flat area, immediately before the text, is a wedge or arrowhead. This represents the pointed end of the manuscript leaf.

Small geometric shapes are built up of square blocks of color, usually the product of four tablets weaving for four picks (single passes of the weft thread through the warp thread). These blocks can be arranged to give diamonds, crosses, circles, and stacks. Such motifs may occur singly or in groups, as spacers between pictorial images or between parts of a text.

Some weavers had a large repertoire of quite complex motifs built up of tiny blocks, and took pride in weaving a sequence of sixty or more without repeating a single one. The best of these geometric motifs are like delicate filigree jewelry, showpieces of the weavers' imagination and skill. But these are the exceptions to the rule: in Burmese art virtually all ornament carries religious meaning. Geometric motifs built up of tiny squares may look abstract, but arranged in groups of three they acquire symbolic significance, for now they stand for the *triratna*, the Three Gems, or the Triple

Consolation, the formulaic prayer so often on the lips of the devout Buddhist: "I take refuge in the Buddha, I take refuge in the Dhamma, I take refuge in the Sangha."[1] Three is a number pregnant with meaning in several religions. The sazigyo was woven to bind part of the "three baskets" of the Theravada Buddhist scriptures, the Tipitaka. Sets of dots in groups of three may encode a text, an idea, and a system of law and morality.

If arrangement in groups can invest geometric motifs with meaning, so can the composition of an individual motif. If it has nine elements, it becomes the ancient *navratna* (Burmese: *nawarat*), the motif of the "nine auspicious gems": ruby, pearl, coral, emerald, topaz, diamond, sapphire, garnet, and cat's eye. In royal times the use of the *nawarat* jewel was restricted to members of the royal family and high officials, and it is still associated with power. The nine-element design derives its peculiar potency less from the minerals of the earth below than from celestial bodies in the sky above—it is a talisman invoking the powerful protection of the nine planets. All Burmese have their tutelary planet governing their "birth-day," the day of the week on which they were born. Even nowadays, when royal sumptuary laws are ignored or forgotten, many ordinary people are reluctant to use the nine-gems ornament, for fear of malign forces. The number nine is sometimes associated with the Nats, and people may go to some lengths to avoid it.[2] But men of serious ambition may wear the *nawarat* as a ring, while women commonly wear it as earrings or a pendant.

In woven *nawarat* motifs the nine elements are arranged either in a rosette, eight in a ring around the ninth in the center, or in a diamond parallelogram, as three rows of three. Both symbolic arrangements, the shape of each motif, and their grouping are beautifully shown in B847, p. 135. Here a wonderful weaver with a very organized mind uses over seventy geometrical motifs as spacers between texts or woven images. Every motif is composed of nine elements, and they are always grouped in threes. Trios of rosettes alternate with trios of diamonds. These spacer motifs carry their own reiterated meaning, like a visible litany.

Flower heads represent the lotus, the chosen flower for offerings at the pagoda, and symbol of the Buddha. The lotus bud emerges from the muddy bed of the lake or pond and reaches upwards into the sunlight, so its blossom symbolizes the process of self-improvement and enlightenment, aspiration to nirvana.

Political logos also occur. Certain block motifs woven in colonial times bear a distinct resemblance to the pattern of the Union flag, and the pointing hand looks like the hand of the colonial authority, complete with stiff cuff and wristwatch.

Plate 64

Geometric motifs as pattern and symbol.

DIAMONDS RIGHT

An attractive diamond pattern often appears at the end of the flat area. Its constant twining reverses prevent the buildup of twist beyond the tablets. *(L08, R118, R038)*

ARROWHEADS BELOW RIGHT

The arrowhead or wedge shape emerging from the cross-stripes at the start of many older sazigyo represents the pointed end of the manuscript leaf. *(L04, MYA070T, R062, R103, R090)*

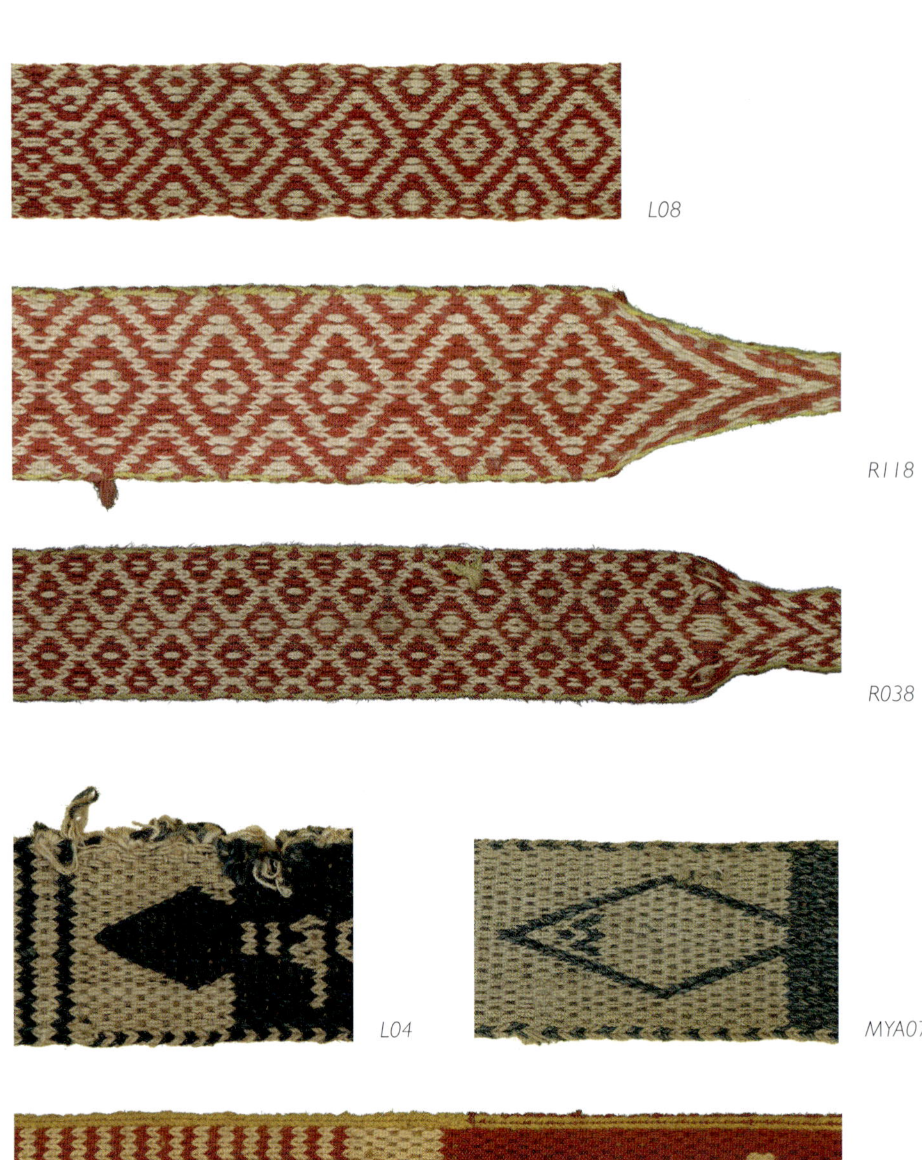

L08

R118

R038

L04

MYA070T

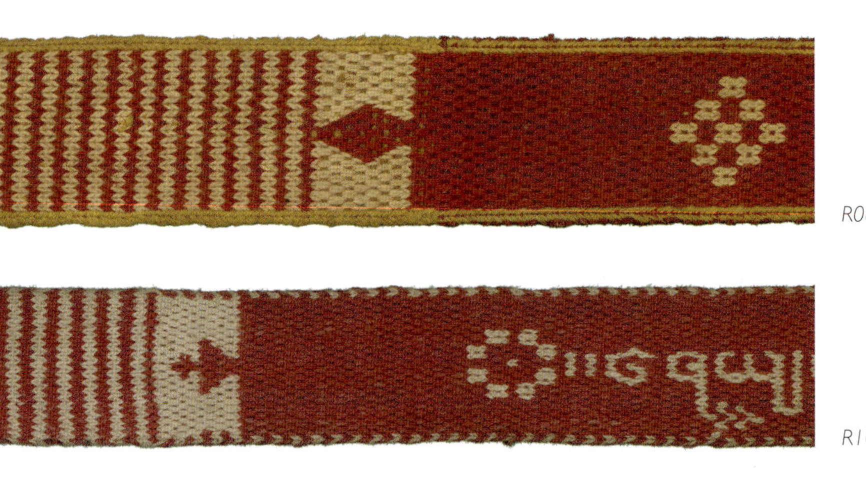

R062

R103

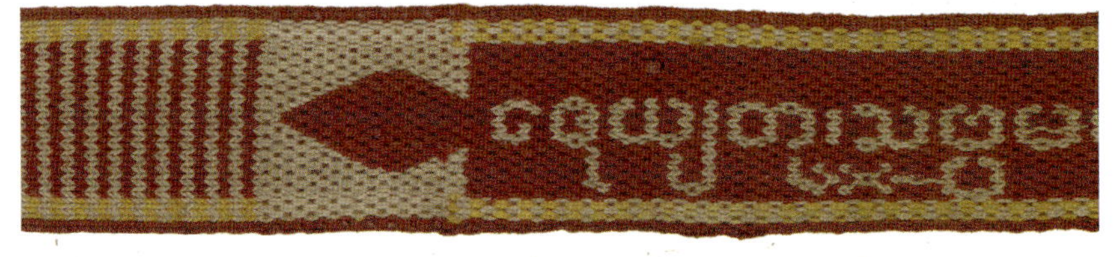

R090

BLOCKS RIGHT

Small geometric shapes built up of square blocks of color, such as diamonds of various types, crosses, circles, and stacks, may occur singly or in groups, as spacers between pictorial images, or between parts of a text. *(B851, B870, MYA070T, R047, R047, R272)*

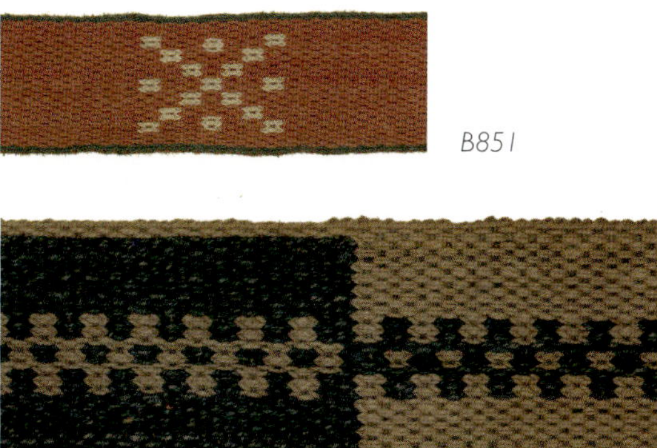

B851

B870

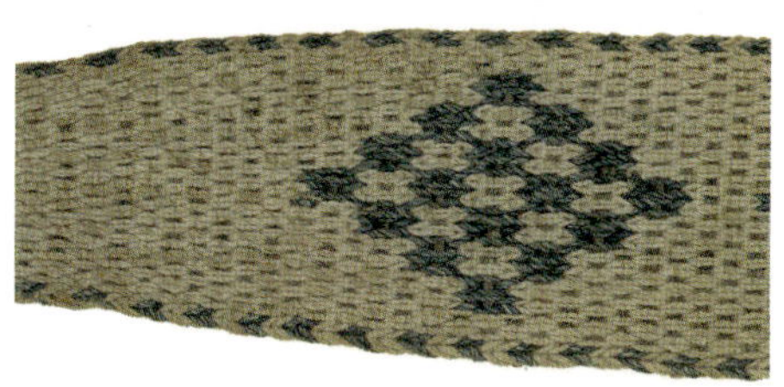

MYA070T

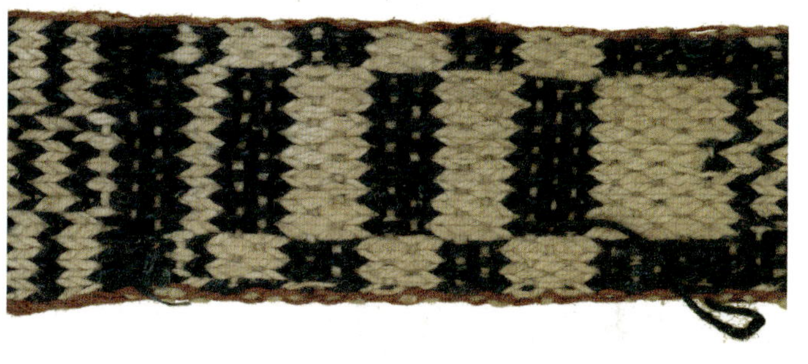

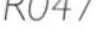

R047

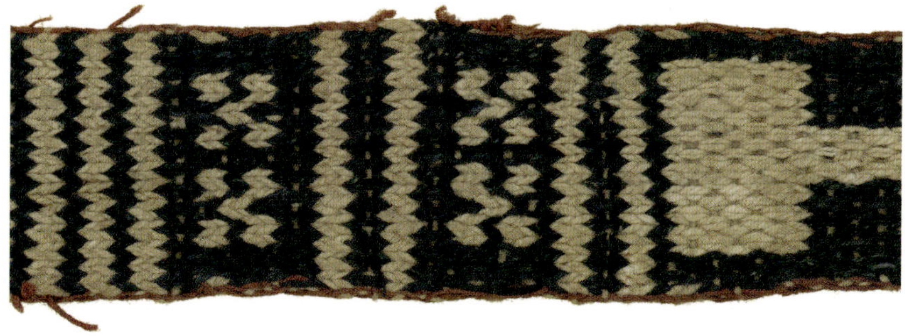

R047

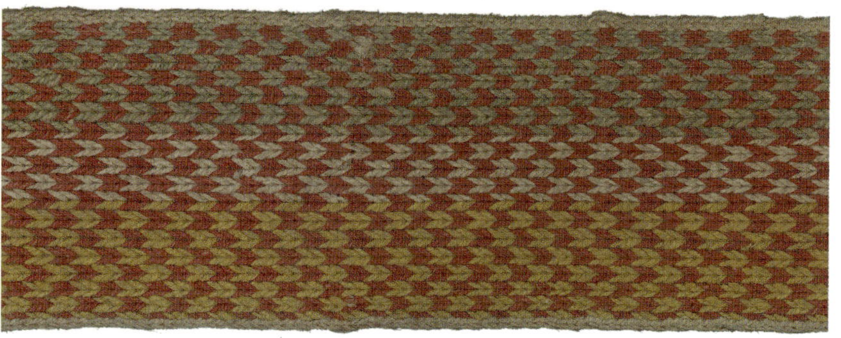

R272 (x2)

COMPLEX BLOCKS

More complex block motifs developed. *(B886, R173)*

Some weavers had a huge repertoire of motifs built up of tiny blocks, and could weave a sequence of sixty or more without repeating a single one. *(R007, R008, R245)*

Some resemble filigree jewelry. *(W93)*

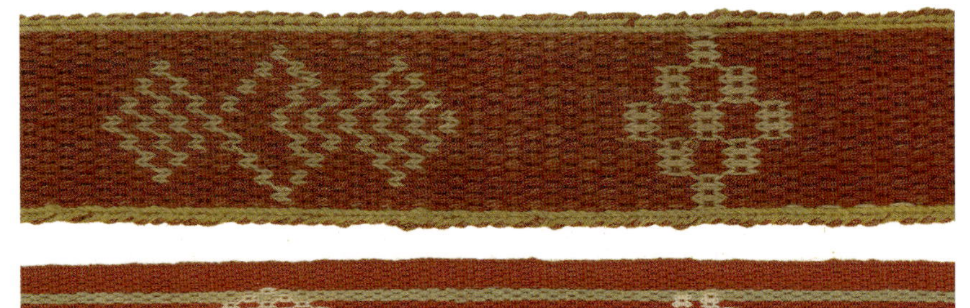

B886

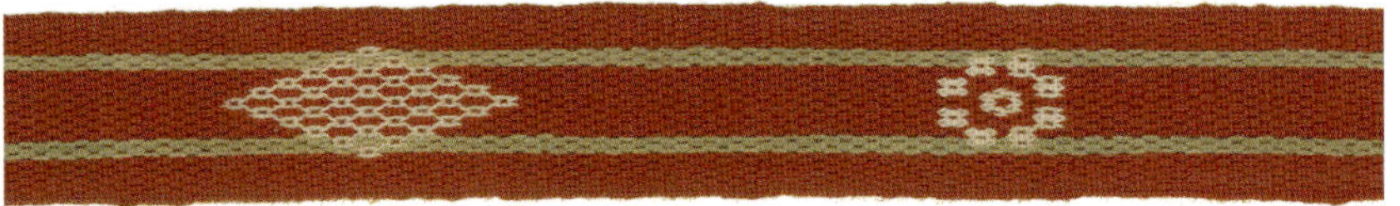

R173

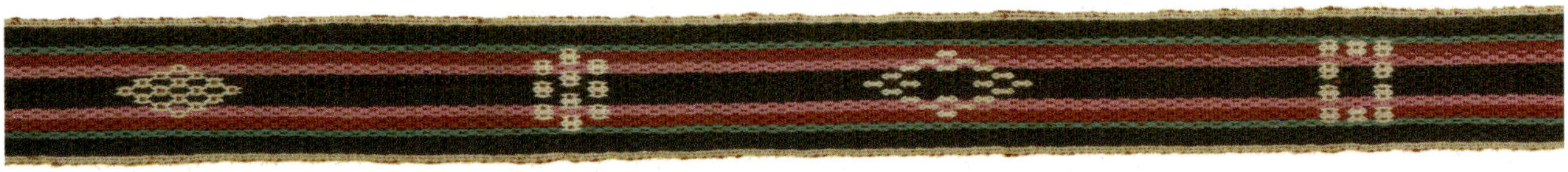

R007

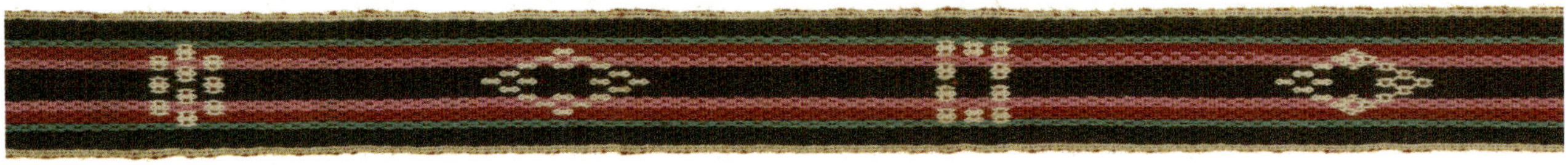

R007

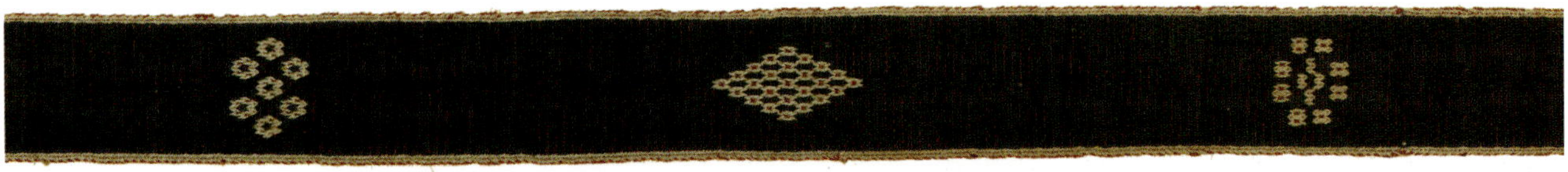

R008

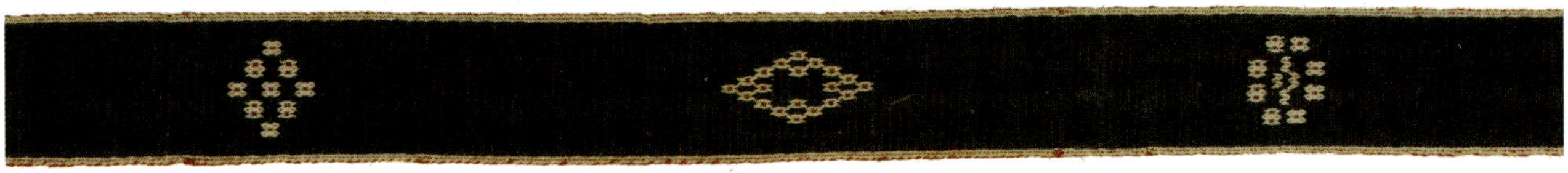

R008

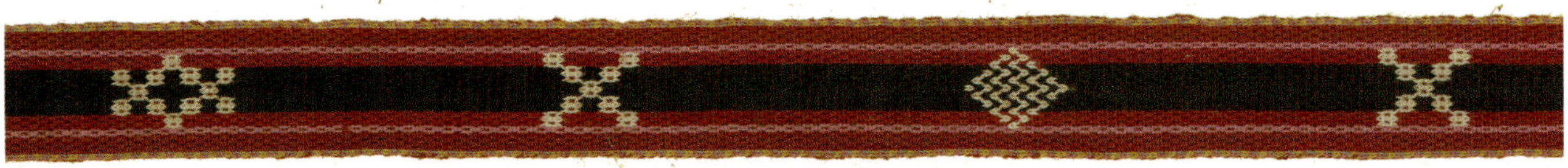

R245

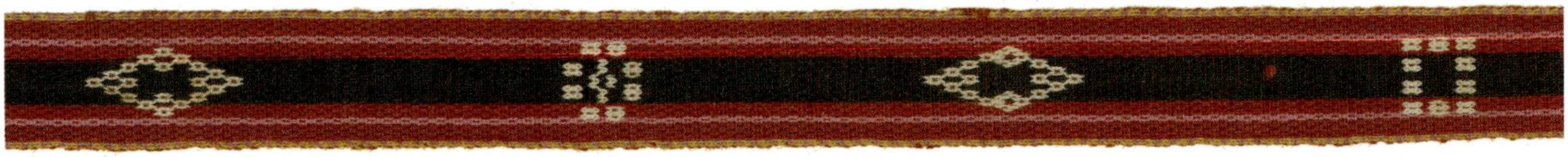

R245

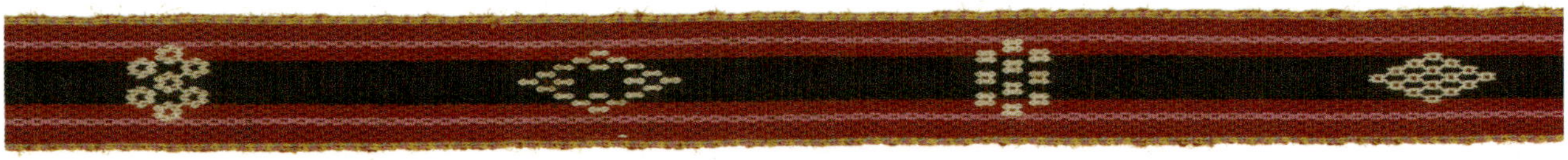

R245

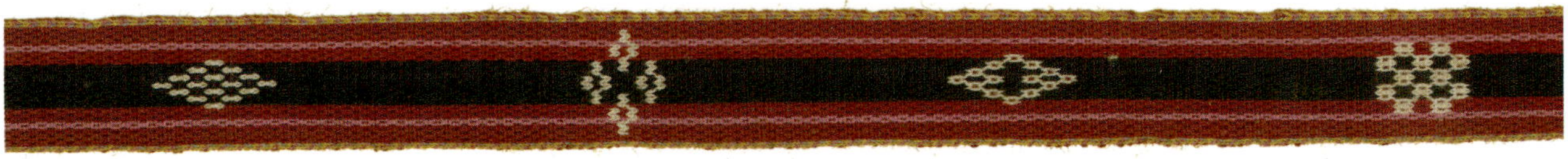

R245

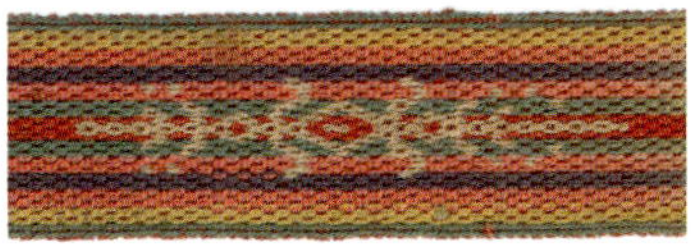

W93

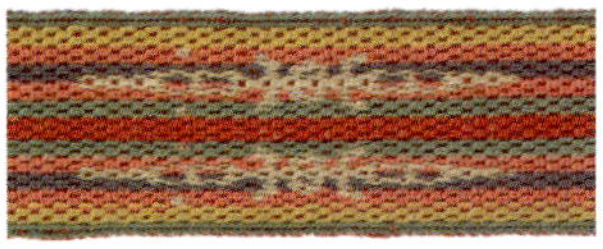

W93

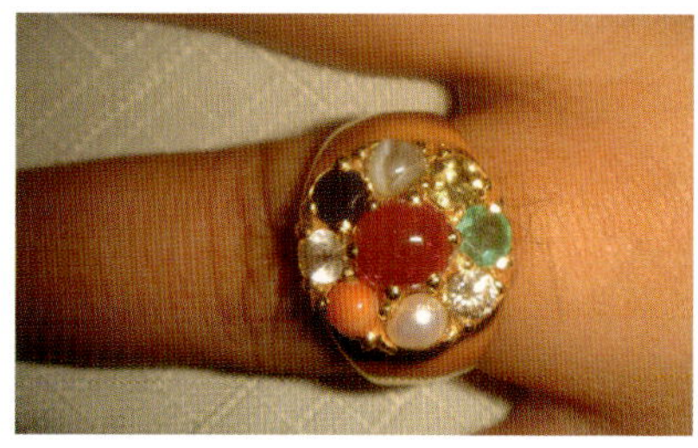

TOP RIGHT

NINE GEMS Geometric motifs composed of nine elements are the *navratna* or nine auspicious gems, a potent symbol of planetary power. *(B874, T467)*

RIGHT

THREE GEMS Geometric motifs arranged in threes symbolize the Triple Gem (Buddha, Dhamma, Sangha). *(B860, M01)* Trios of motifs used as spacers between pictorial images are symbols of the Three Gems, while each component motif is a *navratna*. *(B854, B855, B847)*

BELOW

LOTUS HEADS

Lotus heads symbolize the Buddha. *(R131, R005)*

BOTTOM

UNION JACK

The block motifs used to flank the date of 1290 BE (1928 CE) on this sazigyo bring to mind the banner of the British colonial power, the Union Jack. *(R004)*

Plate 65 TOP

A jeweled finger-ring in the form of a *navratna*.

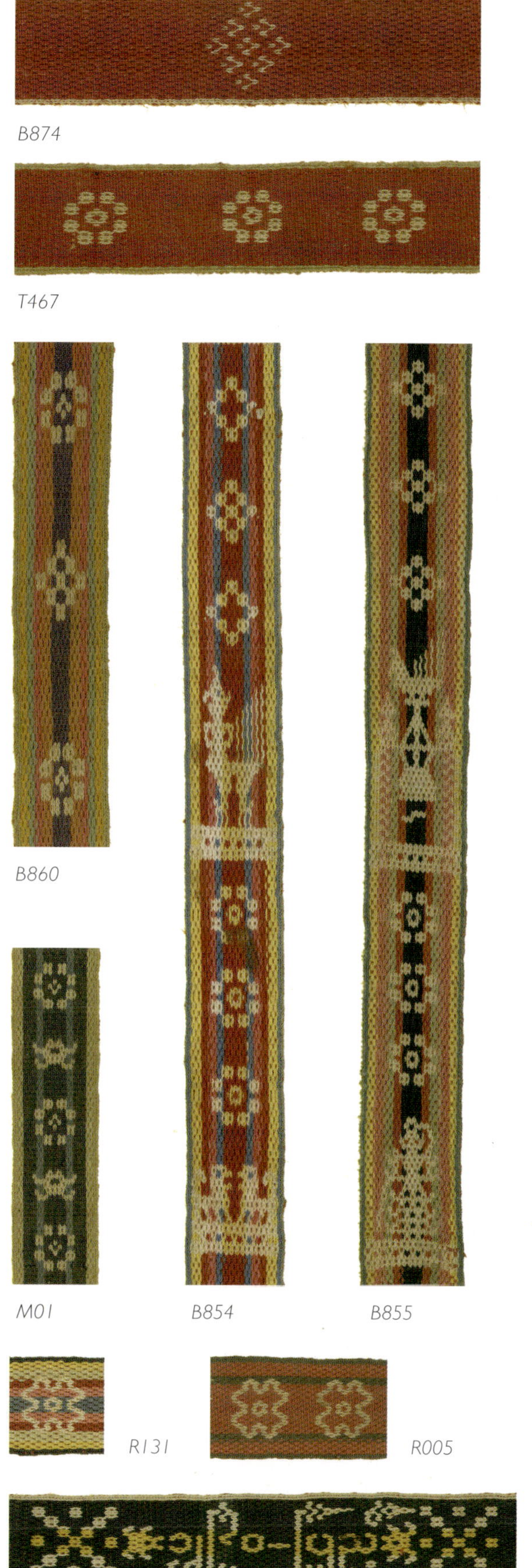

Part IV Chapter 13

The Miniature Woven Images and Their Symbolism

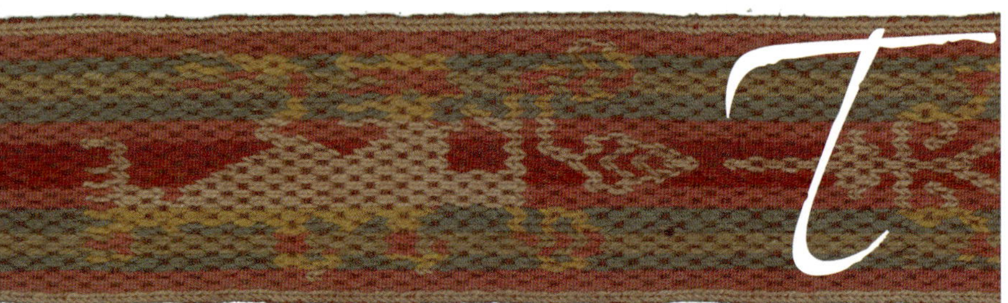

R303

The miniature pictorial images have instant appeal and are perhaps the chief charm of the sazigyo. Certainly they are proof of the weavers' extraordinary virtuosity. And for the great majority of readers who know no Burmese, they may shine out like pinpoints of meaning in a dark sea of impenetrable text in an unfamiliar script. Some birds and beasts are recognizable at a glance, but many of the creatures and objects depicted are not so easily identified, and a closer look brings puzzlement: what do they actually mean? I shall argue that the images are not mere decorative embellishment of the woven text. Many of them function as symbols of big ideas, and relate directly to the sazigyo's purpose as a record of a religious act, the charitable donation of a manuscript to a monastery. Text and pictorial images are aspects of the same message.

In this section of the book the images are identified, and their presence on the sazigyo explained in terms of their symbolic significance. Mythical creatures and real birds and beasts, bells and parasols, thrones and chariots—these can be shown to reflect the complex Burmese system of beliefs and the motives of the Burmese Buddhist donors who commissioned the weave in order to acquire merit for a favorable rebirth, and eventually to reach nirvana.

It was not possible to interview sazigyo weavers about all the images in their repertoire, for they are no longer alive. The one published work on sazigyo in Burmese is mainly an anthology of sazigyo texts, with little discussion of the woven images. Most educated Burmese to whom I showed a sazigyo had never seen one previously. Others admitted that they had never really thought about the meaning of the images, but were glad enough to confirm my interpretations. So the interpretations I offer of the images and of their symbolic significance are my own. That does not make them mere conjecture. Knowledge of Burmese art, life, and custom and close familiarity with the range of images found engraved on Burmese lacquerware are my credentials. The interpretations I have arrived at are offered here to enhance the appeal of these beautiful little woven pictures by placing them in a social and religious context. Their attraction is immediate, but they can also be mystifying, and they will give even more pleasure when properly understood.

Plate 66 NEXT PAGE
Sequences of images before and after the text not only look decorative, they also carry symbolic meanings. *(B842, B847, R027, B854, R247, T261)*

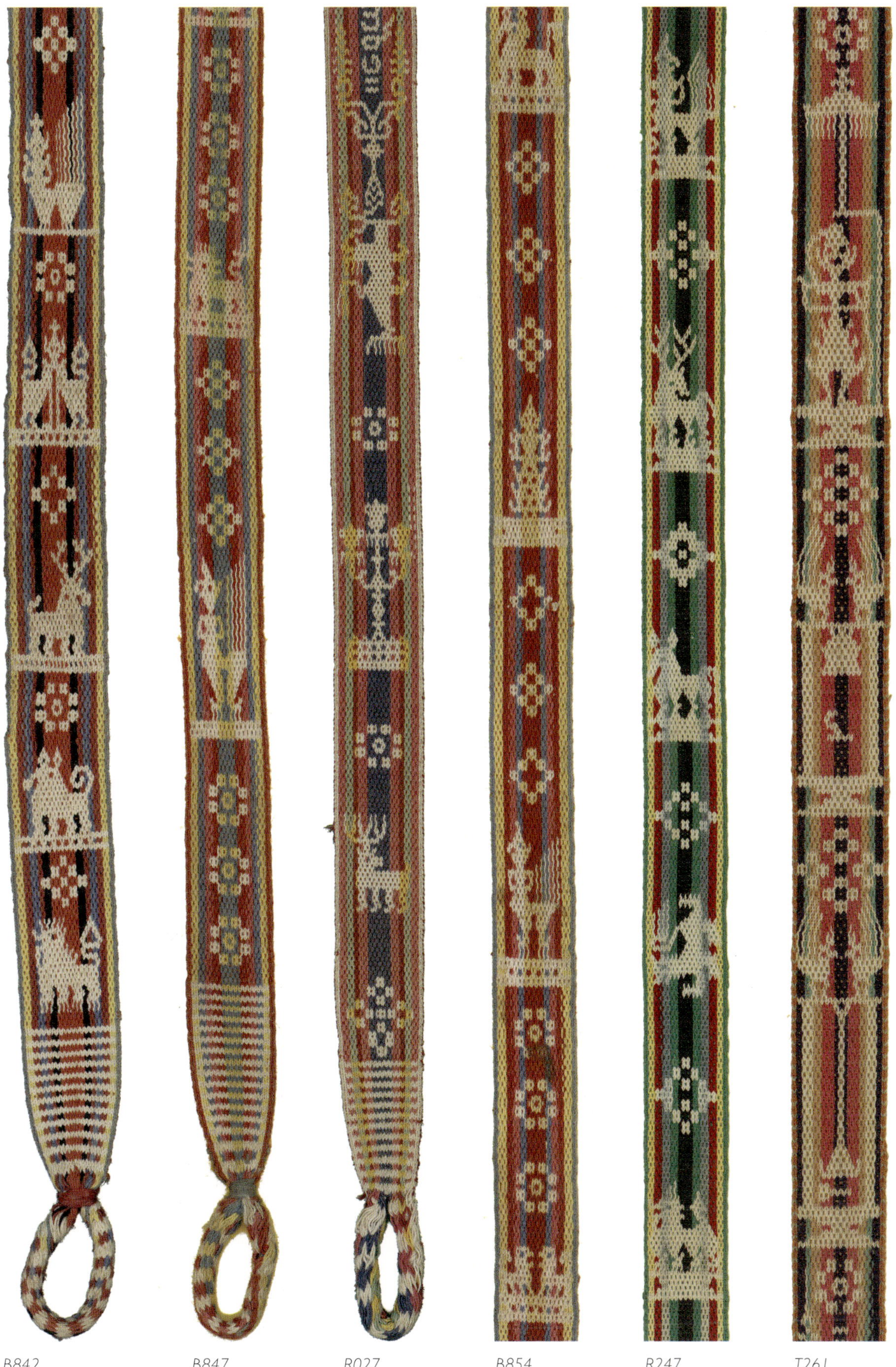

B842 B847 R027 B854 R247 T261

Plate 67 BELOW LEFT
No image of the Buddha ever appears on sazigyo. This Buddha image is of "hollow" or "dry" lacquer. The original sculpted core of clay has been removed, leaving the outer skin of lacquer, gilded.

Plate 68 BELOW RIGHT
In the early centuries of Buddhist art, the so-called "aniconic" period, the Buddha is not depicted as a person. Instead he is represented by various symbols. On this drum slab from a Buddhist stupa at Amaravati, sculpted in the third century CE, no less than four of these symbols appear: the sacred fig tree, the vacant throne itself, a parasol on the throne and a pair of footprints below it.

The Three Gems of Theravada Buddhism—the Buddha, the law, and the order of monks (Buddha, Dhamma, Sangha)—are represented by symbols. Other images reflect Burmese Nat-worship and belief in astrology. The donor's "birthday beast," the animal vehicle of the planet governing the day of his birth, may appear on the sazigyo. So may the zodiac sign of the month when the weave was completed, and the donation made.

Some images have a straightforward, unequivocal symbolism. Others may be multiple symbols. A plant in a pot can have at least three symbolic meanings. As a sacred fig tree it may stand for the Buddha himself. Any growing plant or tree may symbolize the earth, the first of the Four Great Elements, and the zodiac sign Aquarius for the month of Tabodwe is a vase of flowers.

Skeptical readers who may question my system of interpretation will find my defense set out below. I believe that the grouping of images, the galleries, in this chapter will demonstrate to the open-minded reader that most woven images are indeed symbols, and that some have multiple resonance.

Admittedly, a few images defy interpretation, and remain mysterious. We can only speculate that these may have had a private personal significance for the donors who commissioned the sazigyo, or that they were the whimsical creations of the women who wove them a century ago.

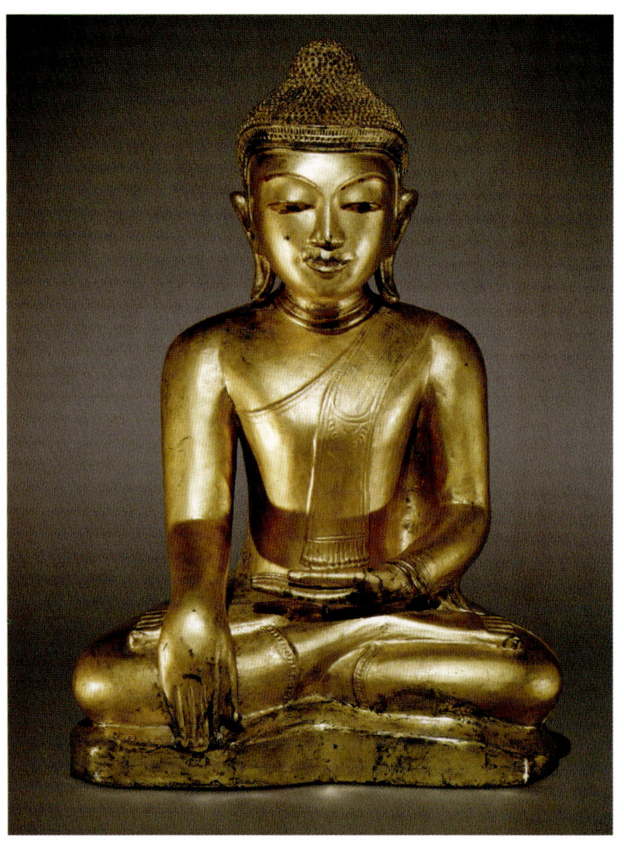

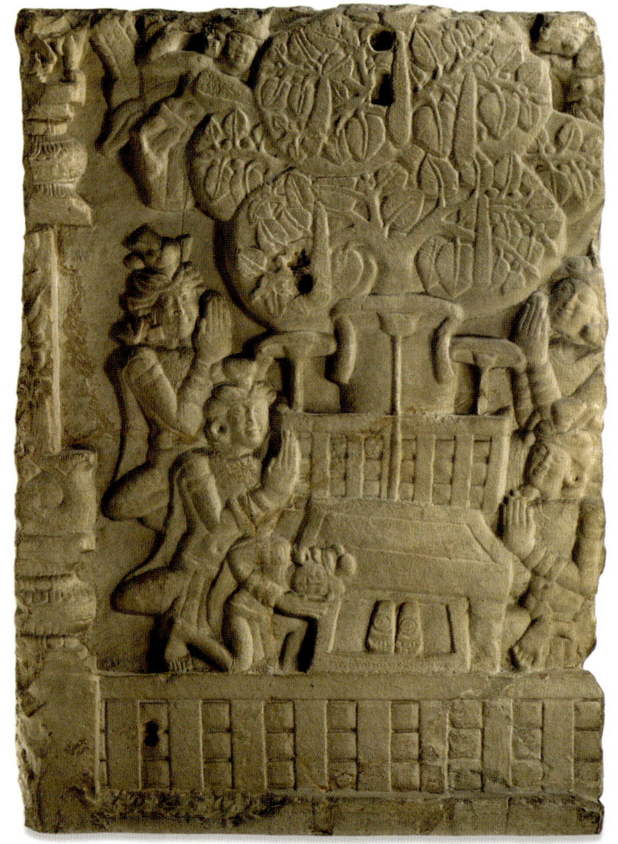

BUDDHA IMAGES

Ironically, the very first room in our gallery, reserved for images of the Buddha, is empty. No Buddha image ever occurs on sazigyo, a striking fact that requires explanation. Buddha images were ubiquitous in Burma in the years when these sazigyo were woven. Long before, in the early centuries of Buddhist art, the so-called "aniconic" period, the person of the Buddha was never depicted. Instead, the Buddha's presence and his powers were symbolized by certain objects. The Buddha's footprint bore the visible marks of Buddhahood. The Bo tree, the sacred fig, stood for his enlightenment. The parasol, emblem of royalty in ancient India, stood for his authority, as did an empty royal throne. The stupa enshrined his bone relics, and stood for his worship.

A carved stone slab from Amaravati in the British Museum shows worshippers revering the Buddha, who is not depicted. Instead he is represented by four of these aniconic symbols together: an empty throne, with a fig tree behind, a parasol above, and a pair of footprints below it. In the Norton Simon Museum in Pasadena, California is a carved stone railing pillar from a stupa, dated to around 100 BCE. It depicts the "Great Departure," Prince Siddhattha riding out of the palace on his horse Kanthaka—but instead of a person, a parasol is depicted in the saddle. Two millennia later, when the conventions of the aniconic period were long abandoned, most of these ancient

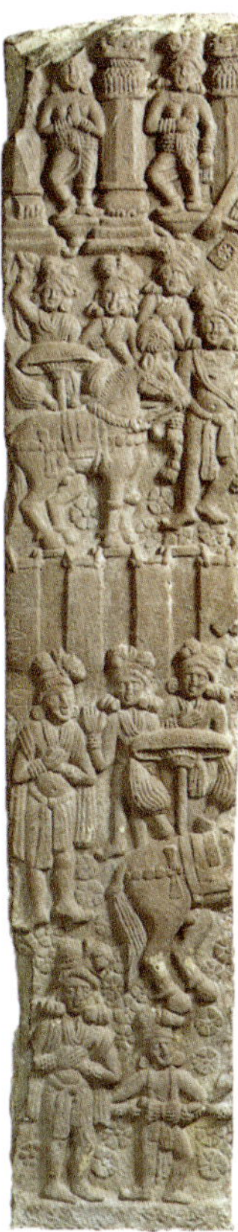

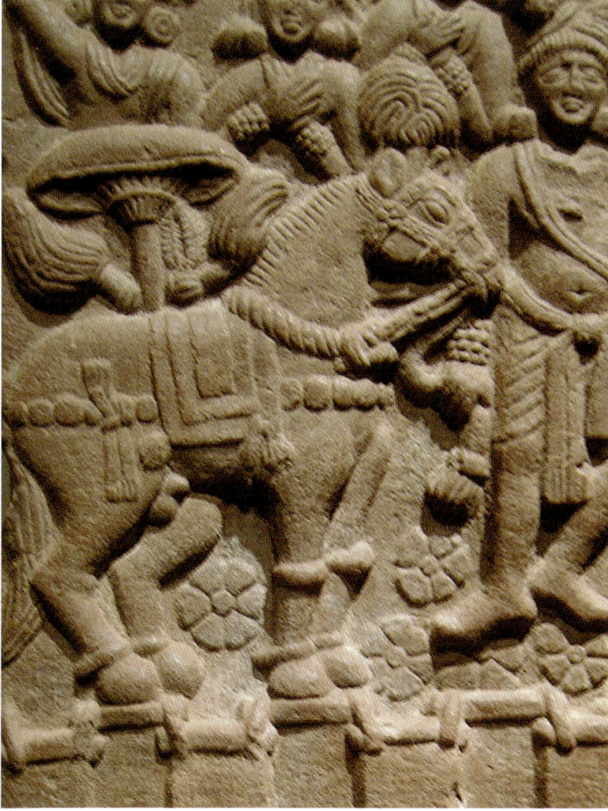

Plate 69 RIGHT
The Buddha is represented by a parasol in this carved stone pillar from around 100 BCE.

Plate 70 FAR RIGHT
The Buddha riding his horse Kanthaka is represented by a parasol in the saddle.

Plate 71 RIGHT
Images of the Buddha appear in the gilt decoration on the covers and margins of the scriptural manuscripts for which the sazigyo were woven, but never on the sazigyo itself.

Plate 72 NEXT PAGE
SYMBOLS OF THE BUDDHA
The Buddha is represented on sazigyo by four symbols: woven images of the Bo tree, parasol, stupa, and empty throne.

FIG TREE
The sacred fig tree symbolizes the Buddha. It was under the Bo tree that Prince Siddhattha attained enlightenment and became a Buddha. *(H004, R008, R026, R130, R192)*

PARASOL
The parasol symbolizes the Buddha. In ancient India, it was the symbol of royal authority, and in royal Burma white parasols were exclusive to the monarchy and senior monks. *(B855, R028, R245, R154)*

STUPA
The stupa or pagoda, which enshrined the Buddha's bone relics, stood for his worship. On the sazigyo, woven images of stupas symbolize the Buddha. In Burmese the same word is used for "pagoda" and "Lord." *(R150, R182, KJ03, B860)*

EMPTY THRONE
The empty throne or empty shrine represents the Buddha. *(T433, R018, R028, R057)*
Sometimes it is not quite empty. An oblong object shaped like a manuscript may lie on it, doubly representing the Buddha. *(R054)*

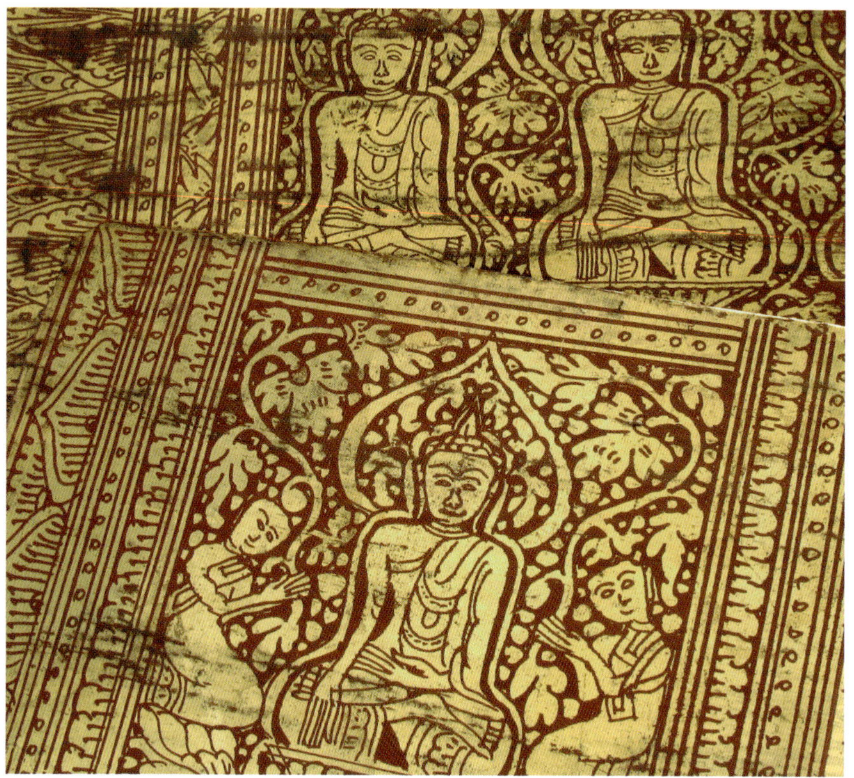

symbols—and yet no images of the Buddha—appear in the Burmese sazigyo weavers' repertoire of images. These women lived, worked, and worshipped surrounded by Buddha images, not only in pagodas and monasteries, but in their own homes, on the domestic shrine or "Buddha shelf," which they tended daily. Images of the Buddha appear in the gilt decoration on the covers and margins of the scriptural manuscripts for which the sazigyo were woven—but never on the sazigyo itself.

A possible explanation for the total absence of images of the Buddha from sazigyo may lie in the gender of the weavers. During the weaving of a sazigyo, the tape almost inevitably brushes against the nether garments of the female weaver. Certainly women are expressly forbidden to rest any scriptural manuscript on their lap. Whether or not woven Buddha images were explicitly banned, women weavers found other ways of representing the Buddha: they did so by the use of symbols.

SYMBOLS OF THE BUDDHA

Woven images of the Bo tree, parasol, stupa, and empty throne all occur on sazigyo. Only the footprints seem to be missing. In addition to these one-to-one symbols, we shall see that several other images also represent the Buddha, but more indirectly. The Bo tree image is often found at the start of the sazigyo, or at the end. Rarely it takes over, like an invasive species of fig tree in nature, and covers the whole flat area: the woven tree illustrated in plate 73 measures 3.5 meters from pot to tip.

The empty throne or shrine is sometimes not quite empty. Oblong objects shaped like a manuscript may lie on it, so that the image doubly represents the Buddha.

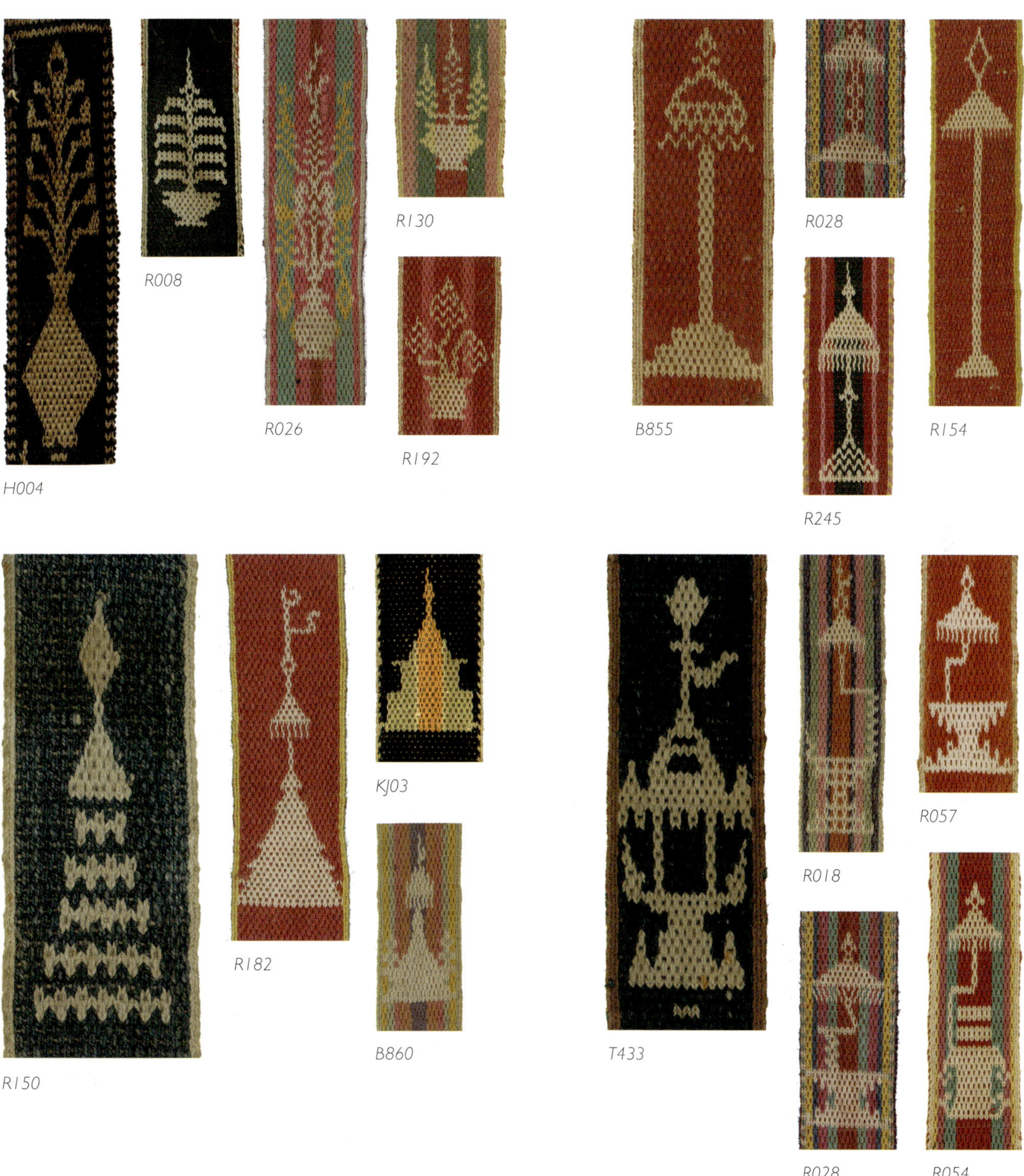

H004 R008 R026 R130 R192 B855 R028 R245 R154

R150 R182 KJ03 B860 T433 R018 R057 R028 R054

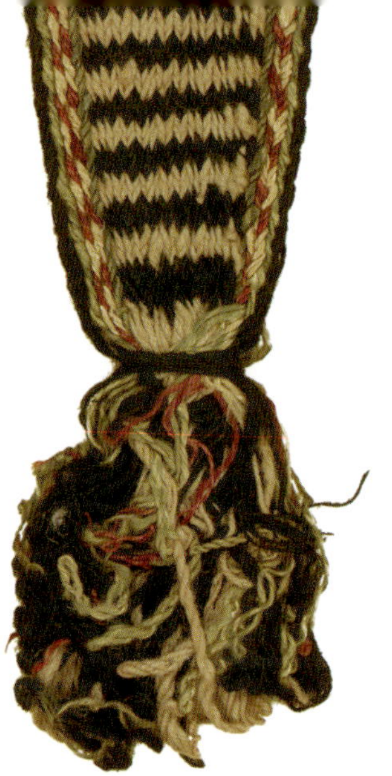

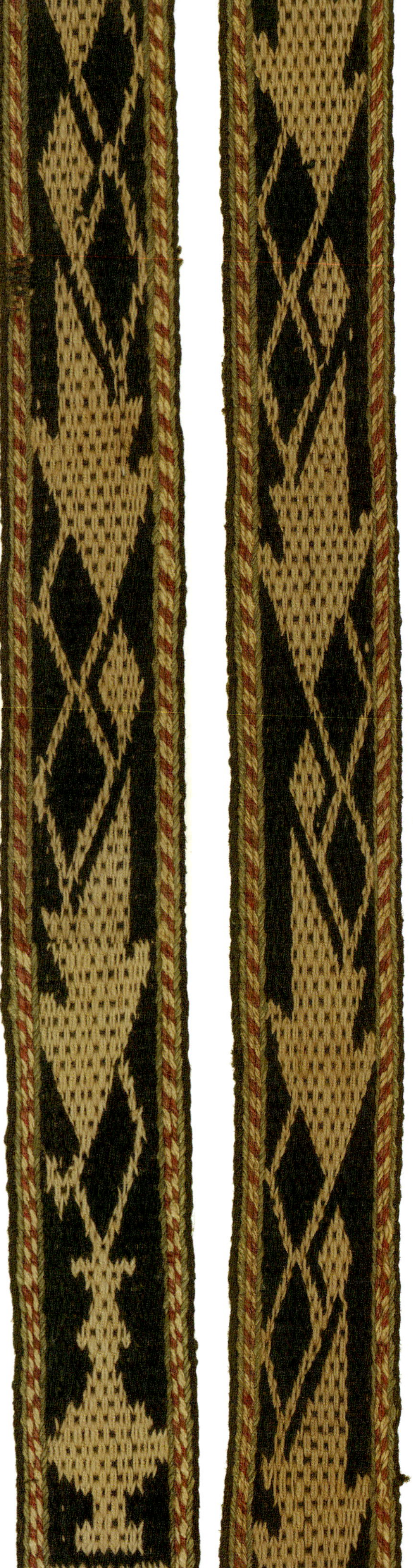

Plate 73 RIGHT, NEXT PAGE, AND FOLLOWING PAGES
This Bo tree grows from a pot at the start of this sazigyo to cover more than three meters of the band. For its entire length this motif represents the Buddha. *(J01)*

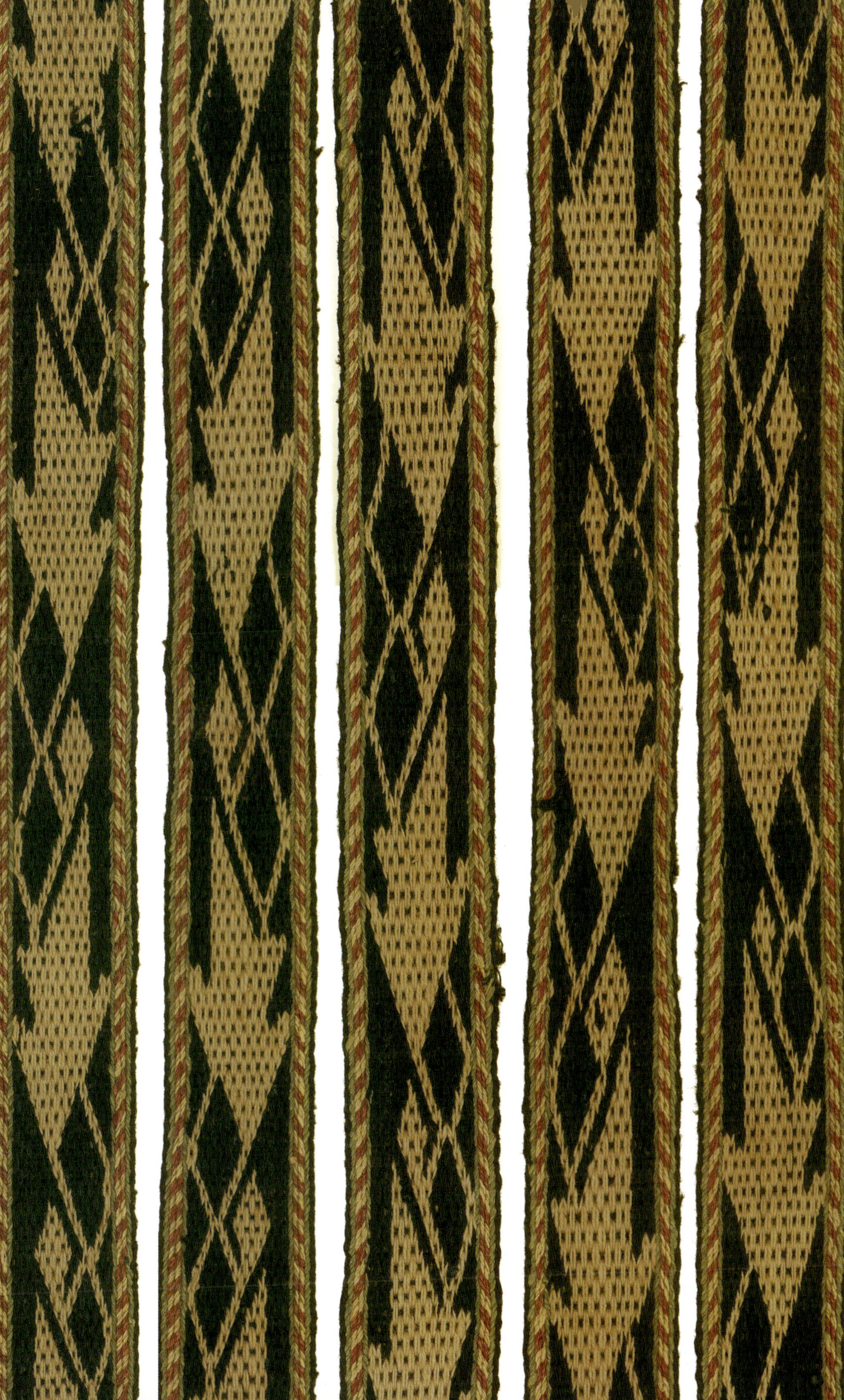

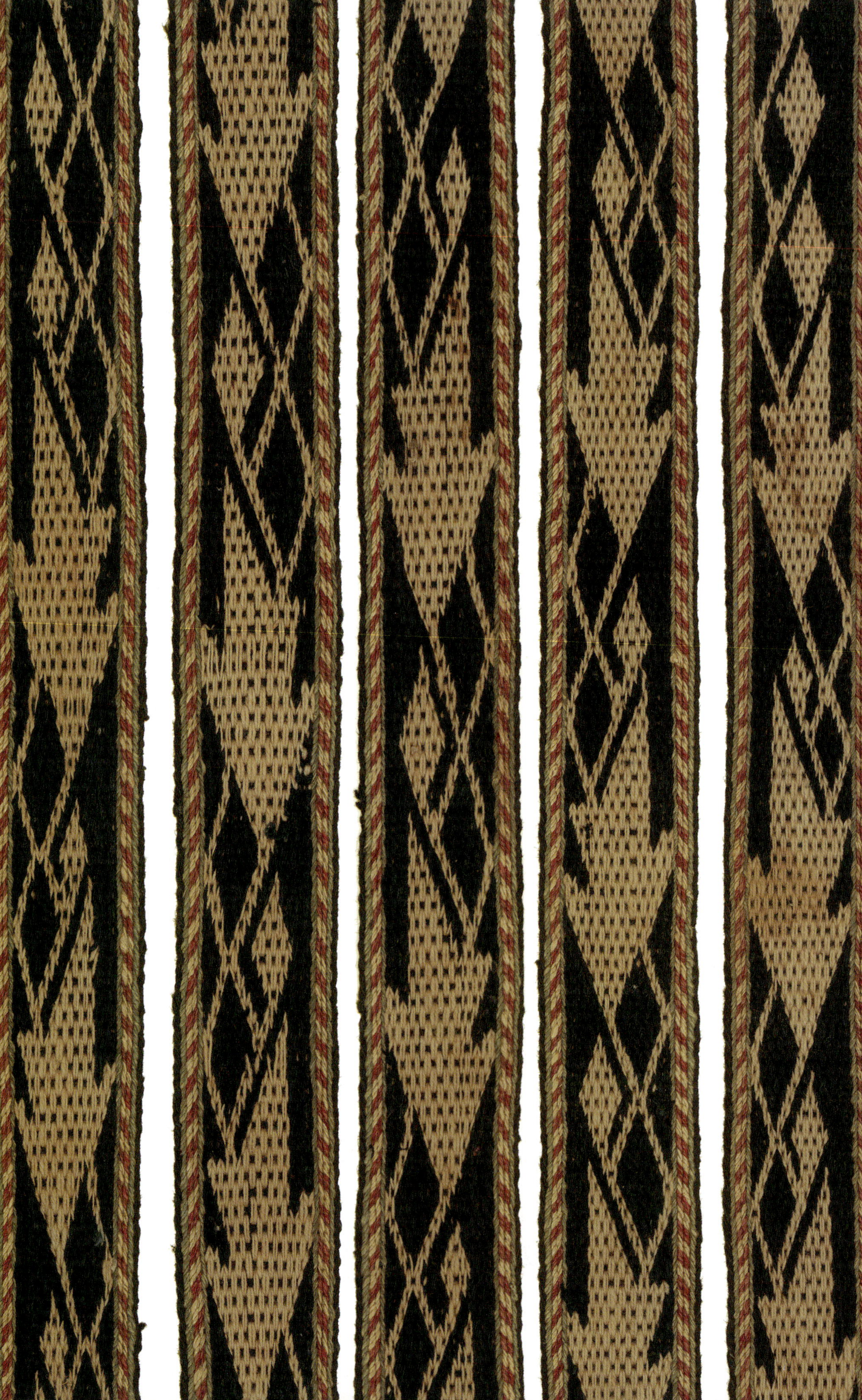

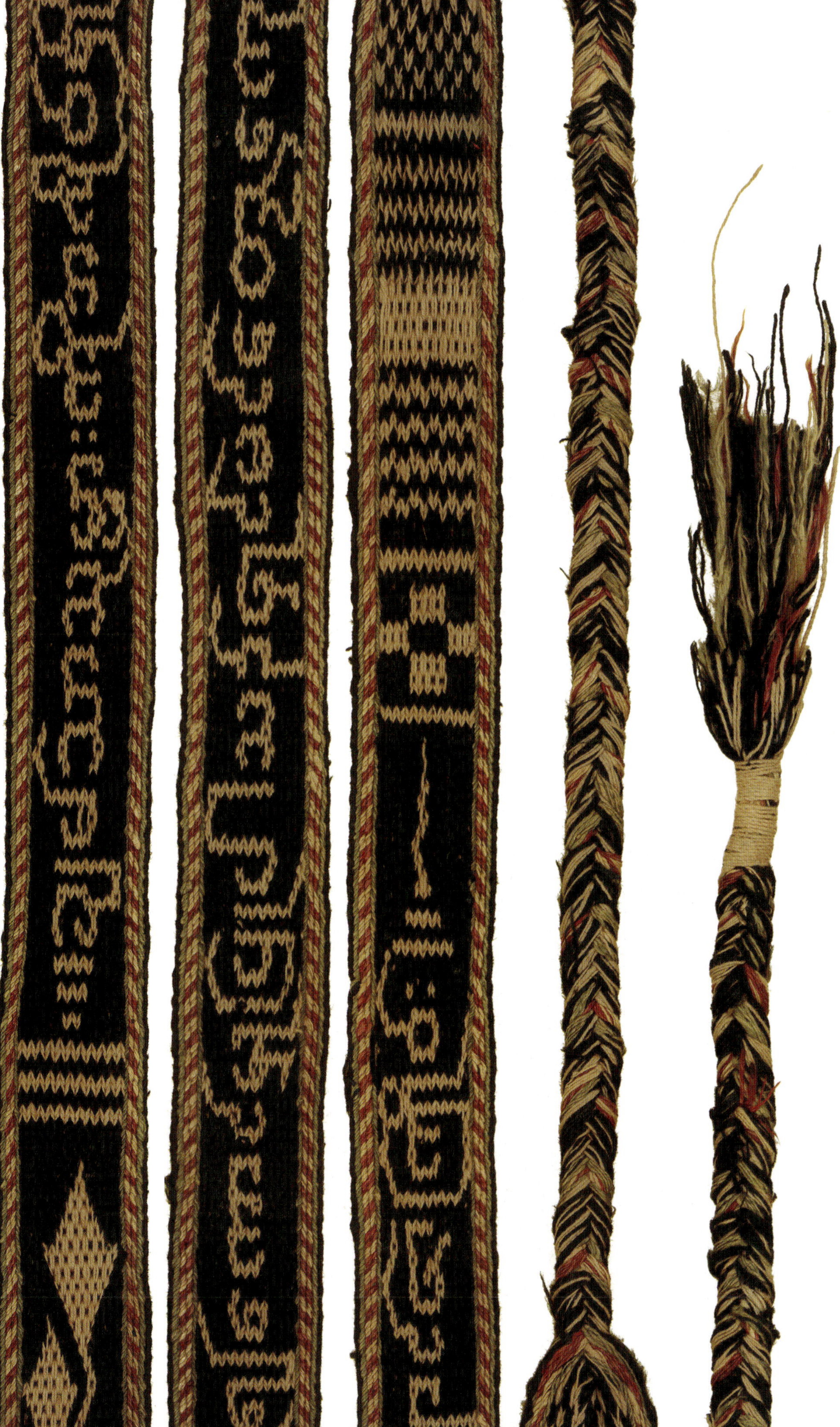

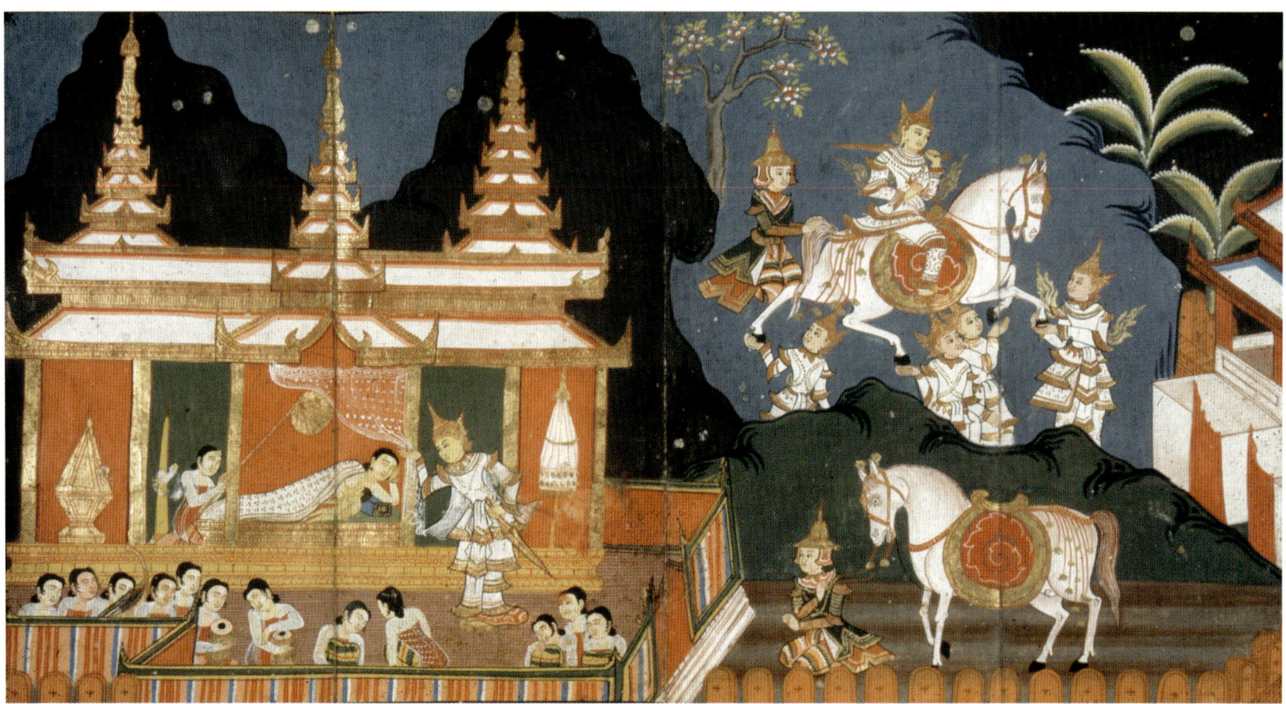

SYMBOLS OF THE LAW AND OF THE MONKS

Burmese Buddhists begin any ritual or religious ceremony by saying three times the *triratna*, the Three Gems: "I take refuge in the Buddha. I take refuge in the Dhamma. I take refuge in the Sangha." It is often on the lips of monks and laity alike. We have seen how this triple formula can be symbolized by trios of abstract geometric motifs, and how several pictorial images symbolize the Buddha. The other members of the Three Gems, the law and the monks, each have their own symbol, and these are depicted in woven images on the sazigyo.

The stag is a frequent image on sazigyo, simple to recognize by its many-branched antlers. First and foremost it represents the Dhamma, the law, because the Buddha preached his first sermon in the deer park at Isipatana near Benares. Next, and by easy synecdoche, the stag may also stand for the individual scriptural manuscript being donated with its sazigyo, since any part of the law may symbolize the whole Tipitaka. Finally, the stag may even represent the Buddha himself, who said "He who sees me sees the Dhamma, and he who sees the Dhamma sees me."[3] At his deathbed, when some of his followers wept at his imminent passing, he said to the monks: "Some of you may think that you have no teacher any more. But when I am gone the Dhamma and the Rule I have taught are to be your teacher."[4] Hence devout Burmese Buddhists believe in the identity of the Buddha and the law. Equating the stag with the Buddha may seem far-fetched, but we learn from the popular Jataka stories that the Buddha-to-be was a great golden stag in several of his previous lives.

Plate 74 ABOVE
Mounted on his white horse Kanthaka, Prince Siddhattha, the Buddha-to-be, rides out of the palace to renounce sensual delights and become an ascetic mendicant. The scene, the "Great Departure," is illustrated in a painted folding book or *parabaik*.

Plate 75 BELOW
A remarkable late nineteenth-century sazigyo in the National Museum, Yangon has two lines of woven text. The donors' immediate motive for their deed of merit was their son's initiation *(shinbyu)* and their daughter's ear-piercing ceremony.

Plate 76 BOTTOM LEFT
"As parents we have . . . adorned the beautiful girls, to look like fairies, with colorful court dress and head wear, for their ear-boring ceremony."
A young girl with her mother, arrayed in her finest, looks a little apprehensive. Music played at ear-boring ceremonies was loud enough to drown the girl's cries.

Plate 77 BOTTOM RIGHT
A procession near Pegu in about 1890 halts for the *shinbyu* boy to strike a pose for photographers Max and Bertha Ferrars.

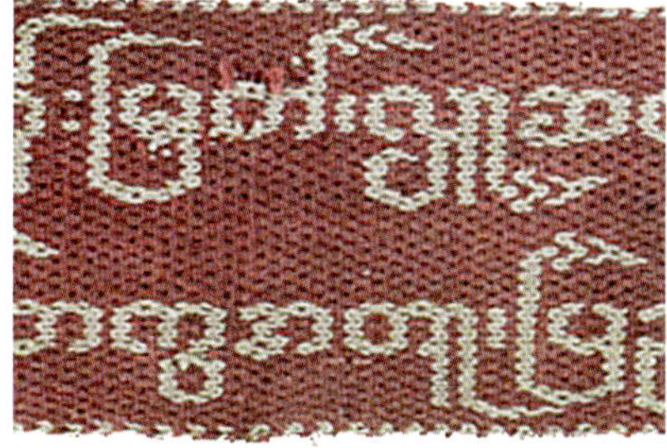

Stag and horse images often occur close together near the start of sazigyo. When they do, they represent two of the Three Gems. The horse, perhaps surprisingly, represents the Sangha, the community of monks. Mounted on his white horse Kanthaka, Prince Siddhattha, the Buddha-to-be, rode out of the palace in the "Great Departure" to renounce sensual delights and become an ascetic mendicant.

This journey is reflected today in the *shinbyu*, the ceremonial initiation into the monkhood of young Burmese Buddhist boys. They ride on horseback to the pagoda, where their heads are shaved and their special princely costume is exchanged for monks' brown robes. This rite of passage is both a religious confirmation and a hugely important family event. Wealthier parents mark it by donations to the monastery where their son is to spend a few days as a monk.

The text of a remarkable late nineteenth-century two-line sazigyo in the National Museum, Yangon records just such a donation by proud parents:

> **We know from ancient literature that Buddhist monks were the guide to the world, acclaimed by Greece and Rome. To celebrate the ear-piercing ceremony of our daughter and ordination (*shinbyu*) of our son, we donated for one hundred monks, three sets of robes including girdle, and a set of a hundred black pottery alms bowls; we also provided a meal of the finest meat curry to monks and to the lay audience.**
> (NMY, translation by Dr. Ye Myint and Ralph Isaacs)

Another family **"celebrates the occasion of introducing the boys into novice-monkhood, to become members in the Buddhist Sasana, and our daughter's ceremonial ear-boring with gold needle."** (MMG, Ch. 7 No. 3)

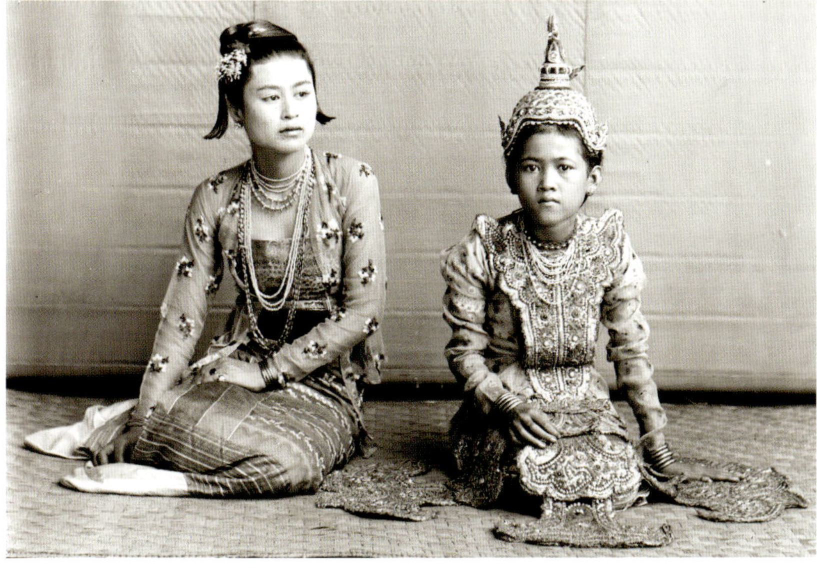

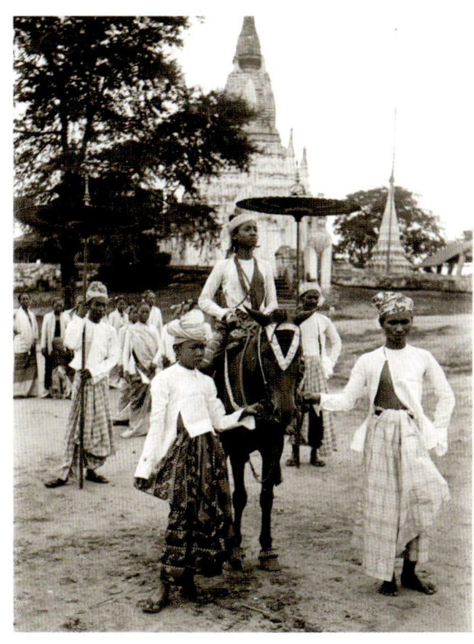

Plate 78 RIGHT

This statue of a Golden Deer in a village monastery near Pagan has real antlers, so it may date back to a time when deer and their antlers could still be found.

Plate 79 BELOW

WOVEN IMAGES OF STAGS

Stags symbolize the Dhamma, the law, because the Buddha's first sermon was preached in a deer park. *(R304, B860, JBT6, BM246, R001, R202, H012, R027, M01)*

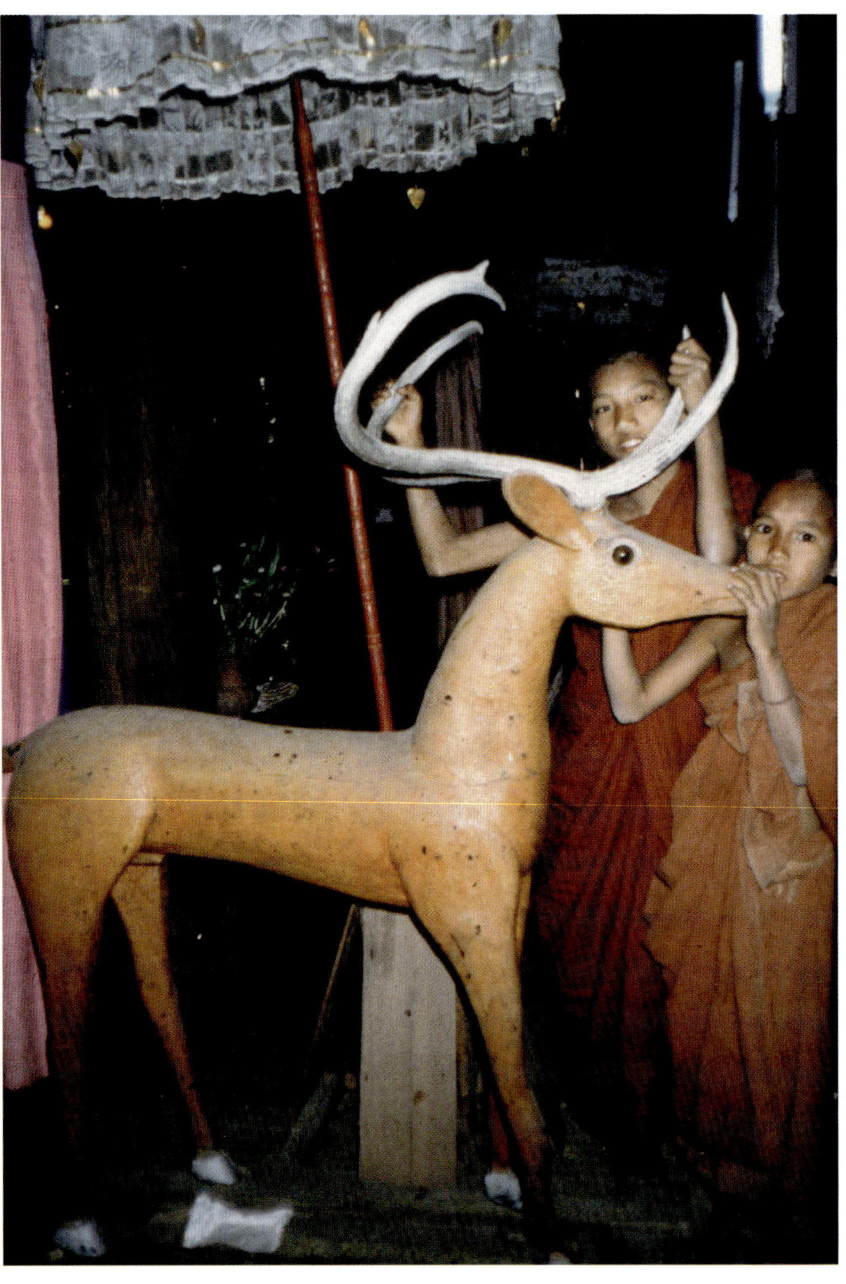

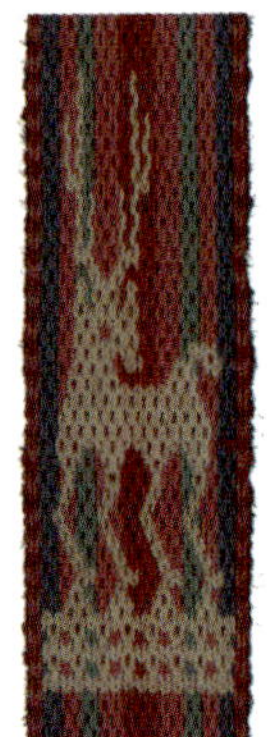

R304

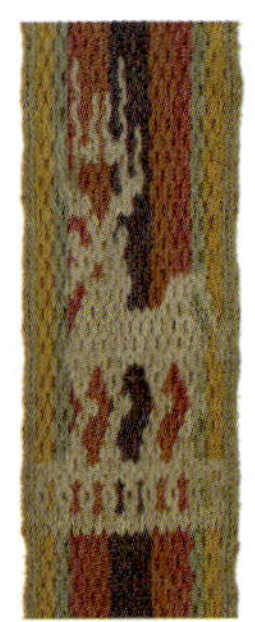

B860

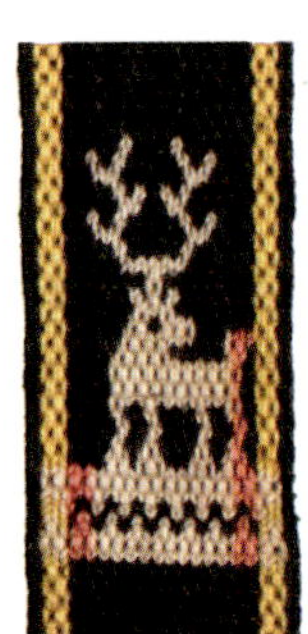

JBT6

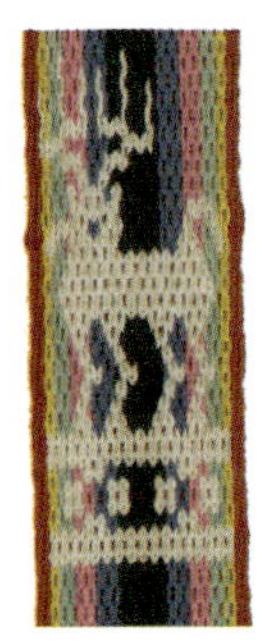

BM246

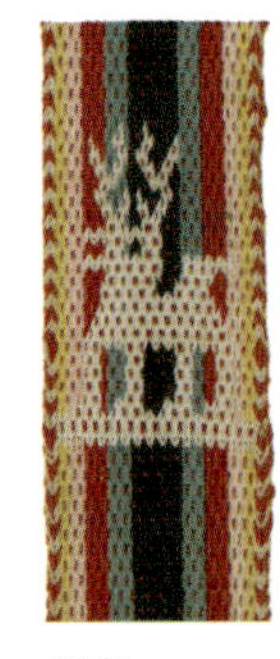

R001

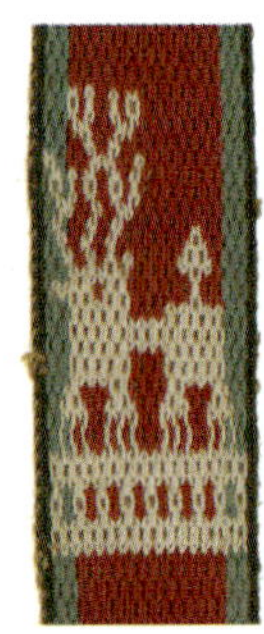

R202

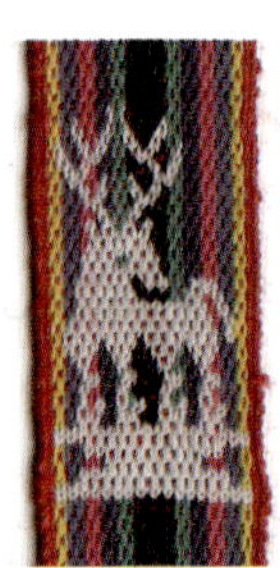

H012

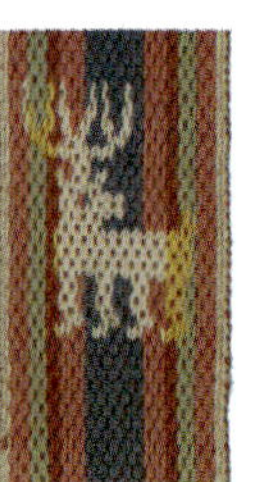

R027

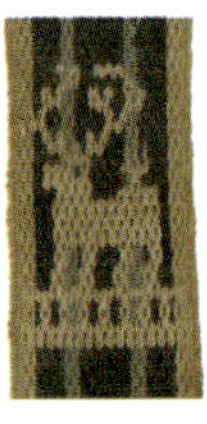

M01

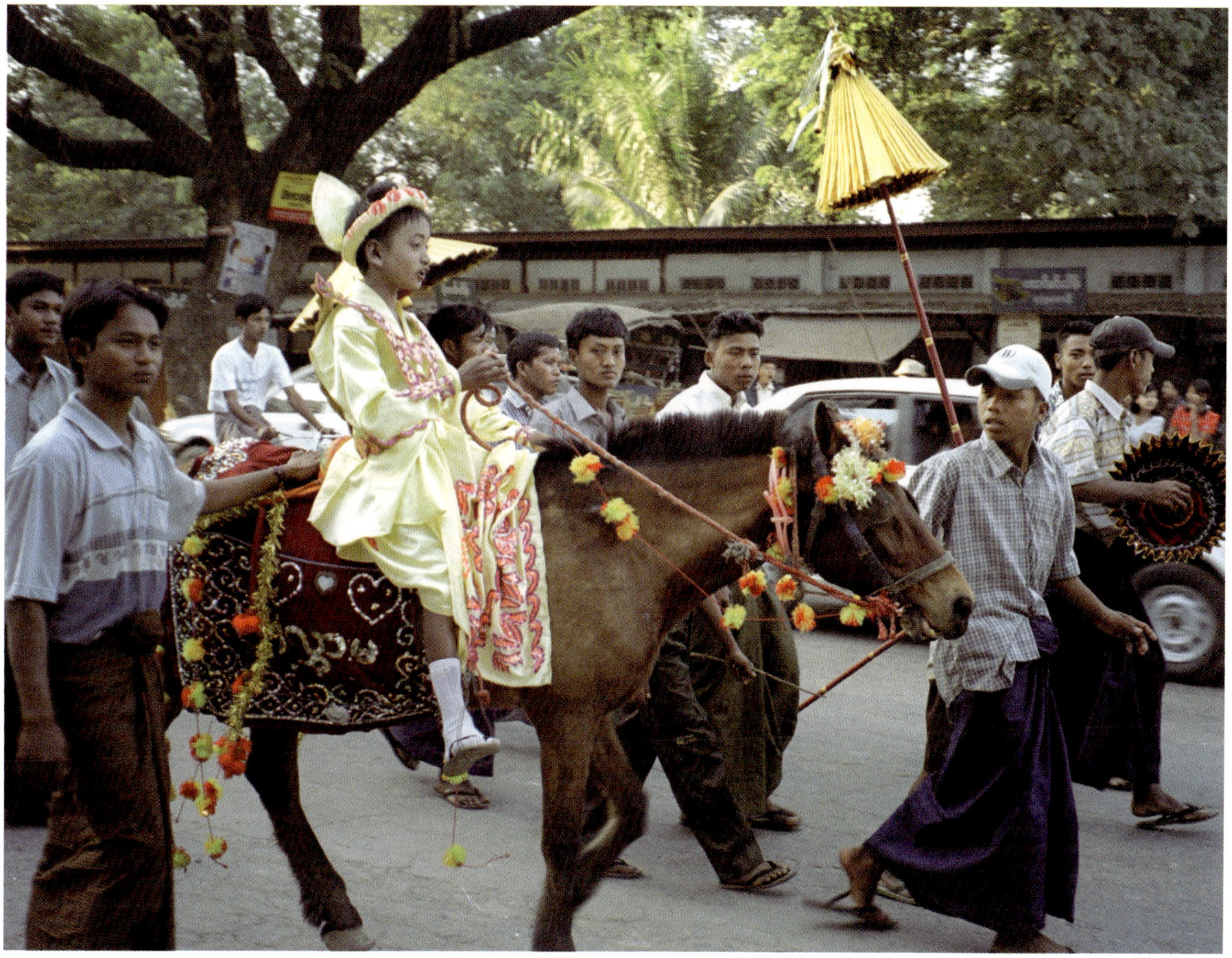

Plate 80 ABOVE
Dressed in princely costume, Burmese boys ride to their *shinbyu* initiation ceremony in Mandalay in 2003, imitating the "Great Departure."

Plate 81 RIGHT
WOVEN IMAGES OF HORSES
Horses symbolize the Sangha, the monks, because a horse carried the Buddha-to-be out of the palace to become an ascetic mendicant. *(R304, B877, R005, B860, H012, B854)*

PAIR, HORSE AND STAG
A stag and horse together symbolize two of the Three Gems, the law and the monks. *(R247)*

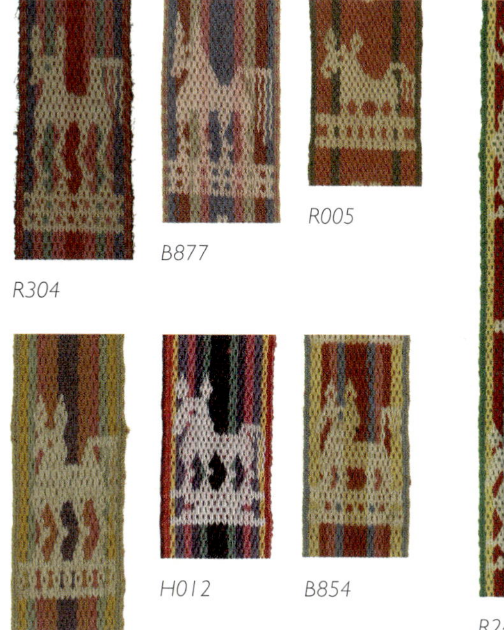

R304 *B877* *R005*

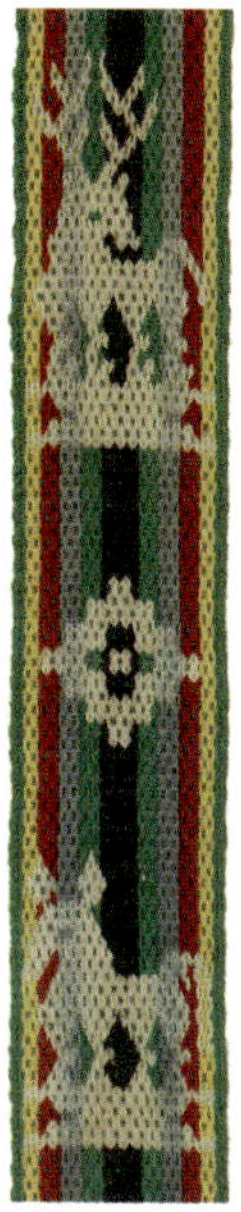

B860 *H012* *B854*

R247

Plate 82 RIGHT
Guardian Nats flank monastery doors.

Plate 83 NEXT PAGE
WOVEN IMAGES OF NATS
Nats are celestial beings whose presence is assumed everywhere in Burma. They abound on sazigyo, where they fill many roles. The King of the Nats, Thagya Min, is invoked at all Burmese Buddhist ceremonies, and his image appears on many sazigyo. Rarely, he may be represented only by his attribute, the *vajra* or thunderbolt.

A SERIES OF NATS *(B847)*

NATS STANDING ALONE *(R023, M02, T467, JBT6.49)*

PAIRS OF NATS *(R251, R028, H031)*

NATS SUPPORTING BELLS *(B843, R192, J05, B877)*

NATS SUPPORTING *DAGUNDAING (KJ02, M01, B889)*

THAGYA MIN, KING OF THE NATS *(B854, T467, M02)*

THAGYA MIN, EYES AND MOUTH IN SUPPLEMENTARY WEFT *(R291)*

THAGYA MIN, *VAJRA* IN EACH HAND *(H031)*

VAJRA Rarely, Thagya Min may be represented by his attribute, the *vajra*. *(B852)*

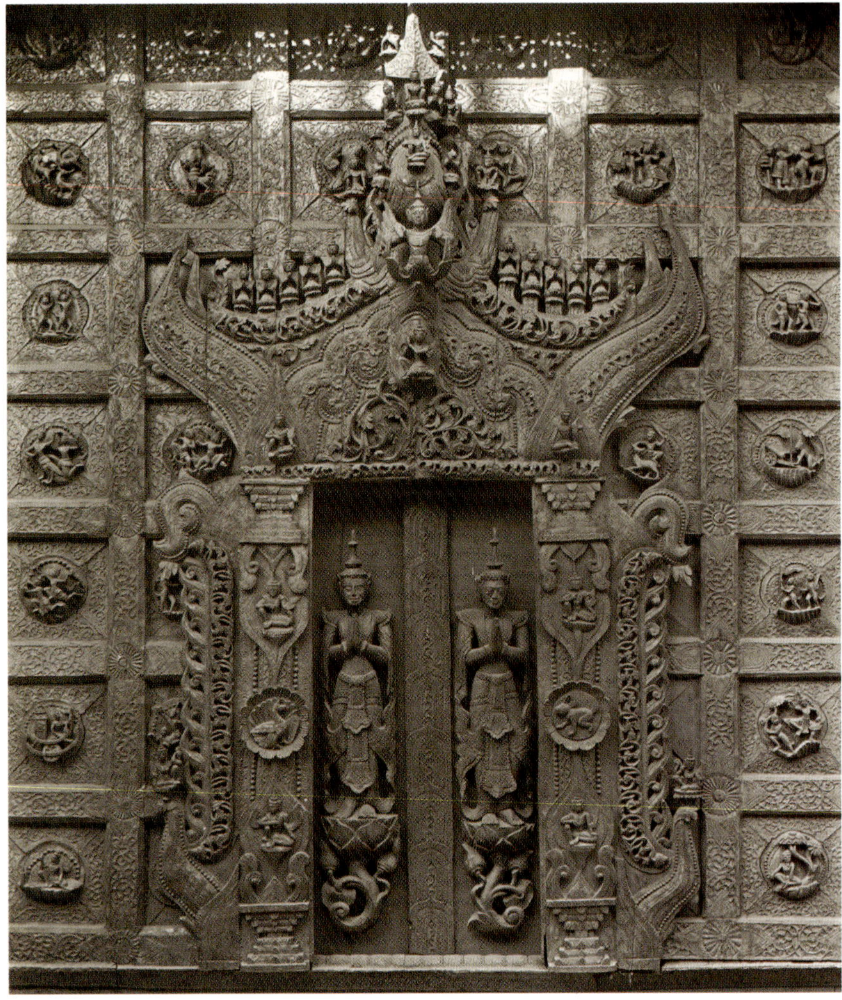

POWERFUL CELESTIAL FORCES

THAGYA MIN, KING OF THE NATS

The complex Burmese belief system embraces an almost infinite range of pre-Buddhist deities, astrological forces, and magical powers. Nats are celestial beings whose presence is assumed everywhere in Burma. Nat guards flank monastery doorways. Nats abound on sazigyo. A single Nat may be found alone and unemployed, but more often a pair of Nats act as supporters for bells and for the *dagundaing*, the tall teak flagpole on the pagoda platform and the final image on most sazigyo.

Thagya Min, the "Lord who knows and hears everything,"[5] is the "King of the Nats." His Sanskrit equivalent is Sakra, the Hindu Indra. Thagya Min is invariably invoked at Burmese Buddhist ceremonies, so his woven image often appears on the sazigyo, which records the performance of a religious act. He is depicted standing on a royal throne, sometimes holding a thunderbolt (*vajra*) in each hand. Rarely, a *vajra* alone represents him. A Burmese Buddhist legend tells how when the Buddha was nearing death he thought of ordaining that his religion should last for 2500 years. But Sakra begged him to increase the period to 5000 years, promising that he would guard it with his thunderbolt during the second 2500 years. This story is not in the Pali canon or the commentaries, but many Burmese still refer to the present era of Buddhism as "Thagya Min's Era of Buddhism."[6]

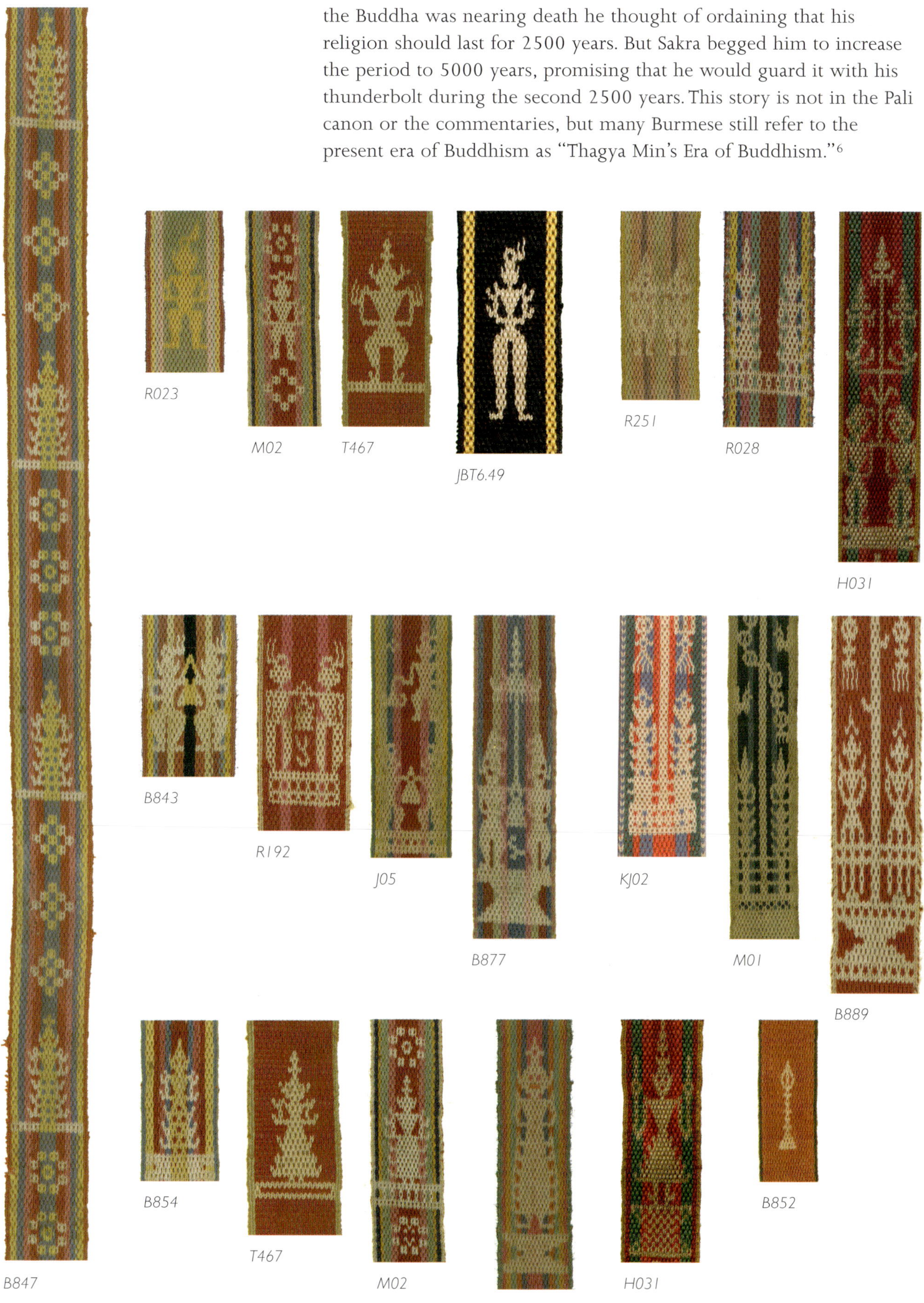

R023 *M02* *T467* *JBT6.49* *R251* *R028* *H031*

B843 *R192* *J05* *B877* *KJ02* *M01* *B889*

B847 *B854* *T467* *M02* *R291* *H031* *B852*

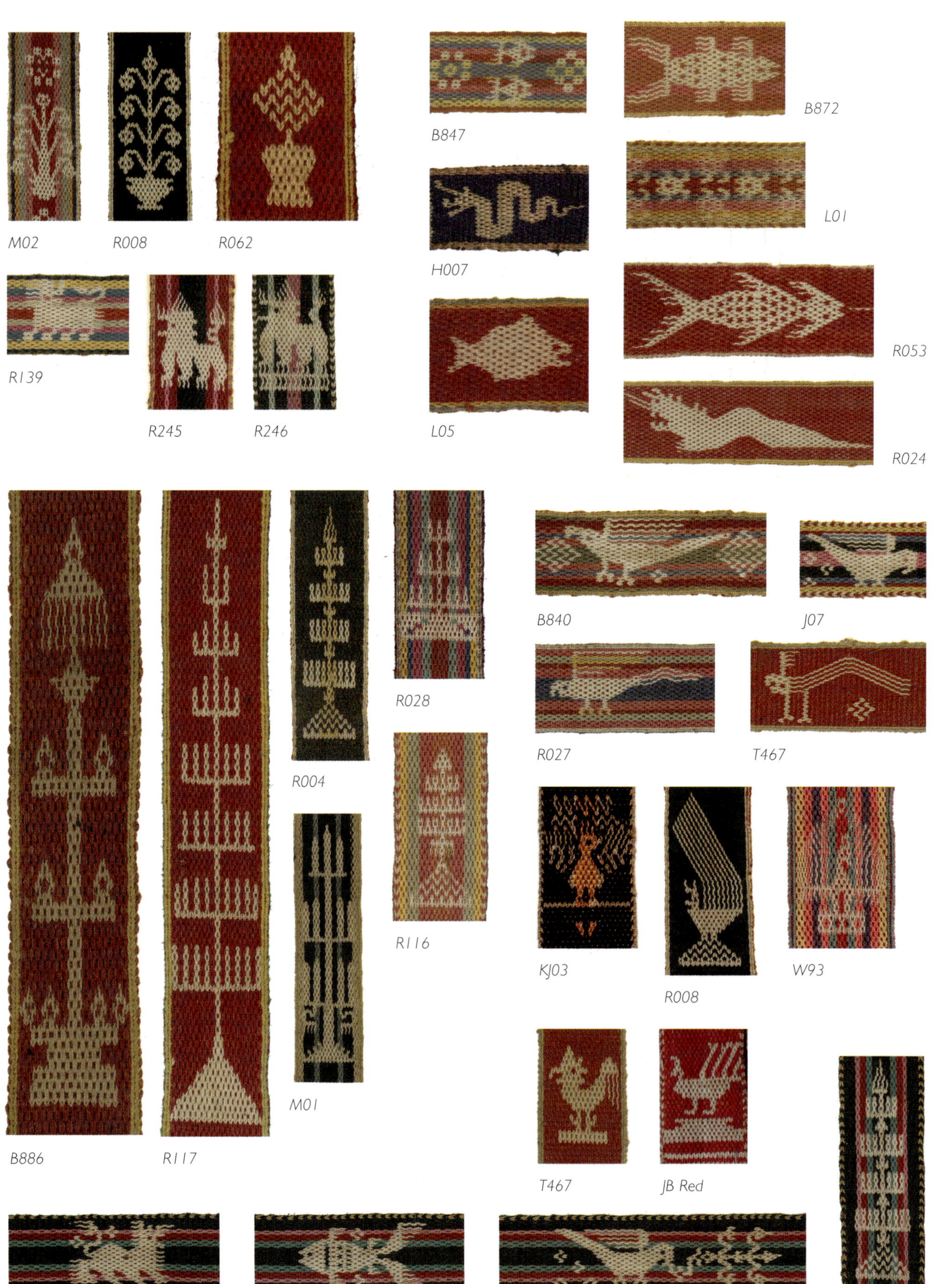

M02 R008 R062 B847 B872 H007 L01 R139 R245 R246 L05 R053 R024

B840 J07 R028 R004 R027 T467 R116 KJ03 R008 W93 M01 B886 R117 T467 JB Red R020

Plate 84 PREVIOUS PAGE
WOVEN IMAGES OF THE FOUR GREAT ELEMENTS
The Four Great Elements are earth, air, fire, and water. Known in Burmese as the Mahabok, they are used by astrologers to select an auspicious date for the donation, and their symbols appear on sazigyo. The earth can be represented by a tree in a pot, or a beast such as a lion. Fish, frogs, or *nagas* stand for the watery element, a candelabrum for fire, and a bird for air. Rarely all four elements of the Mahabok appear in a sequence of four images.

EARTH
Earth can have a tree for its symbol. *(M02, R008, R062)*
Or it can have a beast which walks the earth, such as a lion. *(R139, R245, R246)*

WATER
Water is the element for frogs, fish, and *nagas* (serpent-dragons). *(B847, B872, H007, L01, L05, R053, R024)*

FIRE
Fire is represented by a candelabrum. *(B886, R117, R004, R028, M01, R116)*

AIR
Air is the element of birds such as parrots *(B840, J07, R027, T467)*, peacocks *(KJ03, R008, W93)*, cockerel *(T467)*, or the mythical *hintha* bird. *(JB red)*

THE FOUR GREAT ELEMENTS
All four great elements may appear on a single sazigyo. *(R020)*

SYMBOLS OF THE FOUR GREAT ELEMENTS

The Mahabok (Pali: Mahabhuta) are commonly known as the Four Great or Primary Elements: earth, water, fire, and air. Their remit is wide indeed, encompassing both macrocosm and microcosm. Believed to make up the whole universe, they are the four basic properties of matter—solidity, fluidity, heat, and volatility—but they also cover "external" elements outside the body (mountains, rivers, fire, and wind) and "internal" elements, components, and functions of the human body (such as flesh, blood, ageing, and flatulence). Astrologers use a system based on the Mahabok to cast horoscopes that determine a person's future fortune, and to select an auspicious day and hour for the performance of a religious ritual, such as the donation of a manuscript with its sazigyo. So it is not surprising to find the four powerful elements of the Mahabok represented on sazigyo.

When the symbols of the Four Great Elements appear close together in a series of four woven images they can most clearly be seen to represent the Mahabok. In these sets of four, fire is always a candelabrum, water almost always a fish, and air a bird, though the bird species varies. Earth is sometimes a tree, sometimes a terrestrial beast. When one of these images appears alone, its identification as a symbol of one of the Four Great Elements must be made with caution.

BIRTHDAY BEASTS

Every Burmese man, woman, and child has a weekly "birth-day." The Burmese, like many other cultures, name their days of the week after the planets. There are nine planets in Burmese astrology. The mythical dark planet, Kate, appears only at eclipses. The other eight each govern a day of the Burmese week. The requisite eight-day week is obtained by dividing Wednesday into two "days." Until 6 PM it is Wednesday, but from 6 PM to midnight it is the day of the planet Rahu.

Four planets, those of Monday, Wednesday, Thursday, and Friday, are regarded by astrologers as "benefics," whose influence on the affairs of humans is benign. The other four, those of Sunday, Tuesday, Saturday, and Rahu, are "malefics," capable of wielding a contrary, negative influence. Kate is considered the most powerful planet, and benign, but Kate does not directly govern man's fate. Besides a weekly "birth-day," every Burmese man, woman, and child has a tutelary beast, the vehicle of the planet governing that day of the week. Sunday's planet rides on a *galon*, the Burmese name for garuda. Monday's planet rides on a tiger, Tuesday's on a lion. Wednesday's vehicle is an elephant with tusks, while Rahu's is a tuskless elephant, a *haing*, believed to be more powerful than a tusker. Thursday's planet rides on a rat, and Friday's on a beast called *pu*. This is usually translated into English as "guinea pig," an error which is discussed below. Saturday's planet rides on a *naga*. The

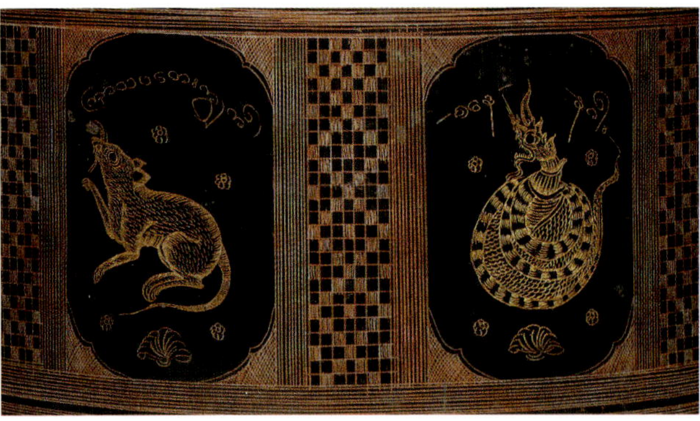

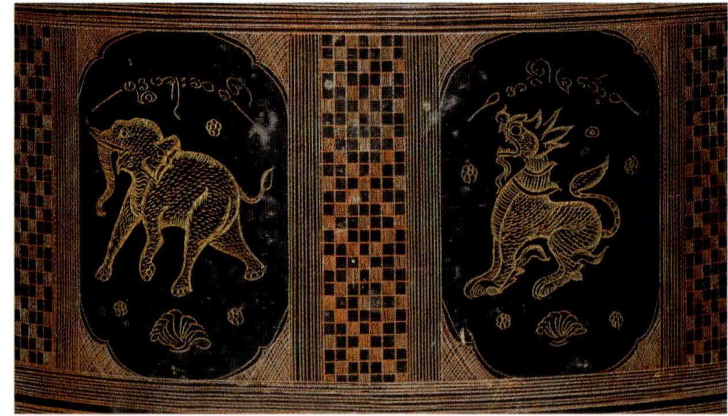

Plate 85 ABOVE LEFT AND RIGHT
The eight birthday beasts commonly appear on lacquer betel-boxes in a ring on the top of the lid, but on this box they occupy large cartouches around the sides of the cover. Thursday's beast is the rat, and Saturday's the *naga* (serpent-dragon) (left). Wednesday's beast is the tusked elephant, and Tuesday's is the *chinthe* bearded lion (right).

Plate 86 BELOW
Eight birthday or planet posts on the pagoda platform mark the eight major points of the compass. A devotee garlands the white marble Buddha image and pours a libation at the planet post for Wednesday. Her birthday beast is the tusked elephant.

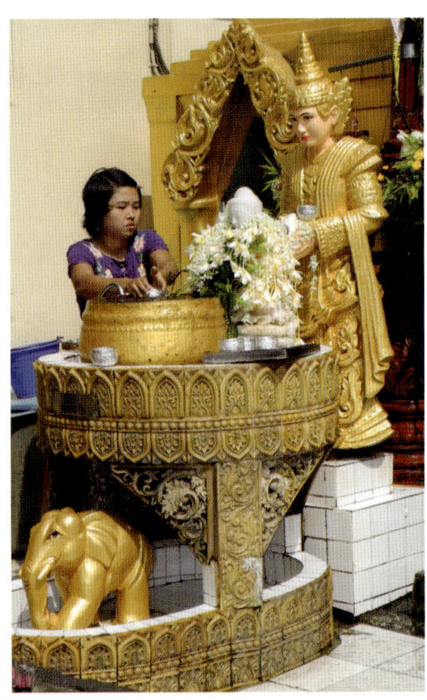

mount for the dark ninth planet, Kate, is the mythical composite *pyinsarupa*, or beast of five body forms, whom we shall meet again later.

Each planet is associated with a compass direction. Planet posts (*gyo-daing*) stand at the cardinal points of the compass around the pagoda platform, each depicting not the god of the planet but his animal vehicle. Devout Buddhists head for their own planet post to pray and to make offerings. However, if their astrologer informs them that they are under the influence of a "malefic" planet, they will also offer special propitiatory prayers at its post.

The eight planetary beasts design, known in Burmese as *gyo-shit-myo*, is common on silver bowls and especially popular on lacquer betel boxes. Many have both a full set of twelve zodiac signs and a set of all eight "birthday beasts." The host would pass his betel box round a social gathering, sure that each of his guests would recognize his own guardian planet and zodiac sign. But though the *gyo-shit-myo* design as a full set of eight birthday beasts is common on lacquerware, it is extremely rare on sazigyo. The only known example is a pink silk sazigyo (T1223), the subject of a special note in appendix 4. Some birthday beasts are frequent on sazigyo, others rare, and some are absent—so donors could not have inserted their birthday beast routinely.

The lion is by far the most common beast on sazigyo, and some of these may be Tuesday's birthday beast. Unless disguised as a lion, Monday's tiger is absent from sazigyo. Wednesday morning's tusked elephant certainly occurs, but the tuskless elephant (Burmese: *haing*) of Wednesday evening makes its single appearance on the pink silk sazigyo (T1223) on which (uniquely) all eight are depicted. A pair of remarkably naturalistic rats face to face on one sazigyo may indicate that both the donor and his wife were Thursday-born. Friday's beast is the round-bottomed tailless beast whose Burmese name is *pu*, commonly translated as "guinea pig." In zoological terms no guinea pig lives in Asia. But the *pu* inhabits the realms of mythology, and in any case it is rare: the only sighting of a woven *pu* is on the pink silk sazigyo mentioned above. If the *pu* has any remote animal ancestor, it could perhaps be one of several species of hamster that live in the lower foothills of the Himalayas. Saturday's *naga*, the serpent-dragon, and Sunday's garuda (Burmese: *galon*) both occur on sazigyo, and may represent the donor's birthday beast.

Plate 87 RIGHT

WOVEN IMAGES OF LIONS

Lions appear on sazigyo in many different forms. Some of these may be the birthday beast for Tuesday-born folk. *(L05, R218, R202, R004, R013, R051)*

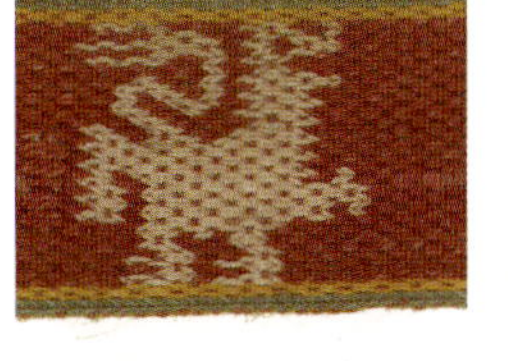

L05

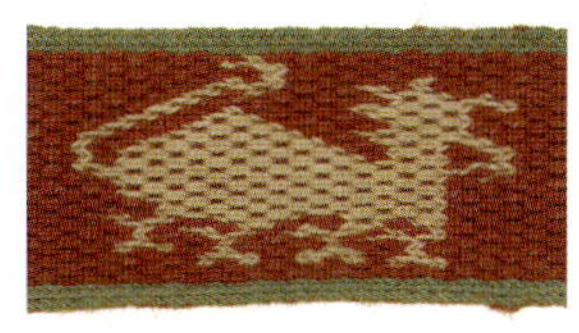

R218

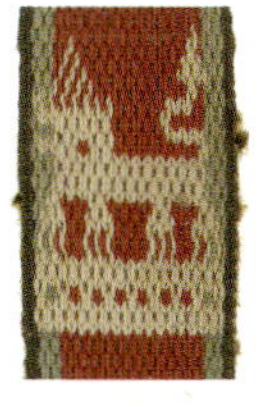

R202

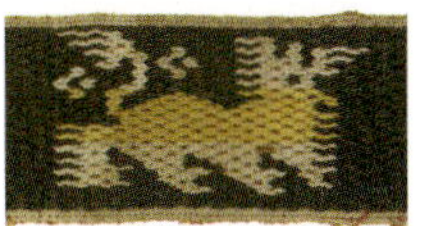

R004

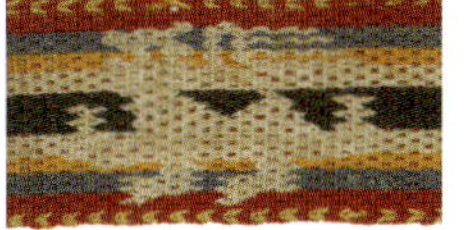

R013

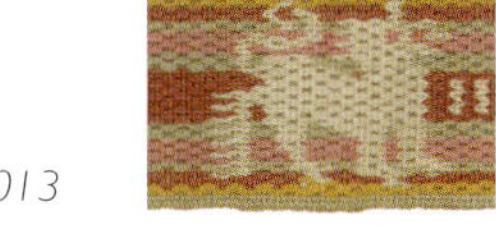

R051

Plate 88 CENTER

THE EIGHT BIRTHDAY BEASTS

Birthday beasts include the *naga* (serpent-dragon) for Saturday-born folk *(H007)*, the tusker, for those born on Wednesday before noon *(B877, H031)*, and the rat, for Thursday-born *(R193)*. Garuda is for the Sunday-born. *(R247, R304, R310)*

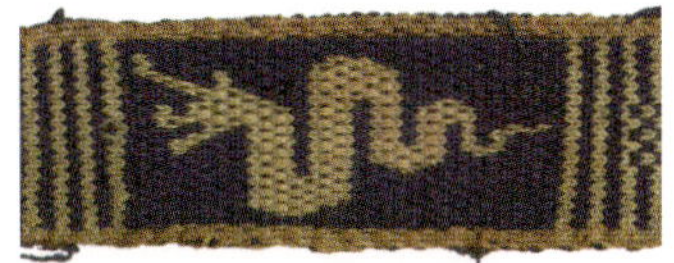

H007

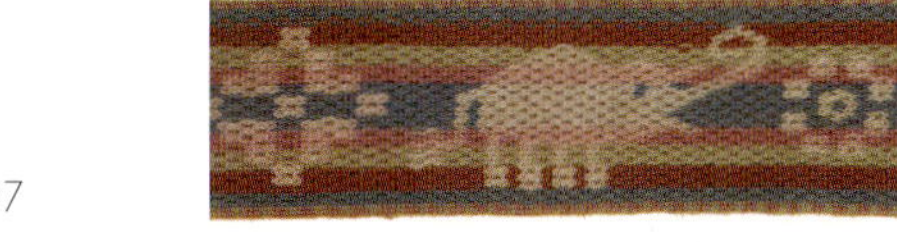

B877

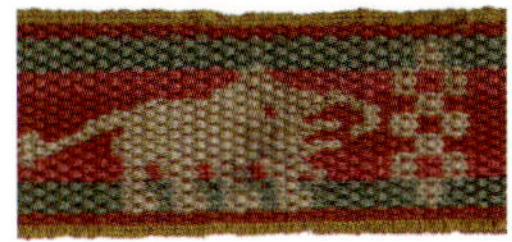

H031

R193

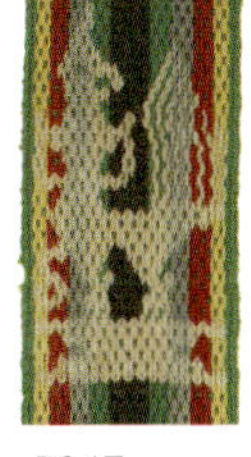

R247

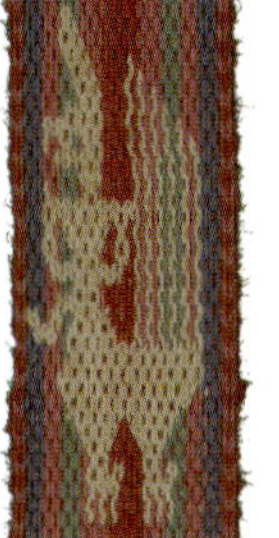

R304

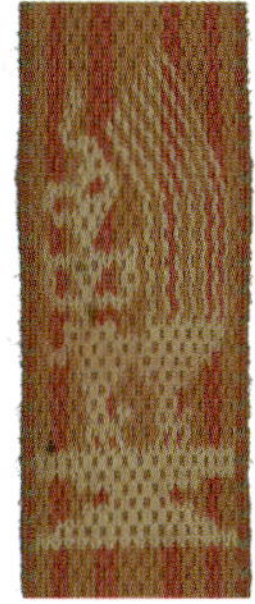

R310

BELOW RIGHT

ALL EIGHT BIRTHDAY BEASTS

All eight birthday beasts appear (uniquely) in the long text of this pink silk sazigyo. They appear one by one in the order of the compass positions they govern, clockwise from northwest, and they act as paragraph markers. *(T1223)*

(1) *Galon* (garuda) for Sunday

(2) Tiger for Monday

(3) *Chinthe* lion for Tuesday

(4) Tusker elephant for Wednesday forenoon

(5) *Naga* (serpent-dragon) for Saturday

(6) Rat for Thursday

(7) Tuskless elephant *(haing)* for Wednesday after noon

(8) *Pu* ("guinea-pig") for Friday

T1223

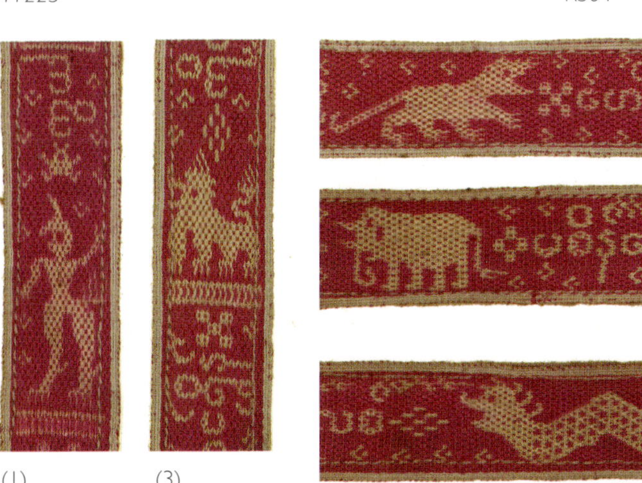

(1) (3) (2) (4) (5)

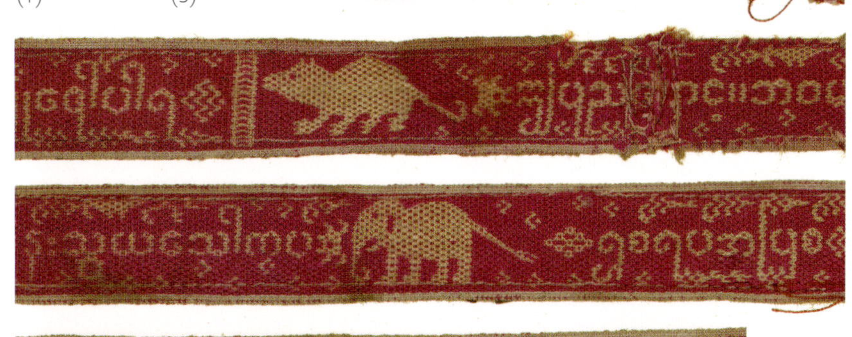

(6) (7)

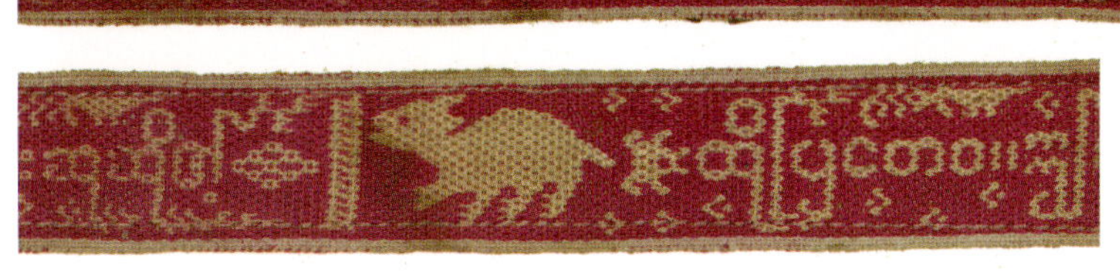

(8)

Plate 89 RIGHT AND BELOW
Signs of the zodiac are a common decorative theme on lacquer and silver vessels, such as this Shan silver bowl (right). The Pagan lacquer betel-box (below) has the twelve signs of the zodiac around the sides of the cover, and the eight planetary animals, or birthday beasts, in a ring on the top of the lid.

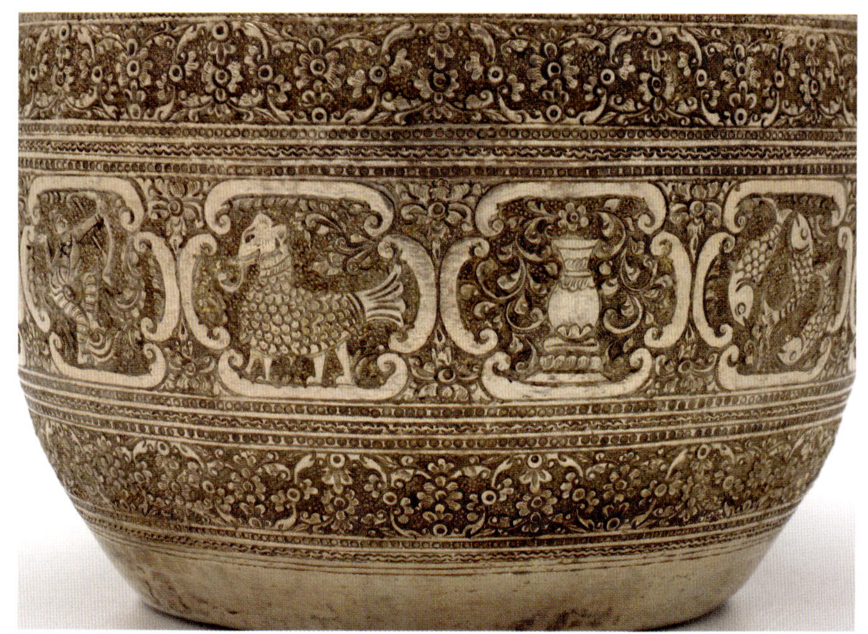

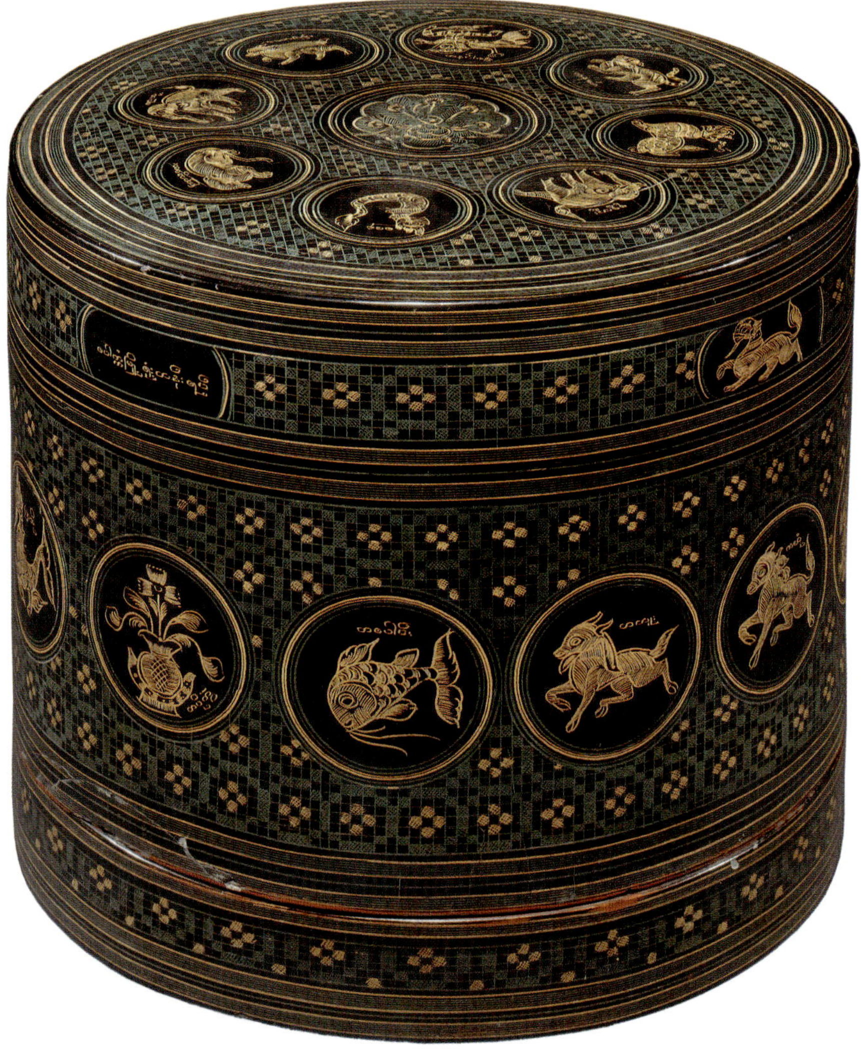

Plate 90 BELOW

WOVEN IMAGES OF ZODIAC SIGNS

Some images on sazigyo are surely zodiac signs. Aries, the ram, is the sign for April. *(M02, R179)*

Gemini, pairs of cranes, or *kinnara*, for June. *(BM246, H031, R173, R247, T467, R311)*

Leo, the lion, for August. *(B884, R020)*

Scorpion for November. *(R005, NIU)*

Capricorn is the *makara*, sea monster, for January. *(H017, R024)*

Aquarius, water pot or plant pot, for February. *(R027, R026)*

Pisces, paired fishes, for March. *(B847, R059, R005)*

ZODIAC SIGNS

Many (but not all) of the twelve signs of the zodiac (*yathi*) can be found among the woven images on sazigyo. Of those that do occur, one is unequivocally a sign of the zodiac: the scorpion, for the month of Tazaungmon. The water pot for Aquarius, the sign for the month of Tabodwe, is often depicted as a vase of flowers. But a plant in a pot need not signify Aquarius: it may symbolize earth, the first of the Four Elements, and if the plant is a Bo tree it may even stand for the Buddha himself. Fish are abundant on sazigyo. Many merely punctuate the text. A single large fish may represent the element of water, but paired fish may be interpreted as Pisces, the sign for the month of Tabaung. Pairs of *kinnara*, man-birds, symbolize constancy and marital fidelity, and may be the zodiac sign of Gemini for the month of Nayon. Some of the numerous lions found prowling on sazigyo may quite possibly represent the zodiac sign Leo, for the month of Wagaung. Zodiac figures absent from sazigyo are the ox of Taurus, crab of Cancer, virgin of Virgo, scales of Libra, and the archer of Sagittarius.

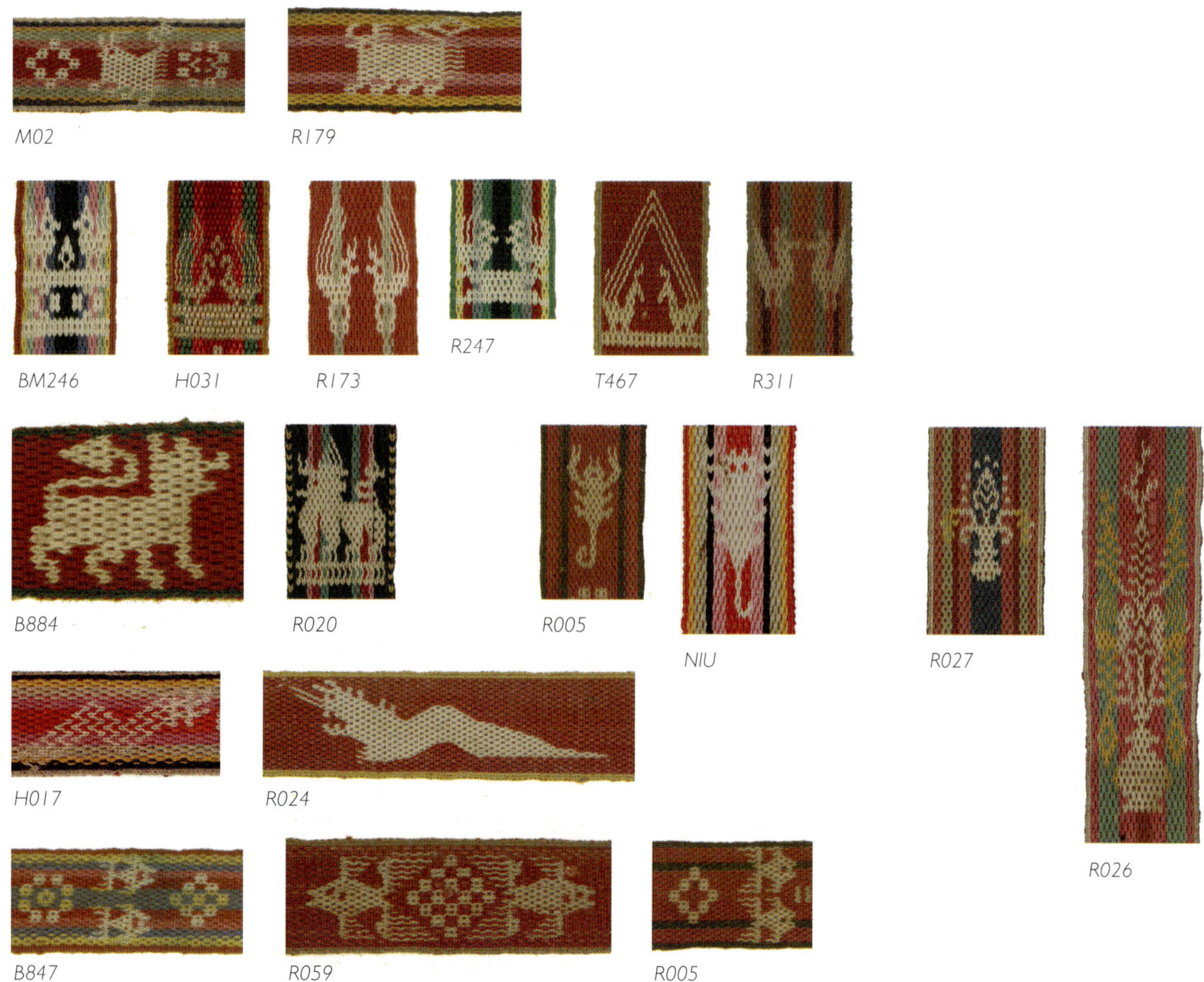

M02 *R179*

BM246 *H031* *R173* *R247* *T467* *R311*

B884 *R020* *R005* *NIU* *R027*

H017 *R024* *R026*

B847 *R059* *R005*

Plate 91 RIGHT

The *hsun-ok* is an offertory vessel with a waisted stem and tall spired cover, shaped rather like a pagoda.

Plate 92 BELOW

WOVEN IMAGES OF *HSUN-OK*

These little woven images of offering vessels symbolize the act of donation, which includes the sazigyo itself. *(B840, R207, R222, R128, H006, R128)*

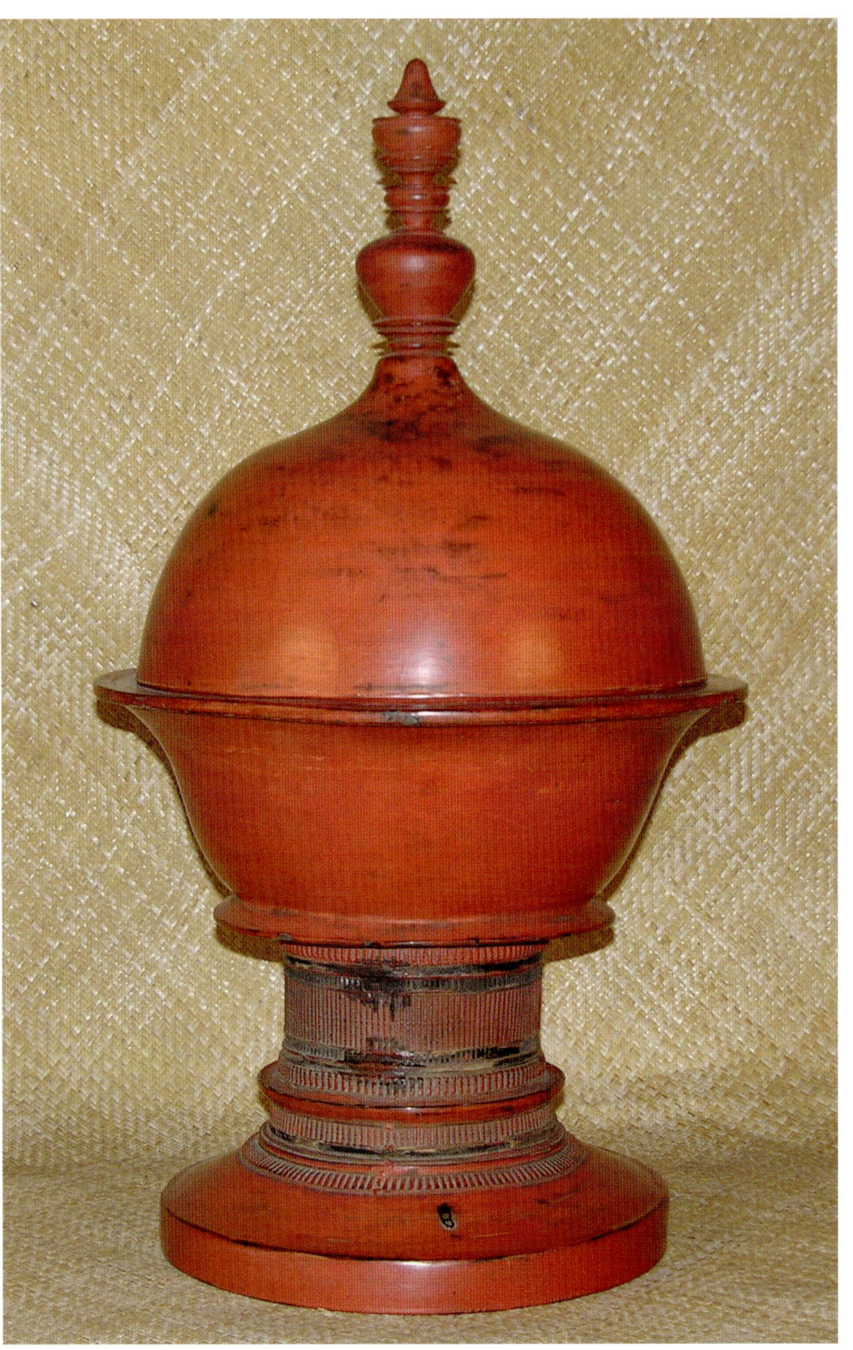

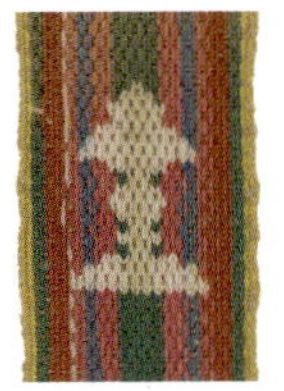

B840

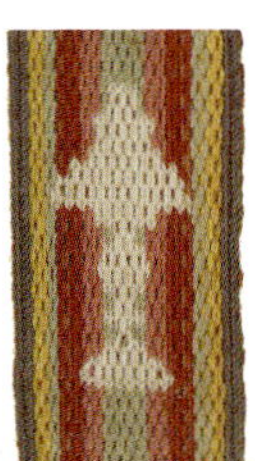

R207

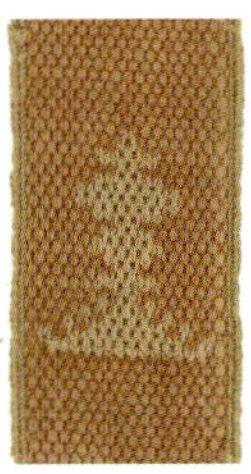

R222

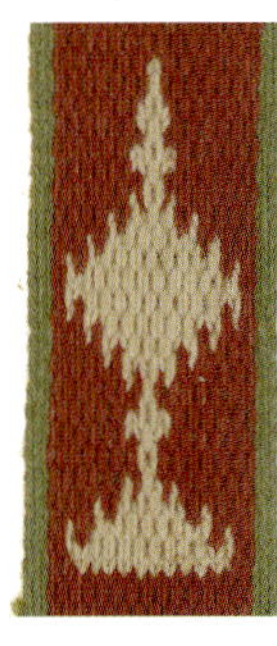

R128

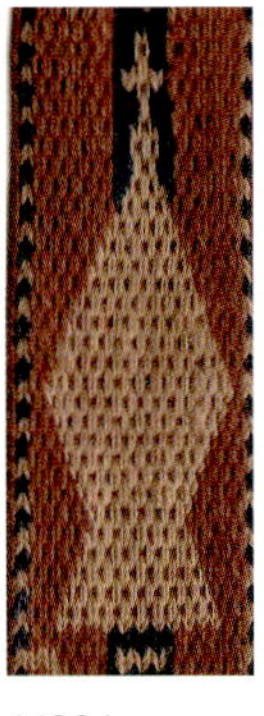

H006

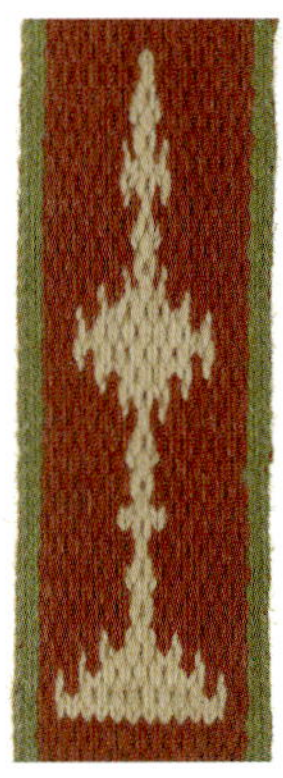

R128

Plate 93 RIGHT
The *kalat* is an open shallow tray on a stand, used mainly for gifts other than food, such as robes or manuscripts.

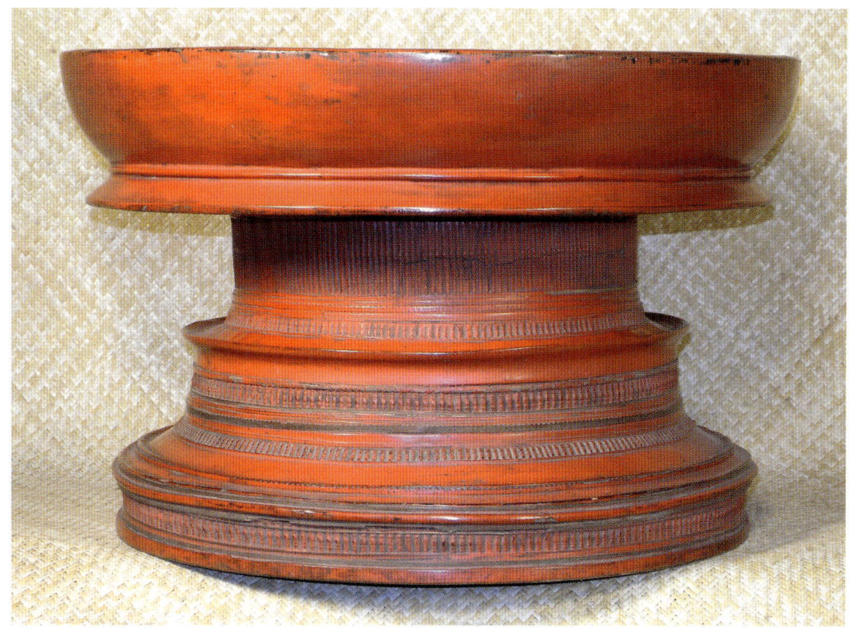

Plate 94 BELOW
WOVEN IMAGES OF *KALAT*
On sazigyo, woven images of *kalat* represent the merit-earning deed of donation. When they appear at the very end of the text, they sum up the donation. Rectangular objects depicted lying upon the tray represent the manuscripts being donated. The fine plump bird sitting on the tray can be read as a symbol of the auspiciousness of the donation. *(R272, B839, JB Red, R103, R128, KJ02)*

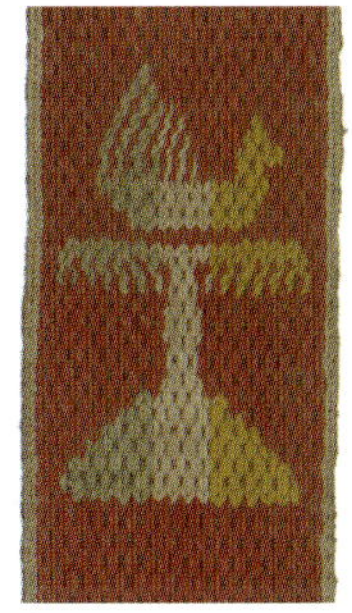
R272

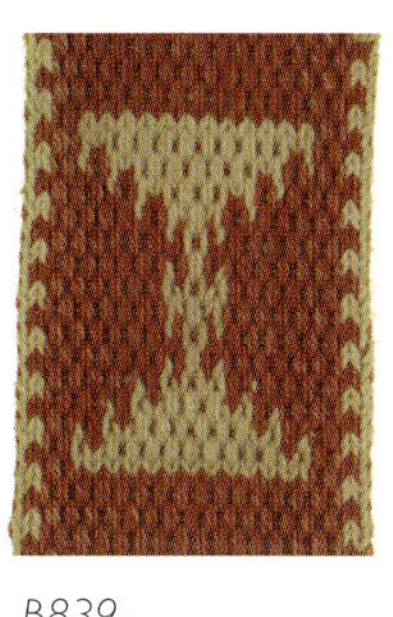
B839

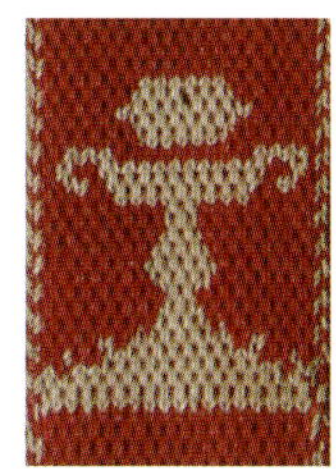
JB Red

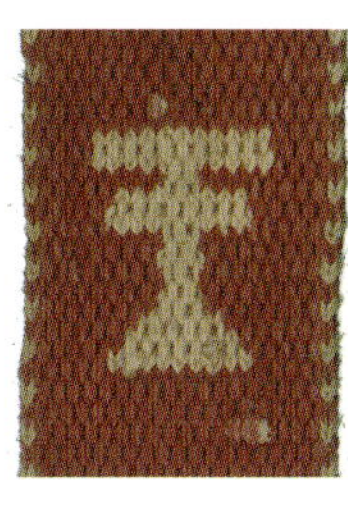
R103

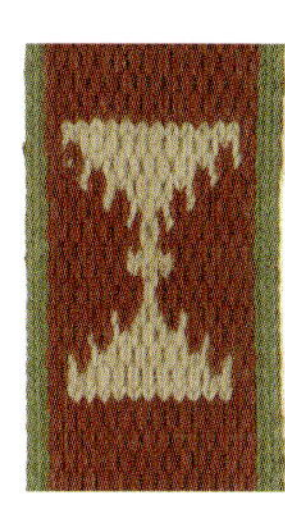
R128

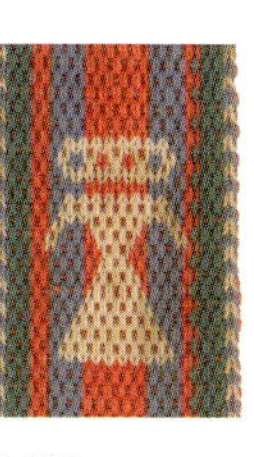
KJ02

SYMBOLS OF DONATION

Leaving the airy realms of astrology, we return to more solid ground. Pure Theravada Buddhist merit-seeking by donation is the right true end of sazigyo. Every sazigyo records a donation, and every sazigyo formed part of that donation. So it is natural that many sazigyo carry woven images symbolizing the meritorious act of *dana*. The objects chosen as symbols of donation are all in some sense containers for the gift. These include two kinds of offertory vessels, "trees-of-plenty" (*padaythabin*), and miniature chariots with multi-tiered *pyatthat* roofs.

Real *hsun-ok* and *kalat* are offertory vessels, containers used exclusively for donations. They are made of wood or bamboo basketry, lacquered black or red, sometimes gilt. The *hsun-ok* consists of a capacious bowl on an integral stand, with a tall spired lid or cover that in profile resembles a stupa. It is used to contain gifts for the monks, usually of food. The *kalat* is an open shallow tray on a stand, like a "dumb waiter." It is used mainly for non-food gifts, such as robes or manuscripts.

Plate 95 RIGHT

Procession of maidens carrying gilt *hsun-ok*.

Plate 96 BELOW RIGHT

A *padaythabin* ("tree of plenty") hung with gifts and equipped with shafts for carrying by four men.

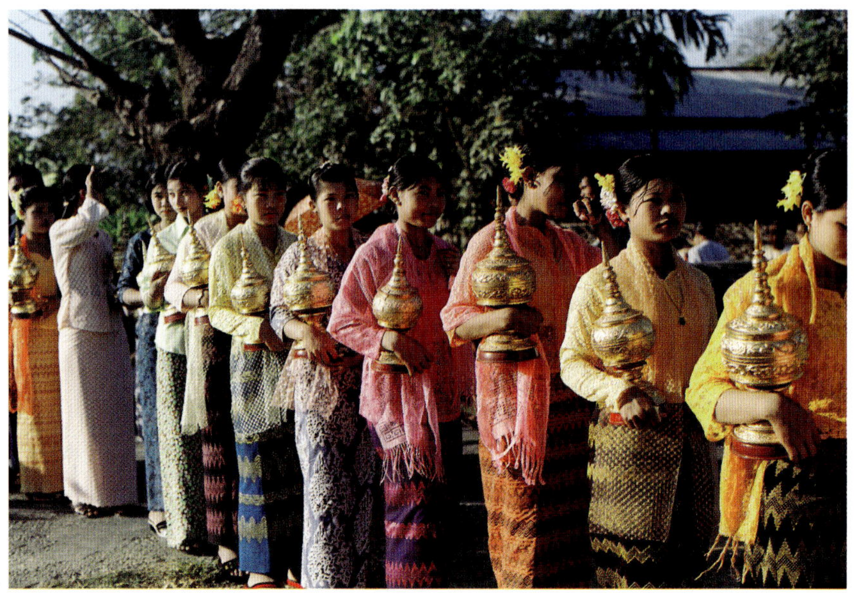

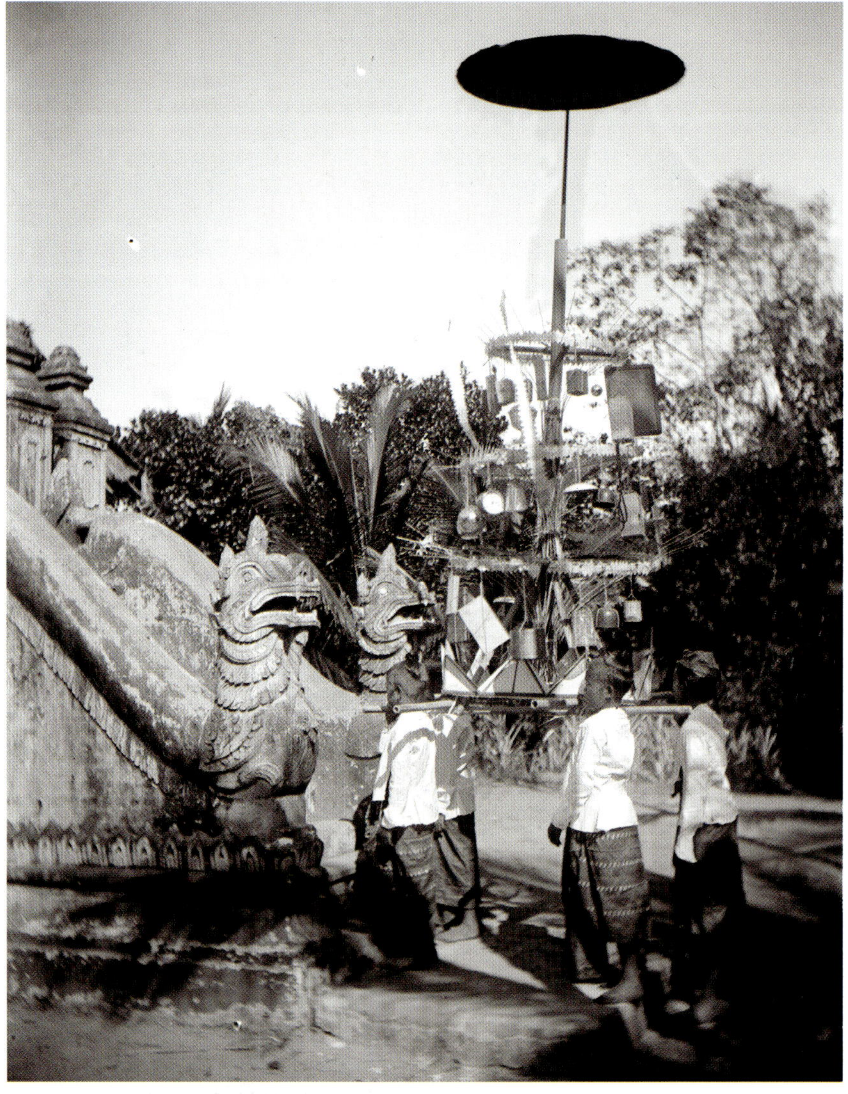

Plate 97 RIGHT

A procession of *padaythabin* at a *pongyibyan*, the elaborate funeral ceremony for a senior monk.

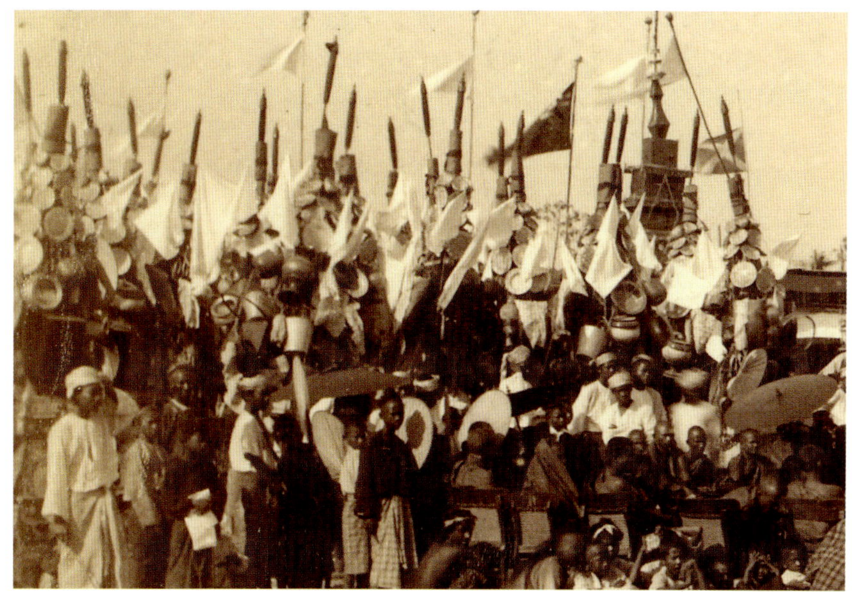

Plate 98 BELOW

WOVEN IMAGES OF *PADAYTHABIN* – TREES OF PLENTY

The most frequent symbols of donation found on sazigyo are *padaythabin*. Weavers enjoy inventing many variations. *(B852, R018, B872, R008, R027, R051, R007, R055, R202, R026, R059)*

The eight birds on a high-rise perch may hold some private meaning for the donor or weaver. *(R270)*

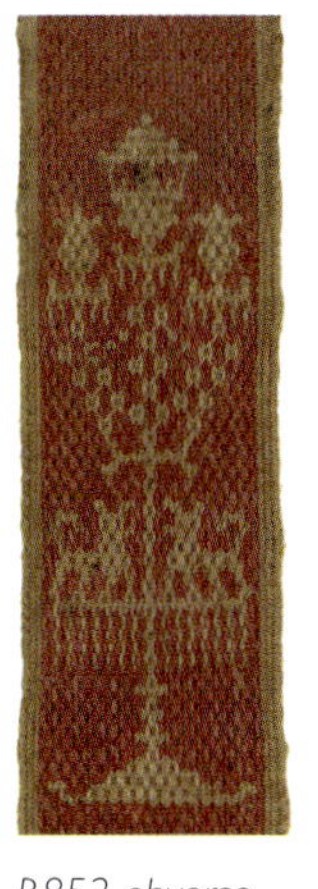

B852 obverse

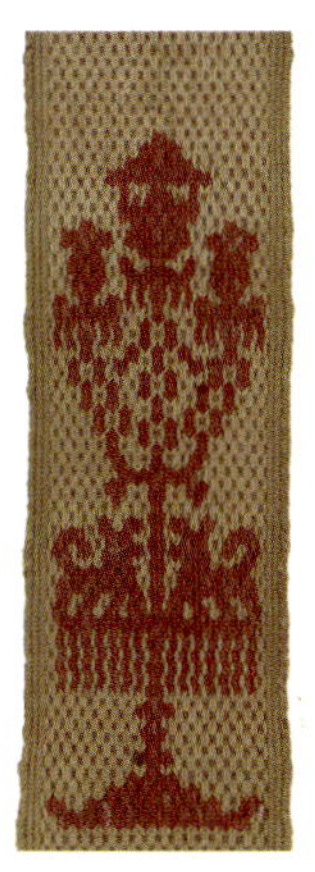

B852 reverse

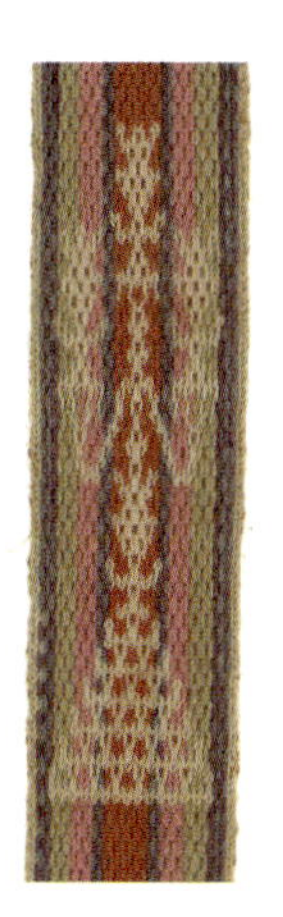

R018

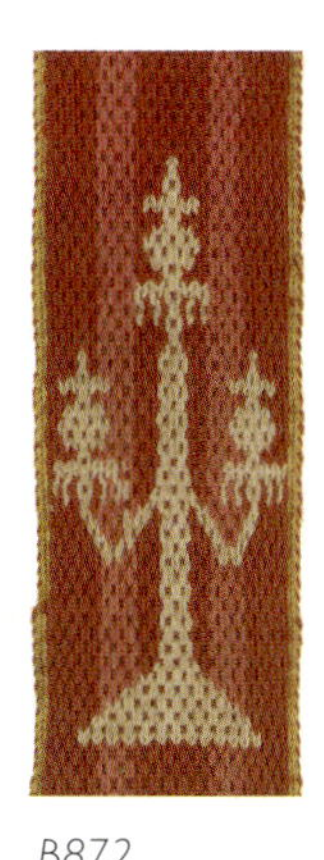

B872

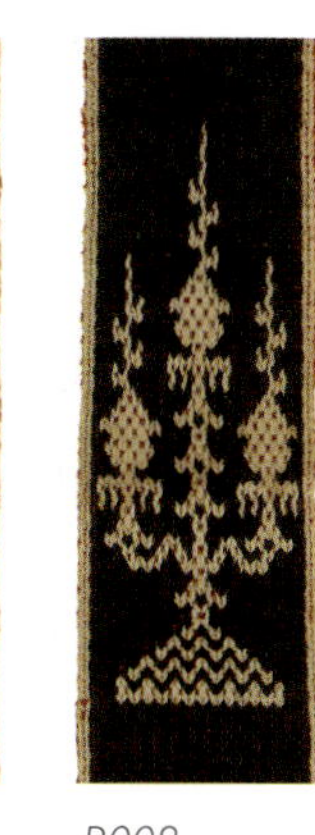

R008

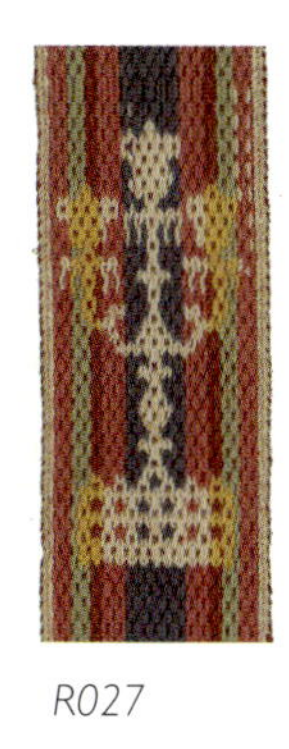

R027

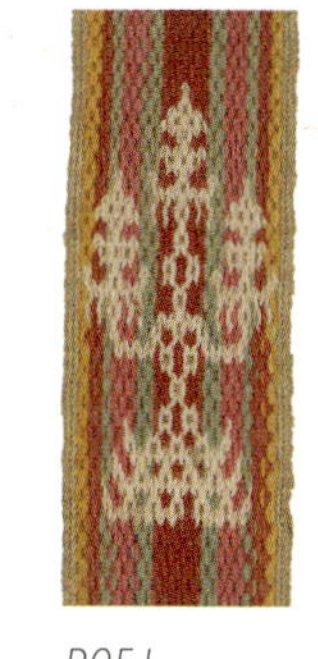

R051

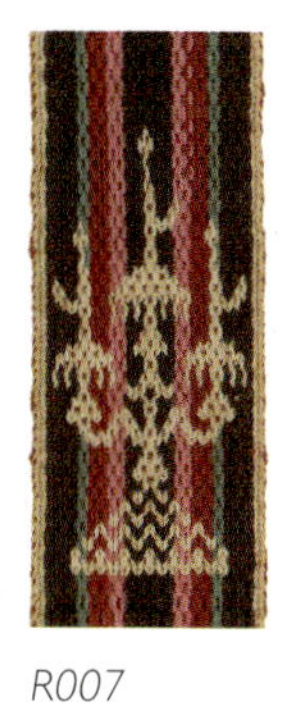

R007

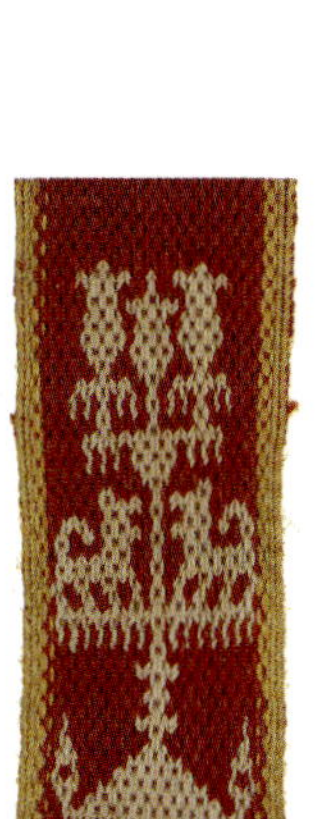

R055

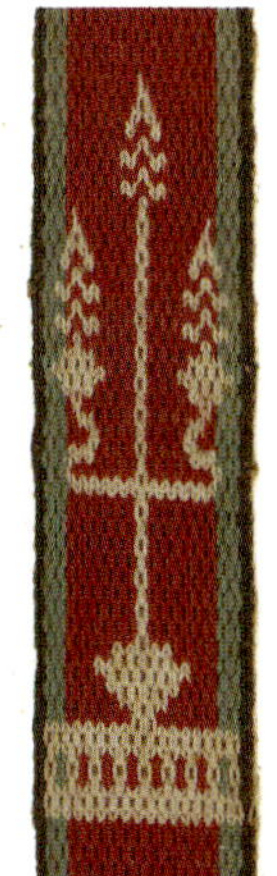

R202

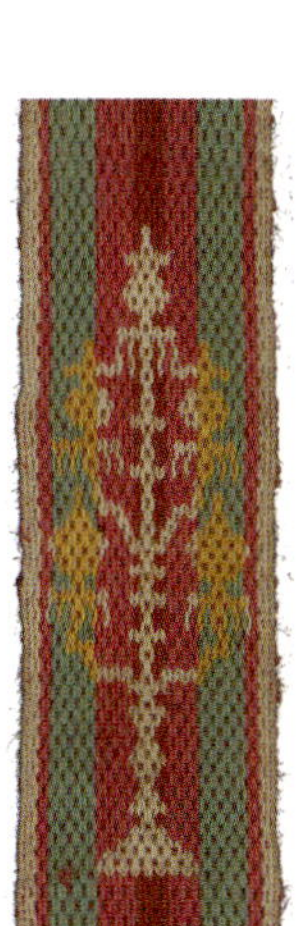

R026

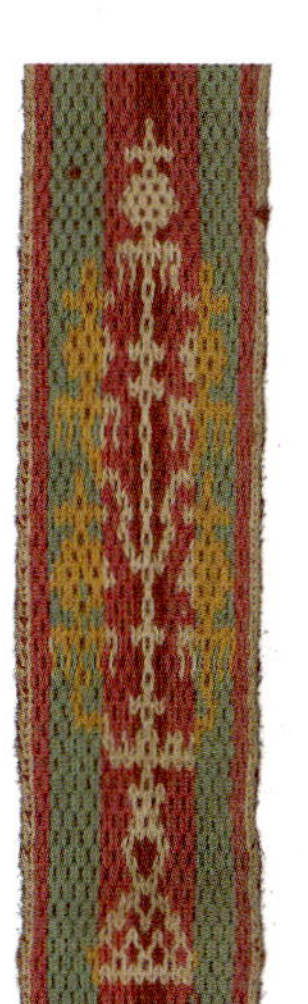

R026

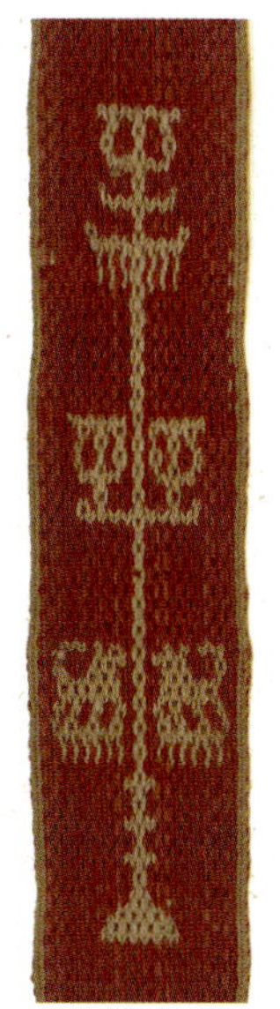

R059

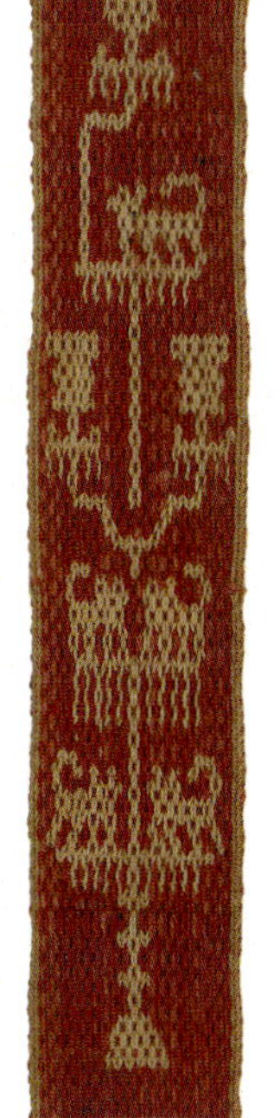

R059

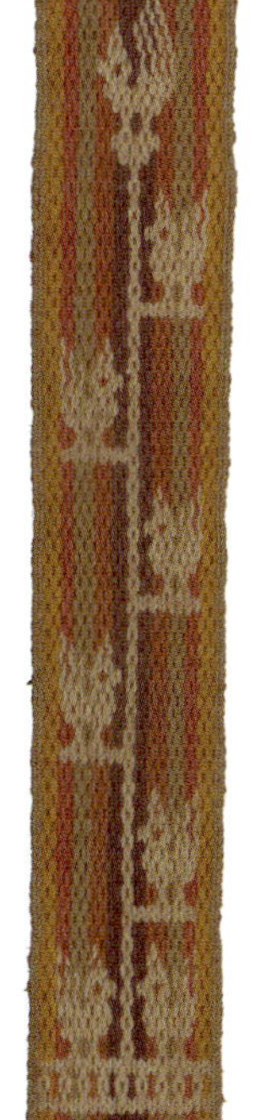

R270

When images of these offertory vessels occur on sazigyo, they are unequivocally symbols of donation, and they have a double significance. They symbolize *dana*, the supreme virtue of generosity; and they also stand for the specific donation of the manuscript with its sazigyo. In some of these images of *kalat* rectangular objects are depicted lying upon the open tray, which surely represent the manuscripts being donated. Quite often this image is the last on the sazigyo, placed just before the cord, a visual summary of the deed of merit.

Most abundant of the many donation symbols on sazigyo are *padaythabin*, or trees of plenty. Tree-like wooden trestles, like huge pyramidal coat stands, are erected in public places during the Kathina festival, when the community organizes the public offering of robes and other gifts for the monks. This festival is of very ancient origins, and may claim to be the only monastic ceremony in which the laity are integrally involved. Daw Khin Myo Chit[7] describes how after the end of the monsoon, in the month of Tazaungmon:

> triangular wooden structures stand in the market places or in decorated marquees by the roadside. Each structure is hung with gifts, such as sets of yellow robes, towels, napkins, cups and other useful items. These are Kathina gifts, and anyone is welcome to hang up whatever he wishes to contribute, a one-kyat note, or a handkerchief or a cake of soap—however small his offering. The structures hung with gifts are called *padaytha* trees. The word *padaytha* is synonymous with inexhaustible wealth. The story of the *padaytha* tree dates back to the beginning of the world when human beings on the Northern Island lived to be a thousand years, but never looked older than eighteen. They were pure of heart. They had a *padaytha* tree which bore everything that a human being could ever wish for. If one felt like eating a special food, one just went and plucked it from the tree. If one wished to wear a beautiful dress, it was right there for the taking. The only rule was that one should take only what one could use for the day, and no more.

But humans were weak. They craved possessions, and would not trust each other to take only what they needed. Hoarding led to quarrels and to fighting, in which the wonderful tree was destroyed.

> The original *padaytha* tree is no more, but during the season of Tazaungdine it grows again in modern Burma . . . Human beings, once again, are generous and loving. They make trees bear all kinds of gifts, great and small. The great moment comes when the gift-laden *padaytha* trees are carried in triumph to the monastery, attended by musicians and dancers and young girls dressed in gorgeous silks.

FLYING CHARIOTS

Plate 99 BOTTOM LEFT
At the regilding of a pagoda, a gilt model chariot in the form of a *karaweik* bird is docked, ready to be loaded with a cargo of booklets of gold leaf.

Plate 100 BOTTOM CENTER
The chariot ascends on ropes and pulleys carrying its precious cargo to the pagoda where the regilding is under way.

Plate 101 BOTTOM RIGHT
The pagoda to be gilded is clad in matting. A slit-shaped doorway allows delivery of gold leaf by flying a chariot to the gilders at work.

This keeps alive the true spirit of offering, as taught by the Buddha.

Capt. Hiram Cox in 1796 witnessed a procession to the Shwedagon pagoda. It "bore pageants in the shape of trees, the branches loaded with clothes, betel and other necessaries for the priests."[8] On a few sazigyo a series of images of *padaythabin*, all slightly different, may represent just such a procession.

On sazigyo the many woven images of *padaytha* trees carry on their branches a triple symbolism: first, they stand for the manuscript donor's current act of donation; then for the virtue of generosity, *dana*, which it exemplifies; and more broadly still for freedom from want and a prosperous future. "Visit any pagoda," writes Daw Khin Myo Chit, "and when you put a coin into the donation box the man sitting with the triangular brass gong will accept the gift and intone a prayer for you, and amongst the things he will wish for you will be: 'May you have a *padaytha* tree right on your doorstep!'" Some of the woven *padaythabin* on sazigyo are depicted with tiny birds or lions perched on the branches. Lions and peacocks probably represent the cash value of the gifts, as we shall see when we consider the next type of woven image.

Perhaps the most charming of all the woven images symbolizing donation are the flying chariots, little model wheeled floats with tall multi-tiered *pyatthat* roofs. At the regilding of a pagoda, stalls sell booklets of gold leaf and offer pilgrims an opportunity to make merit. Their donations are loaded into a gilded miniature chariot modeled like a royal barge, its prow in the form of a *karaweik* bird.[9] This vehicle shoots up, propelled on ropes and pulleys, to deliver its golden cargo to the gilders at work behind a screen of woven matting high up on the pagoda. The flying car ascends to shrieks of delight from the donors' children, and cries of "*Thadu!*" ("Well done!") from bystanders.

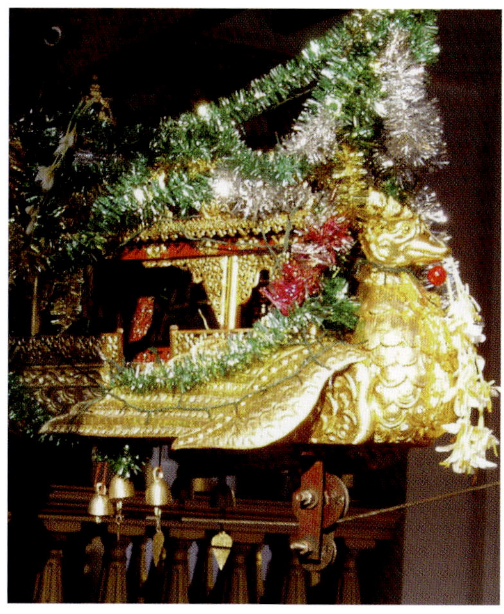

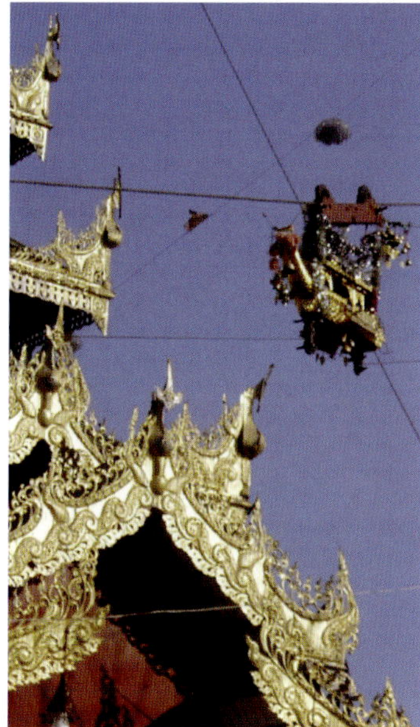

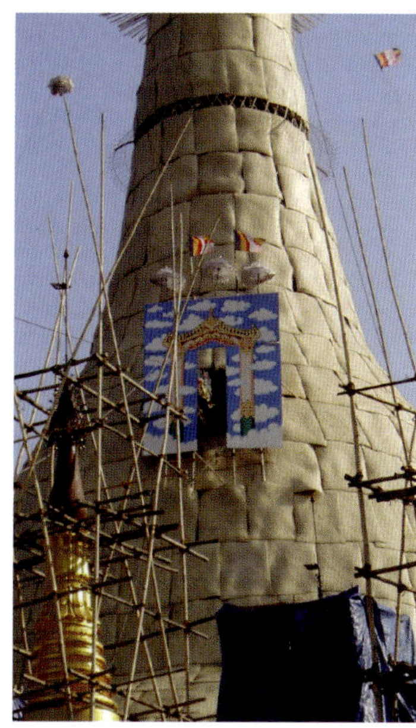

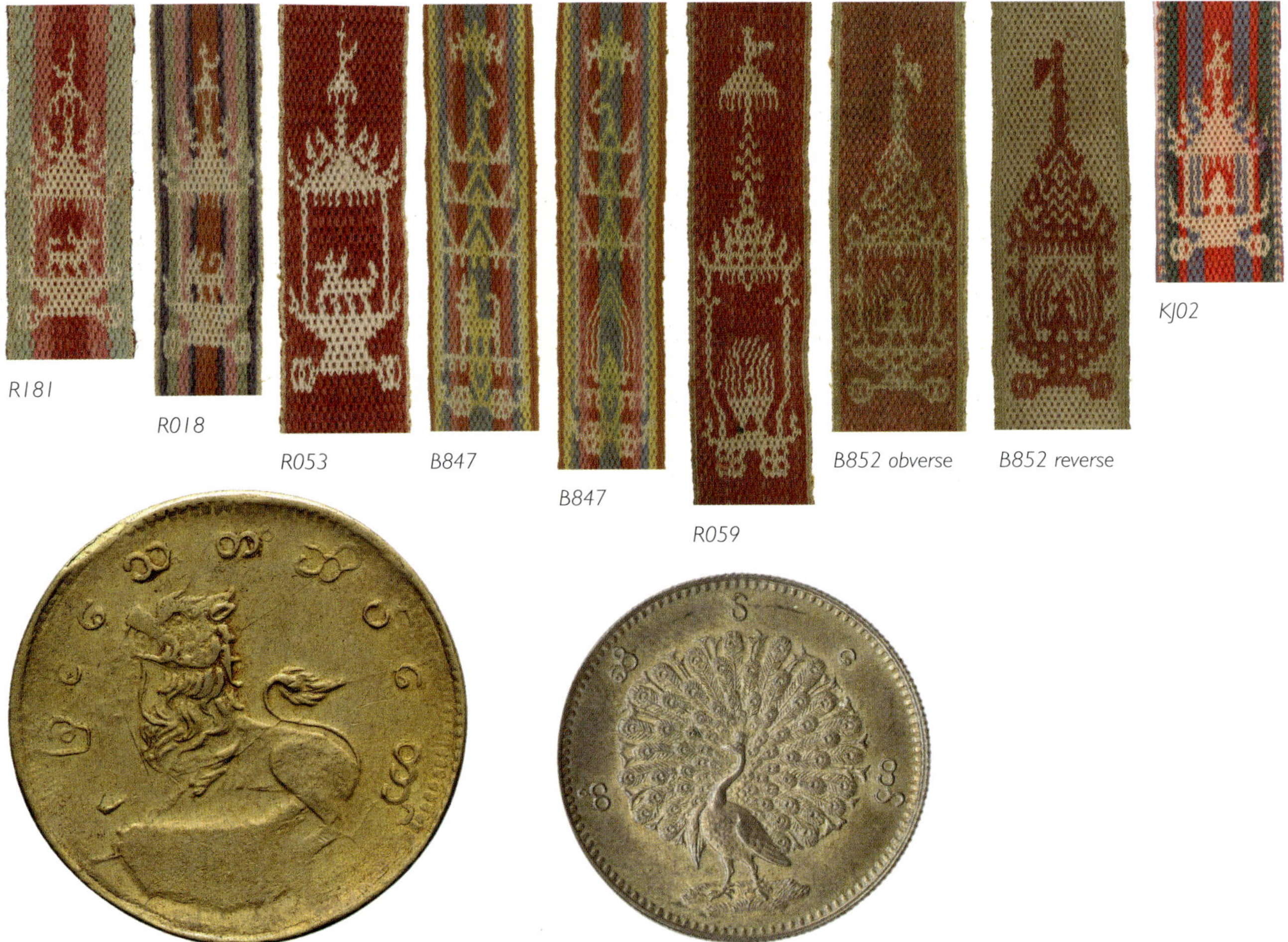

Plate 102 TOP
WOVEN IMAGES OF FLYING CHARIOTS
These little woven chariots are almost always in pairs, one carrying a lion passenger and the other a peacock:
Chariots with lion aboard *(R181, R018, R053)*
Pair of chariots *(B847)*
Chariots with peacock aboard *(R059, B852, KJ02)*

Plate 103 ABOVE
LEFT The lion appears on the gold coin of royal Burma.
RIGHT The peacock appears on the silver coin. Lion and peacock passengers depicted in the woven images of flying chariots on sazigyo represent the cash value of the donation.

Woven images of these flying carriages on the sazigyo symbolize the joy of *dana*, and the generosity of the donors. The chariots usually occur in pairs, and they are never empty: one has a lion aboard, the other a peacock. These passengers may represent the monetary value of the donation: the nineteenth-century coinage of royal Burma had a lion on the gold coin and a peacock on the silver.[10] One sazigyo weaver economized, depicting both passengers, lion and bird, riding together in a single chariot.

Yet another woven image symbolizes donation. The parasol (Burmese: *hti*) is a multiple symbol. In ancient India it signaled royal authority. In the early days of Buddhist art the parasol was one of several symbols used to represent the Buddha. In nineteenth-century royal Burma the number and color of parasols indicated rank in a complex hierarchy of sumptuary rules. White parasols formed part of the royal regalia, and gold was for less exalted ranks. Nowadays white or gilt or colored miniature paper *hti* are sold in stalls near the pagoda platform and included—in numbers and colors prescribed by the worshipper's astrologer—in all pagoda offerings. Their woven images on sazigyo are symbols of the meritorious act of donation.

PARASOLS

Plate 104 TOP RIGHT AND BELOW RIGHT
Gaily colored miniature paper umbrellas are sold in stalls on the pagoda steps.

Plate 105 BELOW LEFT
These little paper parasols form part of most offerings on the pagoda platform.

Plate 106 BOTTOM
WOVEN IMAGES OF PARASOLS
A parasol may symbolize the donation or the Buddha himself. *(R154, R107, R183, T441, W93, R245)*

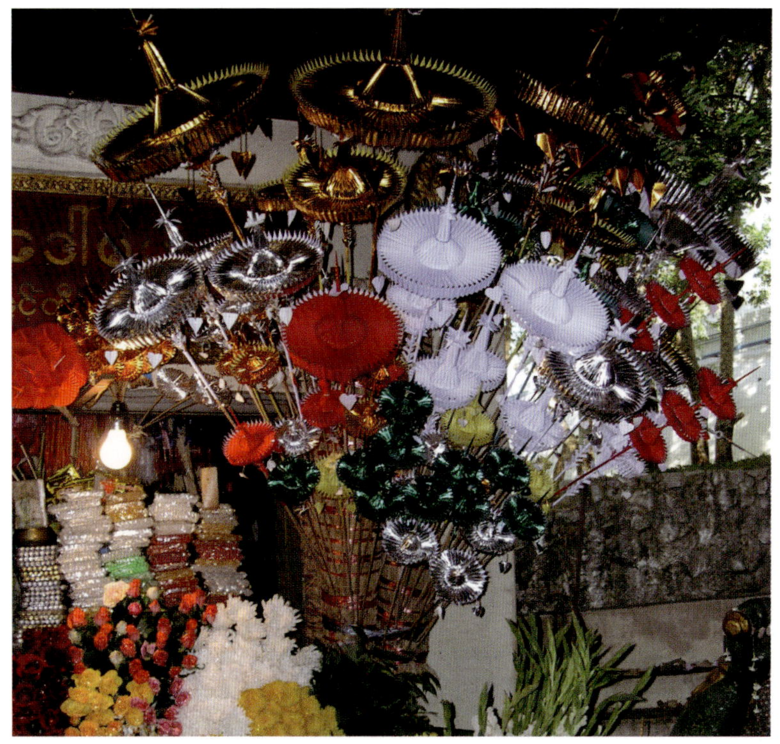

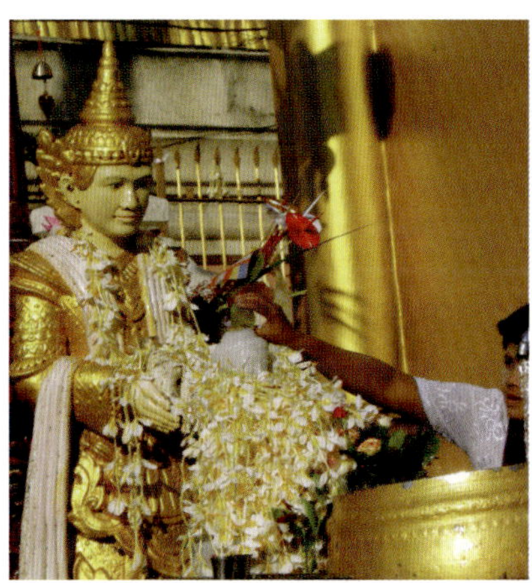

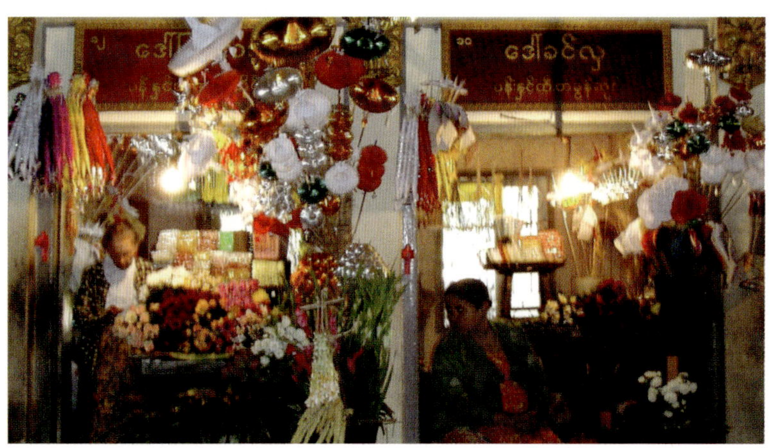

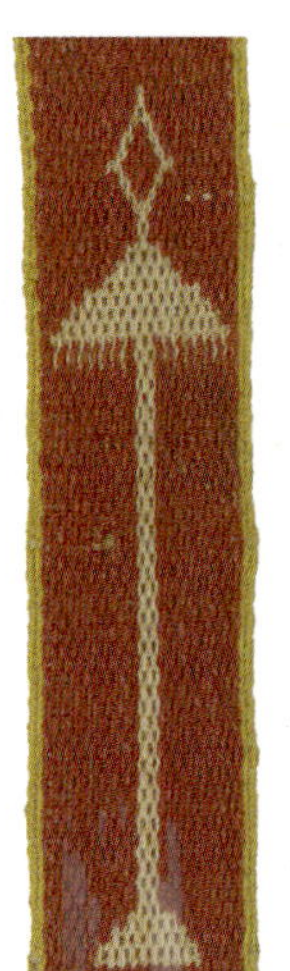

R154

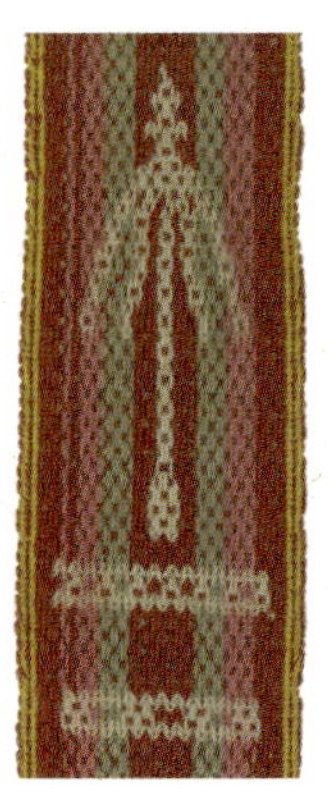

R107

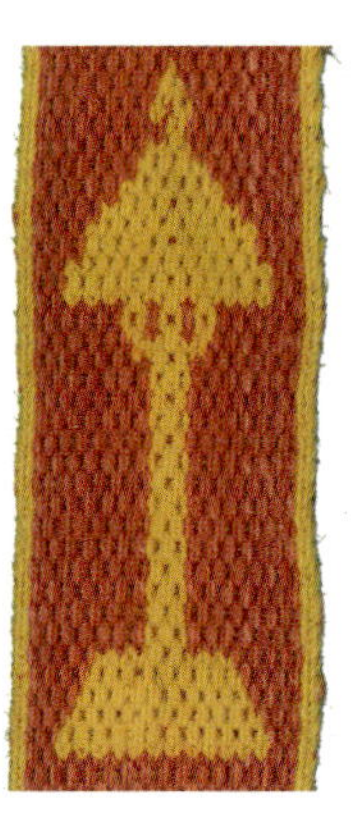

R183

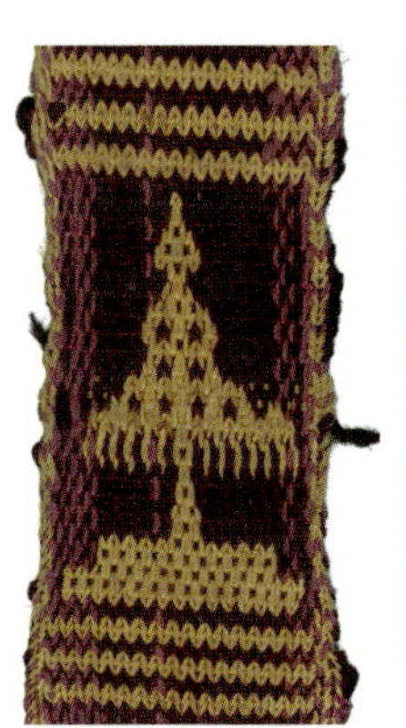

T441

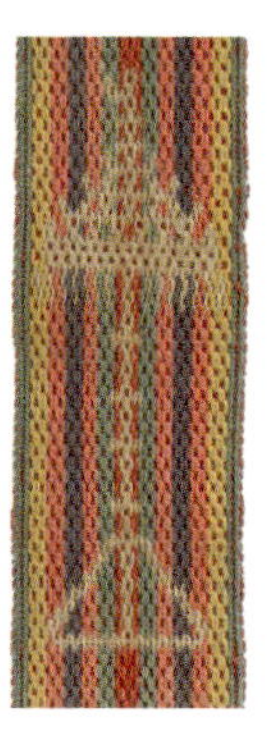

W93

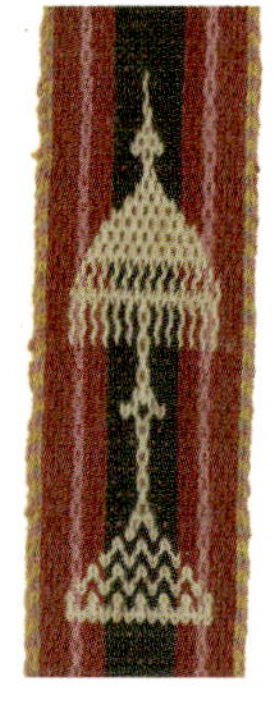

R245

Plate 107 BELOW

WOVEN IMAGES OF LIVING THINGS

Donors offer to share the merit of their donation with every family member, and often also with "all sentient beings in the cycle of existence." This logically includes animal members of the household, such as dogs, cats, horses, and a cockerel. *(Dogs: B844, R005. Cats: R001, R167, R203. Cockerel: T467. Horses: B854)*

The giant spotted gecko lives in house roofs, and its loud cry resounds indoors. *(H002, R075)*

Fish and frogs abound on sazigyo. They live in cool water and symbolize the cooling of the mind, the equanimity necessary to attain nirvana. *(B842, B847)*

The beast that looks "humped like a camel" may be a *samari*, a mythical beast related to the Tibetan yak. *(B872)*

The elephant, admired for its strength, might also be a birthday beast for Wednesday-born. *(H031)*

The peacock is a symbol of royalty. *(R270, KJ03)*

The crane, *kyo kya*, has a loud cry, which Burmese interpret as a shout of victory—but not over military adversaries. The Buddhist seeking nirvana must triumph over spiritual enemies, ignorance, anger, and greed. *(H021)*

OTHER BEASTS, WILD AND DOMESTIC

Donors pray to share the merit of their donation with parents, teachers, every family member, and with "all sentient beings in the cycle of existence." This last is a broad category and logically includes domestic animals, which might explain why woven images of cats and dogs appear on sazigyo. The same might apply to a favorite horse, or to a pair of horses. The giant spotted gecko may also qualify as a member of the household, since it has moved into men's wooden houses from its original forest habitat. It is named *tauk tek* after its loud cry, which is regarded as auspicious if nine times repeated. For four years my wife and I shared a house in Rangoon with a *tauk tek*, and one of our Burmese guests described it as a tree spirit, *yokka soe*. The crane, *kyo kya*, has a loud cry which Burmese interpret as a shout of victory over enemies—not military but spiritual. The Buddhist seeking nirvana must overcome the enemies within—ignorance, anger, greed.

A huge variety of creatures, both real and mythical, occur on sazigyo. There is a single, unexplained, appearance of a *samari*, a mythical beast distantly related to the Tibetan yak. Fish and frogs abound on sazigyo. Frogs have a loud insistent cry, and their use as punctuation in sazigyo texts could be to lend vehemence to the donor's prayer. Fish are silent, but like frogs they live in cool water. Both symbolize the cooling of the mind, in Burmese *tawara aye kyan*, the equanimity necessary to attain nirvana.

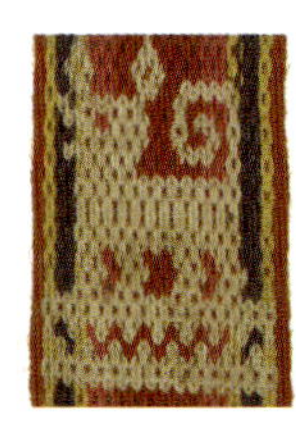
B844

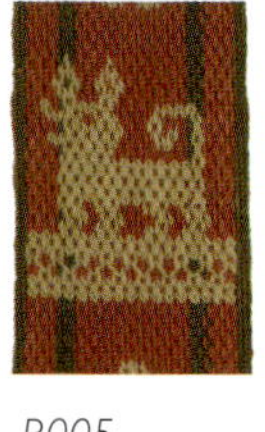
R005

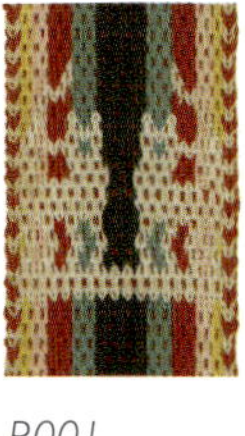
R001

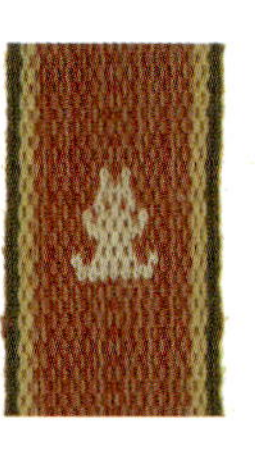
R167

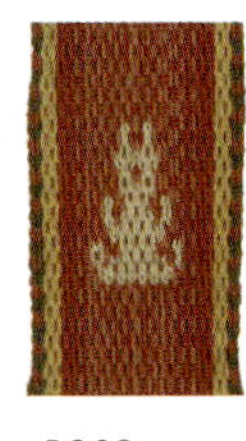
R203

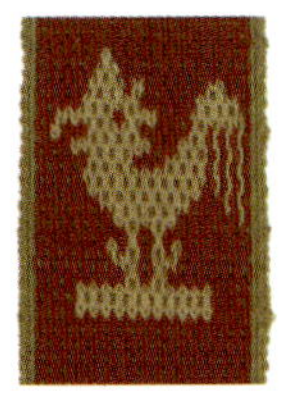
T467

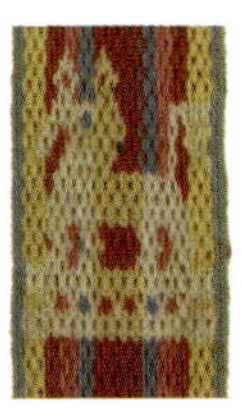
B854

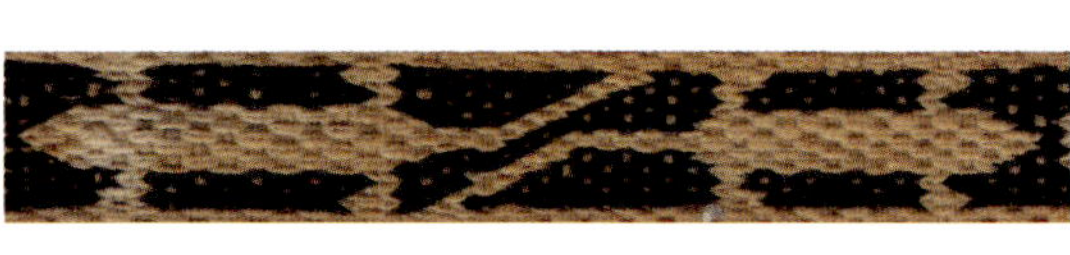
H002

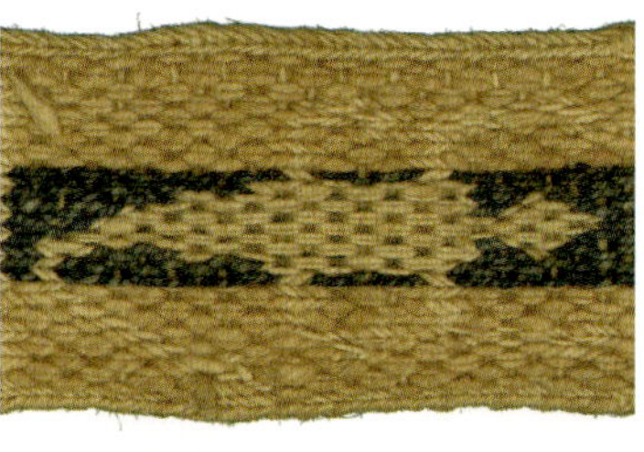
R075

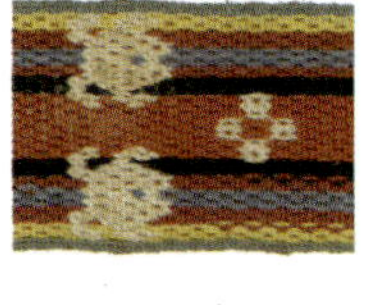
B842

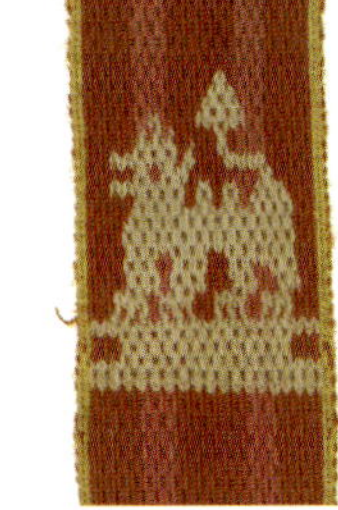
B872

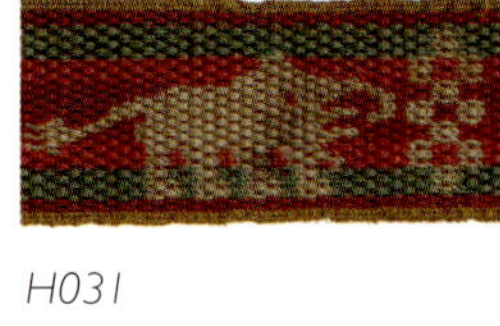
H031

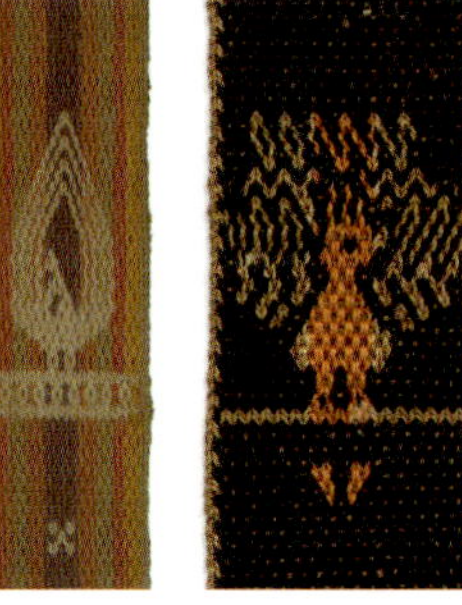
R270 *KJ03*

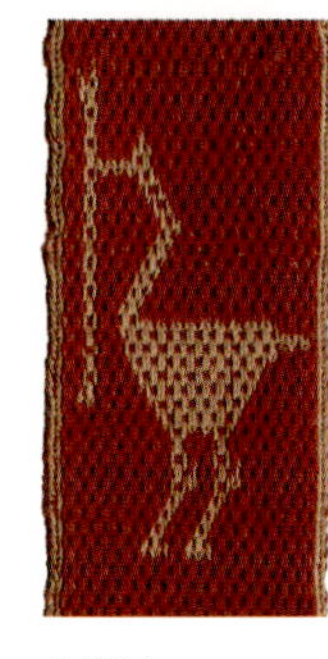
H021

B847

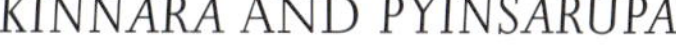

KINNARA AND PYINSARUPA

Two mythical beings carry a particularly rich cargo of symbolism. The *kinnara* is a bird with human head and torso. It is one of the 108 symbols on the footprint of the Buddha. Burmese Buddhists believe that in four of his 136 past animal lives the Buddha was a *kinnara*. In one of these incarnations the Buddha-to-be was Sandakinnara. His spouse Sandakinnari is celebrated for her unwavering fidelity to her husband, and she is one of the four paragons of virtuous womanhood, the *Taw Lay Wa*.[11] The story tells how the couple flew together for

KINNARA and *KINNARI*

Plate 108 CENTER RIGHT
Kinnara and *kinnari* are depicted in a mural in the eighteenth-century Ok-Kyaung (brick-built monastery) in the Ananda pagoda in Pagan.

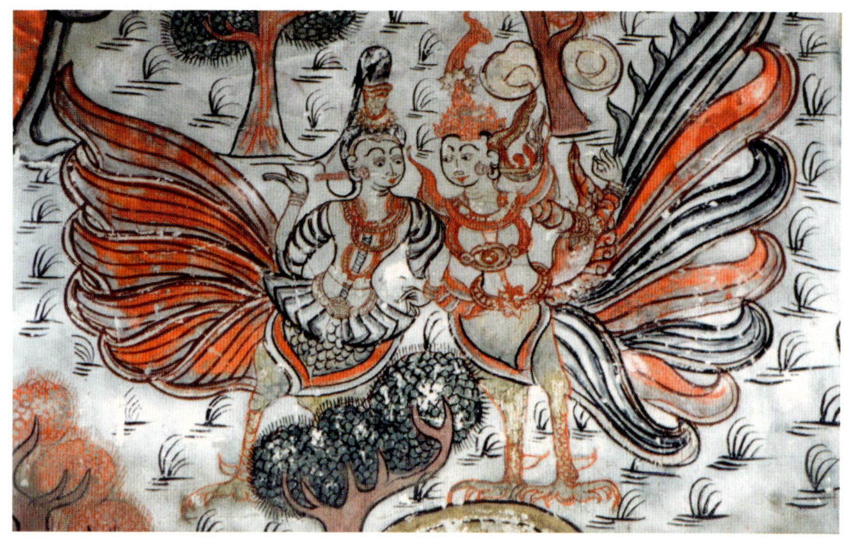

Plate 109 BELOW
WOVEN IMAGES OF *KINNARA*
Singly or in pairs, *kinnara* and *kinnari* symbolize constancy and marital fidelity. *(B842, R251, R004, T467A, R270, T467B, R013, T467C, R296)*
Repetitive patterns made up of tiny *kinnara*. *(R023, JBT 6.49, R285)*

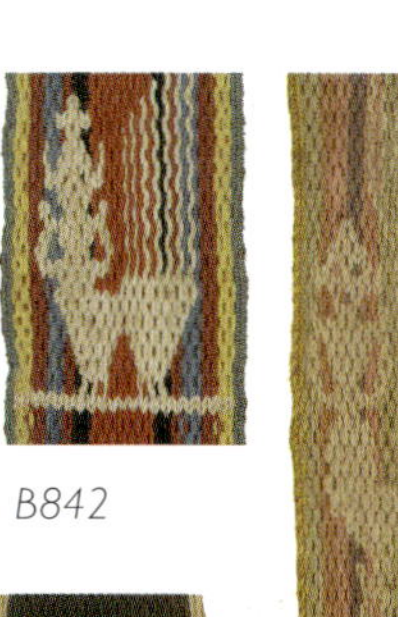

B842 *R251*

R004 *T467 A*

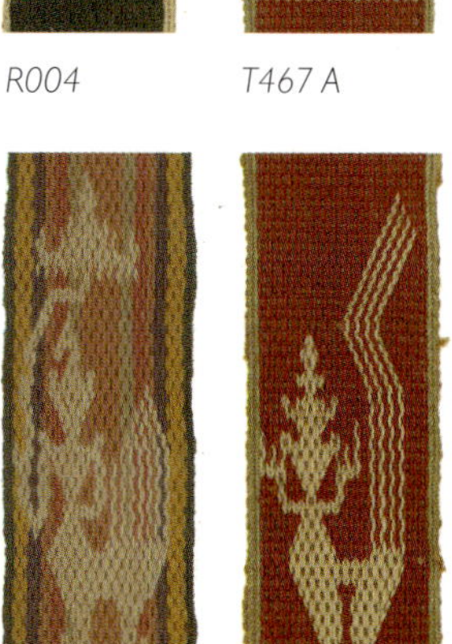

R270 *T467 B*

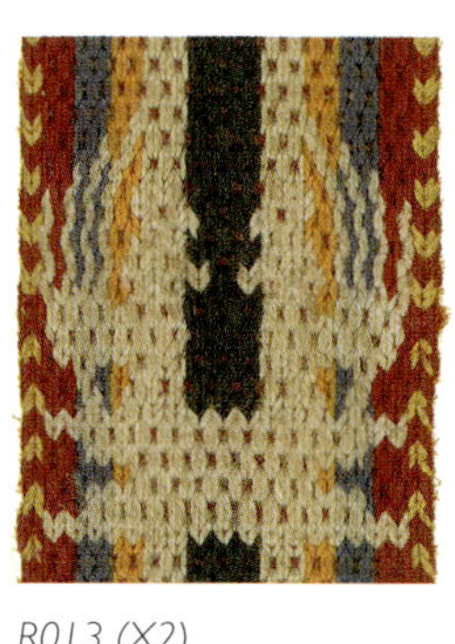

R013 (X2)

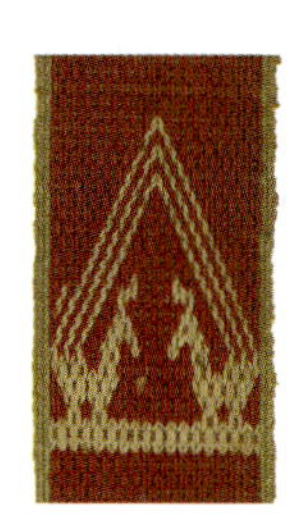

T467 C

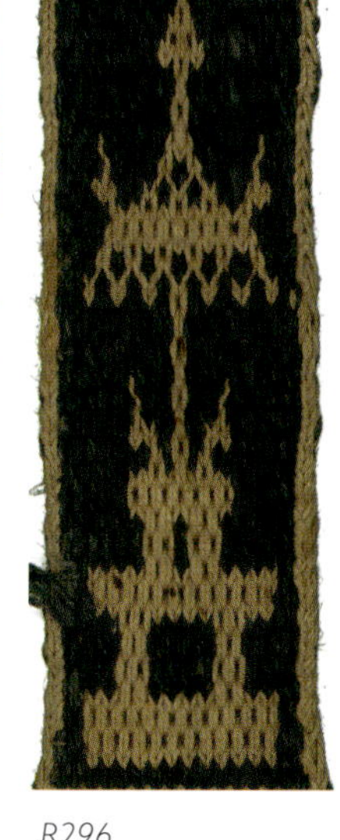

R296

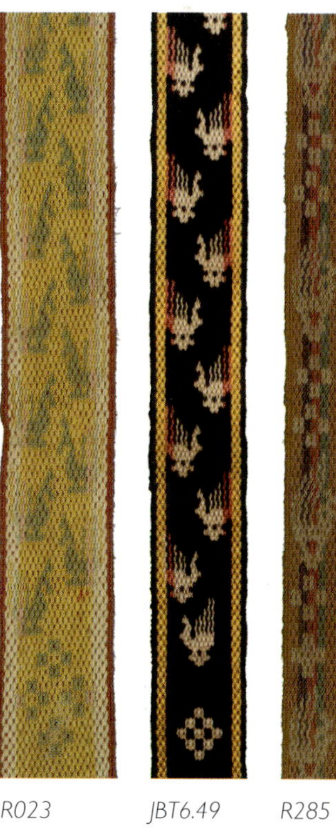

R023 *JBT6.49* *R285*

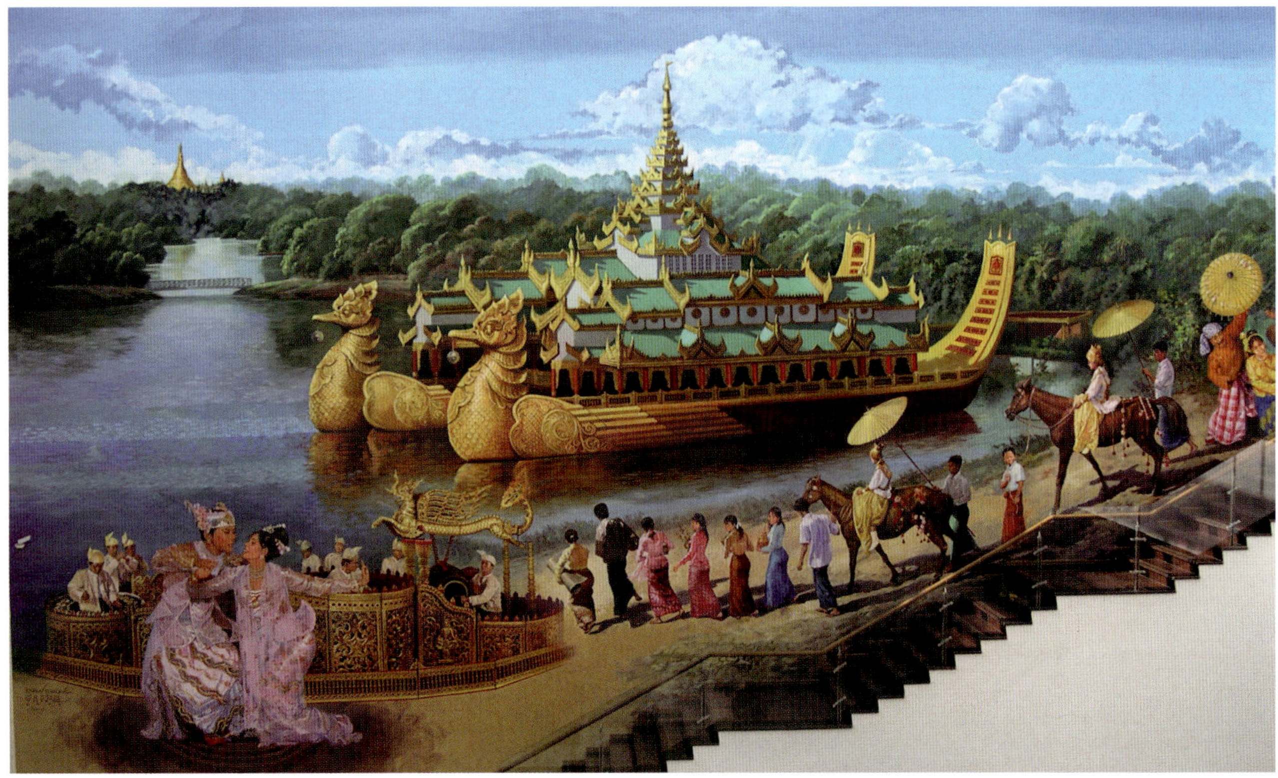

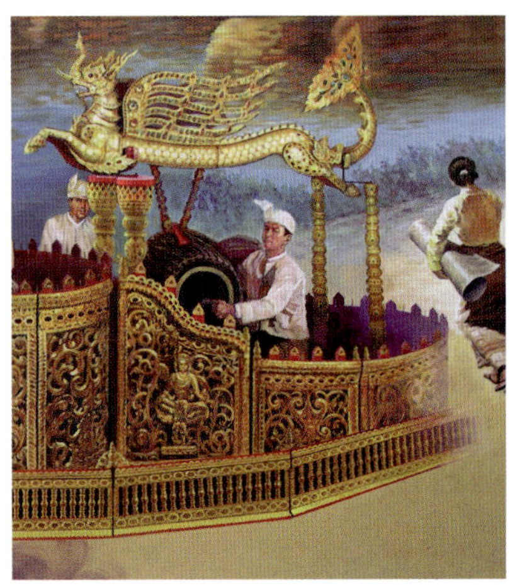

Plate 110 ABOVE
Both photographs are of murals at Yangon's Mingaladon International Airport. ABOVE: In the smaller picture the big drum, the loudest instrument, is shown hanging from the long body of a carved and gilt *pyinsarupa*, the emblem of the modern Burmese orchestra. TOP: The larger picture shows the full orchestra.

aeons. A storm separated them for a single night, and although they were reunited at daybreak, they spent the next 900 years mourning. Now they are inseparable. In the Mahabarata they describe their character in their own words: "We are everlasting lover and beloved. We never separate. We are eternally husband and wife; never do we become mother and father. No offspring is seen in our lap. We are lover and beloved ever-embracing. In between us we do not permit any third creature demanding affection. Our life is a life of perpetual pleasure." Pairs of these winged beings, face to face, are often depicted on sazigyo, as models of devotion and symbols of marital fidelity. This is entirely appropriate, for most manuscript donors were married couples. Cranes, too, are renowned for their lifelong devotion, and their woven images also appear on sazigyo. The usual sign for Gemini in the Burmese zodiac is a pair of *kinnara*.

The *pyinsarupa*, "animal of five body forms," is the mount of the mythical dark planet Kate, King of the Nine Planets. A composite beast, its components vary but they usually include the tusks and trunk of an elephant, antlers and hooves of a deer, neck and mane of a *chinthe* lion, long scaly body of a *naga* dragon, and the tail of a carp fish. Some are also winged. The *pyinsarupa* stands for energy and physical activity. It is also associated with loud noise: cast bronze *pyinsarupa* cling to the hanging loop of bronze bells. Several are to be seen on King Tharawaddi's huge bronze bell on the platform of the Shwedagon pagoda. A carved and gilded *pyinsarupa* is the emblem of the modern Burmese orchestra (*hsaing waing*). Its long scaly body stretched between

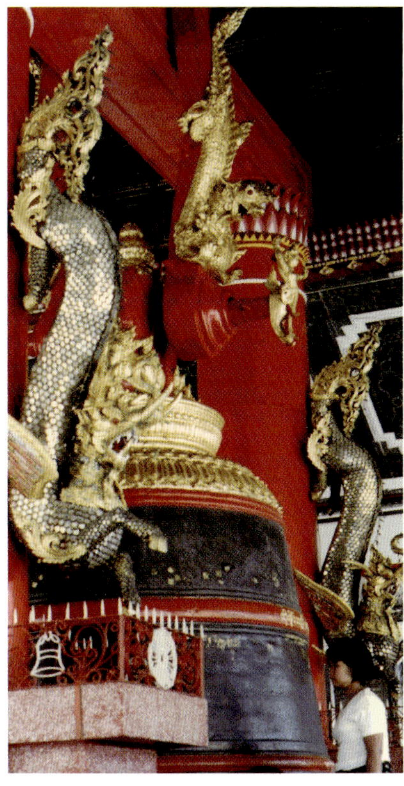

two posts forms the crossbar supporting the loudest instrument, the big drum (*pat ma gyi*).

On sazigyo the *pyinsarupa*'s woven image placed immediately before the main text lends it vehemence, and immediately before images of bells, it acts as a visual amplifier. Examples are shown in Plate 134.

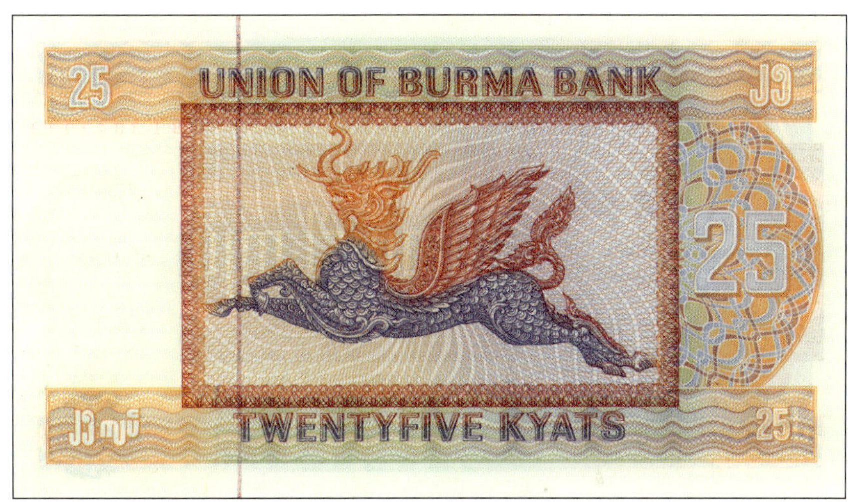

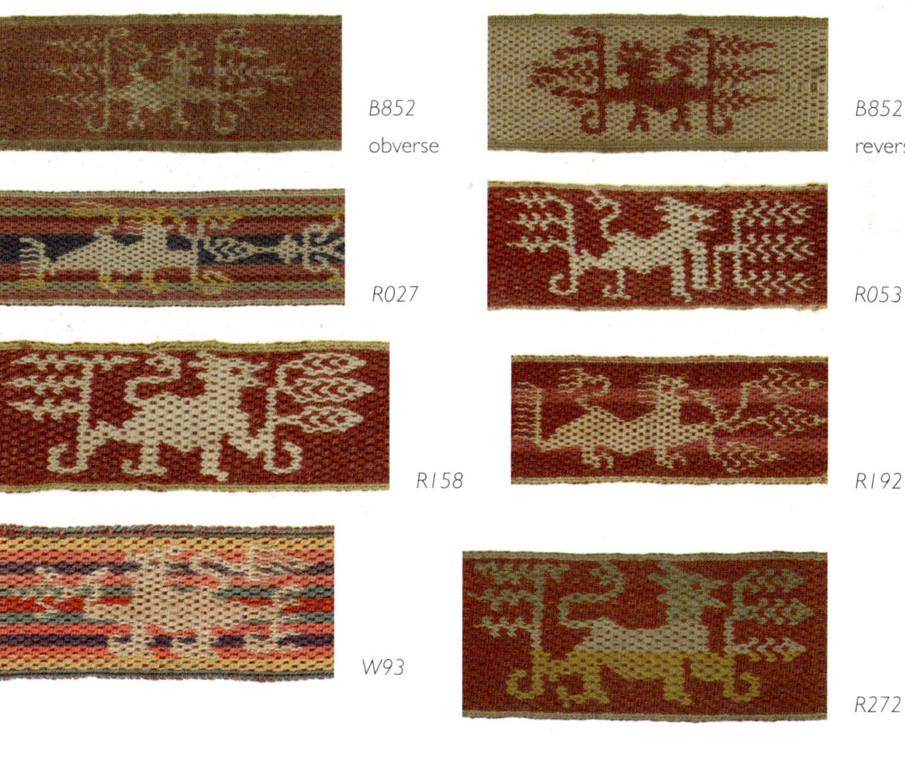

Plate 111 TOP LEFT
PYINSARUPA ON BELL
Bronze figures of *pyinsarupa* cling to the hanging loop of King Tharawaddi's huge Maha Tissada bell on the platform of the Shwedagon pagoda.

Plate 112 TOP RIGHT
PYINSARUPA ON BANKNOTE
The *pyinsarupa* appears on the reverse of the 25-kyat banknote issued by the Union of Burma Bank from 1972 to 1979.

Plate 113 RIGHT
WOVEN IMAGES OF *PYINSARUPA*
Pyinsarupa images on sazigyo may stand alone, but often precede the text as if proclaiming it aloud. *(B852, R027, R053, R158, R192, W93)*
Three colors of warp thread enhance its heraldic pose. *(R272)*
A rare trio of *pyinsarupa*. (R291)

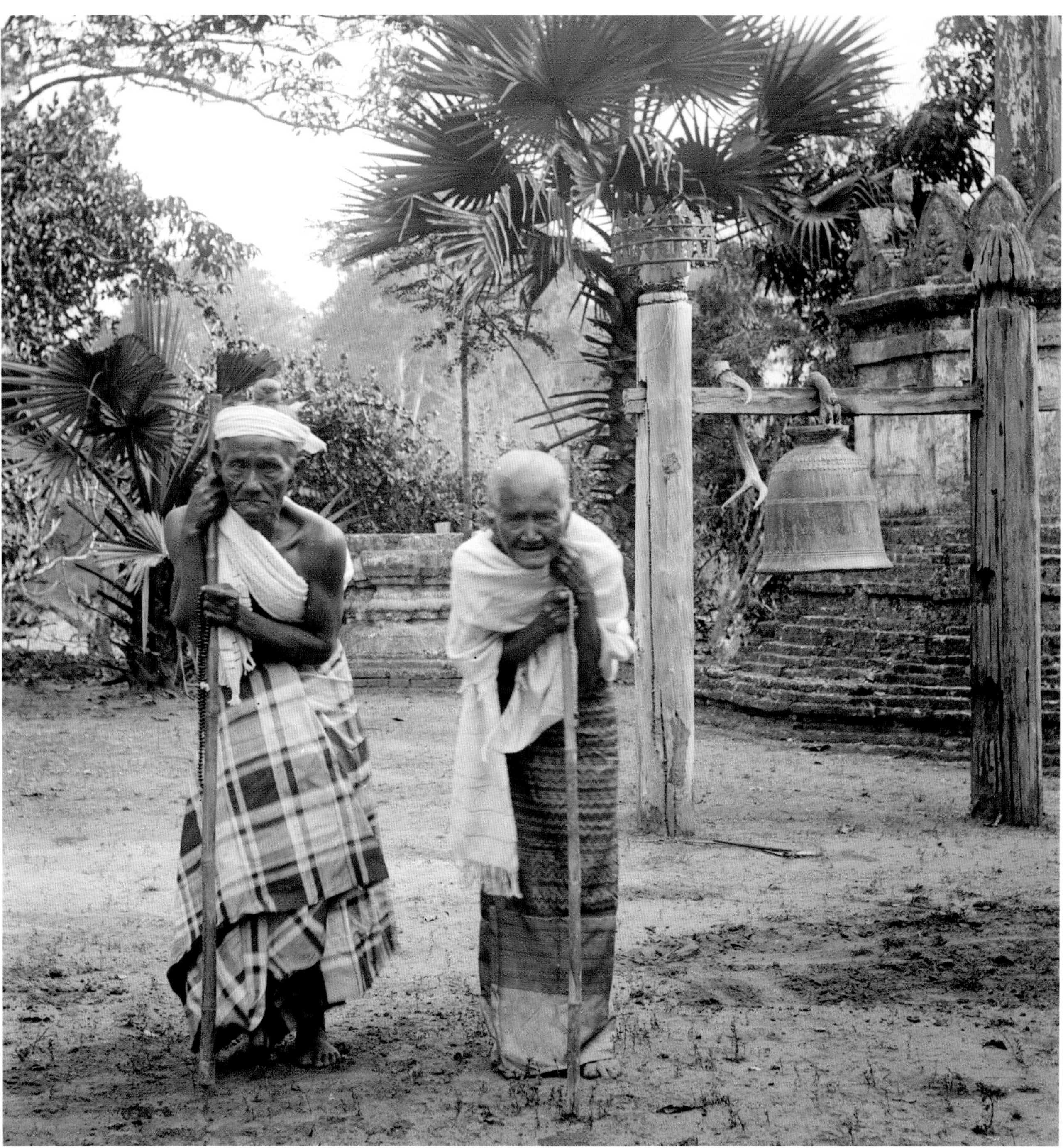

BELLS

Plate 114 ABOVE

A century ago the striker for the round bell was a deer antler, seen here hung by a prong on the bell support. Now that the deer are extinct, a plain billet of wood is used instead, but the crooked or branched antler striker lives on in the woven images on mid-twentieth-century sazigyo.

BROADCASTING THE DONATION, SHARING THE MERIT

The Judeo-Christian ideal of charity by stealth, with donor and recipient decently anonymous, so strongly commended in the Gospel of St. Matthew,[12] finds no place in Burmese Theravada Buddhist practice. There is nothing furtive about charitable donations in Burma. A visitor to the Shwedagon pagoda platform quickly learns that charity here is a very public act, and donation often a noisy business.

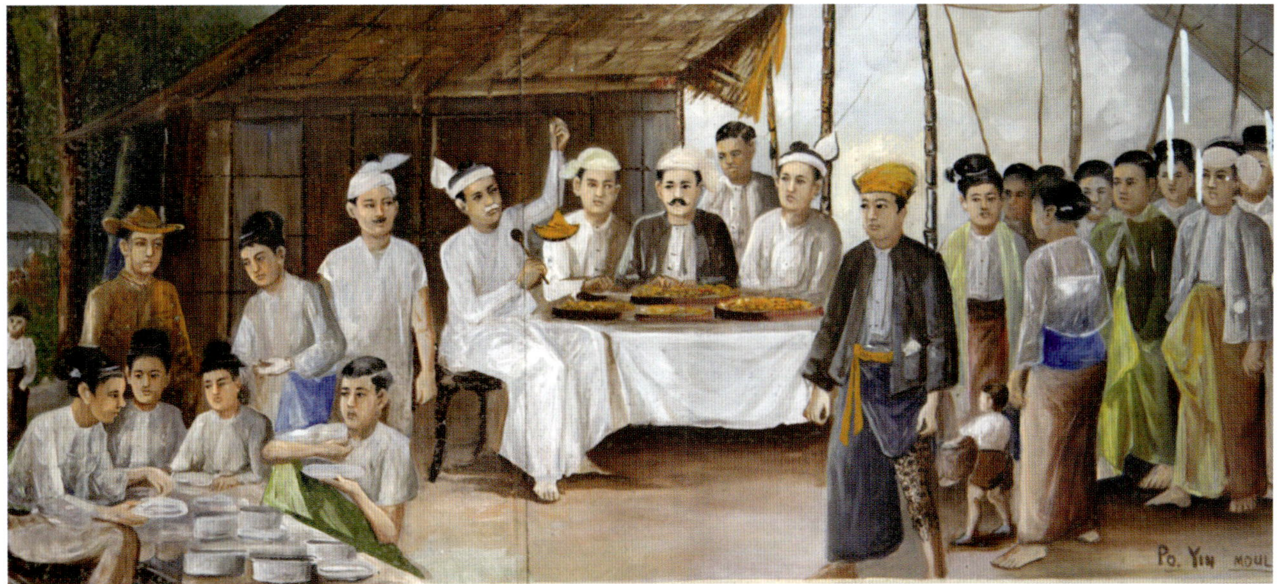

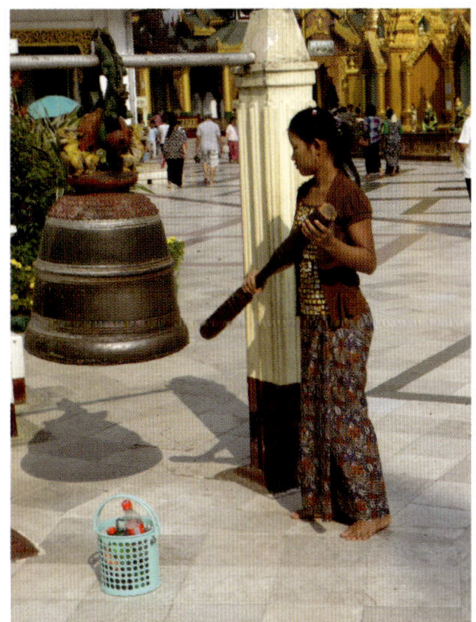

Plate 115 TOP
The *kyizi* is a flat triangular bell which spins when struck on the corner, emitting a surging vibrato note. This painting is one of a series painted on thin metal sheets in about 1935 by the artist Po Yin. It shows donations being received in 1905 for the casting of a large bronze Buddha image in Moulmein.

Plate 116 ABOVE
The donor strikes a bell to invite humans within earshot and the spirits to approve and applaud the deed of merit.

Whenever the devout Buddhist pilgrim hands cash across the counter at any of the dozens of donation stalls, loudspeakers blare out the donor's name and the sum donated, followed by a recorded fanfare. The donor rings a bell to alert the Earth Goddess and all humans within earshot, inviting them to witness, approve, and applaud his deed. Bystanders call out "*Thadu!*" ("Well done!"), whereupon the donor responds "*Ahmya!*"—a single word expressing a complex idea—the equal dissemination of one's merit after performing a charitable deed. It could be rendered: "The merit of this deed is for all of us equally!"

A set sequence of three images that follow the woven text mirror the series of ritual acts, which conclude the religious duty. Two are bells, and the third is the Earth Goddess. First comes the round bell, *hkaung-laung gyi*, with its crooked striker. A century ago the striker for the round bell was the crown end of a deer's antler—obtained without killing, since the living stag shed his antlers annually. Nowadays a plain billet of wood serves instead, but though the deer are extinct their antlers survive in the sazigyo's woven images: the striker depicted below the round bell is always crooked and branched.

Next in the sequence is the *kyizi*, the flat, eared gong. Hung on a twisted cord and struck on the corner with a hammer, the *kyizi* spins, emitting a surging vibrato note. Sir Henry Yule noted in 1855, "The triangular gong (peculiar, I believe, to Burma), which the people strike on holidays as they pass along the streets to worship at the pagodas, is quite remarkable for its musical, prolonged and surging vibrations."[13] A *kyizi* hangs at each donation stall on the pagoda platform, to be rung whenever a donation is received. Both bells are struck three times, for the Three Gems, while three birds perched on the bell posts stand for the three strokes. Sometimes Nats support the bells.

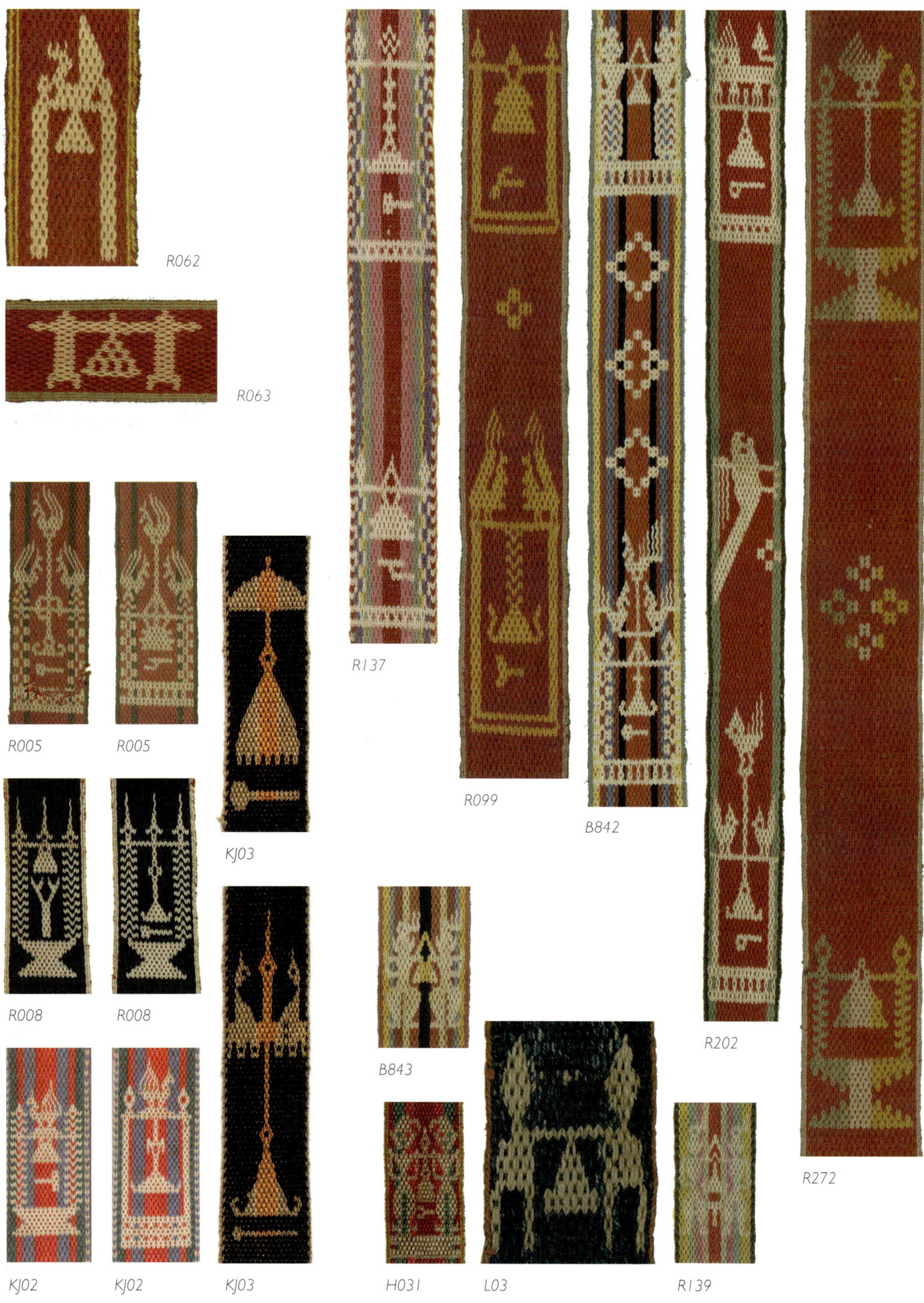
R062
R063
R137
R099
B842
R202
R272
R005
R005
KJ03
R008
R008
B843
KJ02
KJ02
KJ03
H031
L03
R139

Plate 117

PREVIOUS PAGE, RIGHT, AND FOLLOWING PAGE

ROUND BELLS, FLAT BELLS, AND THE EARTH GODDESS

Woven images of two types of bells, round and flat, appear on most sazigyo, always after the main text. They vary from simple to more elaborate.

SINGLE, SIMPLE BELLS

PREVIOUS PAGE TOP LEFT

(R062, R063)

PAIRS OF BELLS

PREVIOUS PAGE BOTTOM LEFT AND TOP RIGHT

Images of bells usually come in pairs: round bell and flat triangular *kyizi*. Some have birds perched on the bell posts. *(R005, R008, KJ02, KJ03, R137, R099, B842, R202, R272)*

BELLS SUPPORTED BY NATS

PREVIOUS PAGE BOTTOM RIGHT

Bells may be supported on the shoulders of Nats. *(B843, H031, L03, R139)*

EARTH GODDESS AS WITNESS

RIGHT AND FOLLOWING PAGE LEFT

The Earth Goddess Waythondaye is summoned by bells to witness the donors' deed of merit and approve it. Her image forms a trio of images with those of the two kinds of bell. *(B850, B855, B877, T883, R192, JBT6.49, R106, R024, R027, R092)*

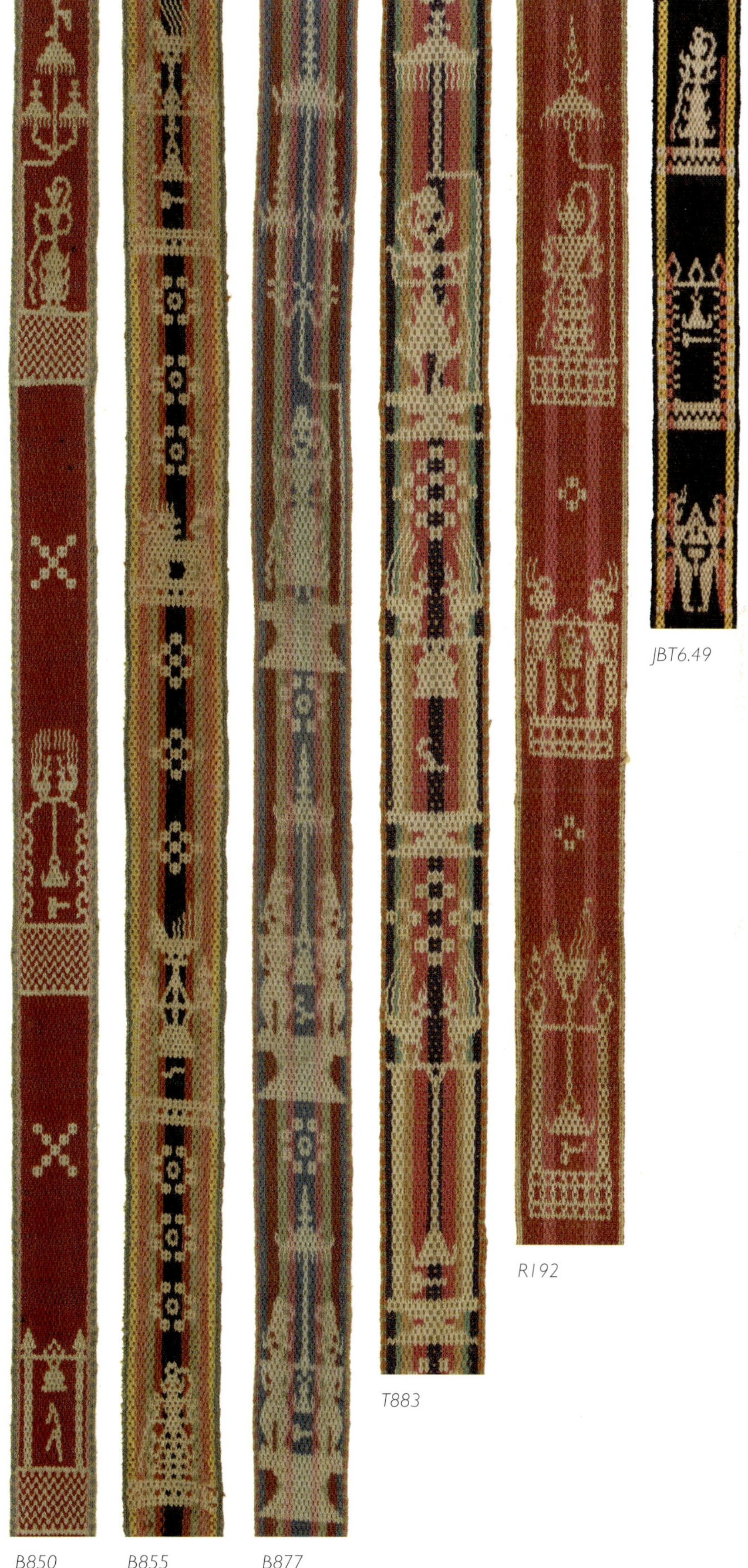

JBT6.49

R192

T883

B850 *B855* *B877*

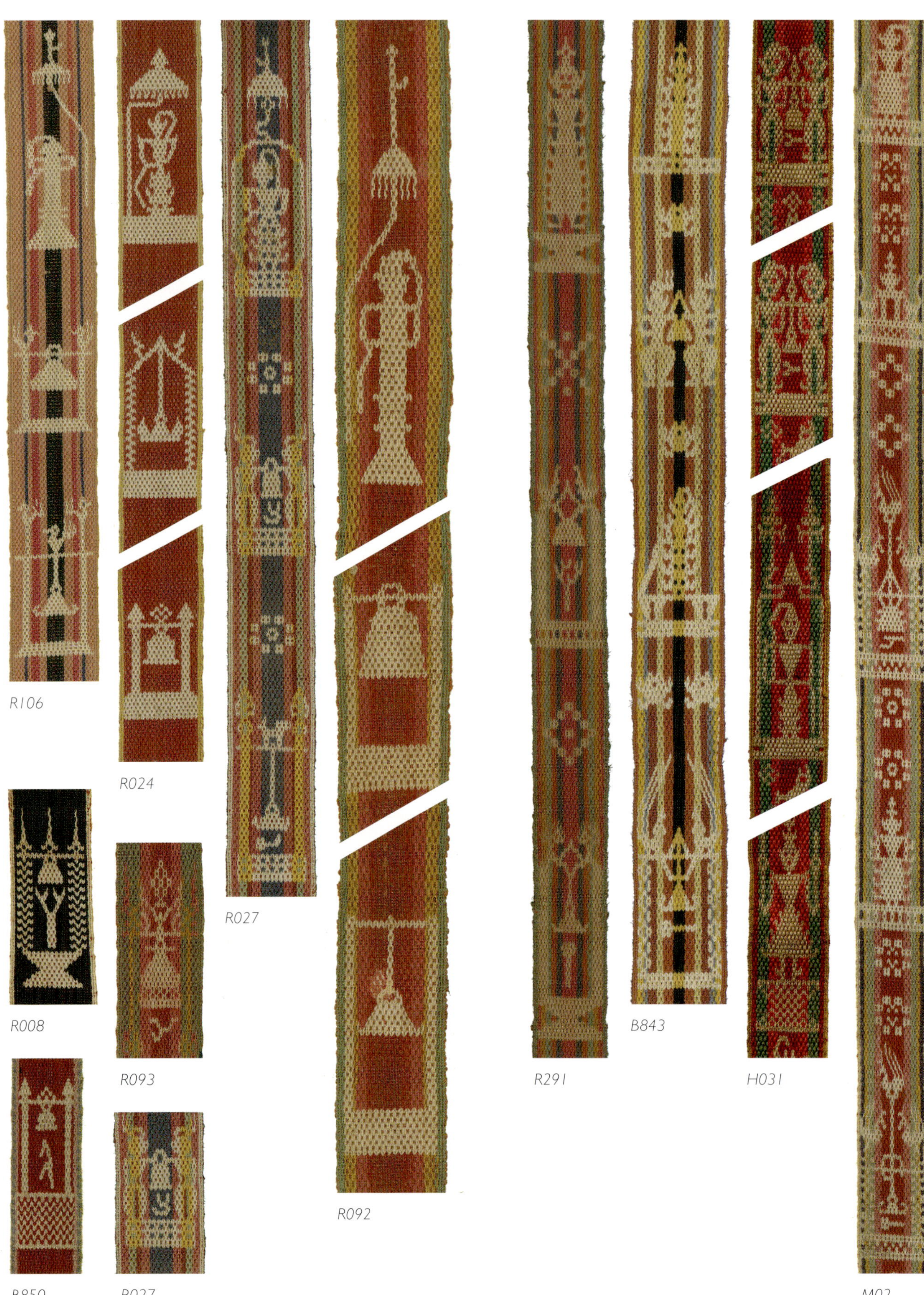
R106
R024
R027
R092
R291
B843
H031
M02
R008
R093
B850
R027

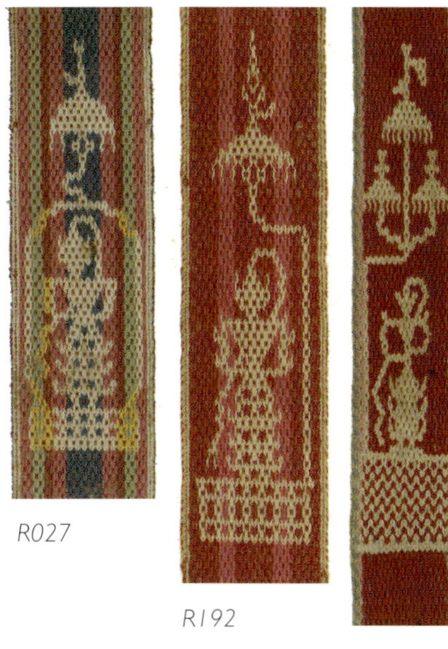

R027

R192

B850

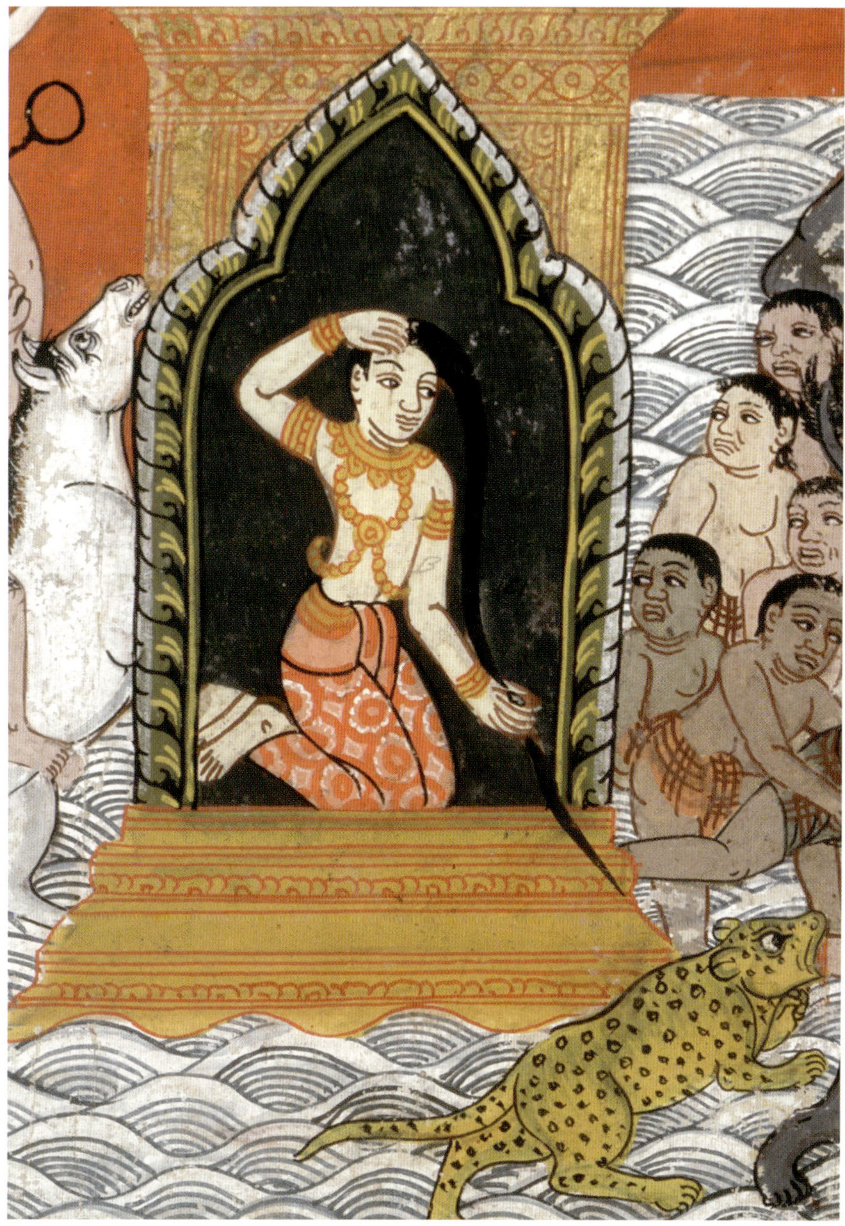

THAGYA MIN, KING OF THE NATS
PREVIOUS PAGE RIGHT
Another powerful celestial witness, Thagya Min, King of the Nats, may replace the Earth Goddess *(R291)* or he may join her, making a strong four. *(B843, H031, M02)*

FORKED OR BRANCHED ANTLER STRIKER PREVIOUS PAGE BELOW LEFT
The striker depicted below the round bell in these woven images is unmistakably the crown end of a deer antler. *(R008, R093, B850, R027)*

WOVEN IMAGES OF EARTH GODDESS WAYTHONDAYE TOP LEFT
On sazigyo Waythondaye is always depicted with long hair, and often with parasols of state. *(R027, R192, B850)*

Plate 118 TOP RIGHT
The Earth Goddess Waythondaye depicted in a painted manuscript wringing out her long wet hair to drown Mara's evil host.

The third image is that of the Earth Goddess. Donors invoke her to witness their deed of merit by ringing the bells, and they may also thump the ground (three times of course) with the same billet of wood. Waythondaye (Sanskrit: Vasundhara) is uniquely qualified as a witness. When he was about to attain enlightenment the Buddha-to-be was assailed by the demon Mara and his evil host. He called on the earth to testify to his fitness to become a Buddha. Thus the Earth Goddess witnessed the enlightenment of the Buddha, and with a flood of water wrung from her long wet hair, she swept away Mara's hosts.[14] Some say her hair was wet with all the libations poured by the Buddha to accompany his donations in all his previous lives. When Burmese kings donated in great public ceremonies, they poured the traditional water dedication, calling the earth to witness.[15]

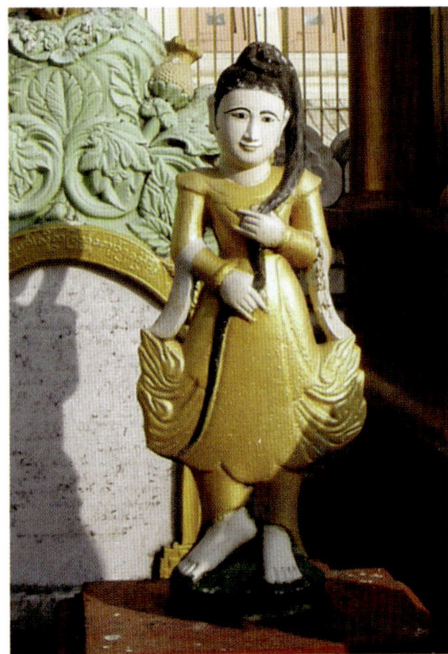

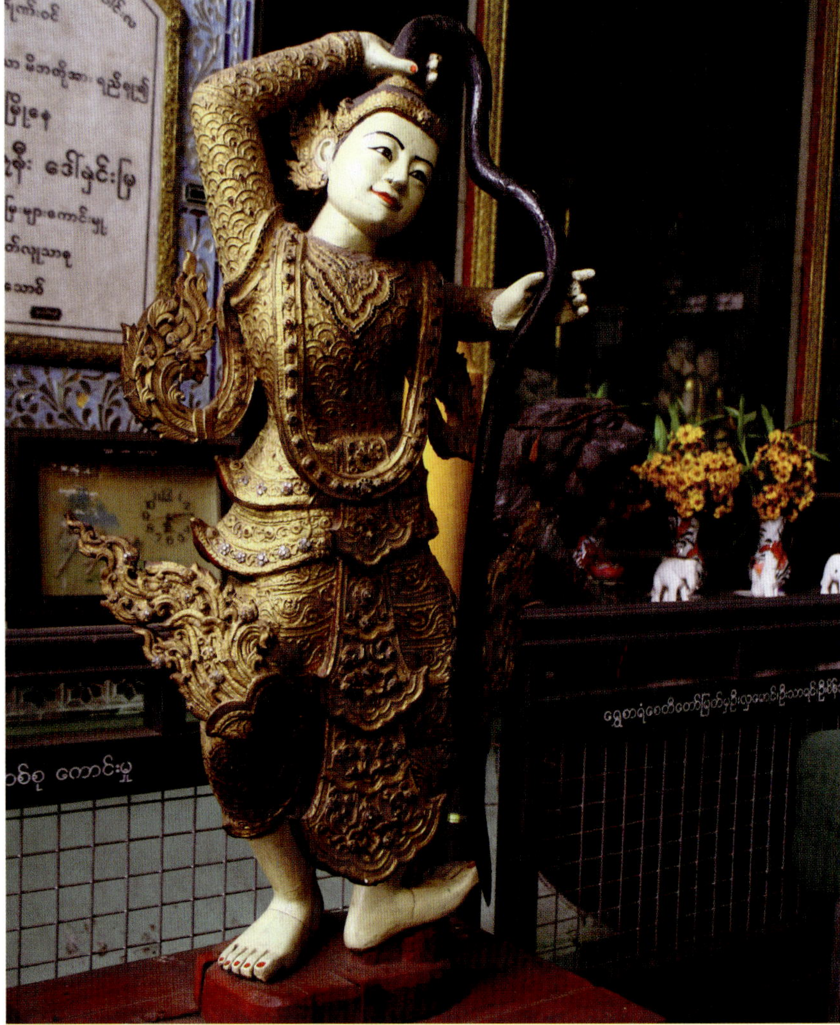

Every woven image of Waythondaye on sazigyo shows her wringing out her long wet hair. Her witness is indispensable for every donation. Some donors address her in the text of their prayer, **"We request Waythondaye, the guardian deity of the earth, to bear witness now and remind us if after long and many lives we forget this good deed."**[16] One couple increased their donation from a single manuscript to a full library chest (*sadaik*). This was recorded in a postscript to the woven text of the sazigyo, and the Earth Goddess had to be recalled to witness the increased donation—so her image appears twice.

In the most elaborate of these images, the Earth Goddess stands on a splendid royal throne, shaded by one or more *hti*, royal parasols and emblems of celestial authority.[17] But the simplest images can be charming, even when the goddess in profile recalls a gasoline pump at an old-style filling station. A few weavers equip her with eyes in special supplementary weft. And on the principle that two celestial witnesses are better than one, Waythondaye and Thagya Min may appear together, close to the bells.

Plate 119 TOP LEFT and
Plate 120 TOP RIGHT
Donors erect statues of the Earth Goddess Waythondaye on the pagoda platform to witness their deed of merit, the donation of a shrine, or Buddha image.

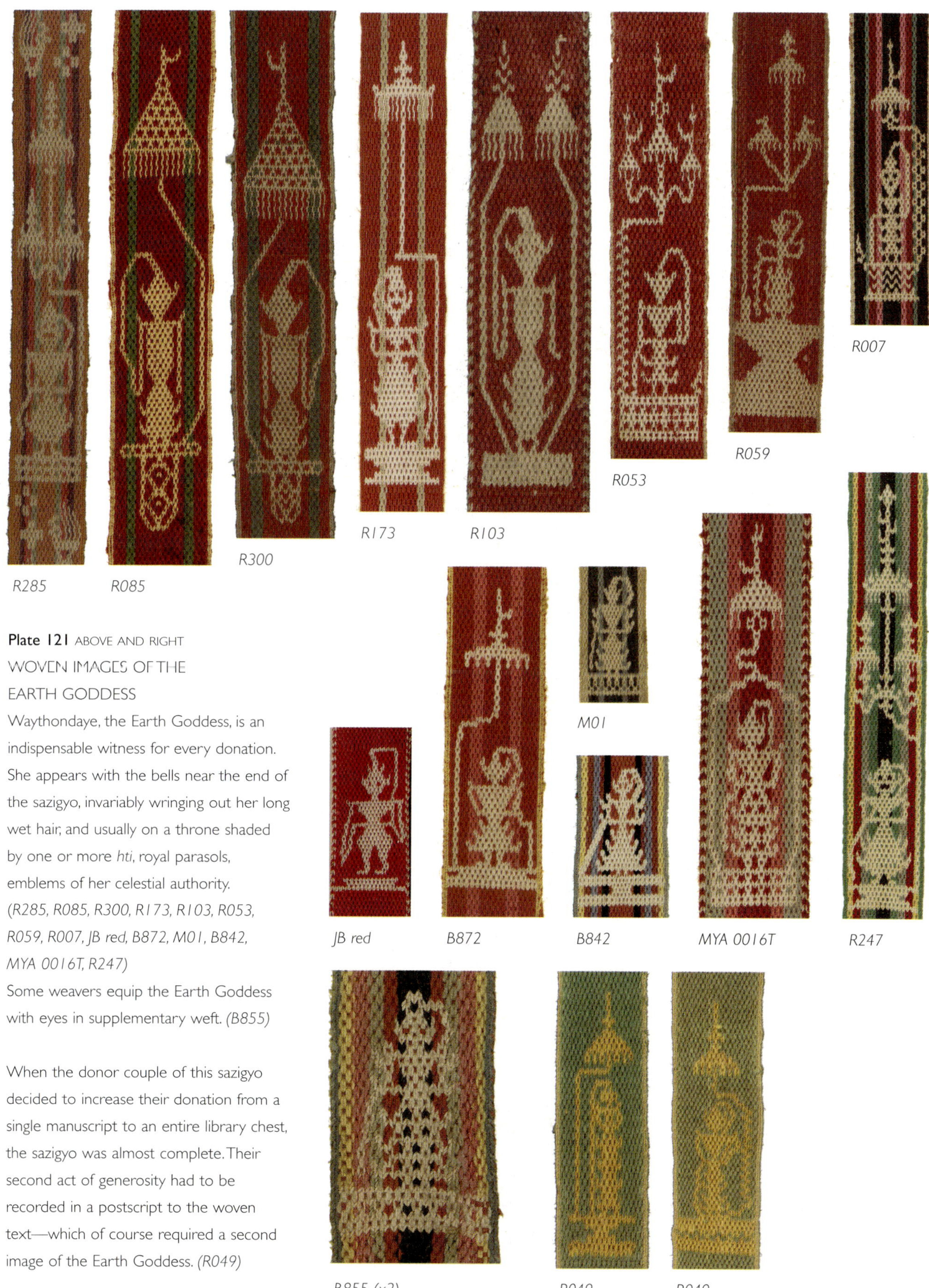

Plate 121 ABOVE AND RIGHT
WOVEN IMAGES OF THE EARTH GODDESS
Waythondaye, the Earth Goddess, is an indispensable witness for every donation. She appears with the bells near the end of the sazigyo, invariably wringing out her long wet hair, and usually on a throne shaded by one or more *hti*, royal parasols, emblems of her celestial authority. *(R285, R085, R300, R173, R103, R053, R059, R007, JB red, B872, M01, B842, MYA 0016T, R247)*
Some weavers equip the Earth Goddess with eyes in supplementary weft. *(B855)*

When the donor couple of this sazigyo decided to increase their donation from a single manuscript to an entire library chest, the sazigyo was almost complete. Their second act of generosity had to be recorded in a postscript to the woven text—which of course required a second image of the Earth Goddess. *(R049)*

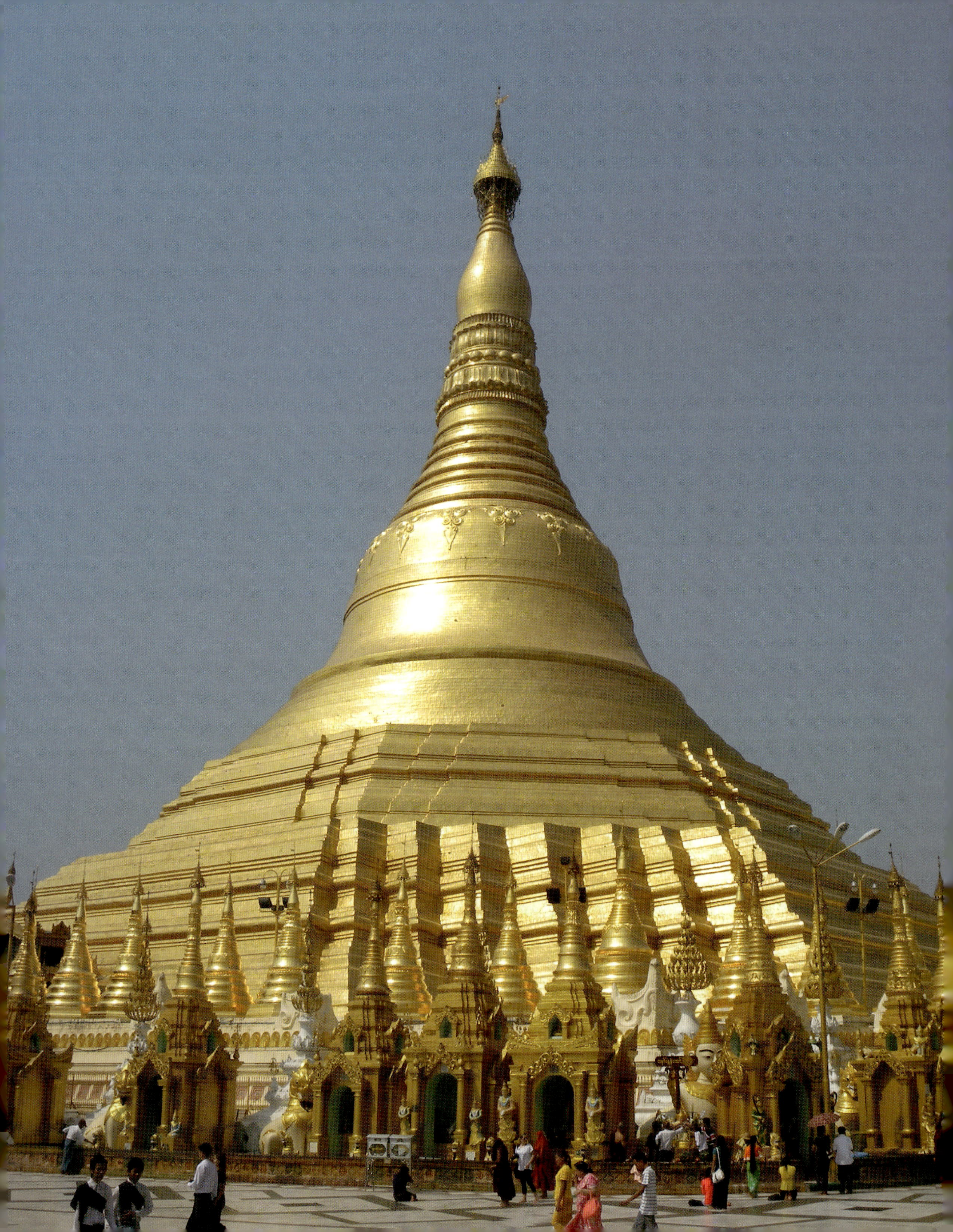

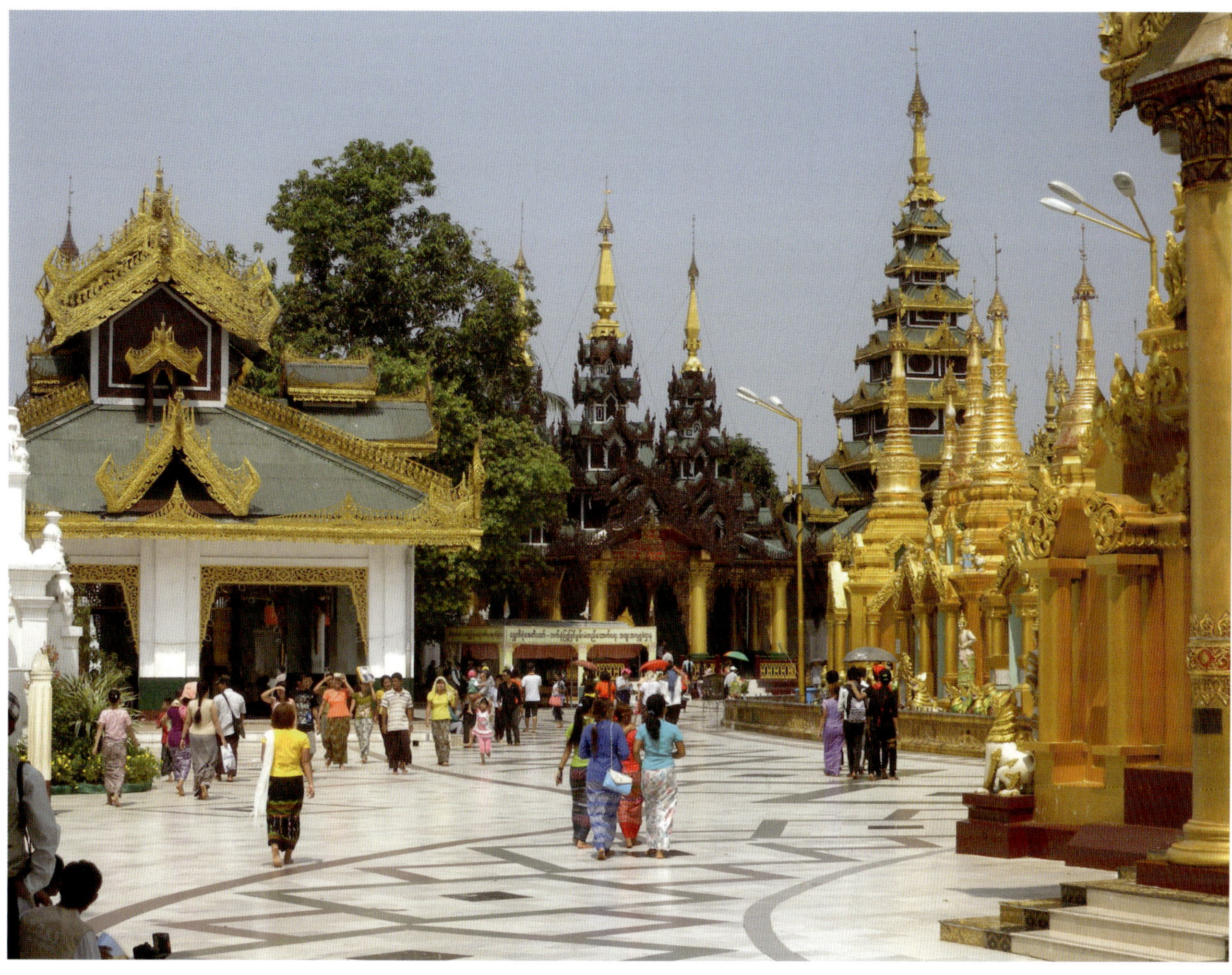

ON THE PAGODA PLATFORM

The act of donation recorded on the sazigyo involves a sequence of religious rituals. An appropriate site for the performance of a religious duty is the platform of the pagoda. The sazigyo weaver may suggest this setting by including in her selection of woven images several depicting architectural features found on the pagoda platform.

A pair of *chinthe*, gryphon-lions, flank the approach to every Burmese pagoda. One or both of these may appear early in the sazigyo sequence. The *manoutthiha* is a mythical man-lion, with a single human torso and twin lion bodies at right angles. This forked body shape neatly fits its architectural function, marking the corners of each level of the pagoda platform. Its formidable appearance frightens off evil spirits.

The fig tree, *nyaung bin*, features in another ritual observed by pilgrims on a duty visit to the pagoda platform: their first act is watering the sacred tree. They may remain in prayer under its shade. "She who waters the sacred fig" is a title of respect for a devout

ON THE PAGODA PLATFORM

Plate 122 PREVIOUS PAGE
The gilded splendor of the Shwedagon pagoda.

Plate 123 ABOVE
The pagoda platform busy with pilgrims intent on their religious duties, often combined with socializing. The tree in the background among the shrines is a sacred fig tree, and is often the first place visited.

Plate 124 RIGHT
Late nineteenth-century view of a pagoda platform, the appropriate stage for the religious act of donation, with a bell frame and two fine tall teak posts *(dagundaing)*.

Plate 125 TOP NEXT PAGE
A pair of *chinthes*, bearded gryphon-lions, flank the approach steps to the Shwedagon pagoda.

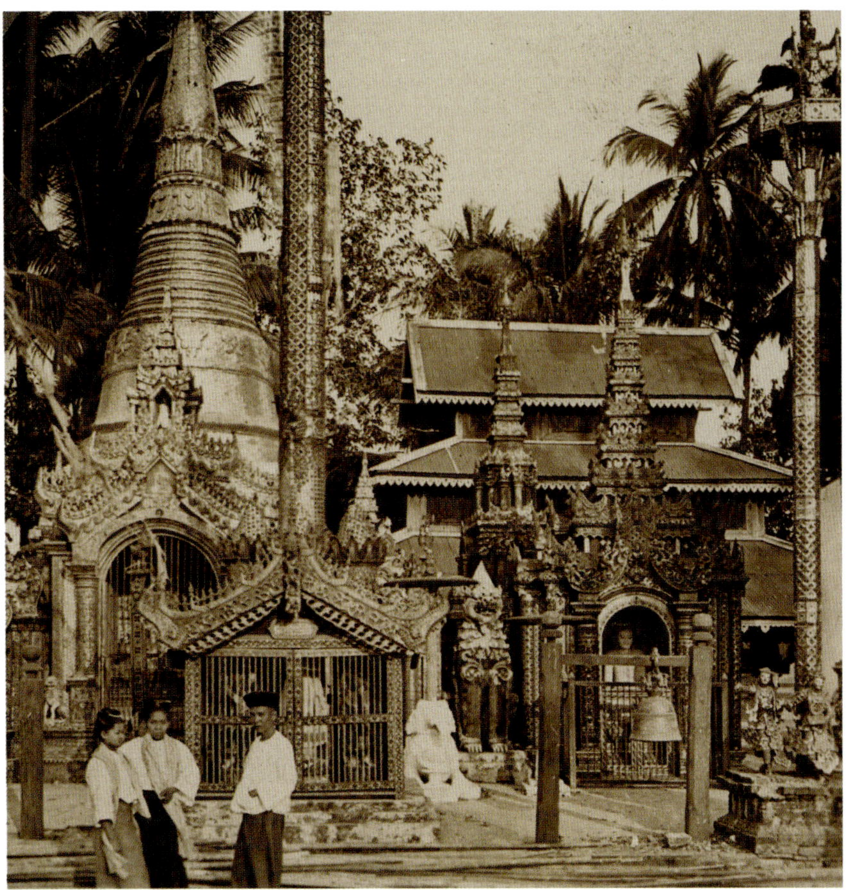

Buddhist, one who conscientiously performs her religious duties. Woven images of the sacred fig tree vary in profile. Some have only three branches, for the Three Gems, a symbol within a symbol. The fig tree may be the very first image on the sazigyo, or the very last.

A stone parasol (*kyauk hti*) stands on the platform and symbolizes the Buddha. In Burmese the phrase *kyauk hti* also has a figurative meaning that would not have escaped some donors: it refers to a person of great distinction, a "pillar of society."

The ritual of the donation is rounded off by the ringing of bells, which hang from teak posts on the pagoda platform. As we have seen, donors ring bells to broadcast their deed of merit, to invite the approval of witnesses (including the Earth Goddess), and to share with them the merit of their deed. This ritual is reflected in the sequence of three images on the sazigyo—two types of bell and the Earth Goddess, Waythondaye.

The last object to remain visible to the departing pilgrim descending from the pagoda platform is the *dagundaing*, the tall teak flagpost with a bird atop and twin tubular pennants hanging down like wind socks. In the past these posts were whole teak tree trunks, up to twenty meters high. The woven image of the *dagundaing* is by far the longest on the sazigyo—and usually the last of all.

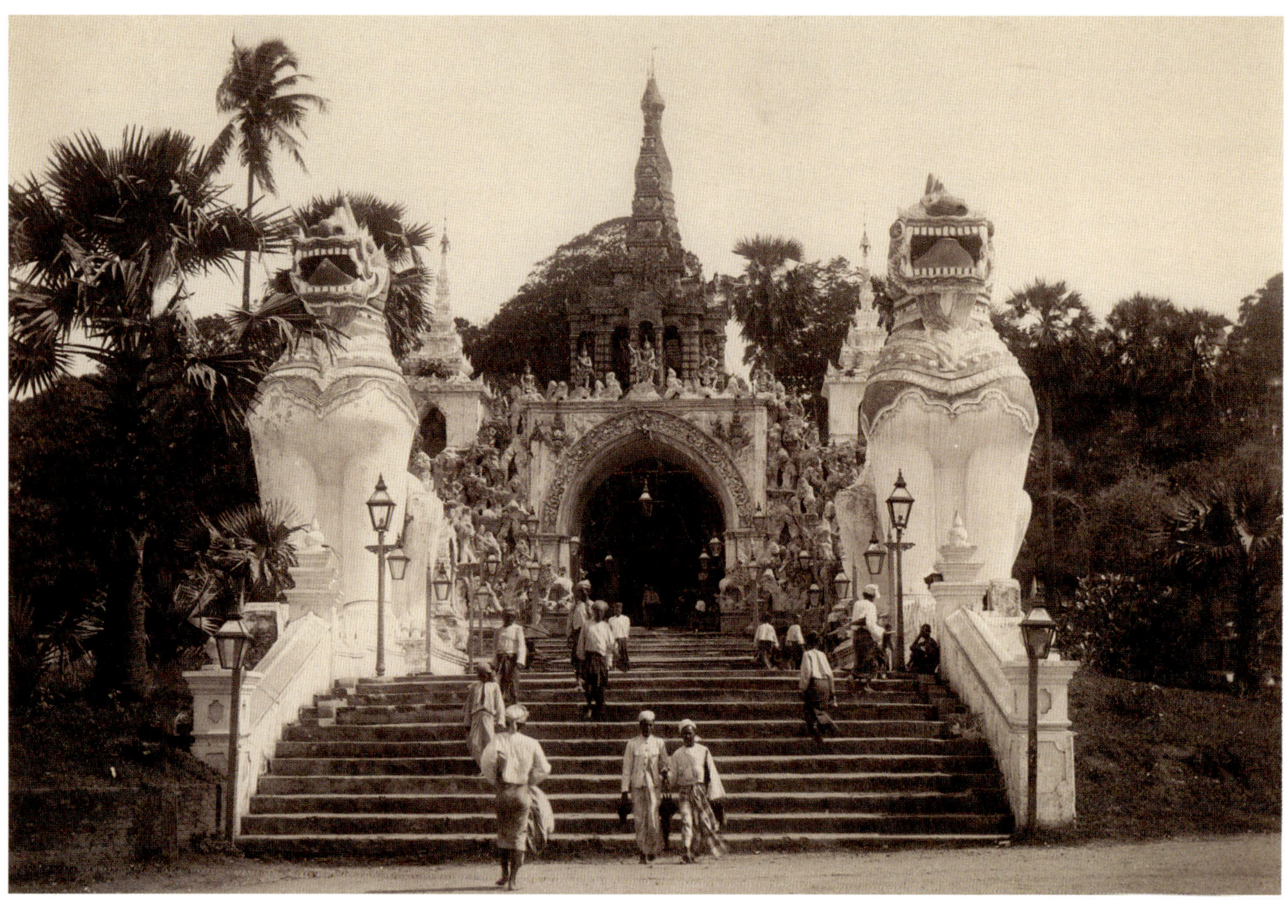

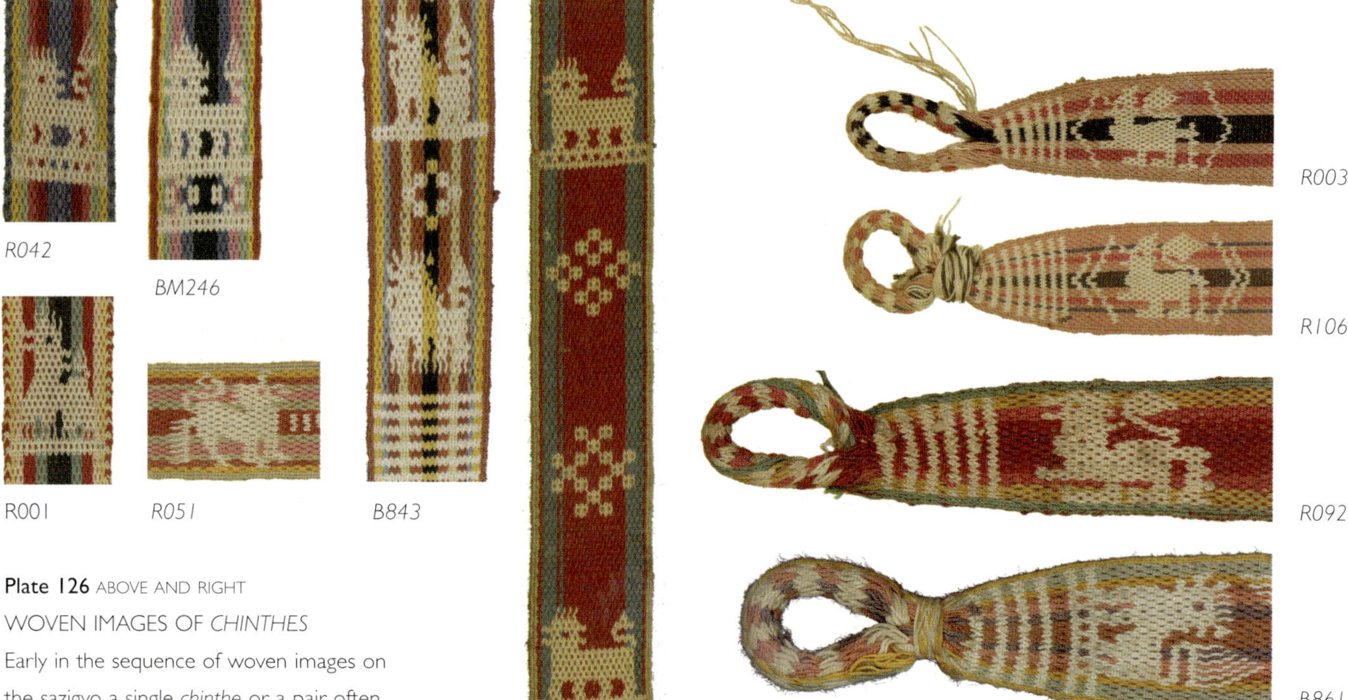

R042 BM246 R001 R051 B843 R076 R003 R106 R092 B861

Plate 126 ABOVE AND RIGHT
WOVEN IMAGES OF *CHINTHES*
Early in the sequence of woven images on the sazigyo a single *chinthe* or a pair often appears. *(R042, BM246, R001, R051, B843, R076, R003, R106, R092, B861)*

Plate 127 RIGHT

Mythical man-lions, *manuthiha*, guard the corners of the pagoda platform, scaring off malevolent spirits. They have a human torso and twin lion bodies, which snugly fit the corners of the masonry.

Plate 128 BELOW RIGHT

WOVEN IMAGES OF *MANUTHIHA*

They protect the sazigyo and the donors' deed of merit from inauspicious influences. *(BM246, R179, B842, B860, M02, R005)*

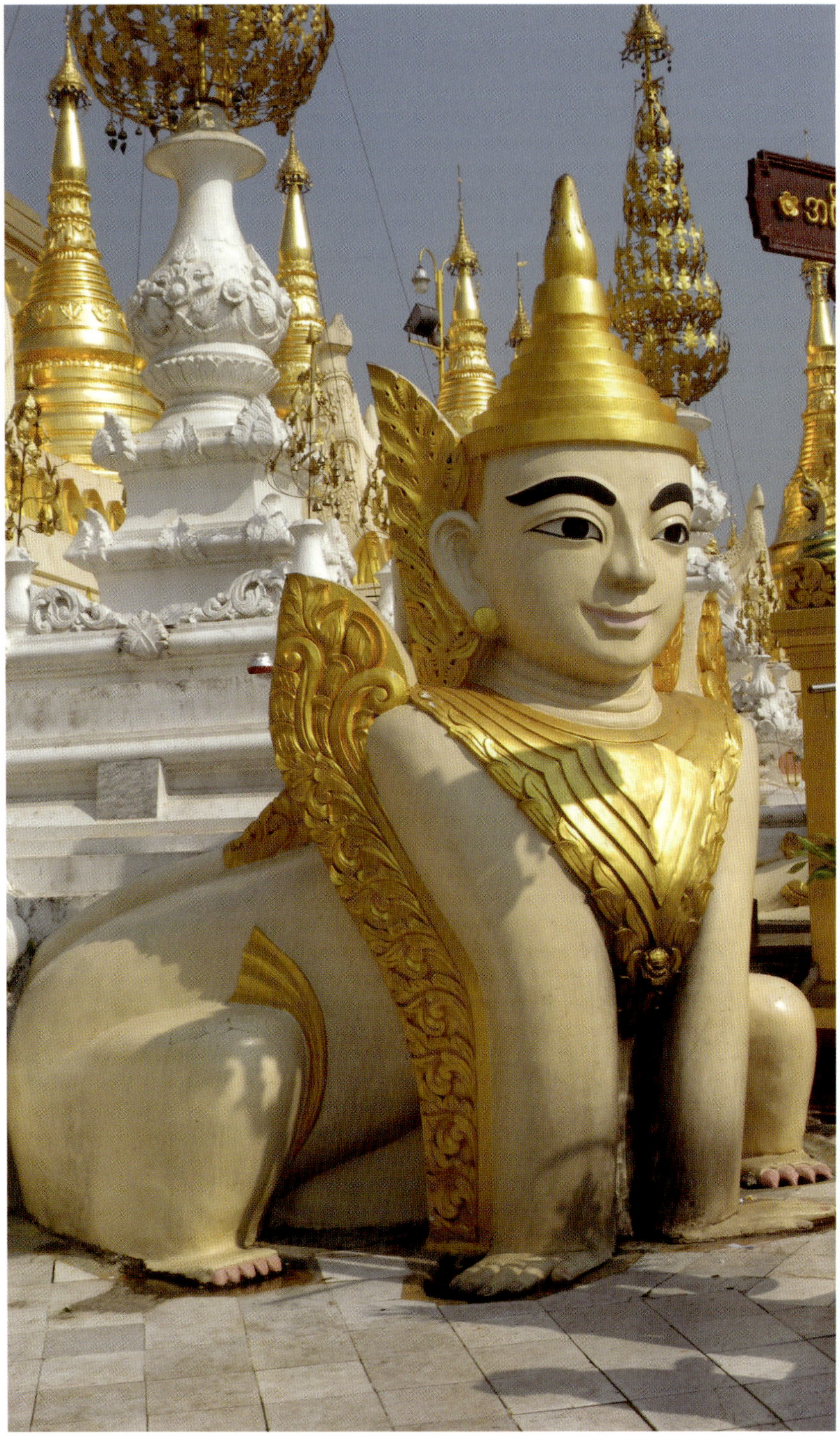

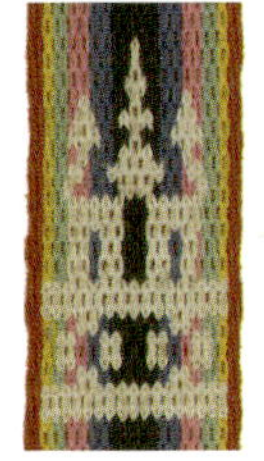

BM246

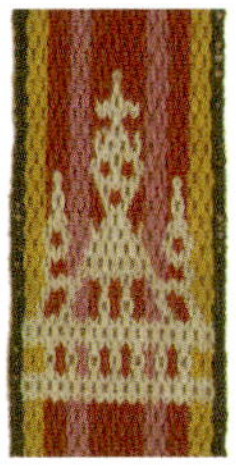

R179

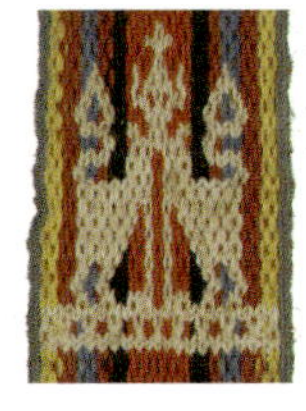

B842

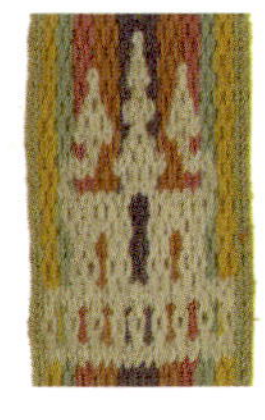

B860

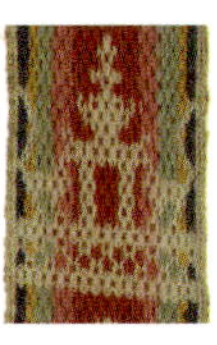

M02

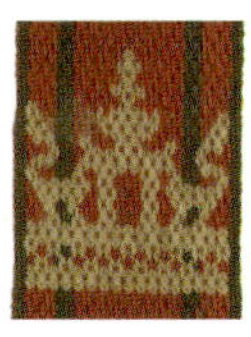

R005

Plate 129 RIGHT

The fig tree on the Shwedagon pagoda platform may be the first stop on the pilgrims' visit. This photograph was taken when, unusually, no worshippers were enjoying its shade.

Plate 130 BELOW

WOVEN IMAGES OF FIG TREES

The first act of pilgrims on a duty visit to the pagoda platform is to water the sacred tree. On many sazigyo the fig tree is the first image. *(J01, H004, R007, R026, R008, R105)*

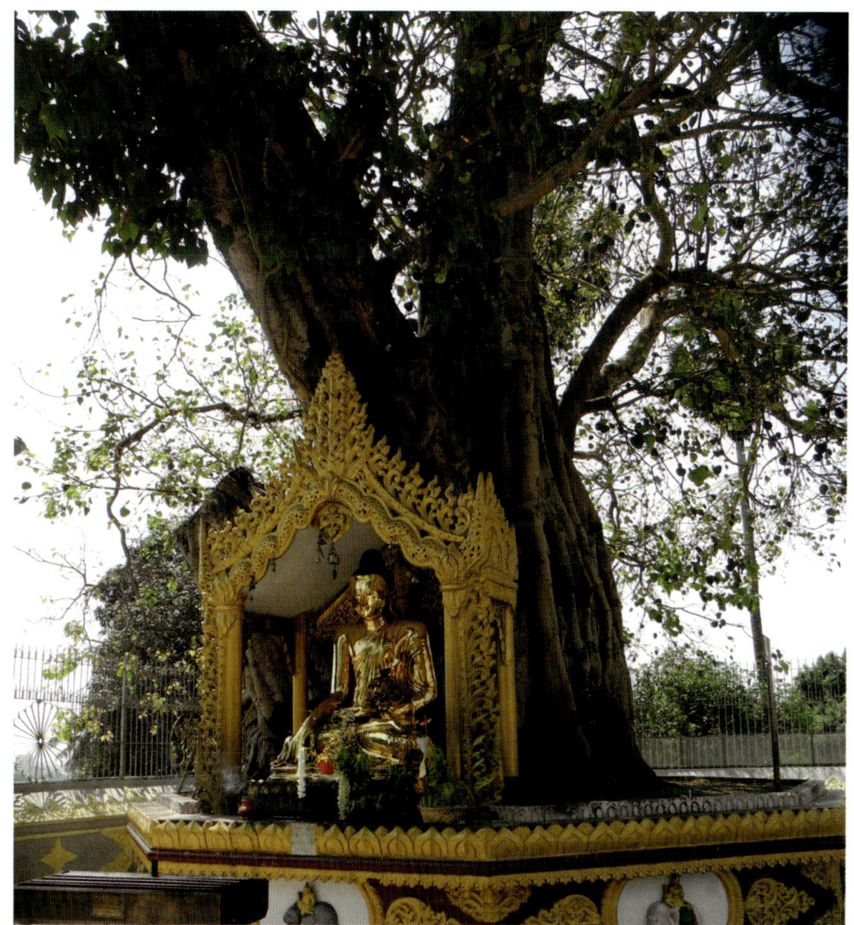

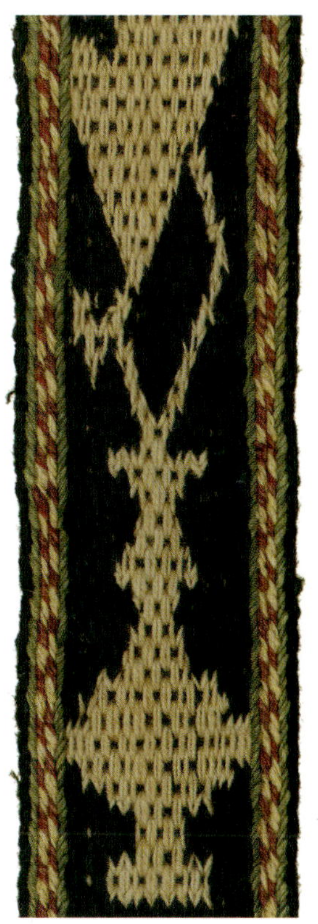

J01

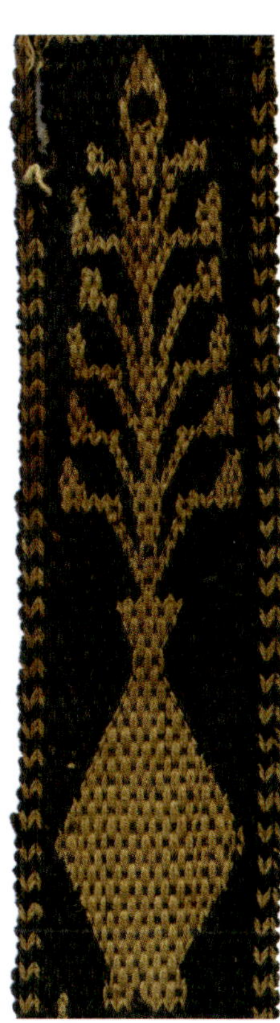

H004

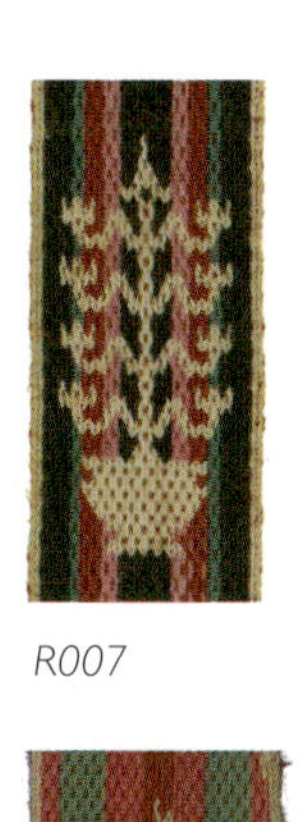

R007

R008

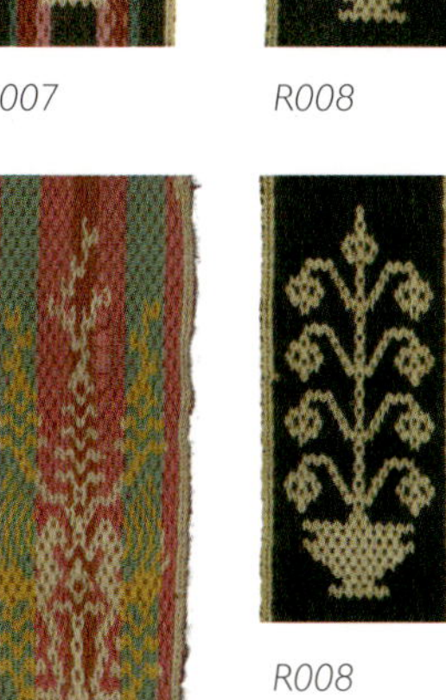

R026

R008

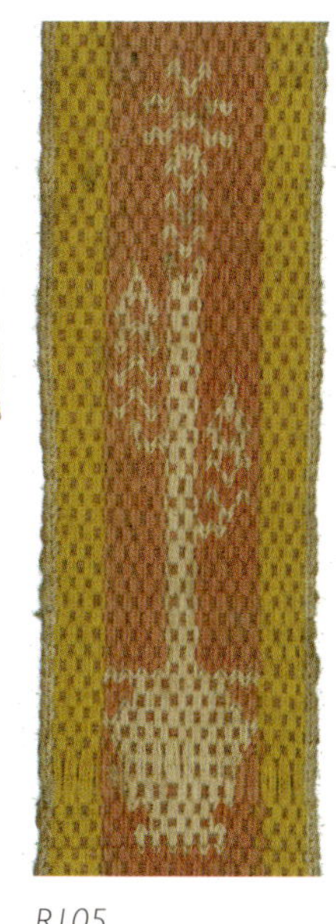

R105

Plate 131 RIGHT
A stone parasol *(kyauk hti)* on the pagoda platform.

Plate 132 BELOW
WOVEN IMAGES OF *KYAUK HTI*
A woven image of a parasol may be the last on the sazigyo, where it symbolizes the Buddha. *(R105, R210, T441, R145)*

Plate 133 NEXT PAGE
SETS OF IMAGES PRECEDING THE TEXT DIFFER FROM THOSE THAT FOLLOW IT
The location of a woven image on the flat part of the sazigyo—before, within, or after the text—matches its function.
At the start of the sazigyo, before the text, images such as the *chinthe* lions, the *manuthiha*, and the sacred Bo tree stand for the donors' arrival on the pagoda platform, and images such as the stag and the horse, symbolizing the law and the monks, reflect the Buddhist donor's devotional intent. *(M02)*
After the text a series of three images, two bells and the Earth Goddess, stand for the donors' broadcasting of their donation, inviting the approval of witnesses, and sharing the merit. The final image on the sazigyo is the *dagundaing*, the tall teak flagpole, symbolizing the conclusion of the donors' duty. *(R106)*

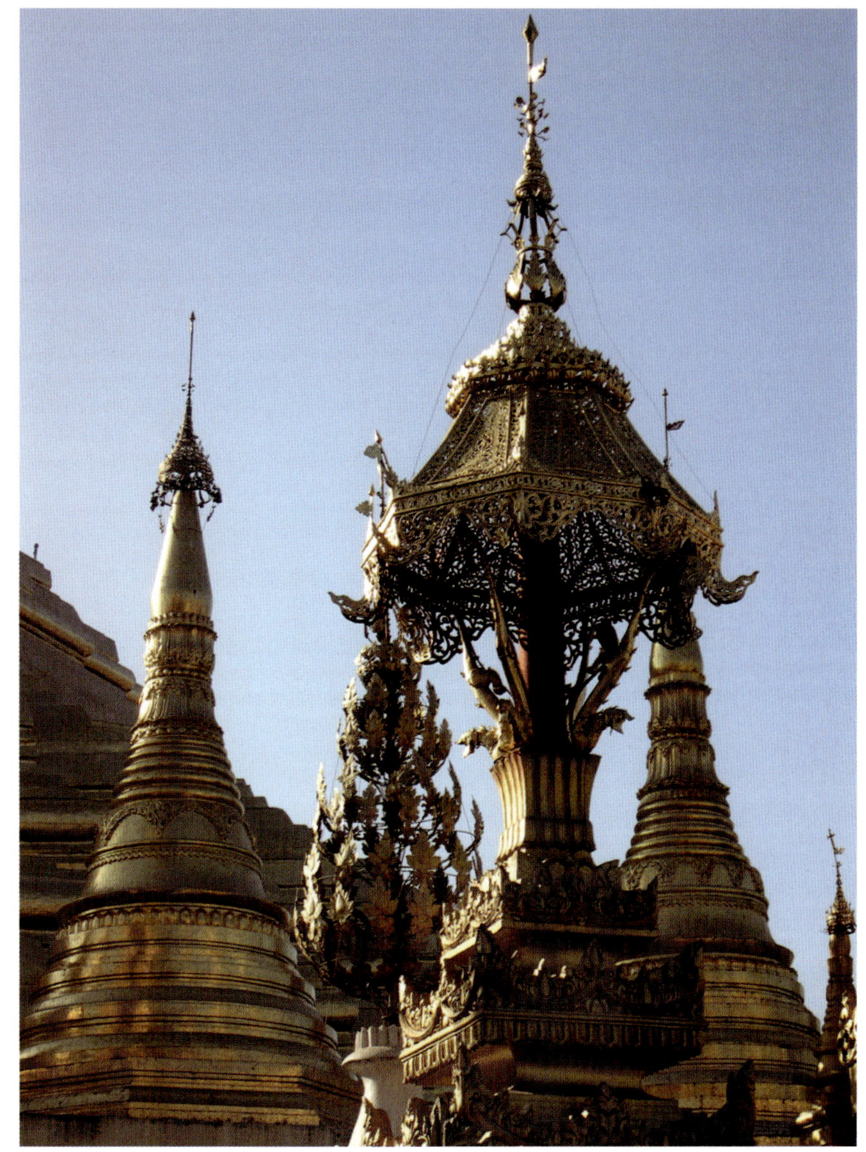

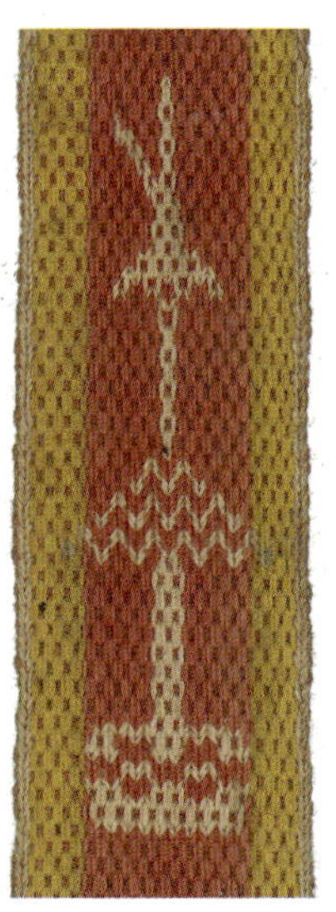

R105

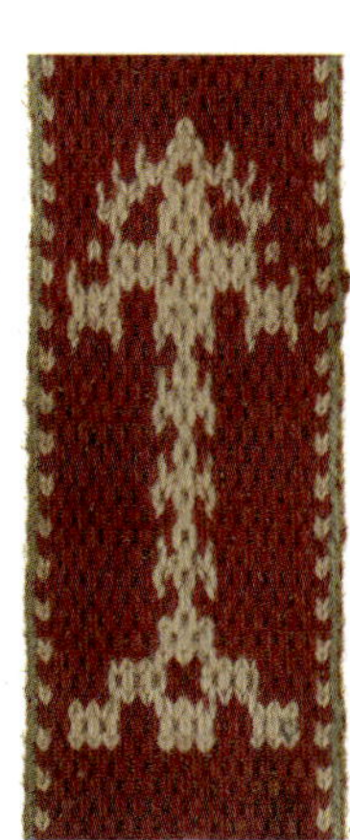

R210

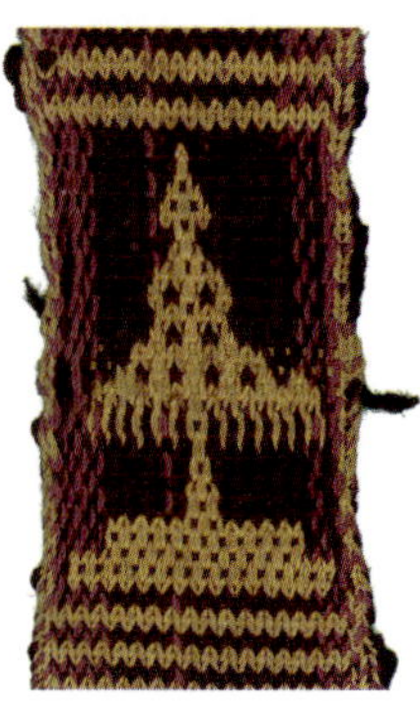

T441

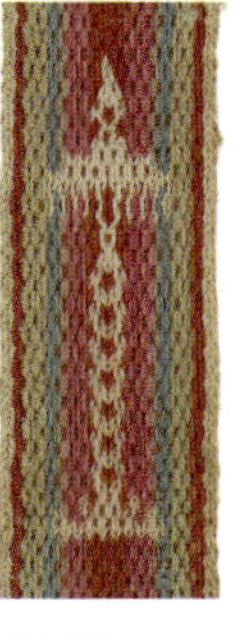

R145

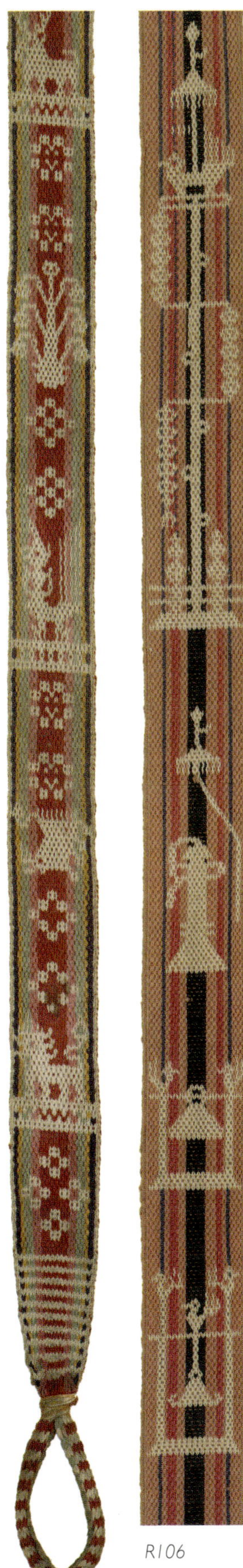

M02 R106

POSITION RELATIVE TO THE TEXT

The position of a woven image on the flat part of the sazigyo—before the text, within it, or after the text—often reflects its ritual function. Some images, such as the Bo tree and *chinthe* lions, appear at the very start of the sazigyo, setting the stage for the act of donation. Vocal birds and beasts immediately precede the text, and long branched processes emerging from their mouths represent the utterance. Pairs of beasts, birds, or fish may act as brackets around the text. Within the text itself, compact little frogs may be enlisted as punctuation marks to mark off the short verses. Some images, like those of bells and of the Earth Goddess Waythondaye, are invariably found after the text, in the space before the end of the tape. They perform their role only after the donors have concluded their prayer. Last and longest of all the images on the sazigyo is the *dagundaing*, the tall teak flagpole.

IMAGES AS "AMPLIFIERS"

The sazigyo is only a tablet-woven cotton tape, not a magnetically recorded audio tape. When we hold it or run it through our fingers to appreciate the beauty of woven script, motifs, and images, we probably do so in silence. And yet silence does not come naturally to the sazigyo. The rhyming verses of the sazigyo text were composed to sound melodious when chanted aloud. The weaver used images of vocal birds, beasts, and bells as visual "amplifiers," to lend resonance to the woven prayer.

The *pyinsarupa*, the animal of five body forms, stands for powerful forces and particularly for loud noise. It could be recruited when a fortissimo was required. Celestial witnesses had to be summoned loudly and clearly. To ensure that the donors' deed was properly recorded, weaver-designers inserted images of vocal birds or beasts, frogs, parrots, and *pyinsarupa*, squeezing them in as close as possible to the round bell (*hkaung-laung gyi*) and flat gong (*kyizi*). They were clearly meant to amplify the sound of the bells, and hammer home their message. The symbols of loud summons almost touch the figures of Thagya Min, King of the Nats, and Waythondaye, the Earth Goddess.

The frog (Burmese *hpa*) has a loud and insistent call. Ancient bronze "frog-drums" (Burmese *hpazi*) were sounded in high ceremonies by the Mon King Manuha. He and his frog-drums were captured by the Burmese King Anawrahta, and the ceremonial beating of the frog-drum became part of Burmese royal ceremonial under King Kyanzitta of Pagan (1084–1113 CE).[18] The emphatic beat of the frog-drum may have its distant echo in the series of woven images of frogs on sazigyo.

Plate 134 RIGHT

VISUAL "AMPLIFIERS"

Some weavers construct a sort of visual amplifier. They position images of very vocal birds and beasts, frogs, parrots, and *pyinsarupa* as close as possible to bells, as if to lend them resonance. They squeeze them in close to the Earth Goddess Waythondaye and to Thagya Min, King of the Nats, making the summons loud and clear. *(B887, T261 A,B,C, R001 A,B,C, H031 A,B,C,D)*

Readers intrigued by this curious device may like details of its use.

In *B887* an elephant attends to the flat bell, and a *pyinsarupa* to the Earth Goddess, but the round bell has only two *navratnas*.

T261 has a *pyinsarupa* for the flat bell *(A)*, a fish (admittedly not a vocalist) for the round bell *(B)*, and a pair of parrots for the Earth Goddess *(C)*.

R001 has a *chinthe* for the flat bell *(A)*, a *pyinsarupa* for the round bell *(B)*, and a single parrot for the Earth Goddess *(C)*.

H031 has a formidable orchestra: *pyinsarupa* and fish for the round bell *(A)*, a second *pyinsarupa* and a pair of parrots for the flat bell *(B)*, a third *pyinsarupa* and another pair of parrots for the Earth Goddess Waythondaye *(C)*, and an elephant for Thagya Min, King of the Nats *(D)*.

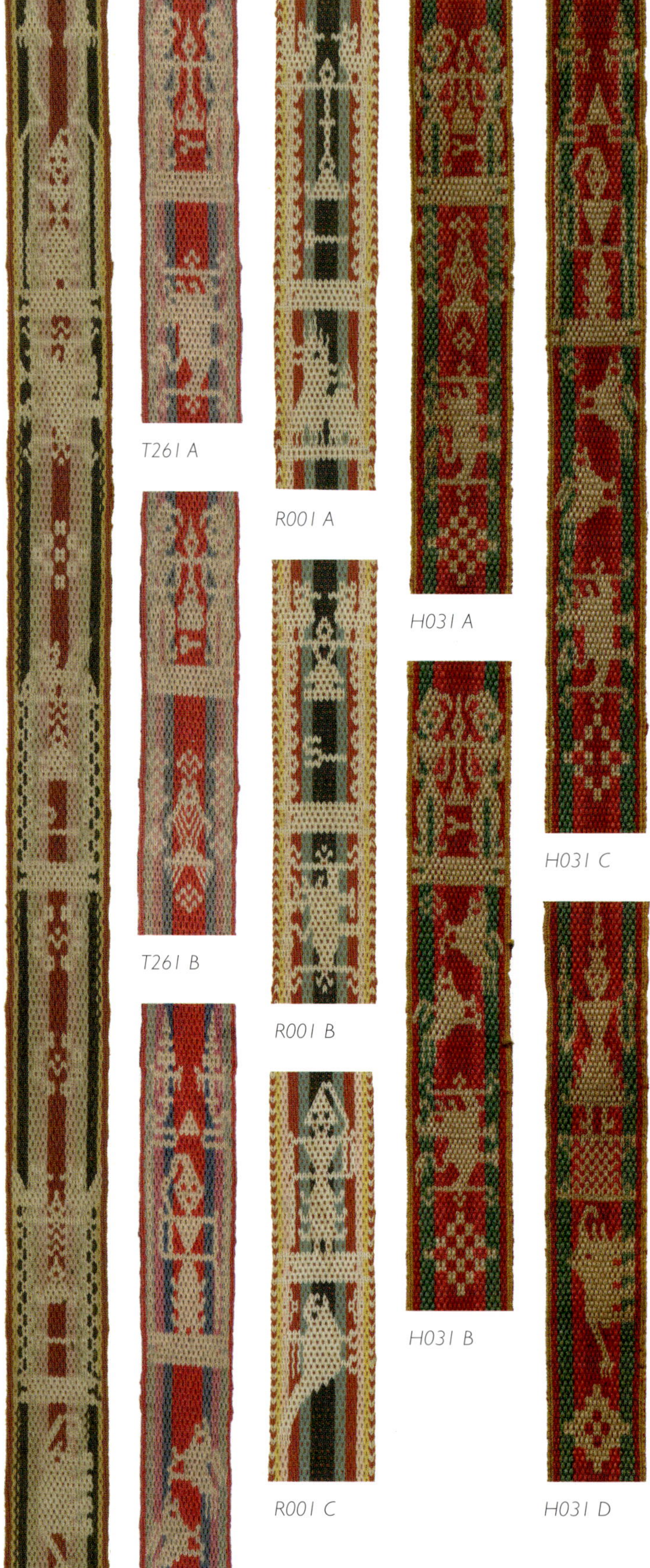

T261 A

R001 A

H031 A

H031 C

T261 B

R001 B

H031 B

R001 C

H031 D

B887

T261 C

Plate 135 BELOW AND FOLLOWING PAGE
EARLY WOVEN TEXT HAS NO PUNCTUATION
The woven text in the mid-nineteeth-century sazigyo below is one long line of letters, with no gaps between words and no punctuation marks. (*B890, J01, R046, R162*)

WOVEN IMAGES AS PUNCTUATION MARKS

In early Burmese script no gaps separate the words. The woven text in mid-nineteenth-century sazigyo is one long succession of letters, with no punctuation marks at all. Later in the nineteenth century punctuation marks appear in sazigyo texts. Each *pada* verse of four single-syllable words is marked off by a single short vertical stroke "I" or (more usually) by a pair "II." In the early twentieth century, at the whim of the weaver, the two vertical strokes might join to form an "H" or intersect in an "X." Later some inventive weavers replaced these conventional punctuation marks with entertaining miniatures of birds and beasts. Little frogs hopped in to mark off the verses of the text.

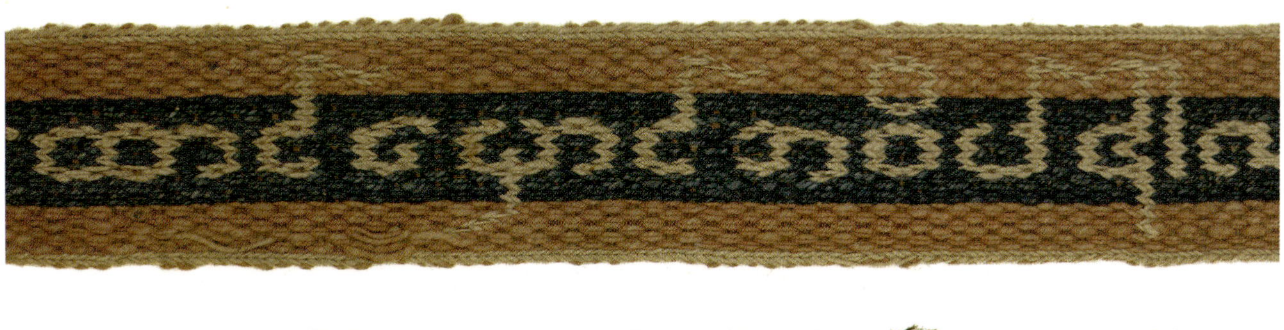

B890

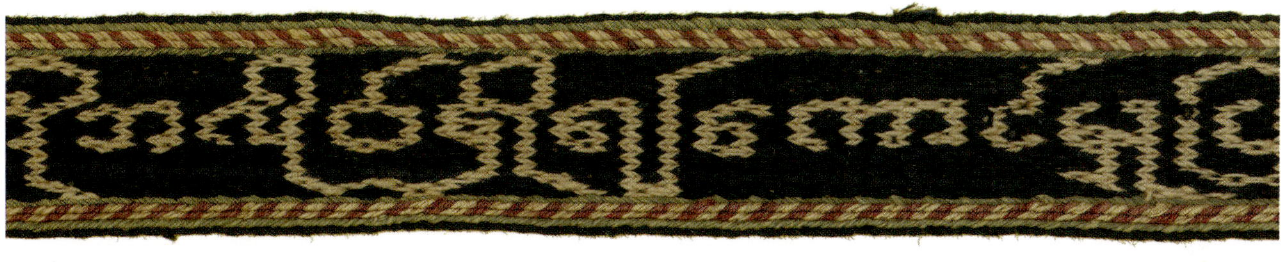

J01

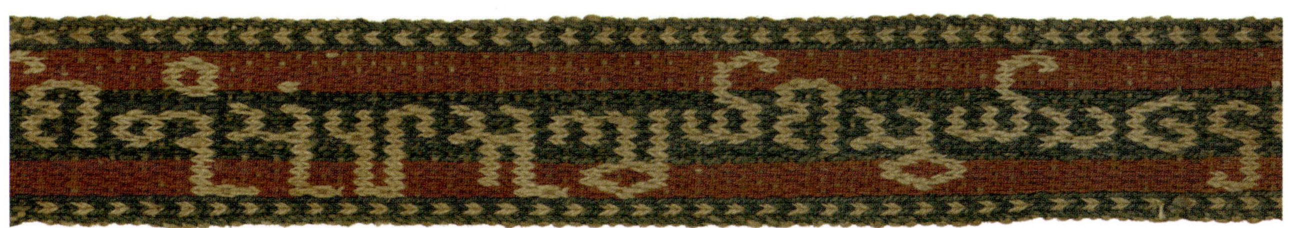

R046

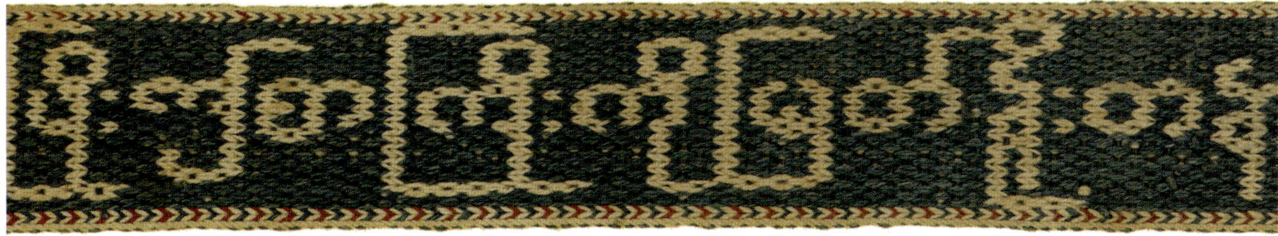

R162

Punctuation marks appear in late nineteenth-century sazigyo texts. Each *pada* verse of four single-syllable words is marked off by a single short vertical stroke (।) *(B846)* or by a pair (॥). *(B840, J07, R247)*

Around the turn of the century, at the whim of the weaver, the two vertical strokes may be joined to form an "H" *(B866, B887)* or intersect in an "X." *(R039)*

In the early twentieth century some inventive weavers replaced conventional punctuation marks with miniatures of birds and beasts. Little frogs hopped in to mark off the verses of the text. *(M01, R245)* The *navratna*, the auspicious nine-gems motif, might also be utilized to mark off the verses. *(T1223)*

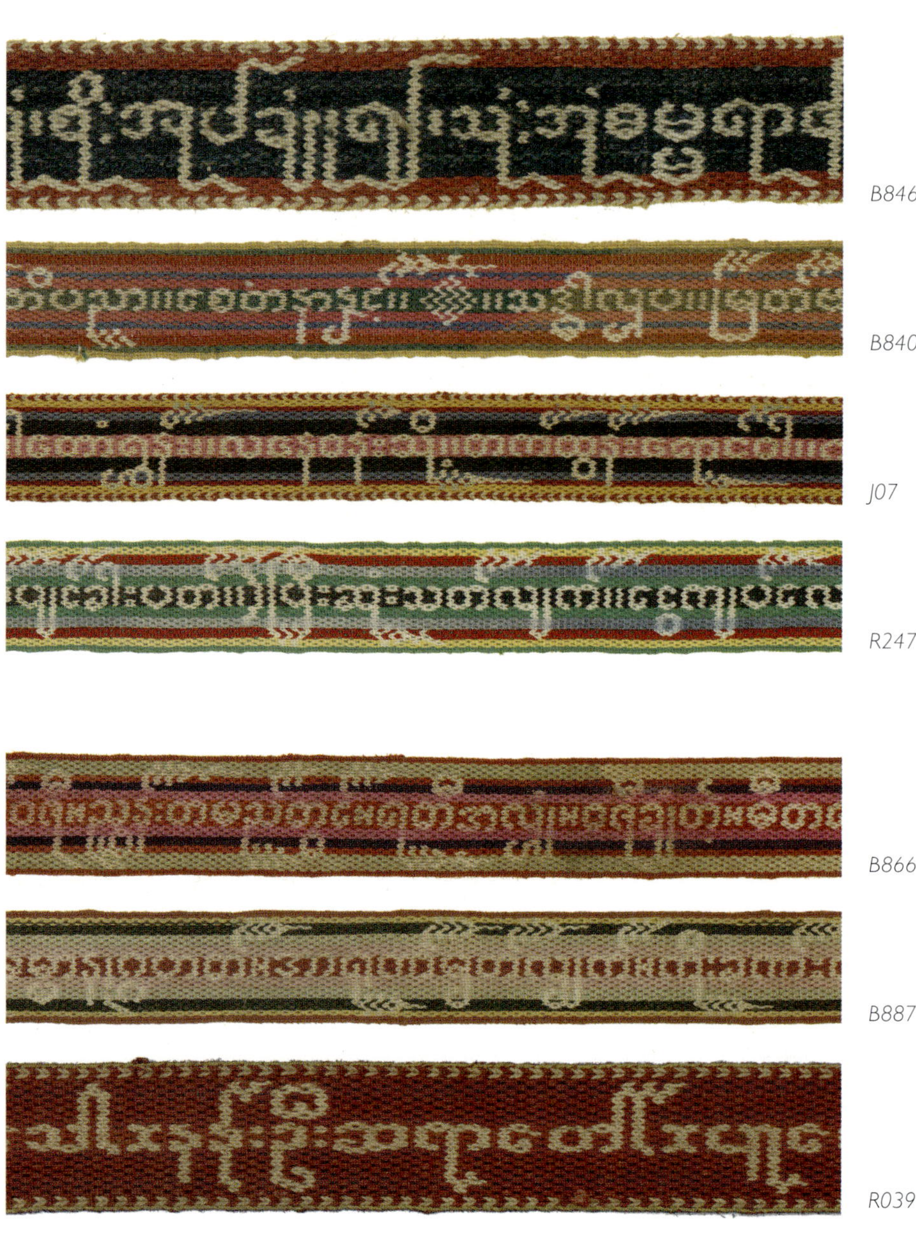

B846

B840

J07

R247

B866

B887

R039

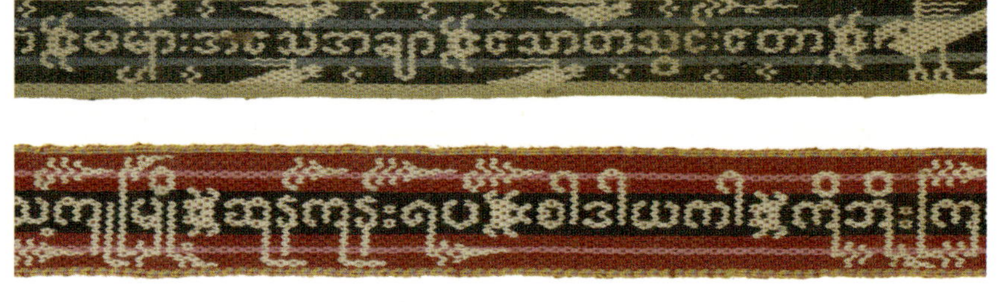

M01

R245

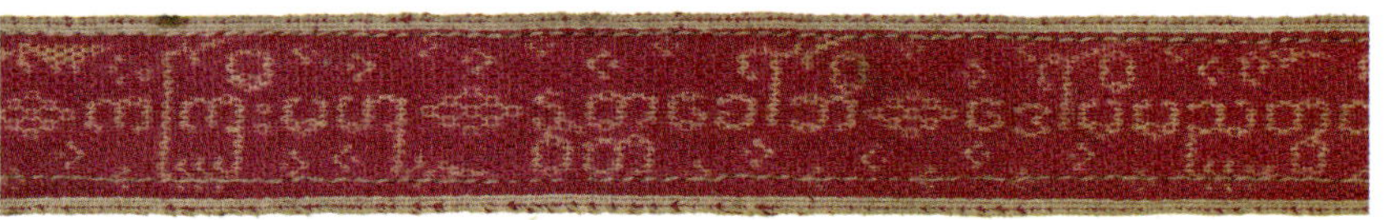

T1223

Plate 136

RIGHT, BELOW, AND FOLLOWING PAGE

FANCY BRACKETS AND FLANKING BEASTS

Elegant decorative brackets may enclose major divisions of the text. *(B874, R082, R082, R130, W93)*

Many weavers favor animated parentheses. Woven images of birds and beasts may introduce and conclude the main text. *(R003, R006, R012, R076, R206)*

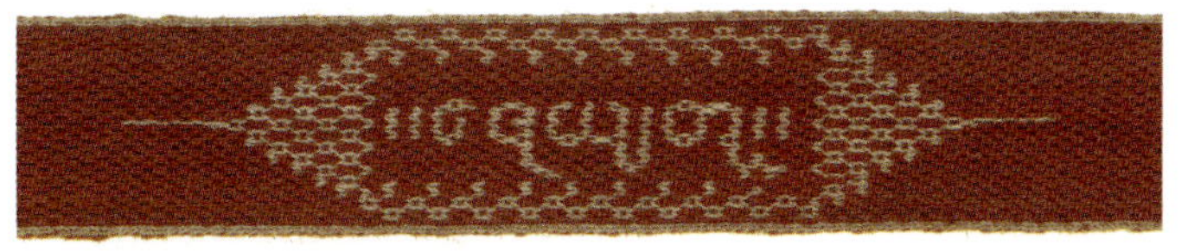
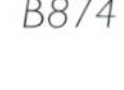

B874

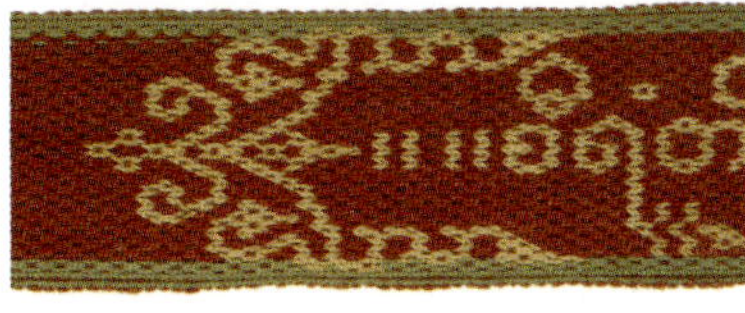
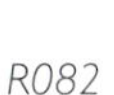

R082

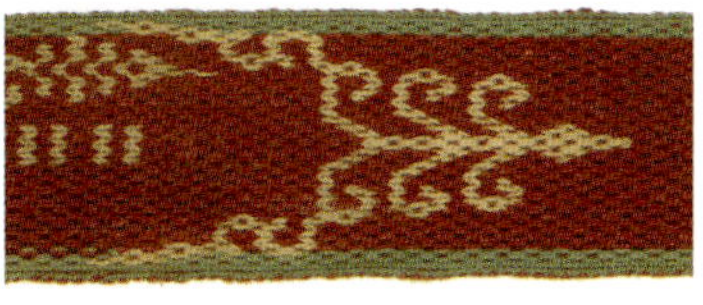

R082

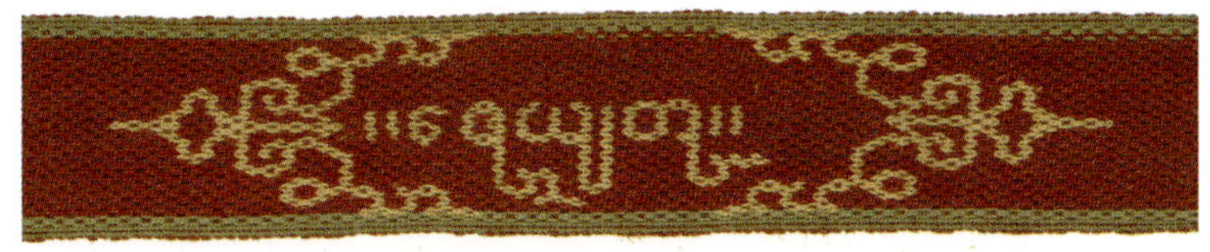

R082

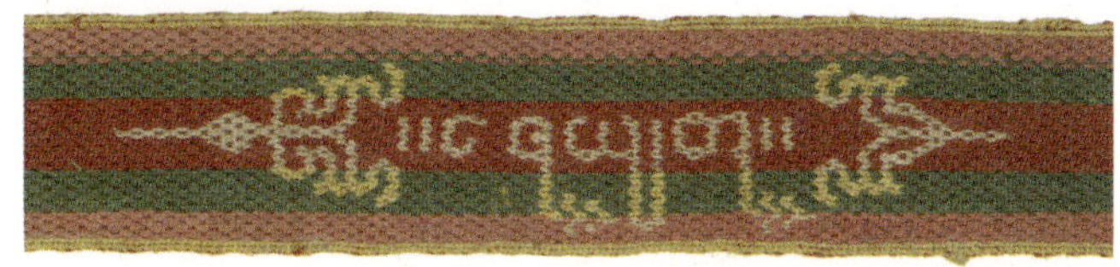

R130

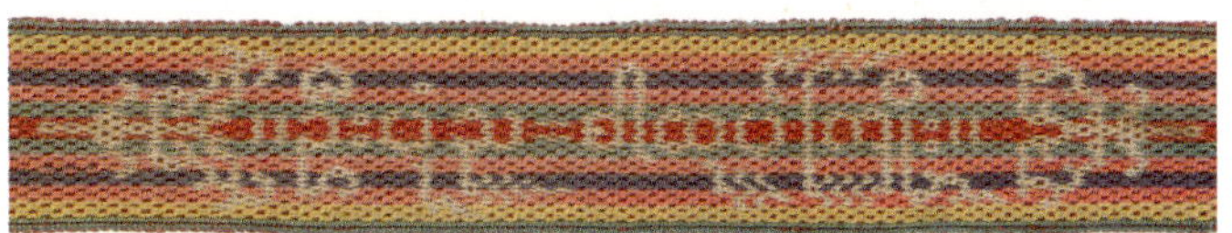

W93

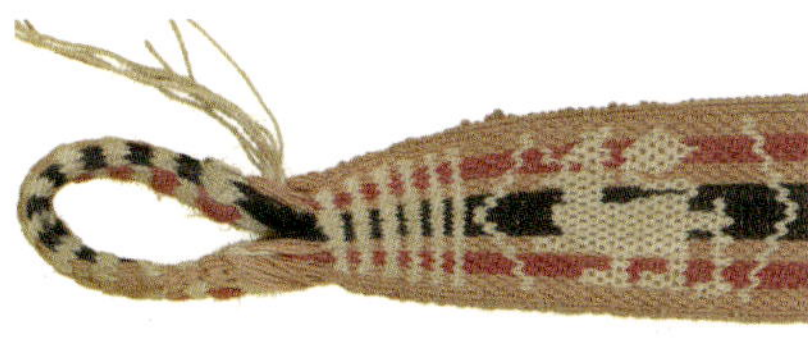

R003

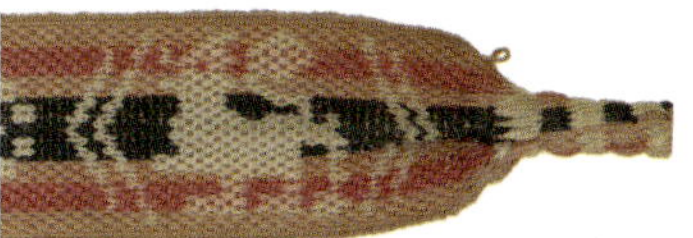

R003

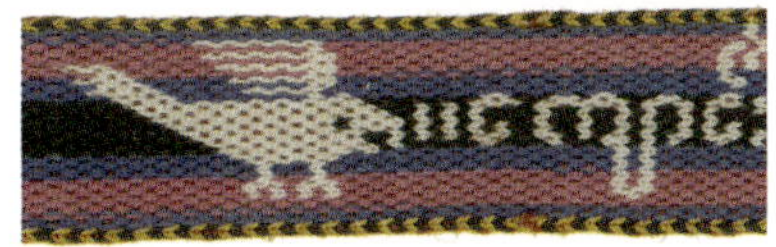

R006

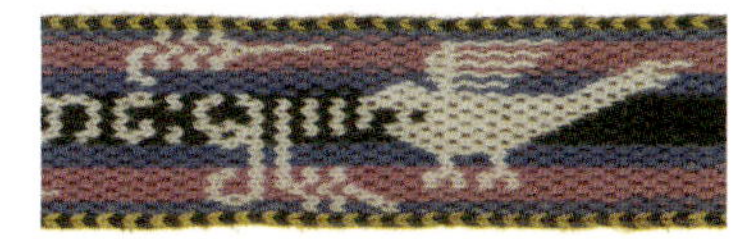

R006

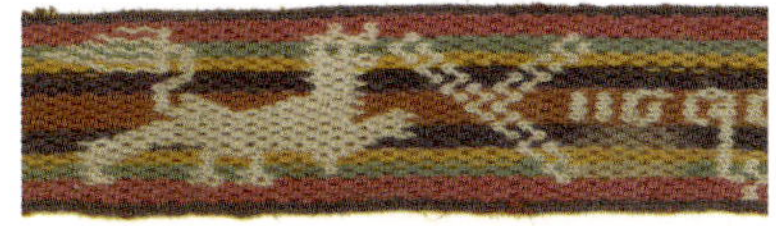

R012

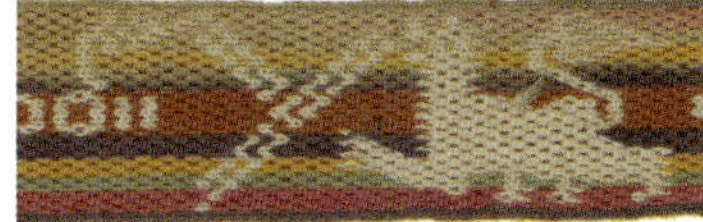

R012

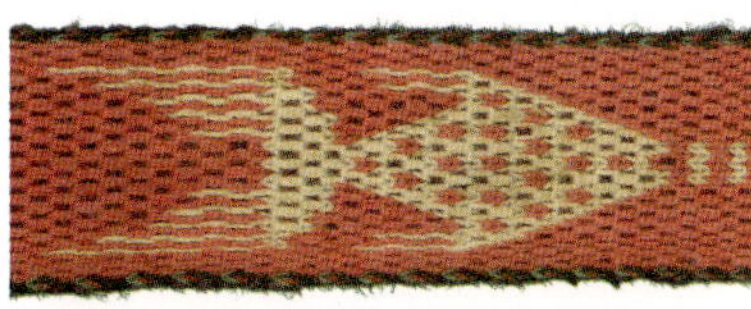

R076

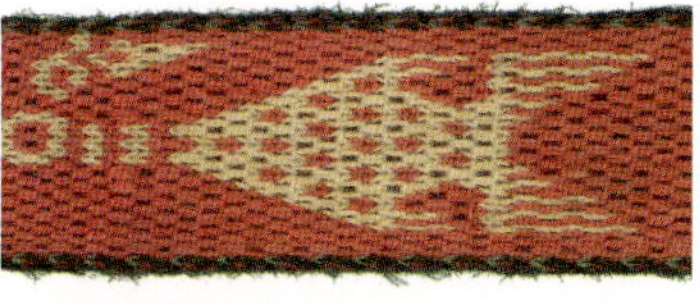

R076

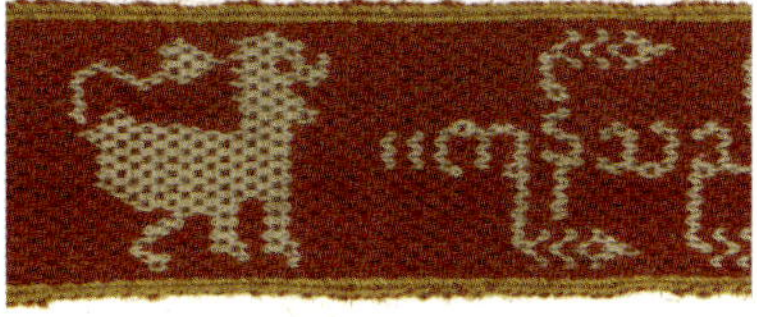

R206

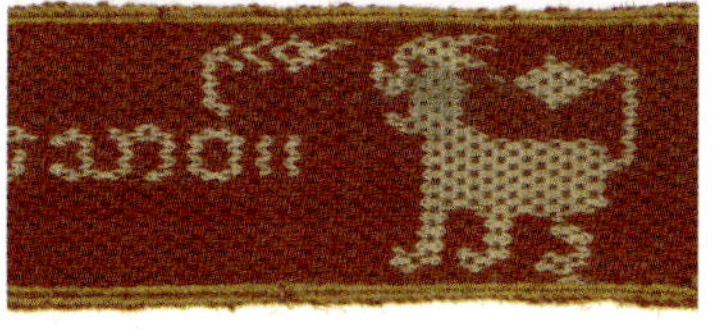

R206

Pairs of birds, beasts, or fish may bracket short "textlets," such as the initial invocation *("Zeyatu!")* or the date of the donation or title of the manuscript. *(R026 , H031, J07, MYA055.T, BL)*
Pointing hands indicate the British colonial influence. *(B860, B851, R054)*

Major divisions of the text may be enclosed in elegant decorative "brackets." Woven images of birds and beasts often make more elaborate, animated parentheses. The main text may be introduced and concluded by a pair of woven images. Burmese script is written from left to right, so when a right-facing lion or parrot immediately precedes the woven text, then a left-facing beast, the mirror image of the first, will follow the last word. When these woven miniatures of birds, beasts, or fish herald the text, appearing to breathe out the first words, they recall the illuminated initial letters in European medieval manuscripts. When the weaver uses two beasts in each position instead of one, a text

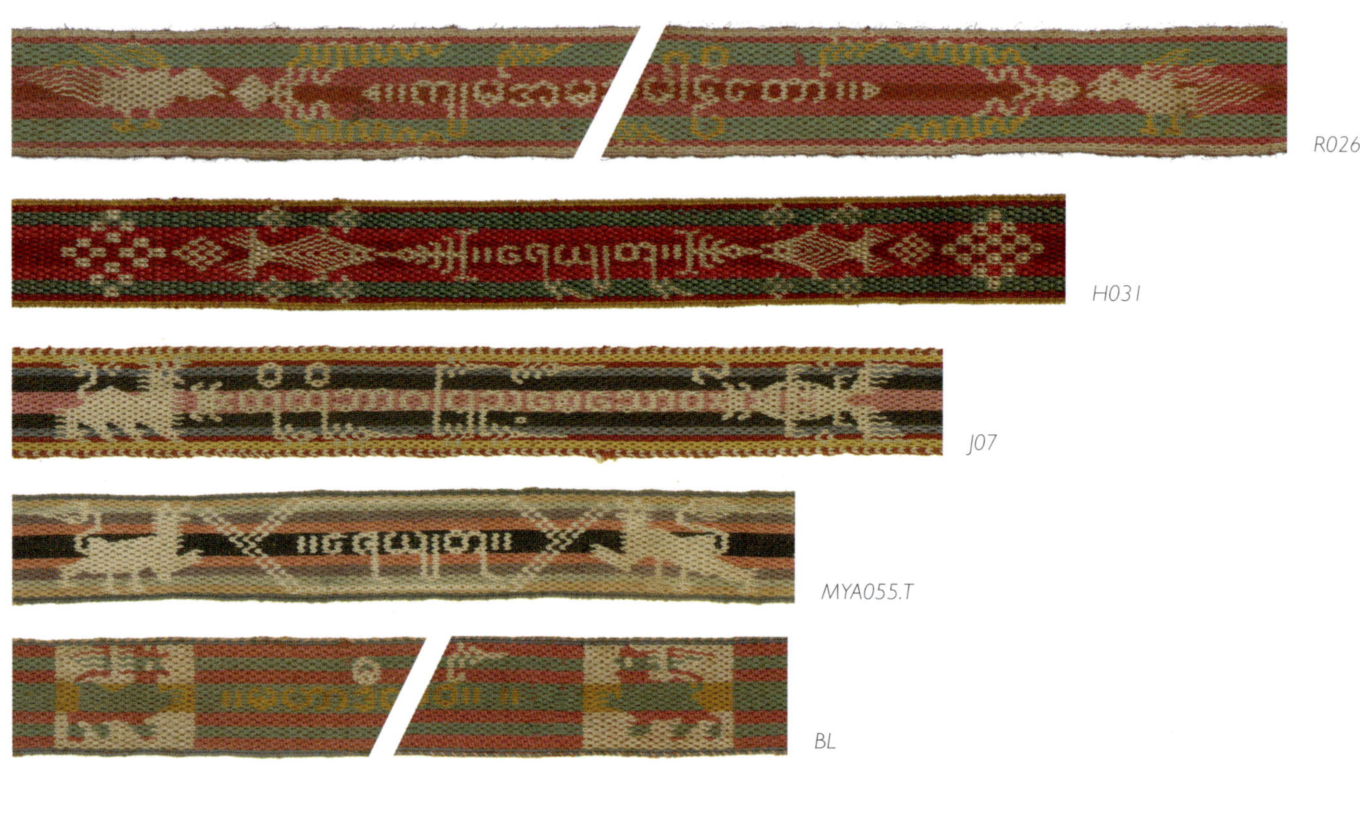

R026

H031

J07

MYA055.T

BL

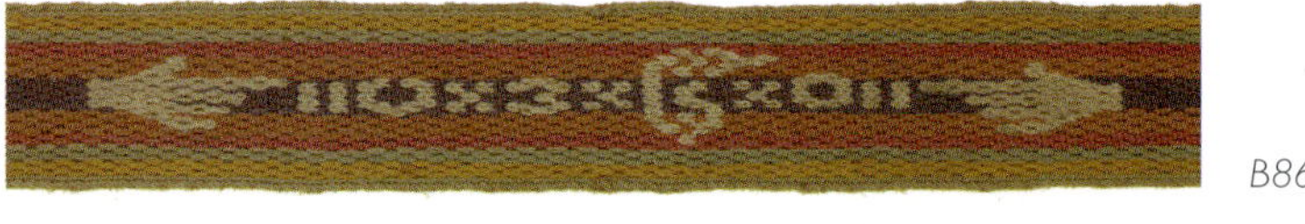

B860

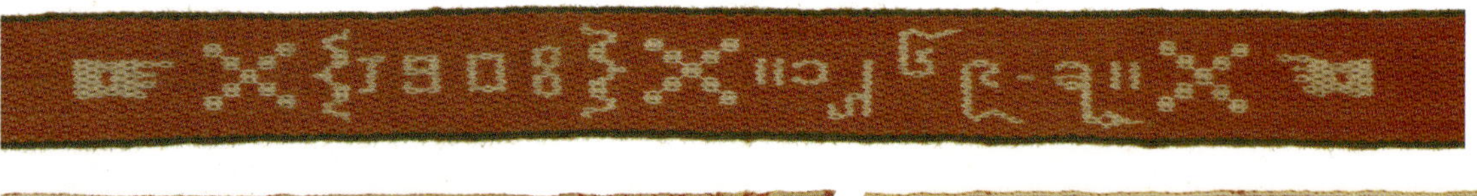

B851

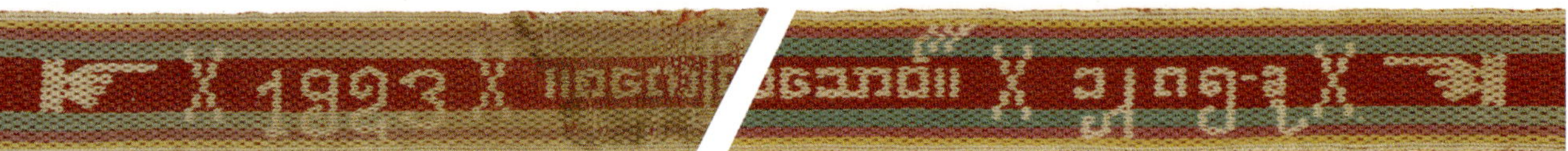

R054

Woven miniatures of birds, beasts, or fish depicted breathing out the first words of the text have their Western counterparts in the pictorial initial letters in medieval illuminated manuscripts. *(R006, H031, B877, R049, R192, R106)*

Heraldic lions support a cartouche. *(R024)*

introduced by a fish and a frog facing right will end with a left-facing frog and fish, in that order.

The very first text on the sazigyo, the single Pali word *"Zeyatu!"* ("Success!"), may be framed in elegant brackets, sometimes enhanced by woven images of beasts or birds, especially parrots. (Parrots are of course talkers.) Other short texts, such as the date of the donation or the signature of the weaver, receive the same highlighting treatment. Occasionally they are completely enclosed in a decorative cartouche in the form of a panel or banner, its long tapes or ribbons held by the supporting beasts or birds, with striking heraldic effect.

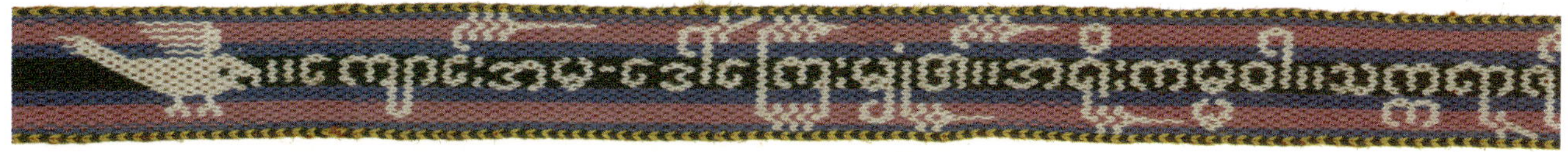

R006

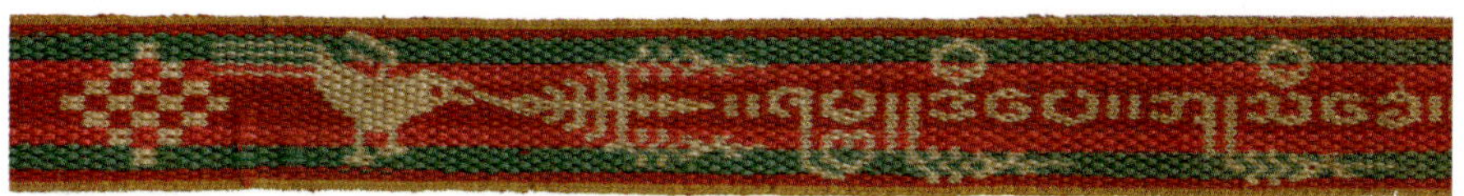

H031

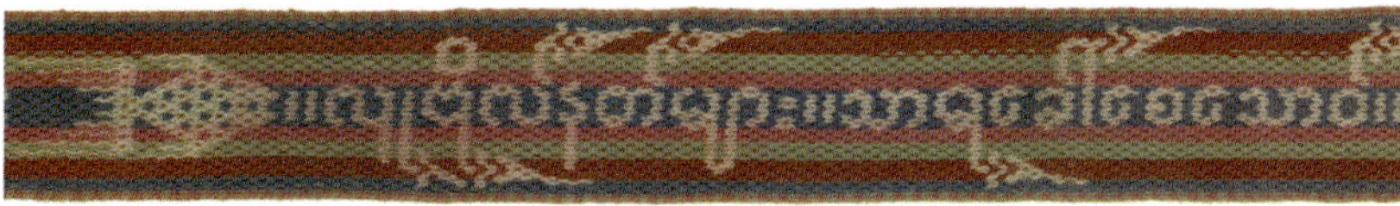

B877

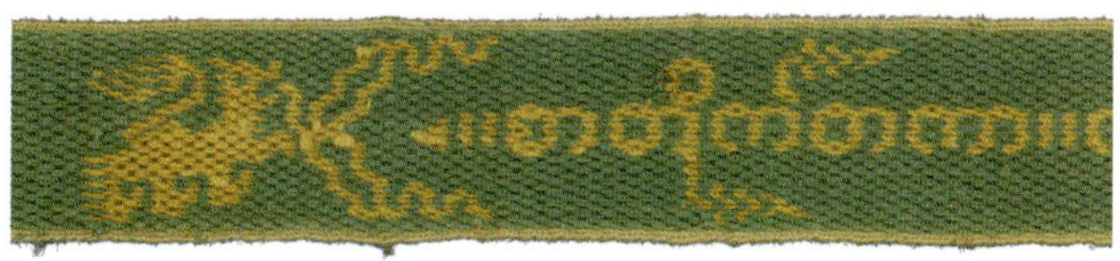

R049

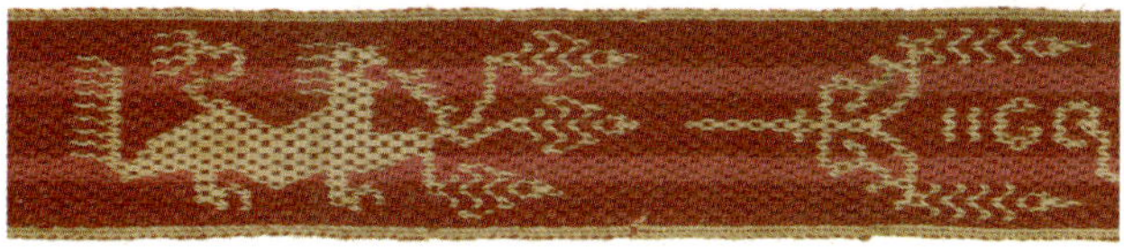

R192

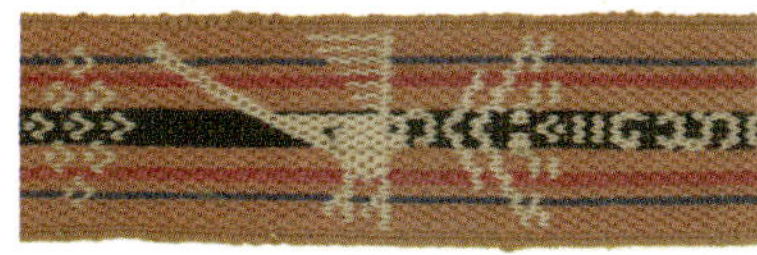

R106

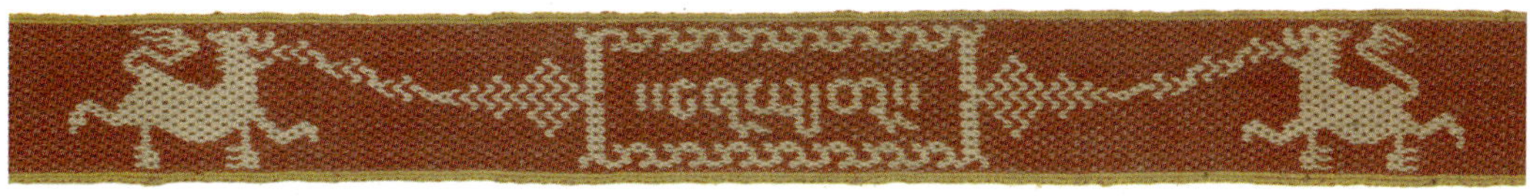

R024

Plate 137 RIGHT
ANIMATED PUNCTUATION
"PARROTGRAPHS"
A single parrot *(B840)* or a pair of parrots tail to tail may be used to mark off major sections of the text (which we could call "parrotgraphs"). *(B843, B877, R106, R160, M01, JBT6.49, R005)*
Fish depicted tail to tail may serve instead. *(R268)*
In long texts these useful birds keep count. They appear after every ten verses, with numerals under their tails to record the cumulative total of verses. *(R030)*

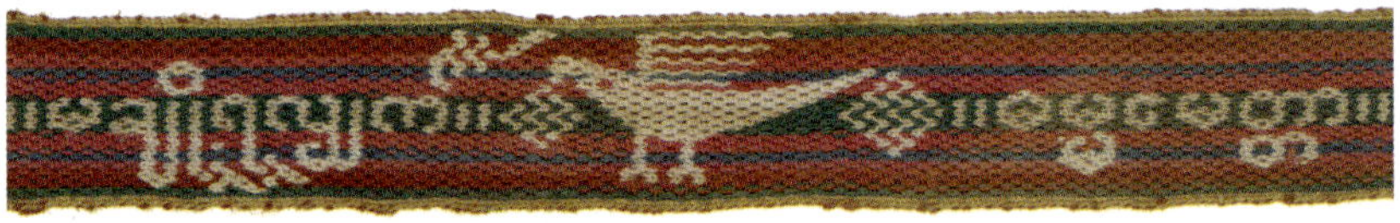

B840

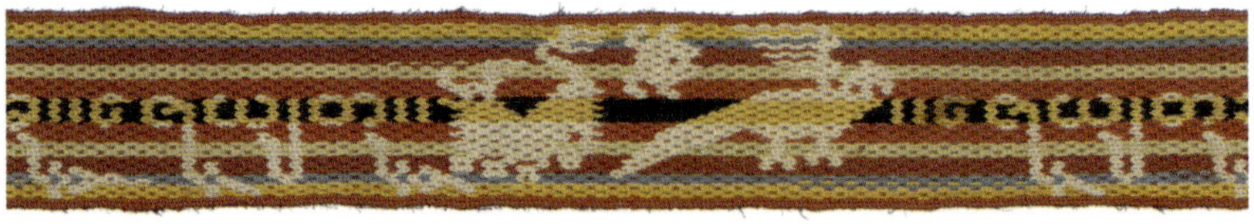

B843

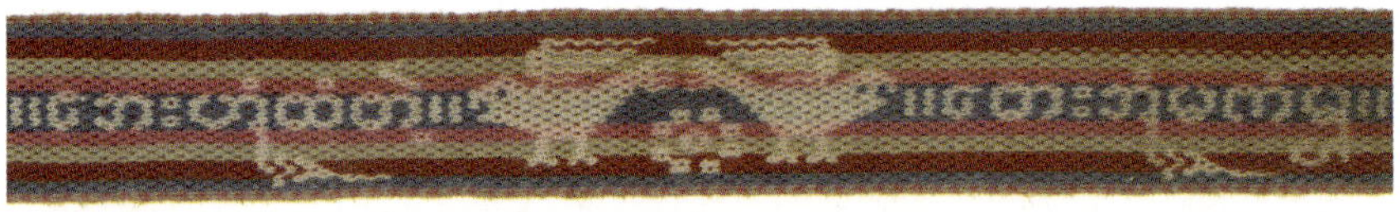

B877

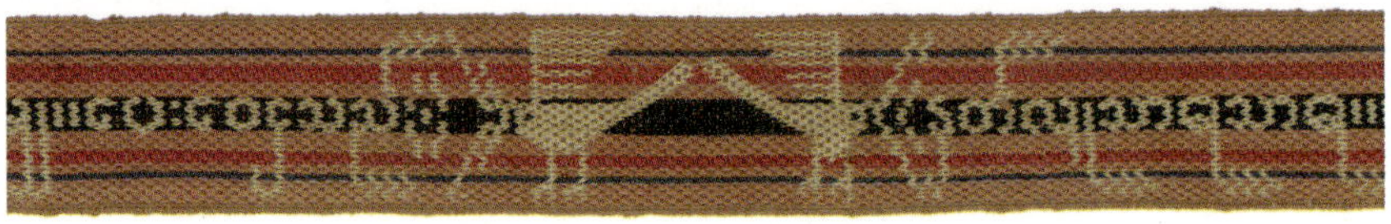

R106

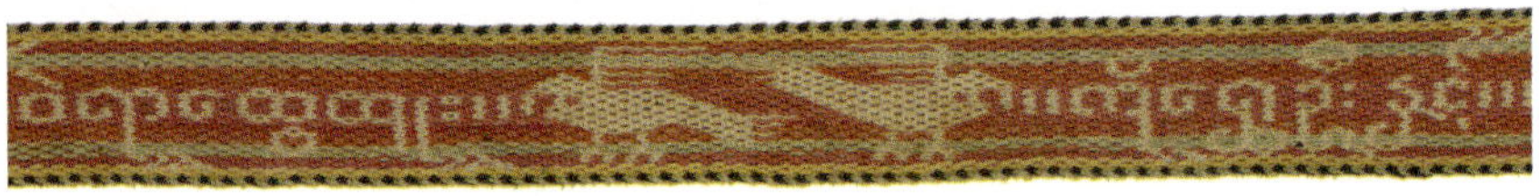

R160

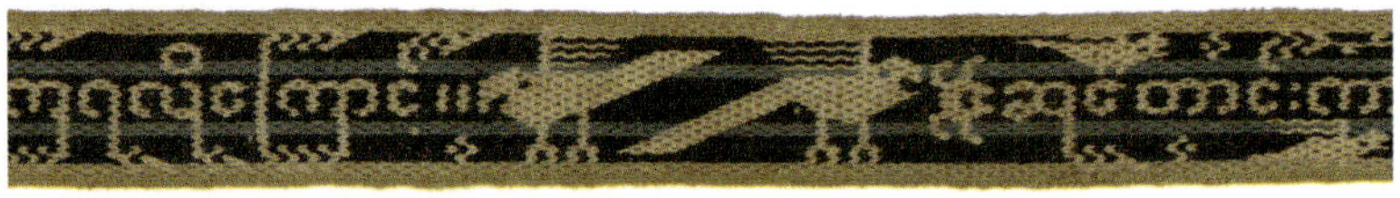

M01

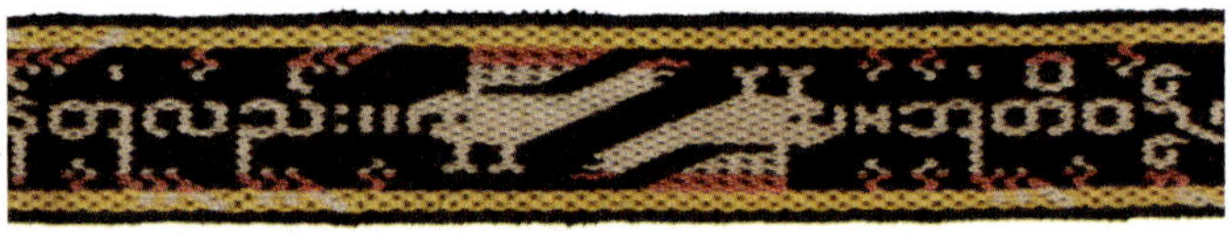

JBT6.49

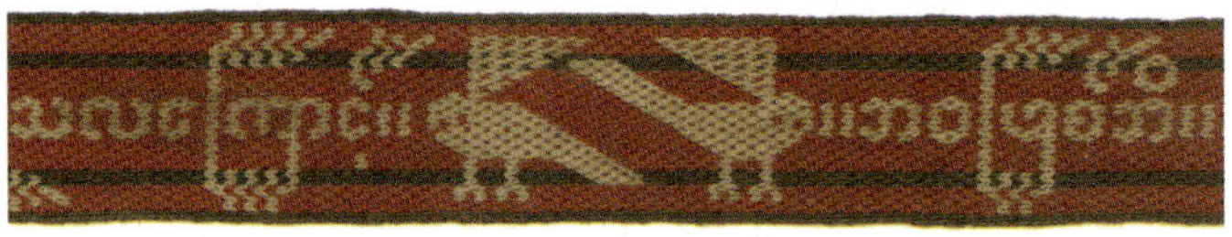

R005

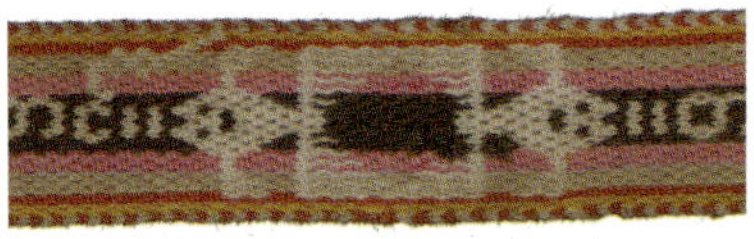

R268

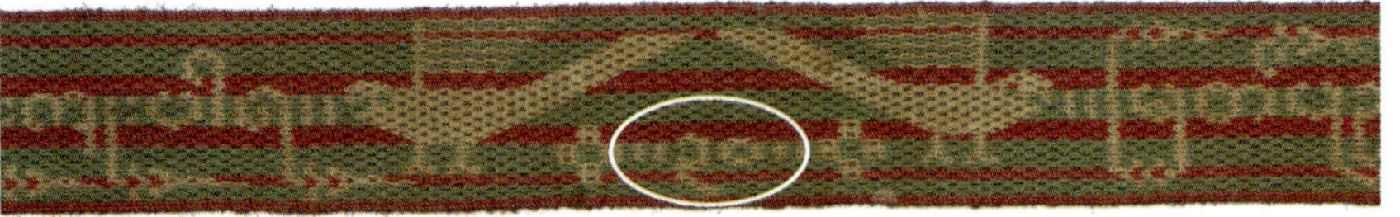

R030

Pairs of parrots, tail to tail, may mark off the major sections of a long main text. They usually appear at intervals of ten verses, to record the cumulative total.

Plate 138 BELOW
Exuberant sequences of images create their own special impact. Here are some from the start and others from the end of beautifully woven sazigyo.
(Start: B842, B843, R005, R247
End: B877, M02, R001, T883)

SEQUENCES OF WOVEN IMAGES

Some sazigyo start or end with an exuberant sequence of miniature woven images. These may be crowded closely together or separated by geometric motifs, often in trios. All symbolize aspects of the donation. Entire sequences, like those shown in plate 138, have more visual impact as a whole than when isolated for analysis of individual images.

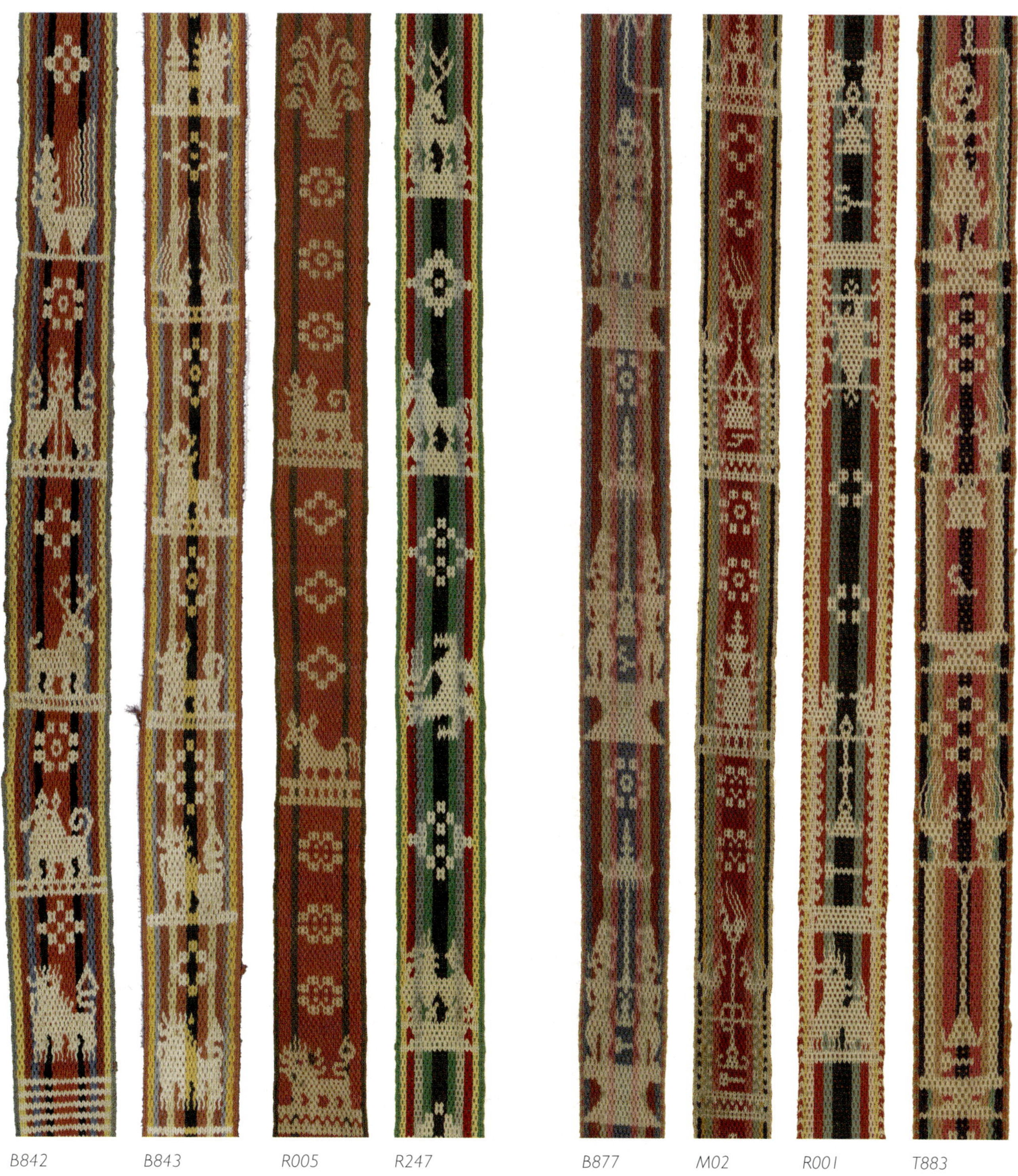

B842 *B843* *R005* *R247* *B877* *M02* *R001* *T883*

Plate 139 RIGHT

Rotate these curious brackets and they are revealed as elongated Nats. *(B879)*
Some images of Nats are thinly disguised as ritual furniture. One example could pass for a baroque lamp-stand, but its blue eyes and pink mouth betray the Nat. *(J05, J06)*

Plate 140 BELOW

Some weavers used a special supplementary weft in a contrasting color to give the Earth Goddess eyes, to equip her for her role as witness of the donors' deed of merit. *(B855, B840, B840, T467)*

Plate 141 NEXT PAGE

TRICK IMAGES AND MYSTERY IMAGES

Mythic *manuthiha* have a human torso and twin lion bodies, but this variant invented by a weaver has the head and chest of a lion, and two lion bodies. *(R007).*
This image may be meant for a bat. *(MYA 055T)*
The lion with a triangular standard is another unique woven image. *(R245)*
This image on an old indigo sazigyo is that of a *thungedaw*, a little naked royal page-boy. Although an exclusively royal symbol, it appears on a sazigyo donated by an ordinary lay couple. *(T410)*
One of a number of startlingly original images on a lovely but sadly faded sazigyo shows a man apparently swinging from a crossbar in a gymnastic exercise. *(R105)*
These two images, a pair of blacksmith's tongs and a smoothing iron, are placed last on a sazigyo, even after the *dagundaing*. Presumably they held personal and private significance for the donor. *(L01)*
A mysterious long and spindly reclining figure appears immediately before the main text on a sazigyo woven about 1920. It cannot be meant for the Buddha, since no images of the Buddha ever appear on sazigyo. *(R107)*

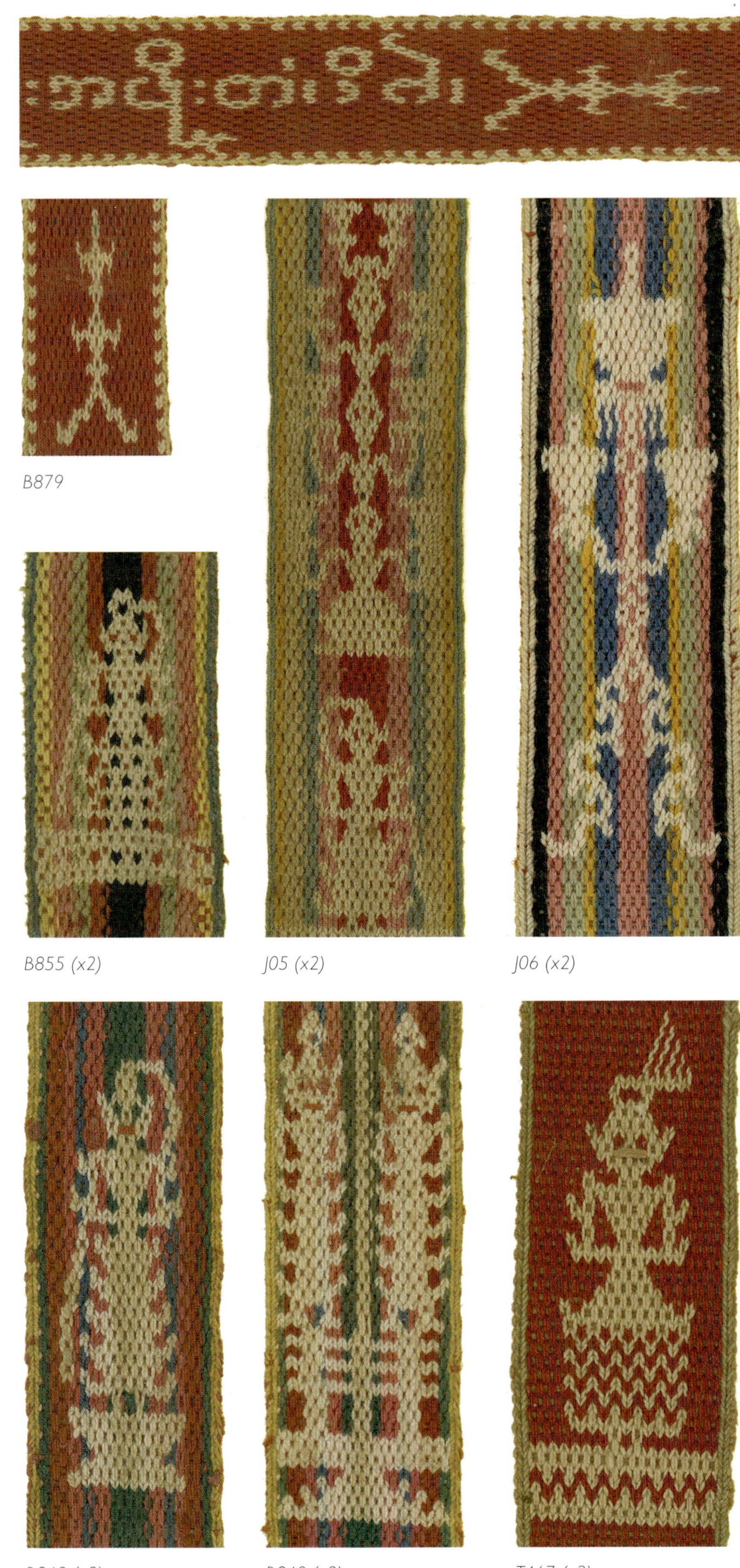

B879

B879

B855 (x2) *J05 (x2)* *J06 (x2)*

B840 (x2) *B840 (x2)* *T467 (x2)*

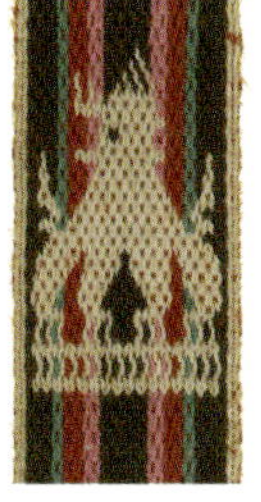

R007

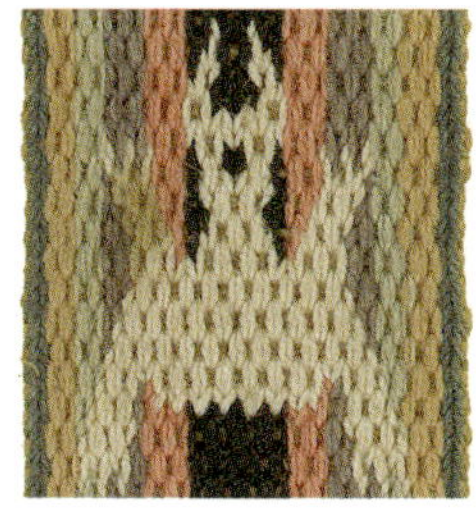

MYA 055T (x2)

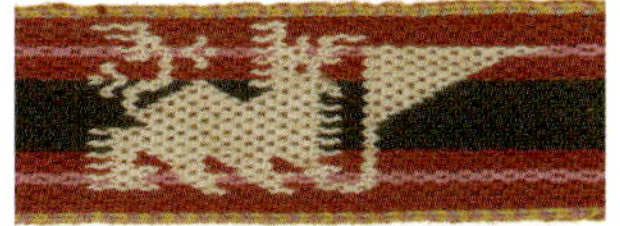

R245

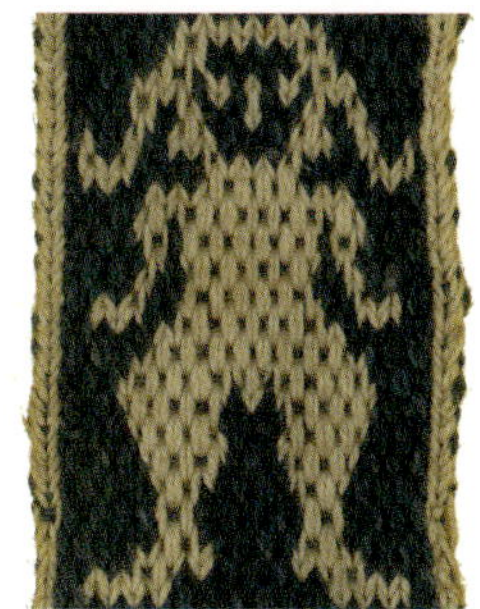

T410

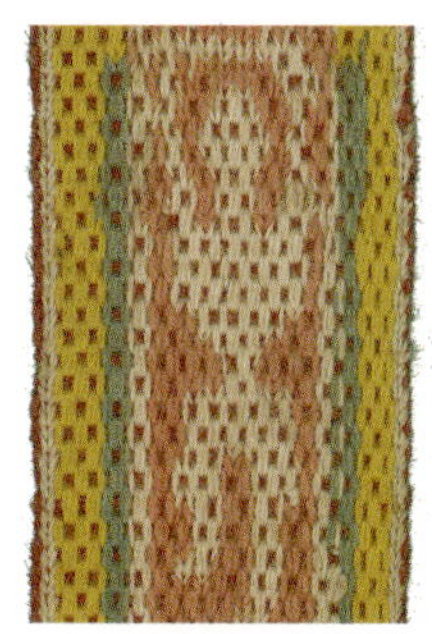

R105

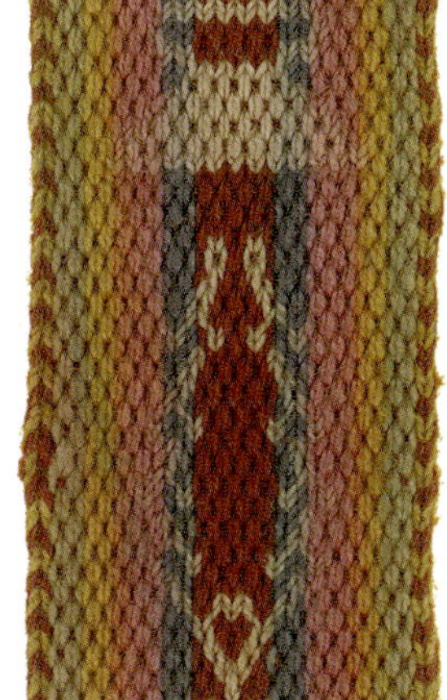

L01 (x2)

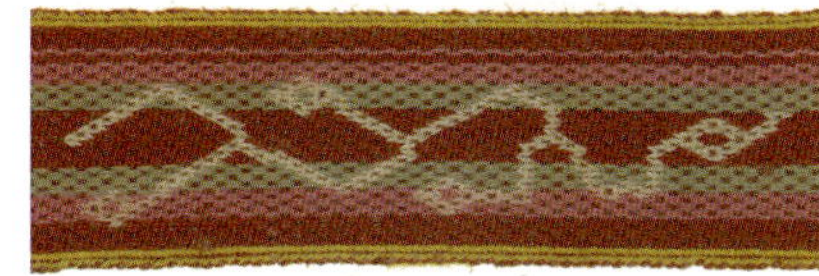

R107

TRICK AND MYSTERY IMAGES

Witty weavers obviously enjoyed inventing playful images. They devised curious brackets, which when rotated to be viewed upright, resemble elongated Nats. Or they disguised Nats as ritual furniture. The fine rollicking example illustrated here might pass for a baroque lamp-stand, but its blue eyes and pink mouth betray the Nat.

Some weavers had their own special technical tricks. A special supplementary weft in a contrasting color endows Waythondaye the Earth Goddess with eyes, vital equipment for her duty as witness of the donors' deed of merit.

Eccentric creatures find a place on sazigyo, and ordinary creatures are liable to behave eccentrically. Mythical *manoutthiha* have a human torso and twin lion bodies, but a variant invented by a weaver is all lion. It has the head and chest of a lion, and two lion bodies.

A few intriguing images defy interpretation, their form or significance (or both) remaining obscure. Perhaps such images were inserted for their personal and private significance to the donor of the sazigyo.

The sole image on an old indigo sazigyo is that of a *thungedaw*. These little royal pageboys are always depicted naked. Carved gilt-wood statues of *thungedaw* stood in groups of eight before each of the nine thrones in the Mandalay palace, their youth symbolizing the growth of the king's power and glory.[19] Their distinctive hairstyle, called *nabansan*, with two tufts hanging from the side of the head above each ear and the rest of the head shaved, can be clearly recognized in this unique woven image (T410).[20] But the donors named in the text were an ordinary lay couple, so it is a mystery why this exclusively royal symbol appears on their sazigyo.

A lovely but sadly faded sazigyo (R105) has a number of startlingly original images, including one of a man apparently swinging from a crossbar in a gymnastic exercise. On another sazigyo (L01) the usual final image, the *dagundaing*, is followed by a pair of blacksmith's tongs and a smoothing iron. We can only guess that these possessed personal and private significance for the donor, who insisted on adding them.

An enigmatic image appears after the "*Zeyatu*" and immediately before the main text on a sazigyo woven about 1920 (R107). It looks human or humanoid, like a long spindly reclining figure, a cross between the sculpture of Giacometti and Henry Moore. It cannot be meant for the Buddha, whose image never appears on sazigyo. And it is not unique, for a similar image appears on a much earlier sazigyo (KJ04). What can it be? Everyone who sees it has a different suggestion. A Burmese friend even suggested it might not be an image at all, but a word in extremely fanciful script, the word "*Thadu*" ("Well done!"). It does indeed begin like the letter "tha." But "*Thadu!*" invariably comes after the main text, never (as here) before it. The mystery remains.

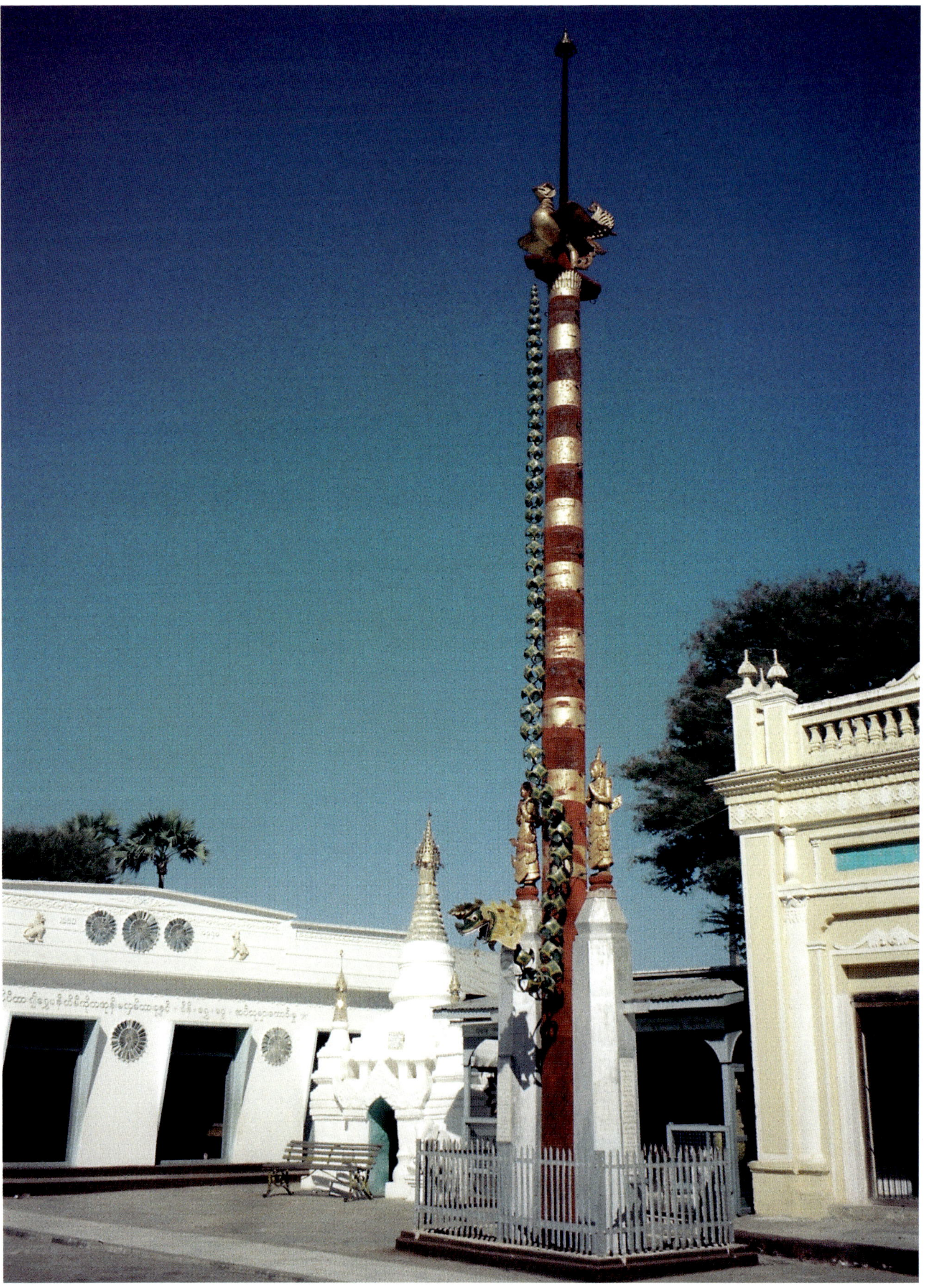

LAST BUT NOT LEAST: THE DAGUNDAING

Plate 142 PREVIOUS PAGE
In the past the *dagundaing* was a teak tree trunk up to twenty meters tall, entirely lacquered and gilded. It was supported at the foot by twin carved figures of Nats, and a gilt bird or *kinnara* perched on a platform at the top. From the bird's beak, or from the platform perch, two tubular cloth pennants dangled to near ground level. In this *dagundaing,* which stands on the platform of the Shwemawdaw pagoda in Bago, the Nat figures are the finials of the twin stout support posts.

Plate 143 RIGHT
Dagundaing on the platform of the Kyaukdawgyi pagoda, Mandalay.

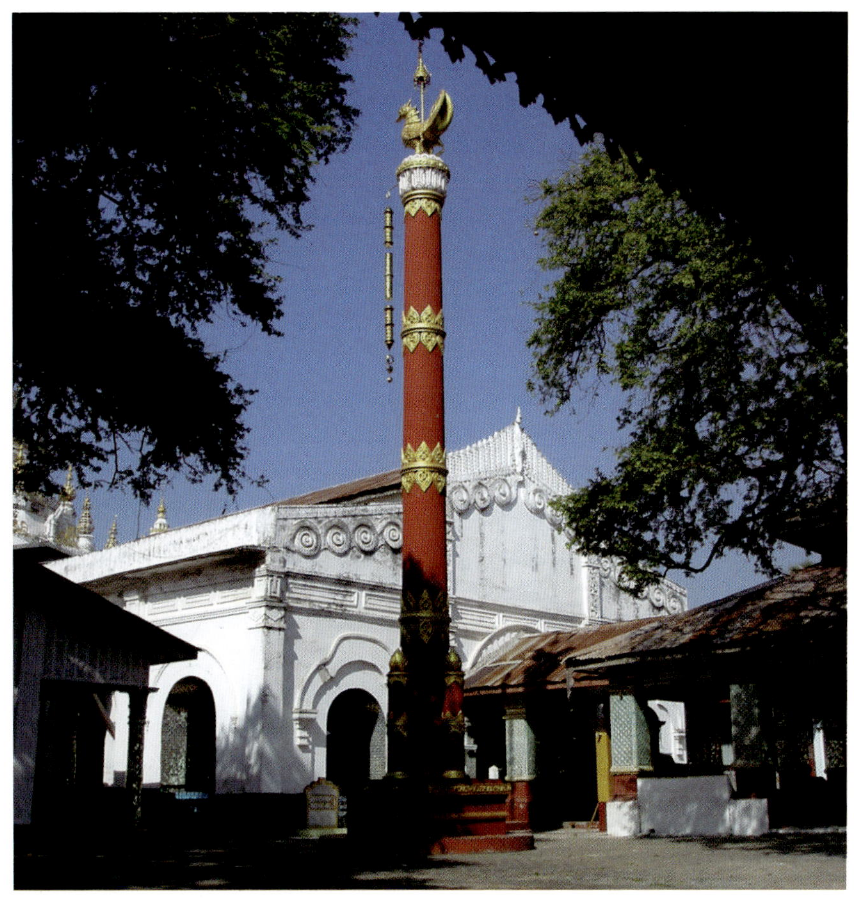

FLAGSTAFF AND PENNANTS: THE *DAGUNDAING*

Last of all the woven images on the sazigyo, and the longest by far, is the *dagundaing*, the tall flagpost on the pagoda platform, which is the last object to remain visible to the departing pilgrim. In the old days the *dagundaing* was a teak tree trunk up to twenty meters tall, entirely lacquered and gilt. Twin carved figures of Nats supported it at the foot, and a gilt *hintha* bird or *kinnara* perched on a platform at the top. From the bird's beak, or from the platform perch, two tubular pennants hung to near ground level. Papered over a light bamboo frame, they were gaily painted and some bore the names of donors and their prayers for merit. A century ago some of these hanging banners were tablet-woven textiles, with the donor's name and prayer in woven script. A rare surviving example of such a *sa dagun* (script-banner) is described in appendix 5.

These tall ornate poles offer sazigyo weavers a wonderful opportunity to show off their skill, and the elaborate woven images of *dagundaing* are a chief glory of sazigyo. They are almost invariably the last image on the sazigyo, and in this conspicuous position they are also among the first to be seen by any reader of the manuscript while untying the cord. They deserve to occupy the final gallery in this section of the book.

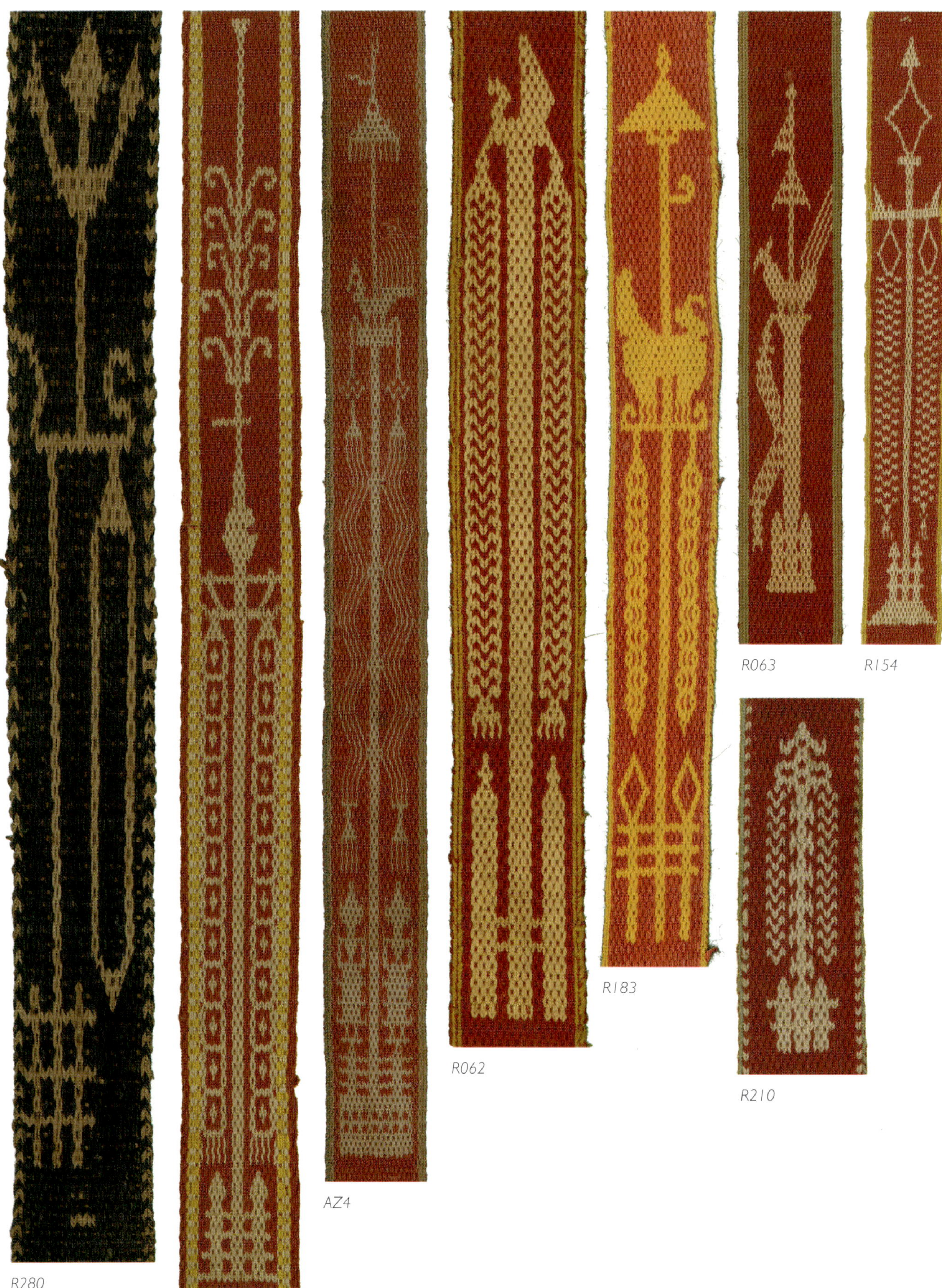

R280

R090

AZ4

R062

R183

R063

R154

R210

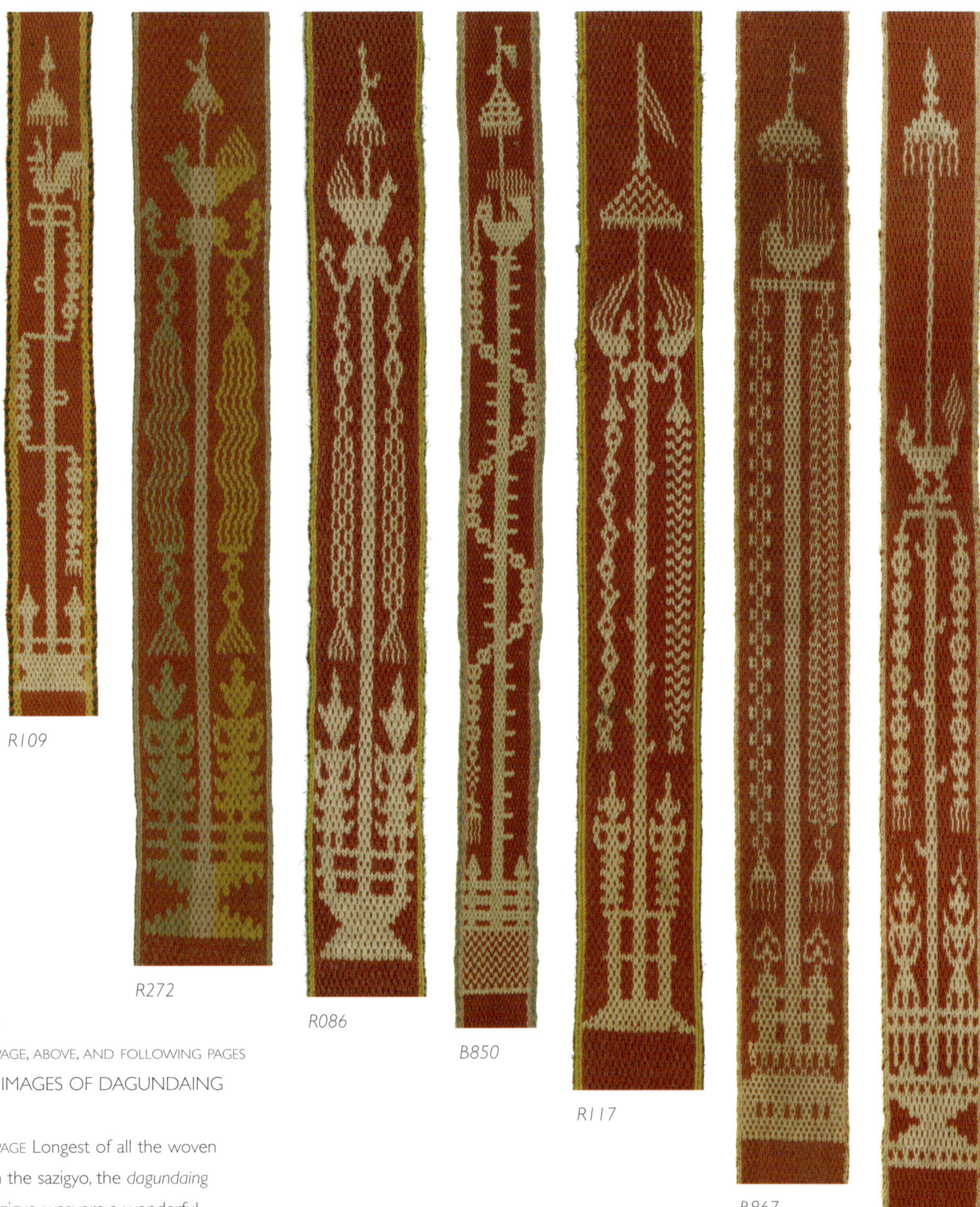

Plate 144

PREVIOUS PAGE, ABOVE, AND FOLLOWING PAGES

WOVEN IMAGES OF DAGUNDAING

PREVIOUS PAGE Longest of all the woven images on the sazigyo, the *dagundaing* offered sazigyo weavers a wonderful opportunity to show off their skill. On some older sazigyo the chunky *dagundaing* recalls a carved wooden totem pole. *(R280, R090, AZ4, R062, R183, R063, R154, R210)*

ABOVE There are some fine examples of *dagundaing* on red and white nineteenth-century sazigyo. *(R109, R272, R086, B850, R117, B867, B889)*

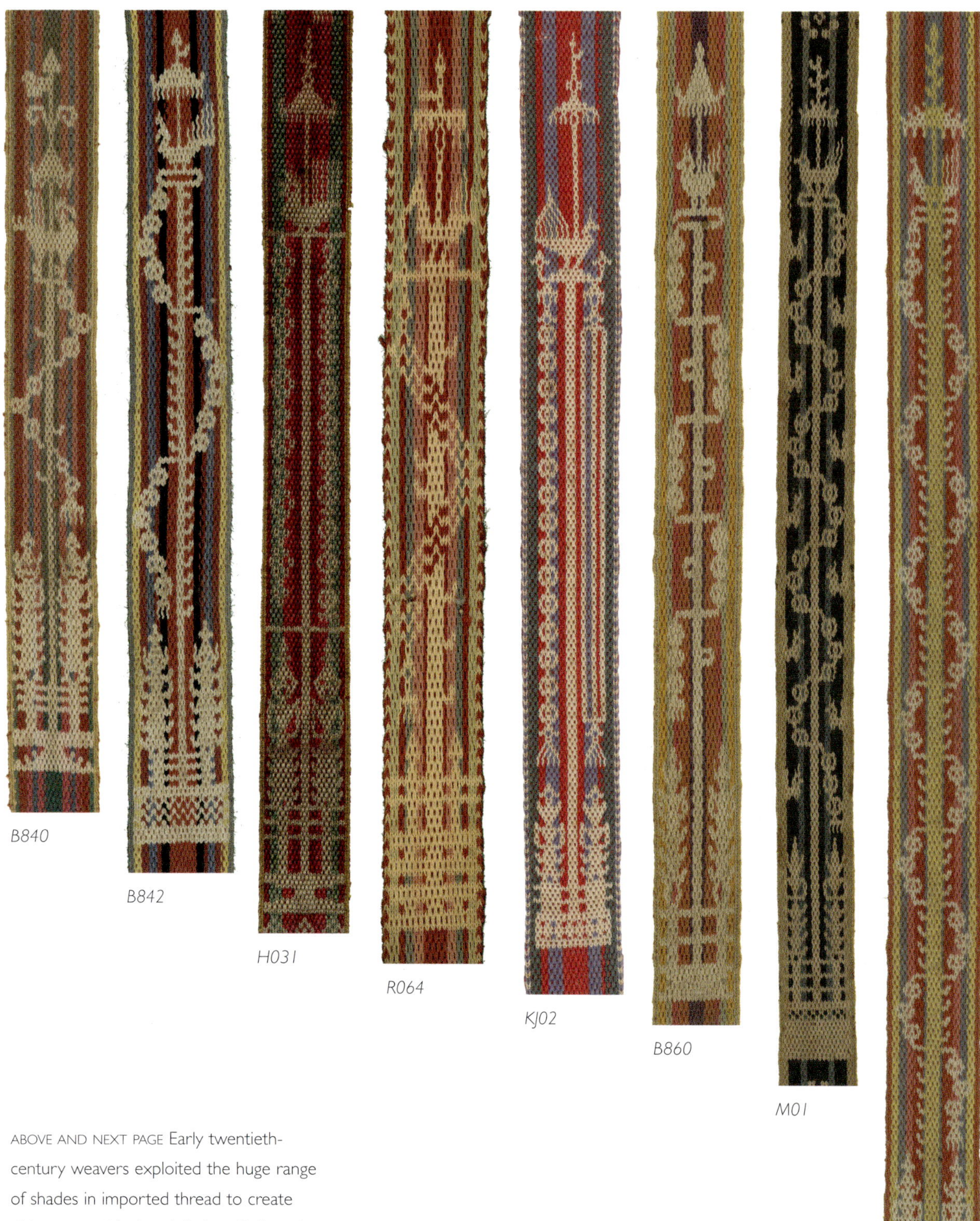

B840

B842

H031

R064

KJ02

B860

M01

B847

ABOVE AND NEXT PAGE Early twentieth-century weavers exploited the huge range of shades in imported thread to create elaborate multicolored designs. Style and degree of stylization vary widely. The hanging banners may be straight or wavy. Twin banners may be identical or very different. *(B840, B842, H031, R064, KJ02, B860, M01, B847, R001, R179, R130, R106, R093)*

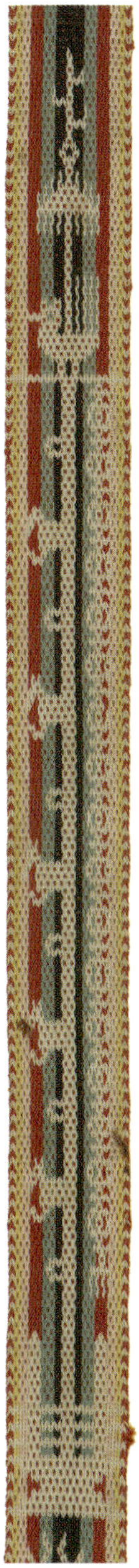

R106

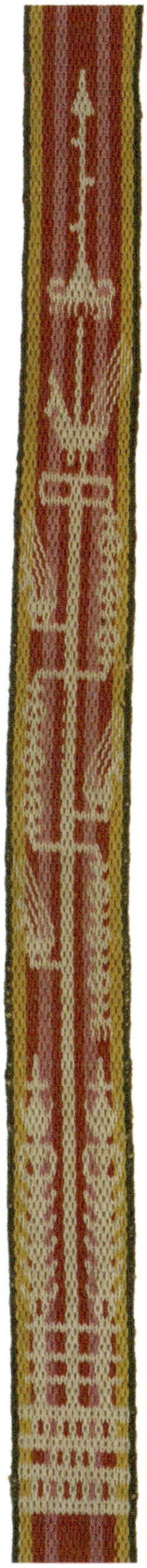

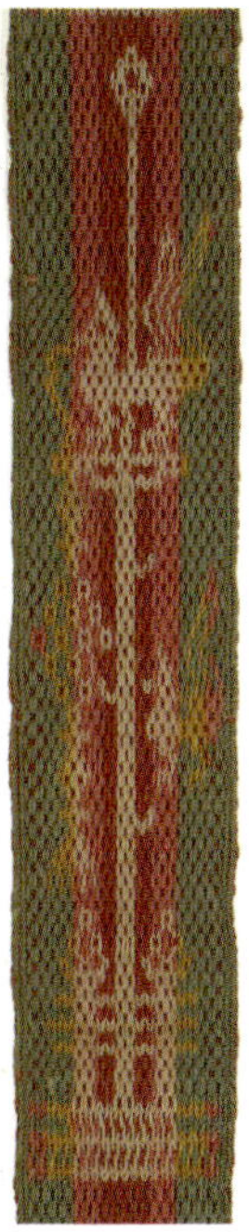

R093

R130

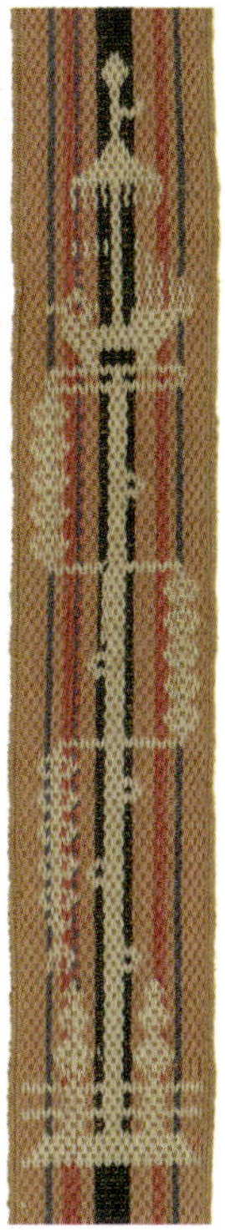

R001 R179

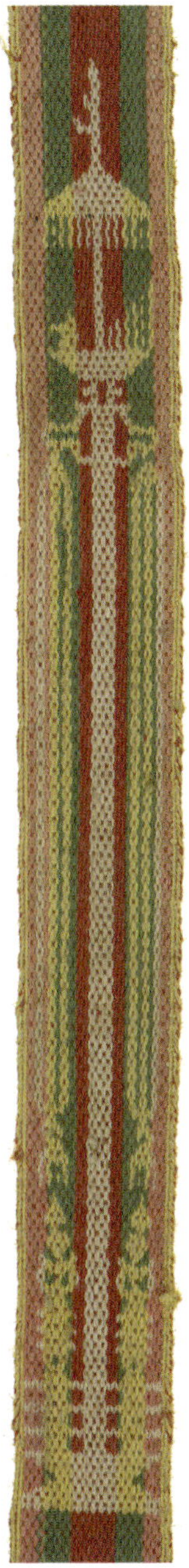

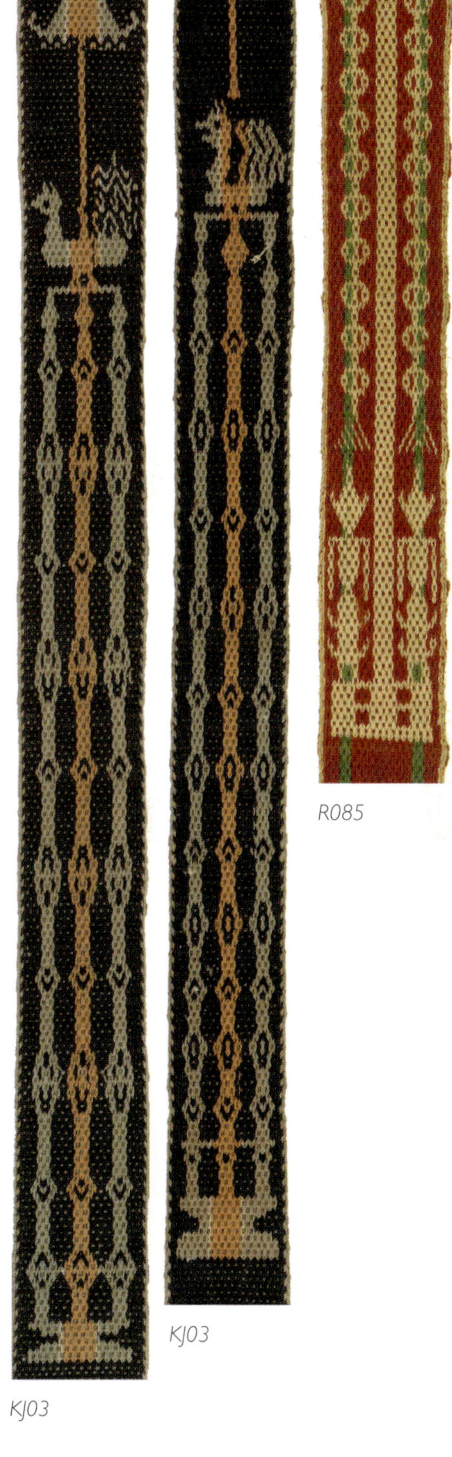

R085

KJ03

KJ03

ABOVE RIGHT Two images with a black background appear on the same sazigyo, the work of an amateur, who wove a sazigyo for a manuscript made with the silk garments of her dead father. The third is rather similar in its geometric abstraction. *(KJ03, R085)*

RIGHT Twin carved figures of Nats supported the *dagundaing* at the foot. *(B889, R086, B840)*

BELOW LEFT A carved and gilt *hintha* bird perches on a little platform at the top of the *dagundaing*. *(R085, R109)* Rarely two birds *(R117)*, and very rarely a *kinnara* perches there. *(HM6618)*

BELOW RIGHT Running short of warp toward the end of this sazigyo, the weaver invented an ingenious space-saving device. She combined the verse-count with the final woven image, inserting the three digits "110" and the two-letter word *"pa-da"* (verses) symmetrically into the rigging of the *dagundaing*—with just four mm of warp left before the flat area ends and the taper begins. *(R160)*

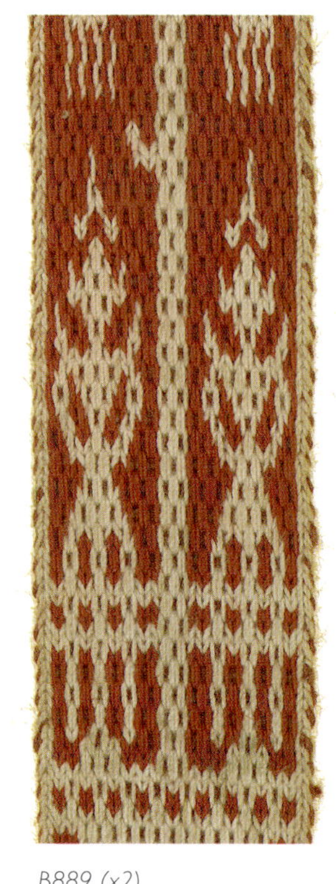

B889 (x2)

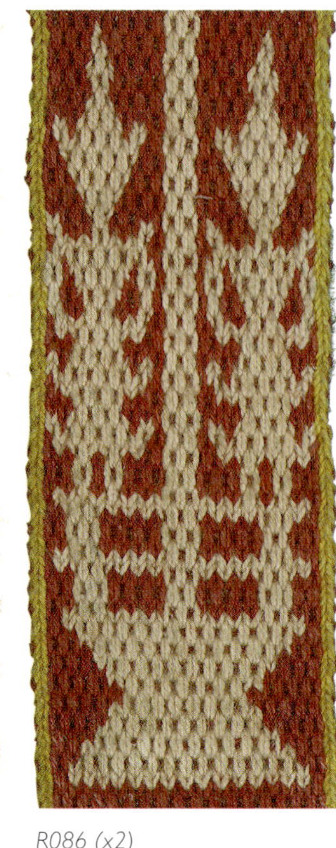

R086 (x2)

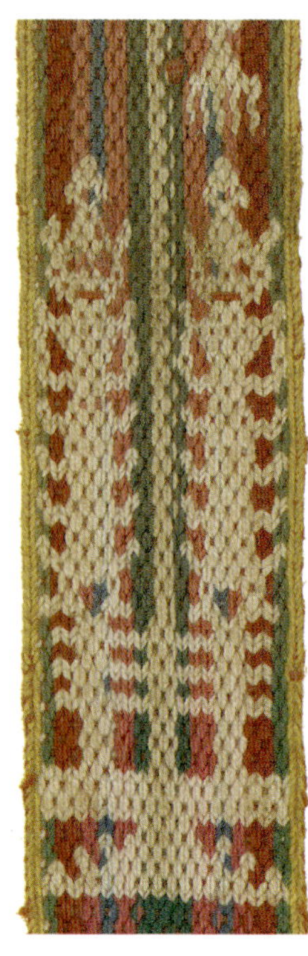

B840 (x2)

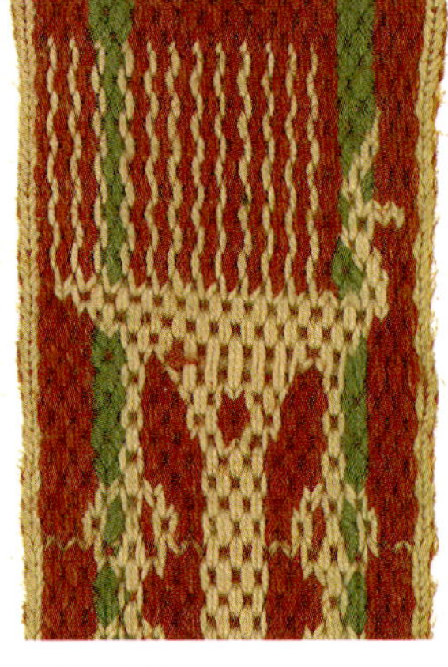

R085 (x2)

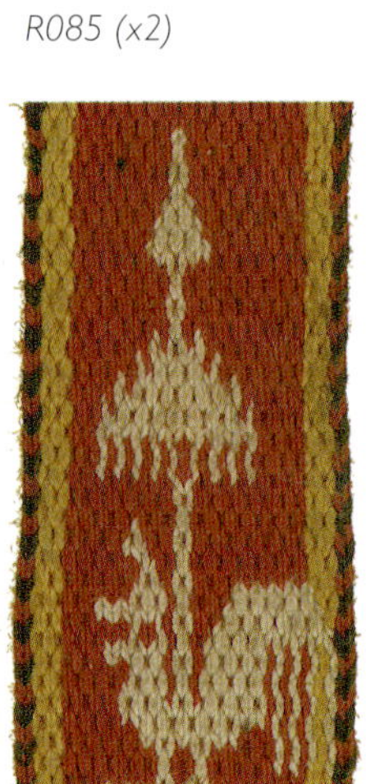

R109 (x2)

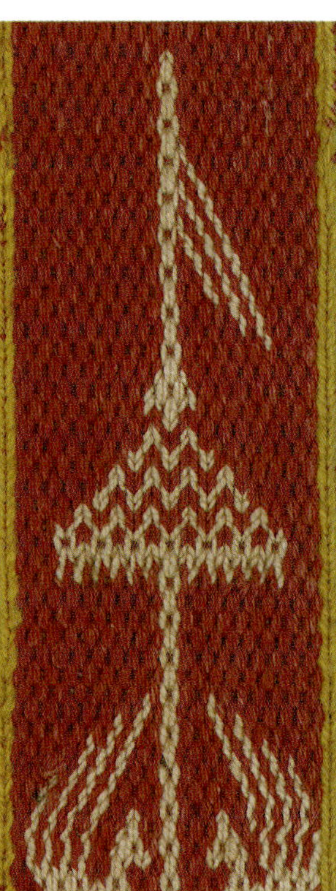

R117 (x2)

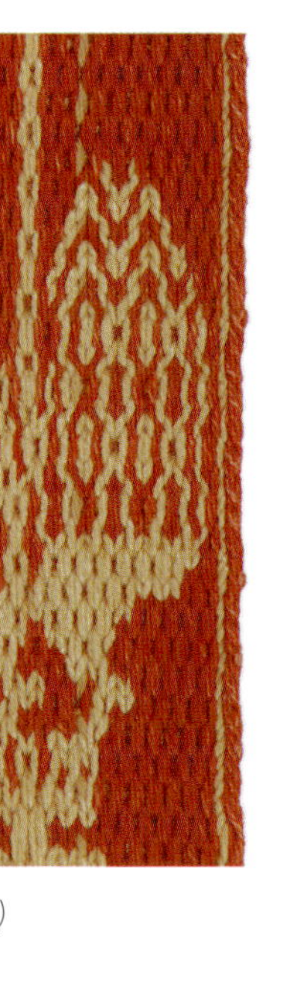

HM6618 (x2)

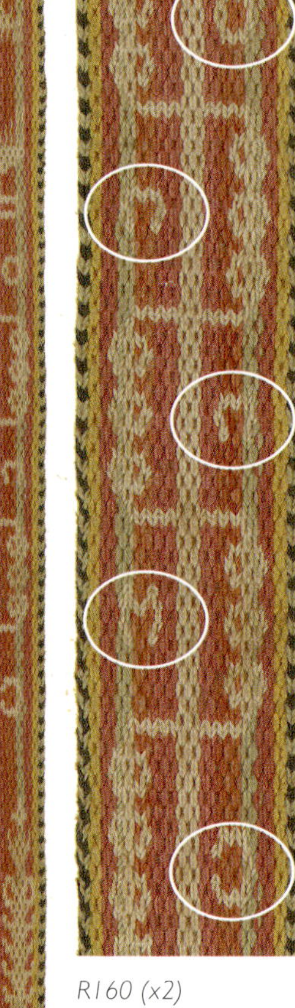

R160 (x2)

R160

Envoi—One Message, One Fabric

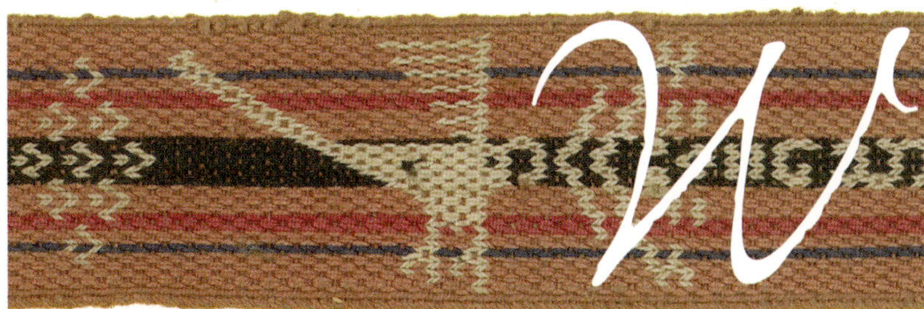

R106

We have seen examples of the sazigyo's woven text and of its woven images. The interplay between these two is one of the most attractive features of sazigyo. It is tempting to draw an analogy between this intimate integration of text and images and the interweaving of warp and weft in the structure of the textile band itself. The sazigyo weaver had to plan and construct a complex pattern, integrating geometric motifs, round Burmese script, and pictorial images into an artifact with a single message. Sequences of images precede the text, and different sequences follow it. Other images are interspersed in the text as punctuation. Pictorial images and text are so intimately related, both spatially and semantically, that they constitute a single fabric, almost as tightly interwoven as the warp and weft of the textile. And this is what gives the sazigyo its special charm and power as a product of the human spirit and of the weaver's art.

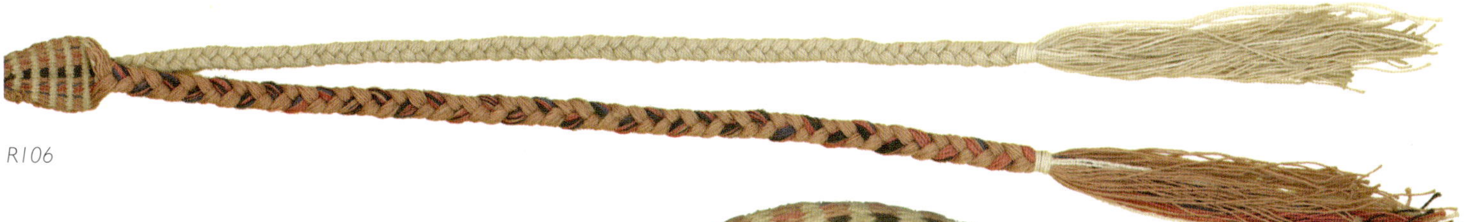

R106

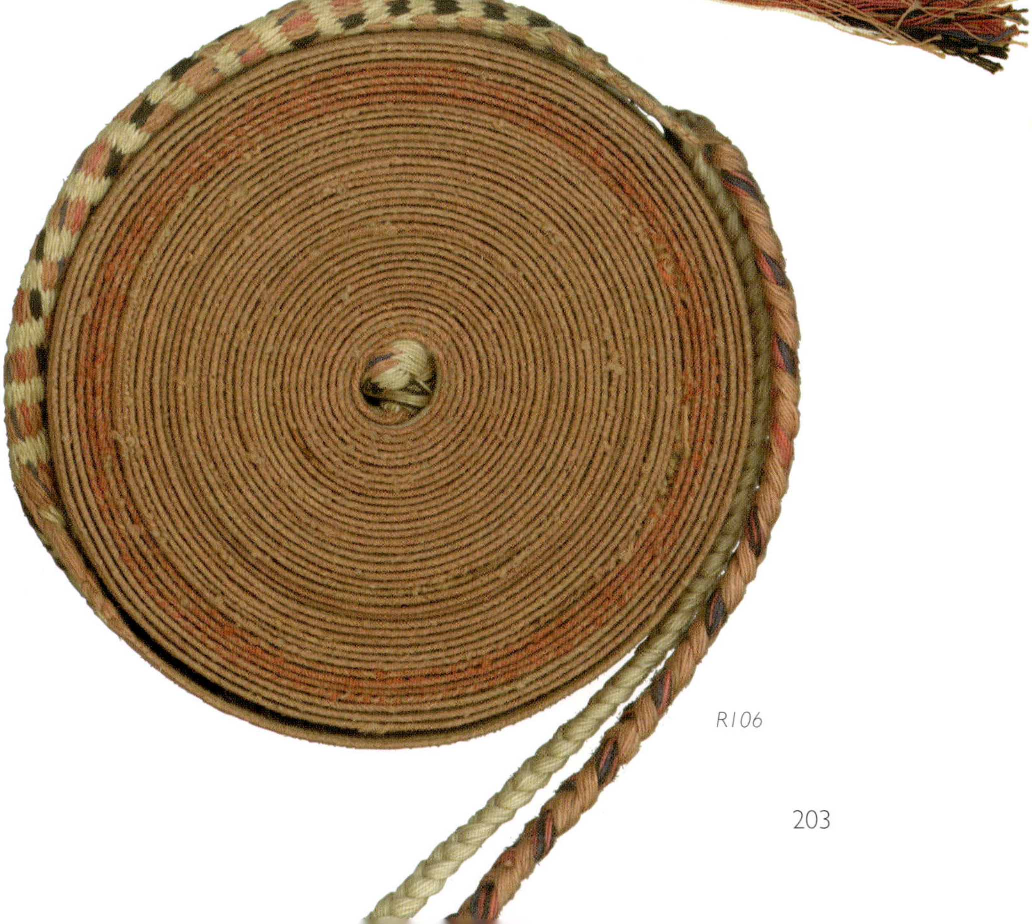

R106

Like a fine new stole of spangled gauze
When you first hold it up, stretched out
And ready to swing on to your shoulders—
So lovely is the round lettering
We North Mandalay girls weave.
The golden verses in our lettered bands
Shine like a row of stars in the sky.

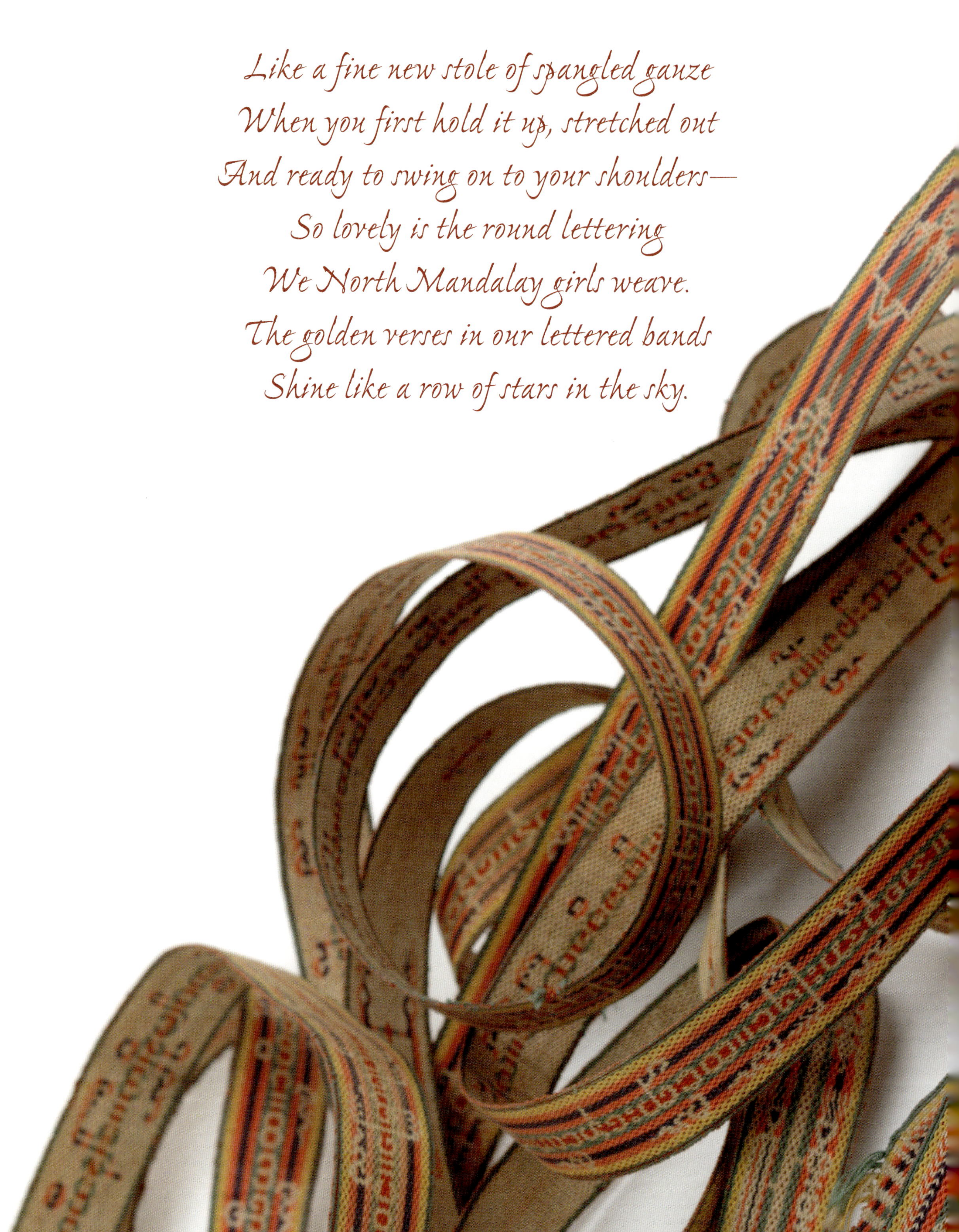

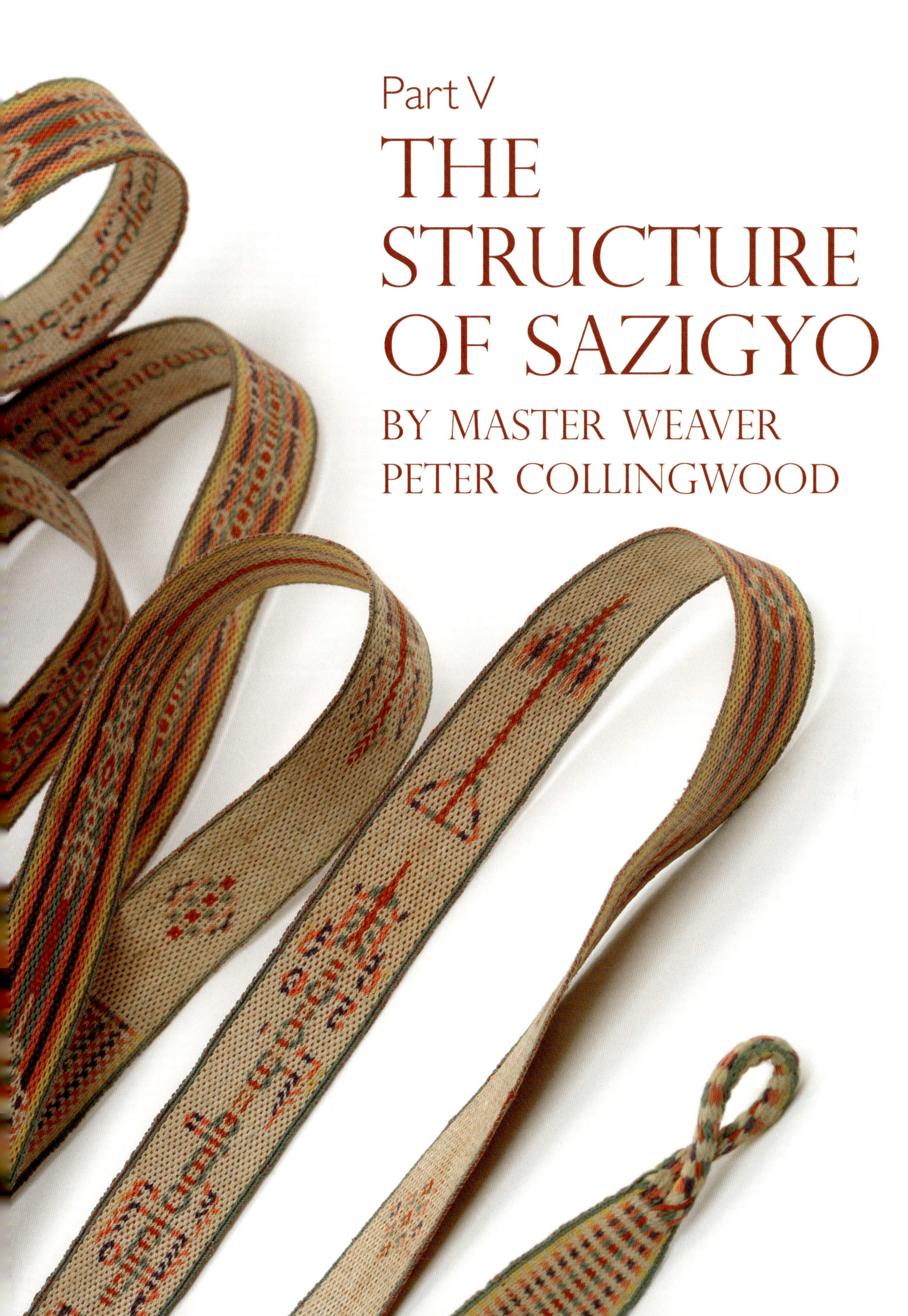

Part V

THE STRUCTURE OF SAZIGYO

BY MASTER WEAVER PETER COLLINGWOOD

Part V Chapter 14

The Brighton Museum Collection of Sazigyo

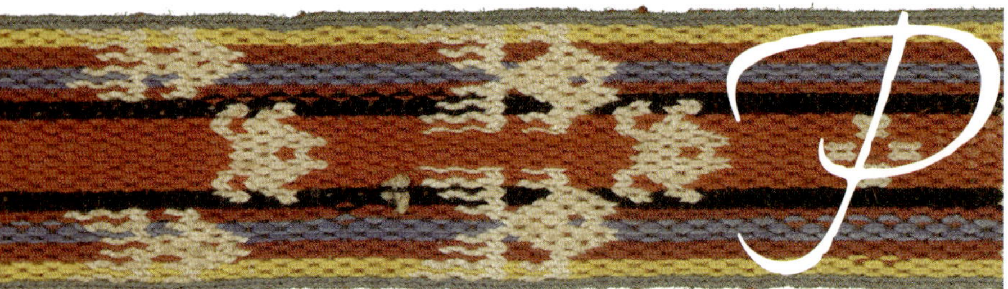

B842

Peter Collingwood's study of sazigyo, published here for the first time, is in three parts. The first describes the tablet-weaving techniques used by the Burmese sazigyo weavers. The second summarizes the details of all sixty bands in the Brighton collection. Both of these appear here with his original explanatory diagrams (the numbered figures), but with the addition of scanned images (plates) to illustrate structural points. In the third part, the sixty bands in the collection are analyzed one by one. These individual "reports" read like a running commentary: Peter seems to sit by the shoulder of the Burmese woman weaver and watch every turn of the cards, every shed and pick she made over a century ago. With his "maker's eye" he is quick to detect the weaver's mistakes, but also to recognize and to praise the great accuracy and imaginative flair that many of these tapes display. Only one of these individual reports has been included in this book (in chap 17). The others can be consulted in the Brighton Museum.

It should be remembered that the sixty tapes that provided the material for this technical analysis are by no means a representative sample of all sazigyo. First, only a single tape in the Brighton collection lacks a woven text, whereas textless tapes such as those illustrated in plate 41 were at least as common as text-woven ones. Next, most of the dated tapes are from 1906 and 1907, and several without a woven date are similar enough to be confidently assigned to the same years. Perhaps this was when the monastery was founded and many of its manuscripts donated. The color schemes, styles of script, and range of images of the sazigyo would naturally reflect those in fashion at that time.

Plate 145 NEXT PAGE
SOME OF THE BRIGHTON SAZIGYO
Most of the dated tapes in the Brighton collection are from 1906 and 1907, so the color schemes and the styles of script and images are typical of those then in fashion. *(B840, B842, B846, B847, B861, B850, B857, B843, B877)*

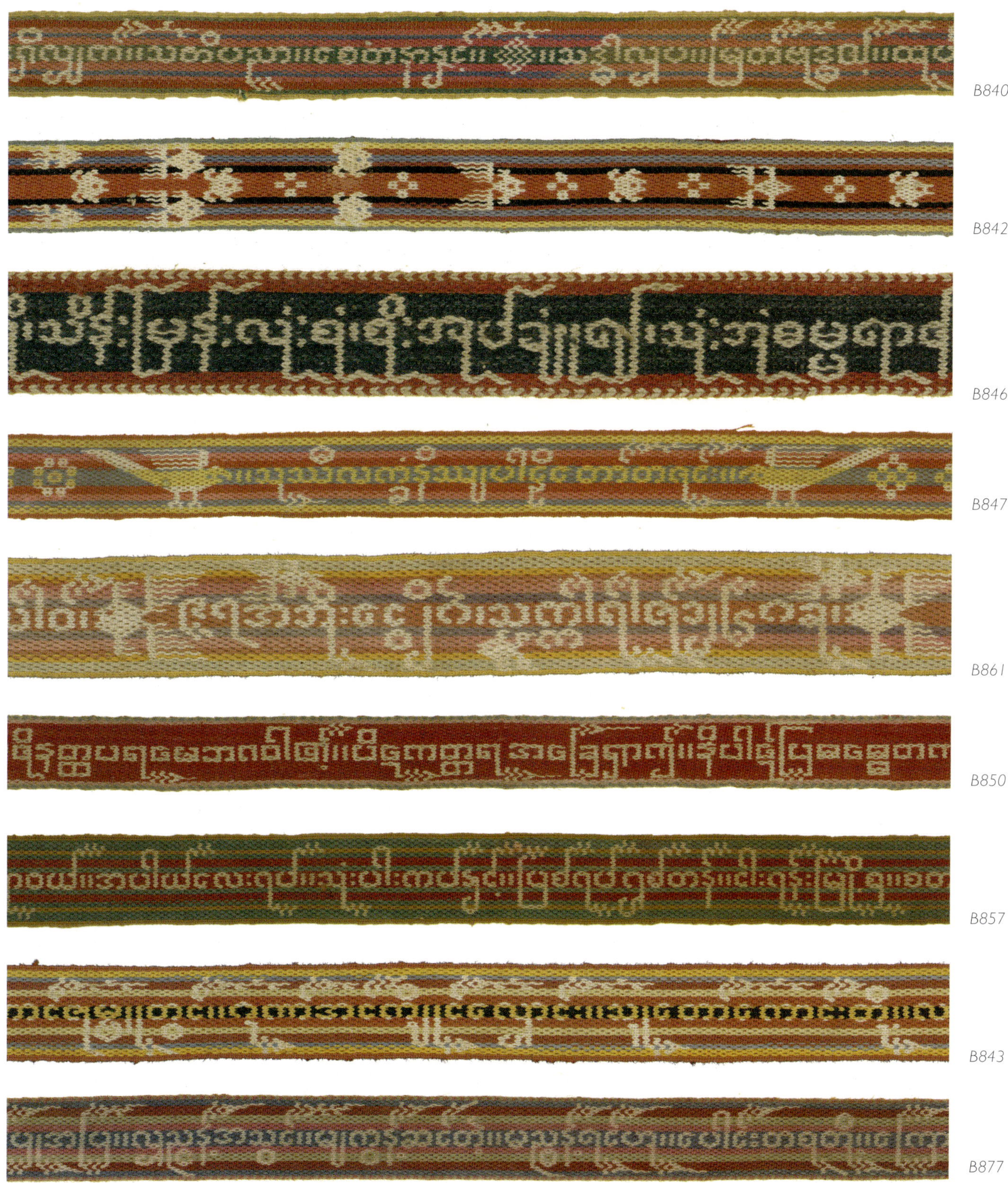
B840
B842
B846
B847
B861
B850
B857
B843
B877

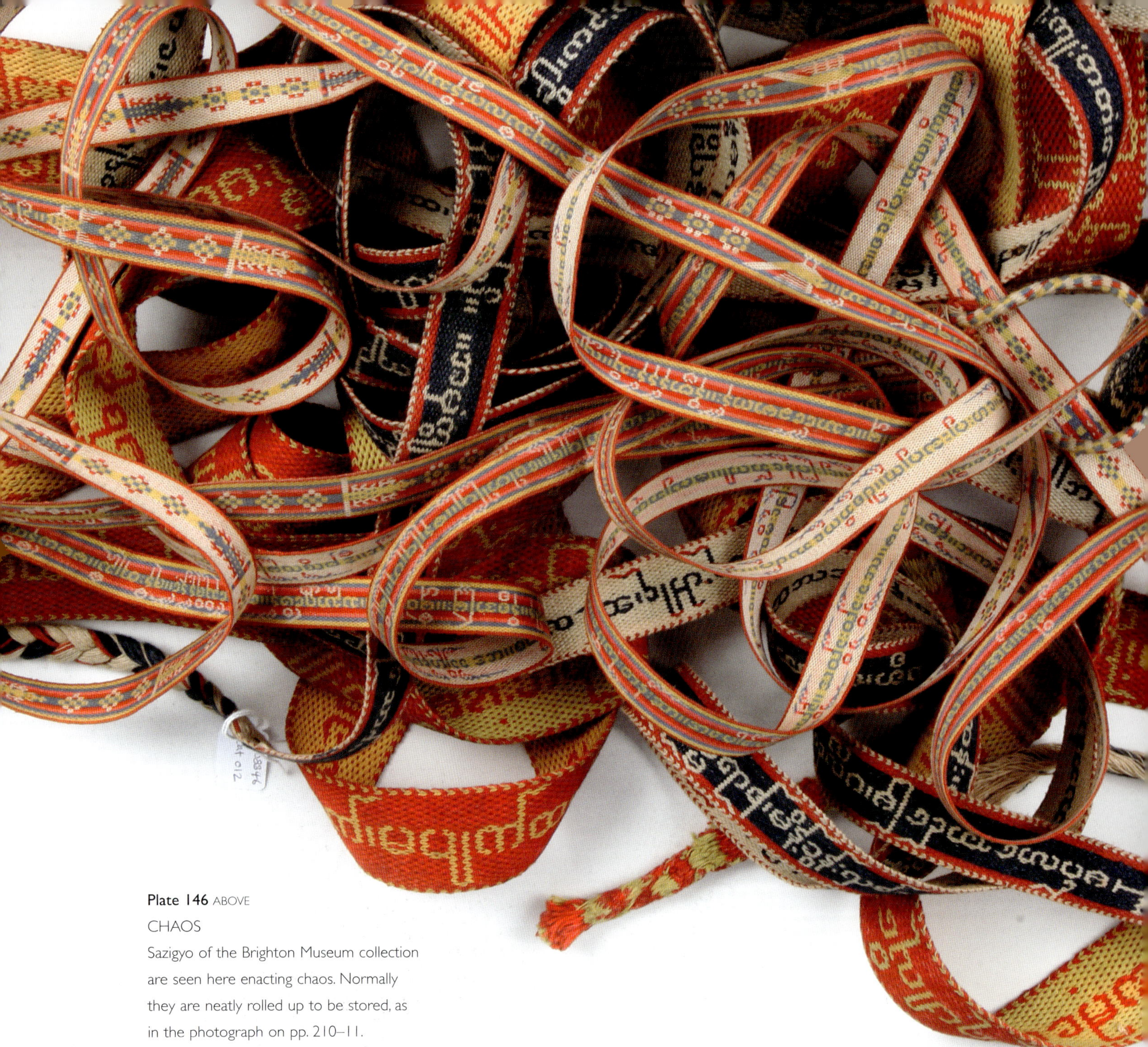

Plate 146 ABOVE
CHAOS
Sazigyo of the Brighton Museum collection are seen here enacting chaos. Normally they are neatly rolled up to be stored, as in the photograph on pp. 210–11.

Plate 147 TOP NEXT PAGE
Peter Collingwood, the great British artist weaver and author of five highly influential books on the techniques of weaving, worked at his looms in Nayland, Suffolk for over forty years till his death in 2008.

Plate 148 BOTTOM NEXT PAGE
The Collingwood "sazigyo-rotor," an essential adjunct for all sazigyo-analysers, sketched by its inventor.

THE COLLINGWOOD "SAZIGYO-ROTOR"—AN ESSENTIAL AID FOR ALL SAZIGYO-ANALYZERS

Peter had undertaken to analyze from loop to cord every sazigyo in the Brighton collection. Each band had to be fully unwound, and each in its turn threatened to add its five or six meters of cotton tape to a great tangled heap. Peter did not grudge the long hours spent examining the weaves pass by pass, but he balked at the drudgery of slow, laborious rewinding by hand. Necessity mothered the invention of a mechanical aid. Here is a sketch of the Collingwood "sazigyo-rotor," sent to me by the inventor. Its effectiveness is shown in the photograph overleaf.

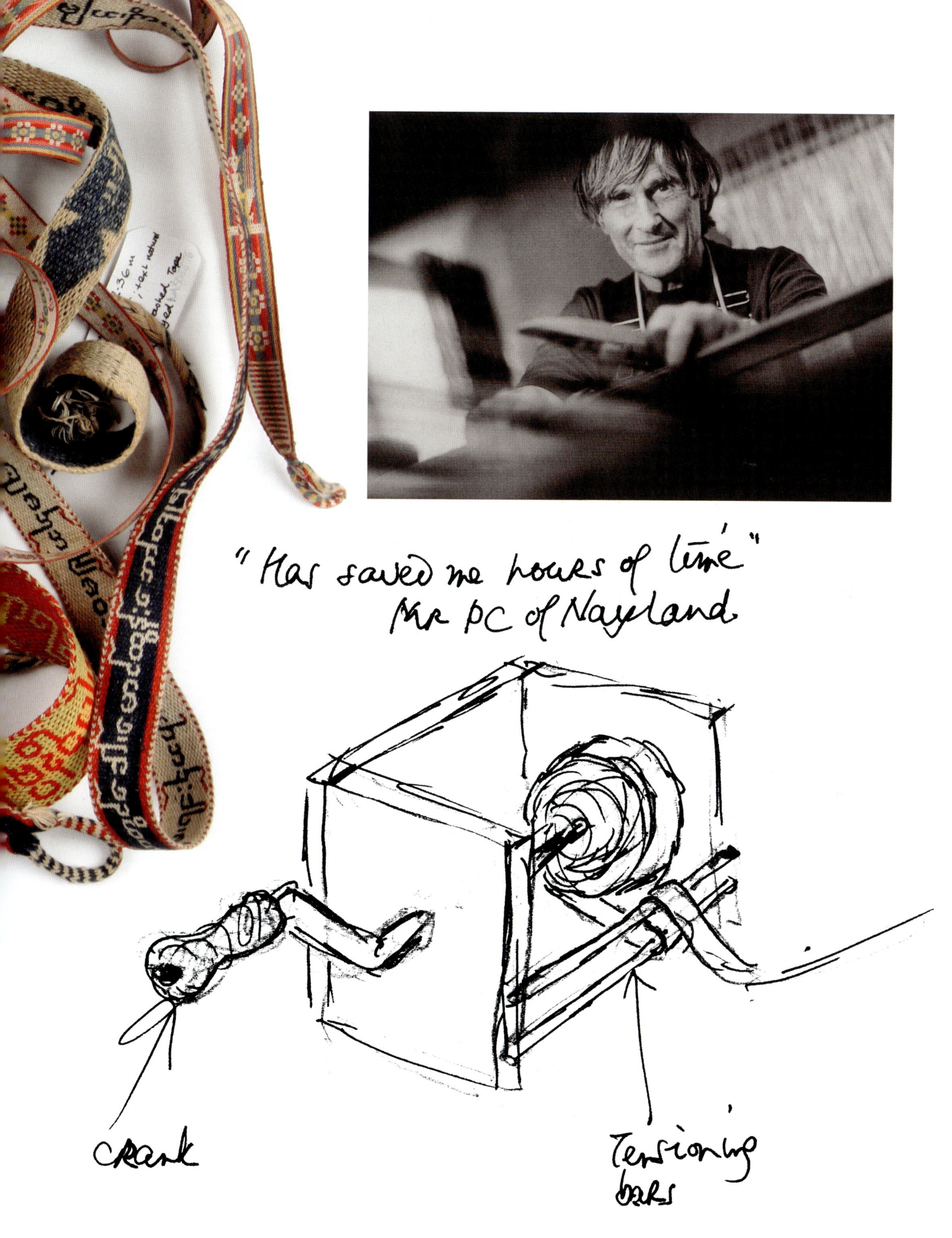
"Has saved me hours of time"
Mr PC of Nayland
Crank
Tensioning bars

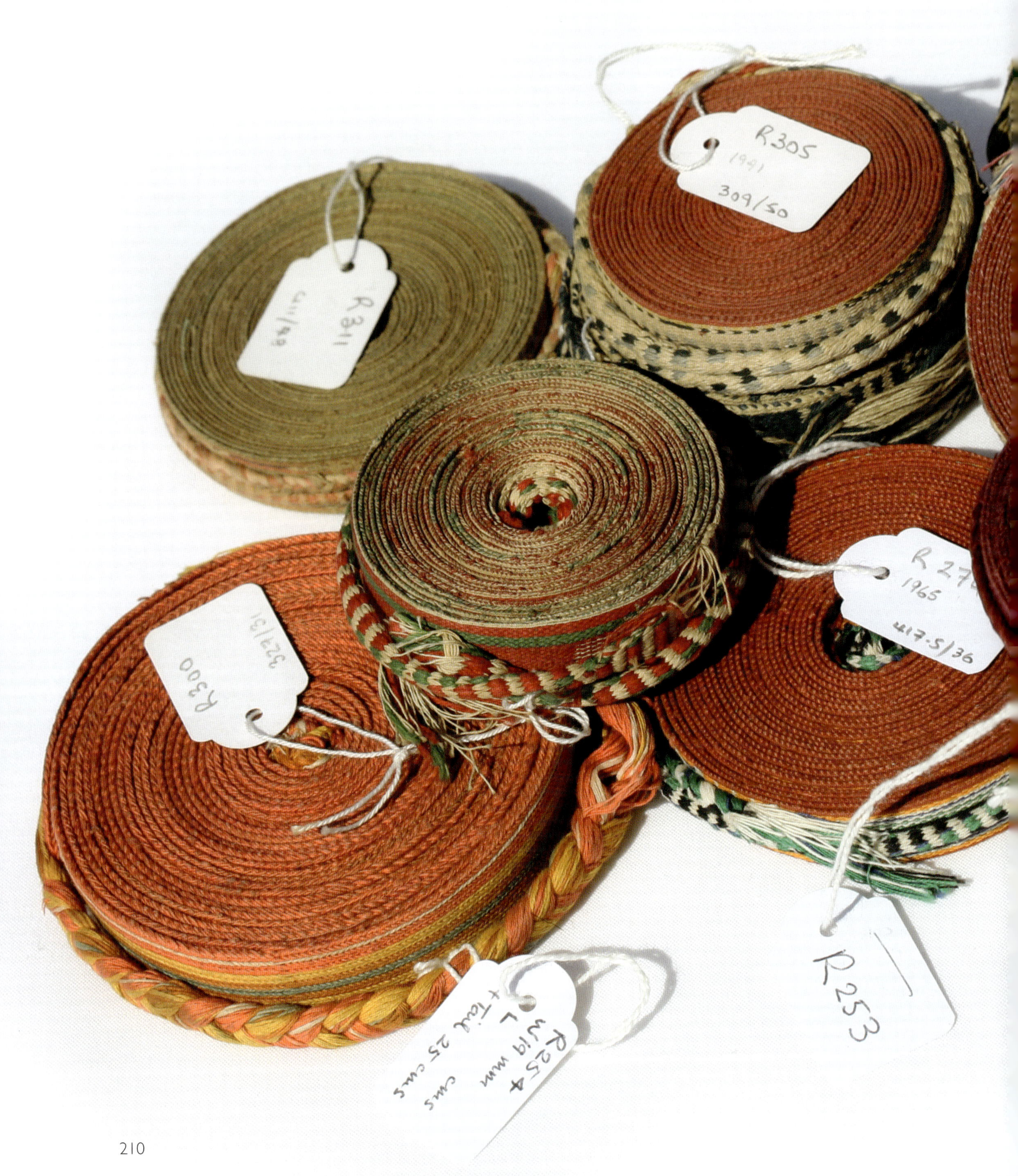
R305
309/50
R300
R253
R254

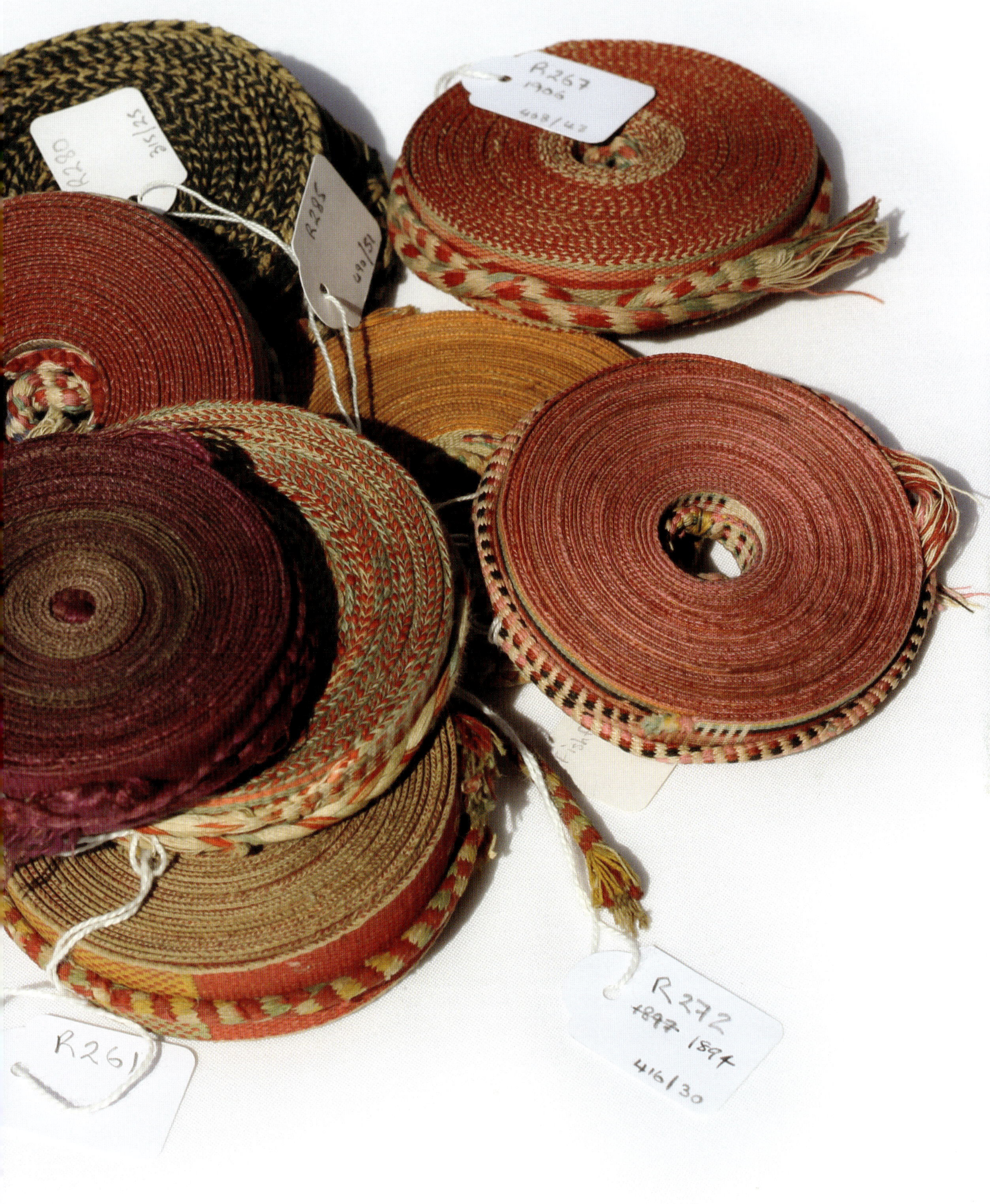
R280
315/25
R285
R267
R272
416/30
R261

Part V Chapter 15

Explanation of Tablet-Weaving Techniques

THE BASICS OF TABLET WEAVING

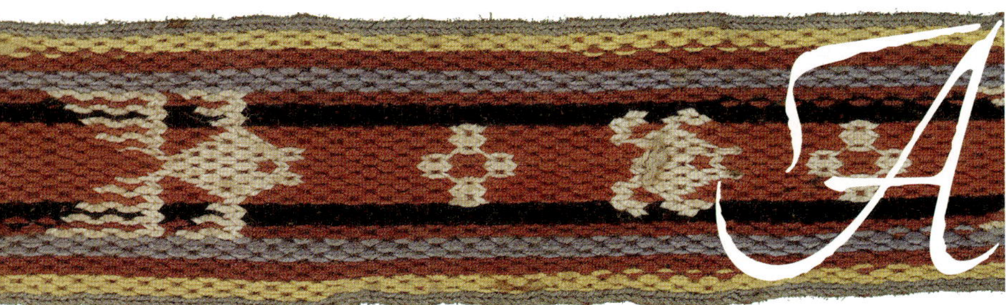

B842

All sazigyo are woven using four-holed tablets. Fig. 1 shows the basic idea and nomenclature of this technique. It shows that the warp threads can pass through a tablet in one of two ways, making it either S-threaded or Z-threaded (see fig. 2). A tablet can be rotated about its vertical axis or "flipped" to convert it from one type of threading direction to the other (fig. 3).

Every sazigyo in the Brighton collection has the tablets alternately S- and Z-threaded all across the width.

Of the many possible structures obtainable with tablets, these bands use only two: namely, warp-twining and a double-faced weave, all bands in the Brighton collection showing both.

Of the many ways of using different colors in the tablets, these bands use only two: either a tablet carries the same color in all four holes, or it carries one color in two adjacent holes and another color in the other two adjacent holes. In sazigyo, the former is always used for the narrow borders (and often for other sections of the band), while the latter is always used for the main central field that carries the text and images.

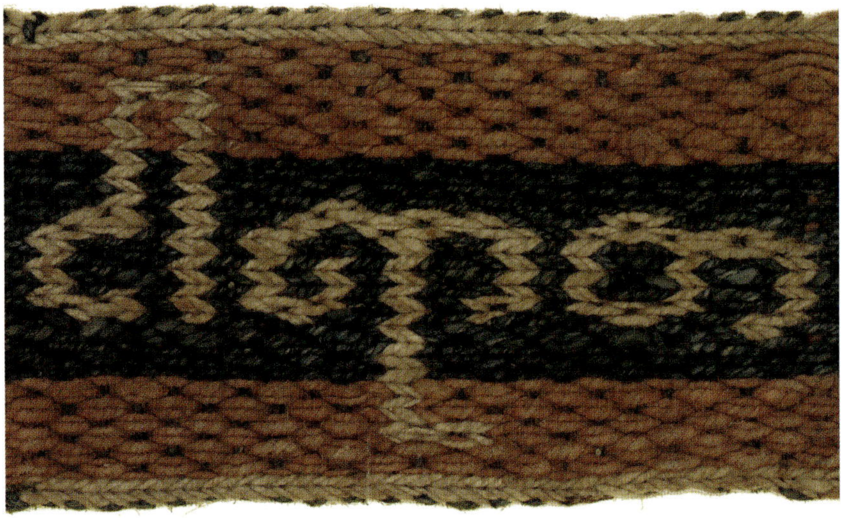

B890 (x2)

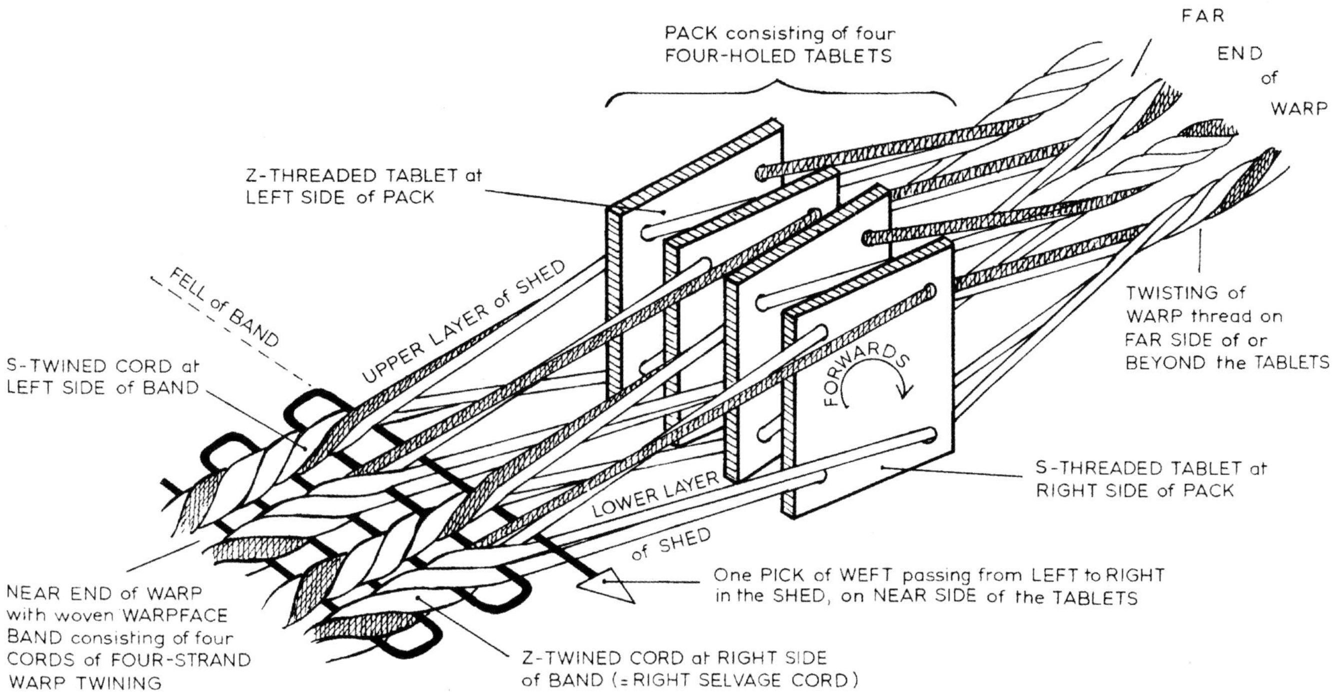

Figure 1

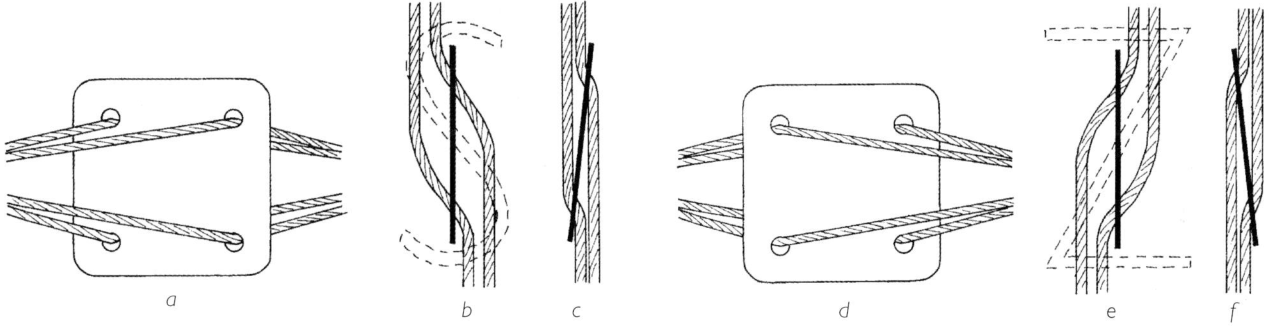

Figure 2

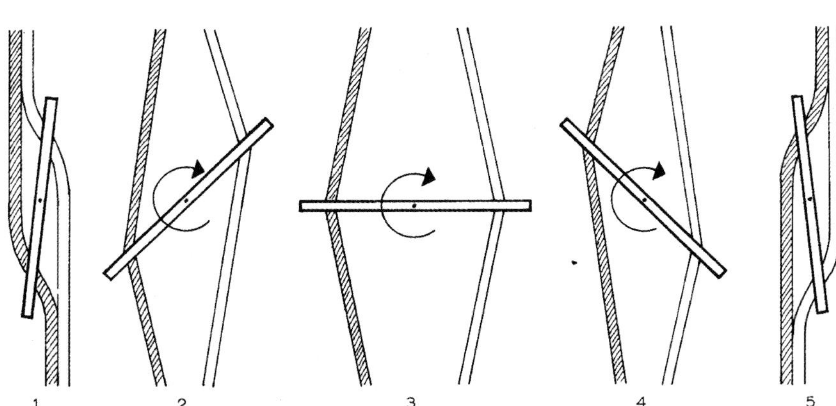

Figure 3

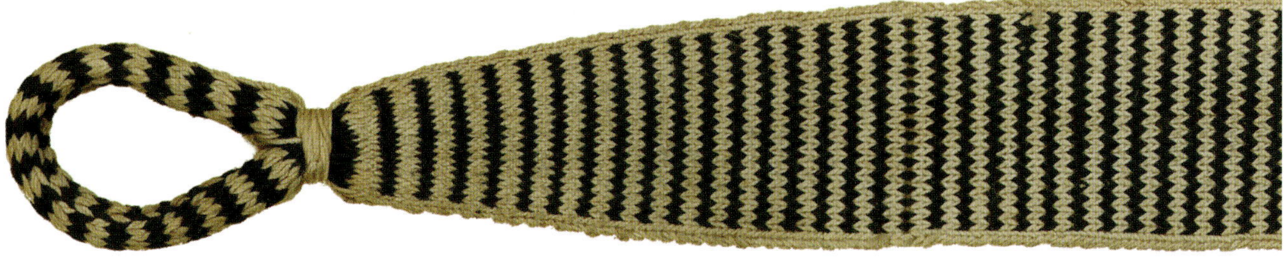

R008 (x2)

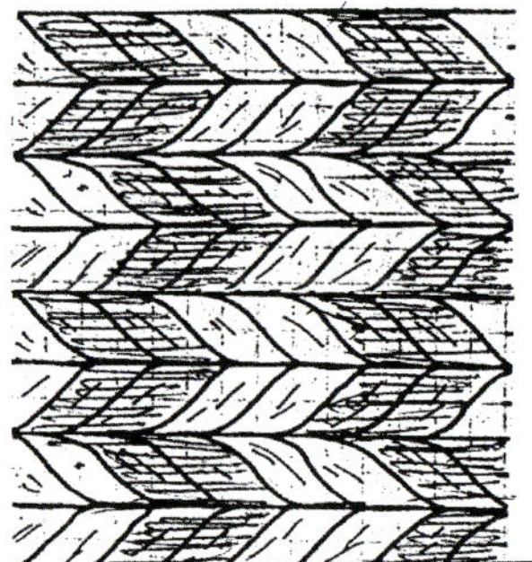

Figure 4

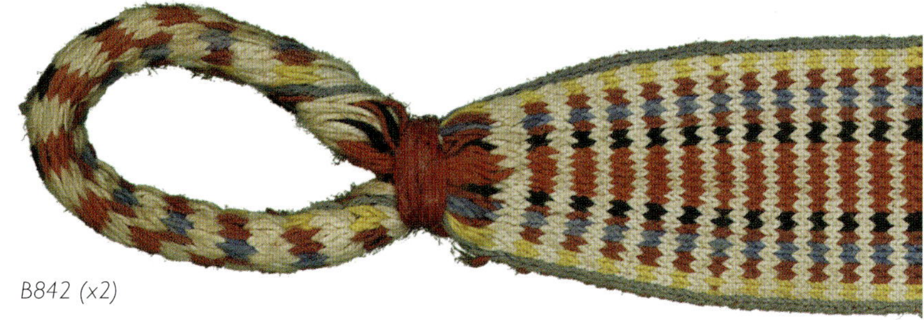

B842 (x2)

Plate 149 ABOVE
CROSS-STRIPES
Bands often begin with these cross-stripes, warp-twining being an efficient way to encourage the band to acquire its full width after the initial loop. *(R008, B842)*

WARP-TWINING

Cross-stripes, one of the patterns made with warp-twining

The tablets, carrying two colors and alternately S- and Z-threaded, are lined up so that they all have their colors similarly placed. Turning the whole pack together, either continuously forwards or backwards, will give very typical cross-stripes with a zigzag outline; these are "warp-twined cross-stripes" (see fig. 4).

Each tablet twists the threads it carries into a four-ply cord, with two plies of color A and two plies of color B; the lining up of the similarly colored plies in all adjacent cords gives the cross-stripes. The invisible weft binds these cords together to make a warp-twined textile.

In the sazigyo one color is always white or natural cotton; the other is often red but can be blue or any color. So the cross-stripes will be alternately white and another color.

Bands often begin with these stripes, warp-twining being an efficient way to encourage the band to acquire its full width after the initial loop.

If tablets only carry one color, they produce the same structure but it will appear as a one-colored cord; this is often used for the narrow borders of these bands.

Twining reversal

A disadvantage of the method of warp-twining is that the tablets also twist the threads into cords beyond the tablets (i.e., between the pack of tablets and the far loom post), though here, of course, they are not held together by a weft. Eventually this buildup of twist makes turning increasingly difficult, so to relieve this the tablets have to be turned in the opposite direction: backwards if the original direction was forwards, and vice versa (see fig. 5).

Plate 150 BELOW LEFT
TWINING REVERSALS
Arrows indicate the "twining reversal" points, which appear as a slight difference in the striping pattern, or in the chevrons at the edge. *(B879, B873)*

Plate 151 BELOW RIGHT
TOP If two tablets are arranged as for cross-stripes, and the next two in the pack have colors in the opposite positions, and so on all across, then turning the tablet pack all together will give small checks. BOTTOM If, instead of working with pairs, the tablets are used in fours, the checks will be twice the size. *(R008, B870)*

Such a "twining reversal" point is almost invariably seen in warp-twined sections in these bands, appearing as a slight difference in the striping pattern.

The fact that it appears almost dead center in the section illustrates how greatly the weavers were concerned about this effect. By this means the twist beyond the tablets is completely undone by the time the section is finished; the weaver starts as it were with a clean slate for the next section, usually in the double-faced weave.

Small checks

If two tablets are arranged as for cross-stripes, and the next two in the pack have colors in the opposite positions, and so on all across, then turning the tablet-pack all together will give small checks (see fig. 6). The cross-stripes have been broken into small chevrons or checks. It is easy to set up this arrangement from the one used above, by "idling" (i.e., not turning) alternate pairs of tablets for two picks, then turning them all together. If instead of working with pairs, they are used in fours, the checks will be twice the size.

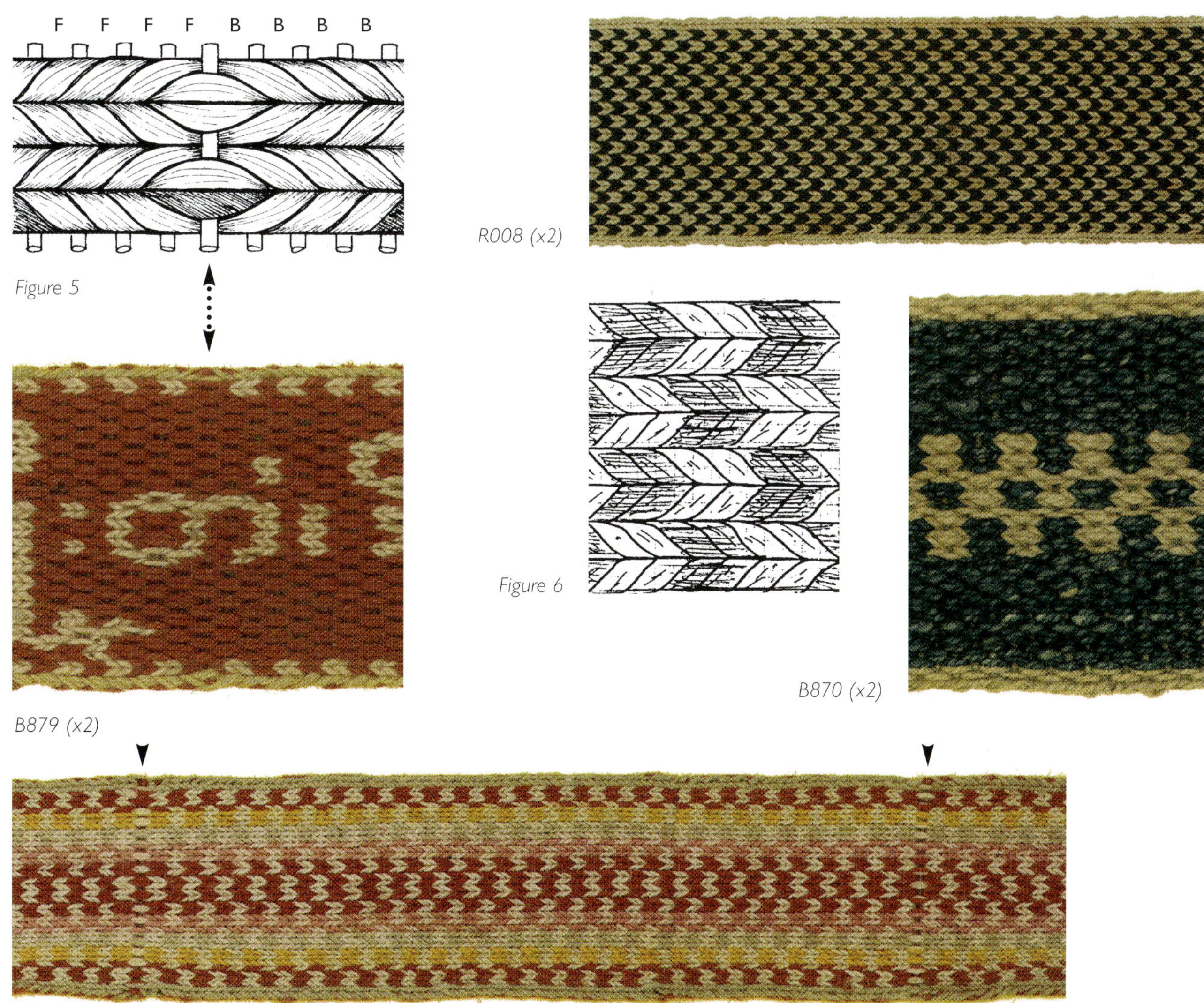

Figure 5

R008 (x2)

Figure 6

B870 (x2)

B879 (x2)

B873 (x2)

Plate 152 BELOW AND NEXT PAGE
DOUBLE-FACED WEAVE
The double-faced weave makes possible the inscriptions, geometric motifs, and the images of animals, birds, and fish that are the chief features of the sazigyo. *(B873 [x2], B852 [x2], B888 [x2])*

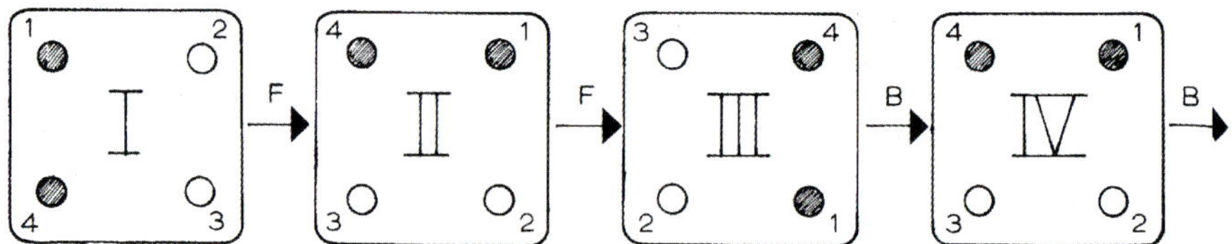

Figure 7

DOUBLE-FACED WEAVE

This is the weave that makes possible the inscriptions, and images of animals, birds, and fish, the chief feature of these bands. The method involves turning tablets individually or in groups, not as a whole pack. The basic turning pattern is two quarter-turns forward, two quarter-turns backward. See fig. 7 at top, where the four positions taken by the tablets are labeled I, II, III, and IV. This turning rhythm naturally has the advantage of eliminating any buildup of twist beyond the tablets.

If the whole pack is treated in this way, then the weave that results is a band with one color, A, on the upper surface and another, B, on the under surface. But if, for example, four tablets are slid forwards out of the main pack and thereafter turned in the opposite direction to those in the main pack, they will produce a block of color B, four tablets wide, on the A-colored background. This block will persist until those four tablets are slid back into the main pack. Naturally, the colors will be seen to be reversed if the underside of the band is inspected: a block of color A on a background of color B.

So all the designs, however complex, depend on moving the correct tablets from the near to the far pack and back again. As well as the free use of the double-faced technique in the text and images, there is a frequent occurrence of small motifs built up of blocks.

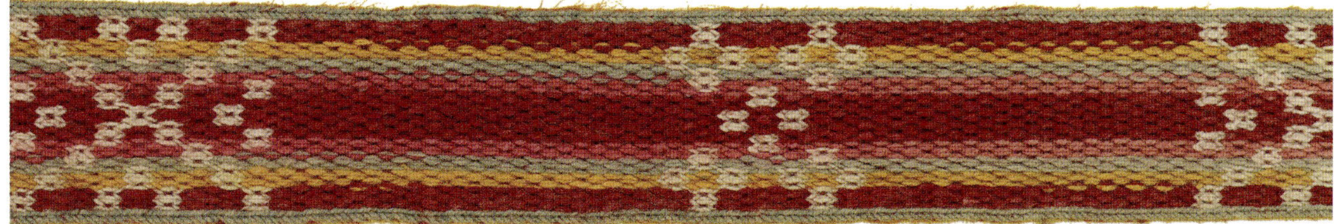

B873 obverse (x2)

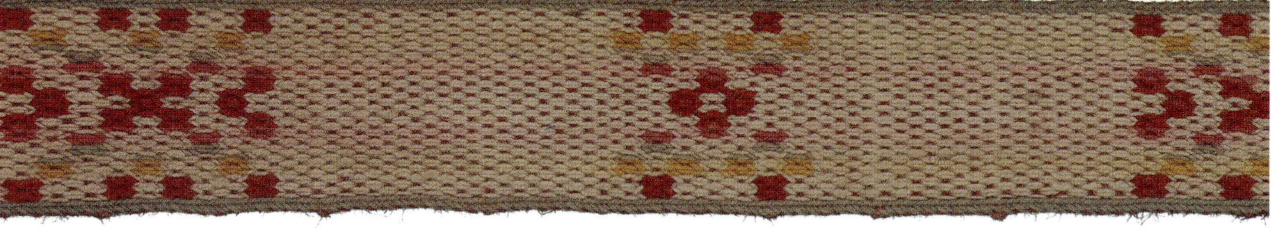

B873 reverse (x2)

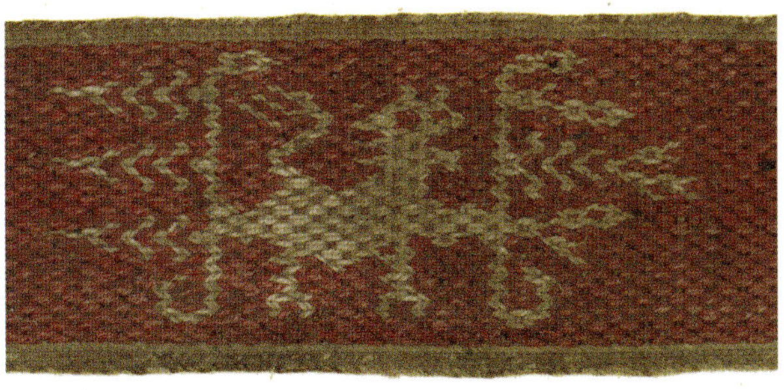

B852 obverse (x2)

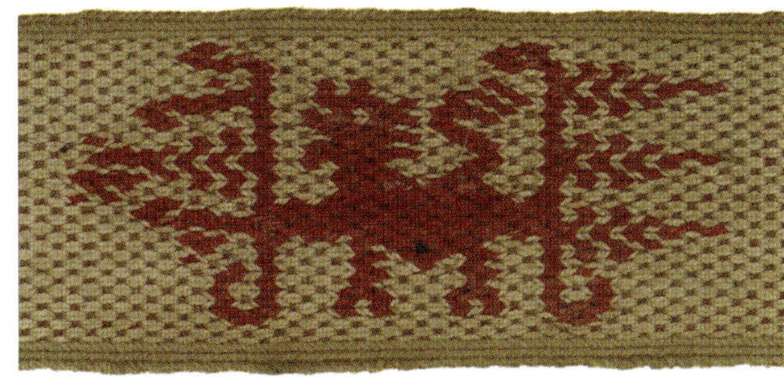

B852 reverse (x2)

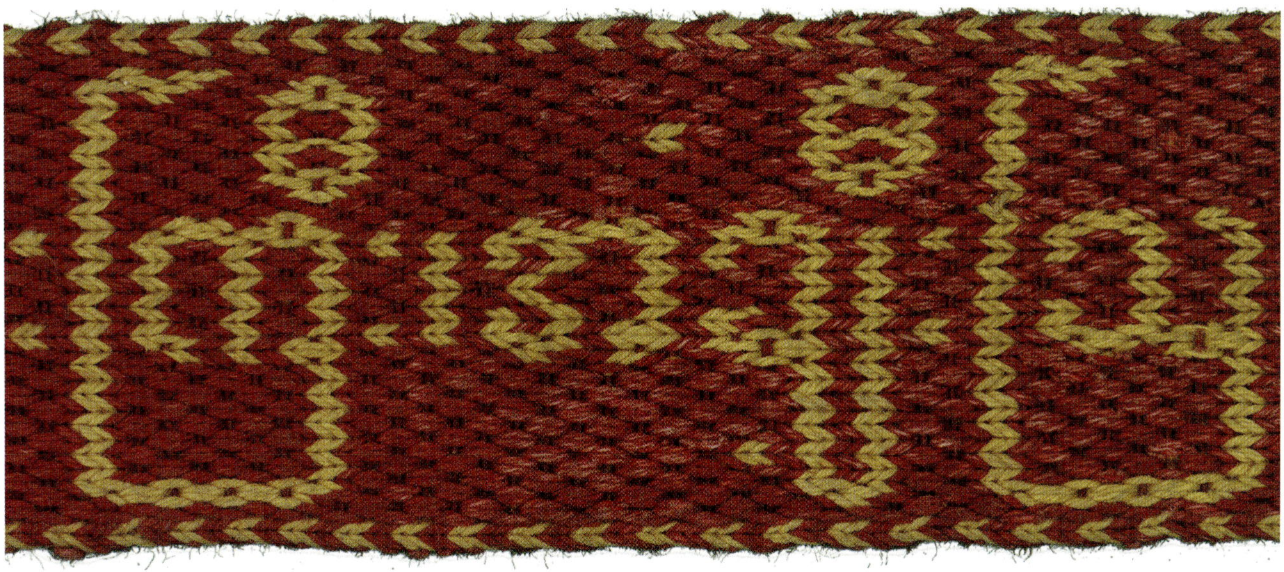

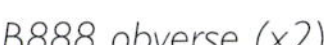

B888 obverse (x2)

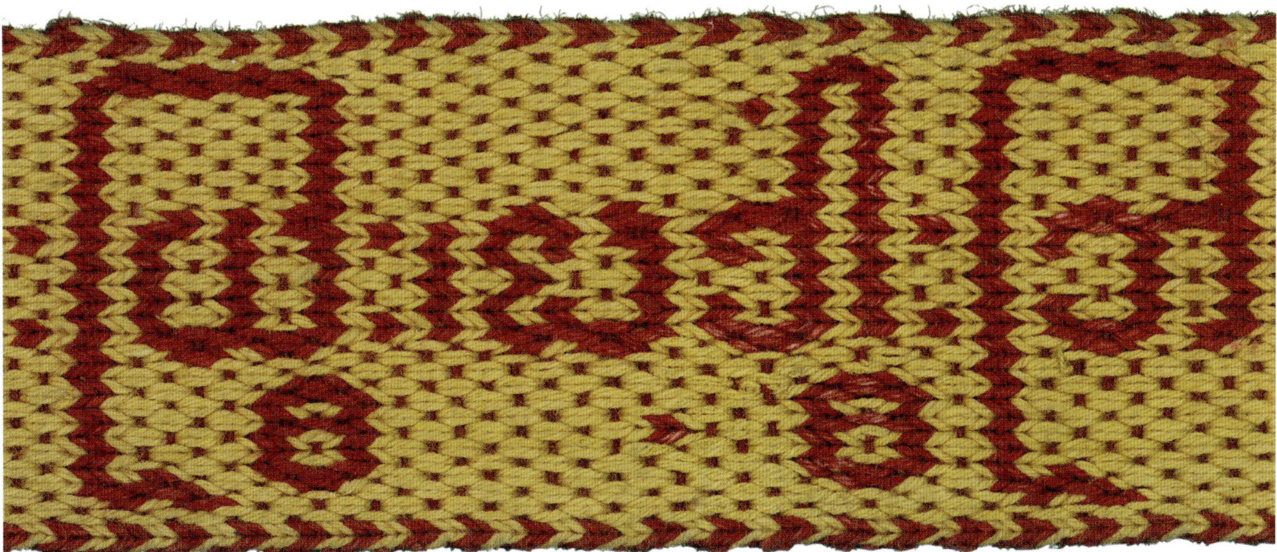

B888 reverse (x2)

Plate 153 TOP NEXT PAGE
Tube formed by method 1. *(B861)*

Plate 154 CENTER NEXT PAGE
Tube formed by method 2. *(R092)*

Plate 155 BOTTOM NEXT PAGE
A simple way to make a loop is to wrap these threads at the starting end using a separate thread, and compressing them into a tight loop. *(B888)*
Bands, which now have only a mass of jumbled thread, were probably wrapped like this, but the wrapping thread wore out. *(MYA070)*

THE STARTING LOOP

A. Woven tube

The loop present at the start of the majority of these bands is a woven tube, made before the weaving of the band proper is started. There are at least three ways of producing this, but only two are found here.

Method 1

The weft is passed from right to left in the shed, carried over the band, then again from right to left in the next shed, and so on. So the band is covered with weft floats (see fig. 8a). When these are pulled up tight, either during the weaving or subsequently, the band curls up until its two selvages touch and a tube is formed (see figs 8b and 10a).

Method 2

The weft is passed from left to right in the left-hand half of the warp threads, then from right to left in the right-hand half (see fig. 9a). Pulling the weft tight forces the left half of the band over the right half, again forming a tube (see fig. 10b). This is by far the commoner method used in these bands.

The numbering of the cords in these two diagrams shows how the color sequence in the tube differs in the two types. So by comparing the colors in the flat band with that in the tubular loop, the method used can be deduced even if the actual start and end of the tube is concealed by a binding tie, as often happens in these bands.

In both methods the tablets are given half-turns, instead of the usual quarter-turns, between the passing of the weft. There is invariably a twining reversal at the center of the loop to avoid twist buildup beyond the tablets.

B. Wrapping the warp threads

As the warp is being made, the threads pass around two posts some distance apart. A simple way to make a loop is to wrap these threads at the starting end using a separate thread, and compressing them into a tight loop. See cat. 055 [here B888].

Maybe the bands which have no loop, only a mass of jumbled thread, were intended to receive this treatment, or did receive it and the wrapping thread wore out.

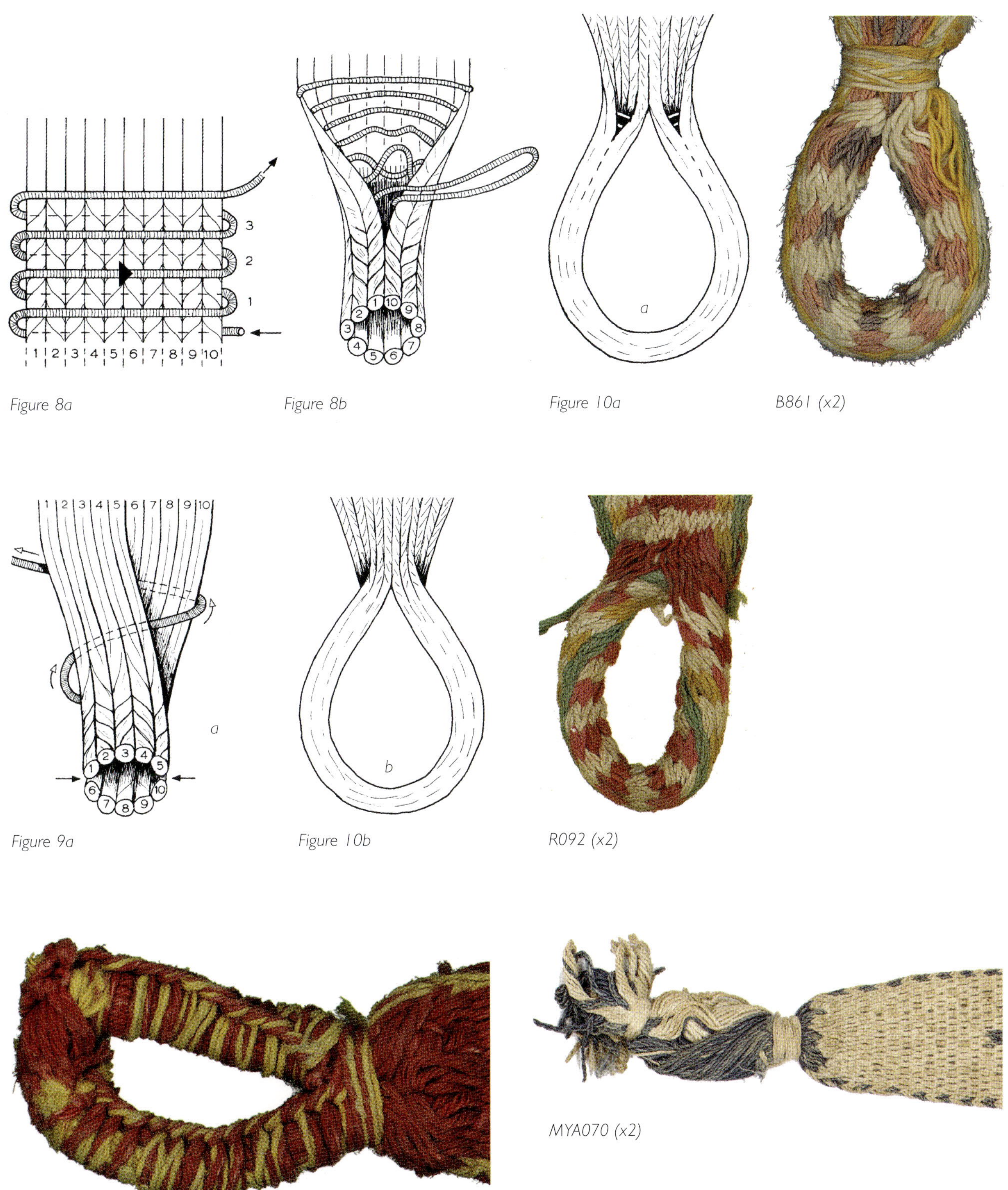

Figure 8a

Figure 8b

Figure 10a

B861 (x2)

Figure 9a

Figure 10b

R092 (x2)

MYA070 (x2)

B888 (x2)

Plate 156 BELOW
In this old sazigyo the band is finished with a simple plait using all the warp threads, without any reduction. *(R150)*

Plate 157 BOTTOM
The taper reduces the number of warp ends before the final tail is made. Gradually cutting the warp ends naturally leads to the band tapering. *(R173)*

THE TAPERED FINISH

The most variation in technique is seen in how the final tapering of the band is accomplished. The purpose of the taper is to reduce the number of warp ends before the final tail is made. If the latter were made, as it frequently is, in tubular form using the full number of ends, it would be too thick, in fact twice as thick as the starting tubular loop.

So the warp ends are gradually cut and eliminated in the following ways. The cutting naturally leads to the band tapering.

1. Cutting the ends from the two (but occasionally three) outermost tablets on both sides and laying them all in the next shed as weft. So this shed carries sixteen warp ends, eight from each side.

They then either protrude from the selvage at the opposite side as a fringe of varying length, or are cut flush. See fig. 11 on the next page for the left-hand side of such a taper.

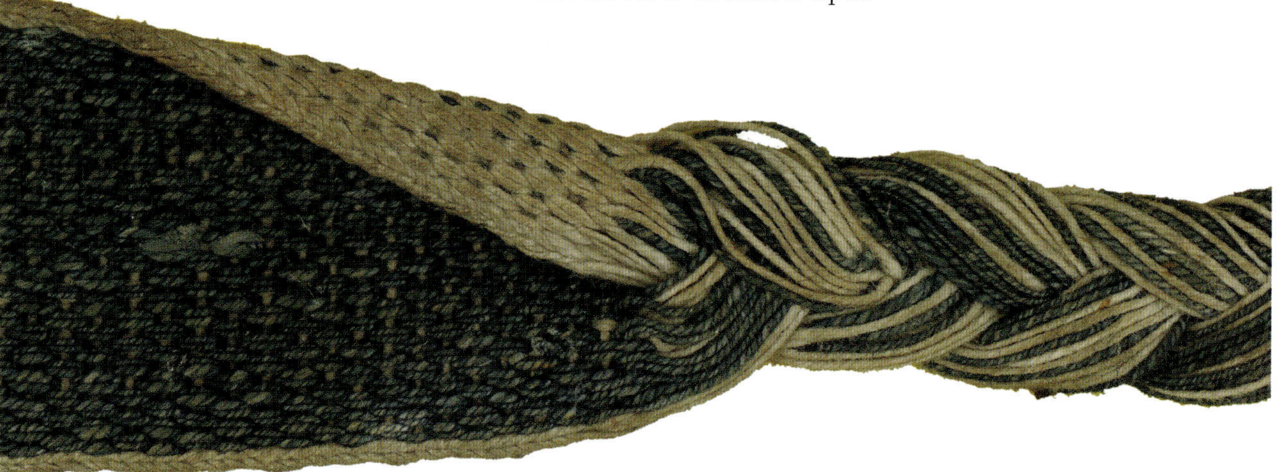

R150 (x2)

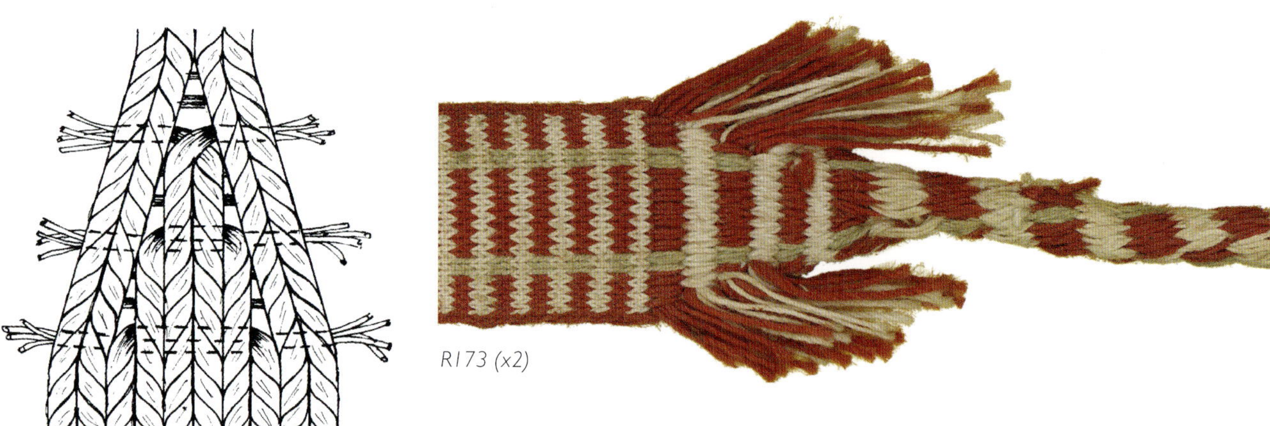

Figure 10c (12a in Peter's orig. report)

R173 (x2)

Plate 158 BELOW
A variation, c, where cut ends pass through the shed and are cut flush. (fig. 11, *B867*)
Method 2, in *B885*, cut ends are taken from inside the selvage. (fig. 12)

Variations:
a. half-turns between successive sheds;
b. quarter-turns between successive sheds;
c. as (b) but cut ends from the right side going in the first shed, those from the left side in the next shed, and so on.
d. Cut ends stop short of the opposite selvage being brought out on to the surface and there cut flush with it. A neat method.

2. Various methods whereby the cut ends do not come from outermost tablets but from those inside the selvage. See fig. 12 for a rough sketch of this in B885.

Sometimes the final bunch of cut ends are used as weft for several picks and pulled tightly to increase the taper.

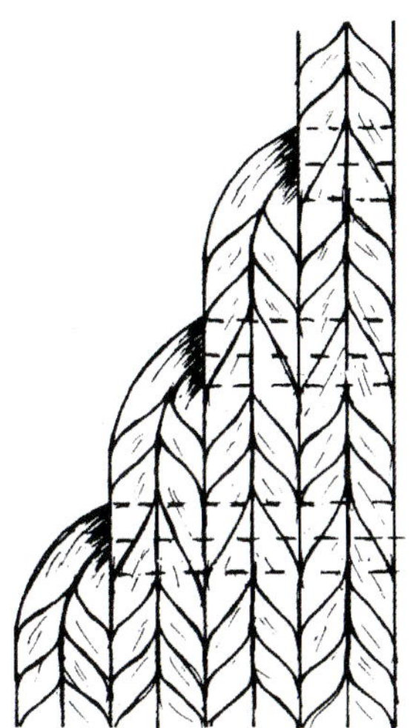

Figure 11

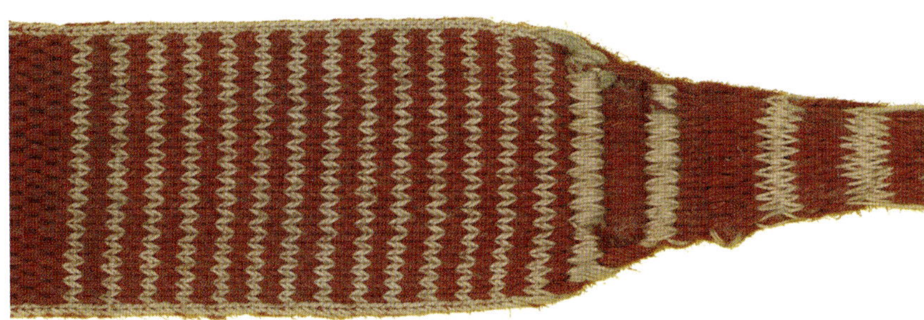

B867 (x2)

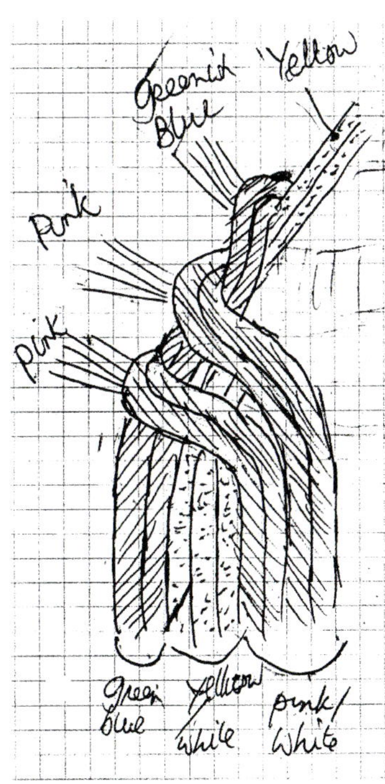

Figure 12

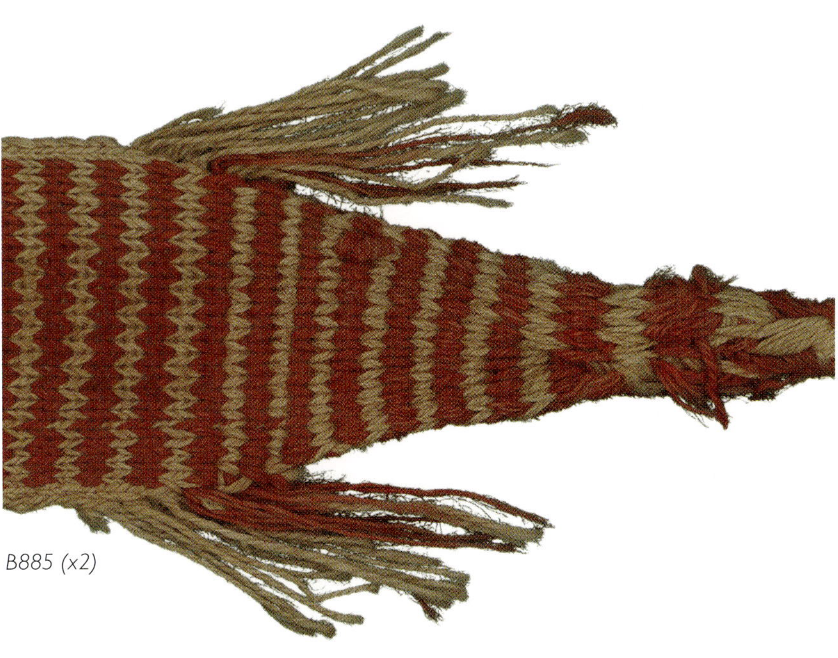

B885 (x2)

Plate 159 BELOW
THE TAIL
Tube (method 2) with flat end. *(R008)*
Tube then plait. *(R173)*
Square plait. *(R082)*
Unfinished simple plaits. *(B861)*

THE TAIL

The final tail or tie is worked either as a tube (method 2), as a three- or eight-strand braid, or as a two-ply cord. It ends with a fringe, sometimes bound, sometimes not.

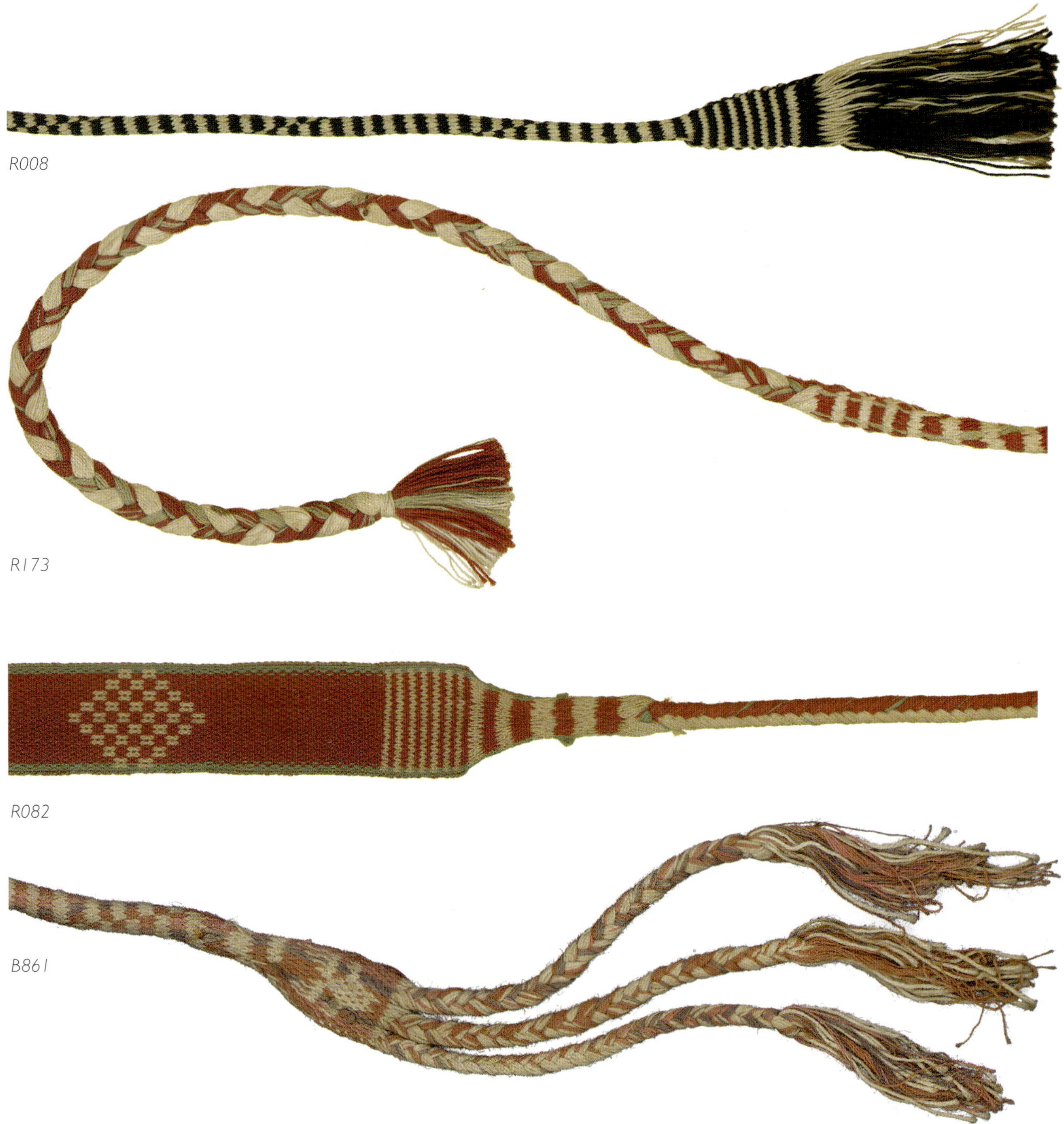

R008

R173

R082

B861

Part V Chapter 16

Summary of Techniques Used by Sazigyo Weavers

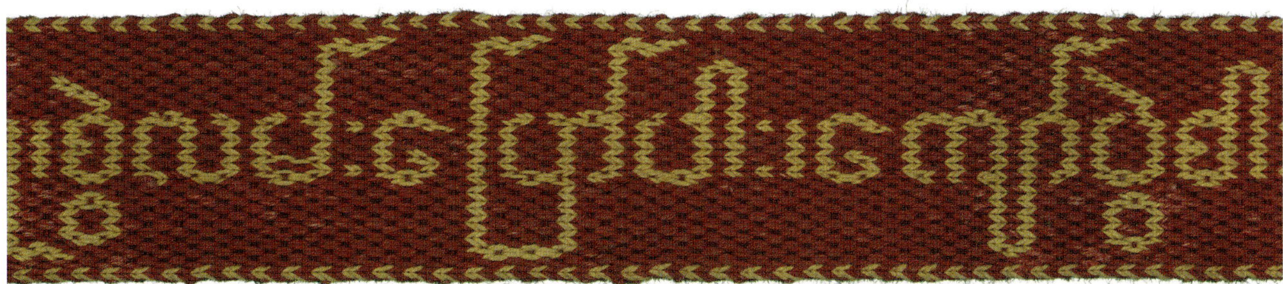

B888

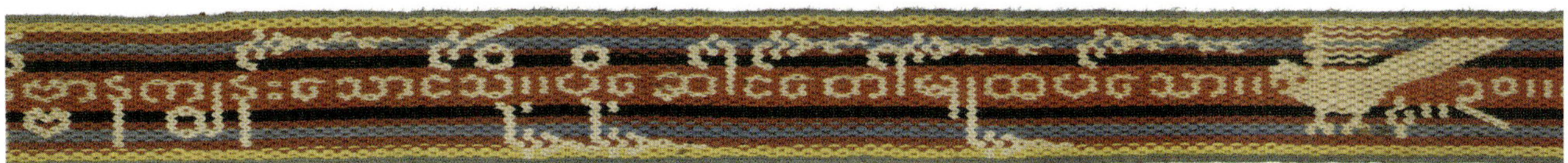

B842

Plate 160 ABOVE

WIDTH AND FINENESS

In this collection, the width ranges from 13 to 30 mm. Fineness varies from 123 ends per centimeter for the finest to as low as 38 ends/cm for the coarsest, a wide range. *(B888, B842)*

Width

Between 13 and 30 mm.

Length

Varies greatly, but almost always over 3 meters, sometimes over 5 meters.[1] The length given includes the loop and the taper, but not the tail, which is given separately.

Material

Always cotton, either two- or three-ply. The thickness count varies. Often yarns of quite different counts are combined in the same band, apparently without any tension problems. The thicker yarn is usually that used for the background. The unevenness of some yarns points to hand-spinning.

Tablet numbers

An even number between twenty-eight and forty-four, most commonly thirty-eight and forty. Only one instance of an odd number, thirty-seven.

Multiplying the number of tablets by four (for the number of warp threads in each) gives the total number of warp ends; then dividing that number by the width gives the count of warp ends per centimeter, a good indication of the fineness of the work.

This varies between 123 ends/cm for the finest, to as low as 38 ends/cm for the coarsest, a wide range.

Plate 161 BELOW
In some sazigyo the weft is the same color as the selvage threads so that it is virtually invisible *(B870)*, but it can also be quite different, giving a "dotted edge" effect. *(B888)*

Warp colors

These are always symmetrical about the mid-line, so they are only listed as far as the center.

The selvage tablets usually carry only one color in all four holes, described as "solid yellow." The rest always carry two colors and are described as "red/white."

The central color stripe is almost always eight, or rarely six, tablets wide; it is on this that the text is centered.

Weft colors

Sometimes the same color as selvage threads so that it is virtually invisible; sometimes quite different, giving a "dotted edge" effect.

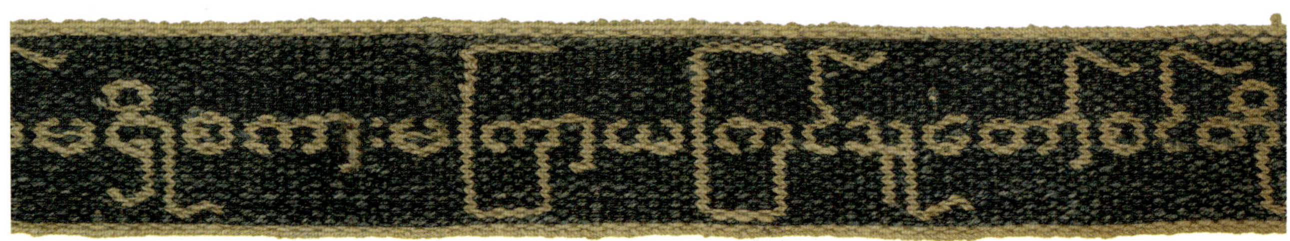

B870

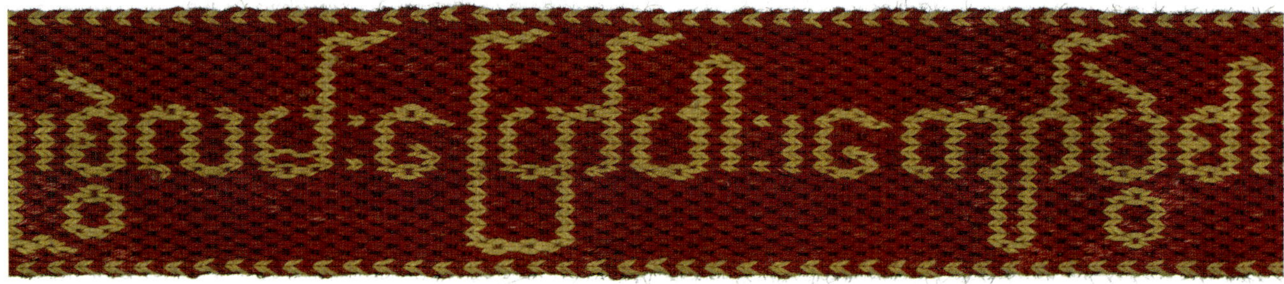

B888

Start

Tubular loop, woven in one of three different methods (see technical notes), method 2 being by the far the commonest.

Often the loose threads found where the loop stops and the band flattens are tightly bound.

BODY OF BAND

Warp-twining

As the band widens from the loop, it usually starts with a section of warp-twining, either as cross-stripes or another simple pattern, like small checks. This invariably has a central twining reversal point.

The lesser used alternative is to start straight in with the double-faced weave.

Plate 162 BELOW
The final fringe can be bound at the end of the plait or braid to prevent unraveling. These braids, which had lost their binding, were expertly rebraided by Jennie Parry. *(R106)*

Double-faced weave

This makes up the majority of the length. It has a warp-twined border usually consisting of two cords, but rarely one or three.

This double-faced section can show various images:

1. Always the inscription itself, exactly centered on the mid-line color stripe. An "O"-shape almost always uses eight tablets (rarely six); verticals are almost always the narrowest possible with tablet weaving. The flourishes to the risers and fallers, most of which in Burmese script point in the direction of the weaving, vary greatly in complexity and could form the basis for a study in themselves.

2. Devices, images. Animals, birds, fish, bells, gongs, umbrellas, "flag masts" are usually placed to be read with the band held vertically; occasionally an animal stands the other way. They can be placed separately or mingled with the text.

3. Block patterns. Small geometric shapes built up of square blocks of color, the product of four tablets weaving for four picks. These can be arranged to give geometric motifs of various types: diamonds, crosses, circles (often with a puzzling central long warp float, obviously intended), and stacks. Less commonly the blocks are three, five, or six tablets wide. Such patterns often separate the pictorial images.

Tapered finish

Many different methods and variations, but all reduce the width of the band and the number of its warp ends. The neatest have no protruding fringes.

Always followed by a tail, either tubular and made as method 2, or a three-strand or eight-strand braid or a two-ply twisted cord, or some combination of these. The final fringe can be bound at the end of the braid to prevent unraveling.

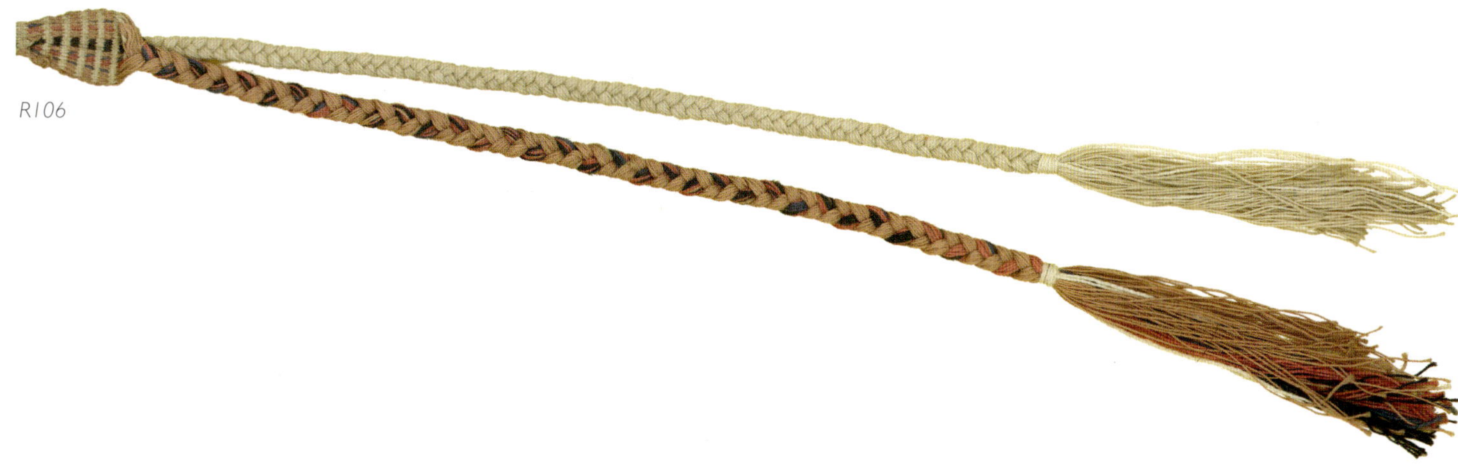

R106

Sample Analysis of a Sazigyo

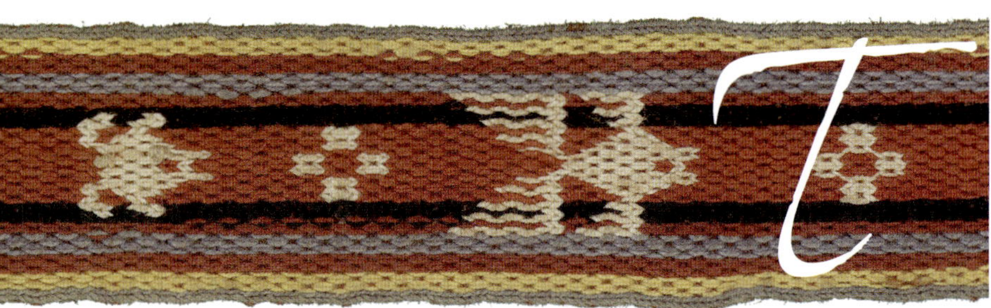

B842

This final chapter consists of two complementary analyses of the same sazigyo. The first, Peter Collingwood's analysis of the weaving techniques, bears his unique authority. It is followed by the present author's parallel analysis, which concentrates on the description and interpretation of the symbolic motifs and pictorial images. The beautiful weave that is the subject of both analytical descriptions is illustrated here in its entirety (plate 165). The English translation of the woven text is given on page 119.

B847 Technical analysis by Peter Collingwood
Width: 14 mm.
Length: 598 cm including loop and taper. Tail 21 cm.
Number of tablets: 38. So total ends = 152, set at 108 ends/cm.

Warp colors:
2 tablets all brown; 3 yellow/white, 3 blue/white; 3 pink/white; 4 dark red/white; 4 blue/yellow to center, then mirror-image to selvage.
Weft: same as outer brown warp.
Start: tubular loop, woven with blue weft using half-turns of tablets. Method 2 can be deduced from colors around tube. A central twining reverse in loop.

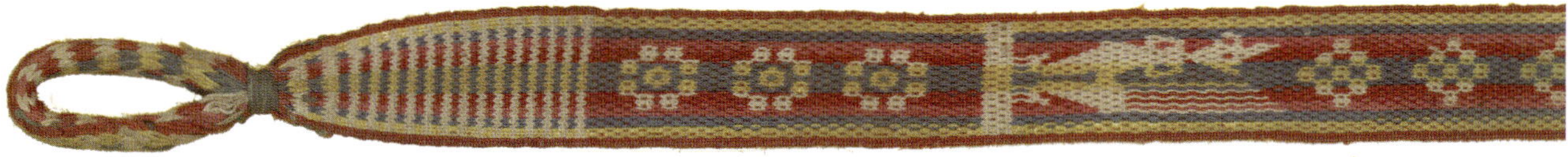

B847

Plate 163 ABOVE
Tubular starting loop. *(B847)*

Body of band: begins with warp-twined cross-stripes, first using a blue thread (from the ones wrapped around the end of the loop) then a brown one. Band quickly broadens with a central twining reverse. After 3.5 cm, the double-faced weave starts with just over a meter of motifs. These twelve motifs (only one is repeated) are separated alternately with three diamonds and with three circles, each made up of blocks of color, four tablets wide. To achieve perfect symmetry in the circles the tablets have to be turned atypically; it is this that gives the long floats visible on back and front at the circles' centers. The two outer tablets give a brown warp-twined border throughout.

Plate 164 BELOW
Taper at the end of the flat area. *(B847)*

The central inscription is punctuated with parrots with two types of wings and gives way to another array of motifs, this time 176 cm long. These are separated as before but mostly show a repeated figure.

After the double-faced weave, 3.5 cm of warp-twined cross-stripes before the taper.

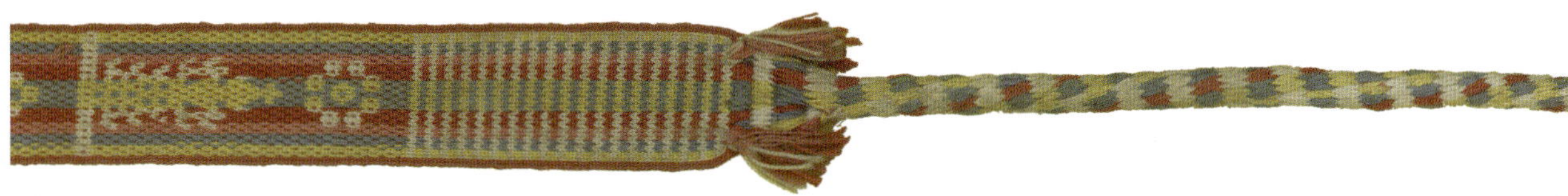

B847

Tapered finish: performed in three untidy stages, with half-turns of the tablets. Then a tubular tail that ends abruptly, probably cut, after 21 cm.
Condition: very good; some worn edges, abraded areas on back (perhaps where wrapped around book). One instance of long warp floats all across.
Comment: beautiful, imaginative, and delicate piece of work, displaying both the weaver's skill and her very ordered mind, concerned with the precise placing of the smallest detail. Unusual for the text to be in yellow and lucky that this has not faded. The motifs amazingly make up only a little short of half the total length. It has the crisp feel of really fine weaving.

B847 Interpretation of motifs and images by Ralph Isaacs
The sequence of woven motifs and images is annotated with comments on their symbolic significance.
Width: 14 mm.
Length: 598 cms + Cord 21 cms (cut).
Dated: 1269 Burmese Era (1907 CE).
Colors: (edge to center, then reverse order to opposite edge) deep pink/yellow/sky blue/rose pink/red/sky blue central warp stripe, with text and images in yellow and white.
Sequence: loop/cross-stripes for 3 cm/series of 12 pictorial images all separated by groups of 3 *navratna* ("nine auspicious gems" motifs symbolizing the nine planets and their powerful influences; each motif is composed of nine small blocks, arranged either in a rosette of eight around the central ninth, or in a diamond of three rows of three blocks. These trios of motifs also stand for the Three Gems: the Buddha, law, and community of monks; alternately all three rosettes or all three diamonds): **1. *Kinnara*** (winged bird-man, symbol of marital fidelity with his consort the *kinnari*, whose image is no. 7); **2. Lion** (*chinthe*, mythical bearded lion, guardian of the approach to the pagoda); **3. Nat** (celestial being who wears the side-knotted silk *gaung baung* headdress and may represent Thagya Min or Sakra, invoked at all Burmese Buddhist ceremonies); **4. Horse** (symbol of the Sangha, the community of monks; the Buddha-to-be Prince Siddhattha rode out of

Plate 165 FOLLOWING PAGES
A FINE SAZIGYO
The subject of Peter Collingwood's technical analysis and of the author's interpretative comments. *(B847)*

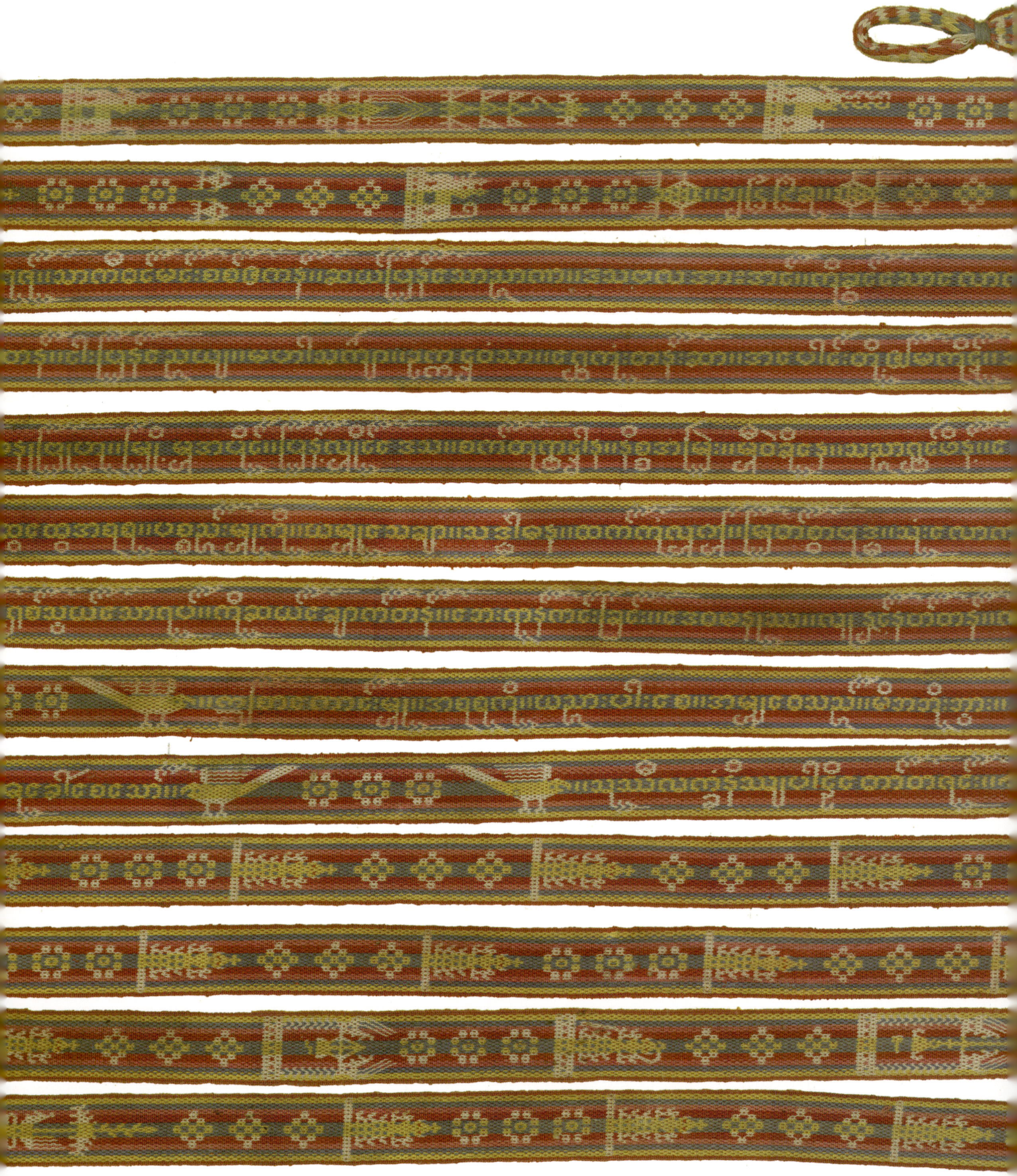

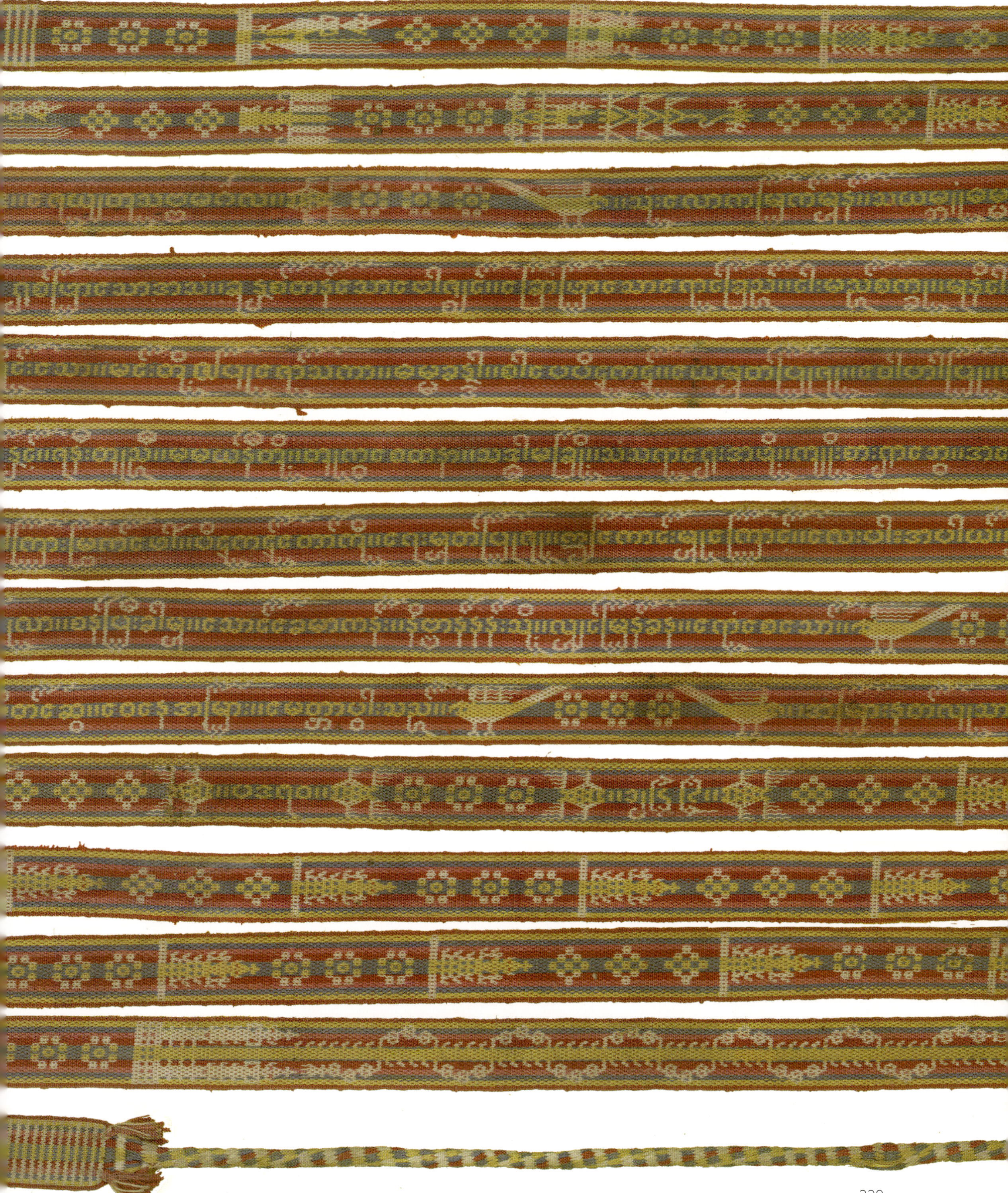

Plate 166 BELOW AND NEXT PAGE
FISH RACE FROGS
Fish and frogs race each other to the end of the flat area (below). A fish wins, by leaping off the end of the sazigyo and reappearing just before the fringe at the very end of the cord. (next page below)

the palace on his white horse Kanthaka to seek enlightenment as an itinerant mendicant); **5. Peacock in chariot** (symbol of *dana*, generosity; these little gilt model chariots with tall tiered *pyatthat* roofs carried donations of gold leaf to the gilders at work regilding the pagoda); **6. Stag** (symbol of the law, Dhamma; the Buddha's first sermon was preached in a deer park); **7. Kinnari** (consort of the *kinnara*; jointly they symbolize marital fidelity, here the constancy of the donor couple); **8. Candelabrum with a row of five candles** (symbol of fire, one of the Four Great Elements, Mahabhuta; often used by astrologers consulted by donors to select an auspicious date for their donation); **9. Lion in chariot** (symbol of *dana*, generosity; the lion and peacock passengers may stand for the cash value of the gold-leaf donation—the nineteenth-century royal coinage had a lion on the gold coin and a peacock on the silver coin); **10. Nat with tall headdress** (Thagya Min, "King of the Nats," is Sakra or Indra); **11. Pair of fish** (possibly the zodiac sign for Pisces); **12. Beast** (dog? If so, its significance is obscure).

After this long series of images, the texts are introduced: **/ 3 N (*navratna*) Fish** (swimming left to right)**> Text (1) date: 1269 Burmese Era** [1907 CE] **<Fish** (swimming to left) **/ 3 N / Fish> Text**

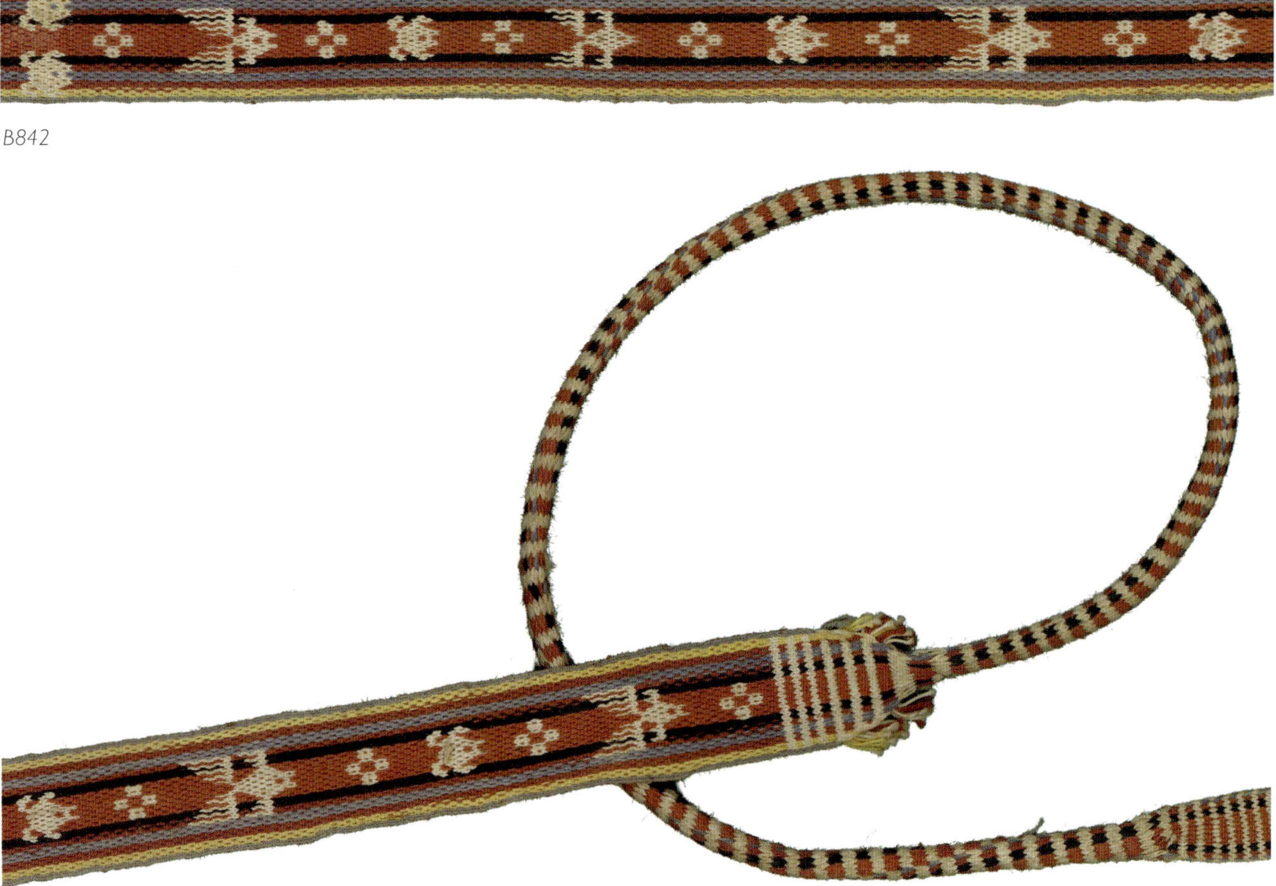

B842

(2) "*Zeyatu!*" [May there be success!] **<Fish / 3 N Parrot** (facing right)**> Text (3) main text** (of 59 four-syllable *pada* verses) **<Parrot** (facing left) **/ 3 N / Parrot> Text (4)** (of eight verses, offering to share merit of the deed of donation) **<Parrot / 3 N / Parrot> Text (5)** (inviting witnesses to call out "*Thadu!*" [Well Done!]) **<Parrot / 3 N / Parrot> Text (6)** (Pali title of scriptural Ms.) **<Parrot / 3 N / Fish> Text (7)** (final verse-count, of 70 verses) **<Fish / 3 N / Fish> Text (8)** (date, repeated, reasons unknown) **<Fish / then 16 repetitions of a group consisting of an image of a Nat followed by 3 N (rosette and diamond-shaped N in alternate groups of three) /** The next three images symbolize the broadcasting of the donation: **round bell, antler striker below, two birds atop** (symbol of broadcast of donation to invite "*Thadu!*" and share merit) **/ 3 N / Waythondaye** (the Earth Goddess, Sanskrit: Vasundhara, called to witness the donors' deed of merit, depicted wringing out her long wet hair) **/ 3 N / kyizi gong, with hammer below and three birds atop** (flat, triangular eared bronze gong, hung on a twisted string and struck on the corner to produce a surging vibrato note; the three birds represent the three strokes) **/ 3 N / *dagundaing*** (tall teak flagpole, with twin tubular pennants, and a *hintha* bird perched atop; the last object the pilgrim would see while descending from the pagoda platform, religious duty accomplished; this woven image measures 19.5 cm) **/ 3 N / Nat with eyes** (the weaver supplies the eyes in a supplementary weft) **/ 3 N / Nat with eyes / 3 N / Nat with no eyes / N / cross-stripes for 3 cm / tubular cord, cut short.**

Brilliantly talented, but also extremely organized, this weaver gives her work satisfying structure by careful controlled repetition of complex groups and by regular alternation of the shape of the geometric motifs. There are no less than eight "texts," each one bracketed off by pairs of beasts or fish.

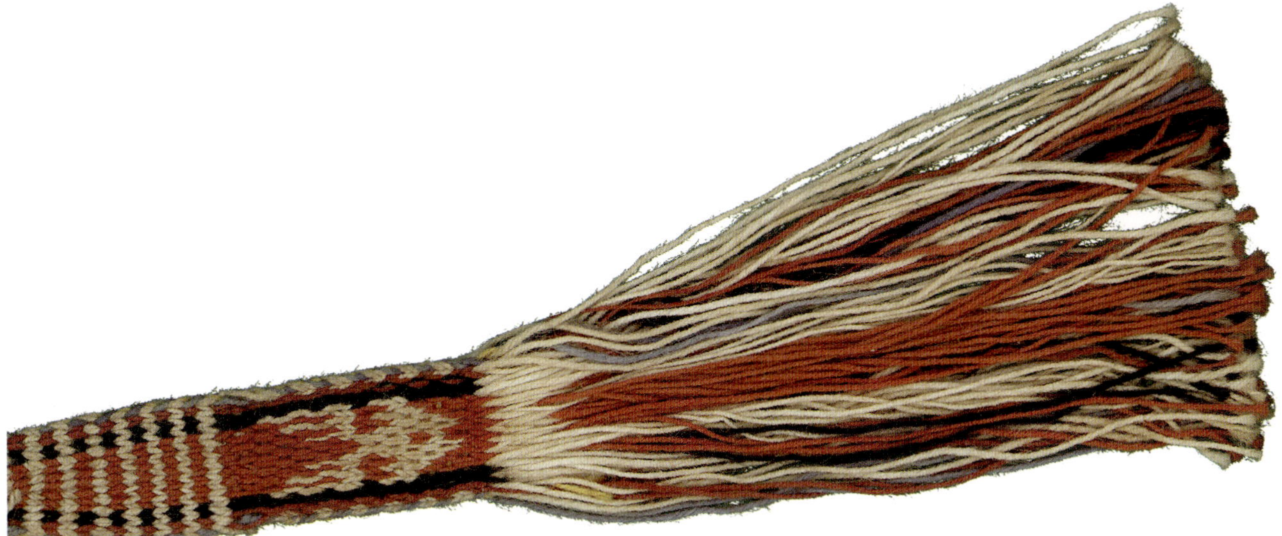

B842 (x2)

Appendixes

Appendix I

SAZIGYO WITH BROCADE BACKING (T1223)

This sazigyo, in the collection of Mrs. Jenny Spancake, has a curious structure that makes it unique. It is 16 mm wide and 483 cm long (incomplete). The loop and start are well preserved, but the tape is broken off near the end.

The upper face is a tablet-woven double-faced weave, in deep petunia pink silk, with text and motifs in white. These are varied and skillfully woven and include a remarkable series of all eight "birthday beasts" (illustrated in plate 88).

Neither the text nor woven images are visible on the reverse because, for virtually its entire length, the sazigyo is backed or lined with an independently woven textile of exactly equal width. This appears to be commercially woven brocade, with yellow silk geometric motifs on a white linen ground. It is not clear how these two fabrics were joined originally, but the stitching shows that at some date a sewing machine had been used.

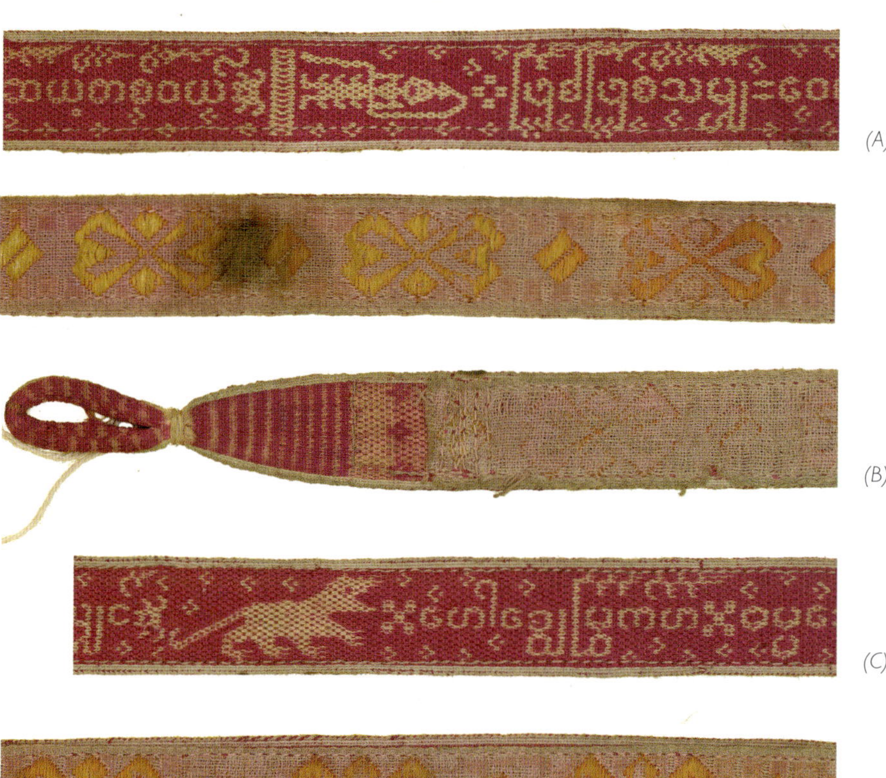

Plate 167 RIGHT
(A) The pink silk sazigyo and its white and yellow brocade backing.
(B) The back of the textile shows the start loop of the sazigyo and the start of the sewn-on backing or lining.
(C) The tiger is the birthday beast for Monday. The stitching attaching the front and back tapes can be clearly seen.
(D) This stretch of the brocade backing shows the edges folded over in places.
(T1223)

Plate 168 RIGHT
This manuscript knife is inscribed with the title of the manuscript on one surface and has the names of the donors on both sides: "The work of merit of pagoda-donors Maung Nandha and Ma Kyay Hmon" and "The third *inga* [bundle of twelve palm-leaf folios], the work of merit of husband and wife."

Plate 169 BELOW RIGHT
This manuscript knife, of plain palm leaf, is securely sewn on to the loop of the sazigyo. One surface is inscribed with the donors' names: "The work of merit of Ko Tu Lu and his wife Ma Lan Thami, of Kywe-lu-aing ["buffalo-wallow-pool"] Village." On the other side is the title of the manuscript: "Tiga-gyaw Nissaya, volume 3."

Appendix II

MANUSCRIPT KNIVES (*GABYIDAN*)

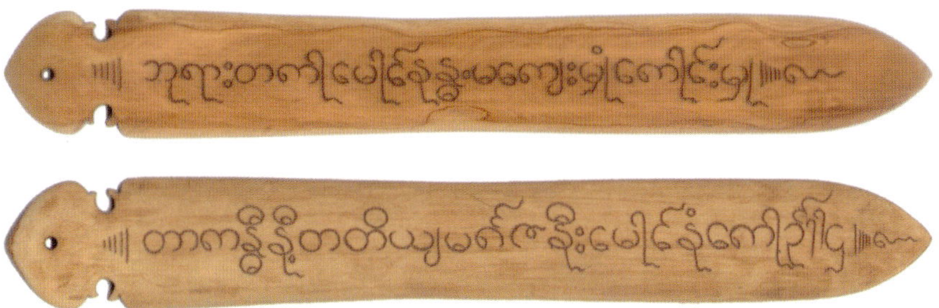

Little slips of palm leaf, more rarely of wood or ivory, often accompanied scriptural manuscripts. The vast majority are rudimentary—simply a short length of a single leaf of undecorated palm leaf. All are pointed at one end, hence their Burmese names *gabyidan* ("inscribed stick") or *than lyet* ("manuscript dagger"). As page-turners they were slipped between the thin palm-leaf folios and used to help turn them. Simple blank book knives might be left in position to act as place markers in a manuscript, probably for teaching purposes.

Book knives were usually separate from the manuscript, tucked into the wrapping cloth or between the overlapping layers of the sazigyo. But a book knife of suitable shape might be inserted at one end into the loop of the sazigyo, and if it was pierced to take a cord the *gabyidan* could be tied securely to the loop of the sazigyo (plate 169).

Some *gabyidan* are inscribed with the title of the manuscript on one surface and the donors' names on the other side (plate 168). Such "inscribed book knives" effectively had two functions. They were descriptive labels for manuscripts, an aid to the monk reader, announcing the title, the length in fascicles, and number of lines per folio; they also identified the manuscript donors. Manuscripts were expensive prestige objects that enjoyed the peculiar status of relics of the Buddha. They did not become the property of the monastery to which the donor had donated them. On the contrary, their legal ownership could revert to the donor following the death of the monastic owner.[1]

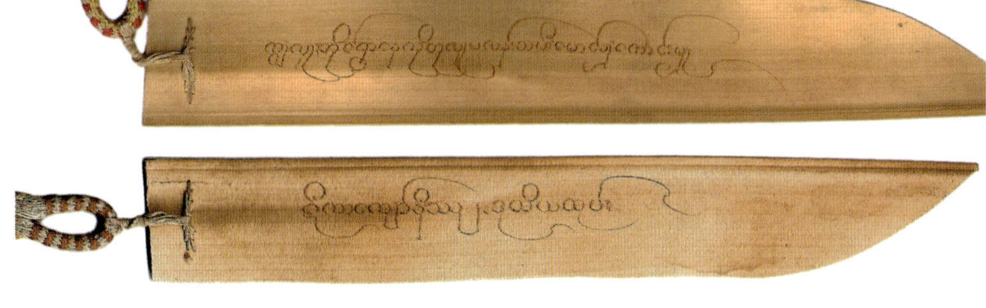

Plate 170 BELOW
The Burmese Pavilion was built in Burma, dismantled, shipped to London, and reassembled with its many-tiered spires to grace the Empire Exhibition at Wembley in 1924.

Appendix III

SAUNDERS WEAVING INSTITUTE, AMARAPURA

The Saunders Weaving Institute, founded in 1914 at Amarapura near Mandalay, not only survives to this day but remarkably retains its name, even in a Burma renamed Myanmar, whose military rulers swept away every place-name and street-name with a "colonial" connection. A tablet-woven band, now in the New Walk Museum in Leicester, was woven in Burma for display at the British Empire Exhibition at Wembley in 1924.[2]

The weave varies in width from 25 to 26 mm. Both selvage and the text and images are in natural yarn, and the colors of the longitudinal stripes, reading from edge to center, are red, pink, turquoise, blue, and red. Like a traditional sazigyo, it begins with a loop, followed by cross-stripes. After an elaborate "baroque" bracket the woven text begins in Burmese script: "Burma, Mandalay District, Saung-Da Loom Weaving School, Amarapura Town . . ." Next comes a woven miniature image of a lion, and the text continues in English block capitals "SAUNDERS WEAVING INSTITUTE [then three

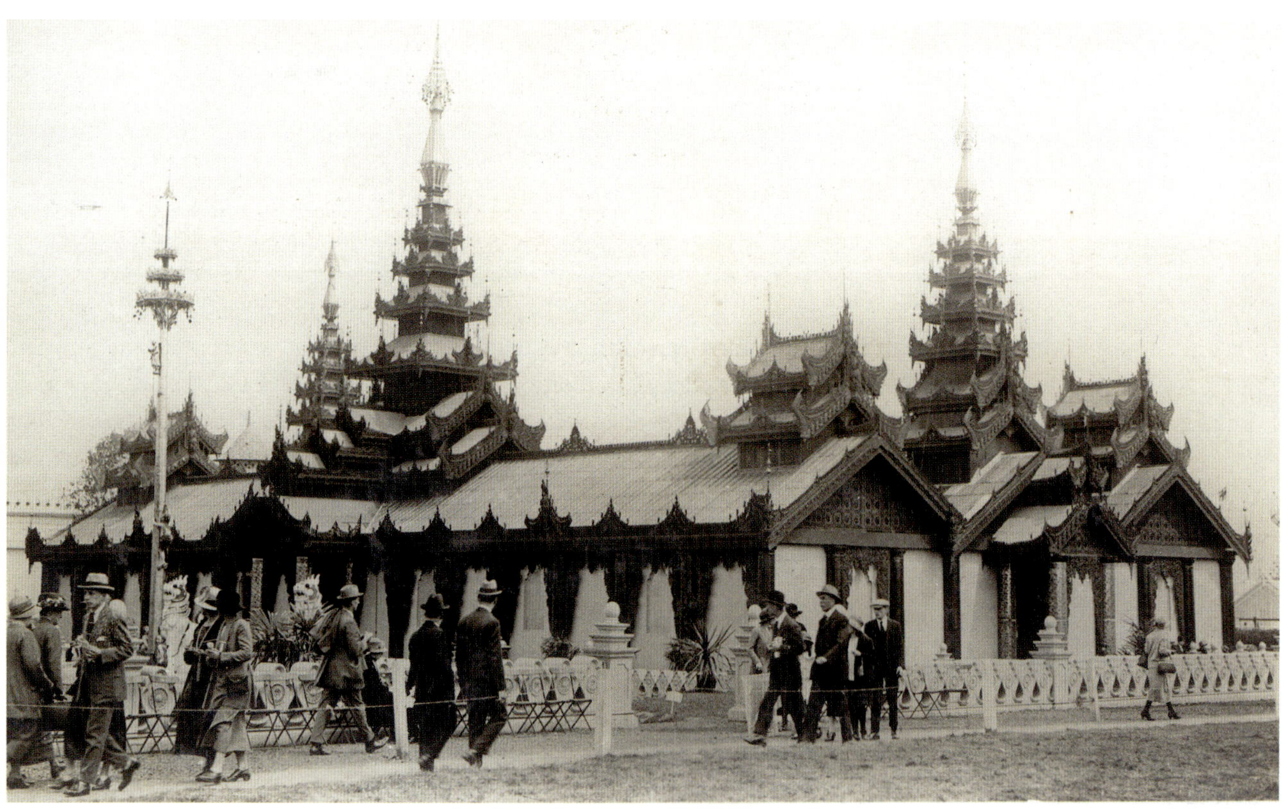

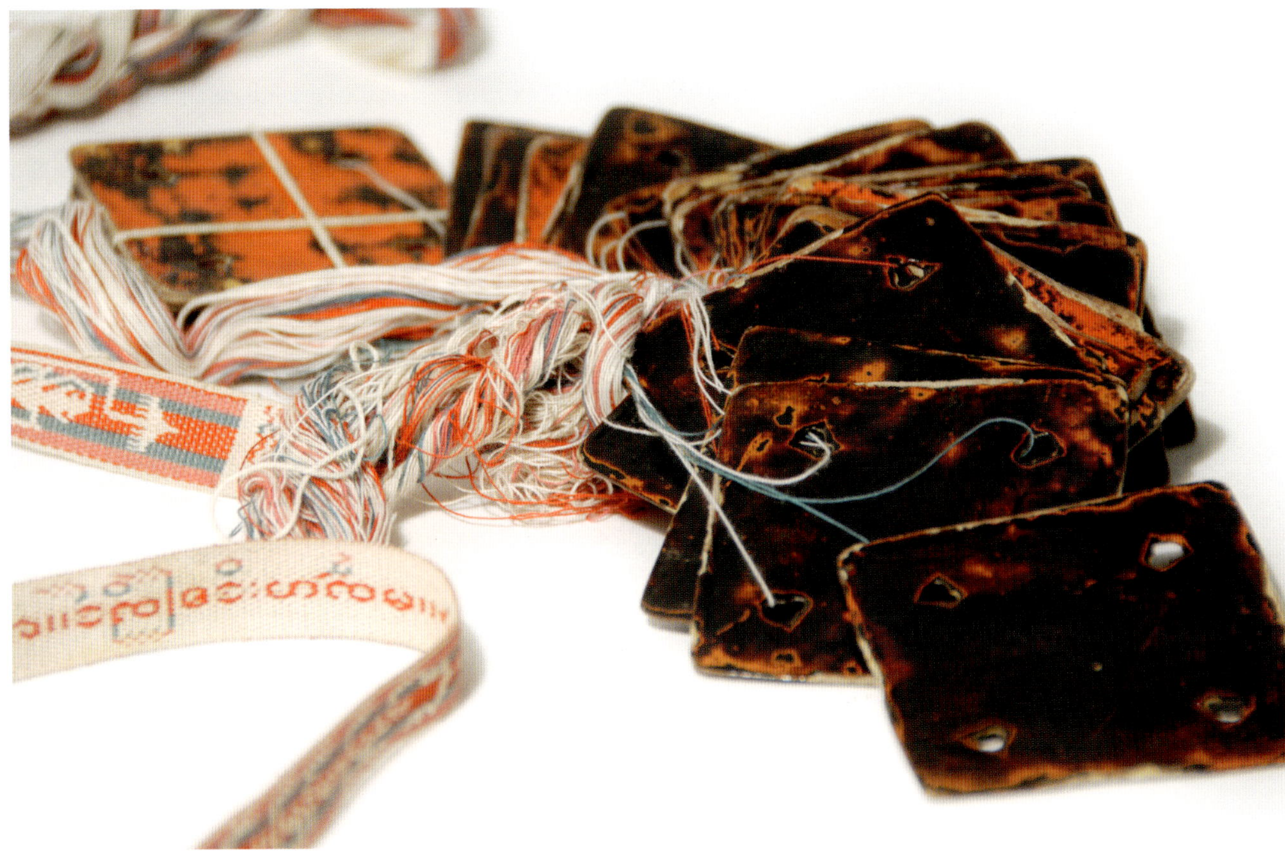

Plate 171 ABOVE
The weave at the British Empire Exhibition at Wembley in 1924 was displayed with tablets still in place on the warp threads.

geometric block motifs] H. B. HOLME ESQR. I.C.S." The final image, of the Earth Goddess Waythondaye, is followed by a pattern of small checks before the warp threads enter the pack of lacquered leather tablets. Beyond these, the warp threads have been loosely plaited and bound at the ends.

The lettering in the Burmese part of the inscription is neatly woven, but there are two bad spelling errors: "Mandalay" and "*yekkan*" (weaving, loom). The English lettering is all upper-case capitals.

The "Britishers" named were both members of the elite Indian Civil Service (ICS). Leslie Harry Saunders arrived in Burma in 1889, and by 1912 was "Commissioner and Additional Judge" in Upper Burma, with responsibility for the general economic welfare of the region. His reasons for taking a particular interest in the weaving industry have not been discovered, but in 1914 he founded the training school that was later named after him. He retired in 1923. In the same year a new post, "Superintendent of Cottage Industries *cum* Provincial Art Officer," was created. It was filled by G. E. Harvey ICS, and the Saunders Weaving Institute came under his wing.

Unfortunately Harvey's health gave way, and he went on leave to Oxford, where he recovered sufficiently to write a pioneering history of Burma.[3] Harvey's superior, the "Director of Industries," H. B. Holme ICS, who was already responsible for arranging the Burma contribution to the Empire Exhibition, assumed responsibility for the Saunders Weaving Institute.

Holme encouraged the establishment of weaving schools in all other districts, though only one district school was set up. From January to July 1922, Holme was on deputation to the British Industries Fair and British Empire Exhibition, and in 1924 he went to London, taking with him craftwork to be displayed in the Burmese Pavilion. This ornate teak structure may, in fact, have traveled on the same ship as Holme—it was built in Burma, dismantled for shipping, and re-assembled in Wembley. Besides lacquer and silver, Holme took this tablet-woven demonstration tape specially commissioned from the Saunders Weaving Institute in Amarapura.

It was purchased from the Wembley exhibition for the Dryad collection, and is now in the New Walk Museum in Leicester (L.E1.1988.418.0 Tablet-weave).

In 1994, a workshop on tablet weaving led by Daw Thein Htay was held at the Saunders Weaving Institute, and a training course in sazigyo weaving was held in June 2013 at the Saunders Institute for weavers from Rakhine state.

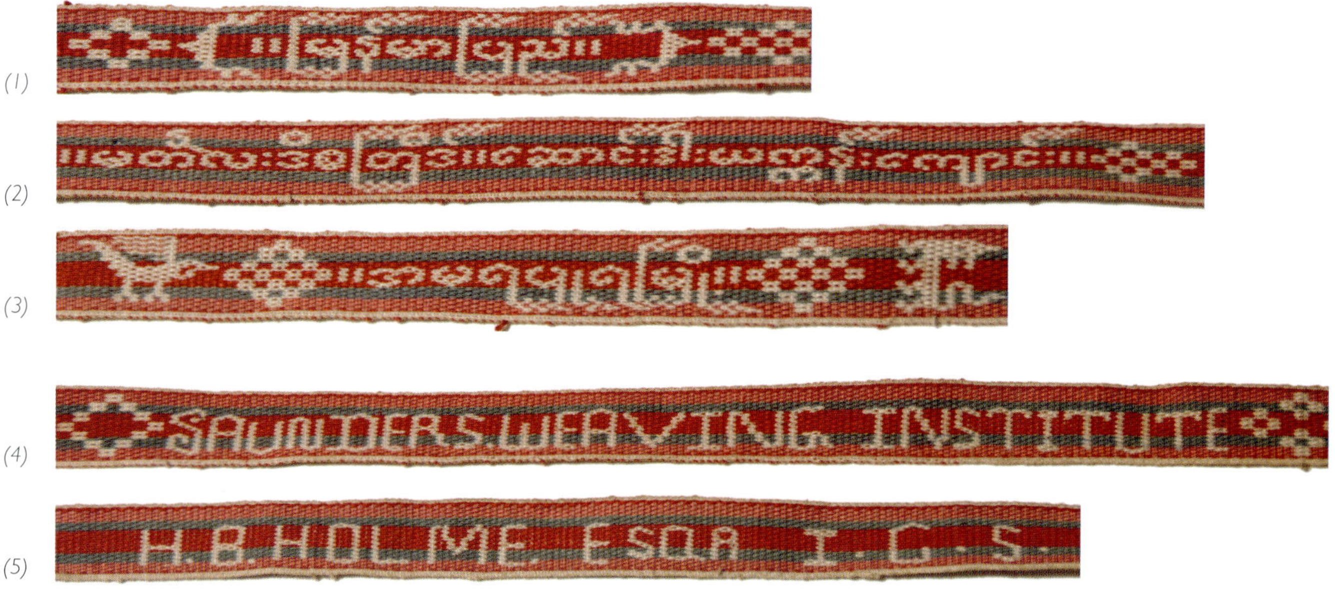

Plate 172 ABOVE
The woven inscription in Burmese and English lettering of the script band exhibited at Wembley.

R128 W 17 mm L 379 cm n. d.
R130 W 18 mm L 515 cm n. d.
R131 W 14 mm L 483 cm d. 1909
R134 W 16 mm L 392 cm n. d.
R137 W 18 mm L 527 cm d. 1919
R139 W 15 mm L 482 cm d. 1907
R142 W 18 mm L 580 cm d. 1900
R143 W 16 mm L 417 cm d. 1883
R145 W 15 mm L 497 cm d. 1912
R150 W 33 mm L 296 cm n. d.
R152 W 18 mm L 366 cm d. 1895
R154 W 17 mm L 432 cm n. d.
R158 W 20 mm L 463 cm n. d.
R160 W 12 mm L 537 cm d. 1911
R162 W 32 mm L 534 cm d. 1854
R167 W 16 mm L 501 cm d. 1917
R173 W 16 mm L 508 cm d. 1921
R177 W 34 mm L 571 cm n. d.
R179 W 14 mm L 485 cm d. 1917
R181 W 17 mm L 466 cm n. d.
R182 W 19 mm L 400 cm n. d.
R183 W 20 mm L 423 cm n. d.
R184 W 26–27 mm L 496 cm n. d.
R189 W 22–23 mm L 407 cm n. d.
R191 W 23 mm L 416 cm n. d.
R192 W 17 mm L 491 cm n. d.
R193 W 15 mm L 471 cm d. 1915
R202 W 15 mm L 473 cm d. 1917
R203 W 14 mm L 503 cm d. 1917
R205 W 23–25 mm L 439 cm d. 1904
R206 W 20 mm L 490 cm d. 1902
R207 W 15–17 mm L 462 cm d. 1904
R208 W 14–15 mm L 491 cm d. 1909
R210 W 23 mm L 370 cm n. d.
R212 W 24 mm L 336 cm d. 1887
R218 W 19 mm L 381 cm n. d.
R222 W 16 mm L 493 cm d. 1908
R223 W 28 mm L 389 cm n. d.
R227 W 17 mm L 424 cm n. d.
R234 W 20–23 mm L 444 cm textless
R235 W 25–28 mm L 436 cm textless
R238 W 16 mm L 495 cm textless
R239 W 21 mm L 383 cm textless
R240 W 20 mm L 376 cm textless
R241 W 19–21 mm L 274 cm textless
R243 W 15 mm L 209 cm n. d.
R244 W 16 mm L 546 cm n. d.
R245 W 14 mm L 500 cm d. 1930
R246 W 15 mm L 487 cm d. 1926
R247 W 14 mm L 473 cm d. 1958
R251 W 16 mm L 545 cm n. d.
R253 W 18 mm L 556 cm textless
R254 W 21 mm L 484 cm textless
R261 W 13 mm L 514 cm n. d.
R266 W 19 mm L 567 cm n. d.
R267 W 18 mm L 556 cm n. d.
R268 W 13 mm L 479 cm d. 1916
R270 W 16 mm L 487 cm d. 1908
R271 W 15 mm L 486 cm d. 1908
R272 W 21 mm L 446 cm d. 1894
R274 W 15 mm L 453 cm d. 1965
R280 W 25 mm L 340 cm n. d.
R285 W 13 mm L 541 cm n. d.
R290 W 21 mm L 504 cm n. d.
R291 W 14 mm L 482 cm d. 1908
R293 W 15 mm L 540 cm n. d.
R296 W 24 mm L 325 cm* n. d.
R300 W 19 mm L 358 cm n. d.
R303 W 18 mm L 536 cm n. d.
R304 W 15 mm L 526 cm n. d.
R305 W 15 mm L 359 cm* d. 1941
R307 W 13 mm L 514 cm d. 1932
R308 W 13 mm L 530 cm d. 1932
R310 W 14 mm L 540 cm n. d.
R311 W 15 mm L 459 cm n. d.

Sazigyo in other public and private collections

I regret that for a few sazigyo some of this data was unavailable.

AZ: Denison Museum; BL: British Library; BM: British Museum; H: collection of Herbert Haar III and Dr. Sathirakorn Pongpanich; HM: Horniman Museum; J: John Lafortune; JBT: James Barker; JP: Jennie Parry; KJ: Mrs. Kathleen Johnson; L: Laurie De Groot; M: Ni Wayan Murni of Bali; MYA: Sue and David Richardson; NIU: North Illinois University; NMY: National Museum, Yangon; PG: Mrs. Pamela Gordon; RAS: Royal Asiatic Society; T: Mrs. Jenny Spancake; VC: Vanessa Chan; W: Wellcome Library, London.

AZ1 W 21 mm L 404 cm d. 1920
AZ3 W 22 mm L 482 cm n. d.
AZ4 W 18 mm L 484 cm n. d.
AZ6 W 18 mm L 447 cm n. d.
BL W 16 mm L 472 cm d. 1904
BM246 W 12 mm L 573 cm d. 1930
H007 W unavailable L unavailable
H008 W unavailable L unavailable
H012 W 15 mm L unavailable d. 1959
H016 W 14 mm L unavailable d. 1917
H021 W unavailable L unavailable d.1884
H031 W 15 mm L 518 cm n. d.
HM12220 W 21 mm L 344 cm d. 1888
HM6618 W 25–30 mm L 140 cm n. d.
J01 W 28 mm L 497 cm n. d.
J02 W 28 mm L 421 cm* n. d.
J03 W 25 mm L 316 cm n. d.
J05 W 16 mm L 340 cm* d. 1908
J06 W 17 mm L 372 cm n. d.
J07 W 13 mm L 519 cm d. 1928
JBT6.49 W 15 mm L 528 cm d. 1911
JBT6.51 W 26 mm L 918 cm d .1876
JP01 W 13 mm L 505 cm n. d.
KJ02 W 16 mm L 515 cm n. d.
KJ03 W 15–19 mm L 494 cm* n. d.
KJ04 W 31 mm L 416 cm* n. d.
L01 W 16 mm L 379 cm* d. 1908
L03 W 33 mm L 361 cm* n. d.
L04 W 27 mm L 308 cm n. d.
L05 W 20 mm L 371 cm n. d.
L06 W 25 mm L 387 cm d. 1879
L07 W 27 mm L 303 cm n. d.
L08 W 22 mm L 403 cm d. 1890
M01 W 13 mm L 329 cm* d. 1911
M02 W 13 mm L 449 cm d. 1915
M03 W 13 mm L 504 cm d. 1913
MYA016 W 20 mm L 597 cm d. 1903
MYA055 W 15 mm L 510 cm n. d.
MYA070 W 28 mm L 232 cm n. d.
NIU W 13 mm L 469 cm d. 1916
RAS W unavailable L unavailable n. d.
NMY W 36 mm L 396 cm* n. d.
PG W 25–27 mm L 338 cm n. d.
T261 W 15 mm L 500 cm n. d.
T405 W 17 mm L 491 cm n. d.
T433 W 22 mm L 357 cm n. d.
T441 W 22–24 mm L 400 cm n. d.
T467 W 16 mm L 562 cm n. d.
T883 W 17 mm L 507 cm n. d.
T1223 W 16 mm L 483 cm* n. d.
W93 W 15 mm L 493 cm n. d.

Appendix VII

SUGGESTIONS FOR FURTHER RESEARCH

The author hopes that researchers will see the text and illustrations as an invitation to further investigations. With this in view, each of the many hundreds of sazigyo illustrated or cited in this book is listed (in appendix 6) with its date where known and its museum acquisition number, to facilitate its being located, identified, and made available for study. Sketched below are some of the many potential areas of work in which researchers could usefully draw on this book's text and illustrations.

Chronological development. Many sazigyo bear a woven date, and others are readily dateable by comparison with these dated pieces. Relating these dates to selected differences (in technique, style of script, imagery, etc.) could throw light on the diachronic development of the art form of sazigyo weaving.

Geographical variation. Many sazigyo texts give the district of Burma where the weave was commissioned and/or woven, and some also give the donors' address. This information could inform a study of regional preferences in sazigyo colors, styles of script, and types of woven images.

Comparison with other art media in Burma. The miniature woven images on Burmese sazigyo could usefully be compared to the imagery found in other Burmese art media, such as wall painting for example. More widely, the use of Buddhist symbols on sazigyo could perhaps be compared to their occurrence in Buddhist art of the Southeast Asian region.

The sazigyo text as a literary genre. Vanessa Chan's translation of the work of the late Shwebo Mi Mi Gyi, and her own collection of sazigyo texts in Burmese original and in English translation, will (when published) together form a basis for the study of the literary merit of the sazigyo text and for a review of this literary genre. The original Burmese texts of all the sazigyo quoted in this book are available for study.

Charity in Burmese Theravada Buddhist practice. The attitudes and beliefs of Burmese Buddhist donors as revealed by the prayers in sazigyo texts, and to a lesser extent, implicitly, by the selection of images might contribute to understanding the range of motives of donation and underlying Burmese ideas, practices, and histories of *dana* (charity).

Colonial influence. A minor but intriguing characteristic of sazigyo imagery and text is the influence of the colonial period. The use of English lettering woven on sazigyo during the colonial period, whole words and dates, invites investigation.

Weaving techniques. Peter Collingwood's description of the tablet-weaving techniques used by Burmese sazigyo weavers (part 5 of this book) offers a solid basis for further study. Many more weaves could be made available for analysis and would certainly exhibit a wider range of variation than the fifty-five sazigyo in Collingwood's study.

Plate 178 BELOW
Otfried Staudigel's pattern (center) for the tablet weaving of a pictorial image of a horse, with (left) the original woven image on a sazigyo (B877), and (right) a replica image woven by the master himself.

Appendix VIII

OTFRIED STAUDIGEL'S PATTERNS FOR WEAVING OF REPLICAS FROM SAZIGYO

Otfried Staudigel, expert lifelong tablet weaver, learned the craft from his mother. She, in turn, was introduced to it by a relative who had seen it practiced in Southeast Asia. Otfried has written two books with text in German and English that provide aspiring tablet weavers with patterns or templates for weaving exact replicas of motifs and pictorial images from tablet-woven textiles from many cultures worldwide. The Brighton Museum collection of Burmese sazigyo was a chief source of material for Otfried's second book, *Woven Images, Unravelled Motifs*, so many of the patterns are for replica weaving of pictorial images in sazigyo illustrated in this book.

One of these patterns is illustrated here, with the corresponding images from the original sazigyo and from a replica textile woven by the master weaver himself.

Many tablet weavers in Germany, the USA, and other countries enjoy using these patterns to weave faithful replicas (choosing their own colors). Readers can obtain these tablet-weaving pattern books direct from the author: Otfried Staudigel, Höppnerstrasse 108, 47809 Krefeld, Germany.

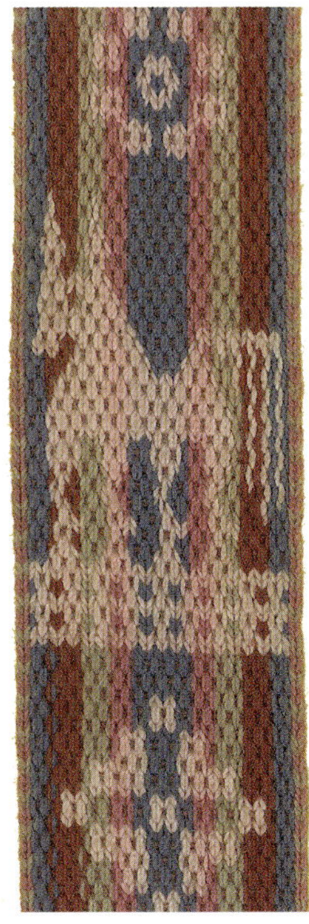

B877 (x2)

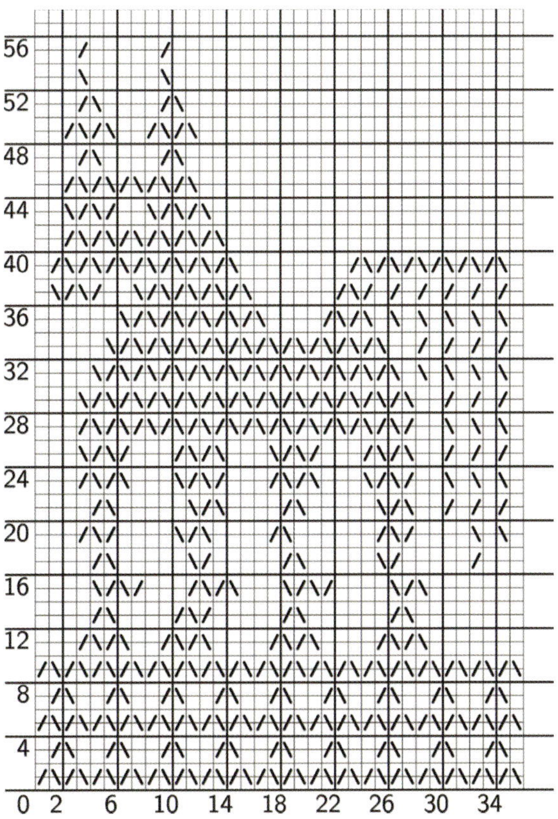

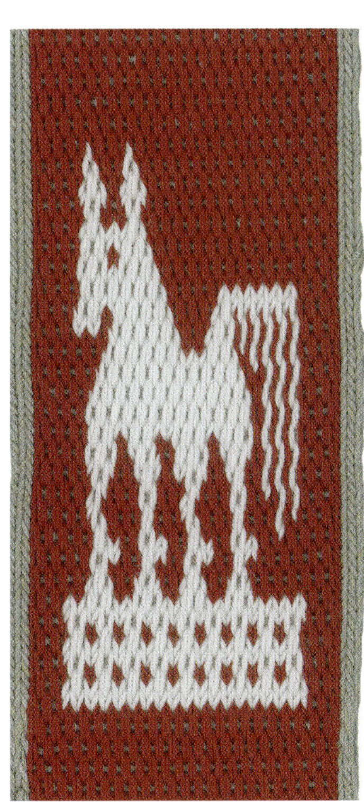

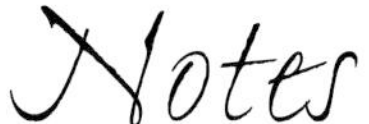

Acknowledgments

1 Elizabeth Dell and Sandra Dudley, eds., *Textiles from Burma*.

Part I

1 *Guardian* Review, October 3, 2009. Hilary Mantel recently recounted her physical reaction to visiting the house where Ralph Sadler had lived centuries ago: "It was then that the shock of the past reached out and jabbed me in the ribs. They were as alive as I am; why can't I touch them? Grieved, I had to stuff my fingers in my mouth, fish out my handkerchief, and do what a novelist has to do: unfreeze antique feeling, unlock the emotion stored and packed tight in paper, brick and stone."

2 T. S. Eliot, *Notes towards the Definition of Culture* (London: Faber, 1948), 92, and *Christianity and Culture* (New York: Harcourt, Brace, 1949), 168.

3 English terms, which translate Buddhist religious technical terms, are here given initial capitals. For explanation and discussion of such terms and of Buddhist doctrine, the reader can consult the books listed in the bibliography. Parentheses indicate relevance of the life story of the Buddha to the text and images found on sazigyo.

4 Rahula, *What the Buddha Taught*, 45.

5 Khin Myo Chit and Paw Oo Thet, *Flowers and Festivals of the Twelve Burmese Seasons*, 84.

6 Maung Htin Aung, *Burmese Monk's Tales*, 6.

7 Scott (Shway Yoe), *The Burman, His Life and Notions*, 129.

8 Ibid, 131.

9 U Thaw Kaung, "Myanmar Traditional Manuscripts and their Preservation and Conservation," 46.

10 Ibid, 54–55.

11 A donor couple mention this costly material in the text of their sazigyo: "It is wonderful that the text has been skillfully written in gold ink on the surface of elephant tusks altogether worth 180 silver coins. It is generously donated with great rapture." (VC38)

12 The vast majority of palm-leaf manuscripts were of the Tipitaka scriptures or commentaries, but royal book gifts might possibly have included works on grammar or history.

13 This text is quoted in the donors' prayer in the text of B850, which was woven in 1907. The translation is by the Ven. Dr. Kammai Dhammasami.

Part II

1 British Museum 1939,1010.181.b.

2 Lehman-Filhes, *Ueber Brettchenweberei*. The first edition of 1901 has a tablet-woven tape as a bookmark.

3 A comprehensive list of these Gujarati terminations follows in the exhibition catalogue. It has been omitted here.

4 RAS Bur. Ms. 86.

5 Pitt Rivers Museum, Oxford, 1889.29.200, presented by Sir Richard Carnac Temple.

6 Singer, "Kammavaca Texts," 106.

7 Dr. Ye Myint (by e-mail). The student was sent to learn from a weaver called Daw Hsint of Mon Ywe Jywe Mon. Vanessa Chan e-mailed me in October 2011: "Sar-si-kyo weaving is in my view still near-extinct, though if I can interest someone in trying to revive it as a commercial proposition, it may yet be retrieved from the dustbin of history. At the very least if our books will raise interest sufficiently, people might consider it worthwhile to start making fakes."

8 In his travel journal Scherman records that he first saw tablet weaving in Pegu in January 1911, and again a few days later in Mandalay, in the courtyard of the house of U Kyaw Yan and his daughter. Here his wife Christine took photographs, and "work and loom" were purchased for the Munich Ethnographic Museum. The photographs have survived, but not the "work and loom." An exhibition of Christine Scherman's photographs of Burma is traveling from Munich to Yangon and Pagan in 2013 (Weigelt, "...'And Saved the State Thousands,'" 12–15).

9 Peter Collingwood, *The Techniques of Tablet Weaving*.

10 This exchange of e-mails is described by the author in two articles published in 2009: "NERDS, or Nayland Express Research Devoted to Sazigyo," in the *Journal for Weavers, Spinners and Dyers*, and "Mr PC of Nayland and Sazigyo: Analysing Burmese Tablet Woven Inscription Bands," in *Strands*, Journal of the Braid Society.

11 Pali-Burmese Ms no. 93 in the Wellcome Library is illustrated on the endpapers and between major sections of this book.

12 Peter Collingwood, e-mail to the author.

13 Yule, "A Narrative of a Mission," 162.

14 Scott (Shway Yoe), *The Burman*, 131.

15 I am grateful to Dr. Ye Myint for obtaining the papers of the 1994 seminar at the Saunders Weaving Institute.

16 Peter Collingwood describes several different types of loop and how they are made in chapter 15.

17 Another sazigyo of mid-nineteenth-century date woven without an integral loop is in the Staatsbibliothek Berlin, Ms Or fol. 927.

Part III

1 Horniman Museum nn 12220, and RAS Bur. Ms 86.

2 Pitt Rivers Museum 1889.29.200.

3 Mi Mi Khaing, *Burmese Family*, 82.

4 This suggestion is that of the late Shwebo Mi Mi Gyi's.

5 Peter Collingwood considered the technique a very tricky one, bringing undesirable tension problems.

6 The sazigyo in the National Museum, Yangon is 36 mm wide and 396 cm in length (both loop and cord are lacking). The text reads: "To celebrate the ear-piercing ceremony of our daughter and ordainment [*shinbyu*] of our son as a novice monk, we donated for each of one hundred monks three sets of robes including girdle, and a set of a hundred black pottery alms bowls; we also provided a meal of the finest meat curry for monks and for the lay audience, residents of east, west, north and south wards in the town of Allagappa, where we had already donated mansions and lakes for public welfare." (Translated by Dr. Ye Myint and the author.)

7 Myat Khine noted in 1986 that in the collections of the Cultural Department of the Ministry for Religious Affairs there were fifty "strings with prayers" and forty "strings without prayers."

8 Brighton Museum WA508839.

9 Pali, a literary language of the Prakrit language family, was probably a living language in Sri Lanka in the first century BCE when the canonical texts were written down. It remains the liturgical language of Theravada Buddhism today. The word Pali itself signifies "line" or "text," and this name for the language seems to have its origins in early written versions of the scriptures, where the core "text" was followed by various commentaries upon it.

10 Monastic property, whether owned by an individual monk or collectively by the monastery, is classified as either "light" (robes and bowls) or "heavy" (furniture, huts, and so on). Manuscripts are a special case. Neither light nor heavy property, they were classified with Buddha images as *cetiya*, relics of the Buddha. I am grateful to Dr. Christian Lammerts of the Nalanda Sriwijaya Centre in the Institute for South East Asian Studies, National University of Singapore, for sharing his knowledge of these "book knives," and of the legal status of manuscripts.

11 Maung Htin Aung, *Folk Elements in Burmese Buddhism*, 18–19.

12 The pains taken by donors to identify themselves unambiguously might be partly explained by the fact that a scriptural manuscript remained the property of the donor, fide Dr. Christian Lammerts (noted above).

13 Prayer of Ko Tet Khaung and Ma Mai Po of Inn-wa (Ava), ca. 1880 CE, in Shwebo Mi Mi Gyi's collected texts, 1993.

14 I am grateful to Vanessa Chan for this information. Her informants were the owners of one of the few remaining Kammava businesses in Mandalay, U Mg Mg Tint (son of U Kyit Myaing) and his wife Daw Tin Tin Oo. This is an example of a sazigyo bearing the name of the owners of the business rather than that of the craftworker who made the piece—which is nearly always the case with lacquer pieces.

15 Isaacs and Blurton, *Visions from the Golden Land*; for a discussion of inscriptions on lacquer see pp. 41–64.

16 Winfield, "Buddhism and Insurrection in Burma, 1886–1890," 345–67.

17 Gombrich, *Theravada Buddhism*, 2.

18 This text is among those collected by Shwebo Mi Mi Gyi, *Pa sa htouk kyo hma hsu taung sa mya*, 18 (ch. 2, no. 9).

19 The "five aggregates" may be labeled form, sensation, perception, volition, and consciousness. These constitute "different aspects of an individual human being's experience of the world." (Gethin)

20 L. E. Bagshawe, *The Kinwun Min-Gyi's London Diary*.

21 Khin Myo Chit and Paw Oo Thet, *Flowers and Festivals of the Twelve Burmese Seasons*, 7–8.

22 Numbered lists of doctrinal points were "a common feature of early Buddhist thought . . . no doubt in order to aid the preservation of teachings in a period of oral transmission." (Wynne) Clock-songs employ a similar device.

23 Maung Htin Aung, *Folk Elements in Burmese Buddhism*, 7–22. A "master" (*saya*) officiates. This in itself, Maung Htin Aung notes, points to the non-Buddhist origin of the ceremony: "That there should be a Saya to perform the ceremony of the Nine Gods is surprising since Burmese Buddhist ceremonies do not need a priest to act as the medium between the worshipper and the worshipped. Burmese *phongyis* are monks and not priests in fact. The Master sets up around a central image of the Buddha, images of the 'eight arahats.' Next he sets up another set of images, those of the nine planets, each on its 'vehicle' beast. All their names are borrowed from Hindu astrology. Then the master sets up the last group of images, those of the Five Great Gods, all Hindu in origin. (They are Saraswati, consort of Brahma; Chandi, consort of Siva; Maha-Peinne, the Burmese name for Ganesh; Peikthano, who is Vishnu; and Gawramanta, or 'he with the horse', who is the ninth and future incarnation of Vishnu.)."

24 Scott (Shway Yoe), *The Burman*, 588, 595–96.

25 David Brindley's 2009 film *Ashes to Diamonds* features a widow having her husband turned into a diamond, and a family putting their father into a steam train's furnace (Minnow Film for Channel 4 TV).

26 Scott (Shway Yoe), *The Burman*, 587 and Max and Bertha Ferrars, *Burma*, 199 both give descriptions of the use of rockets to ignite the funeral pyre at a *pongyibyan*. For collected contemporary accounts see Ralph Isaacs, "Rockets and Ashes," 126–33.

Part IV

1 Mi Mi Khaing, *Burmese Family*, 52–53. "All pills were administered in odd numbers, preferably three. Mother favoured a 'Three Gems' medicine, and would chant 'Baya-hsay, Taya-hsay, Thanga-hsay.'" In English: "Buddha medicine, Law-medicine, Monks-medicine."

2 U Than Htun (Dedaye), *Auspicious Symbols and Ancient Coins of Myanmar*. According to Maung Htin Aung, *Folk Elements in Burmese Buddhism*, 21, the number nine is in some districts of Burma thought to be the property of the Nats, who will be angry if their special number is used by humans. In Kyaukse District men avoid having nine carts in a caravan, and do not build a house on the ninth waxing or waning day of the month.

3 *Samyutta Nikaya*, III, 120.

4 *Digha Nikaya*, II, 154.

5 Maung Htin Aung, *Folk Elements in Burmese Buddhism*, 34.

6 Ibid., 32.

7 Khin Myo Chit and Paw Oo Thet, *Flowers and Festivals of the Twelve Burmese Seasons*, 72–74.

8 Capt. Hiram Cox, *Journal of a Residence in the Burmhan Empire*, 12.

9 One of the thirty-two physical characteristics of the Buddha as a Great Man, listed in the Maha-padana Sutta, is: "He has a Brahma-like voice, like that of the Karawika-bird." Its voice was "sweeter, more beautiful, charming and delightful than all other birds."

10 Robinson and Shaw, *The Coins and Banknotes of Burma*.

11 The *Taw Lay Wa*, four paragons of womanhood, are: (1) Amara, wife of the Bodhisattva during his existence as the wise warrior King Mahodhatta, and who herself was renowned for her perspicacity, courage, and integrity; (2) Sandakinnari, wife of the Bodhisattva during his incarnation as Sandakinnara, celebrated for her unwavering fidelity to her husband even after King Brahmadat slew her husband and offered to make her his queen; (3) Maddidevi, the gentle wife of the Bodhisattva during his incarnation as King Vessantara, who after her husband had to abdicate the throne for his untrammeled charity, dutifully shared his trials and tribulations; (4) Sambula, loyal wife of the Bodhisattva during his incarnation as the leper Prince Sawttisana.

12 Gospel of Matthew 6:2: "When you give alms, do not do it with a flourish of trumpets, as the hypocrites do in the synagogues and streets, so that people may think well of them. . . . But when you practice charity, do not let your left hand know what your right hand is doing, so that your charity may be in secret."

13 Yule, *A Narrative of a Mission*, 157.

14 The story of Vasundhara witnessing the Buddha's Enlightenment and destroying the hosts of Mara by wringing out her long wet hair is popular in Southeast Asia, but does not occur in the Pali canon.

15 Patricia Herbert (in Zwalf, 173, cat. 247) describes a fine painted manuscript (*parabaik*) detailing the donations of King Mindon in 1854 and 1856. The Royal Donation included gilded manuscript chests, palm-leaf manuscripts, and their cloth wrappers. (These can be seen in plate 21). The text states that the king poured the traditional water, calling on the earth to witness, and shared his great merit.

16 Text of a sazigyo collected by Shwebo Mi Mi Gyi, *Pay sa htouk kyo hma hsu taung sa mya*, 83 (ch. 8, no. 5).

17 In Cambodia she is held in high regard by women, who look on her as their champion or protectress, empowering women in a male-dominated society.

18 Fraser-Lu, *Burmese Crafts Past and Present*, 140.

19 Lowry, *Burmese Art*, plate 19.

20 Singer, "Kammavaca Texts."

Part V

1 Peter Collingwood had not seen any sazigyo longer than six meters, but a few exceed nine meters.

Appendixes

1 The help of Dr. Christian Lammerts on the legal status of manuscripts is noted above.

2 It is illustrated in Mabel Peach, *Tablet Weaving*, 19 (lower), and in Peter Collingwood, *The Techniques of Tablet Weaving* (1996 edition), 182, pl. 134.

3 Harvey's *History of Burma: From the Earliest Times to 10 March 1824, the Beginning of the English Conquest* was published in 1925.

4 I am indebted to Jacqueline Filliozat of the EFEO, Paris, for all information about these Thai-Khom title-pieces.

Glossary of Burmese Names and Terms

apaya The four realms of woe: hell, animal rebirth, insatiable craving, rebirth as an anti-god

athat Diacritical sign above a Burmese consonant, often developed into flourishes

Bodhisattva Future Buddha, the "Buddha-to-be" in his previous incarnations

cetiya Literally, relics of the Buddha; object of veneration, such as a manuscript

chinthe Mythical bearded lion, often in pairs guarding approaches to a pagoda

daga Donor, the title by which monks refer to members of the laity

dagundaing Tall pole or flagstaff with long tubular pennants, on pagoda platform

dana Generosity, charity, the foremost of Buddhist virtues; also a specific act of donation

Dhamma The law, the scriptures, the Buddha's teachings; second of the Three Gems

dhammaceti Scriptural manuscript made with cremation ashes of a monk or layman

doun Rocket fired to ignite the funeral pyre of a senior monk at a *pongyibyan*

gabyidan Literally, inscribed stick; spatula or pointer used for turning palm-leaf folios

galon Garuda, mythical bird, enemy of the *naga* (serpent-dragon); birthday beast of Sunday-born

gaung baung Silk headdress tied in a side bow; formal wear for Burmese males

gyo-daing Planet (or "birthday") posts at cardinal compass points on the pagoda platform

gyo-shit-myo The eight planet-vehicles, or birthday beasts; design on lacquer ware

Hinayana "Lesser Vehicle" school of Buddhism, found today in Sri Lanka, Thailand, and Burma

hkana A measure of time equal to "ten snaps of the fingers" or "ten winks of the eye"

hkaung-laung gyi Round bronze bell, hung from teak posts

hsayadaw Most senior monk ("abbot") of a Burmese Buddhist monastery

hsun-ok Offering vessel, like a deep bowl on a stand, with a tall spired cover

hti Parasol, emblem of royalty and of senior monks; also the metal finial of pagodas

inga Bundle of twelve palm leaves; used for recording the size of palm-leaf manuscripts

Jataka Tale of a former life of the Buddha. The last ten of 550 are the Great Jatakas.

kalat Tray on a pedestal, for religious offerings or secular gifts

Kammava Anthology of Vinaya precepts, used at ordination ceremony of monks

kammavaca A manuscript of the Kammava (used interchangeably with Kammava)

karaweik Mythical crane-like bird whose melodious voice is said to be like the Buddha's

Kathina Seasonal festival for offerings of robes and other gifts to monks

kinnara Mythical bird-man or bird-woman, symbols of constancy and marital fidelity

kyauk hti Stone parasol, found on pagoda platforms, representing the Buddha

kyaung Monastery, monastic school, and (nowadays) any school or place of learning

kyizi Flat bronze gong or bell which, when struck on the corner, spins and emits a vibrato note

kyo kya A crane, whose cry is interpreted as a shout of triumph

longyi Men's everyday waistcloth or skirt

Mahayana "Greater Vehicle" school of Buddhist traditions, found in Tibet, China, Korea, and Japan

Maitreya Future Buddha, the next Buddha to appear on earth, who will teach the Dhamma

manuthiha Mythical composite being, with human torso and twin lion bodies

Mara God of sensual pleasure, passion, and death; embodiment of temptation to evil

mingala Auspiciousness, especially of future or planned acts, deeds, and ceremonies

mingala yadu Panegyric of praise chanted at a wedding, naming all family members

naga Serpent-dragon, birthday beast of Saturday-born

Nat Celestial being; Thagya Min is King of Burma's vast population of Nats

navratna (Sanskrit); **nawarat** (Burmese) The nine auspicious gems or nine planets motif

neibban Nirvana, the aim of all donors: to escape from the cycle of birth and rebirth

pada Verses of four syllables, some rhyming with those in previous and following verses

padauk Hard heavy wood, purplish in color, used for loom beaters

padaythabin Branched tree-like stand hung with offerings to monks, such as robes

Pali The language of the "Pali canon," the scriptures of Theravada Buddhism

parabaik Burmese accordion-pleated paper book, often with painted illustrations

paso Men's silk skirt, like the everyday *longyi* but much longer and not sewn into a tube

pat ma gyi Big drum, largest and loudest instrument in the Burmese orchestra

pongyibyan Elaborate ceremonial cremation of a senior monk

pu "Guinea-pig," the birthday beast of Friday-born, perhaps originally a hamster

pyatthat Tiered roof surmounting monasteries, royal buildings, and vehicles

sa dagun Hanging banner with woven text, hung from a post in a shrine

sadaik Container for manuscripts, a chest of lacquered and gilded teak wood

salway Sash of multiple golden chains, worn by Burmese kings and high officials

samari Mythical beast, a hairy quadruped related to the Tibetan yak

samsara The endless cycle of birth, death, and rebirth: suffering

Sangha The community of monks, third of the Three Gems

Sasana The Buddha's teachings preserved by the monks: the Buddhist dispensation

shinbyu Ceremony for a young boy becoming a novice monk

stupa Solid conical building enshrining relics or other offerings; pagoda

tauk tek Giant spotted gecko, living in house roofs; its cry is lucky if repeated nine times

Taw Lay Wa The four paragons of (female) virtue, models of wifely virtue

tazaung Elaborately decorated tectum, canopy, or shrine built around a Buddha image

Thadu "Well done!" Witnesses of a deed of merit congratulate the donors

Thagya Min King of the Nats (Sakra or Indra), invoked at Burmese Buddhist ceremonies

thayo Putty made by mixing raw liquid lacquer with finely sifted bone ash

thein Hall in or near a monastery compound, for ordination rites and other rituals

thok or **thut** Sutra; Buddhist sacred writings, including sermons delivered by the Buddha

Tipitaka (Pali); **Tripitaka** (Sanskrit) The "three baskets" of the Theravada Buddhist scriptures

triratna Three Gems, or Triple Gem: Buddha, Law, and Monks

Vinaya The second of the "three baskets": the rules for monks

Waythondaye Vasundhara, the Earth Goddess, invoked to witness deeds of merit

yathi A sign of the zodiac, adapted in Burma from the Indian version

yokka soe Tree spirit or tree Nat; trees are thought of as living beings

zat Jataka stories of the previous lives of the Buddha; the last ten are the Great Jatakas

Zeyatu "Success!" A Pali invocation, the first word on many sazigyo

Bibliography

Sazigyo

Chan, Vanessa. *Sar-si-kyo: Woven Dedicatory Ribbons of Myanmar.* Singapore: Nalanda Sriwijaya Centre, National University of Singapore, forthcoming.

Collingwood, Peter. "Detailed Technical Report on the Burmese Manuscript Binding Tapes in the Brighton Museum." Unpublished manuscript, James Green Centre for World Art, Brighton Museum & Art Gallery, 2000.

Collingwood, Peter. "Burmese Inscription Bands." *Strands*, Journal of The Braid Society, issue 11 (2004): 6–12.

Hendrickson, Linda. http://www.lindahendrickson.com. Illustrates a fine sazigyo, and lists her instructional books for adult and child weavers.

Isaacs, Ralph. "Textile Texts." In *Textiles from Burma*, edited by Elizabeth Dell and Sandra Dudley, 102–13. London: Philip Wilson, 2003.

Isaacs, Ralph. "NERDS, or Nayland Express Research Devoted to Sazigyo." *Journal for Weavers, Spinners and Dyers* (Summer 2009): 6–11.

Isaacs, Ralph. "Mr PC of Nayland and Sazigyo: Analysing Burmese Tablet Woven Inscription Bands." *Strands*, Journal of The Braid Society (Autumn 2009): 3–8.

Isaacs, Ralph. "Sazigyo: Woven Miniatures of Buddhist Art." *Textiles Asia Journal*, vol. 2, issue 2 (September 2010): 3–7.

Isaacs, Ralph. "Sazigyo: Textile Texts." *Newsletter of the Oxford Asian Textile Group*, no. 34 (June 2006): 16–24.

Isaacs, Ralph. "Woven Texts, Woven Images: The Iconography of the Sazigyo." In *Connecting Empires: Selected Papers from the13th International Conference of the European Association of Southeast Asian Archaeologists*, vol. 2, edited by Mai Lin Tjoa-Bonatz, Andreas Reinecke, and Dominik Bonatz, 179–88. Singapore: NUS Press, 2012.

Johnson, Kathleen F. "Little Masterpieces: The Art of Sazigyo from the Collection of Herbert Haar." In *Sawaddi Asian Arts and Culture*, 34–40. Bangkok: American Womens' Club of Thailand, 2005.

Johnson, Kathleen F., and Tsai Yushan. "The Woven Word: Sasigyo." *Textile Society of America Newsletter*, vol. 21, no. 1 (Winter 2009): 1, 8–9.

Mi Mi Gyi (Shwebo Mi Mi Gyi). *Pay sa htouk kyo hma hsu taung sa mya* [Collected Texts of Manuscript Binding Tapes]. Rangoon: Sarpei Beikman Press, 1993.

Myat Khine. "Prayers from Palm Leave Manuscripts Wrappers [sic]." In *FORWARD*, 27–30. Rangoon: Ministry of Culture, July 1986.

Singer, Noel F. "Kammavaca Texts, Their Covers and Binding Ribbons." *Arts of Asia*, vol. 23, no. 3 (1993): 97–106.

Techniques of Tablet Weaving

Collingwood, Peter. *The Techniques of Tablet Weaving*. London: Faber, 1982. Reprints, McMinnville, Oregon: Robin & Russ Handweavers, 1996, 2002.

Lehman-Filhes, Margarethe. *Ueber Brettchenweberei*. Berlin: Dietrich Reimer (Ernst Vohsen), 1901.

Peach, Mabel W. *Tablet Weaving*. 2nd ed. Leicester: Dryad Press, 1934.

Scherman, Lucian. "Brettchenwebereien aus Birma und den Himalayalandern [Tablet Weaving from Burma]." In *Jahrbuch für Bildenden Kunst*, 223–42. Munich: Münchner Kunstwissenschaftlichen Gesellschaft, 1913.

Staudigel, Otfried. *Der Zauber des Brettchenwebens* [Tablet Weaving Magic: Patterns from Oriental Countries]. Krefeld: O. Staudigel, 2001.

Staudigel, Otfried. *Gewebte Bilder, Entraetselte Motive* [Woven Images, Unravelled Motifs]. Krefeld: O. Staudigel, 2008.

Wardle, Thomas. *Descriptive Catalogue of the Colonial and Indian Exhibition: Indian Silk Culture Court*. London: Clowes, 1886.

Buddhism and Cults

Gethin, Rupert. "The Five *Khandas*: Their Treatment in the Nikayas and Early Abidhamma." *Journal of Indian Philosophy*, vol. 14, no. 1 (1986): 35–53.

Gombrich, Richard. *Theravada Buddhism: A Social History from Ancient Benares to Modern Colombo*. 2nd ed. London: Routledge, 1988.

Herbert, Patricia M. *The Life of the Buddha*. London: British Library, 1992.

Maung Htin Aung, *Burmese Monk's Tales*. New York: Columbia University Press, 1966.

Powell, Andrew, and Graham Harrison. *Living Buddhism*. London: British Museum Press, 1988.

Rahula, Walpola. *What the Buddha Taught*. Bedford: Fraser, 1959.

Temple, Sir Richard Carnac. *The Thirty-Seven Nats: A Phase of Spirit Worship Prevailing in Burma*. London: Griggs, 1906. Reprint, London: Kiscadale, 1991.

Wynne, Alexander. "The Buddha's Skill in Means and the Genesis of the Five Aggregates Teaching." *Journal of the Royal Asiatic Society*, vol. 20, part 2 (April 2010): 191–216.

Zwalf, W. *Buddhism: Art and Faith*. London: British Museum Press, 1985.

Burmese Life, Customs, and Ceremonies

Ferrars, Max, and Bertha Ferrars. *Burma*. London: Sampson Low, 1901. Reprint, Bangkok: AVA, 1996.

Isaacs, Ralph. "Rockets and Ashes: *Pongyibyan* as Depicted in Nineteenth- and Twentieth-Century European Sources." *The Journal of Burma Studies*, vol. 13 (2009): 107–36.

Khin Myo Chit. *Colourful Burma*. 2 vols. Rangoon: University Press, 1983.

Khin Myo Chit and Paw Oo Thet. *Flowers and Festivals of the Twelve Burmese Seasons*. Bangkok: Orchid Press, 2002.

Maung Htin Aung. *Folk Elements in Burmese Buddhism*. Rangoon: Religious Affairs Department Press, 1959.

Mi Mi Khaing. *Burmese Family*. Calcutta: Longmans Green & Co., 1946.

Scott, Sir J. G. (Shway Yoe). *The Burman, His Life and Notions*. London: Macmillan, 1882.

Stadtner, Donald M. *Sacred Sites of Burma*. Bangkok: River Books, 2011.

Weigelt, Uta. " … 'And Saved the State Thousands:' Christine Scherman and the State Museum for Ethnology in Munich." In *Golden Land: Burma/Myanmar 100 Years: Photographs by Christine Scherman and Birgit Neiser*, edited by Wolfgang Stein and Birgit Neiser, 12–17. Munich: State Museum of Ethnology, 2013.

Burmese Art and Artifacts

Fraser-Lu, Sylvia. *Burmese Crafts Past and Present*. Kuala Lumpur: Oxford University Press, 1994.

Gutman, Pamela. *Burma's Lost Kingdoms: Splendours of Arakan*. Bangkok: Orchid Press, 2001.

Herbert, Patricia M. "Burmese Court Manuscripts." In *The Art of Burma: New Studies*, edited by Donald Stadtner, 89–102. Bombay: Marg, 1999.

Isaacs, Ralph, and T. Richard Blurton. *Visions from the Golden Land: Burma and the Art of Lacquer*. London: British Museum Press, 2000.

Lowry, John. *Burmese Art*. London: HMSO, 1974.

Robinson, M., and L. A. Shaw. *The Coins and Banknotes of Burma*. Manchester: M. Robinson, 1980.

U Than Htun (Dedaye). *Auspicious Symbols and Ancient Coins of Myanmar*. Kuala Lumpur: Avahouse, 2007.

U Than Htun (Dedaye). *Lacquerware Journeys: The Untold Story of Burmese Lacquer*. Bangkok: River Books, 2012.

U Thaw Kaung. "Myanmar Traditional Manuscripts and their Preservation and Conservation." In *U Thaw Kaung: Selected Writings*, 255–88. Rangoon: Myanmar Historical Commission, 2004.

Travelers to and from Burma

Bagshawe, L. E. *The Kinwun Min-Gyi's London Diary: The First Mission of a Burmese Minister to Britain, 1872*. Bangkok: Orchid Press, 2006.

Cox, Capt. Hiram. *Journal of a Residence in the Burmhan Empire and More Particularly at the Court of Amarapoorah*, London: Warren and Whittaker, 1821.

Harvey, G. E. *History of Burma: From the Earliest Times to 10 March 1824, the Beginning of the English Conquest*. London: Longmans, 1925. Reprint, London: Cass, 1967.

Scherman, Lucian, and Christine Scherman. *Im Stromgebiet des Irrawaddy, Birma und seine Frauenwelt* [In the Irrawaddy River Basin, Burma and its Women]. Munich: Oskar Schloss Press, 1922.

Symes, Michael. *An Account of an Embassy to the Kingdom of Ava Sent by the Governor-General of India in the Year 1795*. London: Debrett, 1800.

Yule, Sir Henry. *A Narrative of a Mission Sent by the Governor-General of India to the Court of Ava in 1855, with Notices of the Country, Government and People*. London: Smith, Elder, 1858. Reprint, Kuala Lumpur, New York: Oxford University Press, 1968.

List of Illustrations

Index

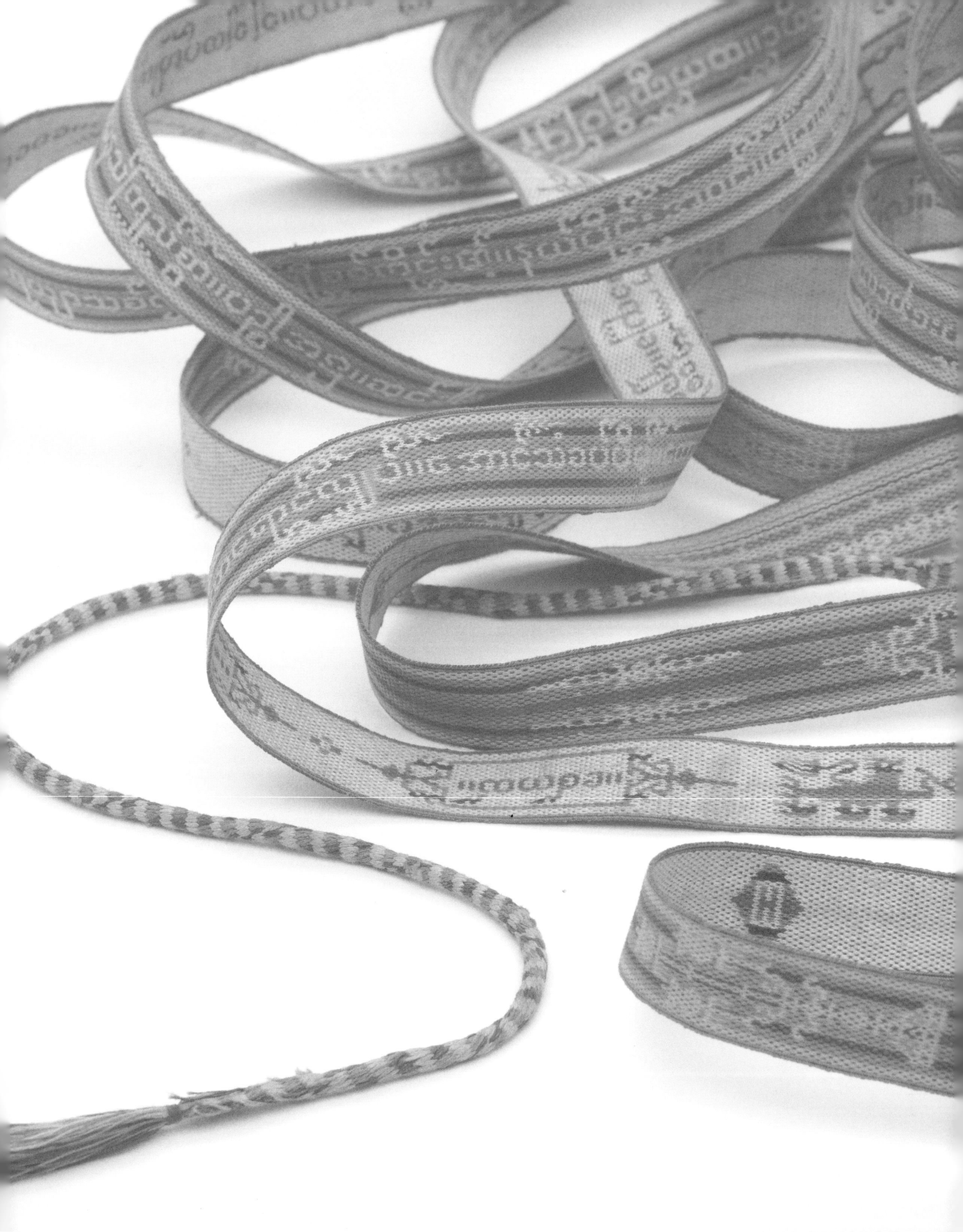